HAROLD TAKOOSHIAN

MENTAL HEALTH IN THE METROPOLIS

(Cover of *Newsweek* Magazine, 1962)

"New York to me is like a huge piece of abstract art. There's a little bit of this here and a little bit of that there. At first it doesn't make much sense. But after a while you see that everything fits."—*a small town Mississippian visitor*

Mental Health
In The Metropolis

The Midtown Manhattan Study

LEO SROLE

THOMAS S. LANGNER • STANLEY T. MICHAEL

PRICE KIRKPATRICK • MARVIN K. OPLER

THOMAS A. C. RENNIE

EDITED BY

LEO SROLE / ANITA KASSEN FISCHER

Revised and Enlarged Edition

NEW YORK UNIVERSITY PRESS • 1978

This monograph was originally published in 1962 by Mc-Graw-Hill Book Company in one hardcover volume. The revised, enlarged, two-book edition was published in softcover format by Harper Torchbooks in 1975, 1977. The senior author has added the following new material to the enlarged editions:

Chapter 1, "Introduction"

Chapter 15, "Parental Socioeconomic Status: Income Adequacy and Offspring Mental Health"

Chapter 20, "The City versus Town and Country: New Evidence on an Ancient Bias, 1975"

Chapter 21, "Summing Up, 1975"

Chapter 23, "Sociologist's Perspectives: Past and Future, 1975"

Appendix F, "Rural-Urban Diagnostic Issues"

Appendix G, "Midtown Critique of Previous Patient Enumeration Studies"

LIBRARY OF CONGRESS CATALOG CARD NUMBER: 77-76507

ISBN: 0-8147-7782-1

Manufactured in the United States of America

Dedicated
To the Memory
of
THOMAS A. C. RENNIE, M.D.
February 28, 1904–May 21, 1956
Late Professor of Psychiatry (Social Psychiatry)
Cornell University Medical College
Founder and First Director
of the
Midtown Manhattan Mental Health Study

PREFACE, 1978

It was an unexpected pleasure to receive and accept the invitation of Mr. Malcolm C. Johnson, Jr., Director of the New York University Press, to reissue the revised and enlarged edition of this work in a durable cloth-cover, single volume format.

It seems especially appropriate that this broad-spectrum research monograph, focussed on what a towering painter of our century, Georgia O'Keefe, has called "my dream metropolis," should now bear the colophon of the university press that is an intrinsic part of the great city for which it is named.

LS

AKF

TABLE OF CONTENTS

TABLES

ILLUSTRATIONS

FIGURES

The Midtown Manhattan Study was funded by a grant (M-515) from the National Institute of Mental Health. Supplementary support was provided by the Grant Foundation, the Corporation Trust, the Lucius N. Littauer Foundation, the Milbank Memorial Fund, the Rockefeller Brothers Fund, and the Samuel Rubin Foundation.

Preparation of this revised and enlarged edition was facilitated by a special grant awarded to the senior author by the Foundation Fund for Research in Psychiatry.

LEO SROLE, PH.D.
Chief of Psychiatric Research, Social Sciences,
New York State Psychiatric Institute
Professor Emeritus of Social Sciences, Department of Psychiatry
College of Physicians and Surgeons
Columbia University

THOMAS S. LANGNER, PH.D.
Professor of Epidemiology
School of Public Health and Administrative Medicine
Columbia University

STANLEY T. MICHAEL, M.D.
Associate Professor of Psychiatry
Cornell University Medical College

PRICE KIRKPATRICK, M.D.
Late Director, Kern County Mental Health Services
Bakersfield, California

MARVIN K. OPLER, PH.D.
Professor of Social Psychiatry, School of Medicine
Professor and Chairman, Department of Anthropology
State University of New York at Buffalo

THOMAS A. C. RENNIE, M.D.
Late Professor of Psychiatry (Social Psychiatry)
Cornell University Medical College

ANITA KASSEN FISCHER, M.A.
Research Associate, Department of Psychiatry
College of Physicians and Surgeons
Columbia University

MENTAL HEALTH IN THE METROPOLIS

Part I

Prologue

CHAPTER I

INTRODUCTION, 1975

LEO SROLE

The stream of new books about New York—like the water in the legend of the Sorcerer's Apprentice—flows without apparent end. Where, within this seemingly boundless main, does the present work find anchor?

Arch-metropolis and mecca of the New World for almost two centuries, New York has drawn a long line of writers, major and minor, wise and otherwise, celebrants, students, and excoriators of what one of them has called "this high-bosomed Mother City." In its streets have gathered storytellers, poets, playwrights, essayists, memoirists, minstrels, town criers, latter-day scholars—itinerant and indigenous.[1] Whatever their purpose, their medium, or their talents, all seemed taxed for words to evoke the City's herculean scale and its protean complexities.

One of the more recent in this motley chorus of voices is the distinguished novelist Saul Bellow. In a piece written for the *New York Times* (December 6, 1970), he addressed himself to his own question: "How do Americans think of New York?" and replied, in part, as follows:

That is perhaps like asking how Scotsmen feel about the Loch Ness monster. It is our legendary phenomenon, our great thing, our world-famous impossibility. Some seem to wish it were nothing more than a persistent rumor. It is, however, as human things go, very real, super real. What is barely hinted in other American cities is condensed and enlarged in New York.

New York is stirring, insupportable, agitated, ungovernable, demonic. No single individual can judge it adequately. Not even Walt Whitman could today embrace it emotionally: the attempt might capsize him. Those who want to

5

contemplate the phenomenon are well advised to assume a contemplative position elsewhere. Those who wish to feel its depths had better be careful. For fifteen years I lived in and with New York. I now reside in Chicago.

Even more hard pressed for words was journalist Gilbert Millstein in his book *New York: True North* (1964). There he concedes:

New York is the endless celebration of everything. . . . Its facts, really, are untranslatable, although the babble of interpretation, of commendation, of condemnation, never stops and is taken up, with insane confidence by everybody from taxicab drivers to teams of scholars minutely measuring the extent of mental disturbance in a midtown Manhattan neighborhood. The facts of New York are as mysterious as Stonehenge; they are concepts like the light year.[2]

In Bellow's "impossible" and Millstein's "untranslatable," the two passages just quoted almost "run the gamut," as critic Dorothy Parker once put it, "from A to B."

The Millstein passage, on double-take, is also an apostrophe about New York's cabbies and a group of scholars who can only be the writers of the present book in its original, hardcover edition.

Taxi drivers are, of course, as indigenous to the urban scene as traffic cops, and, as occupational types, far more articulate. Everywhere, and especially in New York, they are a singularly brass-nerved crew of navigators as well as natural sociologists and critics of the prose they hear and read about "this town."

As for us, "the teams [*sic*] of scholars" dropped into the blue of the Millstein text, we too are a breed native to the metropolis, committed to an offbeat, exploratory exposure of New York for our reader to give heed in the pages ahead.

From what angle has this view been approached? Clearly it cannot be that of the *belle lettrist,* with his freewheeling, often oracular vision, and his license to project, color, and dramatize that highly personal vision as art in search of a captivated audience. Instead, we follow a more prosaic kind of work style, based in part on the collaborative, natural-history life sciences; in particular those, like sociology and anthropology, which scrutinize established societies and groups as significant "experiments of human nature," uncovering insights that at times are strangers to fiction.

This approach requires systematic, critically monitored observation of group behavior within its own setting, precluding, of course, "the contemplative position" from a distant armchair that Bellow urges upon us fellow New York-watchers.

Although the two approaches are far apart in their operating methods and modes of reporting, substantively, of course, they attend segments of the same vast human stage. Recognizing this convergence, Émile Zola, seminal figure in Western literature and adversary of "romanticism," almost a century ago called for "naturalism" in the novel, which he saw leading directly from the field-oriented social sciences. The naturalistic novel, he declared

is in the same path which runs from chemistry to physiology, then to anthropology and sociology. . . . We [novelists] no longer describe for the sake of describing, from a caprice and a pleasure of rhetoricians. We consider that man cannot be separated from his surroundings, that he is completed by his clothes, his house, his city, and his country; and hence we shall not note a single phenomenon of his brain and heart without looking for the causes or the consequences in his surroundings. . . . I should define description: "An account of environment which determines and completes man." . . . In a novel, in a study of humanity, I blame all description which is not according to that definition.[3]

Although his causal claim was overstated,[4] Zola's phrase "study of humanity" is the broad substantive bridge that joins the arts, the psychological and social sciences. From the latter, for example, have come *in vivo* delineations of preliterate, tribal peoples inhabiting such economically marginal areas of the world as Oceania, the American Southwest, the Canadian subpolar zone, and the tropical river basins of Africa and South America.

From societies at higher grades of technological development, these sciences have also contributed a notable series of full-length portraits of communities—rural,[5] suburban, and urban.

At the uppermost reaches of the metropolis,[6] on the other hand, only a scant few have been mounted by a research program of comparable macrosociological scale. These have preeminently included London during the last decades of the nineteenth century,[7] and Chicago during the years between the two world wars (1920–1940).[8]

The metropolis towers over the run of communities like a mountain range over the foothills and plains below. The exploration of such human massifs with social science tools is certainly among the most difficult and costly of all investigative efforts. It is no accident, accordingly, that the London and Chicago research programs each required some twenty years for an outstanding generation of students to conduct and report in a shelf full of volumes.

Although New York has not drawn a comparable kind of encompassing attention, it has by no means been neglected. Recent economists, historians, and political scientists in some numbers have been applying the specialized methods of their trades to this Mount Everest among American cities.[9]

Until the early 1950s, however, no specifically sociological field study had been undertaken here, except that reported in Professor Caroline F. Ware's memorable, but long-neglected monograph *Greenwich Village: 1920–30.* That book is a portrait of a colorful metropolitan enclave (population 40,000 at the time) in the decade following World War I.[10] Rare of its kind, this picture has enduring interest as a fine-grained delineation of one residential neighborhood in the inner metropolis at a relatively early point in the twentieth century.

Beyond this particular fix in space and time, the Ware investigation has two other noteworthy dimensions. First, the social fabric of Greenwich Village is seen as presenting "conditions characteristic of the central sections of older American cities."[11] Second, the scientific purpose was "to throw some light upon the nature of contemporary changes in [these] conditions."[12] The particular was examined, as in all science and most art, for the general significances embedded in it.

The Midtown Manhattan Study, launched several decades later, in certain particular facets is lineal kin to the Greenwich Village investigation, and on a smaller scale, to the Chicago[13] and London field research programs. These facets are here sketched in the Part II chapters entitled: "Midtown: A Sociological Profile." However, in certain other dimensions to be presently outlined, the present Study reaches beyond all three of these monumental predecessors.

For purposes of preliminary identification, Midtown is our code name for a sociologically well-demarcated, wholly residential section (estimated population when studied of 170,000) that adjoins Manhattan's central business district, somewhat as does Greenwich Village. Needless to say, however, the two areas have rather different histories, ecological characteristics, and population mixes.

Also distinguishing the Midtown Study from other sociological investigations of a metropolis is its central concern with mental health differences prevailing within the area's resident (that is, noninstitutional) population. Moreover, among the few studies of communities, large and small, with this general concern, the Midtown investigation remains the only one to explore how such residents are dispersed along the *entire spectrum* of mental health variations, from the incapacitated to the asymptomatic ("the well").

Another unprecedented feature among metropolitan investigations is that the Study was conceived and initiated by a clinical psychiatrist, Thomas A. C. Rennie, its director until his untimely death in 1956. He, of course, was responsible for the Study's primary medicopsychiatric framework. He was also an early example of university-based psychiatrists who add research to their ongoing clinical and training functions, and in such research look beyond the clinic for broader understanding of social forces operating on the generality of people, nonpatients and patients alike. The subspecialty name often accorded this effort to forge closer links between clinic and community is "social psychiatry."

To undertake the kind of inquiry required by this interest, social psychiatrists generally reach out for the collaboration of similarly interested disciplines beyond their own. For example, to man the full-time Midtown Study staff Rennie enlisted a team of veteran field investigators from sociology,[14] anthropology, psychology, and social work, with the present writer as its senior social scientist.

Given these multidisciplinary resources, the Midtown investigation has operated on four substantive levels. (Time: near the midpoint of the century's sixth decade.)

1. Manhattan as Midtown's embracing "mother" borough.
2. Midtown as an area–population–community entity in its own right.
3. Midtown as a multifold patchwork of social subhabitats.
4. Midtown residents' entire range of mental health differences—as these are variously influenced by the third level of group habitats, seen in the perspective of the individual's life history.

Although collaborating on all four of the above levels, the social scientists were primarily responsible for investigating the first three, the psychiatrists primarily the fourth. Both sections of the Study team were equally dedicated to probing the connections between the core third and fourth levels, but with somewhat different first-priority objectives.

For the psychiatrists, knowledge was sought primarily as a basis for realistic planning of psychiatric services in the community. This followed, of course, from Rennie's role as the Study's initiator and director, the Study's sponsorship by the Cornell University Medical College, its funding by the National Institute of Mental Health (M-515) and several private foundations.

While sharing these urgent service objectives, the social scientists regarded the varying group "profiles" of mental health variations as a powerful "X-ray" screen for detecting unsuspected concentrations of pathogenic (and eugenic) social processes. To us, therefore, the study held out the ultimate hope of uncovering clues to the differential quality of various group environments, with potential implications for guiding public policy toward prime targets of preventive intervention and possible social change.

Beyond the chapters of "Midtown: A Sociological Profile" (4, 5, 6), this monograph presents the Study's lines of strategy and tactics in approaching mental health (chapters 7, 8, 9), the findings yielded (chapters 10–19), culminating in the conclusions, implications, and extrapolations of the Epilogue (chapters 20–23). It may be appropriate at this point in the introduction to the enlarged edition of the monograph to first review several stages in the life history of the original edition.

At Rennie's death, the Study's information-gathering had been substantially, but not altogether, completed, data analysis had begun, a provisional chapter outline had been formulated, and several chapters of findings had been written in first draft by the present author.

Professor Alexander H. Leighton* assumed several of Rennie's aca-

---

*Professor of Psychiatry and Preventive Medicine, Dalhousie University, Halifax, Nova Scotia.

demic functions. Leighton, too, is an eminent social psychiatrist, who was already fully engaged at the time in directing a long-term, broadly similar, but essentially independent investigation of mental health in a rural Nova Scotia county.[15] He served in the making of the first edition of this monograph as editorial coordinator, arbitrator, and senior psychiatric advisor. The authors acknowledge their indebtedness to him for both the guidance and the latitude to continue the original work as previously blueprinted through to publication. The final draft of the hardcover monograph was completed late in 1960 and published early in 1962.

The prospective reader of a scientific work, reappearing some years later in a partially new format, may challenge the original edition with two show-me questions: "Now that the book has had a decade of life, what discernible difference has it made? More specifically, what, in documented fact, has been its long-run usefulness, if any, for public and professional purposes?"

Such an accounting is rarely made or put before the new reader to consider as a measure of the book's impact, penetration, and durability. This silence is at least partially prompted by a professional taboo decreeing that discussion of such matters should be left to the book's publishers, early-issue reviewers, and other peers.

Facing the dilemma of serving either the taboo or the new reader's legitimate challenge, the present writer of course opts for the latter, drawing in part on evidence that emerged after the last of the book's many reviews had appeared.

Mental Health in the Metropolis was conceived, designed, and written as a straightforward workers' report to the parent professions of psychiatry and the social sciences, and hopefully, to involved laymen as well.

I cannot say that we ever explicitly formulated our expectations of this book, but had we tried we could hardly have foreseen a number of developments in the course it actually took.

For example, a key finding in our Study population was the overriding relationship of mental disturbance to socioeconomic status (chapter 14), and, most strikingly, to family poverty in the childhood period of life.

By coincidence, the book appeared in the same week as *The Other*

America by journalist Michael Harrington. Although the latter work was based for the most part on secondary, rather than first-hand, evidence, the two books shared this conclusion:

Far from congruence with the popular "happy, carefree" stereotype, those born into a poor family more often than others tend to grow up, in Harrington's incisive phrase, "maimed in body and spirit."

The years after 1962 were followed by the largest outpouring of books on poverty since the Depression years of the 1930s. The combined impact of this tidal literature on public *awareness* of the many bitter fruits of poverty was probably unprecedented in American history.[16] It would seem that each affluent American generation must painfully reawaken to the unrelieved poverty "on the other side of the tracks," and consider anew Cain's primal question, "Am I my brother's keeper?"[17]

Other major findings uncovered in the Midtown volume revealed (1) a frequency of emotional disability far higher than had previously been estimated in any American population; (2) the huge gap between this unexpectedly large call for psychiatric help and the gross quantitative inadequacy of the services available—at that, in the community harboring the nation's highest density of psychiatrists and clinical psychologists; and (3) most revealing of all, the highly discriminatory nature of this gap—those *most* in need of such services had by far the *least* access to them, including in particular the low-income and older age groups in the population.

Filling critical "missing links" in the previous evidence, the book found a place, even before publication, in the research literature that paved the way for the highly influential report *Action for Mental Health,* issued in 1961 by the National Joint Commission on Mental Illness and Health.[18]

The extent of the Midtown investigation's impact was foreshadowed in 1962 when it appeared near the top of a list of "twenty-four research projects considered to be among the most outstanding ones supported through NIMH grants." According to the granting agency, "the Midtown Study represents a major contribution . . . it is not only of general theoretical importance . . . but also provides information with which to anticipate and plan actual treatment needs" (unpublished report of the

NIMH Program Analysis and Evaluation Office, September 1962).

Soon thereafter, *Mental Health in the Metropolis* lent empirical support for Joint Commission recommendations as modified and incorporated into President Kennedy's Community Mental Health Center Act, and passed by Congress in 1963. This legislation was followed by the activation of mental health planning bodies in all fifty states and hundreds of localities.[19] Participants in a number of these bodies have reported personally or in print that the book served such groups as one of their primary resource works. An example is *Psychiatry in the American Community* (1966), a guide to community leaders, by H. G. Whittington. The latter was Director of Community Health Services for the State of Kansas, and in that capacity was involved in establishing ten new community mental health centers in his state. In reporting that experience, his volume cites uses of the Midtown Study at several points.

The upshot of these concerted national, state, and local developments has been a major shift (not without professional controversy) from primary emphasis on big, centralized mental hospitals toward a large-scale expansion and restructuring of psychiatric services around the small, decentralized, *neighborhood-based* community mental health center, particularly in poverty areas. By January 1978, some 650 of these new centers were reported in or nearing operation around the country, serving areas with a total population, in the past largely unserved, of some 90 million people.[20]

By the chances of converging events, then, the data of the Midtown Study, as of several other investigations conducted in the 1950s, surfaced at a time when they could help give impetus and direction to the creation of an institution that in design is new to the American community landscape. Rarely is it given a scientific literature to emerge at the critical time and place to share in such swift and tangible impacts on implemented national policy.

The questioner prompting the present account also presses the author to document any influences of *Mental Health in the Metropolis* in directions other than social policy. One such direction is recent scholarly criticism bearing on the moral quality of the economic foundations underpinning American society. An example is the use of the book to support the case made by philosopher Charles Lichtman in his paper

"Toward Community: A Criticism of Contemporary Capitalism."[21]
Lichtman there asserts:

The meticulous investigations in social psychiatry carried on in the past few years under the title of *The Midtown Manhattan Study* contribute massive support for the thesis of the inverse relationship between socioeconomic status and mental health.

The Midtown Study throws additional light on the issue of the effect of socioeconomic status on the value of psychiatric attention for various classes of patients.

[The Study implies] we are involved in nothing less than distributing the chances for physical and mental well-being on the morally invidious basis of economic class.

In another vein, a leader and critic in the field of public mental health has commented on the same general findings:

The survey methods have produced a very much more sensitive measure of mental health than was available before—sensitive enough to furnish, for the first time, an instrument to relate sociological status of communities to prevalence of symptoms . . . the recognition of the association between social class and the prevalence of mental illnesses as an important factor in the application of treatment methods has brought a new social consciousness to our specialty.[22]

A second direction of influence is the book's visible circulation in the channels of higher education. At the college level, for example, informed observers report that "the massive Midtown Manhattan investigation" is one of three cognate studies since 1939 that "are now required reading in every good undergraduate program in sociology or social psychology throughout the country."[23]

In reduced format, further, one or more chapters of the book have been reprinted in six popular anthologies of selected "readers" published between 1965 and 1970 for both graduate and undergraduate students.

From the total inputs of *Mental Health in the Metropolis* into higher education there is now evidence of penetration to several other academic strata:

1. Questions requiring detailed knowledge of the book's contents have appeared in written examinations prepared for (a) social science candidates for the Ph.D. degree; (b) candidates for Psychiatry Board Certification; (c) certified

psychiatrists voluntarily participating in the Test Program "Self Assessment of Psychiatric Knowledge and Skills," developed by the American Psychiatric Association.

2. In 1964, the computer made possible a new kind of scholarship service: a register of monographs and articles that have been cited in an international series of selected and diverse professional journalists.[24] Through 1976, this service identified a total of some 850 journal articles that have quoted or drawn from the pages of *Mental Health in the Metropolis*.

To my knowledge, no register of this kind exists as yet for similar citations appearing in the *books* of the period. However, from the monographs generated by social scientists, psychologists, psychiatrists, and social workers that have come to my attention, the citations of this Midtown volume in the whole corpus of relevant books are appearing at a correspondingly high rate. Included are the acknowledged influences on a fast-growing number of successor investigations in the United States, Western and Eastern Europe, that in some or other respects have replicated, or have adapted conceptual and technical tools of the Midtown Study, or have used its findings as a standard of comparison.[25]

Beyond such research articulating the sociological and psychological realms, there are the book's beginning signs of influence on physiologists probing the mediation of social processes through the human central nervous system.[26]

Finally, the Midtown Study has been cited by lawyers in several court cases. These center on the status of psychiatric patienthood and its prejudicial consequences for individual civil rights. Relevant here have been the Study's twin findings that (1) persons in ambulatory psychotherapy are not necessarily "mentally ill," either in a de facto or a de jure sense, and (2) others are psychologically disabled but have never come to the attention of a psychiatrist or clinical psychologist. The Study has therefore clarified that treatment status and mental disorder cannot always be equated.

Thus, in length and breadth of lay and professional reach, the first Midtown volume has had a trajectory well beyond its authors' abilities to have foreseen.

In preparing the present edition, the editors were mindful of what had embroiled the national scene in the decade since the original edition was written. It was summed up for us by columnist Tom Wicker in his introduction to the book *Great Songs of the Sixties.*[27] Drawing on a Bob Dylan song for his theme, he wrote:

The times, they were a-changin'—more swiftly and profoundly than ever before —and that was the central experience of the Sixties, whether one urged it on and welcomed it, or resisted and lamented. And it came to us all.

During the period a host of long-simmering domestic problems boiled over with demanding force, among them the deteriorating quality of the social and physical environment, particularly in the cities; the deepening iniquity of large-scale poverty, white as well as black, in the earth's most cornucopian economy; the worsening plight of the aged as a growing minority of socially dispossessed persons; the persisting status inequities between the sexes and between the races; and above all, the rising voice of young people as the insistent conscience of our complacent, "business-as-usual" institutions.

To some of these issues the Midtown Study spoke directly, and to some tangentially, wherever feasible applying as touchstone their possible mental health consequences. Moreover, the passage of time has given the Study two new dimensions as eyewitness history. First, the monograph records a sample of metropolitan Americans as caught "on camera," so to speak, during the mid-fifties. Subsequently, the book was itself caught up in and left its own discernible mark on the mental health currents of the sixties.

Accordingly, the new edition must present the original portrait substantially intact, albeit with some changes and additions[28] to improve its format and freshen its frame. To wit:

1. The Sociological Profile chapters have come forward into the "first act" of the book, ahead of the more technical Research Strategy chapters. They had been partially based on information from the only decennial population and housing census available when they were written, that is, the seventeenth of 1950. Where possible and appropriate these chapters at certain points have been selectively updated to various documented points in subsequent years.[29]

2. Since the pivotal chapters reporting the Midtown mental health findings were completed, new contributions on this front have appeared in the literature. To assess and incorporate all such contributions would require more extensive amplifications of these chapters than would have been practicably possible.

Accordingly, only a selected number of those directly relevant have been woven into the text or the footnote references of the present edition.

3. Five new chapters have been added.

4. Several of the original appendixes have diminished in relevance and have been deleted and a number of new ones have been substituted.

The present edition reemphasizes the vital balance between its sociological and psychological concerns. And to a new generation of readers, committed to viable social change, it now offers a case study of research that continues to speak to some of the unfinished business of American society.

POSTSCRIPT

In the first edition of this book, considerations of building and sustaining narrative tempo led the senior author to sidetrack to the footnotes many issues, observations, digressions, and asides. This practice is continued in the new portions of the present edition. Thus, beyond paying respects to cited sources, the notes at the end of each chapter are addressed to the reader on a large variety of matters pertinent to the Study and its many hundreds of participants.

NOTES

·For an excellent smorgasbord of morsels from the best of this vast literature see E. M. McCullough, ed., *As I Pass, O Manhattan*, 1956.

²Summarizing a major exhibition of paintings gathered thematically "About New York, Night and Day: 1915–1965," art critic John Canaday cryptically observed, "The trouble with the show is that New York turns out to be too big for it" (*New York Times,* October 19, 1965). Indeed, the foreword to the show's program says as much: "An exhibition dedicated like this one, to half a century of such a city, turns out to be an exploration of the unknown and the unknowable."

³*The Experimental Novel*, 1880, pp. 2, 232, 237.

⁴Zola's goal in the naturalistic novel was "to exhibit man living in social conditions . . . which he modifies daily, and in the heart of which he himself experiences a continual transformation. . . . Indeed our great study is just there, in the reciprocal effect of society on the individual, and the individual on society." Ibid., pp. 20, 21.

⁵Men of letters have long provided valuable impressionistic accounts of such places, ranging in recent decades from G. Hicks, *Small Town*, 1946, to R. Blythe, *Akenfield,* 1970, and A. Bailey, *In the Village,* 1971.

⁶To the sociologist, the metropolis best illustrates the relative predominance (over inevitable conflict and potential anarchy) of predictability and coordination in the billions of

seemingly autonomous decisions made by millions of individuals during the course of a single day.

[7]C. Booth, *Life and Labour of the People in London,* 9 vols., 1882–1897. Dickens' works illuminate the milieu of nineteenth-century London through the mirrors of his memorable cast of characters.

[8]J. F. Short, Jr., ed., *The Social Fabric of the Metropolis,* 1971. This is a "reader" of excerpts from numerous studies of highly capsulated aspects of Chicago.

[9]Particularly outstanding, although broadened to cover twenty-two counties in three states, are the nine volumes of the *New York Metropolitan Region Study,* conducted by the Harvard Graduate School of Public Administration during the late 1950s.

[10]For a popular, picture-and-text treatment of this decade on a national scale, see *America 1920–1930,* vol. 3 in *This Fabulous Century* series, 1969. For a scholarly work on a magisterial, worldwide scale see C. W. Ware et al., *The Twentieth Century,* 1966.

[11]C. W. Ware, *Greenwich Village,* 1935, p. 4.

[12]Ibid., p. vii.

[13]See in particular H. W. Zorbaugh, "The Shadow of the Skyscraper," in *The Gold Coast and the Slum,* 1929, pp. 1–16. Parenthetically, it may come as an etymological surprise that the term "skyscraper" was first applied not to the buildings "ascending topless into the bottom of a cloud" that sprang up late in the nineteenth century, but to the topsail furling the highest mast of the clipper ships that flourished early in that century.

[14]Around such scientists, in turn, there has crystallized the newly designated subspecialty of "psychiatric sociology." (L. Srole, "Sociology and Psychiatry: Mapping a Research Terrain"; C. Martins and L. M. DeAssis, eds., *Psiquiatria Social E America Latina,* 1971, pp. 259–267.) For semantic neatness, however, their collaborative undertakings with psychiatrists will here be arbitrarily referred to under the cognate rubric of "social psychiatry."

[15]D. C. Leighton, A. H. Leighton et al., *The Character of Danger,* 1963.

[16]As for impact on public policy, Lyndon Johnson's declared "War on Poverty" was of course an early tragic victim of the "undeclared" War on Vietnam.

[17]See *Poverty Studies in the Sixties,* U.S. Department of Health, Education, and Welfare, 1970. This is a partial, rather than a complete, bibliography of some 600 selected research publications.

[18]Preliminary Midtown findings were made available to the Commission's staff as early as 1956.

[19]Viola W. Bernard describes the activation as "this profound and widespread engagement in processes of change in the mental health area . . .": "Some Principles of Dynamic Psychiatry in Relation to Poverty," *American Journal of Psychiatry* 122 (September 1965): 254.

[20]The Midtown Study continues to highlight the distance still to be covered in this direction. Speaking to this issue, the Acting Director of the National Institute of Mental Health has written us as follows: "We are painfully aware of the need for further [professional] manpower growth in order to bridge the enormous gap between national treatment needs and service capabilities. Your work has been of great help in pointing up the dimensions of this gap." (Private communication dated February 29, 1972.)

[21]"An Occasional Paper on the Role of the Economic Order in the Free Society," published by the Center for the Study of Democratic Institutions, 1966.

[22]P. V. Lemkau, "Editor's Notebook," *American Journal of Psychiatry* 126 (May 1970): 1643–1644.

[23]S. Plog and R. Edgerton, eds., *Changing Perspectives in Mental Illness,* 1969, p. 312.

[24]*Science Citation Index,* "An International, Interdisciplinary Index to the Literatures of Science, Medicine, Agriculture, Technology and the Behavioral and Social Sciences."

[25]Three recent examples are (1) the "ten-years-later" follow-up investigation of mental health in American college students that is reported in the monograph *Youth into Maturity,* 1970, by Rachel Dunaway Cox; (2) *Aging and Mental Disorder in San Francisco,* 1967, by Marjorie Fiske Lowenthal et al.; and (3) *Distress in the City* (Boston), 1969, by William Ryan. See also "Current Research: The Second Polish–Czechoslavic Psychiatric Conference," *Social Science and Medicine* 3 (1969): 259–263.

[26]For a discussion of this overall trend see J. J. Schwab et al., "Psychosomatic Medicine and the Contemporary Social Scene," *American Journal of Psychiatry* 126 (1970): 108–118.

[27]Edited by M. Okun, 1970, p. 12.

[28]The senior author of the 1962 edition of this book, and co-editor of the present edition assumes sole responsibility for all revisions of the 1962 text.

[29]This will make for some shifts in time references across the period just preceding, during, and immediately following the 1952–1960 lifespan of the Midtown Study's original research team.

CHAPTER 2

INTRODUCTION
ALEXANDER H. LEIGHTON

The Rennie Series, of which this volume is the first, is the fruit of a major effort in a new field of psychiatry. Prior to World War II, a few behavioral scientists had for some time been interested in the effects of social and cultural environment on mental health, but within psychiatry itself relatively little attention had been paid to the subject. There were, of course, some exceptions to this, a notable one being Adolf Meyer.

After the war a number of research projects concerned with understanding the sociocultural aspects of etiology in psychiatric disorder came into existence. Some gave emphasis to the significance of cultural differences and some to the patterns of stress and strain in modern living, as exemplified in the industrial setting or as mediated through the family.

This upsurge of interest was undoubtedly influenced by the war. The reasons were manifold: some were diffuse and part of the general shaking up experienced by people everywhere; some reflected greater awareness of the severe emotional problems confronting mankind in a changing society. Another factor was the apparently high prevalence of psychiatric disorder found in the course of selection for military service. Moreover, psychiatrists, in caring for the health of military units rather than individuals only, noticed striking differences evidently due to conditions of living, battle, and morale and were confronted with the problems of rehabilitating those who had been psychiatrically disabled.

Thomas A. C. Rennie was one of those in the forefront of this interest and endeavor. A graduate of Harvard Medical School and with three years of training in internal medicine, he studied psychiatry under Adolf

Meyer at Johns Hopkins in 1931. While at Hopkins he was mainly interested in therapy and teaching, yet he devoted some time to a study of schizophrenia and produced a book on the subject. In 1941 he accepted a position as Associate Professor in the Department of Psychiatry at Cornell University Medical College in New York. Here, in addition to his teaching and clinical duties, he was drawn into activities connected with the war, serving, for example, on the Army Advisory Committee of Greater New York. This led naturally to an interest in veterans, especially in their rehabilitation; and this in turn brought him into contact with many community problems and projects. At one time or another he was Director of the Division of Rehabilitation, National Association for Mental Hygiene; Chairman of the Professional Committee, National Association for Mental Health; Member of the Board of Trustees, American Foundation for Mental Hygiene; Chairman of the New York Community Mental Health Board; Coeditor of the *International Journal of Social Psychiatry;* and Consultant in Psychiatry at the Franklin Delano Roosevelt Veterans Administration Hospital, Montrose, New York. He was coauthor of two books, *Mental Health in Modern Society* and *Jobs and the Man,* as well as of numerous articles that reflected these activities and interests. (References for these publications may be found in Appendix B.)

Under the stimulus of such work, Rennie conceived the Midtown Study and began its planning early in 1950. He was given the full and imaginative support of Professor Oskar Diethelm of the Department of Psychiatry, Cornell University Medical College, and later in the same year he was appointed Professor of Psychiatry (Social Psychiatry), the first such position in the United States, so far as is known. Rennie visualized the project first in very broad terms as aimed at the study of the extent of mental disorder and of resources that might be needed, and as concerned with some experiments in public education. His Charter Day Address at the New York Hospital on May 9, 1950, constituted a preliminary formulation of the project.

It required two years of steady effort before the project was adequately financed and fully under way as a research operation. The fact that such an original, massive, and expensive study came into existence at all is evidence of Rennie's persistence, tact, and enthusiasm. Recognizing the interdisciplinary nature of the task, he turned to a number of consultants. In later years he frequently mentioned the debt he felt he owed to them and, indeed, wrote out a retrospective statement to this effect. The particular individuals are accordingly noted in the authors' acknowledgments (Appendix A of this book), but it seems fair to say here that Rennie himself possessed a rare capacity to make use of the variety of advice and recommendations he received and to synthesize them into something that was his own.

On May 21, 1956, Rennie died from a cerebral hemorrhage. This was a sad loss deeply felt by his many friends. It was also a loss from which the Midtown Manhattan Study could not fully recover. Fortunately, all the field work of the study had been accomplished, so that what remained was a major part of the analysis and the reporting of results and their implications.

The primary members of the Midtown Study who were available to continue the work on a full-time basis were Professor Leo Srole, a sociologist, Professor Marvin K. Opler, an anthropologist, and Professor Thomas S. Langner, a sociologist. Those available only part time were the late Dr. Price Kirkpatrick and Dr. Stanley T. Michael, the two psychiatrists who, with Rennie, had carried out the clinical aspects of the work. Because of my previous association with the project as a consultant to Rennie, and because I was engaged in the Stirling County Study, which had somewhat similar objectives, I was asked by Dr. Diethelm to help finish the work. The position was defined as director and coordinator, rather than as an author.

From 1956 until 1960, the analysis and reporting went forward with the main load of writing being carried by the sociologists. The psychiatrists, particularly Dr. Michael, acted as discussants and critics, especially with reference to the clinical viewpoint. Because of differences in orientation stemming from their various disciplines, the authors had to spend much time in working through to mutual understanding and hammering out acceptable modifications. The completion of this volume is a testimony to their patience and determination.

Implicit in the analysis was the need for many decisions on appropriate targets for investigation. While the design of the field work as established by Rennie defined certain objectives and set limits to subsequent analysis, the range of data obtained was so extensive and the number of possible questions and conclusions that could be investigated so enormous that successive choices had to be made in order to keep the project within the bounds of the attainable. Added to this was the nature of the findings themselves and the promptings they gave to emphasize one rather than another line of thought and interest. As a result of these conditions and influences the work bears the stamp of much that has transpired since Rennie's death. It probably differs in many respects from what he would have done, and it undoubtedly lacks qualities which his genius would have contributed. We hope, however, that he would have been pleased with it and that the volumes as a whole are a suitable memorial to his vision, his zest for living, and his compassion for humanity.

Rennie left behind no specific drafts for any portion of this volume, with the exception of the chapter that follows. Some time in the spring of 1956, knowing that his life might not extend much longer, he wrote out what he intended to say at the beginning of the book. This is not now entirely apposite to the volume, nor can we think of it as what he would write if he were living today. Nevertheless, since it shows many of his outstanding qualities, and since it is the last word we have from him, it is given (substantially) as he set it down.

New York, New York, 1960

CHAPTER 3

INTRODUCTION

Thomas A. C. Rennie

The fact that psychiatrists are now looking to the community for the answer to some of the problems of mental illness and their causation is a logical outgrowth of the development of psychiatry itself. The psychiatrist as a physician is traditionally trained in the intensive study of a given individual—his or her biological makeup, personality structure, family background, and all areas of the person's life, such as education, occupation, marriage, sexual strivings, ambitions, and disappointments. In the study of a given individual, the method used is the biographical one, which gives particular attention to the series of life events beginning with birth and extending throughout the life span. Much attention is given to childhood events as being of major importance in determining the prevailing patterns of reactions, feelings, attitudes, and ways of interpersonal reacting.

As psychiatry has grown in knowledge of general psychopathology and its causation, more and more time is required in the preparation of the psychiatrist for the mastery of this extensive body of data. The young psychiatrist must also develop tools of interviewing and communication and must sharpen his sensitivity to the overtones and undertones of the patient's utterances. He must master an array of techniques for the study of personality, as well as develop skills in the therapy of disturbed persons. He sometimes uses physiologic methods, chemicals, and other procedures, but the main tool with which he must acquire skill is that of psychotherapy. This gives him little time in the three basic years of his training to explore the world beyond the hospital or the clinic or to engage himself in the broader aspects of his eventual role as a member of the community, both as a citizen and as a therapist.

All too soon the average psychiatrist finds himself drawn into a variety of functions in the community wherein his skills are called upon for interpretation, for public education, for preventive services, and for community leadership. He soon finds that a great many people have an intense interest in the problems of mental health and that persons other than psychiatrists have a vital role to play in the promotion of sound mental health, the provision of good hospital treatment, and the increasing creation of preventive services. Very soon he finds that other intelligent and thoughtful people need to profit by his insights so that they may perform their functions more wisely. He soon finds his advice sought by such diverse groups in the community as lawyers and judges seeking to administer the law with constructive wisdom, ministers seeking to advise and counsel with some basic understanding of human behavior, teachers trying to educate the whole person toward the end of sound personality and character development, doctors and public health nurses who must deal every day with sick and emotionally troubled people, and intelligent groups of lay persons bent upon strengthening the adaptive capacities of the people—notably groups such as parent-teacher associations, men's and women's clubs, neighborhood houses, boys' clubs, the Red Cross, and the Travelers Aid Society. As a result of the phenomenal growth of public interest in psychiatry, the enormous number of magazine articles and books written for lay audiences on that subject, and the growing interest of creative artists in the contributions of Freud and other pioneers in psychoanalysis, we in the United States are now witnessing the growth of a great many lay citizen groups banded together for knowledge and action. This development of the mental health movement began with Clifford Beers and progressed for forty years to the establishment of the National Association for Mental Health, together with countless state and community mental health organizations. We have reached the point in psychiatric development where many psychiatrists feel deeply impelled to turn their interest outward from the individual patient to the family, the community, and the total cultural scene. Some of these developments and the way in which allied professional and nonprofessional people can be helpful have been sketched by the author in a prior publication, *Mental Health in Modern Society.*[1]

We are witnessing at present in this country a steady increase in programs for public education in mental health matters. Unfortunately much of this activity is conducted in a vacuum, since we know all too little of what people know and do not know about mental health, what personal anxieties lie behind their resistance, what prejudices and misconceptions stand in the way of their learning, and what anxieties may be stirred up in them by the very attempts at education which are undertaken so enthusiastically and vigorously. In actuality we know that there is an enormous misunderstanding of all matters pertaining to mental health on the part of great segments of the American public. The study conducted in Louisville, Kentucky, by Elmo Roper and associates[2] and a nationwide survey of public attitudes by Shirley Star[3] give clear indication that great confusion prevails, that most people have literally no understanding that mental illness is an illness,[4] and that fewer yet have any idea of when help is needed or where it can be found.

Clearly, mental health educators need to ask themselves a few basic questions: Who is being educated? What do they want and need to know? What is the proper time for the presenting of information? What is the effect of the information given? What are the best tools for the dissemination of mental health information? Much genuine basic research remains to be done in this area.

A second major problem which faces public health officials throughout the country is that of determining what resources are needed for the treatment of mental health problems in a given community. Certainly the most reliable findings are those of Roth and Luton[5] and Lemkau, Tietze, and Cooper[6] in two field studies made to determine the prevalence of mental health disorders. The study undertaken in the Midtown area of Manhattan by the authors should supplement these earlier ones. It indicates that the need for health services is far greater than has been previously realized. Therefore, similar studies should prove valuable in planning the services required by a given population group. They not only should determine this on the basis of the total number of persons likely to need psychiatric help, but should give real indication of the relative amount of help needed by various subgroups.

It is known that frequent physical illness is commonly associated with a high incidence of psychiatric disorder. Furthermore, we have come to know that psychoneurotic and psychosomatic illness occurs in clusters within certain families and that such persons and families can be identified.[7] This clearly points the way to preventive psychiatry at its best. If programs of prevention in the field of psychiatry are to become workable realities, they must be based on family and community studies which indicate the danger areas, the problem persons in families, and the kind of resources needed for a truly preventive program.

We must realize that psychiatric disorder occurs in persons nurtured in a particular family constellation and living in a highly specific sociocultural environment. In the field of delinquency and antisocial behavior this point of view generally prevails, and the research worker in these fields is apt to put stronger emphasis on the understanding of the total cultural environment. However, the fact that certain sociocultural environments may well be conducive to a higher incidence of psychiatric disorder is not generally known. If psychiatry is truly to move into a vigorous period of real preventive work, it must begin to look beyond the individual to the forces within the social environment which contribute to the personal dilemma.

Thus it appears that the time has come to establish a working relationship between the social scientist and the psychiatrist; their cooperation will inevitably lead to new possibilities of research into human behavior.

To set up research projects such as the one reported in this volume in a field so vast, encompassing so many variables, is a formidable task; it has only recently been undertaken by a few investigators determined to define methodologies and come to grips with the endless facets of the problem. The research group faces the difficulty of dealing simultaneously with the whole set of operational forces, while keeping the major ones clearly in mind and attempting to reduce the task to encompassable limits. Such a team must first come to understand each other's discipline and become acquainted with the major theories, hypotheses, and facts of each; they must cross the semantic barrier of technical language which often obscures each member's contribution, even though the team ultimately comes to understand that they are often talking about the same phenomenon obscured by overly specific linguistics.

The next step is the pooling of all relevant data for the formulation of a set of testable hypotheses which can then be reduced to a specific research design. In our project a series of research hypotheses dealing with sociocultural factors and mental illness was derived.

The formula finally arrived at places psychiatric disorder and intra-psychic malfunction as a set of dependent variables. The independent or relatively fixed variables are those of cultural background, socioeconomic status, ethnic identification, and the attributes of urban-rural living. In our own urban study we are concerned with the many variables imposed by urbanism itself—as well as the whole range of unforeseen experiences that befall man in terms of exogenous disease and physical malfunction. We hypothesize that these factors are significant for personality stability or maladjustment.

To forge tools and instruments to accumulate systematically such data on cross sections of the population is one task of a social psychiatrist. In psychiatric practice we see mainly the top of the iceberg—the known sick—those who seek help. Social psychiatry must concern itself also with the submerged part of the iceberg—those persons in society who never seek psychiatric therapy or who find no such help available. To this end, therefore, the social psychiatrist's methodology must include techniques for the systematic psychiatric study of a sample of persons in a given community. Because of the very nature of the task, his psychiatric tools will be less sharp than in the hospital or office, since it is manifestly impossible to conduct deep psychiatric explorations of such a sample. He must rely heavily on validated psychological tests and questions. Furthermore, he must profit by the experience of the statistician, who will help him to draw a workable sample which will presumably be representative of the whole. In our own study a rather far-reaching questionnaire method was utilized for the study of individuals selected at random and of sufficient number to permit generalizations. It was administered by experienced, clinically trained persons with psychiatric social work and clinical psychology backgrounds.

The findings of the various similar researches contemporaneously under way in such different settings as rural Nova Scotia, urban Syracuse, New Haven, New York, and Baltimore and the possibility of sharing and comparing such diverse data should enable us to move forward in the understanding of the total forces significant in human adaptation.

This book, then, is the story of one such community research project which will attempt to define the problem, give a picture of our struggles to arrive at the appropriate methodologies, and report the findings of our community studies in *Midtown,* an area of New York City unequaled for its heterogeneity and diversity of urban living.[8]

New York, New York, 1956

NOTES

[1]Thomas A. C. Rennie and Luther E. Woodward, *Mental Health in Modern Society,* The Commonwealth Fund, 1948.

[2]Elmo Roper, *People's Attitudes Concerning Mental Health: A Study Made in the City of Louisville,* 1950.

[3]Shirley A. Star, "The Public's Ideas About Mental Illness," National Opinion Research Center, mimeographed (University of Chicago: 1955).

[4]From the Editors: That public understanding has changed considerably since these words were written is suggested in Crocetti et al., "Are the Ranks Closed? Attitudinal Social Distance and Mental Illness," *American Journal of Psychiatry* 127 (March 1971): 1121–1127.

[5]William F. Roth and Frank B. Luton, "The Mental Health Program in Tennessee," *American Journal of Psychiatry* 99 (1943).

[6]P. Lemkau, C. Tietze, and M. Cooper, "Mental Hygiene Problems in an Urban District" (three papers), *Mental Hygiene* 26 (January 1942); *Mental Hygiene* 26 (April 1942); *Mental Hygiene* 27 (April 1943).

[7]Jean Downes and Katherine Simon, "Characteristics of Psychoneurotic Patients and Their Families as Revealed in a General Morbidity Study," *Psychosomatic Medicine* 15, (September-October, 1954): 463–476; Jean Downes, "Chronic Disease among Spouses," *Milbank Memorial Fund Quarterly* 25 (October 1947): 334–358; Jean Downes, "Social and Environmental Factors in Illness," *Backgrounds of Social Medicine,* Milbank Memorial Fund, 1949, pp. 64–83.

[8]This chapter is taken in part from Thomas A. C. Rennie, "Social Psychiatry: A Definition," *International Journal of Social Psychiatry* 1 (1955).

Part II

Midtown:
A Sociological
Profile

CHAPTER 4

THE SCENE AND THE PEOPLE
LEO SROLE

PRESCRIPT

The investigation focused upon Midtown can, in a special sense, be likened to an intensive case study. Here a community rather than an individual is the case.

However, if it is to be understood in its mental health innards, this subject must first be grasped in its salient characteristics as a social entity. In other words, we must apprehend it as a rather special sort of population that (1) has many historically differentiated group and subgroup segments, (2) resides in a particular kind of physical locale, (3) interacts, to a certain extent, in its own complicated network of institutions, (4) exhibits diverse life-styles that revolve in "grooves of accelerating change," and (5) is enveloped by the sociopsychological climate pervading the rock-cropped island on which it roots.

The immediate effort here is to portray Midtown to the reader as it strikes the encompassing eye of the sociological observer. This purely descriptive purpose, however, is also a means to a larger end, namely, placing Midtown in the taxonomy of American communities on criteria more weighty than surface appearances. Only when this is done can we perhaps judge what Midtown represents as a community entity, and thereby consider to what population universe the findings of this study can be generalized.

The gathering of data for this purpose was entirely carried out by research aides, sociology students, and a cadre of community volunteers[1] under the direction of the present writer. As responsibilities to other research operations permitted, we adapted two social science traditions of community study. The first is to be found in ecological and demographic investigations conducted in a number of large cities. These projects extract their data principally from documentary sources in federal, state, and municipal government agencies.[2] We too drew from such documents.

The second tradition rests on sociocultural studies of relatively *small* communities, with data collected at first hand by extensive participant observation and interviews with informed residents.[3] The size of our community, as well as the higher-priority claims of our mental health field operations, forced us to compromise with this research model. More specifically, we shortened the reach for direct and informal participation in community circles, and instead drew testimony from two special eyewitness sources. One source was the extensive published works of gifted observer-commentators on the Manhattan scene, some by writers for the incomparable local press.[4] Many of these, in fact, were long-time Midtown residents. The other source was a large representative sample of Midtown adults who were queried on lines relevant both to our community delineation and to exploratory mental health goals. Compared to other studies of this particular kind, therefore, our community profile data are necessarily more selective than comprehensive and more extensive than intensive.

THE CONTEXT

Grasp of a great city in its "unspeakable complexity," as a *New York Times* editorial has phrased it, poses problems even for the observing lifelong resident. Sociologists have also spoken to this point: "It is apparent that the [city's] complexity of physical layout and structure is immense; that [its] social structure is so complicated that even research teams of sociologists can do little more than grasp the outlines of significant groups and their interrelationships. And who ordinarily can hope to know or appreciate the whole social history of a city?"[5]

The editors of a national magazine, dedicating an entire issue to New

York City, caution us in a related vein: "What stuns at first in New York is the overwhelming *number* of small worlds (music, clothing industry, shipping, the United Nations, theater, etc., etc.) which overlap and intertwine in one city, so that for the newcomer who does not recognize the threads, does not see the pattern each world forms for itself, the city is simply megalopolis, confusion compounded, chaos."[6]

A small-town visitor from Mississippi, as quoted by the *Times,* saw through this "confusion" in terms of a highly perceptive image:

New York to me is like a huge piece of abstract art. There's a little bit of this here and a little bit of that there. At first it doesn't make much sense. But after a while you see that everything fits.

Confronting a city less than half the size of New York, as encompassing an observer as John Gunther could concede: "About Chicago itself there is so much to be said that the task of compression becomes hopeless."[7]

This task may seem somewhat more hopeful for Midtown, a single residential world harboring only one-fiftieth part of the New York City population. But Midtown is a flesh and bone segment of the City and cannot possibly be delineated or encompassed apart from it.

Thornton Wilder's memorable drama *Our Town* opens with a monologue by a stage manager-commentator, who identifies the play's locale as "Grover's Corners, New Hampshire, the United States of America, Western Hemisphere, the Earth, the Solar System, the Universe, the Mind of God."

Reversing and telescoping this expanding order somewhat, we might gradually "zero in" on Midtown, starting from a national point of departure. If we were to draw a population map from this vantage point, we could first indicate that peppered thinly across the country at midcentury were farming families aggregating some 25 million people; in small clusters widely scattered among these were another 30 million persons in nonfarming families gathered in thousands of rural villages and "Grover's Corners" towns with fewer than 2,500 inhabitants; both, together, aggregate about 36 percent of the national population.[8]

At the opposite pole from such extreme human dispersion, we could next mark the fourteen *standard metropolitan areas* with highly compact populations exceeding 1 million each.[9] These large metropolitan concentrations, their combined land space figuratively compressible into one of the smallest of the fifty states, held a total of 44 million people, or almost 30 percent of the American populace. Among these, the largest metropolitan complex of all comprised seventeen counties designated by the Census Bureau as the "New York-Northeastern New Jersey area." Here have crowded a population of almost 13 million, its workers representing about one in every ten of the entire United States labor force.

Wedged into this 4,000-square-mile topography is the corporate entity of New York City, covering 8 percent of the area's land, but occupied by 60 percent of its people. The colossus among American cities, New York, within its 320 square miles of land, continues to house a population of nearly 8 million, exceeding that of all but three of the Union's fifty states. This bare statistic, of course, misses the salient fact that the City is functionally a generating, terminating, or put-through point of all manner of traffics, human and symbolic, for the region, the nation, and the world,[10] a fact we need hardly pause to document with details.

Of decisive importance to this network of far-flung traffic confluences is the compression of most of the City's diverse economic functions within its hub borough of Manhattan, an island of twenty-two square miles (one-fourth of it man-made), too small to be separately delineated on any map of the United States. At the time of the Study, the City's working population[11] approached an estimated 4 million people, including the self-employed. Of these, we estimated about 2.5 million, or almost 67 percent, conducted their work in Manhattan. To appreciate the specialized nature of this concentration, we might briefly note a few of the major fields which engaged Manhattan's working (employed and self-employed) population. An estimated 375,000 were in finance, insurance, or real estate. Approximately 325,000 worked in retail shops and department stores, perhaps another 250,000 in wholesale trade. Over 200,000 were employees of government—municipal, state, and federal. Nearly 400,000 were in the "service" category of functions. Employees of manufacturing enterprises numbered 550,000 people, including office personnel as well as factory workers.[12] Obviously, this is not an inclusive list, but it is sufficient to highlight a characteristic common to the core of big cities, and reaching the highest point of specialized development in the

"The towers of Manhattan cast their shadows not only over the entire nation but everywhere on the globe. For New York City has become the crucible and nerve center, the focus and symbol of man's civilization on earth."

Manhattan economy. We refer to the advance to dominance of the administrative, distributive, and services functions and the retreat to outlying areas of all but the lightest forms of factory production. In the imagery of the Manhattan workaday street scene, the leather briefcase has long since displaced the tin lunch box.

We have noted the concentration of the City's working population within Manhattan. However, of the City's total office floor footage in 1970, over 90 percent was confined to an area comprising about 1 percent of its land space, namely, a one-mile-wide strip of Manhattan that we designate the *Central Business Section*.[13] In this narrow belt, which has been called the heart of the national economy, regularly work almost 2.1 million people.

For briefer transient purposes of business, shopping,[14] recreation,[15] or other services, there also converge here throngs of New Yorkers, suburbanites, and out-of-town visitors, numbering on peak days perhaps 1 million persons. All told, about 3 million people commute into this section daily. Taken together with some 500,000 residents within or around its flanks, plus occupants of the section's 100,000 transient-hotel rooms, the total street traffic,[16] in an area of some four square miles, during the average week day exceeds the entire 3.4 million residential population of Chicago in 1970.

Sheltering most of this mass of human beings, during daylight or evening hours, are the section's thousands of commercial buildings. Seen at a distance, these form Manhattan's vaulting skyline, the City's craggy promontory that has probably inspired more graphic art and photography, poetry, and prose[17] than perhaps any other man-made phenomenon in history.

Midtown, our portrait subject and our object of research study, is a Manhattan district almost wholly residential in character. From its position adjoining the midtown portion of the Central Business Section[18] comes the rationale for its pseudonym.[19] That position also defines its general location as more or less midway up the length of Manhattan Island, and through that locus, its stand near the business and traffic vortex of New York City and the New York-Northeastern New Jersey metropolitan region. However, from the inclusive national perspective, Midtown, with its estimated 170,000 residents, at the time roughly equivalent in size to the population of Hartford, Connecticut, or Nashville, Tennessee, can also be viewed as a microscopic slice of the large segment of America that inhabits the biggest metropolitan areas.[20] ·

HOUSING: DENSITY

One direct consequence of its location for Midtown can be read on the yardstick of gross population density. Figured in terms of individuals per square mile, the 1970 population density of the United States as a whole is 60, of the New York-Northeastern New Jersey metropolitan area 3,300, and of New York City proper about 25,000. However, the accessibility of transportation to the pyramiding economic and recreational facilities over the small patch of Manhattan's Central Business Section has had strikingly different consequences for the City's five boroughs. For example, in Staten Island, the borough most distant from Manhattan and until 1965 accessible only by ferryboat ride over a five-mile expanse of harbor, gross population density per square mile in 1970 was 4,800. As the borough that has the most recently constructed rapid transit lines to Manhattan, Queens has a density of 17,000 people per square mile. With the oldest subway arteries to Manhattan, the Bronx and Brooklyn have gross population densities of about 34,000. For Manhattan itself, gross population density figures to about 70,000 per square mile.

Gross population density is calculated on the basis of an area's total land space; the term is an understatement when, as in the case of Manhattan, most of the land is used for purposes other than habitation. *Net population density* is calculated on the basis of total land area in parcels put to residential use. Applied to Manhattan, average net population density is estimated to be 350,000 people per square mile of residential land.[21] Or, stated in terms that can be more readily grasped, on the average 100-by-100-foot residential plot there live about 125 individuals.

Looking out from the observatory of the Empire State Building, towering above Manhattan's Central Business Section, population densities from the City's rim inward can be seen increasing progressively toward Manhattan's core residential areas immediately adjacent. On this panorama, Manhattan's Central Business Section assumes the likeness of a gigantic geodemographic magnet, its population attraction being strongest at its immediate borders and diminishing more or less directly with increasing distance and travel time. This magnetism will repeatedly be found to be a key to understanding the characteristics of Midtown as a locale, as a population, and as a community.

If resident population density climbs with proximity to the office skyscrapers of Manhattan, this of course also reflects the mounting vertical dimension of its residential housing. A partial measure of this dimension is found in a classification of residential structures according to the number of dwelling units they contain. Table 4–1 gives the classification applied and the distributions for the City's boroughs and Midtown at the time of this Study, as estimated by interpolations from the Seventeenth and Eighteenth Decennial Census reports.

TABLE 4–1.   DISTRIBUTION OF RESIDENTIAL BUILDINGS IN MIDTOWN AND THE FIVE BOROUGHS BY NUMBER OF DWELLINGS

	Number of dwellings per building			
	1–2	3–4	5 and over	Total
Staten Island	84%	7%	9%	100%
Queens	56	8	36	100
Brooklyn	32	18	50	100
Bronx	15	7	78	100
Manhattan	2	2	96	100
Midtown	3	2	95	100

We note that at one extreme the populations of Staten Island and Queens lived predominantly in one- or two-family houses; and that at the other extreme, the people of Midtown, like those of Manhattan generally, made their homes almost entirely in buildings with five or more dwellings. The observant visitor to Midtown at that time could fill out the picture in far more graphic detail. He would encounter three- or four-story single-entrance structures, some few occupied by one or two families, many divided into six or more dwellings. The greatest part of the residential land space was occupied, row on row, block after block, by five- and six-story multi-entrance walk-up apartment houses. Of

". . . horizontal compression and vertical stacking . . . unbroken walls of brick, mortar, and glass."

course, these two types of buildings were also found in high-density boroughs like the Bronx and Brooklyn. However, far more prevalent in Midtown and residential Manhattan generally, and not reflected in the Census Bureau's classification, were the elevator-served "cliff-dweller" apartment buildings, in some new instances reaching upward to 50 floors.[22] According to press reports, land for the newest of these structures was acquired at a cost varying between $100 and $225 a square foot, suggesting something of the enormous pressure of demand for living space.

The visitor's eye would catch such additional details as buildings set close to or flush with the front sidewalk, "elbowing" each other at the flanks with little or no intervening space (some occupying 90 percent of the entire site), to form almost unbroken walls of brick, mortar, and glass. If he explored their interiors systematically to check the number of rooms in their dwellings, he would find overall that only about one-fourth of the households had five or more rooms (that is, two or more bedrooms), approximately one-fourth had four rooms,[23] another one-fourth had three rooms, and the remainder were about equally divided between one (or "one and a half") and two rooms. Accordingly, about three in every four dwellings provided no more than one room designed for sleeping purposes.[24] From such observations, the visitor would come away with a vivid sense of record population density achieved by both horizontal compression and vertical "stacking" in Midtown's housing.

HOUSING: SOCIAL CLASS HISTORY

Another striking aspect of Midtown's housing requires a rapid retrospective glance over Manhattan's economic and social history. By way of preliminary, several decisive facts must be taken into account.

First, separated from Brooklyn, Queens, and Staten Island by wide rivers that until 1883 could be crossed only on small ferryboats, Manhattan was by statute an independent city until 1898.[25] Long before that, when the other boroughs were still congeries of scattered rural villages and suburban satellites, Manhattan had become the nation's first city in population size and economic power.

Spirit of Manhattan by Daniel French, formerly on the south pylon at the approach to the Manhattan Bridge, now at the entrance of the Brooklyn Museum. As described in a catalog of works of art owned by the City:

"A colossal draped female figure in granite, seated, wearing a castellated crown, with breastplate indicative of defense, and holding in her right hand a winged globe suggestive of Dominion and Progress, her right foot resting on a treasure box. At her right are emblems of art and material prosperity, and on her left the prows of three ships representing Commerce, and a peacock as a symbol of Pride."

Second, through the whole of the nineteenth century Manhattan's bursting economic expansion created a large class of wealthy families that it held residentially clasped to itself. This group, in turn, placed its indelible stamp upon the Island, to a degree probably unmatched by its counterparts in other American cities.

With enormous economic thrust, Manhattan's population soared from 96,000 in 1810 to 515,000 in 1860 to a high-water mark of 2,300,000 in 1910. This seam-splitting growth was channeled in the only direction open— northward on the tight corridor of the Island, with rather noteworthy consequences.

During the late eighteenth and early nineteenth centuries, most of Manhattan's work places were crowded around the southern point of the Island, and nearby, along the edges of both rivers principally, were gathered the homes of the "gentility."

The harbor's gateway to the hinterland via the new Erie Canal brought a surge in Manhattan's maritime industry, which spread northward, lacing the Island's waterfronts with wharves, shipyards, warehouses, ship chandlers, and the like. These in turn displaced the mansions of the well-to-do, who soon resettled on the nearby northern residential outskirts at a point roughly midway between the East and Hudson rivers.

The business center (of finance, wholesale and retail trade, and related fields) in the meantime was likewise expanding northward, and also on an axis approximately halfway between the bordering rivers. There it soon caught up with and dislodged the second area of "fine homes," often converting the latter for business purposes,[26] now forcing the affluent further north in a leapfrog to the margin where Manhattan's new streets and avenues had not yet leveled the wilderness and primitive rural slums beyond.[27]

This pattern, to be repeated again and again[28] through 150 years, involved two elements: (1) the persistence of wealthy families in resettling more or less cohesively midway between the rivers (of course within easy travel distance of their offices), and (2) the northward drive of the business section on the same axis, to push the "elite" residential district steadily ahead in a compact three-block-wide lane that centered first on lower Broadway, next on lower Fifth Avenue, and then along the reaches of Fifth Avenue progressively above.[29]

When this long migratory trail of the best homes reached Central Park (Fifty-ninth Street) just before the turn of the twentieth century, with the Central Business Section continuing to advance in the rear, the moneyed classes began to move around the Park, first to the west and later to the east, fanning out from there toward the flanking rivers. In the years before World War I, with Manhattan's empty land consumed, this group, for the first time on a large scale, started to abandon the traditional "castle" of the one-family town house and took to the high apartment buildings.[30] This was a development that Bostonian Oliver Wendell Holmes incisively characterized as "intentional domicide."

The historic pattern just reviewed,[31] necessarily in highly simplified form, was of course marked by local deviations arising from special circumstances we cannot pause to describe here. However, their effect was to divert the obliterating movement of the Central Business Section around certain "exclusive" residential "islands" that have survived (now largely converted into apartment houses) behind the front line of its advance.[32]

Moreover, with Manhattan solidly built up, in recent decades we find whole blocks of middle- and even low-rent housing being remodeled or demolished and transformed into high-rent areas. As compared with the situation a century ago, therefore, the residential cohesion of Manhattan's top income group has now been broken into a number of scattered enclaves, large and small, old and new, but all within short travel distance of the Central Business Section.

This summary account has sketched the roots of a central fact about Midtown as it is today, namely, that within its boundaries are to be found a portion of one of the largest of these enclaves and a scattering of several smaller ones, all the end result of a long process in Manhattan's development, and all reflecting the silver cord of nurturance that binds their residents to work places beneath the Business Section's skyline.

To turn the historical view toward the other end of the social spectrum, the "hewers of wood" in the swelling Manhattan community of the early nineteenth century were first provided barracklike quarters in "breweries, old warehouses, or any structure with four walls and a roof"[33] under conditions approximating steerage in the ships that brought most of them to the City.[34] Then, at about mid-century emerged the prototype of the five- to six-floor walk-up tenements devised by jerry-building experts at crowding a parcel of land.[35] These were predominantly constructed on open land adjoining the river frontages of maritime docks and all their appendages. As the laboring population multiplied and remultiplied, the tenements spread steadily northward (in strips several blocks wide), along one river toward the upper reaches of the Island. Needless to say, access to place of employment was a consideration even larger for callused workmen than for the well-groomed businessmen who, in the earlier period, appeared at their offices in top hat and morning coat. In this light, the prodigious nineteenth-century growth of Manhattan's economy—a giant cramped into a procrustean space by natural barriers on all sides—forced poor and rich alike, in an era before the development of rapid transit, to settle hard on the flanks of its habitat. With the coming of new forms of urban transportation, Manhattan's economy by its sheer giantism continued to hold its teeming population density and residential congestion—somewhat changed, to be sure, since 1910, as the land base in residential use has shrunk and the land base in business (and institutional) use has swelled further.

Tenement housing during the period of our field research was still heavily represented in Midtown, although it had been receding since 1930, either to be replaced by apartment buildings or to be remodeled for middle- or high-income occupancy. As to the condition of Midtown's remaining low-rental tenements, we have indications from the United States census of housing reports.

By census criteria a dwelling was substandard if it (1) lacked a private bathroom, or (2) lacked running water, or (3) was dilapidated, that is, "run-down or neglected, or of inadequate original construction, so that it does not provide adequate shelter." By these criteria, 18.7 percent of Midtown's occupied dwellings at the time of the Study were in substandard condition. The corresponding figure for Manhattan as a whole was 18.5 percent. It may also be added that among Midtown's 190 residential blocks, 35 of these had between 20 and 94 percent of their dwellings in such condition, most of them to be found in tenement-type housing dating, in many cases, to the nineteenth-century era of "dismal, claptrap" construction.

In the latter half of the nineteenth century, the prospering middle class was predominantly accommodated in the solid rows of three- or four-floor "brownstone-and-stoop" structures[36] characteristic as well of other seaboard cities during the period. In terms of land space occupied, these were also a highly prevalent type of housing in Midtown during the period of study. However, many had either been remodeled for high-income occupants or had been cut into smaller dwellings for low-income families. By and large, therefore, Midtown (like Manhattan as a whole) in its overall housing shortage relative to demand had, and still has, a shortage of middle-bracket dwellings. Its remaining middle-income group remains scattered among the better-kept brownstones, the older, smaller apartment houses, and the refurbished tenements.

POPULATION COMPOSITION

From the above housing review it can be gathered that within its great population density Midtown, like the rest of Manhattan at the time of the Study, presented a picture of enormous socioeconomic diversity, its residents covering the entire range from families with social-register lineage—some associated with the top fortunes in the land—to families quartered in tenements near or at the slum level.

Originally, these social extremes were settled at opposite sides of the Study area. Subsequently both expanded toward the center. Where their housing converged, the effect was often a juxtaposition, back to back and even side to side, of downgraded brownstones, near-slum tenements, upgraded brownstone townhouses, and luxury apartments.[37] Such cheek-by-jowl contrasts have grown in recent decades. Builders for the wealthy, having discovered the light, air, and vista advantages of the riverfront— once occupied by wharves, warehouses, breweries, and slaughterhouses —have erected "lavish" apartment houses near tenements of the poor.[38]

In this light, Midtown fits the specifications of heterogeneous, high-density residential areas that sociologists have designated as "gold coast and slum" and have found adjoining the central business section in other metropolitan cities such as Chicago, Detroit, New Orleans, Baltimore, Philadelphia, and Boston.[39]

It is generally characteristic of such areas that their inhabitants are almost entirely white, reflecting the residential segregation of the black population in less central sections of the inner city. Sharing this characteristic, Midtown when studied was 99 percent white. Manhattan, on the other hand, was then about 22 percent nonwhite—this population being principally confined to the Harlem section.

Although the metropolitan "gold coasts" are predominantly nurtured by wealth made in the economy of the big city itself, a significant number of their residents have been recruited from families who had created their wealth in smaller centers and then migrated to the metropolis.[40]

This underscores one of the crucial forces in the development of the metropolis, namely the power it generates to draw migrants to itself. Its well-known capacity to attract immigrants from abroad will presently be documented for Midtown. Its pull on the native-born of the American hinterlands, here designated *in-migrants,* lacks such census documentation. However, from our Study sample of 1,660 interviewed adults, we can estimate that among Midtown adults (then in the twenty to fifty-nine age range) approximately three in ten were American-born in-migrants from varying distances beyond New York City's borders. Of these some 30 percent came from families of apparently high socioeconomic status, 53 percent were of middle-range origins, and only 17 percent had fathers who were in the blue-collar occupations.[41] The corresponding proportions for Midtowners age twenty to fifty-nine born in New York City were 11, 31, and 58 percent, respectively.

The gravitation to American metropolitan centers from abroad, particularly during the period 1850 to 1920, helped to recruit indispensable manpower for the expansion of these cities and for the surging industrial growth of the American economy.[42] Hence, the lower-class levels in all big American cities outside the South in time were predominantly occupied by a variety of immigrant groups. Upon arrival in the city, the first area of settlement of these ethnic groups (as we shall refer to the immigrants of each national origin, their children, and grandchildren) was usually on one edge of the original nucleus of the central business section, for example, Manhattan's Lower East Side—once a "rustic suburb for well-to-do Anglo-Saxons"—Chicago's "old" West Side, and Boston's North End. When the pressures of additional newcomers mounted, tenement quarters for them were built outward in other directions. In time, these coalesced with the newer "fashionable" sections that arose in the van of the expanding business section. Thus, heavy ethnic representation and diversity have been characteristic of the laboring class in these metropolitan gold coast and slum areas. An excellent case in point, Midtown has been described in the local press as "a polyglot district which crosses all lines of wealth and nationality."

In both Manhattan and Midtown during the Study period, the foreign-born constituted about one-third[43] of the white population and derived from every country on the map of Europe, predominantly Germany, Austria, Ireland, Italy, Hungary, the United Kingdom, and the Slavic countries of Eastern Europe. Numerically, some of these immigrant groups were represented in the Midtown area in about the same proportions as in the whole of white Manhattan[44] while some were more heavily concentrated and others less so.

Midtown's immigrants in the twenty-to-fifty-nine age range *did not* come predominantly from rural places as did their nineteenth-century predecessors. About one-fourth derived from cities with populations of over 500,000. Approximately 40 percent came from smaller urban areas. And only one-third stemmed from farms or villages. In economic origins, judging by occupational level of the father in the homeland, about 60 percent were from the blue-collar class, 30 percent from the lower white-collar class, and about 10 percent from the business and professional class. Finally, although several of the nationality groups were entirely Catholic in religious background, most were divided among Protestantism, Judaism, and Catholicism. Thus, Midtown's immigrants, in national variety, in rural-urban derivations, in economic origins, and in religious backgrounds, present a picture of considerable heterogeneity.

Of course, the American-born children of immigrants, that is, the second generation, were also well represented in Midtown, numbering at the time of the Study some 29 percent of the area's population. A sizable part of these (about one-third) were ethnically mixed, that is, the two parents were of different national origins. Moreover, a significant number (30 percent) of this generation were not derived from the local ethnic groups as such, but were themselves in-migrants to New York City from other American communities. Given the incisive impress of American acculturation, these children of immigrants added to the overall diversity within the several ethnic groups of Midtown.

We carry classification of the ethnic population to the third generation, that is, to the grandchildren of immigrants. Unfortunately, the United States Census did not specifically identify this element for us. From our Study sample, however, we can estimate that, among Midtown adults between the ages of twenty and fifty-nine, some 4 percent had parents born in the United States and four immigrant grandparents of *like* national roots, and another 12 percent were descended from parents born in the United States and immigrant grandparents of *diverse* national origins, together totaling 16 percent of this population. From diversity of cultural descent and further transmutation by the absorptive processes of American life, this third generation had become largely indistinguishable, except in the religious sphere, from the native, Old American stock. As defined by the operational criterion of families in the country four or more generations, the latter numbered about 14 percent of Midtown's adult population in the twenty-to-fifty-nine age span. It might be added that United States born in-migrants to New York City constituted 30 percent of Midtown's ethnic second generation, 47 percent of the third generation, and 72 percent of the Old American group.

The third generation, by its largely complete sociocultural assimilation, enlarged the patchwork heterogeneity and fragmentation within each ethnic group. The evidence offers no support to inferences either that these groups were culturally homogeneous or socially monolithic communities or that they were residentially insulated in their own quarters of the area, outside the mainstream of American life.

We do not thereby imply that the ethnic element had become invisible on the streets of Midtown. Although every ethnic group had families dispersed through most of the area's 190 blocks, there were separate clusters of blocks where each group—principally its immigrant elders—was more heavily settled than elsewhere in Midtown, but in no case approaching a point where it was in a numerical majority.

Moreover, in the neighborhoods where three of Midtown's largest nationality groups were most heavily represented, the observer would find a gathering of institutions directly or indirectly reflecting the particular ancestral culture, such as restaurants, bakeries, groceries, recreation halls, travel agencies, and the editorial office of its foreign-language newspaper.

The evidence of these institutions should not be misread. In part they served the local group, but they also served group members living in other areas of Manhattan and in adjoining boroughs,[45] as patrons of the newspaper, the restaurants, and recreation halls bore witness. In this respect, they functioned as centers of the dispersed citywide nationality group, rather than as exclusively local institutions of the Midtown group.

Conspicuous in the overall portrait of the Midtown population was its extreme heterogeneity in both socioeconomic status and ethnic background. It need only be noted, further, that these aspects, as elsewhere,[46] were closely intertwined. That is, from immigrants through the second and third generations in our sample population, there had been progressive upward advances from predominantly lower socioeconomic status to predominantly middle-class status, with the Old American group holding the largest representation in the upper class.

Religious background is a demographic characteristic not covered by the decennial United States Census. However, in our age twenty-to-fifty-nine sample of Midtown's adult population, we found that almost half (48 percent) were of Catholic parentage, these predominantly of lower socioeconomic origin, approximately one-third were Protestant in descent, and one-eighth were of Jewish background, both of the latter groups deriving principally from middle-status parents.[47]

The perceptive observer on the streets of Midtown during a good autumn weekend was soon impressed by the number of children he encountered, that is, the *small* number. The impression was confirmed by the Seventeenth Decennial Census report that whereas children under the age of fifteen represented almost 28 percent of the American urban[48] population, they comprised only 15 percent of Midtown's residents.

Several factors were responsible for Midtown's striking deficit of children, a characteristic shared by other metropolitan communities. We would first emphasize that its relatively small proportion of children was not an artifact of an excess of old people. In fact, the proportion of Midtown's population over the age of sixty-four at the time of the Study was estimated as almost identical with that in the white Manhattan population and in American urban places as a whole, that is, about 10 percent.

One of a series of clues to the problem was found in the census report that, relative to the white population over the age of fourteen, never-married individuals numbered an estimated 22 percent in United States urban places and 32 percent in Midtown.[49]

Another facet of this phenomenon was the number of one-occupant dwellings, which we refer to as *singleton* households. In American urban places 11 percent of all households were singleton, as compared with 25 percent in Midtown. Parenthetically, this is a characteristic particularly associated with residential areas adjoining the central business section in metropolitan cities as was observed in sociological studies of Chicago several decades ago.[50] Thus, the small proportion of children in Midtown was in part explained by the large number of unmarried[51] and exmarried adults.

A second clue was discovered in the estimate that 35 percent of its dwellings had two occupants, consisting in largest part of childless couples. Following this lead into the sample of adults studied, and focusing down to the wives between the ages of forty and fifty-nine from whom further births are unlikely, we found that one-third were childless and another 25 percent had only one child,[52] a condition equally prevalent among the younger (age twenty to thirty-nine) wives. Thus, the large proportion of unmarried adults, and the majority of its married couples who had either one offspring or none, together accounted for the relative scarcity of children in the Midtown population.

Linked to this scarcity was another generalized characteristic of the American metropolis, namely, its high proportion of employed females.[53] In Midtown when studied, women were an estimated 44 percent of the resident employed, as compared with 32 percent in the national white labor force employed in nonagricultural work.

Contributing heavily to Midtown's resident employed force were its married women. To judge from our own sample of adults, 53 percent of Midtown wives held either full-time or part-time jobs, as compared with 26 percent among white married women in the national urban population. It can be safely assumed that this contrast was not unrelated to the low birth rate observed among these Midtown wives.

Another condition in the American metropolis associated with the large female representation in its labor force was the sheer fact that here women outnumbered men by a significant margin. At the time of the Study, the Midtown population counted over 125 females for every 100 males. This disparity prevailed not only above the age of sixty, where was reflected the decidedly greater capacity of the "weaker" sex to survive the "stronger"; it appeared as well on every age level between eighteen and sixty. That a local deviation from the Mendelian law of equal sex chances was not involved can be concluded from two facts. First, among Midtown's children (under age fifteen) there were indeed 100 girls to every 100 boys. Second, in our sample of Midtown adults (age twenty to fifty-nine), those born in New York City were almost equally divided between the two sexes (105 females to 100 males). On the other hand, among the sample's foreign-born element the female ratio was 160:100,[54] and 175:100 among its American-born in-migrants. The reasons for such disparities in the sexes are matters to which we shall return in chapter 12.

MIDTOWN: SPECIAL OR GENERIC CASE?

Our overview of Midtown as a locale and a population raises a question whether this community is a special case lacking general significance.[55] This is a many-faceted question that also pervades the mental health chapters in this monograph and therefore must be tentatively held in abeyance.

However, we can here address ourselves to two aspects of the problem posed. In one direction, we have already suggested a number of characteristics that Midtown shares with "gold coast and slum" areas in other of America's largest cities, for example, proximity to the central business section, peak population density, racial homogeneity, great socioeconomic and ethnic heterogeneity, a deficit of children, an excess of single people—particularly of females—and heavy representation of women in the labor force. Further comparative research must determine how far the similarities and differences observed among these core residential areas warrant their classification as a species of the metropolitan genus within the family of American communities. On the basis of present general indications pointing to striking similarities in the historical development of these areas, it seems likely that such warrant exists. In this light, Midtown stands not as a unique case but as a member of a species, to be sure a small and highly specialized species.

In another direction lies a specific query as to how far Midtown, racially almost wholly white, was representative of New York City's white population. To simplify control of the racial factor, we addressed this question to a demographic comparison of Midtown, the white population of Manhattan, and the borough of Queens, itself 97 percent white at the time.

On eleven of the thirteen housing and demographic yardsticks applied to census data, we found Midtown and white Manhattan standing closely arrayed in like distributions, which more or less contrast with those of Queens. Only in its ratio of females to males was Midtown somewhat higher than the two other communities, linked with a corresponding difference between Midtown and white Manhattan in their percentages of employed females. And we would add that all three communities to a certain extent differed among themselves in the nationality composition of their immigrant populations.

All told, we can conclude first that in nearly all respects discernible from census reports, Midtown was decidedly different from Queens (as also, in varying degrees, from Staten Island, the Bronx, and Brooklyn); and second, that with the exceptions just noted, the Midtown population at study was rather strikingly like the estimated 1.25 million Manhattan non-Puerto Rican whites, among whom it was a 14 percent segment.

Accordingly, the question raised can be given the answer that although in demographic respects Midtown was hardly representative of New York City's inclusive white population, on the evidence available it appears, on the whole, to have been quite representative of the white population in its own borough. With that observation as warrant, the next two chapters will draw materials from sources that refer either to Manhattan in general or Midtown in particular.

SUMMARY

Facing the impossibility of catching and projecting the complex character of a city by the devices of words, we first attempted to locate Midtown in a series of spheres to which it intrinsically belongs, namely, metropolitan America, its metropolitan region, the City of New York, and Manhattan.

We reviewed such salient elements in Midtown's human environment as its position astride the City's vast network of economic arteries, its high population density, the horizontal compression and vertical extension of its housing, and the great socioeconomic, ethnic, and religious diversity in its demographic and ecological makeup.

Following the clue offered by its scarcity of children, we uncovered Midtown's large contingent of unmarried adults, the low fertility of its families, the heavy representation of wives in the labor force, and the unbalanced number of its adult males and females. Finally, we noted that on a variety of criteria Midtown seemed to be representative both of similarly located core residential areas in other large American cities and of the large white population in its home borough of Manhattan.

Midtown as here sketched is caught in a still photograph taken at a narrow span of time. However, these outlined characteristics are themselves concatenations of individual and group processes that have moved a variety of people, under a diversity of motives, to live in Midtown rather than anywhere else. The next chapter undertakes to shift from the static to the dynamic view of Midtown's inhabitants as residues of movements from much larger population reservoirs.

"The tide of humanity that sweeps in every weekday morning, swamping its cramped and crooked streets . . . sweeps out again at nightfall . . . to make the Bay of Fundy's tides seem mere ripples."

NOTES

[1] See Appendix A.

[2] Illustrative examples are R. Faris and H. W. Dunham, *Mental Disorders in Urban Areas*, 1939; E. Shevky and W. Bell, *Social Area Analysis*, 1955; and D. W. Timms, *The Urban Mosaic*, 1972.

[3] Among many illustrations are: R. and H. Lynd, *Middletown*, 1929; W. L. Warner, P. S. Lunt, L. Srole, and J. O. Low, *Yankee City Series*, vols. 1–5, 1941–1959; J. R. Seeley et al., *Crestwood Heights*, 1956; H. J. Gans, *The Levittowners*, 1967; and P. Binzen, *Whitetown USA*, 1970.

[4] This press, and those one-of-a-kind magazines, *The New Yorker* and *New York*, are a rich source of grist for the sociologist's mill. In fact, a publisher of one of the city's dailies, referring to his paper's coverage of crime and other ills of the metropolis, commented, "As the *New York Times* reports it, it's sociology."

[5] R. R. Wohl and A. L. Strauss, "Symbolic Representation and the Urban Milieu," *American Journal of Sociology* 63 (March 1958): 523–532.

[6] *Holiday* (October 1959): 49.

[7] *Inside USA*, 1947, p. 369.

[8] The population and housing figures presented on this page have as their source the reports of the Seventeenth Decennial Census.

[9] As defined by the Census Bureau, the standard metropolitan area was composed of (1) a "central city" with more than 50,000 people, and (2) contiguous counties which, by certain criteria, "are essentially metropolitan in character and socially and economically integrated with the central city." We are here arbitrarily applying the 1 million population criterion to differentiate the fourteen largest among the nation's 168 metropolitan areas.

[10] Over a century ago, James Fenimore Cooper observed: "New York is essentially national in interest, position, pursuits. No one thinks of the place as belonging to a particular state, but to the United States." (Quoted in Alexander Klein, ed., *The Empire City*, 1955, p. xxi.) Now we are told: "The towers of Manhattan cast their shadows not only over the entire nation but everywhere on the globe. For New York City has become the crucible and nerve center, the focus and symbol of man's civilization on earth." Ibid., p. xxi.

[11] *Working population* refers to all people who carry on gainful employment within an area, whether domiciled there or not.

[12] The figures in this paragraph are adapted from those provided by New York City Planning Commission publications. However, commission data were confined to wage and salary earners covered by Unemployment Compensation, excluding the self-employed. We have made estimates of the distribution of the self-employed among the several fields named above and have adjusted the commission's figures accordingly.

[13] Actually, this consists of two subsections of commercial concentrations locally often referred to as *downtown* and *midtown*. The latter, as a rough approximation, covers the area southward from 59th to 14th Street, between Ninth and Third Avenues. The former, also by way of approximation, includes the area southward from Houston Street to Battery Park at the end of the Island, between the Hudson River and a line extending southward along LaFayette, Baxter, and Chambers Streets to the East River.

Official city documents employ *Central Business District* to refer as a rule to all of Manhattan south of 60th Street. The lines we have drawn to define the two areas designated together as the Central Business Section exclude most of the 500,000 people who make their homes in the predominantly residential areas south of the 59th Street line.

[14] It has been said that this district contains "the greatest yet most compact shopping bazaar on earth."

[15] It may seem superfluous to note that also concentrated in this section are almost all

of New York's hotels, legitimate theaters, concert halls, first-run movie houses, name night clubs, fine restaurants, etc.

[16]With specific reference to the section's downtown financial district, it has been written: "The tide of humanity that sweeps in every weekday morning, swamping its cramped and crooked streets and surging into its buildings, and then sweeps out again at nightfall leaving almost the whole area enveloped in tomblike silence, is of a magnitude to make the Bay of Fundy's tides seem mere ripples. . . . It is one of the few places in the country where pedestrian traffic jams are worse than vehicular ones." J. Brooks, "Part-time City," *The New Yorker,* January 10, 1959, pp. 76–92.

[17]Approaching the somatic level of reaction, one essayist in a national magazine avows that "this haphazard upthrust panorama is a sight to stir the viscera."

[18]On Midtown's other three sides are a bordering river and two major thoroughfares that set it off from neighboring residential sections with varyingly dissimilar (to the *New York Times,* "sociologically distant") characteristics. By the lines of differentiation marking it off from surrounding districts, Midtown conforms 'in large degree to the criteria applied by sociologists in identifying "natural areas" within a city.

[19]We resort to a pseudonym for three very different reasons. First, to the residents of the area, who contributed so freely of their time in the interests of the Study, we gave assurances of confidentiality and personal anonymity. Anonymity of locale adds to that word of assurance. Second, it is quite possible that further research may be conducted in the area. To identify the area in these pages could compromise local acceptance of such new programs. Third, there are several place names in local use, but none is applied to the study area with geographical consistency either by residents or by the New York press. Accordingly, the misunderstanding and confusion these available names would certainly promote can be avoided by the new designation here adopted.

[20]From another kind of comprehensive vantage point, the nation can be seen in terms of its large regional divisions, such as New England, the South, and the Far West. For a discerning treatment of the Middle Atlantic states as a region and New York City's place within it, see M. Lerner, *America as a Civilization,* 1957, pp. 202–203.

[21]Adapted from the New York City Department of City Planning *Newsletter,* January, 1958.

[22]Plans made in 1967 for "the world's tallest purely residential building"—of eighty stories—were subsequently pared to fifty-seven floors and then to forty. The roof, so to speak, came tumbling down twice in a reversal of the "more, always more" trend in American value orientations.

[23]Suggestive of a recent trend, a City survey found that among newly built apartment houses in Manhattan only 5.5 percent of the units had more than four rooms.

[24]Inquiry would also show, as did the 1960 census, that only 6.8 percent of Midtown's households own their own dwellings—mainly quarters in cooperative apartment houses.

[25]It may be of some interest that prior to this date Manhattan had itself been New York City. In that year its name was changed to Borough of Manhattan as part of the consolidation with the other boroughs under the new rubric of Greater New York. However, the legislation that wrote the new names into law could not counteract the force of local attitudes. Thus, residents of all five boroughs, including their bellwether taxi drivers, to this day continue to use "New York" or merely "the City" to refer specifically to Manhattan.

[26]So rapid was this tide that areas of "elegant" new homes of "rich and socially elect families," within twenty years of construction, often turned into "shabby rooming houses," and within another decade were converted (in many cases with additions of extra floors) into "sweatshop lofts and merchant warehouses."

[27]In the middle of the nineteenth century, by newspaper account, much of the area that later became the focus of the Midtown Study "was still a desolate wilderness of swamps, rocks and brambles. Almost 5,000 squatters lived in its caves and shanties, and 100,000 pigs, goats and sheep foraged for food among rubbish heaps. The area was dotted with stables, piggeries, quarries, swill-mills and bone-boiling works."

[28]As a result, not a few of the newer buildings in Manhattan's .Business Section are the third or fourth structure to occupy their respective sites in a century. Some replaced in the Island's post-World War II construction surge were themselves put up during

the previous boom of the post-World War I years.

[29]With it also moved the theaters, music halls, hotels, hospitals, and, in some instances, churches. However, many of the latter remained on their original sites. Thus, if the extant Protestant churches of denominations associated with the upper class are spotted on a map of Manhattan, they will reveal, in trace outline, the historical course of the northward movement just described.

As a case in point, the Grace Episcopal Church (now on Broadway and Tenth Street) recently observed the hundred-and-fiftieth anniversary of its founding. On that occasion, *The New Yorker* recalled that in its original edifice, Grace Church "attracted what newspaper and magazine accounts for a hundred years afterward were to describe as *'la crème de la crème'* of New York society. Within thirty years, the cream having moved their residences northward, Grace Church decided to move north, too."

An account in the same journal suggests that merchants serving *"la crème"* were more nimble in following their customers. One family dynasty of men's clothiers had a migratory history of 100 years confined entirely to Fifth Avenue. Beginning on 16th Street, this establishment "had a twenty-year stay in that neighborhood, then twenty years at Thirty-Fifth Street, twenty years at Thirty-Ninth Street, twenty years at Forty-Fourth Street, [then] moved to Forty-Ninth Street, where it remained for eighteen years," and today is on 59th Street—and Fifth Avenue still.

[30]Characteristically, the elite of Boston never did follow this example. As an illustration of the general attitudes of this group toward what it regarded as New York's ostentatious use of wealth, there is the anecdote about the Boston dowager who in a tone of resignation commented: "There's no use trying to compare with that New York wealth; all we can do is to be as queer as possible."

[31]This pattern is actively operating to this day. That it may continue in the future to its logical conclusion was envisaged by one of the City's leading businessmen. He noted in 1959 that "the northward march of business [will] move to take over some of Manhattan's best residential areas of today" and that "by the year 2000 we can expect Manhattan's 22 square miles to be entirely occupied by skyscraper offices, other commercial enterprises, and hotels."

That this prophecy was not altogether far-fetched may be gathered from the fact that the shrinkage of Manhattan's population from about 2 million in 1950 to about 1.5 million in 1970 was in part a consequence of the continuing turnover of residential land into commercial and institutional uses. Washington excepted, Manhattan probably leads all other great central cities in the proportion of its land occupied by nonprofit institutions, private and public.

[32]Such survival has been bought at a price of perennial embattlement. The *New York Herald Tribune*, September 15, 1959, editorialized: "The casual stroller through Murray Hill on Sunday night might have been a bit startled at the sight of Revolutionary War soldiers out in full uniform, but he might also have gotten the point that the residents are trying once more to protect their neighborhood. This time of course the enemy is not General Howe but Borough President Hulan Jack. . . . Murray Hill is one of New York's fine old neighborhoods, richly steeped in history (as the Revolutionary uniforms should remind us), long an island of repose in the commercial bustle of mid-Manhattan, the sort of neighborhood the city should do all it can to preserve."

[33]C. Tunnard and H. H. Reed, *American Skyline*, 1953, p. 98.

[34]For a vivid pictorial record of this and other aspects of the period, see the monumental volume: J. A. Kouwenhoven, *The Columbia Historical Portrait of New York: An Essay in Graphic History*, 1953.

[35]Kouwenhoven notes, "Into these tenements human beings were packed more densely than anywhere else in the world—London's worst slums and the rabbit warrens of China and India not excepted. The Tenth Ward (Lower East Side) in 1890 averaged 522 people per acre (330,000 gross density per square mile)." Ibid., p. 381.

[36]For a comprehensive social and architectural history of this genre of New York housing see C. Lockwood, *Bricks and Brownstone*, 1973.

[37]In a more general respect, New York has been characterized as a place where "the extremes make up in their bizarre neighborliness the city itself." Alfred Kazin, "Brooklyn Bridge," in Klein, *The Empire City*, p. 154.

[38]It may be remembered that Sidney Kingsley's play and movie *Dead End* had such a Manhattan riverfront setting.

[39]H. Zorbaugh, *The Gold Coast and Slum,* 1929; and W. Firey, *Land Use in Central Boston,* 1947, pp. 87–135.

[40]The pattern of this migrational sequence can be illustrated by three cities. Wealthy families from the smaller centers of New England have resettled in the Beacon Hill section of Boston. Similar families from Middle Western communities have established themselves in the Lake Front section of Chicago's Near North Side. In turn, older families from these gold coast areas of Boston and Chicago have moved and settled themselves in the "elite" sections of Manhattan. A fictional case in point is to be found in John P. Marquand's most durable novel, *The Late George Apley.*

[41]In our white Midtown population at least, the Horatio Alger image of the poor American youngster going to the big city is not corroborated. And the related picture that such people are drawn in large numbers from the rural areas of America is also not supported. On the contrary, among Midtown's American-born in-migrants, only one in seven has come from a farm or village, whereas almost half are from cities with populations of 100,000 or more.

[42]Foreign migrants to smaller American communities there filled the places of native sons who were migrating to the big cities. Cf. W. L. Warner and L. Srole, *Social Systems of American Ethnic Groups,* 1945, pp. 53–66.

[43]Their proportion in the Midtown population has been steadily dwindling since 1920. Writing about the foreign-born groups, a chronicler of the New York scene (Meyer Berger, *The New York Times,* April 29, 1956) has observed that they are getting "thinner and thinner through the years. Assimilation works in its quiet, mysterious ways, and new generations tend to blend into the national weave."

[44]We use immigration primarily as a criterion of derivation from a country with cultural background different from that of America's indigenous Yankee stock. Puerto Ricans are a special case. They are American citizens in their home island, and therefore they are not immigrants in the usual legal sense when they settle in the continental United States. Nonetheless, they are probably as culturally distinctive as, let us say, immigrants from Spain and face the same problems of personal and group adjustment. For our purposes, therefore, they will be classified as one of the ethnic groups.

This is by way of prelude to the observation that in 1954 Puerto Ricans comprised an estimated 10 and 1.5 percent, respectively, of the Manhattan and Midtown populations.

[45]Reporting a Fifth Avenue parade of 15,000 marchers celebrating General von Steuben Day—resumed in 1958 after a lapse of forty years—*The New York Times* indicated: "The marchers were described as representing every segment of the German-American community in New York, New Jersey, Connecticut and other neighboring areas."

[46]Cf. Warner and Srole, *Social Systems of American Ethnic Groups,* pp. 67–102.

[47]There is no firm evidence on the religious composition of either the Manhattan or New York City populations. However, estimates have been made suggesting that compared to the Midtown sample the overall representation in Manhattan is approximately the same for Catholics, somewhat smaller for Protestants, and somewhat larger for Jews.

[48]By Census Bureau definition, places with populations of 2,500 or over are urban.

[49]Broken marriages are also relevant here. However, available census publications combine the divorced with the widowed and the separated with the married, and they are therefore of little use for our purpose. As a matter of record, in our Midtown age twenty-to-fifty-nine sample, the divorced and separated comprise 11.5 percent of those ever married and the widowed 7.7 percent. No comparable age specific rates in other populations are available.

[50]In the Chicago studies of that earlier period the usual loci of singleton dwellings were rooming houses, in which tenants lacked private cooking facilities. There is evidence that this was also the case several decades ago in Midtown. But in our study area at the time of writing, rooming houses had in most cases been transformed into utility apartment buildings by the expedient of placing a pullman kitchen in a closet or corner of the one-room dwelling unit. More suitable middle-class variants are to be found in Midtown's residence clubs (usually lacking cooking facilities) for unattached women and in one-and-one-half-room apartments of recent construction.

[51]These are in large part younger people, i.e., under the age of forty. But it might be noted from our own sample of Midtown adults that among women between the ages of forty and fifty-nine about 19 percent are unmarried, a rate three times greater than among women of the same age in the national population. As for Midtown males in the forty to fifty-nine age range, 15 percent are unmarried, a rate about twice that of men of like age in the nation at large. These older unmarrieds will get further attention in chapter 12.

[52]It has long been established that urban middle- and upper-class populations are associated with low fertility rates, and families of low socioeconomic status, both urban and rural, with high fertility rates. It is accordingly striking that when these older Midtown wives are analyzed according to socioeconomic levels, there are no appreciable differences among these levels in the proportions of childless or one-child women. On this particular criterion of fertility, Midtown's low-status women appear to be as infertile as their higher-status neighbors. However, when the former do have more than one child, they tend to have larger numbers than do the women of higher station. In fine, large families are far less prevalent among them than has heretofore been observed, but are by no means extinct.

The overall average in 1954 of 1.4 children per ever-married Midtown sample respondent was far below the "zero-growth" reproduction rate of 2.1 children that is nationally being approached in the 1970s. If the metropolis, as it often has in the past, foreshadows future national trends, the "below-zero" population growth rate may be expected to further accelerate downward on a countrywide scale.

[53]"The largest participation by women in the labor force is in the great metropolitan centers. [This] decreases as the size of the city decreases." E. Shevky and M. Williams, *Social Areas of Los Angeles,* 1949, p. 46.

[54]This ratio seems to be contrary to the historical image of immigrants as heavily weighted with males. However, among the 1.3 million immigrants of all ages who entered the United States in the years 1936 to 1950, females outnumbered males by 140 to 100. We estimate that among the adults of this immigrant population the sex ratio approximated 150:100. Thus, the ratio reported here for the foreign-born adults in the Midtown sample may largely reflect the sex composition of immigrants to the United States in the decades preceding the Study.

[55]Even if an affirmative answer were indicated, the present study, needless to say, would have been amply warranted. The special or extreme case, even if *sui generis,* is worthy of investigation in its own right. In that event, the researcher faces an important disadvantage, in that the generalizations he can draw from the findings are severely limited. On the other side of the scale, such findings may generate hypotheses of potentially large significance for investigations of cases having greater generality.

CHAPTER 5

EXILE AND INGATHERING
LEO SROLE

In a long-standing characterization, Manhattan residents are reportedly all settlers from somewhere else. This can be read as implying either that conception, gestation, and birth are processes too delicate to be elicited or sustained in Manhattan's raucous environment, or that children delivered there are quickly transferred for safekeeping to more antiseptic surroundings. Although both inferences, needless to say, are false in the main, the characterization does have a certain large basis in fact. To judge from our cross-section sample of interviewed adults, Midtown's age 20 to 59 population is divided into three more or less equal parts: (1) the immigrants from overseas; (2) the in-migrants "from the lanes and alleys, streets and avenues" of America, as Melville phrased it; (3) the New York City-born. Moreover, one-third of the latter, although "launched" in New York, were raised elsewhere by their *émigré* parents, and therefore, in a strict sense, they also are in-migrants to the City. All told, then, about three in every four of the indicated Midtown population have made the passage from the home town of childhood to an adopted dwelling in the massive, three-dimensional congestion of Manhattan.

From this fact follow two insistent questions: Why did these migrants exile themselves to gather in New York City? Why did they settle in Manhattan in particular?[1] Certainly, a common motif behind the act of migrating to New York, whether overland or by sea, lies in the cultural, ideological realm of what has been called the American Dream. In E. B. White's notable essay on the City, this has been given expression in eloquent form: "[New York] is to the nation what the white church spire is to the village—the visible symbol of aspiration and faith, the white plume saying the way is up."[2]

Economic realities are in part the substance of this symbolic dream role played by New York.[3] Historically, a great metropolis first outpaces competitor cities in population growth by more rapidly expanding its economic accommodations for migrants, then maintains its attractive powers by the larger number and variety of opportunities lodged in the towering size and tempo of its economy.

However, we can be certain that among the vast populations aware of New York's economic largess, only a minute fraction respond by breaking native roots to take the expatriate's lonely road to its gates. When we ask how the migrants differ from their home-town peers who did *not* respond in like fashion, objective factors in New York's economy lose much of their explanatory value. This question is decidedly relevant to the mental health focus of this Study. Yet lack of evidence on the stay-at-home fellows of the migrants leaves the question unanswerable here.

Clues come into reach when we scale the question down to the more modest form: What are the migrants like in their main characteristics? From our sample of Midtown adults, we know that both immigrants and in-migrants predominantly moved to the City when they were at an age ranging from late adolescence to late twenties, that is, they were young, unmarried people at a fledgling and formative stage of their adult careers. Were they more venturesome, more attuned to the American Dream pointing the way up, than their childhood companions who remained behind or who sought lesser plumes? We do not know. But psychological probabilities suggest that perhaps in some part they were.

Essayist E. B. White[4] seems to support this view: "The residents of Manhattan are to a large extent strangers who have pulled up stakes somewhere and come to town seeking sanctuary or fulfillment or some greater or lesser grail. . . . The City is always full of young worshipful beginners."

Drawing from the literature on New York's in-migrants, we know that they include the "talented who make a vital contribution to New York's primacy [in the arts]. . . . Where else but to New York would the gifted . . . hurry to show their wares?"[5] Joining those of specific talent are the bright who go "out and away [from] the towns and smaller cities of America."[6]

We are told that New York also draws to itself "the restless, the dissatisfied and the ambitious, who have demanded more from life than the circumstances of their birth offered them."[7] The phrase *demanding more from life* than parents had given echoes the American Dream that spurs such people to New York.

This prompting is expressed in other phrasings: "For Americans New York symbolizes 'facing life'; it is considered to be our greatest challenge, it is here that people feel they are testing themselves to the limit."[8]

Another major theme in the literature reveals that in the stream of migrants are those for whom New York is more a haven of escape from the place departed than a city sought for its own rewards. On one level it has been suggested that "if Paris is the perfect setting for a romance, New York is the perfect city in which to get over one, to get over anything."[9] More explicit is the observation that "many of its settlers are probably here merely to escape, not to face, reality . . . although many persons are here from some excess of spirit (which caused them to break away from their small town), some, too, are here from a deficiency of spirit, who find in New York a protection, or an easy substitution."[10]

On this plane, Truman Capote sees the City as "a place to hide, to lose or discover oneself, to make a dream wherein you prove that perhaps after all you are not an ugly duckling."[11] The theme of the deviant type among migrants to the city has been elaborated by the pioneer urban sociologist, Robert Park.

In a small community it is the normal man, the man without eccentricity or genius who seems most likely to succeed. The small community often tolerates eccentricity. The city, on the contrary, may reward it. Neither the criminal, the defective, nor the genius has the same opportunity to develop . . . in a small town that he invariably finds in a great city. In the city many of these divergent types now find a milieu in which, for good or for ill, their dispositions and their talents parturiate and bear fruit.[12]

Developing the point, Park adds:

Because of the opportunities it offers, particularly to the exceptional and abnormal types of man, a great city tends to . . . lay bare all the human characteristics and traits which are ordinarily obscured and suppressed in small communities.

Thus, migration to the metropolis of "the strong, the weak, and all shades in between" seems to operate as a selective psychosocial process, flattening diversity of personality variation in the small communities, which are the population tributaries for the big city, and heightening such diversity in the metropolis that receives these self-chosen young people.[13] If so, to the investigator of mental health the metropolis may expose the range of personality differences characterizing the overall national scene, in a form both more comprehensive and more concentrated than do the drained-off populations of smaller communities.

Of course, the selection process is by no means ended with the act of migration. Writers on the city from the ranks of the fine arts have revealed that many migrants are polarized, positively or negatively, by the metropolis. For some, it is mistress in an affair of unadulterated love. John Lardner writes: "For myself, I can only hope that the next world . . . I don't care which branch of it . . . provides another . . . such as New York."[14]

The Englishman Alec Waugh could observe: "I recognized when the time came for me to leave [New York] that I had been placed under a very special bondage. For I had come not only to love New York, but to feel that I belonged there, and that is a feeling a man very rarely has. . . ."[15]

With more transparent symbolism, Thomas Wolfe writes of

. . . the iron-breasted city, [where] one comes closest to the enigma that haunts and curses the whole land. The city is the place where men are constantly seeking to find their door and where they are doomed to wandering forever. Of no place is this more true than of New York. Ridiculously ugly for the most part, one yet remembers it as a place of proud and passionate beauty; the place of everlasting hunger, it is also the place where men feel their lives will gloriously be fulfilled and their hunger fed.[16]

To many, on the other hand, the City is an object of undiluted hate, such as could prompt one nineteenth-century English poet to compose the line "God the first garden made, and the first city Cain."[17]

In counterpoint to Lardner's prayer for the afterlife, it has been ob-

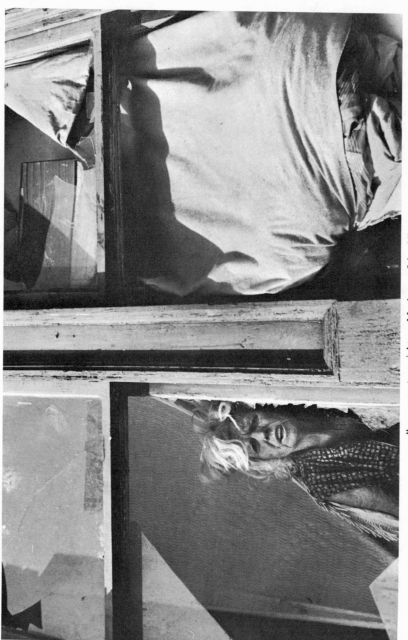

". . . purgatory right on Manhattan Island."

served that "there are some who would say with passion that the only real advantage of living in New York is that all its residents ascend to heaven directly after their deaths, having served their full term in purgatory right on Manhattan island."[18]

Perhaps the ultimate in this attitude was expressed by Frank Lloyd Wright: "Here is a volcanic crater of blind, confused human forces pushing together and grinding upon each other, moved by greed in common exploitation. . . . This mantrap of gigantic dimensions, devouring manhood . . . is as good an example of barbarism as exists."[19]

The literary commentator Alfred Kazin has called attention to these polarities in two of America's greatest writers, both native sons of Manhattan and contemporaries. "Herman Melville's *Pierre* . . . is full of downtown New York . . . the landscape of a certain bitterness. . . . The city which Melville usually describes as a dark place to live in and a good place to leave . . . aroused in Walt Whitman every golden hope. . . . For Whitman America began in the streets of New York."[20]

One explanation for the extreme, enduring dissonance of affect toward the metropolis is suggested by Thomas Wolfe. "The city has a million faces, and . . . no man ever knows just what another means when he tells about the city he sees. For the city that he sees is just the city that he brings with him, that he has within his heart . . . made out of sense but shaped and colored and unalterable from all that he has felt and thought and dreamed about before."[21]

Another element is illuminated in the personal history recorded by John Steinbeck.[22] He delineates four stages in his in-migrant's reactions to New York. First, settlement and retreat: "The city had beaten the pants off me. Whatever it required to get ahead I didn't have. I didn't leave the city in disgust. . . . I left it with the respect plain unadulterated fear gives." Then, brief visits when "I pretended and believed my pretense, that I hated the city and all its smiles and traps . . . and I fled the Whore of Babylon with relief and virtuous satisfaction." Next, reluctant resettlement in a Manhattan apartment: "but even then I kept contact with my prejudices . . . I was going to live in New York but I was going to avoid it. . . ." Finally, sudden conversion: "a kind of mystical experience . . . something burst in my head, a kind of light and a kind of feeling . . . which if it had spoken would have said, 'My God! I belong here'

. . . I was no longer a stranger. I had become a New Yorker!

"Now there may be people who move easily into New York without travail, but most I have talked to about it have had some kind of trial by torture before acceptance."

In the same vein, it has been noted that Manhattan "daunts everyone who comes to it . . . even Americans, perhaps especially Americans. . . . They confront it with some of the emotions recruits feel going to the front, or fliers feel soloing for the first time."[23]

We have earlier suggested that migrants to New York, American and foreign-born, may represent a selective screening from their home populations. But there is also an outbound traffic from the metropolis, consisting of newcomers who were repelled by it, and also of native New Yorkers.

Testimony of highly literate people reveals that migrants to what Sartre has called "the harshest city in the world" undergo a second screening process, arising from the enormously complex depths of individual personality under impact of the enormously complex realities of the City.

As a consequence of this trial, many newcomers find their needs, normal or deviant, fulfilled and fervently adopt New York as their permanent home. Others find their needs and expectations frustrated and, as one writer phrased it, "go down in it, embittered, or flee from it."[24] Still others, in their ambivalence somewhere between the above two types, make a compact with themselves to remain, but with the understanding that it will be temporary. . . . These people have been known to characterize themselves as "carpetbaggers." If they finally leave they can say, as did one of their number: "Once I visited New York for twenty years and I wouldn't live there [again] if you gave me Philadelphia. . . . I'm glad I don't have to cope with New York anymore."[25]

Of those who migrate to New York and sink roots, a further question may be asked: Why do they usually choose to wedge into the overcrowded island that comprises only one-fourteenth of the City's land area? When considering this question it should be recalled that on arrival they are largely young, unmarried people in the early years of forging a career, and are following essentially the same pattern as many natives of the City's other boroughs who move to Manhattan at approximately the same stage of life.

We can infer that by and large their motives for choosing Manhattan are relatively uncomplicated, at least on the surface. First, their careers usually revolve around institutions that are located in or near Manhattan's Central Business Section, and quick transit to and from the job is crucial in budgeting scarce time for the many interests of life. Second, in or near the Business Section are most of the City's wealth of recreational institutions, which uniquely distinguish Manhattan from the home town or home borough. Third, in Manhattan above all can one find the companionship of peers in age, stage of career, and unmarried status. All of these motives are touched in the advertisements of a new apartment house directed to the "Manhattan Miss" who is a "quick-change artist. She can go from fashion designer to dazzling date in the shortest possible time because her elegant street suite is mere minutes from her office. And since it's mere minutes from theaters, shows and clubs she can get home early enough on week-day dates." Finally, to young, native New Yorkers from other areas of the metropolis (as to in-migrants), movement to Manhattan is often a decisive break from parental controls.

As long as these Manhattan settlers remain single, such motives will almost invariably keep them in the hub borough. If they marry and remain childless, by design or otherwise, more or less the same motives usually continue to operate, probably reinforced if both husband and wife are employed. However, when children begin to arrive, a series of complicated problems are delivered with them.

Around these children has raged a perennial debate that has filled programs of Manhattan parents' organizations and columns of the press. The subject of the debate, variously worded, is the proposition that "Manhattan is no place to bring up a child." Defenders of the metropolis in this controversy have usually built their case on the "stimulus" view that to the child it "holds tremendous intellectual challenge, magic, adventure, and beauty."

The impartial visitor in search of relevant facts may begin on the less romantic plane of the child's immediate surroundings. The New York City Housing Authority, administering over 100,000 low-rent dwelling units in public housing projects (over 150,000 in 1970), has applied a formula calibrating family size to size of the dwelling occupied, namely, a limit not exceeding two persons per each dwelling bedroom. With this as a norm, the visitor could inspect the Midtown Study's sample dwellings—all in private housing—that have three or more occupants and should be accommodated with two or more bedrooms. Taking into account socioeconomic level, he would find that 77 percent of lower-status families lack such housing accommodations. Among households of middle and upper status, the corresponding figures are 64 and 34 percent, respectively.[26] Because of the exceptionally high rentals and sheer numerical scarcity of multibedroom Manhattan dwellings, many Midtown families on all socioeconomic levels cannot provide fully adequate sleeping arrangements for their children.

The waking period of the child's day emerges as a problem of even larger proportions. Small in floor space and catch of sunlight,[27] most Midtown dwellings would hardly impress the observer as sufficient play area for the child in the long age range of self-locomotion. A book in the how-to-do-it genre, entitled *Understanding the City Child*[28] and addressed to that child's parents, reveals the situation in the following way:

One thing is certainly safe to say about the average child in the city: he spends more time indoors than does his opposite number in country or suburb. In addition, more of this time is likely to be spent under his parents' feet. The amount of time the apartment dwelling youngster must spend indoors is undoubtedly the greatest drawback to city living. . . . If possible, some indoor arrangement should be devised to give youngsters . . . an opportunity for climbing, hanging by their hands, or otherwise working off accumulated physical steam in an acceptable way.

Nevertheless, children must have outside space for unhampered play and free access to the company of others their age. To this point, the book just quoted strikes another indoor note when it suggests to the city child that "social life can flourish up and down the stair well or elevator shaft of an apartment house as easily as in the backyards of happy memory. Differently, perhaps, but easily."[29]

But the child insists, "I want out!" The observer notes in Midtown that an open play area connected with a residential building is a rarity and parks and playgrounds are few, with one exception small and overcrowded, and for most children too distant for ready use. Available, therefore, is only the cement and asphalt street area, consisting of narrow sidewalks and a "nightmarish congestion" of cars, bumper to bumper, both parked and moving.

One pictorial magazine article that celebrated the "glamour" of Manhattan evaluated these elements of the child's environment in an apparently serious vein:

To be a boy in New York is to be free . . . to be a man before you're out of boyhood. . . . Who needs a pasture? [A boy] has a whole street . . . a whole city of streets . . . where he can run about, learning nimbleness by dodging through traffic. Who needs nine men on a ball team? It's a better game with three. . . . There's no fat on him, and since he has breathed exhaust fumes all his life, he can endure anywhere. . . . He wouldn't swap New York for all the fresh air in the West.[30]

That this view is less than universal is indicated by the local mother who affirmed that "it's hard on children to be shut away in town." Another Manhattan mother briefly amplified with the explanation, "I can't just let them run out the door to play here." Truman Capote, recalling the metropolis where he grew up, concludes that "for a child it is a joyless place."

There is evidence suggesting that this is a matter of considerable disquiet both to Manhattan parents and the civic conscience. A newspaper account of a PTA conference on "The Urban Child" reported, in part, as follows: "How can city-minded parents 'sell' the city to their young and still avoid the pangs of guilt that stab so sharply when boys and girls complain about urban living?" The article indirectly tries to allay this guilt by observing: "Countless influences from Mark Twain's books to television's Westerns conspire to convince youngsters that life outside the city limits is one sparkling adventure after another. . . . Under the influence of these subtle 'commercials' for non-city living[31] many a youngster wails long and loud against the fate that keeps him dry-gulched in concrete canyons."

However, the piece goes on to quote a mother in a postmeeting interview who revealingly commented: "We've reached the point where we can take it fine when a four-year-old says 'I hate you!' But let him say 'I hate it here!' and we get all tied up in knots. In the first instance we know that his anger is just part of a passing mood. . . . In the second,

"The Fate that keeps youngsters dry-gulched in concrete canyons."

we react as if his expression of irritation carried the weight of a Supreme Court decision."

The heavy civic conscience is manifest in the local voluntary organizations which try vainly to sweep the children "off the city streets." It is manifest in the newspapers which regularly and waspishly call attention to "the shortage of recreational facilities for our children." It breaks through, sometimes tinged with anguish, in their editorial lapses from civic optimism, such as in the following examples:

1. From an editorial on efforts to plant trees on the streets of Manhattan: "It is interesting to envisage New York turned into a forest. The Indians may yet be persuaded to take it back."

2. From an editorial entitled "Chaos in Microcosm": "The state of disorganization into which this overorganized civilization of ours is falling shows itself in little as well as in big ways. . . . New York City, for example, is probably the most highly developed and complex urban organism in the world. Yet the mechanistic structure we have built is getting to be so intricate that . . . we seem to be losing the art of living with the monster our mechanical and industrial genius has created."

3. From an editorial on financial support for new schools: "Maybe it is a mistake to build cities as vast as this one. But the flesh and blood that goes to school in such cities is essentially just the same as that which long ago walked bare foot to the little red schoolhouse."

The issue was also opened to our interviewed sample of Midtown adults. Although their views are being held for discussion in a later context, it can be indicated here that they strongly support the proposition that "Manhattan is no place to bring up a child."

Accordingly, on this and other evidence, limitations of the Manhattan environment for the child's well-being are judged to be both subjectively and objectively real. We can assume that if this were the only consideration pressing upon parents there would be a nearly complete exodus from Manhattan and Midtown of couples with children. Indeed, for many decades, but in particular since 1946, "the greatest migration since the days of the covered wagon," as a local journalist put it, has been the evacuation of millions of American families from metropolitan centers to the suburbs and exurbs. The prominence of children among these exmetropolites is one of the most striking aspects of the movement.[32] The magnitude of this movement locally is indicated by the report of the New York City Board of Education that in the years 1961–1966 about 215,000 pupils, equivalent to 22 percent of the total 1961 public system registration, transferred to out-of-city schools. Nevertheless, that about one-half (47 percent) of all married people in our Midtown sample have one or more children under the age of eighteen documents the degree to which this exodus has been considerably less than complete.[33]

It can plausibly be assumed that these Midtown parents are different, in certain respects, from those who departed. For the latter, it seems clear, the well-being of their children was a dominant motive for making the considerable change in environment. Although the interests of their children were doubtless no less weighty to the parents resisting the pressures for removal to suburbia, we must assume that other, stronger values took precedence in keeping them anchored in the Midtown area. It is not possible, nor altogether necessary here, to explore these other values systematically. However, it is possible, at least inferentially, to discern a common thread carried over from the central motive that brought these people to Manhattan in the first place, namely, an overriding commitment to the way up, or the "glory road" that runs through the Central Business Section.

In the case of the white-collar Midtowner, there are a number of indicators pointing in this direction. For example, economically they "travel light" by severely restricting the number of children they produce. By employment of the wife, in many cases, they increase family income. Moreover, from the writings of middle-class Manhattanites we cull characterizations of the Island as a place "geared to adult ambitions," and tailored "for the type of people with get-ahead-or-else drives."

That the City is the natural habitat of this type of individual is revealed in an official brochure[34] where he is baited with

. . . that subtle, pervading, and often determining factor: *being in the swim!* To be associated with success; to rub elbows with the pace-setters; to be so close to sources as to get the latest ideas by word of mouth; to look around and *see* that you are shoulder to shoulder with competition, if not ahead of it—these are privileges that go with a New York location and automatically confer CONFIDENCE and spell PRESTIGE.

Above all, there seems to be reflected the need to mobilize leisure time and social relationships around "the job." To this end we are told, each by a separate writer, that it is necessary (1) "to do the right thing with the right people in the right places," (2) "to keep in touch socially with old business friends and new business contacts," (3) "to work harder and hustle more than anybody else," (4) "to keep on top of the whole picture by collecting information all day long."

As capstone we have the testimony of a rising business executive known to us who had lived in Midtown, moved to the suburbs, and before long returned to Midtown. Explaining the return: "The headquarters of my firm are here. If I am to go to the top Manhattan is where I should be—to entertain business associates and customers." A returnee wife has said: "My husband was so busy that *if I wanted to see him* I had to live in town."

Here we seem to see the mandate of the American Dream carried to its farthest point of development, in which one's leisure, comfort, cronies, wife, and children are transcended in a sense by the higher value placed upon the climb to the top, or at least to the ever-present next rung. Apparently, residential proximity to the Central Business Section is inescapable because one's home and private life have in effect become annexes to one's office.

If these people appear to fit certain specifications of the "organization man" as drawn by W. H. Whyte, Jr., surely the resemblance is no mere coincidence. Whyte, however, tracked his man to a family house in the suburbs and almost completely overlooked his psychosocial "twin" in the high-rise apartment buildings of Manhattan.[35]

The precise line dividing such Midtowners from their suburban twins is suggested by the comment of one of the latter that "I'm anchored to my office but that's no reason my family should be near it."

There is little in the available literature to indicate whether a comparable orientation exists among Manhattan people who are in the blue-collar occupations. Although these are probably not mobilized in their get-ahead drives as are their white-collar neighbors, there are intimations from our Midtown sample that such aspirations are by no means absent. For example, we earlier noted that a surprising number of such couples have only one child or none, the middle-class pattern of "traveling light" (in number of offspring) for the upward climb. Also, many of these wives are employed, suggesting diversion of their domestic roles for enhancement of family income toward the middle-class range. During their work histories, far from remaining frozen in one occupation, these men have shifted their line of work to about the same considerable extent as have the middle-class males. Finally, on a question relating to "worries about getting ahead," as large a majority of the blue-collar men expressed such a concern as did the white-collar males.

Thus, if these working-class families are different, in ways we cannot specify, from their peers who left the crowded Midtown tenements for more open sections of the City and its suburbs, they appear, in respect to certain basic values, not unlike the neighboring higher-status families who for certain ends have also elected to remain within the cramped confines of Midtown.

Amid the great socioeconomic differences we can discern a common core of values by which a Manhattan residence is often a means to *future* goals, rather than that key *current* end: adequate family *lebensraum.* Pressing upon us from the observation just made were these questions: How do its people actually regard Manhattan as a human habitat? Will we find here the predominant tendency to consider one's community at the very least "as good to live in as any other place"?[36]

The issue was put to our sample of interviewed Midtown adults in several different ways. One query asked the respondent: "For *yourself,* do you think it is better to live on a farm, in a small town, in a small city, or in a big city like New York?" By their replies 53 percent of the sample indicated their feeling that they would be better off living elsewhere than in the kind of big city they now occupy.

This interview question was preceded by two more pointed inquiries. One, asked much earlier in the interview session, offered health effects as a criterion for assessing the local environment. Here respondents could react to the opinion that "the big city is just as healthy to live in as any other place." A total of 57 percent flatly disagreed with the proposition.

Applying a third criterion, immediately preceding the "for yourself" query, the respondent was asked: "For *growing children,* do you think it is better to be brought up on a farm, in a small town, in a small city, or in a big city like New York?"

In reply, 85 percent of the sample respondents with varying degrees of intensity recommended any place other than a big city like New York as a place for raising children. Of course, we expected that these particular replies would vary decisively with the rural-urban backgrounds of respondents. This proved not to be the case. Native New Yorkers were as overwhelmingly disapproving of their city in this respect as were the immigrants and in-migrants from smaller home towns.[37]

Let us now classify these respondents according to the major combinations of their replies to the two questions soliciting perceptions of the metropolis as a home setting for themselves and for children. Exactly half of the sample population were consistent in rejecting Manhattan, on both counts, in favor of other alternatives. Doubtless some of these are of the "carpetbagger" type, long-term transients who look forward to ultimate breaking of the chains of career that keep them anchored to Manhattan. Some are parents of young children and are likely candidates for suburbia.[38] Others are probably the defeated and embittered who are too encumbered to take the course of flight.

Another 13 percent of the sample adults were consistent in upholding the metropolis on both counts in preference to other alternatives. These are probably the people who see Manhattan as the best of all possible worlds, avow they would live nowhere else, and emphasize, as did George M. Cohan, that "When you're away from Broadway, you're only camping out," or, as did one British expatriate-repatriate upon celebrating his permanent resettlement in New York: "For anyone who has lived in New York for seven years, anywhere else is a village—even London." On the same point, Theodore Dreiser quotes an old, "half-demented" Manhattan seamstress and slum dweller to the resolute effect that "I would rather live in my [single] hall-bedroom in New York than in any fifteen-room house in the country that I ever saw!"[39]

With characteristic flourish, Alexander Woollcott writes: "Since God lifted this continent above the waters and so clad its plains and valleys that it could be a homestead for a numberless multitude, it must fill Him at times with mingled surprise, amusement and exasperation to note how many of us are perversely scrounged together in a monstrous determination to live crowded on Manhattan Island

and there only—there or not at all."[40]

Perhaps most interesting of all in the dissensus of our Midtown sample population is the 37 percent segment that revealed mixed feelings of one pattern or other by rejecting the metropolis as the milieu of choice for growing children, but approving it for themselves despite its acknowledged shortcomings.[41] The literature gives ample voice to this kind of orientation in its many variants.

Relevant is the following excerpt from E. B. White's essay:

By rights New York should have destroyed itself long ago, from panic or fire or rioting or failure of some vital supply line. . . . New Yorkers meet confusion and congestion with patience and grit—a sort of perpetual muddling through. Every facility is inadequate—the hospitals and schools and playgrounds are over-crowded . . . there is not enough air and not enough light. . . . But the city makes up for its hazards and deficiencies by supplying its citizens with massive doses of a supplementary vitamin—the sense of belonging to something unique, cosmopolitan, mighty and unparalleled. . . . The city is uncomfortable and inconvenient, but New Yorkers temperamentally do not crave comfort and convenience —if they did they would live elsewhere.[42]

Steinbeck elaborates the theme:

New York is an ugly city, a dirty city, its climate is a scandal, its politics are used to frighten children, its traffic is madness, its competition is murderous. But there is one thing about it—once you have lived in New York and it has become your home, no place else is good enough. All of everything is concentrated here. . . . It is tireless and its air is charged with energy. . . . Every once in a while we go away for several months and we always come back with a "Thank God I'm home" feeling. For New York is the world with every vice and blemish and beauty. . . . What more could you ask?[43]

Ada Louise Huxtable, architectural critic, emphasizes the two sides of New York's character in rather different terms:

New York usually seems to be an all-is-for-the-worst-in-the-worst-of-all-possi-ble-worlds city. But when it is good, New York is very, very good, which is why New Yorkers put up with so much that is bad.

When it is good, this is a city of fantastic strength, sophistication and beauty. It is like no other city in time or place. Visitors and even natives rarely use the words "urban character" or "environmental style," but that is what they are reacting to with awe in the presence of massed, concentrated steel, stone, power and life. It is a quality of urban greatness that may not solve racial or social tensions, or the human or economic crises to which a city is prone, but it survives them.[44]

A more clear-cut stage of unreconciled conflict may be discerned in the book *Manhattan and Me*[45] by Oriana Atkinson, herself a Manhattanite. To cite some scattered illustrative comments:

Walking about the streets and observing the state of dwelling houses in general, you get the uncomfortable feeling that this is a doomed city.

New York is no place to live, no place to bring up a child. So people say; so many New Yorkers admit.

What would be the answer from all the young who inhabit this mammoth cave? . . . I think I know without asking. Everything I have said about this vexatious city is true. And yet everything I have told you is a lie. . . . New York [is] the city whose ultimate boon is youthfulness of spirit. . . . I knew, deeply, that New Yorkers are really a happy people. . . . We [New Yorkers] are a young and vigorous race, geared to excitement, contradictory, emotional, ready for whatever the next hour may bring.

It seems like a dismal shame that a city like this one, with everything in the world necessary for the health, happiness, and general welfare of its citizens, should have degenerated into such a slovenly, mean, uncomfortable place to be.

It has been said, and perhaps with truth, that anyone who has ever lived in New York cannot be happy living anywhere else. Speaking for myself, I know I'm very tired of this city; yet, when I think over the other places where I might choose to end my days, I am always doubtful that I'd be happy there.

In the seventies, physical insecurity descended upon New Yorkers as a constant specter. Defying the lure of the suburbs, this is how one Brooklyn mother poignantly reconciled herself to the new hazards and tensions:

We have two locks and a chain on our apartment door. . . . In the streets I'm always conscious of my pocketbook. [People] are afraid to travel in the subways. . . . But every once in a while I feel an inexplicable sense of camaraderie because of all of us in it, all going to and from work to try to keep our lives pieced together, all trying to live and find, each in his own way, some of the same things.

I would like to feel safer in New York. I would like the air and the streets to be cleaner. . . . But I am not going to run away. If there is no safety, no comfort here in New York, where will I find it? The problems of New York City are the problems of the world in which I live. I do not expect to be absolved from them. . . .

But why pretend that my choice not to run is cerebral? There is no place else, in the deepest place in my heart, where I want to live. Love, I suppose, is like that. . . .

As soon as I can afford to, the only suburb I'll ever consider is Manhattan.[46]

Whether they perceive Manhattan's blemishes or not, whether they affirm or deny it as an adequate place to live, most schools of thought testify to the Island's "youthful spirit," "excitement," and "exhilaration." We approach here an intangible, elusive quality of the metropolis, that seems to elicit in its residents a heightened sense of vitality.[47] Although self-consuming, this brand of *élan* persuades that one's life energies burn brighter and higher while it lasts. Such seeming surcharge of personal energy, vistas of the steep but open way up, proximity to the arena of career battles, and immediate access to a huge array of recreational facilities, together, we infer, bind to Manhattan people who in the strict logic of family comfort and well-being would otherwise settle, as one exmetropolite deftly put it, "for the airier way to live."

Here, perhaps, we can discern two polar types of human beings: (1) those restlessly bent on maximizing their latent sensibilities[48] and potentialities who are irresistibly drawn to the polytonic metropolis, as moth to the flame, despite its discomforts, insecurities, risks, and costs,[49] and (2) those settled and at ease in the steady rhythm of monotonic, smaller places, who look upon the metropolis with distaste for its hurly-burly, carnival image, and its "vaulting ambitions."

To recapitulate, then, the population of Midtown, like that of Manhattan, is the distillate of a three-stage process of selection. First, from the large American and foreign populations there is selection of the few, relatively speaking, who leave their childhood homestead to build new lives in the vastly different environment of New York City. From all these, and also from people native to other parts of the metropolis, there is a screening out, in the second stage, of those who elect to reside in a Manhattan section like Midtown. Finally, from those who settle in Manhattan there is a winnowing of those who elect to remain, when the best interests of self and family urge removal to more spacious sections of the metropolitan region.

After the centennial of Charles Darwin's revolutionary book,[50] it may be relevant to recall his emphasis on the process of biological selection in the evolution of species, as each adapted to the environment and its changes. By way of rough analogy, there are discernible in Midtown processes of psychosocial selection. From vastly diverse human populations, these processes operate to draw individuals into the highly specialized cliff-dweller habitats of the great city.

And we suggest that the Midtown population, for all its great heterogeneity, can be viewed as an emergent of a relatively new, localized species of American. This is the species that is adapted, albeit in an uneasy fashion, to its chosen environment at the vortex of the one city to have been saluted as "the world's supreme metropolis."

NOTES

[1]Given the extreme length of the Study sample interview, evidence bearing on these particular questions could not be secured from our sample adults. However, other kinds of testimony are available to us.

[2]E. B. White, *Here Is New York*, 1949, p. 23.

[3]There are specific limiting sides to these realities, as are revealed in two facts. When New York's economy was expanding in its "heavy work" sectors both immigrants and in-migrants were predominantly males. When, as in recent decades, these sectors contracted and growth shifted to the "paper work" functions, the sex balance shifted toward females among both types of migrants.

[4]White, *Here Is New York*, pp. 9 and 32.

[5]H. Taubman, *The New York Times Magazine*, April 29, 1956.

In explaining why his company had decided to remain in New York and construct a new skyscraper-headquarters, the president of the nation's largest publishing house announced: "New York is the cultural and entertainment capital of the nation, as well as the commercial, financial and communications capital. The quality of the city's cultural life serves as a magnet to attract the creative people who are vital to our business. We could not find the talent anywhere else in the nation." (*New York Times*, August 6, 1971).

[6]Granville Hicks, *Small Town*, 1946, p. 25.

[7]Alec Waugh, *The New York Times Magazine*, April 29, 1956.

[8]Editors, *Holiday* (October 1959): p. 49.

[9]Cyril Connolly, *Ideas and Places*, 1959, p. 176.

[10]White, *Here Is New York*, pp. 16 and 17.

[11]Truman Capote, *Local Color*, 1946, pp. 13–14.

[12]Robert E. Park, *The City*, 1925, pp. 1–46.

[13]Grayson Kirk has observed of New York that "here in almost complete cross-section are representations of virtually every social, racial and economic problem America knows" (*The New York Times*, April 26, 1956). To this roster of problems can probably be added those in the realm of personality.

[14]John Lardner, "The Case for Living Here," *The New York Times Magazine*, April 29, 1956.

[15]Waugh, *The New York Times Magazine*, April 29, 1956.

[16]Thomas Wolfe, *The Web and the Rock*, 1939, p. 229.

[17]Abraham Cowley, "The Garden."

[18]A. Klein, ed., *The Empire City*, 1955, p. xxi.

[19]Frank Lloyd Wright, *The Disappearing City*, 1932, pp. 435–436.

[20]Alfred Kazin, "Writing: The Voice of the City," *Holiday* (October 1959): 88–89.

[21]Wolfe, *The Web and the Rock*, p. 223.

[22]John Steinbeck, "The Making of a New Yorker," *The New York Times Magazine,* February 1, 1953.

[23]Editors, *Holiday,* (October 1959): 49.

[24]Meyer Berger, "Preface," in Klein, *The Empire City,* p. xx.

[25]Frank Sullivan, "The Case for Just Visiting," *The New York Times Magazine,* April 29, 1956.

[26]A newspaper article reports a Manhattan luxury-housing survey to the effect that "high income, high-rent tenants spend their shelter dollars not on added space but on quality and location." On the other hand, a critic of Manhattan's recent residential construction observes as a trend that "luxury apartments become smaller, shoddier and more stereotyped."

[27]One critic arraigns the skyscraper that "has destroyed light, space and air, and turned sunshine into a special privilege."

[28]Dorothy Barclay, *Understanding the City Child,* 1959, pp. 50, 56, and 150.

[29]Ibid., p. 150.

[30]In 1972, with assaults on school children having become a frequent occurrence the same magazine had an article on "big-city boyhood" entitled, "It's scary sometimes, but it's a lot of fun."

[31]With remarkable prescience, Mark Twain put this warning notice at the head of *The Adventures of Huckleberry Finn:* "Persons attempting to find a motive in this narrative will be prosecuted . . . persons attempting to find a plot in it will be shot."

[32]"The exurbs and all exurban life are primarily centered around the children. A couple may have had all sorts of bemused reasons for moving so far from the city, but the wife had one compelling one: her children are out of the city." A. C. Spectorsky, *The Exurbanites,* 1955, p. 248.

Referring to critics of the city-to-suburb movement, one ex-Manhattan mother wrote in a letter to the editor: "[Have they] stopped to consider that parents who made the change from city to country were not necessarily seeking 'Suburbia.' The real reason for moving was the desire for freedom from a confined city apartment . . . the houses beckoned and the people went."

[33]Tailored to the market of these parents is the book F. Weiner, *How to Survive in New York with Children,* 1969.

[34]*What's So Big about New York?,* New York City Department of Commerce and Public Events, undated.

[35]Furthermore, we do not view the Manhattan variant of the "climbing man" type as specific to rising executives but as covering more or less the entire range of white-collar jobs, both in corporations and out. Thus, Whyte's model of the organization man appears to be a subtype of the climber species (pinpointed in these words of one specimen: "You can't save money here, the competition is fierce, but the job opportunities are as huge as the skyscrapers"). W. H. Whyte, Jr., *The Organization Man,* 1956.

[36]A. Kornhauser, *Detroit as the People See It,* 1952, pp. 5–18.

[37]Least approving were the childless group of never-married and married-but-infertile respondents (10.7 percent), as compared with the parent group (19.5 percent).

[38]In fact, about 30 percent of the entire sample indicated they have thought of moving out of "this section of town."

[39]Theodore Dreiser, *The Color of a Great City,* 1923, p. 2.

[40]Alexander Woollcott, "No Yesterdays," in Klein, *The Empire City,* p. 420.

[41]Stated differently, of all respondents who said they regarded the big city as the best place for themselves, only 24 percent expressed the opinion that it is similarly suitable for the young. Focusing on the good-for-me group exclusively, we find that good-for-children replies were given by 37 percent of the low socioeconomic stratum in the group, 28 percent of the middle stratum, and 17 percent of the upper.

On the surface, these data appear somewhat surprising. Of course, the financial resources of the high-status people are translated for the child into larger living quarters, domestic help to expand mother's free time, private schools, special recreational advantages, and so forth. On the other hand, the lower-SES adults see their children without any of these buffers to the metropolitan environment. Accordingly, we could expect the high group to be more prone than the low to favor the big city as a home base for the young.

That the reverse is the case, among those apparently committed to Manhattan for themselves, suggests the following as one possibility: The upper-SES group, predominantly also of higher education, may be more critically aware of and concerned about the potential impact of the metropolitan milieu as it bears, *even at its very best,* on their children.

[42] White, *Here Is New York,* pp. 24–26 and 50.

[43] Steinbeck, *The New York Times Magazine,* February 1, 1953.

[44] *New York Times,* March 31, 1968.

[45] Oriana Atkinson, 1954, pp. 28, 39, 41–42, 132, and 265–266.

[46] Marie J. Lederman, "New York," *City* magazine, Summer 1972.

[47] One suburbanite exiled from Manhattan, on a return visit was quoted in the local press: "You're alive here. In Fairlawn you just exist."

[48] British novelist J. B. Priestly touched this vein in a newspaper interview, when he observed: "Among the mass of New Yorkers I sense a great eagerness for new experience."

[49] Maslow's formulation of the "self-actualizing" personality may be an extreme and relatively rare variant of this broader type. A. H. Maslow, *Toward a Psychology of Being,* 1962.

[50] *The Descent of Man,* 1871.

CHAPTER 6

COMMUNITY INSTITUTIONS AND PSYCHOSOCIAL CLIMATE

LEO SROLE

"A house," in the professional accent of Madam Polly Adler, "is not a home." On the same principle, a metropolitan area and its people do not necessarily make a community, as Manhattan's Bowery district and its flophouse tenants need hardly testify.

How far Midtown warrants accreditation as a full-fledged community or falls short of that estate is one of several questions to be considered in this chapter. The issue is entangled in complexities that require a more extensive use of conceptual instruments than has been necessary hitherto in this book. Moreover, we move here on ground where our literary witnesses, so illuminating in the preceding chapter, are decidedly less articulate.

To avoid possible misunderstandings of our key notions, let us fix as one working definition that a population occupying a circumscribed locale is a community to the extent that it satisfies this major criterion among others: The full variety of its human needs—both common and special—are adequately met by ongoing social arrangements, such as have been established in the gamut of extrafamilial institutions. *Institution,* in turn, is here treated as a generic term[1] referring to more or less enduring organizations that, within the communal division of social labor, have specialized functions and specialized personnel, for example, church, corporation, hospital, and school.

Of course, for a residential section of a city the criterion of human needs locally served cannot apply as strictly as it does to the far more self-contained and self-sufficient entity of the city itself. Nevertheless, our interest here is in discerning the extent to which Midtown, at the time of the Study, was institutionally organized relative to its own needs, problems, and capabilities. Furthermore, this goal is itself only a means to our larger purpose, namely, that of conveying to the reader a sense of the general nature and texture of the human environment in which the people of Midtown carried on a considerable portion of their daily lives. A case study of a population that omits delineation of the communal aspects of its environment is in a sense as incomplete as a case study of a patient that overlooks his familial environment. With this observation, we would emphasize again the limitations of the present group portrayal made from the bird's-eye view, rather than from a close-up vantage point.

INSTITUTIONS: TYPES

For descriptive convenience, we might start on the most elementary level of services performed by Midtown's economic institutions. It must be indicated, parenthetically, that the area is free of industrial establishments, except for a few small factories in loft buildings at scattered points near its borders. Thus, its internal economy consists almost entirely of small retail shops and service enterprises in considerable number and variety. Some of these, highly specialized in kind, draw customers from surrounding Manhattan and from other boroughs. In largest numbers, however, they serve either their immediately adjoining neighborhood alone or get the trade of residents from other parts of the Midtown area. Retail stores of the latter type are particularly concentrated along the length of one of the major thoroughfares, which is locally regarded as something of a "Main Street" shopping center.

Despite the proximity of Manhattan's Central Business Section and its unparalleled shopping facilities, to an important degree Midtown residents satisfy their consumer and service wants within local establishments, many of which are long-settled fixtures of the scene. Indeed, the latter and the relatively few inroads of national retail chains, so conspicuous in smaller cities, contribute to the overall impression of rooted stability in this sector of Midtown's economy.

Turning to the field of professional services, we might compare Midtown with the rest of Manhattan on the yardstick of number or rate of professionals per 100,000 population. For example, Midtown and Manhattan were almost identical in their rates of locally practicing dentists, chiropractors, and morticians. However, a striking divergence was encountered in the medical profession. In 1954, practicing physicians with offices in or overlooking Midtown numbered 1,180 per 100,000 local population (up to 1,330 in 1969), as compared with rates in the rest of Manhattan and the urban United States of 285 and 132 (in 1969, 320 and 160) per 100,000, respectively. Midtown's unprecedented rate reflects the fact that the area is a base for heavy concentration of medical specialists serving not only Manhattan and the City at large, but the entire metropolitan region and, occasionally, beyond. As a highly relevant example, we might focus on the psychiatrists among these physicians. Those who were members of the American Psychiatric Association[2] in 1954 and had offices in or adjoining Midtown numbered about 250 per 100,000 of the local population (up to 440 in 1969), as compared with corresponding rates for the rest of Manhattan and for the City's other four boroughs of 18 and 16 (in 1969, 40 and 7), respectively.

In many American metropolitan centers, privately practicing medical specialists (like specializing lawyers) predominantly tend to establish their offices within the central business district. It is not relevant here to explore the particular factors that might explain why a residential area like Midtown, rather than Manhattan's main business hub, has acquired this centralized service function. It is pertinent to note one corollary, namely, the fact that Midtown is also a center for hospital institutions, voluntary (i.e., nonprofit), municipal, and proprietary—general as well as specialized. In 1954 these hospitals were eighteen in number, and all told provided over 2,100 beds per 100,000 Midtown population, as against 1,100 and 990 beds per 100,000 in the rest of Manhattan and the United States, respectively. (By 1969 these eighteen hospitals had expanded to 3,300 beds per 100,000.) Also operating were twenty-five other medical research and service organizations. It might be added that Midtown exhibits the pattern, seen in other big cities, of major medical institutions congregating in residential areas that adjoin the central business section. Of course, Midtown is only one of a number of Manhattan areas with such concentrations of hospitals.

Two further points about these medical institutions should be noted. First, the largest ones, accounting for most of the beds, are not local in geographical range of their reputations, their supporting funds, or their patients—who come not only from Midtown and the entire metropolitan region, but in some instances from the country at large and even from abroad. These hospitals did not spring into being at the initiative of the Midtown community acting out of felt local needs. In most instances they had long been established elsewhere in the City and had migrated "uptown" to Midtown because of their own internal growth and external ecological forces that pressed for a more central and accessible location.

Nonetheless, at-hand availability of medical services in a locality is often a decisive factor in their utilization when need arises or looms on the horizon. Accordingly, in number and quality of hospitals, as in private specialists, Midtown appears to be one of the best-equipped residential areas, medically speaking, in the world.

Out of our specific mental health interest, it should also be added that in 1954 Manhattan had 90 psychiatric outpatient clinics (138 in 1969), large and small.[3] Although few of these low-fee facilities are in Midtown proper, its residents are within relatively easy transit access to many of them.

All told, in terms of creature, medical, and specifically psychiatric needs, Midtown gives the appearance of being institutionally well served. This appearance, in its psychiatric aspects, is a matter to which we shall return in a later chapter. Now we might proceed further into the larger, encompassing framework of Midtown institutions.

There are a variety of human needs that can be met in a democratic society only by the voluntary, collaborative action of local citizens working through the instruments of their own self-created and self-supported organizations. These fall into two major types: organizations created by and for one of the several constituent groups or *segments* of the local population, and those established to serve the overarching, common, or general welfare of the *entire* population. For purposes of convenience we shall designate these two categories of institutions as *segmental* and *central,* respectively.

Perhaps the most conspicuous of Midtown's segmental organizations are its many institutions of worship, including over thirty (by 1969 down to twenty-five) Protestant churches (predominantly Episcopal, Presbyterian, Baptist, Lutheran, and Methodist), approximately fifteen Catholic parishes, a number of synagogues representing the Orthodox, Conservative, and Reform wings of Judaism, and several Eastern Orthodox churches.[4] In size of congregation these vary considerably, among the Protestant churches, for example, in a range from under 100 to well over 2,000. However, there are reasons to believe, on the one hand, that the parishioners of the Catholic churches are almost exclusively Midtowners,· and on the other that the Protestant and Jewish congregations include not a few ex-residents of the area.

Of course, neither the number of institutions of worship nor the absolute number of their local adherents give any clue to the vitality of institutional participation by the population at large. For such a clue we can look to the sample of Midtown adults interviewed for this Study. Among them, slightly less than one-half (45 percent) report attending religious services more than the gestural three times a year. About one-fourth go infrequently (that is, two or three times a year); and approximately 30 percent indicate they never or rarely attend. Thus, hardly one-half of the adult Midtown population can be regarded as having more than a nominal identification with an institution of worship. On the other hand, it must be emphasized that these institutions have gone far beyond their central function of providing for religious worship. Indeed, they are also serving adherents of their own faith through a large and complex network of auxiliary institutions.

Segmental institutions, religious or otherwise, which have adult membership bodies can be further differentiated according to the major kind of function they perform: (1) the "self-service" function, that is, the organization serves the needs of its own face-to-face membership; and (2) the "serve-others" function, that is, the institution is primarily dedicated to the needs of nonmembers, although usually within the same segmental group.[5]

A church or synagogue is primarily a self-service institution in that it is directed to the religious needs of its congregants. However, in the many auxiliary institutions created by the Midtown churches and synagogues, or by their parent bodies, we see in conspicuous form the serve-others motive. These creations include not only systems of day schools, to be reviewed below, but also the following: nurseries for very young children; homes for the orphaned, the handicapped, the aged; recreation centers and associations for adolescents and young people; residence "clubs" for young adults away from home; and adult-education programs. Finally, for its adult members each congregation or parish is sponsor and guide to a series of laity associations that have both self-service and serve-others functions.

Another important source of segmental institutions in Midtown is its large group of high-income residents. Although Midtown has a number of institutions of worship with upper-status congregations, from our Study sample of adults it appears that attendance of religious services, within each major denomination, tends to be inversely correlated with socioeconomic standing. The higher the status, that is, the less frequent is participation and affiliation. It seems, therefore, that the social activity of Midtown's upper-status group revolves predominantly around its characteristic secular clubs and organizations,[6] including separate associations of descendants of Dutch and English "old families." Some of these have quite limited self-service functions, as in the case of the street associations, each created for cooperative planting and maintenance of trees on one or more block fronts of townhouse residences. Many organizations appear to combine a primary self-service function of get-together recreation and an incidental serve-others function of contributing to one of a large variety of philanthropies. For other organizations, on the other hand, the dominant emphasis is on supporting a specific service agency or program, local, citywide, national, or overseas, and social affairs are basically part of the fund-raising strategy. Among the Midtown nonsectarian, serve-others agencies so supported are its voluntary hospitals, its several long-established and professionally staffed settlement houses in tenement neighborhoods, and a number of limited programs and organizations directed, for example, to getting the youth of such neighborhoods off the local streets.[7]

Except for church auxiliaries, the middle-class associations, so active and vocal on the social landscape of smaller American communities, in Midtown appear conspicuous by their scarcity, quietism, and primarily self-service orientations. In 1954 they included a chamber of commerce, a Lions Club, several geographically limited businessmen's associations, a few posts of the major national veterans' organizations, a number of neighborhood political clubs affiliated with one or another of the political parties, the PTAs of public elementary schools, a League of Women Voters, and a chapter of Alcoholics Anonymous.

The working-class segment of Midtown for the most part is divided into a number of ethnic groups. As we have noted, certain churches serving this particular segment tend to follow national-origin lines of division. Although for some people in these ethnic groups primary participation centers on the church and its auxiliary organizations, for others it revolves around the group's secular associations that are largely recreational·in their activities.[8] The latter appear in a variety of special-interest forms. Some carry the word *literary* or *democratic* or *independent political* after the national designation in their titles. Others refer to themselves as gymnastic, athletic, or singing societies.

The smaller of Midtown's major ethnic groups have no local associations of their own in the area but have nationality organizations available elsewhere in the City. On the other hand, several groups have two or more locally based, secular recreational associations that also attract members from other sections of the City. In each of three of these groups there is also a local community hall that is the focus of much of its organized recreational activity.

Conspicuous as these secular associations may be to the observer, the test of the range of group participation is as relevant to them as to the churches. Interviewing our sample of Midtown adults, we asked individuals with ethnic backgrounds whether they had "any interest at all" in the recreational organizations of their particular nationality group. Responding affirmatively were 24 percent of the immigrant (first) generation, and 10 percent of the second generation. *Participating* to any degree in meetings or social affairs of such organizations, whether as members or not, were 18 and 6 percent in the first and second generations, respectively.

Of course, there are wide differences among the Midtown ethnic groups on indices of adult interest and participation in their secular associations. However, in none have we found participants representing more than a minority of the group's adult element.

In this review of Midtown's institutional aspects as a community, we can hardly overlook its schools. The area has three separate educational "systems" each covering the entire span from the nursery level through colleges granting the bachelor degree. We shall not touch upon the latter, nor upon the many high schools (which are of both the college preparatory and vocational types) because in all three systems their student bodies are drawn from Manhattan or New York City at large. As for the elementary schools, serving Midtown almost exclusively, in 1954 there were twelve in the public system (six in 1969), ten (twelve in 1969) in the Catholic system (as well as several Protestant and Jewish parochial schools), and twenty "private," nonsectarian schools for children of high-income families (twenty in 1969).[9] The trichotomy of public, parochial, and private schools highlights for us in summary fashion the institutional segmentation of Midtown along the cross-cutting lines of socioeconomic and religious differentiation. This follows the general pattern of all large, heterogeneous American cities, a pattern deeply rooted in the fundamental democratic rights of freedom of worship and freedom of association.

INSTITUTIONS: CENTRAL

As has often been emphasized, the other side of the coin of democratic freedoms that support group segmentation is the citizen's share in the general welfare, in the community as a common enterprise, and more specifically in those local conditions that are beyond the resources and authority of the separate segmented groups to resolve. The responsibility that adheres to this share of course transcends individual commitments to a segmental group and its institutions and can only be discharged through what we call central institutions. These are of two main types. One is to be seen as prototype in the voluntary citizens' council, which we shall discuss below. The other appears in the City's overarching municipal government, which for Midtown performs certain "housekeeping" functions, like providing water supply and police, fire, and sanitation services. Of course, it also administers the local public schools. And its departments of health and hospitals maintain special institutions in the Study area.

Not yet given due mention is the City's Welfare (now "Social Services") Department. Under economic conditions of full employment, as in the Study period, this department primarily extended public aid to three main categories of nonemployable people, namely, children, the aged, and the disabled. For the City as a whole we know that in 1954 over 300,000 individuals were given help to an aggregate of about $220 million. (Fifteen years later the number so assisted had almost quadrupled, reflecting changes that had occurred in the nonemployable and unemployed population of New York and most other large American cities.)[10]

This particular function of government as a central institution, whatever its form, must be seen in conjunction with the City's complicated apparatus of social-service agencies that were established by the voluntary, i.e., segmental, type of institutions previously discussed. If one carefully examines the biennial *Directory of Social and Health Agencies of New York City,*[11] he will find many hundreds of social agencies identified and grouped under such headings as Adoption, Correctional Care, Employment and Vocational Guidance, Family Service, Homeless and Unattached, Recreation, and Shelters: Temporary, for Children.

Confronting the City's governmental and voluntary institutions functioning in this field of *special* human needs, one magazine writer declared that "the picture emerges of a huge welfare and eleemosynary setup—one of the largest ever known to man."

Even if this setup were the very largest in history, its sheer size is secondary to the question of its adequacy, that is, its capacity relative to the magnitude of urgent needs to be met in the population it serves. First, in the interest of brevity, let us circumscribe the question by arbitrarily limiting ourselves to the needs of children in certain critical circumstances. Then, let us attend the measured words of a state authority in the social service field, speaking with specific reference to foster care of children who are the debris of irreparably shattered families:[12]

I think everyone is agreed that New York City faces a critical situation with respect to the care of such children. . . . The voluntary agencies are putting forth their best efforts but the size of the problem is greater than the current facilities and resources to deal with it. . . . A large area of unmet need remains and unless some positive steps to reverse this trend are made, the gap will continue to widen. I think the time has arrived when all the forces interested in the welfare of children should subscribe to an unequivocal policy that no child accepted as a public charge by the [City's] Department of Welfare should be denied care, of the kind needed and when needed, because of any limitation in the facilities or policies of voluntary child-caring agencies.

The last sentence cited suggests the nature of a service failure in unmistakable terms. (Press reports in 1970 suggest that this "distressing" default has not been significantly corrected.)

Focusing down to a second group of New York children, namely, juvenile delinquents, we read the following query in a New York newspaper: "No other city can boast of police forces more numerous, corrective institutions so progressive and such a structure of municipal, state, Federal and private services dealing with almost every social problem known to man. Why then are juvenile delinquency and the phenomena associated with it measurably on the increase in New York?"

As if in reply to this question, John Dollard, writing in the same newspaper, commented on New York's delinquency problem: "The main trouble is that there is not enough of anything: institutions, social workers, religious workers, probation officers, settlement-house staffs, psychiatrists, teachers, judges, police. . . . The heroic few now working are solving the problem in principle, but they cannot contend with it in fact."

A newspaper article discussed the understaffed Juvenile Aid Bureau in the City's Police Department and noted that this bureau, with jurisdiction for wayward youths under the age of sixteen, continues its unwanted "social work function only because there is a vacuum—the private agencies won't take most of these [young delinquents] and there is no public agency equipped to deal with them." For delinquent adolescents over the age of fifteen the vacuum seemingly is total.

In its Declaration on the Rights of the Child, the United Nations has codified the universal principle that "mankind owes to the child the best it has to give." It seems, however, that two categories of New York children, both in catastrophic predicaments, are rather beyond the combined management capabilities of the sprawling municipal welfare and service apparatus and the multitude of voluntary social agencies. Against this citywide background of partial default in meeting the crises of the homeless and the delinquent children, we can now return to Midtown for further consideration of its particular effectiveness as a community in serving certain special local needs. For this purpose, we shall first place in evidence the indicators provided by a series of human pathologies. Quantified in the form of frequency rates, these can also be read as sociologically symptomatic of conditions in the area and its people. Table 6-1 presents Midtown's rates of known juvenile delinquency, tuberculosis morbidity, and four selected types of mortality among its residents, during the year preceding the inception of the Study. As baselines for comparison, rates are also given for the matching (white, non-Puerto Rican) resident populations of Manhattan and four outer boroughs of the City.[13]

TABLE 6–1. RATES OF SIX PATHOLOGIES IN THREE WHITE, NON-PUERTO RICAN POPULATIONS OF NEW YORK CITY

Pathology	Midtown	Manhattan	Outer boroughs
A. Juvenile delinquents* in fiscal year March 1951–1952 (annual rates per 100,000 youths age 5–20)	2,460	2,294	1,569
B. Active tuberculosis cases† on Dec. 31, 1951 (prevalence rates per 100,000 total population)	284	283	138
C. Infant mortality‡ in calendar year 1951 (annual rates per 1,000 live births) . . .	27	25	20
D. Three other mortalities in calendar year 1951 (annual rates per 100,000 total population):			
Alcoholism	17	10	6
Suicide	15	15	9
Accidents—nonvehicular	48	45	25

*From Central Registration files of the New York City Youth Board, generously made available by its Research Director, Mrs. Maud Craig, to Dr. Alfred Parsell and his staff of City College of New York sociology students.

†From A. M. Lowell, *Socio-economic Conditions and TB Prevalence in New York City, 1949–51,* 1956.

‡Sources for the four forms of mortality are:

For Midtown, tabulations especially made for this Study by Dr. Carl Erhardt and his staff in the Bureau of Records and Statistics, New York City Department of Health, to whom we acknowledge our gratitude.

For the boroughs, *Vital Statistics by Health Areas and Health Center Districts, 1951,* Bureau of Records and Statistics, New York City Department of Health.

First, we note that juvenile delinquency in Midtown, and in its parent borough as well, was approximately half again higher than in the rest of the City's white health areas. Even more striking is that the prevalence of known, active tubercular cases in Midtown, as among Manhattan whites, was twice larger than that in the outer boroughs. In rates of infant mortality, the differences among the three populations, although not so marked, were in the same direction as observed above.[14]

Turning to the three predominantly adult forms of mortality, we again see relatively sharp differences, especially in deaths due to alcoholism and nonvehicular accidents.[15] If in suicide rates the differences are not so pronounced, it will be remembered that the motivational line of demarcation between deaths appearing to be accidental and those certifiable as suicide is often difficult to draw. In cases where the evidence is equivocal, the benefit of the doubt upon certification by the family physician usually falls toward the former alternative. Rather more clearly, alcoholic fatalities are generally motivated by self-destructive tendencies. On these grounds, if we combine the three forms of adult mortality in section D of table 6–1, the aggregate rate for Midtown was eighty, for white Manhattan seventy, and for the outer boroughs forty.

The Midtown frequencies appearing in table 6–1 can be followed further. As we have seen, this residential section is at a far extreme from homogeneity, and the six types of pathology reported above are not distributed at random in its population.

Rates for these pathologies were available to us only by health-area units that the New York Health Department uses administratively to divide the City. As a next step, let us cull out the Midtown health areas with the lowest and the highest rate for each type of pathology in turn.

Following the specifications indicated in table 6–1, the range in these health area rates are:

TABLE 6–2. RANGE IN HEALTH AREA RATES

Pathology	Lowest rate	Highest rate
Juvenile delinquency	360	5,010
Tuberculosis: morbidity.	106	321
Infant mortality	14	45
Alcoholism: mortality.	4	37
Suicide	8	25
Accidents: nonvehicular mortality . . .	26	79

Thus, the frequency differences among Midtown's health-area units are substantial indeed. But such units are themselves highly heterogeneous in population composition. For three of these pathologies, however, we were able to secure the home addresses of the victims. When delinquency, tuberculosis morbidity, and infant fatality cases are spotted by residence on separate block maps of Midtown, an identical pattern emerges, namely, overwhelming concentration in the belt of blocks covered by five- and six-story walk-up tenements that were slum housing when they were newly reared by speculative builders around the turn of the century.

It is not necessary to make the simplistic assumption that such housing *breeds* the kind of pathologies concerning us in these immediate pages. If slums create an environment that in some part aggravates, magnifies, or triggers the complex conditions which issue in the above pathologies, there is sufficient warrant for including them in the overall picture of ecological contamination.

These objective criteria aside, under the democratic conscience the inequities of maintaining such housing have to be ultimately redressed. In point of fact, this has been implicit in the City government's actions between 1936 and 1961. With municipal, state, and federal funds aggregating several billion dollars, the City in this period carried out a record housing program, constructing some 150,000 dwelling units. Manhattan alone secured about one-third of all these low-rent dwellings. Nor does this take into account the Island's substantial low-rent housing projects built by private institutions with one of several types of cost-reducing assistance from the municipality.

As far back as 1938, the Mayor's Committee on City Planning surveyed the Midtown area, declared that its principal problem was housing, and recommended its core tenement belt to "demolition or rehabilitation." By 1961, when Midtown held 10 percent of Manhattan's entire resident population, the public funds poured into housing had not found their way to build one residential structure in the area. The conception and design of most public housing, like public welfare generated in the innovating New Deal period, has also come under severe and largely justified, albeit hindsight, criticism. What is not at issue, however, is that adequate housing can be provided low-income families on the necessary scale only with contributory funds from the public sector.

Midtown's lack of such publicly supported housing during the Study period has relevance here to a matter mentioned earlier in this chapter. We refer to the necessity in a segmented population for central, integrating institutions of the voluntary, citizens' council type that addresses itself to overarching needs and problems in its own communal edifice. One of its minimal functions, in a residential section like Midtown, is to communicate its local requirements to the larger, governmental type of central institution. As a matter of fact, the highest elected authority in the municipal government at that time explicitly voiced this principle: "From the beginning, this administration has not only shown willingness to listen to suggestions of community groups concerning matters of government policy and practice, but has actively solicited the aid of these groups."[16]

Midtown had not been without a voluntary central organization of its own. Indeed, for some years it had a housing council, but this expired without trace before the present Study began. A civic council, representing substantially the same territory as is covered in this Study, was formed in the years after World War I. From objectives such as furthering the installation of traffic lights, it shifted during the Depression years to gathering private funds for relief and again, during the 1940s, to coordinating citizens' groups and voluntary agencies in the social service field. In 1952 it was reorganized as a constituent of the citywide Welfare and Health Council.

It was not our purpose to evaluate this central institution. However, perusal of minutes of the predecessor body, attendance at several meetings by the present investigators, and reports from knowledgeable local informants were made possible. All these sources added to the impression that the Midtown Welfare and Health Council on the one hand was relatively strong in professional participants from local social agencies, including nationally known figures in the social work field versed in the skills of community organization. On the other hand, there was the decided impression that the Council was weak in representation and participation of segmental groups and of citizens-at-large. This contrast seemed to parallel a difference in perceptions of Midtown's housing problems and their consequences.[17] Apparently, the Council was thereby left voiceless and powerless to secure for Midtown's tenement belt the public rehabilitation program long recommended by municipal planning authorities themselves.

For a diagnosis of the difficulty in Midtown's sole voluntary central institution, a parallel may be found in the *New York Times*'s notable series of articles on factors behind the City's chronic juvenile delinquency problem:

Lack of vigorous civic effort can unquestionably be proved. But it would seem that the roots of the problem lie deeper—in the feeble participation by ordinary citizens in political life, in an increasing concentration by the community's most able leaders upon the more distant horizons of business, banking and national politics. . . . The plain truth seems to be that . . . the city and most of its inhabitants have been content to drift and make do. "Let George do it" has been a convenient motto for too many. . . . Too many persons have stood by idly, content and confident that the city's multiform social agencies are handling the problem. . . . Today the fearsome harvest is being reaped.[18]

Lack of a broad base of citizen interest and support seemed to account for the impotence of Midtown's own central institution in relation to its inadequate housing and derivative problems. However, this condition is not inherent in the metropolis. Through the City's alert press, it has been possible to keep an observant eye on other of Manhattan's residential sections as they contend with their own local problems.

One extremely heterogeneous Manhattan area has a vigorous neighborhood association that has received attention in national magazines. Its "purpose is nothing less ambitious than to unite all the social, civic and religious groups in the area into one body that works for common goals." According to a newspaper account, this federation of four neighborhood councils is "a citizens' self-help association organized to improve [its area]. It conducts a youth division to combat juvenile delinquency, sponsors an art show and open-air concerts, and operates a job-finding office for hard-to-place youth; as well as other activities."

Another Manhattan residential section formed a community council, consisting of seventy-nine religious, civic, business, labor, veterans', and parent-teacher organizations. Its goal was to combat the area's "deteriorated housing and other problems." Within months of its formal organization City officials were engaged with the council in working out a large-scale redevelopment plan that included a low-rent public housing project. The plan is now well advanced toward implementation.

The central citizens' organization in a third Manhattan area successfully fought determined official efforts to cut up a local park for auto traffic purposes. Explaining this outcome, a resident wrote a local newspaper editor: "Most people never know the feeling of community in the hugeness of New York City. This lack of community feeling is a basic cause of many New York City problems. [This district] is a rare exception—a community whose inhabitants have a feeling of belonging."

A striking point in Midtown's absence from this small company of exceptional Manhattan areas is that its assets in resident financial wealth, leadership resources, and segmented institutional strength are probably not exceeded anywhere else in the borough or the City. The large default of Midtown's middle- and high-income groups in not assuming their share of the common responsibility seems to differentiate this area from the exceptional districts with records of problem-solving accomplishment.

All in all, the Midtown adult population is partially organized within its group segments, principally around religious and secular recreational institutions. It has struggled, so far unsuccessfully, to sustain voluntary, areawide institutions that could act to correct certain glaring, long-standing environmental conditions with public funds directly at hand. In the sociological view, this is a failure to meet the final criterion of a full-fledged, integrated, and need-responsive community. To be sure, for a residential section of a great metropolis, such fulfillment is beset with real difficulties, but elsewhere in the same city it has proved to be not in the realm of the impossible.

THE PSYCHOSOCIAL CLIMATE

Up to this point, we have been regarding Midtown from the sociological perspective of its extrafamily institutions as these constitute the organized, communal edifice of its human environment. However, there are more subtle aspects in the psychosocial climate of informal interpersonal relationships that are relevant to our descriptive purposes. For evidence on several of these aspects we shall turn principally to the writers on Manhattan, many of them Midtown residents.

One of the most persistent themes in the literature on Manhattan, sounded in many variations, refers to its hustle, frantic speed, breakneck pace, etc. One newspaperman wryly quoted "a sociologist who works for a living running a night club" to the effect that "New Yorkers are perpetually drunk—not with whiskey, but with motion." Doubtless this quality in Manhattan led Christopher Morley to characterize it as "the nation's thyroid gland," and expatriate Frank Sullivan to taunt its residents: "Where are they all hurrying to so frantically? . . . What's biting them? Are they afraid they'll be late for that coronary they think they must have at fifty?"[19]

One observation offered about this phenomenon is: "You'll find, if you're in New York for more than a few days, that the mill-race way of living gets to be a habit. You're a human ship in a fast-moving tide and by and by, without meaning to, you find you're accommodating your pace to the common tempo."[20]

Another interpretation emphasizes the competition, seen as tough, fierce, or fantastic, in a population "seething with determination to forge ahead," and in an environment where "one has to work harder, hustle more than anywhere else." Involved here is a way of life set to a tempo that many writers epitomize with the phrase "the rat race of the job."

Of course, the metropolis is preeminently the place offering opportunities for economic and social advancement. In drawing to itself a migrant population largely motivated to actualize these opportunities, a hypercompetitive society is created of people "on the way," who at the very least, we are told, "must hurry even to remain where they are."

Manhattan's tempo appears to have its origin at least partially in the work and career areas of life. On the other hand, its quality of personal anonymity seems to derive from other social sectors of metropolitan existence. This facet can perhaps be best identified from the perspective of the small community. Describing the New England village in which he lives, Granville Hicks comments:

No one can write about such a place as Roxborough without emphasizing patterns of thought and action that distinguish the small town from urban life.

" . . . you'll find . . . you're a human ship in a fast-moving tide . . . accommodating your pace to the common tempo."

"A City of Strangers"

. . . In the small town you know everybody or nearly everybody, and, what is more, you know a considerable number of persons in a considerable number of ways. [Here] no local event . . . birth, illness, change of job, real estate transaction . . . is likely to go unremarked. [You discover] the simple fact of interdependence: you need your neighbor and he needs you. Whatever its origins, neighborliness has gone deep into the grain.[21]

The contrasting situation of "a city of strangers"[22] is drawn by John Steinbeck through the eyes of the City's new recruit from the hinterland:

A young man in a small town, a frog in a small puddle, if he kicks his feet is able to make waves, get mud in his neighbor's eyes—make some impression. He is known. His family is known. People watch him with some interest, whether kindly or maliciously. He comes to New York and no matter what he does no one is impressed. He challenges the city to fight and it licks him without being aware of him.

Offering another vantage point is the novel[23] in which the chief character, Anson Page, a New York resident, muses as follows:

The [suburban] world of Eugene Hollister was not one in which he [Anson] would choose to live, but at least it provided Eugene with the illusion of having a place. That was more than he could say for himself. There were times when he felt that he did not belong anywhere, and this was one of the times. He had not felt that he belonged anywhere since he left Pompey's Head. Nor could it be said that he had failed with his group. He had no group. Sometimes he wondered if anyone in New York had. There were circles and cliques in New York, people drawn together by the same profession or a loose collection of momentarily shared interests . . . but these were temporary associations at best. The interests were always changing, and the faces with them, and there was always the feeling that everybody you met in New York was just passing through, or else on an extended visit, so that there were times when you had the impression that it was not so much a city as a big, endless game of musical chairs.

Phillip Greene once remarked to him that although New York was a collection of neighborhoods it was a place where nobody had any neighbors. "Some people say that this is one of the fine things about the city, but I don't think so," Greene went on. "A man wants neighbors. He may want to put a fence between himself and them, but he wants them just the same. The trouble with New York is that it imposes a set of unnatural conditions. Nobody knows anybody, even when they live next door to each other. You can make your home here for fifty years and still feel a stranger. I know I do."

Though Anson was barely acquainted with Phillip Greene at the time, he was surprised to hear him voice a set of feelings that were so close to his own. Greene was one of the people whom he had imagined as being completely at home in New York.[24]

John McNulty generalizes the point in the following words:

There are afflictions called "Parkinson's Disease" and "Bright's Disease," and so on, but loneliness is "Everybody's Disease." It is especially rife, and there is no serum handy, in cities like New York.[25]

Anonymity is a form of isolation; one's defense against the rejection implied in the isolating, impersonal behavior of others is to insulate himself from them. This mechanism was observed by a local newspaper columnist in the City's restaurants and lunch counters, where he identified among diners the phenomenon of "luncheons anonymous." "The basic essential of the whole concept is the elimination of all communication beyond the absolute minimum needed to obtain food; where this can be done without affirming choices by voice or asking simple questions of an attendant, so much the better."

When a visiting Italian monk suggested that New Yorkers "are hermits at heart," the same newspaperman further developed the reechoing theme that New York can be the loneliest place in the world: "When our solitude is clothed in that mantle of impersonality we tend to be brusque when we might better be kind, or thoughtless when we should be considerate, or even downright rude when we know we should be polite. The solitude of hermitage, improperly used, tends to harden the soul and the face as well—if one may judge by some of the unhappy expressions worn by the people on our streets."

Here we have testimony that the casual interpersonal relationships of the metropolis carry not merely the neutral or cold aspect of indifference; to the normally sensitive individual, they are frequently tinged with bruising harshness. Spreading by disaffection into more intimate kinds of relationships, this quality can produce a partial breakdown in the person-to-person private lines of communication. Such a social process can turn out to be psychologically impoverishing, pushing the individual toward a state that the present writer has elsewhere identified as *anomia*.[26]

On this theme, it has been observed by one of New York's major social agencies: "In a big city like New York, sickness, loneliness, trouble, a

". . . sickness, loneliness, trouble, a need for help, can be inches away from you . . . on the other side of the wall . . . and you may never know."

". . . only one in twenty" (p. 210)

need for help, can be inches away from you . . . on the other side of the wall . . . and you may never know."[27]

The blocked need to be an object of sympathetic communication may be discerned in local commercial uses of the telephone, not as a mechanical medium but rather as a robot communicator. One arrangement is actually designated "Sympathy Service," and is specifically directed to women who, upon calling a given telephone number, can pour out their troubles to a male who, according to a newspaper account, "makes comforting noises at the other end of the line."[28] A parallel but independent telephone service for men plays a recording of a sultry female reciting a flirtatious monologue. As another case in point, several Manhattan churches sponsor a "Dial-a-Prayer" telephone service "for troubled people" who can hear a recording of a prayer uttered by an anonymous clergyman.

Without challenging the facts about this element of anonymity in the social climate of the metropolis, many writers have evaluated it positively. For example, John Lardner notes the high value Manhattanites place on privacy and adds: "Privacy is the rarest condition in modern life, and New Yorkers, for all the physical crowding that exists in their city, have achieved it to a degree beyond the powers of people in other places."[29]

Alec Waugh[30] elaborates the point: "It is the charm of all great cities that you are not supervised, that your every movement is not watched and commented upon . . . that you can lead your own life undisturbed."[31]

Addressing New York specifically, another literate British sojourner observed, "Here one is enfolded in a sense of privacy, of intimate living as one might be in an oasis."

Certainly it cannot be overlooked that the freedom to be yourself in the private sectors of one's life, and the opportunities to realize one's abilities, talents, and interests, arise from the tolerant anonymity and the vast economic and cultural diversity of the city, justifying its characterization as the natural environment of free men. A letter "To the Editor" of the *New York Times* (November 22, 1970) put it this way: "Give me noisy, dirty, crowded Manhattan, where the body suffereth . . . but the mind is free!" Going further, philosopher Irwin Edman has noted that in Manhattan "the spirit has many mansions and there are many incitements to the spirit. For all its distractions, its rush, its brashness, there is hardly a place in the world where there are so many nourishments for the life of the imagination and the mind."[32]

Showing both sides of the coin on this element in Manhattan's social climate is E. B. White's observation: "On any person who desires such queer prizes, New York will bestow the gift of loneliness and the gift of privacy. It is this largess that accounts for the presence within the city's walls of a considerable section of the population. . . . The capacity to make such dubious gifts is a mysterious quality of New York. It can destroy an individual, or it can fulfill him, depending a good deal on luck."[33]

Under ordinary circumstances of life, in our view, people of more or less sound personality thrive on balance in the freedom and privacy of metropolitan anonymity, as no doubt do many deviants and disturbed personalities who find in the metropolis "sanctuary from the prying eyes and clacking tongues of small-town neighbors."[34] Most people who remain in Manhattan by choice have probably come to terms, as did John Steinbeck, with its characteristic of ignoring and looking through the individual's claim to personal identity, worth, and attention. If this should evoke a sense of isolation and loneliness, they can accept it as the price to be paid for more important values found only in the metropolitan environment. It is in this sense that Heywood Broun could comment that "Manhattan is the place of sacrifice. It is only for those who can subsist on locusts and honey."[35]

However, under personal circumstances that are extraordinary and potentially damaging (for example, the crises of prolonged illness, death, disability in one's family, or unemployment), the response of town and metropolis would likely be somewhat different. That is, the town, with its highly developed sense of person-to-person interdependence and social mechanisms of mutual aid, as delineated by Granville Hicks, would probably rise spontaneously to provide the afflicted with group supports that tend to be psychologically stabilizing because they operate to share and absorb the shock. In the indifference and isolation of the metropolis, on the other hand, the same crisis often rallies relatively few intimates around the distressed.[36] To discern the full import of this difference, one need only note in town and metropolis the very different mobilization of others around families that have suffered a death. This has been sharply revealed to the present writer by comparative observation of funerals in the two kinds of communities. Thus, sociologists have emphasized that "one effect of the urban environment is to intensify the effects of crisis."[37] A somewhat dissenting view is held by Anthony Burgess, British author and professor at City College (of New York): "New York is full of helpful people, and I consider, has more saints than any other city of comparable eminence. This is to restore the balance."[38]

Our literary sources are not wanting in observations about the resulting psychological condition of metropolitan man. Frank Lloyd Wright sees the metropolis as "forcing anxiety upon all life." From the perspective of long residence, E. B. White concludes: "New York has changed in tempo and temper during the years I have known it. There is greater tension, increased irritability. You encounter it in many places, in many faces. The normal frustrations of modern life are here multiplied and amplified."[39] Newspaperman Brooks Atkinson hears in New York "the nervous beat of a taut community." In one of his plays Thornton Wilder, creator of Grover's Corners, describes New York as "a tired out, nervous collection of ants." The inimitable *New Yorker* magazine has run this item of "appraisal": "A pal of ours just had his annual medical checkup, and informed us that the doctor who went over him was disturbed about his blood pressure, his pulse rate, his basal metabolism, and a lot of other things. 'I thought you ought to know,' said our friend, 'that after all his muttering about the poor shape I was in, he told me I was 'New York normal.' " One young ex-New Yorker, in the lexicon of the seventies, has it that "everyone's some kind of freak in New York."

And, of course, there is a whole genre of essays with content suggested by the title of one: "The Crack-up City."[40] However, caution is here urged against generalizing from these sensitive observers and arriving at premature conclusions about the psychologically noxious characteristics of Midtown's physical and social environment, not, at least, until comparable research data become available on populations in other kinds of American communities.

Granville Hicks, as journalist, does not attempt to measure the prevalence of mental disturbance in his New England place that houses a population numbering less than a thousand individuals. Yet his perceptions of this village community offer a sobering hint that we suspend judgment on Midtown until we have a larger base for comparison. He writes:[41] "Roxborough . . . has its share of neurotics. . . . I cannot be absolutely sure that in any particular instance the condition is related, one way or another, to small-town life. The chief point is that even a small town has its instances of nervous disorder. . . . We have our neurotics, our drunkards, our 'bums.' And what is more, we know we have them."

Closing this attempt to portray the Study area in certain salient characteristics, the author concludes from a personal history of a lifetime divided among three of America's largest cities, from a professional background of investigations in several small American communities, and from years of research immersion in Midtown, that he stands neither with the advocates of Manhattan as the penultimate stage of the heavenly city nor with those who regard it as a preview of purgatory.

Rather, from outside that frame of values, he views it developmentally as the summit in the long, upgrade evolution of urban civilization. Whether the rarefied, turbulent atmosphere and slippery footing at this peak are in themselves psychologically eugenic or pathogenic for those willful, hardy people who have climbed to it—and remained—is a question that this report can touch only peripherally. We must look to successor studies, conducted at other points on the grade, for the larger clarifications of the comparative perspective.

NOTES

[1]The term has so few synonyms that its overworked use in the following pages is unavoidable.

[2]Nationally, an estimated 25 percent of all psychiatrists have not been members of the American Psychiatric Association.

[3]*Directory of Social and Health Agencies of New York City,* 1956–57 and 1969–70 editions.

[4]Some of the churches are identifiable by the character of their names as being associated with a particular ethnic, i.e., nationality, group, and others, while lacking such designation, are in membership predominantly drawn from one of these groups.

[5]It is possible, in turn, to distinguish between the serve-others association of laymen and the serve-others agency with a professional staff that the former creates and is committed to support.

[6]From notices in the society pages of the city newspapers, it is clear that the members of these organizations are largely, but by no means exclusively, drawn from the Midtown area.

[7]Cf. B. Rudofsky, *Streets for People*, 1969, an excellent historical account of cities abroad that have made "streets into oases rather than deserts" for children.

[8]As is usually the case even for lower-class Old American secular organizations, the serve-others function is negligible, being channeled by financial necessity into self-service and mutual aid shared among the members.

[9]Of course, the numbers of institutions of each type are no indicators of their respective enrollments, which are unknown to us. In New York City at large we know that about 35 percent of school-age children attend parochial or private schools. We have grounds to assume that in Midtown this figure may now fall in the 40 to 45 percent range.

[10]The federally guaranteed annual income for families in poverty has become a major political issue. The problem is to build an income floor that will be sufficiently supportive to eliminate the obscenity of want and malnutrition from the American scene.

[11]Published for the Community Council of Greater New York, Inc., by Columbia University Press.

[12]R. W. Houston, commissioner, New York State Department of Social Welfare, "Why All This Welfare?" Address to the annual meeting of the New York City Federation of Protestant Welfare Agencies, February 25, 1958.

[13]For the six pathologies in the series, case frequencies are available in common only for the City's "health areas," each a Health Department administrative unit comprising several United States Census tracts and a population usually approximating 25,000. The frequencies reported derive from official records and have obvious limitations which we need not define here.

To match the two comparison populations to Midtown, we have included only those health areas in Manhattan and the outer boroughs with populations in 1950 that were 90 to 100 percent white, non-Puerto Rican in composition.

Rates have been calculated for each of the outer boroughs separately, i.e., Bronx, Brooklyn, Queens, and Staten Island. However, there were no significant differences among these four boroughs; as a result, we can more efficiently present them as a unit.

[14]Of course, infant mortality rates vary inversely with amount of prenatal medical care received. The latter in turn varies to a certain extent with the local availability of medical services. Accordingly, it is plausible to assume that if the outer boroughs' population had the same advantages in this respect as have Midtown's and Manhattan's, their infant mortality rate would have been even lower than that observed.

[15]There are no differences among the three populations in rates of automobile fatalities.

[16]Hon. Robert E. Wagner, "Address of the Mayor of New York City to the City Council upon Presenting his Annual Report for 1955."

[17]At one well-advertised Council meeting attended by the writer, a local realtor gave an informal address advancing the theme that Midtown's housing is "in excellent shape." He was followed by a municipal housing expert who took a dissenting view and chided his forty listeners that Midtown had no specific organization concerned with its housing problem or its shortage of playgrounds. "You can't sit by and let George do it," he pointedly declared. "You have to work with citywide bodies and local citizen groups."

[18]Harrison E. Salisbury, "The Shook-up Generation," March 30, 1958.

[19]*The New York Times Magazine*, April 29, 1956.

[20]Meyer Berger, *The New York Times Magazine*, April 29, 1956.

[21]Granville Hicks, *Small Town*, 1946, p. 13.

[22]John Steinbeck, "The Making of a New Yorker," *The New York Times Magazine*, February 1, 1953.

[23]*The View from Pompey's Head*, pp. 117–118. Copyright 1954 by Hamilton Basso. Reprinted by permission of Doubleday and Company, Inc.

[24]We can test the impression of Phillip Greene (a character from Basso, *The View from Pompey's Head*) that New Yorkers predominantly share the almost universal want for friendly neighbors. To our Midtown sample respondents we put this question: "People say that in smaller cities neighbors are helpful and interested in each other. Is this something you would like or dislike?" Only one-sixth of these Midtowners replied "dislike," another 9 percent gave a qualified "like" response, and three-fourths indicated unequivocal approval.

[25]John McNulty, "Search for the Perfect Bar," *The New York Times Magazine,* October 10, 1955.

[26]L. Srole, "Social Integration and Certain Corollaries," *American Sociological Review* 21 (December 1956): 709–716.

[27]*The Greater New York Fund Bulletin,* 1957.

[28]The enterprising young organizer of this service has detected the gulf between New Yorkers and their intimates in what they *do not* reveal to each other. He has said: "It's a moving, distressing experience. The only trouble is, I've begun to wonder what my girl friend really thinks of me."

[29]John Lardner, "The Case for Living Here," *The New York Times Magazine,* April 29, 1956.

[30]Alec Waugh, *The New York Times Magazine,* April 29, 1956.

[31]It is important to emphasize that although this consequence of anonymity applies to places like Manhattan, there are sections of the metropolis with far lesser population densities, where personal visibility differs little from that characteristic of the small community. For example, dramatist Arthur Miller writes of his boyhood neighborhood in Brooklyn: "It was a village. . . . I don't recall a time when the cops had to be called. Everyone was so well and thoroughly known that the frown of his neighbors was enough to keep things in line." "A Boy Grew in Brooklyn," *Holiday* (March 1955).

In a similar vein, Gilbert Sorrentino, author of the novel *Steelwork* (1970), has written of his Brooklyn neighborhood: "When I was growing up, people lived lives as inevitable as those in a tribal society."

[32]Irwin Edman, *The New York Times Magazine,* February 1, 1953.

[33]E. B. White, *Here Is New York* 1949, pp. 9–10.

[34]Meyer Berger, in A. Klein, ed., *The Empire City,* 1955, p. xx.

[35]Heywood Broun, in A. Klein, ed., *The Empire City,* 1955, p. 450.

[36]As substitutes for such "intimates" the metropolis may provide, under certain limited, qualifying conditions and upon formal application, the professional and bureaucratized services of a social agency. Such services are not to be minimized if they are sought; if resources, eligibility policies, and case load of the agency allow response in time; and if help extended is adequate to the need. Such multiple contingencies probably explain facts earlier noted that the unserved needs may be large indeed.

[37]Robert E. Park, *The City,* 1925, pp. 1–46.

[38]Anthony Burgess, "Cucarachas and Exiles, Potential Death and Life Enhancement," *The New York Times Magazine,* October 29, 1972.

[39]White, *Here Is New York,* p. 48.

[40]Helen Lawrenson, "New York: Crack-up City," *Esquire,* July, 1953.

[41]Hicks, *Small Town,* pp. 149–152.

Part III

Research Strategy
And Tactics

CHAPTER 7

GOALS AND GUIDELINES
LEO SROLE

In his Special Message of February 5, 1963, to Congress, President Kennedy declared:

Mental illness and mental retardation are among our most critical health problems. They occur more frequently, affect more people, require more prolonged treatment, cause more suffering by the families of the afflicted, waste more of our human resources, and constitute more financial drain upon both the public treasury and the personal finances of the individual families than any other single condition.

The magnitude of the drain, at least in tangibles that can be measured, is currently estimated by the National Institute of Mental Health as $21 billion annually, over $4 billion for direct costs of treatment and prevention, and almost $17 billion from loss of the affected families' productive capacity.[1] It is ironical, in this light, that mental disorder continues to be one of the most refractory and least understood of our public health problems.

These observations may suggest something of the pressures upon science to engage the problem on an all-out alarm basis. The Midtown Manhattan Study represents one among many research responses to those pressures.

The reader, whether layman or professional, is here invited to participate in that response retrospectively. Sharing this experience, we will present not only certain findings of the Study, but also the operations that produced these results, and even the scientists' caveats on the imperfections and limitations of their data. To adapt Cervantes' analogy, "proof of the pudding" is not in the eating alone, but also in the review of the chef's recipe and how it was actually followed.

From the general reader we ask forbearance for shoptalk that is of interest mainly to the student and is confined in large part to chapters 7, 8, and 9. From the professional reader, on the other hand, we ask understanding for our attempt to distill fundamentals of his field, necessarily simplified, for those of other backgrounds. Reflected in the fare here set out, then, is diversity among the expected guests.

The challenge before science to confront, contain, and ultimately prevent the genera of psychological dysfunctions sometimes called "mental illness" ("disorder" or "disturbance") is urgent and many-sided indeed. From one direction comes the insistent call for *program research* to guide public and professional policy in mobilizing the treatment fronts of the problem. This need was spelled in deceptively elementary terms by the former Medical Director of the National Institute of Mental Health.

How many people in the United States actually are mentally ill? How many mental health clinics do we need? How many psychiatrists? How many psychiatric nurses? All of these questions are reasonable and important. Yet to none of them can we give a firm answer, based on tried and tested facts.

It may be argued that, since the deficiencies in service personnel and facilities in this field are so obvious and so great, why bother collecting data to prove what is already known?

This argument is not valid. We have the problem of allocating scarce resources and must find areas of greatest need. The very complexity and vastness of the problem make it imperative that we get the best possible data upon which to base our action programs. ... Our great need is for facts—many facts, accurate facts. ...[2]

From another direction comes the equally insistent demand for *basic research,* to wrest new knowledge, without regard to instant program utility, about the still-elusive mainsprings of most mental-disorder processes.

Both calls were cardinal points of orientation to Rennie, to the writer, and to our research colleagues through the entire course of the Midtown Study. However, the need for basic research claimed by far the greater part of available energies and resources and will receive corresponding attention in the pages of this monograph. Even on this level, pressures of priorities force us to give far less attention to the favorable end of the whole mental health spectrum that we ranged across than to the unfavorable segment.

As with the still-unknown causes (pathogenesis, etiology) of most cancer types, the magnitude and complexity of mental disorder dictate an overall strategy of probing attacks along the entire horizon of theoretically promising approaches. Rennie's choice of specific approach to be taken in the Midtown Study is suggested by the composition of the research staff which he, as directing clinical psychiatrist, assembled in June 1952. Joining him originally were representatives from the fields of sociology, psychiatric social work, clinical psychology, and anthropology.

For over a year, this multiprofessional team functioned as a committee of the whole and through special subcommittees in the processes of decision making on two levels of project planning. On the first level, the Study's objectives, working concepts, and test hypotheses were provisionally formulated to steer the investigation on its course. The general outlines of the conceptual framework which was developed, and the problems it posed, along with analytical schemes later elaborated to order the data, are sketched in the present chapter.[3]

On the second level of planning, the research design, procedures, and instruments were forged to implement the conceptual framework adopted. These are outlined in the two chapters that follow.

During the conceptualizing phase of staff planning, interdisciplinary difficulties inevitably arose. Several of these are worthy of brief mention here, only because the resolutions reached are suffused through the pages of this monograph. One problem hinged on the specialized technical terminology employed by each scientific discipline and the tendency to view the professional language of every other science but one's own as jargon. It was decidedly our experience that in most instances team collaboration ultimately bridged such gulfs.[4]

Nonetheless, as a collaborative product of several sciences the present monograph of course draws upon the technical vocabularies of all participating disciplines. It does so by the sheer necessities of its diverse tasks.

Semantics aside, among its collaborating disciplines the research group also encountered inevitable differences in theoretical points of emphasis. Such divergences among more distantly related disciplines were further complicated by differences, sometimes striking, between representatives of the same or closely related disciplines. The principle underlying the effort to overcome such barriers on the part of Rennie and most team members has been expressed in a notable paper that happened to touch on intradisciplinary contention in psychiatric research. The relevant observation is this: "It is earnestly to be desired that in this difficult field, questions of absolute truth and universal validity be set aside and attention concentrated upon the experimental study of working hypotheses and provisional concepts."[5]

Bounding this and all subsequent chapters is this qualification: *the goals sought and concepts applied in the Midtown Study were provisionally tailored to the limiting realities of what was operationally achievable,* rather than to what would have been theoretically ideal in the emphatic view of one or another scheme of thought. For this reason, among others, the Midtown Study must affirm that it is an *exploratory,* rather than a *definitive* venture in basic research. For its large questions it can secure only qualified answers, but these, hopefully, may provide grounds for framing new or more specific research questions.

The results of this exploratory effort await the reader's judgment. Those who wish to "leap frog" over the following "tooling up" chapters (7, 8, 9) of the book will find that each of these and all subsequent chapters concludes with a brief outline of its main highlights.

RESEARCH APPROACH AND FOCUS

The multifaceted research approach brought to bear in the Midtown Study is hardly novel. Historically viewed, however, it is seen to represent a convergence of three independent streams of scientific development.

One strong current in this confluence flowed from the discipline of medical epidemiology, a research arm of preventive medicine. In briefest compass, medical epidemiology can be defined by its focus on "the origin and course that disease takes in population groups."[6]

A historian of the field records that, although "originally concerned only with epidemics, its scope was extended first to include infectious diseases which do not ordinarily occur in epidemic form, such as leprosy, syphilis, and tuberculosis, and later to noninfectious diseases."[7] The latter included the diseases of nutritional deficiency (beriberi, pellagra, and scurvy), metabolic disorders, and cancer, among others.

Epidemiology traditionally has rested on the concept of *ecology,* under which disease is observed from the perspective of populations as they are affected by their environments. However, Gordon[8] adds that until nearly the end of the period of sole concern with the infectious diseases, roughly coinciding with World War I, epidemiology was heavily preoccupied with the bacteriological agents to the neglect of research into other environmental contributions to disease. The turning point came when it was realized that with this one-sided emphasis, "the question of why epidemics come and why they go was little better defined than before." Doull[9] describes the shift as a recognition that, although "the occurrence of an infectious disease is determined by a dosage of pathogen sufficient to overwhelm resistance of the human host, there are social and economic factors which may cause, augment or prevent exposure and which may raise or lower resistance." Evidence has been noted, for example, that while tubercle bacilli are widely disseminated in the population, the disease itself tends to be narrowly concentrated in certain small social segments of the community.

With the push of epidemiological research into the noninfectious chronic disorders came greater awareness of "the social component of environment [as] that part which results from the association of man with his fellow man [including] the attainments, beliefs, customs, traditions, and like features of a people [that] range from housing to food supply; and from education to the provisions made for medical care."[10] The more specific contributions of medical epidemiology to the evolution under review here will be considered presently.

Psychiatry has historically followed two main avenues of research development. The first moved into the organic preconditions and corollaries of mental disorder from various separate points of departure in the human system, including heredity, neurology, endocrine function, metabolism, and electrophysiology.

To a certain extent independent of this biological or somatogenic approach, the second avenue of psychiatric investigation examined the dynamic interplay of psychological processes and life experiences. However, with certain notable exceptions, the sociocultural environment that structures the family unit and envelops individual experience was not systematically taken into account and conceptualized within this psychogenic approach. Redlich, for example, has commented that in historical perspective "psychiatry has paid relatively little attention to the social environment and concentrated more on the exploration of organic and intrapersonal factors."[11]

Nonetheless, increasingly in recent years representatives of the psychogenic approach in psychiatry, like the medical epidemiologists, have been moving in this new direction, where they have met and joined the third scientific stream—itself with diverse origins in the social sciences. Included were sociology, with its long-pursued interest in the links between social-system pathology and such behavioral deviations as delinquency, suicide, and crime; anthropology, with its own particular emphasis on the global, normative view of both culture and personality; and social psychology, with its focus on the full range of behavior variability as related to specified interpersonal settings. In all three instances, these sciences had breached their original disciplinary dikes and were descending together on areas of direct concern to the expanding psychogenic approach in psychiatry and to the rather elementary sociogenic approach developing within medical epidemiology.

This convergence of psychiatry, medical epidemiology, and social science upon a common ground has recently evolved into a working partnership between social psychiatry, psychiatric sociology, and psychiatric epidemiology.[12]

Some clinical psychiatrists, to be sure, have greeted social psychiatry as a "term full of sound and fury, signifying little." The present volume, like its research predecessors, attempts to define what one facet of social psychiatry actually signifies, at least in the operational terms of the research behaviors and output of one set of investigators. Also relevant is the literature that has been accumulating in the new field. For example, we now have accounts of early gropings by major figures in both psychiatry and the social sciences toward the untenanted no man's land stretching between them.[13] Adolf Meyer's part in this development was of particular importance, both directly[14] and through his students. Included among the latter are the psychiatrists Diethelm, Gruenberg, Leighton, Lemkau, and Rennie, all research contributors to the advancement of the new field. From another direction in psychiatry has come the weighty impact of such neo-Freudian theorists as Horney, Sullivan, Erikson, and Fromm. There are also the significant crystallizations of thought in the work of the Committee on Social Issues of the Group for the Advancement of Psychiatry,[15] and of the Committee on Research in Psychiatry and the Social Sciences appointed by the national Social Science Research Council.[16]

In the light of these convergences, the Midtown Study phrases the following general proposition as its most fundamental postulate: *sociocultural conditions, in both their normative and their deviant forms, operating in intrafamily and extrafamily settings during childhood and adulthood have measurable consequences reflected in the mental health differences[17] to be observed within a population.*

The Midtown investigators were acutely aware of the obstacles that awaited them on the scientific borderland marked by the above postulate, as well as of the limited objectives they could accomplish in the time available for the Study's mission. In a similar vein, Franz Alexander has commented: "The understanding of the dynamic interaction of the self with the social environment is in itself a goal [that] could occupy the productive capacities of generations to come."[18]

Before venturing into the far reaches of the social environment, the researcher, having rather less than one professional lifetime remaining to him, must first conceptually stake out the specific boundaries of the terrain he intends to explore. As a step in this direction, be it noted that the family, both to social science and to psychiatry, is the basic social unit and one of decisive relevance to their respective concerns. Placed in a larger frame of observation, however, the family is seen functioning in the nurturing medium of the surrounding community and its complex system of neighborhoods, groups, institutions, and friendship circles. Communities of course have their similarities and their differences. These differences become weighty indeed when communities are classified, among other possible ways, by the index of population size, for example, on the rural-urban continuum ranging from the prairie "four corners" hamlet to the giant world metropolis.

Even in its presumably private functioning, the family presents open doors to the influences of the community which serves many of its elementary needs. Hence, it is a plausible postulate that any given big-city family is different, in gross and subtle respects significant for its members, from what it would have been had it settled in a small town.

Because it penetrates into the most intimate affairs of the family through direct impact on each member in extrafamily spheres of daily living, the local community in effect is forced upon social psychiatry as a necessary focus of collaborative study.

In so accompanying sociology into the community, social psychiatry is also following the example of epidemiology, its senior sibling research field. In the words of a medical epidemiologist, the community "extends the boundaries in which disease can be viewed beyond the ward or clinic. It provides a third dimension to the understanding of disease by creating awareness of the environment in which the disability arises, of the factors in the community which contribute to its causation, and in turn, its effect upon the community."[19]

In larger perspective, it has also been urged that "to attain a true concept of the national [mental health] problem we need studies . . . of as many individual communities as possible . . . to be able to make comparisons between various geographic, socioeconomic and cultural areas of the country."[20]

The community population chosen for study here has been described, and its larger significance considered in chapters 4 to 6. We designate it by the descriptive code name of *Midtown* and need only recall now that in 1954 it numbered an estimated 170,000 individuals settled in a socio-geographically well-delineated residential area near the epicenter of New York City's hub borough of Manhattan.

Our subject of study, then, was narrowed down to this particular metropolitan community, and the objective was to assess the fundamental but as yet generalized and seemingly obvious premise that socio-cultural conditionings of its people are somehow implicated in their subsequent mental health fate.

The terrain marked out, the researcher starting toward such an objective finds himself immediately caught in the enormously tangled and slippery underbrush problems of causation. To guide his course over such treacherous ground, he usually carries in his equipment a general *modus operandi* for discerning antecedent-consequent links, if not direct cause and effect. Usually left implicit, this mode of inference deserves to be made explicit more often, at least in terms of its key assumptions.

The view applied here is essentially that developed in medical epidemiology and rests on the bedrock axiom that illness is an aberrant "output" reaction emerging from a complex of "input" conditions. More specifically, like hurricane weather,[21] it is the resultant of a number of factors that often vary independently of each other and converge to initiate, facilitate, or perpetuate a chain of atypical processes. Since the interactions among the several responsible factors upon convergence are often obscure, the specific traces of these factors in the dysfunctional process tend to be concealed from direct observation.[22] This is especially the case in the chronic types of disorders. For example, we are told that of the factors conducive to "hypertensive or arteriosclerotic cardiovascular disease almost nothing is known, although these two account for the great bulk of deaths from cardiovascular disease."[23]

Within such etiological darkness, the first "alert" signal that a particular factor may be implicated is evidence that in population groups where it is known to be operating the frequency of the disorder is significantly higher than in groups where it is known to be absent. That is, the specific factor, when present, increases the risk that the dysfunction will occur.[24] Such telltale evidence, if confirmed, establishes a relationship between factor and disorder that is of the utmost importance, although remaining temporarily unknown may be (1) the specific mechanisms linking the two, and (2) the roles of other factors.[25] An illuminating case in point is provided by recent cancer studies: "It has been repeatedly shown that the greater the exposure to certain environmental factors the greater the risk of developing certain types of cancer. Though these factors may not be the only agents responsible for the induction of these cancers, *in their absence the cancer incidence is greatly reduced.*"[26]

When several factors are separately found to be responsible for furthering a dysfunctional development, they may next be investigated for the pattern of their interactions in the pathogenic process.

Two general types of etiological patterns in somatic disorders have been discerned. The first type seems to characterize the infectious diseases, where a microorganism, the responsible disease agent, requires several accessory conditions. Such accessory conditions would include circumstances in the physical environment facilitating or inhibiting the multiplication of the microorganism (for example, climate), conditions in the social environment favoring or blocking its spread (for example, sanitation) or affecting exposure (for example, population density), susceptibility-immunity of individuals, and other factors.

Here each factor is a *necessary* but *not sufficient* condition, by itself, to produce the disease. This constellation might be characterized as *stable* in that more or less the same pathogenic conditions tend to recur in eliciting the disorder.

The second type of pattern, probably involved in the degenerative conditions, is more fluid, in the sense that the same kind of malfunction and symptoms may be induced by different factors in diverse combinations. "That similar diseases may arise from dissimilar causes is established principle. . . . Examples are cirrhosis of the liver [and] appendicitis."[27]

In this type of configuration, the pathogenic factors may include one, or more, that is indispensable to the dysfunctional process, such as individual susceptibility. However, the remaining factors in the pattern are interchangeable, in the sense that preconditions A, B, and C may be operative in certain cases, D, E, and F in others, and so on. Compared to the stable type, with its relatively few pathogenic factors, this pattern appears to be characterized by potential preconditions in larger number, variety, and combinations. Since many mental disorders seem likely to arise from this more fluid kind of emergent pattern, the analytical problems posed are of course far more complex.

In dealing with situation-response phenomena, it is customary to designate the antecedent conditions as the presumed *independent* variables and the consequence that follows, in this instance mental health, as the *dependent* variable, a distinction involving issues that will be considered presently. As to criteria and classification of mental health[28] itself, these are being reserved for special discussion in chapters 8 and 9.

The two major orders of independent variables potentially capable of influencing mental health are the somatic and the sociocultural. The question about the relative contributions of these two large sets of independent factors has long been a special case of the nature-versus-nurture controversy. The question has too often been addressed in the past, not as an empirical issue of extreme complexity, but as a debate from prefabricated platforms.

Our own tentative views on the matter can be briefly outlined in terms of the following assumptions:

1. In the individual patient it is etiologically important, of course, to delineate any organic foundations for the disorder. However, in the most prevalent, so-called functional conditions this is often impossible.

2. In the population at large we can assume for mental morbidity that predisposition varies on a wide arc and may have diverse organic roots that will ultimately be uncovered.

3. In the population at large we can assume for mental morbidity that intensification of predisposition and actual precipitation of disability vary in a wide span with the magnitude and character of pathogenic environmental intrusions.

4. Accordingly, it would follow that the mentally disturbed are etiologically heterogeneous to a high degree. At one extreme would be those in whom somatic vulnerability is maximal and the environmental contribution minimal. Bounding the other extreme would be those in whom organic vulnerability is minimal and the environmental impact maximal, as in certain traumas of military combat that can produce severe anxiety and pseudopsychotic reactions of a transitory nature. And stretching between would be all manner of balances in relative pathogenic weights.

Ultimately, research may be able to focus down to the interactions between specific somatic conditions and circumscribed sociocultural factors, as these jointly interpenetrate in the deeps of psychological processes. But it was our view that to make this possible, it is necessary *first* to isolate and identify such specific factors in each order of independent variable *separately*. This position led to the strategic decision to concentrate our research efforts on one of these orders.

In fixing on the social environment as the realm to be explored in the Midtown Study, the investigators, needless to say, did not thereby reflect a position of environmental determinism. In part, the decision grew out of an awareness of the fragmentary state of our knowledge both about the somatic realm as it shapes mental health[29]—including the psychosomatic disorders[30]—and about specific influences emanating from the sociocultural realm.[31]

Thus, the major limitation imposed on our data by this decision is that the contributory role of predisposing somatic factors in mental health has been largely untouched. This limitation, it may be added, represents a lack of analytical completeness that in one degree or other is inherent in most exploratory investigations with the etiologies of disorder as their goal and a relatively short working life to reach it.[32]

THE TEST FACTORS

Under the limited time available to it, the Midtown mental health research project was planned as a cross-sectional investigation. That is, in its major aspect a large sample of the adult population was studied at one point in time, with highly selected information about each subject gathered retrospectively along the life-history axis applied in clinical psychiatry.

In such a study, a further issue for decision is this: What factors of a sociocultural nature should be tested for their relationship to mental health? The interpersonal environment, as a concept applied to a metropolitan population in particular, refers to a social universe of enormous proportions and complexity. To search this enormity for clues and leads to conditions associated with mental disturbance can be a sightless groping if conducted in haphazard fashion. The only practical alternative is purposively to select from this universe a few theoretically promising (and technically researchable) landmarks for exploration. Prerequisite for such selection is a taxonomic ordering of potential (and testable) etiological factors to which every individual is exposed in varying ways. The taxonomy applied here is based on several simple, cross-cutting distinctions.

One distinction dichotomizes potential or suspected or test factors into two types, designated the *demographic* and the *component*. A demographic factor is a culturally significant property or condition, differentially manifested by all individuals, that provides a basis for classifying a population into a limited series of social segments or groups. We can view demographic factors as falling into two major divisions, namely, the *biosocial* and the *sociocultural*. Under the biosocial rubric belong groups differentiated by sex, by age—or position in the life cycle—and by marital status—or position relative to family formation during the adult phase of the life cycle.[33]

Under the sociocultural rubric we place groups differentiated (1) by socioeconomic status,[34] (2) by religion, (3) by generation in this country,[35] (4) by ethnic or national origin of immigrants and their descendants, including Old American, and (5) by rural-urban origin, that is, the kind of community in which the individual grew up.

The elementary distinction between the biosocial and sociocultural rubrics aside, an analytically more significant consideration requires that we distinguish between *independent* and *reciprocal* types of demographic variables. For present purposes, let us assume that one or more of the demographic factors are found to be related to mental health differences, the Study's *dependent* or *response* variable. Given such a relationship, for a demographic factor to be considered etiologically *independent,* it must satisfy a pivotal criterion, namely, that it is not open to reciprocating influence from, or choice by, the individual and the psychological processes subsumed under the dependent variable, that is, his mental health. If a factor fulfills this requirement, then we can be reasonably confident that its relationship to the dependent variable proceeds dynamically in a single direction, that is, as one possible input contributing to the final output.

Examples of the independent type of demographic factor are age[36] and sex, both of which are beyond any possibility of influence or change by processes of individual choice. Other examples we assumed were (1) ethnic origin, as determined by descent, and (2) generation in this country.[37]

Demographic factors that clearly do not meet the criterion of independence in Midtown's adult population are marital status, socioeconomic standing, religious affiliation, and migration from a rural-urban range of childhood communities. Variations in all four may be self-determined, and as such may well be *consequences* rather than independent antecedents of mental health.

To focus on marital status, by way of example, a further observation is in order. Although this factor may be determined in the first instance by psychological characteristics that belong under the umbrella concept of mental health, among newly adult individuals of *like* mental health, differences in marital status may subsequently have disparate effects on their mental well-being. Given this "circular" or "spiraling" interaction through time,[38] if a relationship is found between marital status and mental health in a single point-of-time study such as this, it would necessarily remain ambiguous in its etiological significance. For purposes of the present study, therefore, we postulate that such demographic factors stand to mental health as *interdependent* or *reciprocal* variables.[39]

It should be emphasized, nevertheless, that a correlation established between a reciprocal factor and mental health may potentially have values in its own right. First, the finding that certain marital status groups, for example, represent high risks of mental disorder could have important program-planning implications. Second, the ambiguity of direction in the correlation may provide impetus for bringing together scattered bits of evidence that fall into place, as in a jigsaw puzzle, to partially illuminate the relationship, or at least to suggest more refined hypotheses about its nature.[40] And third, appropriate longitudinal studies would be stimulated to lift the ambiguity by following the spiraling course of the interaction through time.

In this monograph, present socioeconomic status and religious identification of adults, like marital status, belong in the category of reciprocal variables. But unlike marital status, there was a simple expedient at hand to capture these demographic factors in a form that would qualify them as independent variables. This expedient was information secured from our adult subjects that permitted classification of each individual in terms of his *parents'* socioeconomic status and religious identification *during his childhood.* With rare exceptions, such early conditions were certainly beyond his capacity to select or influence. Therefore, any relationship found between either of these two kinds of demographic *origins* and mental health can be assumed to be unidirectional or independent, rather than mutually interactive or reciprocal.

In all, four demographic factors of the sociocultural type were considered available for testing as independent variables potentially related in a unidirectional manner to adult mental health. These were (1) parental socioeconomic status, (2) generation-in-USA, (3) ethnic origin, and (4) parental religion. It remains to consider more closely how these factors are dynamically relevant to the crucial childhood stage of individual development.

As a point of departure, it may be noted that clinical psychiatry often assesses members of the patient's family during childhood as potential pathogenic agents, generally in terms of their behavior tendencies and interpersonal patterns. As suggested earlier, however, the family must be seen in the larger setting of the community, itself a heterogeneous social system composed of a variety of cross-cutting sociocultural groups, such as those principally defined by our above four demographic factors.

Families, of course, vary in their positions or affiliations relative to each of these four demographic axes of group segmentation. Associated with different group contexts, we assumed, are variations in intrafamily functioning. These variations, we postulated, may ultimately be seen (1) in behavior patterns culturally enjoined or inhibited, through the definition of normative roles; (2) in bonds among the several kinds of family members; (3) in cohesion as this affects the family's emotional economy, stability, flexibility, and control of behavioral disruptions; and (4) in family life styles and social resourcefulness. These may affect the frequency with which families internally generate noxious or crisis situations, as well as their immunity-vulnerability in the face of stressful external conditions.

Sociologists have properly charged that "demographic variables, all too frequently, are used as independent variables in a mechanical way."[41] In our formulation, the independent, sociocultural type of demographic factor is seen as one potential key to intergroup differences in intrafamily dynamics.

A psychiatrist has recently expressed views pointing in this general direction:

One of the great deficiencies in the epidemiological study of all behavioral disease ... has been the failure to particularize adequately the position ... of individuals in the various social systems through which they act. . . . Unless we can do a better job of defining the individual in relation to the various primary groups to which he belongs, we shall not know how to find and to control pathogenic stress, particularly when it may arise in the social and cultural systems.[42]

From the start of the Midtown Study planning process, the writer viewed the demographic variables of the sociocultural type as multiple location points that help identify the specific network of group alignments held by a family in a heterogeneous and complex community. By isolating the independent demographic alignments of the individual's parents during his formative years, we could take the indispensable first step toward testing for possible links between (1) a variety of childhood family settings and (2) various kinds of outcomes for the mental health of their offspring, now adults engaged in the life of a great metropolis.[43]

In this view, the independent sociocultural type of demographic variable may provide guidelines to family-to-family differences in functioning which, as Clausen has since phrased it, "are internalized [by children] in such a way as to produce differing response tendencies to later situations, different ways of coping with one's environment, different self-conceptions and modes of defense."[44] Or, as Stainbrook has trenchantly added, such family alignments permit us to "comprehend . . . the social and cultural world which is not only around [the individual] but which, to a significant extent, is organized within him."[45]

To recapitulate, the typology of demographic factors here advanced for testing in relation to Midtown's adult subjects of study can be summarily outlined in table 7–1.

TABLE 7–1.   DEMOGRAPHIC FACTOR TYPES

	Independent	*Reciprocal*
Biosocial	Age Sex	Marital status
Sociocultural	Parental SES* Generation-in-U.S. Religious origin Ethnic origin	Own SES Rural-urban background Own religion

*SES is the established abbreviation of socioeconomic status.

Having outlined the structure and potential significance of the demographic variables, we might recall that earlier in this discussion the latter were paired with those we called *component* variables. Since the distinction was not there defined, we can take as point of departure our observation that the demographic factors allow us to probe for connections between certain *kinds* of childhood families and certain variants of adult mental health. However, assume that such connections *are* discovered. In that case, with the family itself functioning as a complex social system, we will not know which of the many elements operating in this system specifically differentiate the pathogenic and the eugenic types of family structures.

These specific differentials of experience we designate as *component* variables. By way of single concrete example, the element of interparental harmony-discord is a childhood experience we place in the rubric of component factor. Some 160 of such items were covered in the Study as potentially relevant to mental health, more or less evenly divided between experiences during childhood and during recent adult life.

Assuming that correlations would be established between some demographic variables and mental health, we originally hoped that the component factors would perform an explanatory or "bridging" role by showing a correlation on the one hand with the implicated demographic variables and, on the other, with the mental health variable.

For purposes of illustration, suppose demographically defined family type Q1 is found to be low in mental morbidity rate and family type Q3 is found to be high in this rate. Taking our previous example of a component factor, it was our hypothesis that interparental harmony would characterize the former family type and interparental discord the latter. If this should prove to be the case, then we would be able to infer that, among other possible respects, the Q3 family type is pathogenic for its children in the specific sense that it tends to be loaded with interparental conflict.

Given the quantity of data secured by the Midtown Study, several monographs are necessary for their presentation. The division of contents initially adopted called for concentrated coverage in this first volume of our findings on the demographic variables, both of the independent and the reciprocal types. Suggestive data on the component variables are offered in the second monograph.[46]

SUMMARY

In its mission to treat and prevent mental disturbance, psychiatry, like general medicine of which it is part, has necessarily fixed its attention and energies upon pathology. Going beyond the clinic into the community at large, social psychiatry encounters the well, the disabled, and all grades in between. Accordingly, the Midtown Study directed its attention to mental health both sound and impaired, although the latter called for primary emphasis, as we shall see in the two chapters that follow. By the same token, our search for etiological clues was turned not only to pathogenic factors deriving from the social environment but also to the eugenic or "contrapathic" factors contributing to mental well-being.

In the scientific and humane tasks to which the mental health problem calls, the several perspectives must be steadily kept in sight. In the short view, the current untreated afflicted must be identified, reached, and helped. In the middle-range view, those representing high risks of *future* disturbance should have ready access to preventive measures. In the long view, finally, society must prevent the environmental blights that keep children from maturing to pursue and achieve the two values Yehudi Menuhin finds in making music, namely, "the pleasure of being of use *both* to oneself and to the community."

From its inception, the Midtown Study was intended to serve the purposes of both program and basic research. Project planning by a multidisciplinary team was carried out at length, on both the conceptual and the technical levels of design.

Of the several alternative directions available, the one undertaken in this investigation represents a recent convergence of medical epidemiology, clinical psychiatry, and the social sciences upon a common borderland of research. This conjoint approach advances the general postulate that sociocultural forces hold good or ill potentialities for mental health. It rests, moreover, on a general logic of situation-response evidence and inference derived from medical epidemiology. The relationship of this approach to the biological theories of mental disorder was discussed, and the limitations upon the Midtown data were indicated.

The chapter also attempts to specify and classify orders of elements in the sociocultural realm as test factors that are potentially relevant to mental health. With the family unit as the crux, these orders range downward in magnitude from the community social system, at one extreme, to detailed patterns of intrafamily functioning (the component variables) at the other. Intermediate were the demographic variables, which were arranged in a typological schema on several taxonomic criteria.

The demographic variables are the principal foci of the present monograph and are a possible first step toward isolating the kinds of families that are respectively pathogenic and eugenic for the mental health of their members. In fine, the Midtown Study seeks to bring into its broad purview both mental well-being and mental morbidity and such sociocultural conditions as may be associated with each.

NOTES

[1] Report of NIMH Office of Program Planning and Evaluation, Biometry Branch, 1971.

[2] R. H. Felix (with M. Kramer), "Research in Epidemiology of Mental Illness," *Public Health Reports (U.S.)* 67 (February 1952): 152.

[3] It should be added that the initial, tentative formulations, together with assumptions implicit in our decisions, far from remaining "frozen," at certain points followed an evolutionary course of refinement and elaboration through the years of field work and data analysis. Accordingly, this chapter outlines provisional thinking and assumptions in the first year of operations, as subsequently clarified and systematized by the present author.

[4] Of course, each discipline is in a continuous process of conceptual evolution, and special shorthand words must be adapted or invented to fit the new refinements in thought with greater specificity than is usually possible in the popular lexicon. Hence the professional "language" of each discipline, far from being a deliberately esoteric obfuscation of the obvious (as literary critics tend to insist), instead reflects a pressing need, paralleling that of each handicraft, for specialized tools appropriate to its specialized functions. Although this need is usually conceded to the physical sciences, the same prerequisite in the behavioral sciences is not generally recognized.

[5] John Whitehorn and Gregory Zilboorg, "Present Trends in American Psychiatry," *American Journal of Psychiatry* 13 (1933): 303–312.

[6] J. E. Gordon, "The Twentieth Century (1920–   )," in C. E. A. Winslow et al., *The History of American Epidemiology*, 1952, p. 120.

[7] J. A. Doull, "The Bacteriological Era (1876–1920)," in Winslow, ibid., p. 76.

[8] Gordon, "The Twentieth Century," p. 115.

[9] Doull, "The Bacteriological Era (1876–1920)," p. 108.

[10] Gordon, "The Twentieth Century," pp. 124–125.

[11] F. C. Redlich, "The Influence of Environment on Mental Health," *Bulletin of the New York Academy of Medicine* 30 (August 1954): 614.

[12] For a discussion of the emergence of these fields as collaborating subdisciplines see L. Srole, "Social Psychiatry: A Case of the Babel Syndrome," in *Social Psychiatry*, J. Zubin

and F. A. Freyhan, eds., 1968, pp. 56–68. Compilations of work from these linked fields are also to be found in S. K. Weinberg, ed., *The Sociology of Mental Disorders,* 1967; F. C. Redlich, ed., *Social Psychiatry,* 1969; and S. C. Plog and R. B. Edgerton, eds., *Changing Perspectives in Mental Illness,* 1969.

[13]Cf. H. W. Dunham, "The Field of Social Psychiatry," *American Sociological Review* 13 (April 1948): 183–197; T. D. Eliot, "Interactions of Psychiatric and Social Theory Prior to 1940," in A. M. Rose, ed., *Mental Health and Mental Disorder,* 1955, pp. 18–41; C. Kluckhohn, "The Influence of Psychiatry on Anthropology in America during the Past One Hundred Years," in J. K. Hall et al., eds., *One Hundred Years of American Psychiatry,* 1944, pp. 489–618.

[14]See A. H. Leighton's "Introduction," in A. H. Leighton, ed., *The Collected Papers of Adolf Meyer,* vol. 4, 1952.

[15]*The Social Responsibility of Psychiatry: A Statement of Orientation,* report no. 13, July 1957.

[16]A. H. Leighton, J. A. Clausen, and R. N. Wilson, eds., *Explorations in Social Psychiatry,* 1957.

[17]Hereafter, the two-word phrase "mental health" is used only in this specific sense of differences along the entire range from "well" or "sound" to "incapacitated." Specifications of the concept, in operational terms, will be presented in chapters 8, 9, 10. See also note 28 below.

[18]Franz Alexander, "Psychoanalysis in Western Culture," *American Journal of Psychiatry* 112 (March 1956): 699.

[19]Thomas Francis, Jr., "The Teaching of Epidemiology," *Journal of Medical Education* 29 (October 1957): 622.

[20]Jack R. Ewalt, "A Case for the Community Self Survey," *Public Health Reports (U.S.)* 72 (July 1957): 622.

[21]For parallels between meteorological and human causation, see Hans Reichenbach, "Probability Methods in Social Science," in D. Lerner and H. Lasswell, eds., *The Policy Sciences,* 1951, pp. 121–128.

[22]Historically, the factors in the etiological complex of a given disorder are often separately isolated and identified, each, in many cases, after years of exploration by a host of investigators. Even so, for few disorders can it be definitively said that most of the contributing factors have been moved from the rubric of *suspected* to the status of *established.*

[23]T. R. Dawber, G. F. Meadows, and F. E. Moore, Jr., "Epidemiological Approaches to Heart Disease: The Framingham Study," *American Journal of Public Health* 41 (March 1951): 280. See also their monograph, *The Framingham Study: 16-Year Follow-Up,* 1971.

[24]Note that a quantitative, actuarial criterion of risk, namely differences in the occurrence of a disorder within whole populations, is the decisive clue tracked in the detective hunt to expose it. Given that "the statistical approach is essentially alien to the psychiatrist's thinking" (Redlich, "The Influence of Environment on Mental Health," p. 613), some clinicians tend to quote Adolf Meyer to the effect that "statistics do not explain the individual case." They may have overlooked the fact that Meyer directly followed this observation with the unanswerable question "Why should they?" (*The Collected Papers of Adolf Meyer,* vol. 4, p. 393). The point implied is that morbidity rates, operationally speaking, are properties of *groups,* not of any given individual, and that potentially they can lead us to endemic conditions in their populations otherwise hidden to the eye.

[25]The remaining unknowns of course may call for further research of different kinds. Etiological "boxing in" of a disease, like all science, proceeds by the pyramiding of progressive refinements and enlargements of knowledge, method, and theory.

[26]E. L. Wynder, I. J. Bross, and E. Day, "Epidemiological Approach to the Etiology of Cancer of the Larynx," *Journal of the American Medical Association* 160 (April 21, 1956): 1384.

[27]J. E. Gordon, E. O'Rourke, S. L. W. Richardson, Jr., and E. Lindemann, "The Biological and Social Sciences in an Epidemiology of Mental Disorders," *American Journal of Medical Science* 223 (March 1952): 319.

[28]The term *mental* in itself usually refers to the cognitive processes. On the other hand, with the sanction of professional usage the phrase *mental health* is accepted as denoting the states of affective-cognitive-interpersonal functioning. It is in this broad, conventional

sense that the phrase is being used in this monograph.

[29]Cf. S. S. Kety, "Biochemical Theories of Schizophrenia," *Science* 129 (June 5 and 12, 1959): 1528–1532 and 1590–1596.

[30]With specific reference to the psychosomatic disorders, Henry H. W. Miles has observed that "the problems of assessing, evaluating and measuring the genetic and constitutional factors are among the most basic in all medicine and their solution will be a job for future generations of investigators." In P. Hoch and J. Zubin, eds., *Current Problems in Psychiatric Diagnosis*, 1953, p. 268.

[31]A. Anastasi, "Heredity, Environment and the Question 'How?' " *Psychological Review* 65 (1958): 197–208.

[32]Marie Jahoda has commented on this point: "What research and experiment can do is certainly not to solve the problem of mental health and disease. Biological, cultural and situational factors are inextricably interwoven in every human being. For scientific purposes each of these factors has to be singled out for scrutiny, and the result will inevitably be answers to isolated questions, which must be treated with caution when considering the complex of factors which affect the functioning of the whole personality. Provided this is borne in mind, however, such research can be expected to contribute increasingly to a better understanding of mental health problems." In "Environment and Mental Health," *International Social Science Journal* 2 (1959): 23.

[33]Racially differentiated groups presumably also belong in the biosocial category. However, the Midtown population, being racially homogeneous (99 percent white), does not offer a test of the racial factor.

[34]Specifications of this factor will be found in chapter 13 of this monograph.

[35]This factor encompasses as its groups: immigrants, or first generation; children of immigrants as the second generation; grandchildren of immigrants as the third generation, and so on.

[36]It should be added that age is an independent variable in a sense different from the other demographic factors, in that one's present age level is not strictly speaking antecedent to his current mental health. Nevertheless, by the certainty that chronological age level (if not reported years) is beyond individual choice or influence, we can consider that it qualifies under this criterion of independence.

[37]The sole apparent exception is confined to immigrants who came to the United States of their own volition, i.e., for the most part as adults, rather than as children brought by parents.

[38]An earthy illustration of a spiraling chain of interactions was reported in the New York press. When a waiter was asked the reasons for closing down Lindy's, a major Broadway restaurant, he replied in these cryptic words: "A number of things. A cause leads to an effect, and an effect to a cause, and a cause to an effect, and then you're kaput."

[39]The distinction here drawn between independent and reciprocal variables approximates but does not completely parallel the distinction made between "exogenous" and "endogenous" variables by K. Arrow, "Mathematical Models in the Social Sciences," in Lerner and Lasswell, *The Policy Sciences*, p. 151, and between *ambient* and *membership* variables suggested by W. G. Cochran et al., *Statistical Problems of the Kinsey Report on Sexual Behavior*, 1954, p. 296. The former "describes aspects of the surroundings or background of the subject over which the subject has had little or no choice," the latter "referring to a variable where subject's choice is very important."

[40]Cf. E. McCaffery and J. Downing, "The Usefulness of Ecological Relationships in Mental Disease Epidemiology," *American Journal of Psychiatry* 113 (June 1957): 1065.

[41]J. B. Lansing and L. Kish, "Family Life Cycle as an Independent Variable," *American Sociological Review* 22 (October 1957): 512.

[42]E. Stainbrook, "Research on the Epidemiology by Psychosomatic Disease," in C. H. Branch et al., eds., *The Epidemiology of Mental Health*, University of Utah, Salt Lake City, 1955, p. 47 (mimeographed).

[43]Often emphasized as limitations of single point-of-time, or "synchronic," studies is that (1) they can only provide correlations between concurrent variables, and (2) if correlations emerge, they provide no firm basis for discriminating antecedent and consequence. By concentrating primarily on demographic factors characterizing one's childhood family and their linkages to adult mental health, we have in effect converted the Midtown investigation

from a synchronic kind of study into one that is at least partially of the general longitudinal-retrospective type. Obviously if a relationship is established between an encompassing characteristic of one's childhood family and his current mental health, there is presumptive ground for inferring the direction of influence from the temporal sequence.

⁴¹J. A. Clausen, *Sociology and the Field of Mental Health*, 1956, p. 28.
⁴²Stainbrook, "Research on the Epidemiology of Psychosomatic Disease," p. 59.
⁴³T. S. Langner and S. T. Michael, *Life Stress and Mental Health*, 1963.

CHAPTER 8

OVERALL STUDY DESIGN
LEO SROLE

Setting his goals and conceptual guidelines, the investigator narrows the
ground to be explored and fixes general bearings for his course. In a
multidisciplinary study this is likely to entail a complex and painful
process of syncretism. Even so, it is hardly more than a brief prelude to
the prolonged labors of hammering out the overall research design and
procedural apparatus—field tactics and instrumental equipment—in the
great number of fine details necessary to the Study's mission.

The specifics of this "tooling-up" process are of little interest to the
general reader. On the other hand they are of critical relevance to those
who wish to gauge the degree to which the Study's findings can be
generalized and to judge the "grains of salt" dosage required by limitations in its methods. Hence, an account of the Study's technical apparatus cannot responsibly be withheld from the published record, although it is offered with a reminder that it is briefly outlined in the
chapter's concluding section.

Given the weight of accumulated technical details, the reporting scientist is inevitably driven to condense such an account—sometimes, unfortunately, to a point of extreme capsulation. We are pressed for such a
summary exposition here. However, in this account we shall pause to
note points of significant conflict, where planning of Study methods
encountered dilemmas of choice between disparate alternatives or no-
choice decisions forced by such facts of life as limited resources, refractory field realities, and committed study goals.

Without the tempering awareness of these behind-the-scenes problems, the student may regard certain research procedures as unwarranted, or at least eccentric, departures from technical canon in his field.[1] This reaction can be especially elicited by an investigation that is multidisciplinary in scope and audience and eclectic in method by the sheer demands of its objectives.

In this light the present chapter and the one to follow have been prepared. Compact in form, they fall far short of providing a full bill of technical particulars.[2] Nonetheless, they go beyond usual practice by reporting the Study's research design in its main features as these took form in the drafting process.

Certain general issues pervaded the "tooling" phase. One we might briefly discuss here centered on the degree of precision we could expect from our research instruments. The issue is rooted in certain study variables that are not of the either-or type characterized, as in the sex factor, by sharply differentiated classes. Rather, they are of the continuous type, in which variations shade into each other in unbroken array, as in the chromatic spectrum. Some of these, like age, sibling order, and family income, can be expressed in numerical units that permit arbitrary but reasonably accurate discrimination of classes.[3]

For many continuum variables, on the other hand, numerically expressed classification is not yet achievable. Such classification, however crude, is possible now for performance on the IQ test but not for mental health, to offer one relevant illustration.[4] Where this is not possible, discrimination of classes is beset with difficulties of isolating and standardizing operational criteria for consistent and objective definition of such classes. Such definition is what we mean by the terms *precise* and *accurate.* In general, numerically phrased classification is more characteristic of the physical disciplines than of the behavioral sciences, but is not intrinsically peculiar to the former. Evolution in both genera of sciences has been marked by advances in this mode of classification as their bodies of knowledge and technology have expanded.

Our own outlook on this matter, from a vantage point on the new ground of social psychiatry, paralleled that of a contemporary group of investigators working on the epidemiology of cardiovascular disease: "In a state of ignorance, we are willing to accept data with many qualifications. . . . In our field we have so little exact data about most problems that relatively crude approximations are still in order."[5]

Similarly, for the Midtown Study we must disclaim that our available base of knowledge and working tools permit anything more than broad, rough, or crude forms of classification in certain key study variables.[6] On this plane also we can qualify only as an exploratory, rather than as a definitive, investigation.

A second side of the problem raised by nonmetric factors derives from the nature of the analysis to be performed on the data secured. One alternative is statistical analysis, which for certain purposes entails two fundamental kinds of determinations: (1) the scatter of the study population among classes of each investigated variable, and (2) the correlation between distributions on separate variables. Only by these means is the way opened to systematic, standardized testing of the network of interrelationships among qualitative variables.

The other alternative is to forgo statistical analysis in favor of a purely descriptive mode of ordering and reporting the phenomena studied. This is appropriate for certain purposes where interest in correlations among variables is not germane or must rely, at least temporarily, on the investigator's impression of the interlacings among the factors.

In general, the second alternative is indicated when the focus of investigation is a limited number of cases, whereas statistical analysis is required to discern trends and their interconnections within a large population of cases—as in the instance of the Midtown Study.

Working with roughly categorized nonmetric variables, however, the researcher may be lured into the use of elaborate statistical measures—often on the assumption that their algebraic elegance will compensate for looseness in classification of the study factors. Taking the contrary view, we hold that as a rule such variables do not warrant the application of more than elementary quantification techniques.[7] Even more important, such elementary techniques keep the analysis fixed on the distribution data. They thereby offer a more sensitive picture of a complex relationship than do advanced statistical measures that can conceal more of significance than they reveal.[8] This position between the extremes of purely descriptive exposition and high-order statistical computation will be manifest in all chapters that follow chapter 9. It is emphasized, in short, that we operate in a field which can muster few claims to the status of exact science.

Responsible for the mental health data reported here were two research programs or operations that were radically different in their implementing procedures and in their calls upon team resources and energies. The larger of these by far, and the keystone of the entire Study, was the Home Interview Survey. Playing a secondary role was the Treatment Census operation, to which we turn first.

TREATMENT CENSUS OPERATION: THE PATIENT POPULATION

The Home Interview Survey, presently to be discussed, could not cover Midtown residents who were in psychiatric hospitals. And we assumed that it would reach too few residents in outpatient care to allow credible analysis. Both types of patients were germane, not to our search for clues to sociocultural etiologies, but rather to our concern with the human traffic moving through the psychiatric facilities and its practical implications for social policy.

To serve this purpose, the specific mission of the Treatment Census was to enumerate Midtown residents who were patients in the four standard kinds of psychiatric facilities,[9] namely:

1. Publicly supported mental hospitals in New York State—municipal, state, and federal (that is, Veterans Administration)
2. Licensed private mental hospitals in New York and adjoining states and major private institutions in more distant states
3. Licensed outpatient clinics in Manhattan—private, and those supported by municipal, state, or federal funds
4. Psychiatrists and clinical psychologists in private office practice within Manhattan

To Mrs. Freeda Taran and Dr. Margaret Bailey, the team's psychiatric social workers, were assigned the manifold responsibilities[10] of carrying out this operation. Sought from the files of the many treatment services covered were data on all bona fide Midtown residents[11] who were being carried on the records of these facilities as "open case" patients, including hospital patients placed in convalescent care status.

By such means the frequency or rate of *treated* mental disorder can be determined relative to the Midtown population as a whole and to its various separate demographic groups. However, two standard patient rate yardsticks are available, and their selection depends in part on the time span to be used. One yardstick requires a count of all patients who *enter* treatment over an extended period, usually a year, and disregards people in treatment during that period who became patients *prior* to its opening date. This is referred to as the *incidence rate*.

The other yardstick requires a count of all patients who are open cases at a specific point of time, usually on one particular day, and disregards the length of time since they entered treatment. This is referred to as the *prevalence rate* and expresses the proportion of a population in treatment at any one time.

A spirited controversy between partisans of the two yardsticks livens the epidemiological literature.[12] Without entering into the limitations specific to each measure or common to the two, we can indicate that our Treatment Census operation applied *both* yardsticks. Its "prevalence day" was *prospectively* fixed for May 1, 1953. Its "incidence year" was *prospectively* fixed for May 2, 1953, through May 1, 1954. Furthermore, for patients of the publicly supported hospitals, the incidence reach was extended *retrospectively* to cover patients previously admitted during the period from May 1, 1948, through April 31, 1953.

Subsequently, when prevalence and incidence data were put through preliminary analysis, several conclusions emerged: (1) The prevalence yardstick not only was more pertinent to our overall research design, but for our purposes was beset with fewer questionable assumptions than was the alternative measure; and (2) while both yardsticks were subject to errors of underreporting, the incidence rate seemed to be beset by the larger margin of such error.[13] With the incidence data revealed to be questionable, if not misleading, we decided their presentation in the monograph served no purpose beyond supporting the hindsight view that this aspect of the operation had been unnecessary.[14]

It should be added, finally, that our plan for using the patients prevalence data also changed considerably during the analysis phase of the Study.[15] Under the influence of insights from evidence gleaned by the other research operations, the Treatment Census prevalence findings are accorded a relatively limited place in the monograph proper, and then only as they could be woven into the more comprehensive scope of the Home Interview Survey.

THE HOME INTERVIEW SURVEY: THE GENERAL POPULATION

The Survey's Mission

The primary goal of the Midtown Study was to test the general hypothesis that biosocial and sociocultural factors leave imprints on mental health which are discernible when viewed from the panoramic perspectives provided by a large population. One kind of evidence suggesting such imprints takes the form of intergroup differences in the frequency of mental morbidity. It was our literal-minded position (1) that the Treatment Census operation could strictly tell us only what it counted, namely, the frequency of *treated* mental disorder, (2) that the latter had to be distinguished from *overall* or total frequency of such disturbance among nonpatients as well as patients—just as the visible portion of an iceberg must be viewed as only a fraction of its total mass, and (3) that there was no evidence available to indicate that *treated* frequency rates and *overall* frequency rates are related in a consistent fashion such as to allow the former to be accepted as an *indirect* but reliable indicator of the latter.

Since an adequate test of the Study's central hypothesis demanded *direct* evidence on the *overall* occurrence of mental disturbance, research of a radically different kind was clearly required—research that cuts away from dependence on institutional records and systematically moves out into the open community for face-to-face assessments of its residents and their individual differences in mental health. This extremely difficult mission was implemented in a Study research operation of such intricacy as to stretch available methods to rather far limits.

The Crucial Decision

The goal of the Home Interview Survey to study the mental health of Midtown residents through direct observation could of course be accomplished only with a sample of its population.

The question of the size of the sample to be encompassed was the obverse face of another question: By what method of mental health assessment shall these people be studied?

The dilemma in effect turned on which question had claim to higher priority in terms of advancing the Study's main goal. On the one hand, if it were demanded that the methods of study should above all else follow the model of intensive clinical examination and diagnosis, then realities would operate to keep the sample small. On the other hand, if the Study's objectives demanded that the sample be large, then realities would compel the adoption of research methods which departed considerably from the intensity of the clinical model.

Given his background in clinical psychiatry, Rennie originally leaned to the first alternative, as was manifest in his initial proposal for intensive examination of a random sample numbering approximately 100 Midtown households. In team discussion of this plan it was pointed out that if the survey's goal was solely to compare *overall* mental morbidity in Midtown as a unit with that in other communities as units, then the sample size proposed could conceivably (but not confidently) be an absolute minimum for the purpose. However, if the Study's objective went beyond this narrow analytical range into group-to-group comparisons of Midtown's cross-cutting demographic segments, then the suggested sample size would be altogether inadequate. Specifically, to have some of the many subgroups large enough for elementary statistical treatment would require a study sample of 1,500 to 1,600 individuals as an irreducible minimum.

Here came directly into play our view of the special significance of the demographic variables discussed in the preceding chapter. In this light, it was the unanimous decision of Rennie and his research associates that the large sample be the chosen alternative. From this decision followed many inexorable consequences, as we shall see presently.

Sample Design and Participation

Necessary to the selection of a sample are specifications, as precise as possible, of the population universe to be covered. The major specification for inclusion in the Midtown universe was that the individual be a resident for whom a Midtown dwelling is both his primary "home base" and the place he now actually occupies:

1. This included, of course, people in residential hotels and residence clubs but excluded those in transient hotels and clubs.

2. It included living-in staff members of Midtown institutions but excluded the patients and charges in those institutions.

3. It included non-kin members of households, like boarders and living-in servants, but excluded members of a family who, during the period of the survey's interviewing program, were away on extended or indefinite leave, for example, occupied in military service, domiciled at college, engaged in foreign travel or distant work assignment, or confined in institutions.

4. It also excluded people who had their home base elsewhere, usually out of New York City, but maintained a year-round Midtown dwelling for use on a sporadic or part-time basis. These were designated *secondary residents.*

Requirements of intergroup analysis may dictate a paring down of the universe to be investigated in order to increase sample homogeneity. This reduces the number of subgroups that contend for representation in a sample that is uncomfortably large in administrative respects but uncomfortably small for the investigator's analytical purposes.

On a number of grounds, we scaled the survey's universe down along the axis of age differences. In one direction we decided to confine the survey to Midtowners beyond the formative, relatively protected years of adolescence and at least initially launched in the swim of mature life with its various cross currents and undertows. At the other extreme, we decided to exclude adults in the declining years of life, a period when aging and its organic concomitants can complicate the mental health picture and obscure its sociocultural traces. By these boundary definitions the population universe to be sampled was narrowed to people in the prime-of-life range spanning the ages of twenty through fifty-nine.[16] By estimate from U.S. Census reports of 1950 and 1960, the Midtown population in this age range numbered somewhat over 100,000 individuals during the Study year 1954.

Out of this host of people, leading largely unexceptional daily lives from the anchoring base of their Midtown dwellings, we had to find subjects for person-to-person study. There are of course a variety of possible methods for securing such subjects. All methods seeking to draw from special categories in the population that are self-defined by reason of the voluntary nature of their actions, for example members of an organization, clients of a social service, patients of a medical institution, subscribers in the telephone directory, or volunteers responding to an appeal for study subjects, will almost certainly produce an unbalanced or biased sample that is unrepresentative of the far more numerous individuals who do not take such actions. This is known as a self-selected or *subjective* type of sample.[17]

At the opposite extreme are the methods of *objective* sampling, developed principally by the U.S. Census Bureau. These methods permit no self-selection by the subject and, equally important, no option in selection to the investigator with his unwitting potential for biased screening of subjects.

In one of its several variants, objective sampling proceeds in essence as if it systematically assigned to every individual in the population universe one in a consecutive series of numbers. All these numbers are then given the same known chance of being selected in a process designated as *systematic drawing from a random start*. In a drawing from these numbers chance alone determines which individuals are chosen. Hence this is also referred to as *probability sampling*. Even the investigator's part in this determination is solely one of following rigorously defined rules to bring chance into play while ensuring that he himself does not intrude in this operation of chance. By mathematically established laws such a sampling plan, if rigorously executed, produces a representative cross section, in miniature, of its population universe— with a *known*, small margin of possible variance, that is, deviation due to fluctuations inherent in the play of chance.[18]

As applied to a population like Midtown's, the details in the design of probability sampling are highly technical. Suffice it to record that a three-stage area sampling type of design[19] was used in the Home Interview Survey. The stages were as follows: (1) From all city blocks in the Midtown area was first chosen a systematic sample of blocks; (2) from the latter blocks was next chosen a systematic sample of dwellings; and (3) from age-eligible occupants of the latter dwellings finally was chosen a systematic sample of adults. Each objectively selected and specifically identified individual was next assigned to an interviewer, who was barred from accepting any substitute source of information. We would add that by such methods 1,911 Midtowners in the twenty to fifty-nine age range were selected from the same number of dwellings, representing a sampling ratio of 19 per 1,000 individuals in the defined population universe.

Ideally, of course, every individual so chosen should participate in the study. Actually this ideal is never fulfilled, because some individuals are impossible to contact during the study period and others who *are* reached exercise their right to decline participation. Of course, if the nonparticipants are relatively few in number, their absence can have no significant effect on the representative character of the study findings. On the other hand, if the nonparticipants are many, then the investigator must acknowledge that the representative integrity of his sample may have been compromised.

Acting in a form of negative self-selection (that is, self-exclusion), the nonparticipants may well differ from the participants in various ways crucial to the study's findings, for example, in mental health. But given that the nonparticipants are unstudied, the investigator is in an untenable state of ignorance about the degree and kind of bias left to the studied sample by the defection of nonparticipants in some numbers. This unenviable and by no means rare predicament leaves a study's findings hanging in several senses at "a point of no return."

As we assembled our list of 1,911 sample Midtown dwellings and their occupants, we were acutely aware of this risk: whether they would yield few or many nonparticipants was a contingency which would largely turn on our own management of preliminaries to the interview encounter that was our chosen method of face-to-face study.

This risk was one of several overriding considerations in developing tactics for meeting with our sample people. But before we unfold this phase, perhaps we can jump ahead in chronological sequence to conclude our discussion of the nonparticipation problem. This can be accomplished by reporting the response to our approach for an interview that was made by the 1,911 Midtown adults drafted for our complete sample.

To frame a realistic norm for judging these results, previous sample survey experience is certainly germane. National opinion surveys have found that, on the whole, the larger the community, the higher is the nonparticipation rate.[20] Although these usually manage to hold nationwide nonparticipation to about 10 percent, in one well-conducted citywide Detroit study[21] this rate came to 19 percent. Suggesting perhaps the metropolitan outer limit in this respect is the sample survey of health in the five boroughs of New York City that has reported data reflecting a nonparticipation rate at the 34 percent level.[22]

Moreover, opinion-survey experience has also shown that, among sections within big cities, the larger the proportion of apartment house dwellings, the greater is sample nonparticipation. As we have already noted, Midtown is one of the New York areas with greatest density of apartment buildings.

In the light of these experiences we can report that nonparticipation in the complete Midtown sample was kept to an acceptable 13 percent level,[23] a figure close to the national norm for surveys touching substantive areas considerably less sensitive than mental health. Stated differently, we were able to interview 1,660 individuals, or 87 percent of all those selected, involving a sampling ratio of 16 per 1,000 persons in the specified population universe[24] drawn from 24 per 1,000 of all Midtown households.

The skeptical reader may well demand assurances more solid than faith that the 1,660 interviewed individuals or *respondents* are indeed representative of the 100,000 adults from whom they were systematically drawn. To meet this "show me" stopper we might inspect these respondents in terms of their age composition. First, we can compare them in this respect with their population universe. The necessary data for the latter can be estimated by interpolation from U.S. Census information for 1950 and 1960. Given the uneven tempo of population changes during the decade, the approximations inherent in all estimates, and normal small fluctuations in sampling results, we obviously cannot expect this comparison to show absolute identity of age distributions.

Second, we will enlarge this comparison by also introducing the age composition of the complete sample of 1,911 individuals.[25] The three sets of age distributions for each sex appear in table 8–1.

TABLE 8–1. AGE DISTRIBUTIONS BY SEX IN THREE OVERLAPPING POPULATIONS

Age groups	Interviewed sample (1954) N = 1,660	Complete sample (1954) N = 1,911	Midtown universe (1954) N = 100,000 (estimated)
Males:			
20–29	20.6%	19.4%	21.8%
30–39	23.9	23.4	24.4
40–49	28.7	29.4	26.5
50–59	26.8	27.8	27.3
Total	100.0%	100.0%	100.0%
Females:			
20–29	23.0%	22.2%	23.9%
30–39	23.0	22.8	22.9
40–49	27.7	27.8	26.2
50–59	26.3	27.2	27.0
Total	100.0%	100.0%	100.0%

With respect to age composition in both sexes, the triangulation (table 8–1) shows that the interviewed sample[26] achieves practical identity with the complete sample, as does the latter with the population universe. Although still providing less than an ironclad guarantee, which would have required the U.S. Census to be conducted in the year of the interviewing, these latter two populations, in age and other demographic characteristics, offer warrant for a high degree of confidence that the Midtown sample of 1,660 interviewed adults (respondents) are in fact representative of the population from which they were drawn.[27] On this plane, at least, the survey reaches a known approximation to precision. Without such solidity in the survey's sample foundations, the effects of unavoidable imprecision in its substantive variables might have been grossly magnified.

Methods of Interviewing

Our purpose with each drafted sample adult was to elicit intimate information on certain sectors of his private life: on signs and symptoms relating to both his general and mental health—present and past—on his demographic alignments and social roles, and on central areas of experience during his preadult and adult years. This is an interview task of extreme delicacy, yet one that had to be projected on a large-sample scale. Clearly, great care had to be exercised in planning this "chips down," climactic phase of the survey operation.

One aspect of the problem revolved around the staging of the interview, and here emerged four principal conflicts between the ideal *should* and the practical *must*. These can now be indicated only summarily:

1. In the interest of strict privacy, the interview should have been conducted at a place other than the respondent's home, preferably in the psychiatric clinic where Study personnel were based. However, it seemed certain that the inconvenience and time required for such travel from home would convert a sizable number of sample draftees into nonparticipants.[28]

Here maximal sample participation and complete privacy of conversation were mutually exclusive alternatives. Ideally we required both. Realistically we could have only one, and in the end the interest of sample integrity prevailed. In compensation, the interviewers made every tactful effort at the home to interrogate the respondent out of earshot of others.[29]

2. To maximize the volume of information secured, several sessions with each respondent would have been desirable. However, previous survey experience warned that under this avowed plan some potential participants would turn into nonparticipants at first approach, and some respondents seen in the first session would not be available for a second. Here maximal individual information and maximal sample participation were mutually exclusive alternatives. In the choice between more data from a biased sample of respondents and fewer data from a representative sample of respondents, the latter was felt to be the transcending interest. Accordingly, it was decided to confine the interview to one session.

3. Ideally, perhaps, interviewing should have been done by psychiatrists. However, to see so many sample people, at the specific time and place of their convenience, over the short operating span of several months allotted to the interviewing program, was far beyond the capabilities of the limited and overworked supply of psychiatric personnel. Accordingly, the responsibility was

delegated to allied professionals who have technical experience in the methods of intimate interrogation. These included psychiatric social workers, clinical psychologists, social caseworkers, and social scientists.

4. Ideally, the interview should have been conducted along the lines of what we might call the open style of interrogation, which allows the interviewer complete freedom to decide the substance, sequence, and wording of questions to be asked in each case. Two considerations argued instead for a structured line of personal inquiry in which the interviewer follows a carefully prepared and standardized schedule of questions; these considerations arose in spite of our awareness that, as Clausen has phrased it, "Psychiatrists tend to have a profound distrust of data secured by questionnaires or by structured interviews."[30]

First, it was in the survey's interest to secure the largest systematic coverage of information that was possible within the tight compass of a single session. And it appeared likely that the sharply focused, preplanned interview can, on the whole, cover more pinpointed information in a strictly limited period of time than could alternative methods.

Second, and even more important, the structured inquiry minimizes idiosyncratic skewing of the respondent data as a result of the varying personal equations and skills of the interviewers, whereas under open-style interviewing this is maximized. In the latter instance, such "interviewer effect" can variously intrude to undermine the validity and comparability of data obtained from respondent to respondent.[31] Above all, this is a probability in eliciting mental health information.

On the other side of the coin, the obvious risk in the questionnaire-guided inquiry is its capacity to turn into a perfunctory routine. This real danger was directly faced in the construction of the interview instrument itself, in the determination of the kinds of professionals to be invited to apply for the interviewing task, in the careful selection of applicants, and in the planning of the special training program to which they were exposed. There they were placed under a specific mandate not only to record the respondent's answer to each prepared question and his spontaneous elaborations and asides, but to report observations of his behavior and to probe replies and comments that were either ambiguous or suggestive as possible openings to matters of further significance. We would note a rough procedural parallel between the interviewer's role as just defined and that of the trained administrator of a projective test like the Rorschach. Both start with standardized stimuli, uniformly administered, and both follow responses with the disciplined inquiry or probe technique.

Thus, if the interview as designed was in structure less fluid than a psychotherapy session, it was certainly more freewheeling than the systematic but hasty review of possible symptoms that often characterize medical intake interviews. Testifying in part to the interview's flexibility in the face of the respondent was this fact: Although minimum time for administration of the questionnaire was about seventy-five minutes, actual individual interviewing time ranged from that lower limit to an upper limit beyond four hours, the average for the respondent sample being about two hours. As an exemplar in clinic case-history recording, Rennie was himself agreeably surprised at the "individual richness of information that comes through in the interview protocols."

Interview Development

If one set of planning problems revolved around the staging of the interview, other problems centered on the contents of the questionnaire that would steer the inquiry in a like pattern for all respondents.

As preliminary, however, we might briefly outline the sequence of steps that had to be taken before the interview instrument was finally ready for oral communication to the first Midtown sample respondent.

It is relevant to note that all members of the Midtown Study team during its planning period were professionally experienced in the open mode of interrogation. Unquestionably, this kind of interviewing, when mastered, is a fine personal art but one difficult to codify beyond its general principles. It therefore offers few specifics that can be transferred to the task of designing a long questionnaire as a detailed and complete entity—itself an exacting, specialized art that conceals endless traps and pitfalls for the unwary novice designer.[32]

As it happened, two team members additionally had an aggregate of about twenty years' experience in questionnaire development for sample surveys in a variety of fields, mental and general health included.[33] Designated by Rennie as the Questionnaire Committee, these members were given assignments (1) to comb the literature on all previous relevant instruments for potentially useful mental health "items" (that is, symptom questions), and (2) to draft the first version of the survey questionnaire in a form consistent with the Study's outlined framework of concepts and hypotheses.

After months of intensive work the committee submitted its first draft of the instrument for critical discussion by the team sitting *in camera*. On the strength of these meetings and consultations with Rennie and Kirkpatrick, the Study psychiatrists in that period, the committee prepared a second version of the questionnaire for further team discussion and consultation. This interactive process was repeated for nine drafts in all, after which the writer, assisted by Langner as newly added team and committee member, composed the tenth and final form of the survey questionnaire.[34]

It is important to add that three of the nine preliminary drafts were subjected to pretests under field conditions. Used as subjects in these tryout interviews were a total of 145 previously unknown adults living in areas adjacent to Midtown, some drawn from the outpatient rosters of a psychiatric clinic. These pretests were of decisive importance in the development of the survey questionnaire. By reviewing the data produced, and evaluating subjects' and interviewers' reactions to the instrument and interview situation, the committee developed a wide variety of refinements that were carried into the structure, content,[35] and administration of the instrument and into the subsequent training program for the staff of professional interviewers.

Interview Content

On the questionnaire as communicated by sensitive, psychologically knowledgeable interviewers depended the survey's entire framework of concepts and hypotheses.

To do its work this information-moving vehicle was equipped with some 200 questions pointing to the Study's test factors—demographic and component, independent and reciprocal.

During the development of the questionnaire, these factors posed far fewer problems than did the dependent variable, namely, mental health. Therefore, it is to the latter, as the Study's decisive cutting edge, that this section will look exclusively.

It is necessary to clarify first how the detailed mental health signs and symptoms elicited from the respondent were to be summarized, evaluated, and classified for purposes of hypothesis testing. Of two major alternatives open, the most expeditious would have permitted translation of these details into the psychometric form of numerical scores and profiles. The ideal course, on the other hand, would have one or more psychiatrists concentrate on the interview protocol of each respondent in turn for a global judgment of his mental health condition.

In point of fact, this was at no time a real issue. To Rennie the latter course, although raising a variety of knotty problems, was strategically the only alternative that could be defended before the imperatives of the Study's goals. With Rennie as their preceptor and supervisor, Kirkpatrick and Michael were designated to sit in separate psychiatric judgment on the mental health evidence secured from each sample respondent.

It was under the relatively broad latitude of this strategic decision that the Questionnaire Committee, in collaboration with the team psychiatrists, worked to structure the mental health content of the interview instrument.

As finally evolved, the brief on each respondent provided each of the two psychiatric judges with information that included the following:

1. The respondent's free-association elaborations and asides, spontaneous or elicited by the interviewer's probes. In many cases, these were voluminous, in other cases sparse. But in either instance, such added comments often proved to be significant in the clinical judgments of the psychiatrists.

2. The observations garnered by the interviewer during the course of several hours of sustained interaction with the respondent. These the interviewer systematically reported in a prepared outline. The latter covered various aspects of the respondent's behavior, including manifestations of ease or tension, affect or mood, appropriateness of replies, apparent level of intelligence, dress and grooming habits, the presence or absence of muscular tics, stutter or stammer in speech, memory difficulties, and physical deviations or disabilities. This report was descriptive, rather than diagnostic, and was specifically prepared by the interviewer as a communication to the team psychiatrists.

3. Data derived from our Treatment Census files relating to psychiatric care, if any, during the time span covered by this census (namely, six years for mental hospitals and one year for outpatient facilities).

4. Results of a check made of the records of the New York City Social Service Exchange for a history of personal or family problems brought or reported to

one or more of the City's many social agencies, including those attached to the civil courts.[36]

Although important in their own right, these four kinds of information were supplementary to the symptom questions put to all respondents during the course of the interview session. Of course, we could cover only a sample of the universe of possible signs and symptoms. Accordingly, it was our effort to include in this sample such symptoms as would demonstrably represent the most salient and *generalized* indicators of mental pathology.[37] As might be expected, the final series of symptoms covered were heterogeneous in substantive character. To simplify description here, the author finds it convenient to group them under a limited number of rubrics.

One heuristic category is based on behavioral evidence of five types. In type I fall the respondent's replies to queries about a history of epilepsy, of "nervous breakdown," or of seeking psychotherapy. This information, together with data from the Treatment Census and Social Service Exchange files, provides evidence suggesting mental pathology and when it occurred.

To type II are assigned the results of reviewing with the respondent a series of ten gross somatic disorders that, with varying probabilities, are often attributed to a psychogenic basis. These included arthritis-rheumatism, asthma, colitis, diabetes, hay fever, heart condition, high blood pressure, hives or rashes, neuralgia-sciatica, and stomach ulcer.

What we might designate as *psychophysiologic manifestations* of emotional disturbance[38] are placed in type III and were covered in the interview by twenty-four questionnaire items referring to nervousness, restlessness, dizziness, fainting spells, headaches, back pains, hand tremors, cold sweats, damp hands, feeling hot all over, insomnia, appetite and digestive disturbances, shortness of breath, heart palpitations, neurasthenia, and excessive intake of coffee, food, tobacco, or liquor.

Type IV behavior relates to memory difficulties reflected in the respondent's negative response to the questionnaire statement suggesting that his memory "seems to be all right," a point on which the interviewer reported his own independent observation.

The fifth type of behavioral sign emerged from eighteen questionnaire items focused on current interpersonal functioning within the social settings of family, work, and peer groups.[39] Also important on this level were the respondent's elaborations about these settings, extreme deviations in relating himself to the interview situation, and a problem history on the records of the Social Service Exchange.

Of course, psychiatric evaluation of behavioral symptoms required the sounding of forces potentially underlying them. For this purpose, the questionnaire included thirty items relating to seven selected areas or dimensions of current intrapsychic functioning, designated anxiety, inadequacy, depression, rigidity, immaturity, withdrawal, and suspiciousness.

To convey how soundings were taken in these areas, we might illustrate with the series of anxiety items. These included such statements of self-characterization as "I am the worrying type" and "I have personal worries that get me down physically" and also a series of specific kinds of worries, for example, cost of living, marriage, overwork, children, old age, atom bomb, enemies, and personal health.[40]

Supplementing the questionnaire's coverage of these dimensions were the interviewer's observations of the respondent bearing on four of the areas, namely, anxiety, depression, suspiciousness, and withdrawal. In addition, the respondent's spontaneous remarks were often revealing in terms of one or more of the seven intrapsychic dimensions.

In all, ninety-two structured questions related to behavioral or intrapsychic symptoms of malfunction during recent adulthood. Also included in the instrument, for purposes of developmental perspective, were twenty-eight selected signs of disturbance during childhood, of course reported retrospectively. These referred to the five types of behavioral indicators and to one intrapsychic area, namely, anxiety.

It remains to indicate that a core series of the symptom items, consisting principally of the psychophysiologic manifestations and those tapping the anxiety, depression, and inadequacy dimensions, were drawn from two previous instruments, namely, the experimental version of the Army's Neuropsychiatric Screening Adjunct (NSA)[41] and the Minnesota Multiphasic Personality Inventory (MMPI). These symptom inventories had demonstrated high reliability and validity in discriminating between groups of psychiatric patients and controls. For the Midtown Study, the symptom items selected from these sources were tested in a pilot validation experiment conducted by Weider. Suffice it here to note briefly that it involved two small samples of Manhattan adults, one a criterion group of 139 diagnosed neurotic and remitted psychotic patients, and the other a control group of 72 people judged to be "well" by an examining Study psychiatrist. From this limited test, almost all the NSA and MMPI symptom questions emerged with validity confirmed.

In this modest validation check, as in the Army NSA investigation, the core series of "psychophysiologic manifestations of emotional disturbance," *eighteen items in all,*[42] when taken *alone* and expressed in the psychometric form of a numerical count, defined a "critical score" of sufficient discriminatory power to identify correctly about 90 percent of the criterion group of patients.

It should be emphasized that clinical experience, as well as statistical evidence of validity, was a consideration in selecting the larger sample of symptoms covered in the Midtown questionnaire. By application of the validity criterion, selection in part hinged on evidence that the symptom appears *far more often* among nosologically heterogeneous psychiatric patients than among psychologically heterogeneous nonpatients. Thus, through a statistical form of guilt by association, such a single symptom can serve as a flag warning that a large reservoir of underlying pathologic disturbance may be present at a level usually found in psychiatric patients. In general, the larger the number of such warning signs systematically canvassed, the greater are the probabilities that mental morbidity will not go undetected among those studied. Viewing the symptom items singly, Rennie was originally skeptical about the discrete value of each for mental health assessment. However, with intensive exposure to the pretest interview protocols his views changed decisively. Weighing the 120 structured "signs and symptoms" items, backed in depth by the four types of supplementary information, Rennie regarded the combined body of information as a highly useful yardstick for global psychiatric judgments about the relative current mental health status of each Midtown respondent.

Two important qualifications must now be entered on the record. First, it is considered virtually impossible that the Midtown questionnaire, or any other instrument of this type, or for that matter any single-session psychiatric examination, can be 100 percent accurate in detecting all cases with significant symptomatology in a community sample.[43] Rennie did not doubt that certain kinds of individuals, for example those in the early stages of alcoholism or drug addiction, can slip the net of warning signals built into the survey questionnaire. Thus, whatever estimated mental morbidity rate emerges for the Midtown sample as a whole must be considered to be a *minimal* estimate, one that is an understatement by an unknown but hardly large margin.

Second, it must also be emphasized that other researchers implementing the same goals, working with the same respondents, and otherwise employing the same methods might conceivably have chosen a substantially different sample of symptoms for assessment of mental health. Accordingly, the findings that have emerged from the psychiatrists' evaluation of Midtown respondents are bound to the specific body of symptomatic information collected for the purpose. In this sense, the psychiatrists' classifications of mental health must be strictly considered as in the nature of *operational* definitions geared to these particular data.

Orientation of Respondents

The qualifications just entered are linked to another basic issue, namely, the orientation of the sample respondent to the interview itself —a matter bearing directly on the quality of his answers to the questions asked him. The psychiatric patient is often in treatment through motivated self-selection, thereby disposing him to accept professional questioning as a necessary part of the sick role and therapeutic process. This disposition is of course lacking when the objectively sampled individual is being questioned, posing for us the most thorny of all problems in managing the interview encounters with the Midtown respondents.

To a certain extent we can agree that "the quality and quantity of information secured probably depend far more upon the competence of the interviewer than upon the respondent."[44] It was on this conviction that we selected and trained our staff of interviewers, and so far as possible, furthermore, assigned them to match the specific ethnic, social class, and age characteristics of the prospective respondent.[45] But we also recognized that the effectiveness of the most competent and culturally congenial interviewer, standing as he initially does in the role of stranger to the respondent, is in large measure dependent upon the terms in which the interview situation is initially framed for and accepted by the respondent.[46]

In this recognition, we were called upon to define the interview situation in terms of a model that is acceptable because it is familiar and also comfortable, or at least nonthreatening. It is clear, for example, that an interview explicitly defined from the start as being focused on mental health[47] could not possibly serve as such a model. Because this would have cast us as netting candidates for a psychiatric tag, it was almost certain to provoke large-scale nonparticipation[48] and to elicit from participants information of dubious value.

The model actually brought into play was composed of a number of elements, each more or less familiar in itself, but combined in a new pattern. This was conveyed in Dr. Rennie's introductory letter of explanation to the sample household and during a subsequent call at the home by a field staff member to arrange an appointment for the interview session itself. In brief, these elements consisted of (1) communication of the institutional image of the Cornell Medical College, (2) identification of the survey as one focused on community health, (3) specification of method as that of a census, generally known to require a call at the home for individual information asked of many people on prescribed lines,[49] and (4) reinforcement of the professional image in the prearrangement of an appointment, and in Dr. Rennie's written assurance that individual information, like all medical data, would be kept confidential and anonymous.

By opening the interview proper with a bloc of questions bearing on general health and somatic symptoms, we expected that the model would be quickly crystallized as conforming to the familiar medical symptoms review,[50] one that generally reinforces the individual's motivation to give all requested information at his best level of accuracy. This, we believe, gave the interview the momentum to carry, without perceptible resistance, into the subsequent more sensitive areas of mental health symptoms. Moreover, by cutting this large symptom series into a number of smaller clusters of items and by interspersing these clusters through the longer blocs of sociocultural background questions, we felt that attention would not be fixed long enough on the sensitive -matter to mobilize censoring anxieties or "response sets."

It seems likely not only that the indicated model provided a motivating role for intimate information giving, but further that, by avoidance of sharply focused attention on mental health, two potential tendencies of an opposite character were more or less kept in check. These were (1) censored denial of existing behavioral and emotional symptoms, and (2) stimulation to report nonexisting symptoms under the suggestion of the research interest itself—the spurious "no" response set and the spurious "yes" response set, respectively.

We hasten to add that our avoidance of sharp focus on mental health substance does not imply that we neglected to acknowledge the actual nature of the inquiry to sample respondents. Instead, through the interview we sought to convey, explicitly or implicitly, that mental health is a medical concern and in the domain of our research interest. For example, within the interview's opening bloc of questions on specific somatic conditions, we also asked whether the respondent had ever had a nervous breakdown. Another early bloc, reviewing specific kinds of medical specialists previously consulted, included "nerve specialist" and psychiatrist. More pointedly, a third bloc of questions was introduced by the interviewer with the comment: "The thing that interests us very much in this research is how city life and city conditions affect people's health, physical and emotional."

This is not to claim by any means that the sample respondent in the role defined was raised to the same self-revealing plane as the self-selected psychiatric patient. On the other hand, we shall soon review evidence suggesting that, with rare exceptions, he was lacking in the hostility or negativism of the "reluctant" patient entered in treatment at the instance of others.[51] More positively, the respondent generally conveyed an initial approach of engaged curiosity, tinged in varying degrees with the sense that the research was professionally responsive to the common interest and therefore to his own self-interest. This orientation was by no means unfavorable to the survey's immediate interest in maximizing the accuracy of the respondent's information.

Assessment of the Interview Results

No effort was spared in designing and executing the rigorous process of selecting the survey sample. Similarly, no effort was spared in designing and executing the high-stakes program of interviewing the sampled individuals.

The results of the sampling process can be and have been assessed. Comparison of the 1,660 sample respondents on almost every available demographic criterion has shown them to correspond to a remarkable degree with the population they were intended to represent and with the smaller population of 251 nonparticipants.

The results of the interviewing program, in terms of its three separable aspects, namely, (1) form and content of the questionnaire instrument, (2) structuring of the interview model for the respondent, and (3) actual performances of interviewers and respondents, would require assessment against their common objective: procurement of information from the sample respondents that was at a reasonably high level of accuracy.

Unfortunately, direct and systematic evidence of this particular type would require that a separate investigation be superimposed on our research design, at a cost prohibitively beyond remaining resources. However, we can marshal some indirect, suggestive evidence bearing on this issue:

1. In sample surveys of the opinion-poll type, it is the usual experience that about 1 percent of the respondents will break off the interview before it is completed.[52] Such opinion-poll interviews are generally about thirty minutes long and relatively shallow in psychological penetration. By comparison, our interview sessions took an average of approximately two hours, far beyond the limits of even the usual medical or psychotherapeutic session. And in subject content it touched on many potentially painful points across the span of the respondent's life history. We could therefore plausibly expect breakoffs substantially above the 1 percent level. In fact, our breakoff rate was slightly under 1 percent, and most of these cases had proceeded far enough into the questionnaire to permit mental health evaluation by the Study psychiatrists.

2. Information about family income is a sensitive personal matter that in opinion polls is often refused by 5 to 10 percent or more of the respondent sample.

In the U.S. Census of 1950, 8 percent of the Midtown households refused to report family income.[53] Without the Census Bureau's backing of congressional legislation, we could have expected an income refusal rate around the 10 percent level. The actual rate of such refusal among our sample respondents was 3.5 percent.

3. In the sensitive area of private religious beliefs ("To what religious faith do you now belong?") about 0.5 percent of the respondents withheld an answer. In a 1958 national sample survey of religious affiliation, conducted by the U.S. Census Bureau, this rate was approximately the same as the income refusal rate. Thus, in Midtown it would predictably have been about 8 percent.

4. Another item that could readily elicit the answer "It's my private affair" was the pair of questions: "Do you drink liquor, beer, or wine?" and, if this was answered affirmatively, "Like a lot of people, do you sometimes drink more than is good for you?" To either or both of these questions, only thirteen respondents (0.8 percent of the sample) stood on their constitutionally sanctioned rights of privacy.

The above bits of evidence in themselves offer no guarantees that respondents who did not terminate the interview or who did not refuse the requested information necessarily answered the questions correctly. But the low breakoff rate and infrequent refusals to answer delicate queries can be plausibly considered as clues reflecting the positive orientation of the sample respondents to the overall interview situation. That is, it can be assumed that the same factors which kept these rates at very low frequencies also operated to maintain the respondents' motivation to give answers at a relatively high level of accuracy.

Another type of indirect evidence is provided by the interviewer's observations of the respondent during the course of the session on the criteria of apparent interest in the interview and of tension level. Specifically, he was asked to classify the respondent on each criterion at two points of time, namely, soon after the opening of the session and near the close.

By analyzing the sample for the overall trend of change in interest and tension, we can make certain inferences. Of course, given the exceptional duration and content of the interview, we could plausibly expect change in the unfavorable, rather than the favorable, direction. To judge from the interviewers' observations, as summarized in table 8–2, this expectation is not fulfilled.

TABLE 8-2. INTERVIEWERS' OBSERVATIONS ON 1660 SAMPLE RESPONDENTS
DURING THE INTERVIEW SESSION (AS RECORDED AFTER THE SESSION)

Respondents' interest in the interview		
Interest	After start	Near close
Lacking	7%	4%
Mild	42	35
High	51	61
Total.	100%	100%

Respondents' tension level during interview		
Tension level	After start	Near close
Nervous, fidgety.	10%	6%
Sporadic nervousness	27	21
Mostly relaxed	63	73
Total.	100%	100%

Instead of the unfavorable change we reasonably could have expected,
we note for both criteria a small but definite change in the other direction. Thus, if our definition of the interview situation had the effect of
creating a more or less positive initial orientation among previously
unmotivated individuals, then the conduct of the interview inferribly
counteracted the attrition to be expected from its unusual length and
substance.

From all the above clues it can be judged likely that the sustained,
predominantly positive orientation of respondents to the interview, as
basically modeled after the patient role in the medical situation, operated
on the whole to elicit information at an adequate, if hardly perfect, level
of validity.

JUDGMENTAL BIAS IN PSYCHIATRIC CLASSIFICATION

It has been a major purpose of this chapter to indicate potential sources of error and bias that the Midtown investigators recognized and attempted to control in drafting their research design. One such source was anticipated at the point of classifying the respondent's mental health from the data record assembled about him. Although the details of the psychiatrists' classification procedures are discussed in chapters 9 and 10, the methodological concerns of the sociologists about such techniques can briefly be summarized here.

Of course, mental health is a nonmetric, constellational variable and as yet can only be qualitatively classified by refraction through the lens of the psychiatrist's perceptual and judgmental processes. Such processes are hardly impervious to influences from the judge's particular theoretical preconceptions and leanings, or from his empirical impressions and hunches, or from his personal values and projections. These uncontrolled influences on professional judgments of "fact" are not readily isolated or quarantined. Therefore, in investigations involving judgmentally classified variables their intrusion must be assumed and controlled by appropriate measures in the research design.

The effects of this intrusion are maximal when such classification is dependent upon a single judge. Such effects are reduced when several judges perform the operation. For qualitative classification the principle has long been accepted that "two heads are better than one," on the ground that each tends more or less to balance the errors of the other.[54] This would especially seem to be the case if each judge forms his opinion without knowledge of the other's, and above all if the two differ in professional training, experiences, and theoretical leanings. By Rennie's design both of these conditions applied to the two psychiatrists he chose to evaluate mental health in the Midtown sample.

However, the possibility remained open that *both* psychiatrists unwittingly would operate under certain shared tendencies toward the same kinds of errors. If so, these would be mutually reinforcing, rather than mutually canceling errors, thereby introducing a systematic distortion in the Study findings. This possibility seemed to be magnified by a well-established procedural point in clinic usage.

By way of background, in clinical diagnosis, psychiatrists customarily "operate" on the patient's case history record as a global whole. It was accordingly taken for granted that the Midtown psychiatrists would do likewise with the sample respondent's assembled record. However, the Study's social scientists pointed out that in the transfer of this universal practice from the therapeutic to the research setting a difficulty of some seriousness would be created. Specifically, the Study was attempting to test the relationship of a series of sociocultural factors to mental health. If the two evaluating psychiatrists were to have the entire record for each respondent, their classifications of mental health would be made with full knowledge of the sociocultural information in each case.

It is not suggested that these Midtown psychiatrists were in danger of premature commitment, on theoretical grounds, to the Study's hypotheses linking specific sociocultural variables and mental health. Both were of course physicians medically trained in a perspective that systematically emphasized the biological foundations of human pathologies. However, a risk of shared bias loomed from another, and less obvious, direction. For example, it was entirely possible that in the course of clinical experience *both* psychiatrists had encountered demographic group Z patients principally as psychotics in hospitals and group Y patients mainly as neurotics in ambulatory facilities.

This kind of professional observation that Z patients seen clinically tend to be sicker than Y patients could readily become an adjudicating criterion in the psychiatrist's judgmental processes when he confronted the sample respondents' records. Specifically, a Z-group respondent and a Y respondent symptomatically may both be borderline cases difficult to classify. However, the felt necessity to push them "off the fence" could lead the psychiatrist to fall back on his clinical observations of patients and accordingly place the Z respondent in the less favorable category and the Y respondent in the more favorable.

With this tendency operating as a systematic bias in *both* psychiatrists, the entire group Z sample could emerge as significantly more impaired than the group Y sample. This might happen despite the fact that the same psychiatrists, judging the same respondents "blind," that is, without benefit of information on their group affiliations, could yield data subsequently showing that Z and Y respondents are not significantly different in mental health composition. That is, the pathognomonic picture in the selected aggregate of *known* psychiatric patients may be inadvertently projected on the cross-section representatives of the *unknown* community population, with effects that distort the facts.[55]

On this general rationale, the Study sociologists urged that psychiatric classification of respondents be made blind to the sociocultural data on each sample individual. On their part, the Midtown psychiatrists emphasized that they could not weigh the mental health import of a set of symptoms which were disembodied from the social characteristics that are an integral part of the individual's identity and life history.

Acknowledging the force of this point, the social scientists countered that, nonetheless, if such information were admitted to the psychiatrists' judgmental process, any findings bearing on the relationships between the independent demographic variables and the so-classified mental health factor, *whatever their nature,* would be left in a completely suspended state of ambiguity. The objective nature of these relationships being the Study's terminus, posed here was the issue of compromising this central goal.

Out of this impasse a procedural formula emerged, somewhat complicated in detail but serving *both* sets of interests. It took the following lines:

1. From each respondent's record a two-part Summary was prepared as the psychiatrist's working document.

2. Into Part A was transcribed all symptomatic information (with several important exceptions to be noted below), including items provided by respondent, interviewer, and several documentary sources. Also recorded here were the respondent's age, sex, and marital status. These biosocial demographic data were included on the insistence of the psychiatrists that they had to visualize what manner of human frame went with the symptoms being evaluated.

3. On the basis of Part A information alone each psychiatrist-judge, operating independently of the other, placed the respondent in one of seven categories (later telescoped into six), representing a graded scale of manifest symptom formation and inferred "emotional disability," as Rennie phrased it, for performing the roles of adult life. This classification was designated Rating I.

4. Rating I completed, the psychiatrist turned for the first time to Part B of

the Summary. Transcribed here was the type V evidence of interpersonal functioning (cf. pages 152–153) and all other items of respondent information that were coopted by the psychiatrists as germane to their interest in his social history and interpersonal functioning. Included of course were respondent data bearing on the demographic variables (other than age, sex, and marital status) and on the component factors reported in the Langner-Michael monograph.

Also included were a number of information items highly suggestive of mental pathology but withheld from Part A because they offered clues of a demographic nature that were capable of contaminating classificatory judgment. One example is a problem history in one or more social agencies, often associated with the lower reaches of the socioeconomic range. Another is a history as a psychiatric outpatient, which is usually associated with other than the lower socioeconomic brackets.

5. With Part B of the Interview Summary reviewed in the context of Part A, the psychiatrist now had substantially all of the respondent's record of immediate interest to him. In this more comprehensive light, Rating II could be formed by the psychiatrist as his most global judgment of the respondent's mental health —framed in terms of the same seven-category gradient scale as he had used in making Rating I.[56]

6. Of course, in reaching Rating II, the psychiatrist was not bound by the particular grade he had assigned to the respondent as Rating I. However, if a change was made, he was required to inscribe the information items in Part B of the record that prompted the change. In point of fact, changes in both directions were made for about one-fourth of all respondents, so that the sample's Rating II distribution deviates somewhat from that of the Rating I scatter.

Although cumbersome, these procedures permitted us to assay the possibility that the psychiatrists' knowledge of a given demographic fact, for example, socioeconomic origin, as presented in the Summary Part B document, had contaminated their classifications of respondent mental health. With Rating I as the "before socioeconomic status (SES) knowledge" judgment and Rating II as the "after SES knowledge" judgment, we could compare the distributions of the two ratings on our sample SES-origin categories. If the net changes made in Rating II were similar in direction and magnitude for all sample socioeconomic groups, it could reasonably be assumed that no systematic SES bias had operated as a result of information in the Part B document.

On the other hand, if such changes in one socioeconomic group were loaded toward more favorable classifications, and in another group toward the opposite direction, then the possibility of systematic bias could not be dismissed. Means to further check this possibility were at hand in the specific Part B evidence cited by each psychiatrist as warranting all changes made between his Rating I and Rating II evaluations.

The latter step proved to be unnecessary. Comparisons of Rating I and II distributions, on each of four independent demographic variables of the sociocultural type, yielded grounds for confidence that in none of the four had judgmental bias visibly entered to skew the morbidity findings.[57] For purposes of testing the Study's major hypotheses it is possible, on the basis of this experiment, to shelve the Rating I results in favor of the evidence from the more complete and psychiatrically preferred Rating II classification. With age, sex, and marital status data excluded from the above experiment, we cannot check the possibility that knowledge of these facts had a distorting effect on the psychiatrists' judgments of respondent mental health. However, we shall return to the problem in the appropriate data chapters ahead.

With Rating II serving as the definitive classification of mental health in the Home Survey sample, we should indicate finally that it belongs to the species of yardstick called *prevalence.* More specifically, for each respondent it essentially refers to his relative mental health status as judged operative during the period he was interviewed.

Further discussions of the rating process continue in the two chapters that follow.

SUMMARY

In planning the Study's technical design we confronted certain general problems. Among them was the degree of classificatory precision that realistically could be expected. Another was the nature of the analysis to be used in testing hypotheses. These were part of a larger series of dilemmas imposed by conflicting technical alternatives.

The Study's Treatment Census operation was assigned to determine the size and demographic composition of Midtown's psychiatric patients, both hospitalized and ambulatory. It was undertaken to illuminate the use of psychiatric services as a problem in institutional traffic and followed certain procedures developed in previous studies of patient populations.

The Study's central goals were entrusted to the Home Interview Survey. As its main features (1) a representative sample of 1,660 adults in the twenty to fifty-nine age range was objectively selected; (2) each sample individual was interrogated for two hours, on the average, by a professional person trained and experienced in the intimate interviewing role; (3) the interviewer was guided by a questionnaire that was about one year in preparation.

Planning this survey, the Midtown investigators sought throughout to anticipate potential error and bias in the resulting data and to control these at their several sources by appropriate measures in the procedural design. The three major potential sources were (1) a respondent sample unrepresentative of its population universe; (2) on the part of the respondents, an interview situation not conducive in a number of possible respects to information-giving at a level of motivation adequate to Study standards and purposes; (3) on the part of the survey psychiatrists in their role of evaluating respondent mental health, observations derived from clinical or other experiences that could systematically bias their classifications and distort the evidence necessary to test the Study's hypotheses.

Direct evidence was secured assuring that potentialities 1 and 3 were successfully kept in check. As to fruition of potentiality 2, direct information could not have been acquired except with massive diversions of the staff's energies and resources. However, indirect data on respondents' orientations to the interview situation point toward adequate, if hardly maximal, motivation for reliability in their self-reporting role.

In the light of all the indicated evidence, direct and indirect, the investigators can offer their considered opinion that the results of the survey's tests, to be reported in later chapters do not significantly misrepresent the facts about Midtown.

It has been a major purpose of the present technical chapter to share with the reader the extensive grounds for this opinion.

NOTES

[1] The reality of this possibility has been noted by Lemkau: "Epidemiological methods in psychiatry have already contributed much to our understanding. In all probability they will continue to receive the stinging criticism of psychiatrists and others who believe that to compare even two cases is to violate the concept of the complete individuality of man and who contend that the most, if not the only, important researches in this field are intensive studies of individuals or, at most, very small groups of individuals. We can agree with them to some extent; it appears to me to be true that most of the hypotheses to be tested by epidemiological methods originate in clinical studies. On the other hand, if we are to reach any justifiable generalizations in our field, we shall certainly be dependent upon some techniques for testing hypotheses against a larger population than a single case. To be sure in the process some truths about individuals will be lost, but by complementing individual studies, these population investigations will give us a better grasp of the factors in human living that can be changed for the betterment of the mental health of all men." In "The Epidemiological Study of Mental Illness and Mental Health," *American Journal of Psychiatry* 111 (May 1955): 801–809.

[2] Such complete specifications would require a volume in their own right. Some of these details are being reserved for parenthetic discussion in the appropriate data chapters. Certain other technical specifications appear in the Appendixes.

[3] In the broad view, measurement is of course one of several modes of scientific classification.

[4] Discussing one among many proffered definitions of mental health, Marie Jahoda comments: "From a purely logical point of view this definition leaves loopholes. . . . Yet for the practical purposes of the mental health professions, for scientific discussion, for research and even for therapy, this type of definition serves its purpose; notwithstanding its generally recognized inadequacy, it provides a starting point from which knowledge can be gathered that may lead to more accurate formulation." In "Environment and Mental Health," *International Social Science Journal* 11 (1959): 15–16.

[5] F. E. Moore, Jr., "Problems in the Selection of a Universe for the Study of Chronic Illness," *Milbank Memorial Fund Quarterly* 31 (July 1953): 28.

[6] This will be more fully elaborated in chapters 9 and 10.

[7] For a general elaboration of this view see H. C. Selvin, "A Critique of Tests of Significance in Survey Research," *American Sociological Review* 22 (October 1957): 519–527. With specific reference to statistical tests of significance, Jerome Frank has made the pertinent observation that "statistical measures of significance may be misleading in that a statistically significant finding need not be significant in the nontechnical sense of the term." J. D. Frank, "Problems of Controls in Psychotherapy as Exemplified by the Psychotherapy Research Project of the Phipps Clinic," in E. A. Rubinstein and M. B. Parloff, eds., *Research in Psychotherapy,* 1959, p. 23. On the other hand, Stouffer adds, "Even when no individual pair of percentages is significantly different [by statistical test], a pattern of such differences, most of them in the same direction, may be highly significant." S. Stouffer, *Communism, Conformity and Civil Liberties,* 1955, p. 273.

[8] David Gold, "Statistical Tests and Substantive Significance," *The American Sociologist* 4 (February 1969): 45, 46.

[9] These cover the entire psychiatric treatment "waterfront" (exclusive of special institutions for the mentally retarded), but they represent a compromise with Rennie's original hope to also include troubled people in nonpsychiatric but "corrective" organizations and institutions, for example, certain civil and criminal courts. As is true of other relevant institutions of this type, the enormous administrative complexity of the New York City courts made systematic screening of their records for Midtown residents a burden impossible to assume along with coverage of the complex system of psychiatric facilities.

[10] These included the function of soliciting the cooperation of all of the above treatment

units. For extending such help, acknowledgements are here gratefully accorded to Dr. Henry Brill and his staff in the research section of the New York State Department of Mental Hygiene, as also to the private therapists and clinic and hospital administrators in numbers far too large to identify individually here.

It should be noted parenthetically that the cooperation solicited carried assurance from the Study director and the Cornell Medical College department of psychiatry, guaranteeing the complete professional confidentiality of the patient data made available for the scientific purposes of the Midtown Study.

Also assigned to the team social workers were the tasks of transferring data on hospital patients directly from official files and processing patient reports prepared and submitted by the other kinds of treatment services.

[11]The phrase "bona fide" was defined to exclude people listed as last domiciled at a Midtown address but hospitalized continuously for five or more years.

[12]Since the controversy is a recurrent one and is revived with each new Study monograph, it is important that our minority position on the issue be clarified. This technical discussion appears in Appendix C.

[13]Although lacking documentary proof, we believe that Midtown's *incidence* patients reported quarterly by clinics and office therapists were less complete than the patients they reported for our one-day *prevalence* count.

[14]For the benefit of the student, this can be properly identified as the "waste motion" phenomenon that undoubtedly comes to roost in many investigations, but is publicly acknowledged by few.

As to the principle involved in such acknowledgments it has been observed: "It is truly unfortunate that . . . there is not more opportunity for the thoughtful and honest airing of the dilemmas, compromises and problems of carrying out research. . . . Most research is described as if it went off perfectly according to plan. There is little chance to learn from the mistakes of others. . . ." Joan K. Jackson, in a book review, *Journal of Health and Human Behavior* 2 (Summer 1961): 161.

[15]The statistical analysis was carried out by Thomas S. Langner and his staff under the direction of the author of this chapter.

[16]These particular age cutoff points were selected for the Home Interview Survey to conform with the age classifications of the U.S. Census Bureau. Thereby, it would be possible to check the sample in terms of age composition and related criteria against its population universe as determined by the Census Bureau.

It should be noted, on the other hand, that the Treatment Census operation set no limits on its age coverage.

[17]One consequence of this type of sampling has been noted in the literature on cardiovascular disorders. "Numerous hypotheses have been proposed relating many factors, both host and environmental, to the development of coronary heart disease or hypertension. Controversy exists regarding practically all such hypotheses. A great deal of controversy has been due to the difficulty of obtaining a population free of bias in which to test the hypothesis." T. R. Dawber and W. B. Kannell, "An Epidemiological Study of Heart Disease: The Framingham Study," *Nutrition Review* 16 (January 1958): 1–4. See also Cochran et al., *Statistical Problems of the Kinsey Report on Sexual Behavior,* 1954, pp. 55, 262, and 265.

[18]The larger the sample in absolute members, the smaller is the margin of such "random error" deviation or "sampling variance."

[19]M. H. Hansen and P. M. Hauser, "Area Sampling—Some Principles of Sample Design," *Public Opinion Quarterly* 9 (Summer 1945): 183–193.

[20]Stouffer, *Communism, Conformity and Civil Liberties,* pp. 242 and 244.

[21]A. Kornhauser, *Detroit As The People See It,* 1952, p. 194.

[22]*Health and Medical Care in New York City,* Committee for the Special Research Project in the Health Insurance Plan of Greater New York, 1957, p. 211.

[23]Of the 1,911 selected individuals, only 2.3 percent were in the "never contacted" category of nonparticipation, reflecting the survey policy of no specific upper limit to the number of possible return calls to sample dwellings. Another 7.2 percent were "contacted refusals," many revisited after the initial refusal. The final 3.5 percent consisted of "contacted miscellany," none refusing to be interviewed, but all being unable (or unwilling) to

arrange the necessary appointment during the period of the interviewing program. Cf. H. Sharp and A. Feldt, "Some Factors in a Probability Sample Survey of a Metropolitan Community," *American Sociological Review* 24 (October 1959): 650–661.

[24]With 1,660 individuals the range of sampling variance can be suggested through this example: If 25 percent of these individuals were found to have blue eyes, then the probabilities would be very high (95 in 100) that the proportion of blue-eyed people in the population universe stands somewhere between 23 and 27 percent.

[25]This was made possible by securing pertinent demographic and other information, through direct or indirect means, on all the sample nonparticipants.

[26]For purpose of convenience, this will hereafter be referred to as *the sample.*

[27]It remains theoretically possible, of course, that sample nonparticipants and interviewed respondents are essentially alike in demographic composition but different in mental health composition. If so, the latter would be a biased sample in this specific respect. To test this possibility, at least partially, we can compare the two groups on frequency of psychiatric histories as independently uncovered by our Treatment Census operation. The latter found that among the interviewed respondents 3.4 percent appeared on its records as having been a patient of a mental hospital, clinic, or office therapist within certain specific time periods. The corresponding figure for the nonparticipants was 3.2 percent. Thus, the two groups do not appear to differ with specific respect to institutionally known and reported mental pathology.

[28]Epidemiological studies of community samples that involved free medical examinations in the clinic have actually encountered this problem on a large scale. See T. R. Dawber, F. R. Moore, Jr., and G. V. Mann, "Coronary Heart Disease in the Framingham Study," *American Journal of Public Health* 47 (April, 1957): 4; and *Chronic Illness in a Large City,* Commission on Chronic Illness, 1957, pp. 208–216.

[29]To judge from interviewers' regular reports on this point in the protocol, close to half of the sessions were held under "ideal" conditions of privacy, another 40 percent with some brief interruptions—including telephone calls, ringing doorbells, or children demanding attention. The remainder involved small children or a radio operating somewhere in the house as a prolonged distraction. With few exceptions the interviews appear to have been conducted beyond the hearing of another adult.

[30]J. Clausen, *Sociology and the Field of Mental Health,* Russell Sage Foundation, 1956, p. 49.

[31]"It is clear that interviewer effect is a fundamental problem faced by all the social sciences which make use of the interview method in the collection of data. . . . Interviewer effects in all these fields have their parallel in the errors of observation and measurement or interpretation found in other sciences. When we note that there are observer differences in reading chest X-ray films or in interpreting the results of laboratory tests of syphilis or in appraising the malnutrition of children from medical examinations . . . or in noting the transit of stars in a telescope, we must acknowledge the fact that interviewing is not uniquely vulnerable." H. Hyman, *Interviewing in Social Research,* 1954, pp. 13 and 14. (See also Hyman's discussions of research on psychiatric interviewing, pp. 9, 94, 121, and 383–384.)

[32]H. Hyman, "Interviewing as a Scientific Procedure," in D. Lerner and H. D. Laswell, eds., *The Policy Sciences,* 1951, pp. 203–218; and R. L. Kahn and C. F. Cannell, *The Dynamics of Interviewing,* 1957, pp. 131–165; and L. J. Bauman et al, "Respondent-Interviewer Interaction in the Research Interview," Columbia Bureau of Applied Social Research, 1971 (mimeographed).

[33]These were Arthur Weider, clinical psychologist, and the present writer, with wartime service as military psychologist in AAF rehabilitation hospitals.

[34]Approximately a year of work intervened between formation of the committee and completion of the final instrument.

[35]It has often been observed that uniform wording of a question may have different meanings for different respondents. Of course, this is less likely to happen if the established rules of questionnaire construction are respected. Above all, the procedure of the field pretesting of a questionnaire has as one of its main purposes the detection and correction of unanticipated difficulties among respondents in understanding or interpreting questions.

[36]Experience indicated that such a history would be found in the upper-income groups

in too few instances to warrant the high cost required to check the entire sample. Accordingly, only respondents in the lower 60 percent of the sample's socioeconomic range, approximately, were so checked.

³⁷Kubie has defined a similar sampling process in clinical practice: "Good history taking is extremely difficult. . . . You can't take it all. You have to sample, selectively rather than randomly." In a lecture to Payne Whitney Clinic staff, February 14, 1957.

³⁸See R. C. Cowden and J. E. Brown, "The Use of a Physical Symptom as a Defense against Psychosis," *Journal of Abnormal and Social Psychology* 53 (July 1956): 133–135.

³⁹It should be noted that the area of interpersonal and role functioning originally had a somewhat secondary place in the framework of signs and symptoms covered. However, when the team psychiatrists began their trial assessment of the sample interview protocols, this area, although less thoroughly explored than would have been possible, assumed a more central position.

⁴⁰For questionnaires designed by psychiatrists to tap the anxiety area, see G. Saslow, R. Counts, and P. DuBois, "Evaluation of a New Psychiatric Screening Test," *Psychosomatic Medicine* 13 (July 1951): 242–253; and H. Basowitz, H. Persky, S. Korchin, and R. Grinker, *Anxiety and Stress,* 1954, p. 31.

⁴¹See Shirley Star's account in S. A. Stouffer et al., *The American Soldier,* 1949, vol. 2, pp. 411–455; vol. 4, pp. 486–567.

⁴²In the interview summary form presented in Appendix D, these core symptom items can be identified by their code number as follows: R5-1, R6-1, R6-6, R7-1, R7-6, R8-1, R8-6, R9-1, R9-7,8, R10-6, R17-6, R18-1, R18-5, R19-1, R19-5, R20-5, R45-2, and G9-3, 4. Among those items which did *not* discriminate Weider's particular criterion group (of patients), some were included in the Midtown questionnaire on the strength of the psychiatrists' knowledgeable judgment that they *were* clinically significant nonetheless.

⁴³For the closely related field of mental retardation, it has been observed: "Research cannot wait upon the development of diagnostic tools of 100 percent accuracy in the detection of pathology, particularly of the central nervous system." S. B. Sarason and T. Gladwin, *Psychological and Cultural Problems in Mental Subnormality: A Review of Research,* 1957, p. 9.

⁴⁴T. Caplow, "The Dynamics of Information Interviewing," *American Journal of Sociology* 62 (September 1956): 169.

⁴⁵These three characteristics, among others, were approximately known to us through contact with the household prior to the interview.

⁴⁶"The 'depth' of any item of information depends upon its meaning for the respondent, which, in turn, depends upon how he perceives the relationship between the information and the total social context in which it is given. What is in one social situation a mere 'objective fact' . . . may be a devastating threat in another. . . . Deep information is presumed to be accessible to the interviewer under certain conditions, and his hope for success depends upon his manipulating the respondent's definition of the situation in such a way as to make what would ordinarily be deep information come to the surface. The word 'ordinarily' is important as recognizing the norms regarding what should be communicated to whom under what conditions, as well as how the communication is to be carried out." Raymond L. Gorden, "Dimensions of the Depth Interview," *American Journal of Sociology* 62 (September 1956): 158–159.

⁴⁷Or, as being conducted by a psychiatrist.

⁴⁸This would likely happen more often among the mentally disturbed than among the well, in that event seriously biasing the sample of participants.

⁴⁹This also served the important function of keeping the interview situation free of any implication that professional treatment, consultation, or advice would conclude the process. However, if such help was requested by a respondent, the interviewer had instructions to arrange a no-charge consultation session with a Study psychiatrist.

⁵⁰We would note a relevant publication in the series reporting methods and results of the nationwide study of chronic somatic illness and disability being conducted by the National Health Survey as a continuing program of the U.S. Public Health Service. This publication presents findings from a special investigation to evaluate "the effectiveness and reliability in a [sample] survey of the medical-history-taking procedure." Reported as a central finding was this: "It seemed clear that it would be possible to develop a standardized

series of special purpose medical-history-taking questions, and that survey respondents do not hesitate to answer such questions. In fact, people seemed delighted to have the opportunity to talk about their symptoms and illnesses. The answer to the first question under study—namely, would people freely discuss their medical history in a situation in which they had not taken the initiative in seeking medical care—seemed obvious. There were no apparent major barriers to obtaining medical-history data for research purposes. Subsequent interviews sustained this general conclusion." "A Study of Special Purpose Medical History Techniques," *Health Statistics from the U.S. National Health Survey*, ser. D, no. 1, 1960, pp. ii and 4.

[51] S. E. Dean, "Treatment of the Reluctant Client," *American Psychologist* 13 (November 1958): 627–630.

[52] Cf. Stouffer, *Communism, Conformity and Civil Liberties*, p. 241.

[53] This refusal rate reached 33 percent in a 1968 sample survey of 36,000 families conducted by the Census Bureau. Reported in *New York Times*, February 23, 1969.

[54] R. Taft, "Multiple Methods of Personality Assessment," *Psychological Bulletin* 56 (September 1959): 349.

[55] For a study tending to confirm this possibility see W. Haase, "Rorschach Diagnosis, Socio-economic Class and Examiner Bias" (Ph.D. dissertation, New York University, 1956).

[56] The psychiatrist next applied two other kinds of classificatory schemes to the respondent's full record. But since these are only put to the most peripheral use in this monograph they need not detain us here.

[57] It is beyond our purview to speculate about the explanations for this result, except to note three obvious possibilities: (1) The two psychiatrists had no preconceptions about the mental health of Midtown's sociocultural groups; (2) they had such preconceptions, but these differed and in effect balanced each other out; (3) they had like preconceptions, but the procedure of citing the evidence justifying their changes in Rating II may have made them aware of such prejudgments in a form leading to restraint in their expression.

CHAPTER 9

THE MENTAL HEALTH RATINGS

STANLEY T. MICHAEL AND PRICE KIRKPATRICK

The authors of this chapter are two of the three psychiatrists concerned in the mental health ratings. The third was Thomas Rennie, whose death prevented his participation. Our aim is to give, in synoptic fashion, our viewpoint as we approached the interview instrument, helped in its design, and applied the mental health ratings. We will describe the judging process, and the complexities and perplexities with which we wrestled as we converted our raw interview information to overall impressions and formulations of the mental health ratings.[1]

As indicated in chapter 7, the Midtown Study had from its inception the problem of communication among the several disciplines involved. Beyond communication, however, there has also been the problem of orientation; by this we mean that different disciplines tend to view the phenomena of nature differently. Thus, the psychiatrist, as he learns about social theory and the methods of sociology, may still not come to see human behavior altogether in the same terms and with the same flavor and frame of reference as the sociologist. Similarly, the sociologist, even though he may become well versed in psychiatric concepts and able to employ its technical language, may still not see people and the way they behave in quite the same light as does the clinician. Although there is sympathetic recognition by each of the other's ideas, there remains a difference in training, experience, orientation, and attitudes toward the nature of the scientific method itself.

Up to a point, it is possible to achieve reconciliation of these divergences. On the other hand, there is something to be said for letting some contrasts in orientation stand as they are. Most of those which we have experienced are certainly not peculiar to the Midtown investigation but are to be found in many other places where research in social psychiatry is attempted. Setting down our clinical views separately from those of the social scientists allows the reader to evaluate the areas of congruence and divergence in orientation. The presentation of even such limited diversity may enrich the opportunity for advancement of knowledge as well as to make this study more meaningful. Certainly, in our working together, the clarification and recognition of some of the interdisciplinary issues have been beneficial to us.

In the beginning Rennie gave careful thought to the question whether the Midtown sample should be examined directly by psychiatrists, and diagnosis made on each individual, or whether the psychiatric assessment should be made indirectly through the medium of a structured interview conducted by professionals in related fields. Although there are certain advantages in having the psychiatrist talk directly with and observe his subject, the decision was made in favor of the structured interview. A principal and well-grounded consideration for this decision was the methodological requirement of ensuring reasonable uniformity of inquiry and of classificatory criteria.

Of the two authors of the present chapter, Kirkpatrick joined the Midtown Study at the time candidate mental health items were being gathered for the interview instrument. He and Rennie reviewed all the symptom questions proposed by other members of the team, in terms of their appropriateness to the interview as a whole and their usefulness for our clinical judgment. They proposed a series of additional questions, bearing particularly on psychosomatic symptoms, phobic reactions, and mood.

After three field tests of the instrument in trial drafts, the final decision on each proposed symptom question was made by Rennie. We do not feel it would be proper to attempt to speak for him on the rationale behind all his decisions. Time has passed since that stage, but certain general points can be made with the conviction that these do represent lines of thought in which the clinicians shared.

First it should be noted that the primary basis for the psychiatrists' choice and decision regarding the items was clinical experience. By this is meant each rater's years of work in internal medicine, his training in psychiatry, and his years of work in the diagnosis and treatment of psychiatric patients. Knowledge acquired by reading and discussion with colleagues had, of course, a place in this, but it was fused into the general experience; much in the foreground was the learning derived from interaction with patients.

We hoped to include symptom questions in sufficient quantity and range to allow assessment of the presence or absence of malfunctions that might be of clinical importance. Such symptoms were not viewed as if each were a discrete, unrelated behavioral item, but as *reticulated, patterned complexes in which each symptom has meaning only in relation to the other symptoms present,* and *in which the meaning of the whole depends on the interrelationship of the symptoms with each other.*[1]

The individual human being was regarded as a functional unit, with adaptation to life's circumstances as an important theme in his existence. In psychiatry *function* has a rather specific meaning. This can be seen in the distinction commonly made between functional and organic mental disorders. Modern chemistry and biophysics suggest that even though functional disorders do not involve obvious structural damage to the brain, or gross toxicity such as can be observed in organic disorders, in one way or another there is an accompanying physiologic disturbance, even if it is only at the molecular level. For pragmatic and descriptive purposes, however, the functional-organic distinction continues to be useful. *Organic* disorder is used here in its traditional sense as descriptive of gross structural change. *Functional* disorder, by contrast, characterizes impairment of activity quite out of proportion to any evident structural pathology. Such impairment may affect not only observable physical activity but also feeling states and thought processes.

A comparison can be made between psychological and physical functioning. Both in physical and in mental health, there is an extended gradation from sound health to severe morbidity. But whereas physical illness may be precisely defined by observable impairments in bodily structure and function, mental illness involves behaviors that are dysfunctional both for the individual and for others. Good mental health might accordingly be defined as the freedom from psychiatric symptomatology and the optimal functioning of the individual in his social setting.

In evaluating respondent mental health, we were obviously dealing not with clinical cases but with a population of community residents, predominantly nonpatients. Rennie was of course aware that the preoccupation of the physician is primarily with pathology and secondarily with sound health, and that the pathologic, whether physical or mental, has a way of making itself much more obvious than the more "pedestrian" normal. Manifesting his own orientation to both the assets and liabilities of the individual, Rennie outlined for his colleagues the following criteria of positive mental health.

Independence of action, thought, and standards . . . freedom from undue anxiety, freedom from crippling inferiority and guilt feelings, from excessive egotism, and from competitiveness and unbridled hostility . . . concern for others, a respect for differing religions and ethics, an appreciation of one's own liabilities and assets . . . the assumption of adult responsibilities [including] the obligation to find and sustain a satisfying job, to recognize the need for play and rest, and to find satisfaction in one's role as an individual in relation to family, social, and civic life . . . the establishment and maintenance of a home . . . loving and giving to mate and children . . . a capacity to accept illness, disappointments, bereavements, even death and all that which is largely beyond our own control [as well as] our own make-up and individuality, the perfection and imperfections of self and others, success and failure, sportsmanship, and the social comparisons which we call advice, criticism, and authority . . . a philosophy of objectivity about the past and a vision of creative opportunity for the present and the future . . . the capacity to create and participate in a consensus based on understanding others and on making one's self understood.[2]

The final interview form necessarily focused on the presence or absence of a sample of 120 narrowly specific symptoms from a much larger universe of overt symptoms underlying psychological distress and dysfunction. The above "capacities" outlined by Rennie represent large areas of the total personality that could not possibly be covered systematically, within the limits of a single prestructured interview session.

On the other hand, two sets of clues from these areas were available, the first from the respondent's behaviors during the session as observed and systematically reported by the interviewer. The second set of clues often emerged in the respondent's spontaneous comments, elaborations, and asides. The interviewers were alert to the importance of such spontaneous information, and we as psychiatrists were of course sensitive to their significance in arriving at each mental health rating.

To all the interview evidence, needless to say, we applied our separate clinical judgments to the best of our individual abilities. It would be a mistake, however, to overlook the fact that there remain some aspects of the process which are not altogether in our awareness. In this our activity shares with many other kinds of human judgment; otherwise court procedures and art criticism, as well as medical diagnosis, could be performed by machines.

A major problem confronting the study psychiatrists hinged on classifying the heterogeneous data secured on each individual respondent. We were aware that we could not make a diagnosis, in the usual clinical sense of the word, on the basis of this material. Complexes of symptoms could be appraised as possible diagnostic categories, but the nature of the data led us more in the direction of some kind of overall evaluation of mental health functioning. This could be done quite independently of the various psychiatric categories of symptom patterns and their implied etiologies. It was as if one were going to rate a population with many different kinds of ill-defined physical disorders: in such a situation he could place each individual somewhere on a linear scale of functional impairment.[3]

As reported in chapter 8, a two-part Summary of each respondent interview was prepared. Part A of the Summary included such data as the respondent's age, sex, marital status, health history, subjective psychological symptoms, psychosomatic complaints, self-evaluation of health in recent months and also five years earlier, interpersonal orientations, and the interviewer's systematic observations about the respondent's behaviors during the interview.

On the basis of this material each psychiatrist separately assigned the respondent to one of seven graded categories of symptom formation. This was called Mental Health Rating I, and was based essentially on symptomatological evidence. The aim was to provide one rating of mental health for each respondent that would reduce as far as possible any bias that might enter through knowledge of socioeconomic level or other independent sociocultural variables.

Part B of the Summary contained information bearing on the respondent's life functioning and sociocultural environment. Rating II, also divided into seven levels, was formulated after review and study of Part B of the respondent's Summary form pertaining to social functioning.[4] A record of hospitalization, social service assistance, or application ot other welfare agencies added to the available information.

TABLE 9–1. KEY TO MENTAL HEALTH (SYMPTOM FORMATION) CATEGORIES

Independent ordinal ratings	Definitions	Combined* ordinal rating score	Final category of symptom formation
0	No significant symptom formation (symptom free)	0 1	Well
1	Mild symptom formation, *but* functioning adequately	2 3	Mild
2	Moderate symptom formation with *no* apparent interference in life adjustment	4 5	Moderate
3	Moderate symptom formation with *some* interference in life adjustment	6 7	Marked
4	Serious symptom formation, and functioning with *some* difficulty	8 9	Severe
5	Serious symptom formation, and functioning with *great* difficulty	10 11	Incapacitated (partial or total)
6	Seriously incapacitated, unable to function	12	

The "Marked", "Severe", and "Incapacitated (partial or total)" categories are bracketed together as **Impaired**.

*Since the two raters independently assigned ordinal ratings from 0 to 6 to each respondent, the two independent ratings for each respondent were numerically joined to form combined ordinal scores in a 0 to 12 range. One-step differences between the raters account for the odd numbered scores in the combined ratings column. For example, if one judge rated a person 1 (Mild) and the other rated him 2 (Moderate), he received a combined rating score of 3, placing him in the final category of Mild.

The *final* Mental Health Scale assigned to a respondent, representing the combined and adjudicated judgments of the two rating psychiatrists, is presented in the table above. New designations for the final categories have been created to replace the more cumbersome original definitions and also to arrange a serial gradation of severity of symptom formation by the use of one-word labels more easily referred to in the text.

Respondents with a combined ordinal rating score of 12 were so few in number that they were merged with those in the 10–11 score range, together forming the Incapacitated (partial or total) category, and reducing the total number of Final categories to six. The bottom three of these in the table 9–1 entailed interference in life adjustment and impairment in social functioning. Consequently, when they are considered together they carry the collective rubric of "Impaired."

While it might seem that the Summary protocol could fail to communicate the features of the respondent as a human being, the corpus of data secured was of course specifically designed to facilitate the evaluation of the respondent's mental health status. The interview instrument was the product of months spent by social scientists and psychiatrists in selecting symptom items that had survived the screening of validation studies. Many of these items had the discriminatory power of high correlations with treated psychopathologic conditions. Thus, when a Summary protocol, complete with answers of the respondent, was presented to the psychiatrist, a substantial part of the rating was already embodied in the structure of the document, and the latter's task was to further coordinate, synthesize, and evaluate the constellation of symptoms elicited by it.

We recognized that in individual cases we were probably missing and perhaps misinterpreting some evidence bearing on both mental disturbance and mental wellness. On the other hand, when in their separate deliberations one of the psychiatrists thought respondent Z was a "fence case" (that is, seemed to fall roughly on the border between two adjoining categories), the psychiatrist regularly gave Z the benefit of the doubt by according him the *less severe* of the ratings.

This was the tendency for each psychiatrist in arriving at his independent rating for each respondent. Moreover, if it emerged that the psychiatrists' separate ratings for respondent Y had fallen one step apart in the classification scheme, then the difference was systematically adjudicated by finally assigning Y to the *less severe* of the two independent ratings.

By these conservative procedures, clearly the final ratings for respondents like Y and Z leaned in the direction of understating, rather than overstating, the degree of disturbance present. Where the psychiatrists' ratings for a respondent were in accord, as most were, there can be some confidence in the consistency and reliability of the allocated rating.

When the data on social functioning (in Part B of the Summary form) led a psychiatrist to change the Mental Health II Rating (that is, from Rating I), he indicated the considerations influencing the change on the rating sheet. When the Series II ratings of the two psychiatrists were one level apart, the respondent was given the *healthier* rating. When the psychiatrists' separate Series II ratings for a respondent were two levels apart (for example, Mild and Marked), the category intermediate (that is, Moderate) was assigned to him. In the few cases where the separate ratings were three levels apart, it was assumed that unusual problems of interpretation or comprehension of the record were involved, and adjudication was reached in a conference review of the respondent's record with Rennie.

To be sure, we each subjectively graded symptom constellations with greatest confidence at the two extremes of the rating scale; there the evidence appeared overwhelming and not open to reasonable doubt. We were reasonably certain if the respondent gave little or no evidence of symptoms, in which case an "asymptomatic" mental health rating was inescapable. At the other extreme of the scale, definite, disabling psychotic symptoms and behavior, apparent in answers to the interview questions, in spontaneous comments of the respondent himself, or in the observations of the interviewer, provided evidence suggesting severe disturbance and functional incapacitation. But the grades of mental health in between these extremes offered few firm boundary landmarks and left considerable latitude to the judgment of the psychiatrist and to his estimate of the severity of symptom formation. At the "fence" points of the rating scheme, symptom clusters of "borderline" nature had to be weighed with utmost care; and the personal judgment of the rater was frequently strained to arrive at a single concise rating from quantitatively imprecise symptoms.

In essence, the final mental health distribution reported is based on a statistical summation of the 1660 independent judgments of each of the two rating psychiatrists. These were judgments applied to a corpus of symptom information secured in the privacy of a home interview that uncovered a wide range of expressions of psychopathology.

For purposes of reliability checks Rennie himself reviewed and rated the interview protocols of some 320 respondents. (These, however, did not enter into their final ratings.) Concordances and discordances were discussed and judgmental criteria clarified with the co-authors of this chapter. As this clarification sequence of processes continued, all three of us grew in our conviction that what we were doing had meaning. However, we also came to feel strongly that this meaning was a subtle and complex matter, and that interpretation based on statistical treatment of the ratings needed to be made with great care. Throughout chapters 10–18 of this two-book monograph, the dependent variable is a rating of mental health based on the two psychiatrists' independent perceptions and judgments, operating on the information obtained in a prestructured interview with the respondent.

Thus, the psychiatrists writing this chapter agree with our sociological collaborators that the associations between the mental health ratings and the various tested sociocultural factors do not yet offer unequivocal proof —rare in all areas of psychiatric research—about the etiology of mental disorder. What these relationships do offer, however, are bases for some exceedingly suggestive interpretations, for defining new research questions to be attacked in a more refined and specific manner, and finally, for offering a number of promising propositions and hypotheses.

NOTES

[1]The editors have here merged chapter 4 and parts of Appendix F from the original edition.

[2]T. A. C. Rennie, "Motivation in Health Education," in I. Galdston, ed., *Psychological Dynamics of Health Education*, 1951, pp. 26–42.

[3]This does not imply that the standard nosological types of mental disorder can be accorded a fixed position on a scale. The raters did not intend that a scale be drawn with graded points such as psychotic, psychopathic, neurotic, compulsive, psychosomatic, and mildly depressed. On the contrary, some patients with a depression or an obsessive-conpulsive reaction could be more functionally impaired than many ambulatory schizophrenics.

[4]For a full listing of information presented to the raters, see Appendix D.

Part IV

Mental Health Composition
And Psychiatric Care
In The Community
And Its Biosocial Groups

CHAPTER 10

MIDTOWN AND SEVERAL OTHER POPULATIONS

LEO SROLE

On the broad canvas of the sociological profile chapters we sketched Midtown as a local habitat, as a population, and as a community. In the long national perspective, it appeared neither typical of the American scene nor unique to it. Instead, Midtown was seen to be representative in most demographic respects of the inclusive (non-Puerto Rican) white population of Manhattan during the mid-fifties and apparently of populations in similar high-density, core residential sections found in other major American metropolitan centers. Beyond these special characteristics, it can also be surmised that our study area and the people who settle it express certain basic tendencies in American life, carried, however, to an extreme point of development. To adapt an aphorism from another context, Midtown in this respect may be like the rest of America—only in a decisively more concentrated form.

Against this descriptive backdrop, our primary purpose in this chapter is to draw upon Study findings that reveal something about mental health and psychiatric care behind the façade of Midtown as a social entity, and second, so far as possible to compare these revelations with results yielded by studies of other American populations.

TREATMENT CENSUS FINDINGS

On the principle that the known is a convenient point of departure in the search for an unknown, we might start with Midtown's residents who were known to psychotherapists (that is, psychiatrists or clinical psychologists) as "patients." It was one task of our Treatment Census operation to enumerate all bona fide Midtowners *of all ages* who on our census day, May 1, 1953, were on the "active" rosters of the following inpatient facilities available to the Manhattan population:[1]

Eight state mental hospitals
Two Veterans Administration psychiatric hospitals
Two Veterans Administration general hospitals with psychiatric divisions
One municipal psychiatric hospital (short-term care only)
Seven voluntary (nonprofit) general hospitals with psychiatric divisions in Manhattan
Twenty-three licensed, private (proprietary) psychiatric hospitals and sanitoriums in New York State
Eleven private (proprietary) psychiatric hospitals in adjoining states

In table 10–1, the 864 inpatients distributed among the several types of hospitals are expressed in one-day prevalence rates per 100,000 of Midtown's total resident population. In brief, for every 1,000 people having a Midtown residence as their home base, five, according to our criterion, were confined in psychiatric hospitals.

TABLE 10–1.   TREATMENT CENSUS (AGE INCLUSIVE) PREVALENCE RATES
OF MIDTOWN INPATIENTS* (PER 100,000 POPULATION)
BY TYPE OF HOSPITAL

Publicly supported hospitals:		
State	435	
Municipal	12	
Federal (VA)	9	
Total public hospitals		456
Privately supported hospitals.	46	
Total all hospitals		502

*Hospitalized less than five continuous years. Includes undischarged patients in family or convalescent care.

By separate inspection of the Treatment Census patients in private hospitals, we find that 20 percent had been hospitalized between twelve and sixty months, whereas the corresponding figure for the Midtown patients in public hospitals was 64 percent. Calculated differently, the former had been in the institution for ten months on the average, and the latter about two years.[2]

If length of hospitalization in these two patient groups is strikingly different, in another respect the groups are identical: about one-third of both were readmissions, that is, hospitalized at least for the second time.[3] It would appear, therefore, that if private hospitals more quickly return their patients home, their results in preventing relapse and rehospitalization are not perceptibly better.

Because no previous prevalence study of inpatients has employed our limiting criterion (that is, under five years of hospitalization), it is not possible here to place the above data in the comparative perspective of other hospital populations.

However, no such limitation was indicated for or applied to Midtowners in ambulant treatment (on our census day) while continuing to live at home, including 290 reported on the rosters of some fifty psychiatric clinics.[4]

Solicited through personal letters from Rennie were the patient reports of 798 psychiatrists and 316 clinical psychologists known to have private offices in Manhattan.[5] About 10 percent of these therapists explicitly refused their cooperation or did not reply to the several Rennie letters. The cooperating therapists, on the other hand, reported 959 Midtown residents as patients on May 1, 1953.[6] The error of understatement due to the noncooperating therapists could be objectively estimated and corrected accordingly.[7] With this correction introduced, table 10–2 below presents the clinic and office patient prevalence rates per 100,000 Midtown population, together with comparable rates calculated from percentaged data reported by the New Haven study.[8]

Let us focus first on the Midtown side of the picture. Combining hospital and ambulant patients, we arrive at a total reported patient rate,[9] on our census day, of 1,290 per 100,000 of the entire Midtown population. Since the average Midtown residential block housed about 1,000 people, this combined rate can be stated in a more concrete form: In each Midtown block on any given day there were an average of thirteen individuals reported in the care of a psychiatric service, with eight of the

TABLE 10–2. TREATMENT CENSUS (AGE INCLUSIVE) PREVALENCE RATES
OF MIDTOWN OUT PATIENTS* (PER 100,000 POPULATION)
BY TYPE OF SERVICE WITH COMPARABLE NEW HAVEN "PSYCHIATRIC CENSUS RATES"

	Midtown (May 1, 1953)	New Haven (Dec. 1, 1950)
Clinic.	168*	67‡
Office.	620†	157‡
Total.	788	224

*Estimated by Midtown Study social workers to be about 95% complete.
†Corrected by estimation for noncooperating therapists but not for underreporting by cooperating therapists.
‡Estimated by New Haven investigators to be about 98% complete.

thirteen known to be in an outpatient facility and five in a hospital.

Nothing was known directly concerning the nature of the treatment received by these outpatients. However, indirect suggestive evidence has been reported by a nationwide study of 380 psychiatric clinics and their patients. About these clinics we are told that "of each ten patients terminated during the year [ending June 30, 1955], three received diagnosis and treatment, four received diagnosis only," the remainder apparently getting even briefer types of service. Only 20 percent of all terminated patients had been seen in ten or more clinic sessions.[10] Whether these findings also apply in exact detail to Midtown clinic patients is uncertain. But even had *all* of these listed patients begun actual treatment, the benefits resulting may be suggested by a study made several years earlier, involving 288 patients of New York City clinics.[11] In summary statement, "only about one-fourth of the patients *accepted for treatment* [author's italics] were rated as having received significant help."

Together with evidence that four in five of all New York state hospital patients (in 1955) were receiving custodial care only (see note 2), these indications from the psychiatric clinics warn against any generalizations about the therapeutic significance of patient status in a psychiatric facility.

Table 10–2 also includes the outpatient rates we have computed from the parallel prevalence study earlier conducted in New Haven, Connecticut. Comparison of the two sets of rates in the table immediately evokes this question: How are we to account for the intercommunity differences there revealed?

Before addressing ourselves to this question, we might briefly consider the diagnostic range among the ambulant patients. Previous hospital investigations in many instances viewed inpatient rates as reflecting the frequency of psychotic conditions in the general population, with the outpatient rates inferred as representing the frequency of less disabling, nonpsychotic disorders. Analysis of the diagnostic composition of the reported New Haven and Midtown outpatients reveals that the proportion of psychotics in each[12] stood at 24 and 15 percent, respectively.[13] Focusing on specific psychotic conditions among all reported Midtown patients, we learn that in ambulant care were 40 percent of the manic-depressive cases, 36 percent of the nonparanoid schizophrenics, 25 percent of the nonsenile chronic organic conditions, 14 percent of the paranoid schizophrenics, and 22 percent of all other psychotics exclusive of the seniles.

In both communities, it is clear, substantial fractions of the diagnosed psychotic group were ambulant patients. Accommodations for psychotics in local outpatient facilities have undoubtedly diverted not a few of them from their respective state hospital systems—both known to be overcrowded at the time by margins of about 25 to 30 percent beyond their certified bed capacities. In this light, inpatients certainly do not qualify as a reliable index of the frequency of "treated" psychosis in an urban population. Actually, it is highly probable that intercommunity differences of inpatient rates partially reflect variations in bed capacities and admission policies[14] in the mental hospital systems serving different states and communities, as well as differential availability of alternative services.

If we now focus only on the reported nonpsychotic conditions (principally neuroses and personality disorders) in the care of outpatient facilities, we find a prevalence rate per 100,000 population of 616 in Midtown and 164 in New Haven,[15] a difference of about 3.7:1. Is it possible to assume that this disparity reflected a like difference between the two populations in the *overall* frequency of the nonpsychotic disorders? Were these conditions really three to four times more prevalent in Midtown than in New Haven? Before this possibility can be seriously entertained, other alternatives should certainly be considered. One plausible alternative open to testing is that the observed difference is related to variations in the treatment capacities of the psychiatric outpatient facilities accessible to each population.

Taking into account only the *number* of locally based outpatient clinics, we find that per 100,000 population Manhattan at the time of our Treatment Census had 2.2 times as many clinics as did New Haven when it was being studied. Hardly by coincidence Midtown's clinic patient rate stands to New Haven's in a ratio of 2.5:1 (table 10–2). Next, marshaling psychiatrists and clinical psychologists[16] locally in office practice (full-time or part) during the two investigations, we calculate their number per 100,000 population as fifty-seven in Manhattan and thirteen in New Haven, a difference in the magnitude of 4.4:1.[17] Again by no coincidence, the office patient rates of Midtown and New Haven stand to each other as 4.0:1. It is accordingly difficult to reject the simple inference that clinic and office patient rates are to a considerable degree determined by size of treatment capacities supplied by local outpatient services.

A two-part principle of supply and demand can here be stated to fit the situation just observed. First, the *supply* of treatment services made available in a community is undoubtedly influenced in the long run by the pressures of local need and *demand* for such services. However, at any given time if such supply in two communities is at different removes *below* current demand, then their respective outpatient rates will inevitably reflect their differences in supply level, rather than in demand level as influenced by the mounting local backlog of untreated pathology.

Under the leavening influence, direct and indirect, of Yale University and its medical school, New Haven stands well above the national average and above sister cities of its state in supply of psychiatric outpatient services relative to population size. In turn, Manhattan stands well above New Haven in this particular respect, at a point perhaps unmatched anywhere else in the nation.

Yet, in neither place is there evidence that this supply is even approaching saturation relative to manifest local demand. In both communities the steady growth in number of office therapists[18] bears witness to a supply situation that was far from sighting demand at the time of the respective studies.

Even more hard pressed are the psychiatric clinics. Of New Haven we are told that, "the demand for [clinic] treatment far exceeds its availability."[19] In Midtown, the phrase *"very lucky,"* as frequently applied to a successful applicant for admission to clinic treatment, is itself a symptom of deep undersupply. By way of one concrete instance, a new private, low-cost Manhattan clinic for adults opened in 1955. During its first twenty-one months of operation it received almost 11,000 applications for help. It could not extend psychiatric service of any kind to more than 500 of these. Thus, even in this new institution lacking the barrier of an initial waiting list, the chances of acceptance over this span of time were no better than one in twenty-two.

As we shall see in the next chapter, clinic services for children in New York have been *relatively* more plentiful than for adults. Yet at the time of the Study the director of the City's Bureau of Child Welfare announced a large backlog of preadolescent children "needing treatment for emotional disturbances [who] may have to wait one or two years before they can enter one of the seven available agencies here." He added that the chances for disturbed adolescents were "even less promising." Finally, one citizens' organization, for evidence of "overwhelming demand for service," pointed to "the long waiting lists at treatment agencies, with frequent closure of intake [that] often adds to the aggravation of the patient's original problem."[20]

That facilities for ambulant psychotherapy (as for hospitalization also) in both Manhattan and New Haven were clogged bottlenecks relative to immediate needs cannot possibly be questioned. How far they fell below the respective local demand levels was unknown while the studies were being conducted. Thus, the line of reasoning just developed in no way precludes the possibility that a real difference *does* exist between Midtown and New Haven in the overall prevalence of nonpsychotic disorders. Precluded, however, is this: If such an intercommunity difference should happen to exist, neither the direction nor the magnitude of the difference can be inferred from the nonpsychotic outpatient rates. Precluded earlier was this: from the hospitalized psychotic rate cannot be inferred the total psychotic *patient* rate, and even less does it lend itself to inferences about the *overall* frequency of psychotic conditions in a community population.

In short, the very bottleneck constriction of psychiatric services, relative to the mounting backlog of unserved local need for treatment, has this inevitable effect: It renders *number* of patients almost worthless as an indicator measure of *overall* mental morbidity in a population. The latter is the elementary but elusive unknown sought fruitlessly in numerous epidemiological studies of psychiatric patients.

THE HOME INTERVIEW SURVEY: PROCEDURES REVIEWED

The shortened, unstable shadow of the above unknown is cast on institutional records. To proceed toward its substance requires a far bolder research strategy, one pointed directly at representative people in the community rather than at the records of patients registered in psychiatric care.

Before indicating the toll paid to follow this course, it will be recalled (chapters 7 and 8) that its execution was entrusted to the Study's Home Survey operation.

At this point it may be useful to review our bearings by highlighting the differences between the Home Survey and Treatment Census operations of the Midtown Study. Since certain results of these twin field projects are sometimes reported in tandem fashion, clarity may be enhanced by reemphasizing the features that give each operation its distinct identity. These are set forth in table 10–3 below.

Psychiatric patients as the focus of epidemiological study are unreliable indicators of the complete extent of mental morbidity in a general population. However, they do offer a specific, or at least an official, diagnosis for each patient, one that the investigator need only copy from the institutional file.

By contrast, the epidemiological study focused on a community population may be on the only direct path that can lead to a competent estimate of overall prevalence therein of mental morbidity. However, this

TABLE 10-3.   DIFFERENCES BETWEEN MIDTOWN HOME SURVEY
AND TREATMENT CENSUS

	Treatment Census	Home Interview Survey
Date of coverage	May 1, 1953	November, 1953–July, 1954
Number of people covered .	2,240*	1,660
Age range of these people .	Entire treated age span	Age 20–59 adults only
Mode of selection	Enumeration of psychiatric patients on rosters of treatment services	Probability sampling of Midtown resident population in indicated age range
Proportion of universe from which drawn	Approximates entire universe of Midtown psychiatric patients on Census day	16 per 1,000 of *all* adult Midtown residents in the indicated age range
Source of information. . . .	Records of treatment facilities only	Face-to-face two-hour interview and secondary sources

*Corrected for patients of noncooperating office therapists and excluding inpatients hospitalized more than five years.

kind of investigation must first itself secure basic data on symptoms of morbidity from each sample respondent, and then by its own devices it must also synthesize the information about each individual in terms of a limited number of psychiatrically relevant categories. Because of the particular nature of the symptom data secured and the special character of the assessment situation, each deviating far from its optimal counterpart in the treatment setting, psychiatric classification of the sample Midtown respondent could not be safely modeled on the diagnostic specificity ultimately entered on the record of the patient.

The sacrifice of such nosological refinement is the price often exacted from large-scale epidemiological investigations of this kind. Clausen defines the elementary dilemma faced by a researcher in such a field: "If he wishes reasonably well-diagnosed cases he must, by and large, work with patients who are hospitalized or under treatment, recognizing that they constitute only a part of the total group suffering from a given illness. If, on the other hand, he wishes to approximate a total count of disturbed persons in some limited group he must accept less reliable diagnosis."[21]

Planning his overall prevalence study of mental illness among the aged population of Syracuse, Gruenberg confronted this dilemma and concluded: "For various reasons no attempt was thought to be feasible in this particular study to differentiate [nosologically specific] mental disorders from one another."[22]

Elsewhere, he has offered partial amplification:[23] "We would like to be very scientific and concentrate on etiologically defined disease entities. . . . Unfortunately, in psychiatry such entities have not yet been defined for the most part."[24]

Another consideration pointing community surveys in the same direction is indicated by Clausen:

Unfortunately, the standard diagnostic nomenclature is designed for classifying full-blown pathology. There is no evidence that high reliability of diagnosis can be achieved in the early stages of illness. Indeed, the frequency with which changes are made in provisional diagnosis given when the patient is admitted to a mental hospital suggests that a period of observation is often necessary to check on the course of the disturbance. Therefore, few clinicians feel any enthusiasm for assigning a diagnostic label to persons about whom their information is limited.[25]

Chapter 8 documents the carefully selected sample of signs and symptoms covered in the Home Survey interview, many serving as validated indicators associated with depths of pathology characterizing psychiatric patients. Nevertheless, it was Rennie's position that symptomatic information of this kind offered the psychiatrist no firm perceptual footing to discern intrapsychic dynamics. The latter, of course, are the *sine qua non* of operable data for diagnosis within psychiatry's rapidly evolving nosological framework.

The unavailability of this framework for the Home Survey sample created a heavy problem for the Study's psychiatrists, namely, that of formulating a classification scheme that (1) would be appropriate to the Midtown respondent's interview data and (2) would be psychiatrically meaningful as well.

The ultimate solution to the problem can here be summarized for nonpsychiatrists, as it was viewed by the Study's senior sociologist (a participating observer of the problem solving), on lines of one generic kind of scientific categorization. The classification system finally devised by Rennie, with the assistance of Kirkpatrick, has already been discussed in chapter 9. Comparison is possible with certain investigations of somatic disease providing a roughly equivalent mode of classification. Instead of assigning a population's chronic somatic illness cases to one or another rubric among the large series of specific disease entities, this medical equivalent grades the stricken people along a single heuristic dimension according to severity of their symptoms and the disability they entail. Classification on these lines has been applied in the largest investigation of somatic illness ever undertaken, namely, the National Health Survey conducted by the United States Public Health Service.[26]

The phenomenological grounds for such categorization of chronic somatic disease have been stated by Sartwell:[27] "Most diseases manifest themselves in a continuous range of severity or extent going all the way from an unrecognizable or subclinical level, on to a maximal severity which may be incompatible with life. This range is sometimes referred to as the spectrum of clinical severity."[28]

Karl Menninger and his associates have sketched the historical development of a like classificatory perspective in psychiatry, emphasizing also its recent revival and current usefulness in clinical practice.[29] Summarizing the scientific literature on the etiology of mental disorders, Felix and Bowers conclude that "the trend has been twofold. First, to see mental health and mental illness as *differing in degree rather than in kind* [italics added], and second to take increasing cognizance of the life history and the socio-environmental context of the life history."[30]

From chapters 8 and 9 it will be remembered that the mental health rating scale on which the Midtown respondents were *finally* placed[31] for purposes of this monograph takes the form of six categories graded by *severity* of symptom formation. The favorable end of this continuum is occupied by respondents regarded by Rennie as "free of significant symptoms." In the sole interest of brevity in our reports, "asymptomatic" or the four-letter code word "well" were later applied in place of this four-word operational criterion.

The counterpart of this criterion is not the seeming twin of the label-of-convenience "well" (that is, *not* the label "sick"), but rather the criterion statement "presenting significant symptoms." This criterion covers an enormous number of variations ranging from minimal symptoms to

maximal. As already suggested, this range has been cut into five progressive *symptomatic* classes (categories, strata, ratings).

Beyond the Asymptomatic group are the Mild and Moderate categories, covering respondents with signs of emotional disturbance in different
weights of psychological significance but free of apparent constrictions
or deficits in discharging the necessary functions or roles of adulthood.

The three categories beyond these on the symptomatic spectrum are
all characterized by symptom configurations that tend to reflect halting,
laming, or crippling effects on the performance of one's daily life roles
—in gradient levels now designated *Marked, Severe,* and *Incapacitated.*

Relevant as background at this point is the issue that "mental illness"
is a rubric of troublesome semantic elasticity, stretched especially since
the work of Freud. In fact, after decades of concerted effort for urgent
purposes of epidemiological standardization, psychiatrists have been unable to agree on criteria for defining a "case" of it. (Reflecting recent
trends, a leading textbook in psychiatry eschews the use of "mental
disease" and "mental illness," preferring instead "to speak of behavior
disorder."[32])

Thus, in placing a respondent in one of the five *symptomatic* categories, the Midtown psychiatrists did so, under Rennie's direction and
supervision, without making any judgment as to "ill" or "not ill." After
this rating process was completed, however, the present writer prepared
plans for statistical analysis of the data, and indicated to Rennie the
desirability for this purpose of sorting out—from the "symptomatics"—
the category or categories that could serve the analysis as a useful anchoring group of "clinically significant pathology."

Rennie had before him at that time the distributions of the entire
Midtown sample on the final mental health (that is, symptom formation)
scale. Moreover, as part of a reliability control check on the rating
psychiatrists he had himself reviewed and rated the interview summaries
of several hundred sample respondents.

Faced now with the alternative of making a decision on arbitrary, *a
priori* grounds, Rennie made essentially an *operational* distinction, based
on his knowledgeable view that impairment in social functioning ("more
than one suffer from it")[33] is a salient criterion of clinically significant
pathology ("morbidity").

Moreover, in the light of his own extensive clinical and teaching experience, both in Baltimore and in New York City, it was Rennie's view that Midtown respondents assigned to the Marked and Severe categories appeared to be more or less symptomatic counterparts of metropolitan patients in ambulant psychiatric treatment. Similarly, he noted that respondents placed in the extreme Incapacitated category had symptomatic counterparts among patients in the Veterans Administration and private psychiatric hospitals he had served. (Although he did not make the point explicit, we can infer by exclusion that he probably would have equated the Mild and Moderate categories of the classification spectrum with the subclinical band of symptom phenomena.)

The research usefulness of these clinical insights is, of course, that it permitted Rennie—without in any way claiming precision—to calibrate a relatively new gradient scheme of classification to the imperfect but only available yardstick accessible to him, namely, institutionally differentiated orders of treated mental impairment.

Obviously, what he knew about these patients was far greater in volume and depth than the carefully sampled information available on the Impaired Midtown respondents. There were, however, congruencies in the two sets of information, and it was on this plane that he saw resemblances—not identities—between the composite, symptomatological "pictures" of patients and the Marked, Severe, and Incapacitated respondents *as groups* (together comprising the Impaired).[34]

It may also deserve mention in the present context that although the Rennie classification scheme overlooks important differences in *kinds* of pathology, this fact does not necessarily rule out its potential descriptive or epidemiological significance. Gruenberg, in a similar connection, has pointed out that "there is a vast range of diagnoses, etiological as well as descriptive, associated with suicide. Yet suicide is a vitally important symptom and many studies attest to the fact that this symptom has epidemiological characteristics rather independent of the distribution of psychiatric diagnoses. The same may be said for juvenile delinquency, alcohol addiction, opium addicition . . . paranoid thinking, phobias, etc."[35] To Gruenberg's symptom list, the Midtown Study would provisionally add impairment in adult life functioning. Subsequent chapters of this monograph will presently bear out that if suicide has certain definite demographic affinities, so also has mental impairment as defined.

A final disclaimer to be recorded is that the Midtown symptom-formation scheme, as it finally evolved, was not altogether an innovation, either in conception or research application. Perhaps the most direct parallel of the Midtown classification is to be found in the postwar studies of psychiatric selection conducted for the Office of Naval Research and reported in a series of papers by C. L. Wittson and W. A. Hunt.[36] Underlying these studies were "three basic assumptions—that emotional adjustment exists on a quantitative continuum . . . that trained psychiatrists or clinical psychologists are able to place an individual in his position on this continuum, and that from this placement valid predictions can be made concerning the individual's future behavior [in the military setting]."

In the research undertaken to test these assumptions,

. . . the basic design . . . involved samples of [Navy] recruits who came to psychiatric observation during basic training but were subsequently judged able to render satisfactory service and were sent to duty. The psychiatric observation made it possible to classify these men in terms of the nature and severity of their maladjustment. Subsequent survey of their health and service records made it possible to check the accuracy of the classification, using both the criterion of discharge rate and that of incidence of hospitalization. In every study, the validity of the original classifications were confirmed.

Of particular interest is one of the Navy studies in which 944 seamen who had come under psychiatric observation were classified according to degree of maladjustment among three categories, namely, Mild or nonexistent, Moderate, and Severe. The independent validity criterion was the rate of neuropsychiatric discharge during the twelve months following. While the overall psychiatric discharge rate in the Navy was 1.6 percent per year, the discharge rates for the above three categories were 6.5, 20.2, and 89.7 percent, respectively.

These results, of course, offer a supporting foundation to the validity of the Navy classification in predicting the outcome of psychiatric discharge. In the case of the more finely divided Midtown scheme of mental health gradations a direct test of its validity would require a follow-up study of our sample respondents and their subsequent development. For a variety of reasons, such an extended longitudinal study is not now within realistic reach.[37] Nevertheless, by the demonstrated validity of their classification system on an independent psychiatric criterion, the Navy studies indirectly reinforce the usefulness that Rennie attached to the parallel system devised and applied in the Midtown Home Interview Survey.

HOME SURVEY SAMPLE: MENTAL HEALTH DISTRIBUTIONS

With this review of the main technical features of the Home Interview Survey, we can now turn to the sample of 1,660 Midtown adults for a first report on their standing within the gradient classification of symptom formation.

In table 10–4 we see that roughly one in five (18.5 percent) respondents were viewed by the team psychiatrists as free of other than inconsequential symptoms and can be regarded as essentially Well.

TABLE 10–4. HOME SURVEY SAMPLE (AGE 20–59), RESPONDENTS' DISTRIBUTION ON SYMPTOM-FORMATION CLASSIFICATION OF MENTAL HEALTH

Well	18.5%	
Mild symptom formation.	36.3	
Moderate symptom formation	21.8	
Marked symptom formation	13.2	
Severe symptom formation	7.5	
Incapacitated	2.7	
Impaired*		23.4
N = 100%.	(1,660)	

*Marked, Severe, and Incapacitated combined.

The Mild and Moderate categories are the most populous strata (36.3 and 21.8 percent, respectively), together holding a 58.1 percent majority of the Midtown sample. It will be remembered that these represent people who to all appearances are performing their adult responsibilities passably or better, although they carry varyingly significant loads of pathology-denoting symptoms. It seems, therefore, that these subclinical strata define the most frequent conditions in the Midtown population, and probably in the inclusive Manhattan white population as well. Whether these are also the most prevalent mental health conditions in more comprehensive segments of the American people is a question rather beyond the capabilities of the Midtown data to answer.

Although separately they are the least populated, the three Impaired categories add up to a sizable 23.4 percent slice of the Midtown respondents.[38] Had we also sampled Midtown's absentee mental hospital patients in the twenty to fifty-nine age range, they would have raised the Incapacitated category (by 0.5 percent) to 3.2 percent and the Impaired proportion to 23.9 percent. Applying the necessary margin for sampling error,[39] we estimate with 95 percent confidence that in the Midtown population universe the mental morbidity rate stands in a range somewhere between 21.9 and 25.9 percent. Next, on the basis of our earlier indication that this estimate probably involves an error of understatement,[40] it seems likely that the true rate stands closer to the high point in this range.

To those who may take exception to the breadth of the impairment criterion, and prefer to concentrate on a smaller, more pathology-weighted group, the combination of the Severe and Incapacitated categories is of course available as the "More Impaired," with a joint prevalence of 10.2 percent in the Midtown sample. However, were we to use this subgroup in place of the totality of Impaired in the data chapters ahead, the directions in the trends there reported, on the separate *relationships* between mental health and the ten demographic factors, would not substantially be altered.

Incidentally important, the size of the inclusive Impaired group offers us this advantage: it permits us to carry the analysis of mental health against a greater number of demographic factors *simultaneously* than would otherwise have been possible to us, or has been possible in any predecessor or successor investigation to this date. As we shall presently see, such multicontrolled analysis has led us to uncover spurious or unanticipated relationships (and nonrelationships) that would otherwise have escaped detection. We cannot overemphasize the usefulness of this leverage in maximizing the yield from the Study's analytic potentials.

With the particular kinds of respondent data that were secured, the symptom-formation classification could be readily applied by the Study's psychiatrists. For reasons already discussed, such confidence could not be extended to classification of sample respondents in terms of the established psychiatric nomenclature. Nonetheless, at the beginning of the evaluation process the ultimate workability of the symptom-formation mode of classification was still uncertain. In short, it entailed an unknown risk of losing invaluable, irreplaceable time. As a form of insurance, therefore, Rennie instructed the evaluating psychiatrists to apply as best they could a second, supplementary classification system, designated the *gross typology*. This involved nosological categories familiar in psychiatry, but their qualification with the term *probable* (more strictly speaking: *possible*) reflects the recognition that they were based on a very large leverage of psychiatric impression and intuition applied on a fulcrum of data not designed for this purpose. With the utility of the symptom-severity rating system subsequently established, the reserve use of the gross typology scheme is obviated in this monograph. However, we yield one exception at this point, for whatever suggestive value there may be in sensing the diverse make-up of the impaired group as delineated under the symptom-formation mode of classification. Thus, analysis of the gross typology composition of the sample's 389 Impaired respondents suggests that about one in twenty (5.7 percent) falls in the probable organic (damage or deficiency) type, one in four (26.5 percent) in the probable psychotic type, and the remaining two-thirds (67.8 percent) in the probable neurotic or probable personality disorder types. Of course, the latter two types are concentrated most heavily in the Marked category of symptom formation.

MENTAL MORBIDITY RATES AND CRITERIA IN OTHER STUDIES

The 23.4 percent impairment rate found in the noninstitutional, in-residence sample population of Midtown may be viewed by some students as staggering in magnitude, and of dubious credibility.

We must address ourselves to such skepticism as potentially justifiable. Specifically, the credibility of the finding may be questioned on two different planes. On one level, the question may imply that the morbidity rate reported is beyond serious technical reproach, but the study population in its loading of mental pathology may be an extreme, local deviant on the American scene. On another level, the study population may not be grossly atypical, but the Midtown psychiatrists' criterion of mental morbidity could be faulty in its excessive breadth.

To get purchase on the first level, a nationwide study of mental health applying the Midtown classification of symptom formation is lacking to us. However, the Midtown interview instrument included a series of "signs and symptoms" questions that had previously been used in the development of the Army's Neuropsychiatric Screening Adjunct questionnaire. Toward this development in 1944, a cross-section control sample of 3,501 white enlisted men on active duty, with no overseas service (and almost entirely between the ages of eighteen and thirty-six), anonymously filled out the experimental questionnaire. Compared to the Midtown sample, this Army sample was of course more homogeneous in age, sex, and socioeconomic status, more heterogeneous in rural-urban and regional origins, and in general more representative of the white population in the nation at large.

Despite these differences, if Midtown adults in mental health respects are an atypical population, we would expect them to show consistently larger frequencies of specific pathognomonic signs than did the Army sample. For purposes of this comparison we have confined ourselves to the eighteen symptom questions that were used in both studies with identical wordings. Only in two of these items did the Midtown sample appreciably exceed the Army's frequencies of "symptom positive" answers. On eight questions, it was the Army sample that exceeded Midtown's in this respect. And in eight other items, the two samples were more or less identical in their replies. Particularly significant in the latter series was the query: "Are you ever bothered by nervousness?" "Yes, often" rejoinders were given by 17 percent of the Army men and by 18 percent of the Midtown respondents.

Nothing can be extracted from this limited analysis to support the inference that the Midtown population was any more deviant than the comparison population of relatively selected,[41] able-bodied, young, white enlisted men. A lesser but related clue may be offered by the 2,252 New

Yorkers who applied for treatment to a new, unopened, low-cost psychiatric clinic. Scattered through the five boroughs, they comprised a city-wide rate of 26 per 100,000 population. Midtowners among these applicants represented an area rate of 23 per 100,000. In this expressed need for psychiatric help, Midtown hardly appeared atypical of New York City at large.

A second basis for questioning the magnitude of the Midtown impairment rate can turn on the possibility that the criterion of impairment it reflects was stretched beyond resemblance to clinical realities. Rennie's calibration of the Midtown impaired categories to the outpatients and hospital patients in his metropolitan experience lessens this specific possibility.

The skeptics can insist, nonetheless, that the Midtown morbidity rate is out of line with previous knowledge, drawn principally from studies of patients. Even more to their case, they can point to two other studies involving professional evaluation of mental health in a large metropolitan sample and producing morbidity rates patently well below that of Midtown's in both cases. One of these was the investigation in Baltimore conducted by the Commission on Chronic Illness.[42] The other was the wartime study of Selective Service examinees in the Boston induction station, as reported by Hyde and Kingsley.[43]

To meet such evidence it is possible, of course, to marshal counterindications, for example, the various estimates that 10 to 60 percent of patients seen by general practitioners and internists are "psychiatric cases."[44] Or there is the morbidity rate of 32 percent uncovered in a Salt Lake City sample of 175 households, by methods exemplifying rather less than the most advanced standards of sampling.[45]

Even if these rates were defensible, however, they would still be irrelevant to the challenge offered the Midtown Study by the Baltimore and Boston investigations, to which we must now detour for careful examination.

The Baltimore investigation consisted of three different research operations, the only one of pertinence here being that designated the *clinical evaluation.* Focused on a broad spectrum of chronic and acute somatic illnesses, and also mental disorder, this particular operation started with a drawn sample of 1,292 persons in an age range defined as reaching from "under fifteen to over sixty-five." Of these, 809 individuals, or 62.6 percent all told, appeared in clinic for (1) a battery of laboratory tests and (2) thorough physical examinations by one of a staff of thirty-one physicians, internists in the main. From this sample of participating examinees a "weighted" estimate of 10.9 percent was derived as the prevalence rate for mental disorder.[46] This figure has not only been extrapolated to the city of Baltimore and quoted in federal publications addressed to the general public, but in a variety of publications has also been projected on the American population at large.

The basic fact that need concern us here is that between the reported Baltimore mental disorder frequency of 10.9 percent and Midtown's 23.4 percent impairment rate stretches a seemingly unbridgeable gulf. Before we accept this difference as lending credence to views that the Midtown Study's criterion of mental morbidity was overextended, we must first determine whether the two studies are comparable in other relevant respects.

First, the studied populations are far from demographic comparability, but this can be partially corrected by isolating the segment of the Baltimore sample that most nearly matches the Midtown respondents, at least in race and age composition. The closest Baltimore age approximation reported in the source volume[47] is the fifteen to sixty-four age range, where the morbidity frequency is 14 percent. We are not told the disorder rate for examined sample people of this age span who are white, numbering 371 individuals. However, we are told that for the whites of all ages the morbidity rate is almost three-fourths again higher than for nonwhites. Setting aside the nonwhites brings the mental illness frequency among the indicated subsample of 371 white persons, by our calculation, to about the 16 percent point.

Attention is next drawn to the Baltimore classification process. For one thing, the complete examination in clinic was made by internists (rather than psychiatrists), who had many somatic conditions to check systematically, and apparently were short both in clinic time for focused psychiatric inquiry and in prior training for secure psychiatric observation, reporting, and evaluation. Explicit at least is that the Baltimore mental disorder rate is beset with potentially serious problems of underreporting, as the monograph authors are at some pains to indicate in the following passages:

1. It was recognized that the number of cases of a particular disease uncovered is closely related to the thoroughness of the examination.[48]

2. With a large number of physicians participating . . . it was not feasible to develop rules governing the recording of diagnoses. . . . The physicians were therefore asked to record all conditions, acute or chronic. . . . Under this general directive there was, as anticipated, a very wide variation in the kinds of conditions which physicians recorded [and presumably did not record] as diagnoses.[49]

3. The method of arriving at diagnoses probably is a more significant factor [affecting] the prevalence [rate] of mental disorders than . . . most other diseases discussed in this report. The examining internists diagnosed a mental disorder as they chose, with or without a psychiatric consultation or psychometric testing.[50] It was recognized that there would be differences in physicians' *interest in and willingness to diagnose mental disorders.* The records, therefore, were subsequently reviewed by a psychiatrist and classified by diagnosis and severity of impairment. . . . In this review, there became apparent substantial differences among examining physicians in the *completeness of recording of information* bearing on mental disorders. The review resulted in the deletion of about one-third of the cases which had been diagnosed [as mental disorders] by examining physicians, on the basis that the information *recorded* did not adequately support the diagnosis. To the extent that the deletion of cases by the reviewing psychiatrist was due to *incomplete recording of evidence* by the examining physician, the data presented here *understate the prevalence* [all italics added].[51]

Thus, in the Baltimore clinical study, the recording of psychiatric diagnoses and supporting evidence depended entirely upon the motivations of the examining internists to venture a diagnosis beyond their professional competence and, if they so ventured, to inscribe the evidence in sufficient volume and detail to satisfy the specialized and exacting, but previously undefined, criteria of the reviewing psychiatrist.

Under these circumstances, it appears likely, first, that cases of mental pathology in the Baltimore sample examined went unrecognized by the physician, or, if recognized, were unrecorded. Their number is of course unknown. Second, among the many cases of recorded pathology that were subsequently rejected by the reviewing psychiatrist, it is likely that a number reflected inadequate probing for or recording of supporting details, rather than absence of mental illness. On the base of a 16 percent mental morbidity rate above derived for the subsample of Baltimore age fifteen to sixty-four whites, we can estimate that prior to such review and rejection this morbidity rate stood at about 24 percent.[52] Represented in the latter rate would be the "false positives" correctly rejected by the reviewing psychiatrist, but *not* the "false negatives" that were over-looked or maldiagnosed or left unrecorded by the examining internists (and unreviewed by the reviewing psychiatrist). If these two different kinds of errors should happen more or less to cancel each other out, a matter on which evidence is lacking, the estimated 24 percent morbidity rate would seem to stand as approximately accurate.

The original mental disorder rate of 10.9 percent reported for the Baltimore sample examined in clinic appears to be distant indeed from the Midtown sample finding of mental impairment in a frequency of 23.4 percent. We have now demonstrated that the apparent discrepancy between the two studies is not real. When the Baltimore sample is demographically matched to the Midtown sample, the illness rate, on evidence reported, must be adjusted from 10.9 to 16 percent. And if identifiable errors of underreporting and overreporting of mental pathology should balance out, it appears possible that the true frequency might approach 24 percent, or near identity with the Midtown rate.

However, any Baltimore frequency would suffer from the further damaging fact that 44 percent of the Baltimore sample whites originally selected for clinical examination did *not* participate in the study.[53] With so large a defection, the bias potential in the studied sample itself is serious indeed. The Baltimore investigators' method of applying "weights" in an effort to compensate for observed biases in age, sex, and racial composition[54] altogether fails to correct for the possibility that participants in the underrepresented groups may be unrepresentative of the many nonparticipants on the crucial index of mental pathology rate. Specifically, if the mentally ill predominantly chose not to submit to the requested medical examination in clinic, then the 24 percent morbidity frequency estimated above as possible—for the Baltimore age fifteen to sixty-four white subsample actually studied—may be an understatement by a considerable margin. All in all, in the face of this haunting unknown, it must be submitted that the Baltimore mental disorder rate is altogether too inconclusive to be used in judging the tenability of the mental morbidity finding of the Midtown Study.

A more promising bench mark may be elicited from America's World War II experience with military-age men. In the most comprehensive review of that experience made available to the date of this writing, Brill and Beebe[55] focus on "the manpower pool of about 26 million men who were in the ages eighteen to thirty-seven in 1941, plus those reaching their eighteenth birthday in the succeeding four years." The quoted authors divide this pool of men into three segments: (1) served in Armed Forces, (2) medically disqualified for such service, and (3) granted occupational or other deferment from such service. For each segment they estimate the prevalence of "psychoneurosis, pathological personality and other psychiatric disorders" and "psychiatric defects, mental or educational deficiency." In the three indicated segments, these total 4.7 million men (excluding the category "neurological defects") or 18.1 percent of the entire pool.

This datum, of course, refers to the entire national population of military-age men. A closer match to the Midtown male population can be drawn from wartime Selective Service rejections on psychiatric grounds at the well-documented Boston Regional Induction Station.[56] Relative to all examinees, we know that the station's psychiatric rejection rate was 10.6 percent during the early months of the war[57] and 21.3 percent in August 1945.[58]

We also know that the national psychiatric rejection rate fluctuated appreciably through the war years with shifts in standards and military demands for manpower. We can assume that the Boston station's rate fluctuated similarly, probably around 16 percent—the middle point in the above range. On the basis of a 1942 study of the station's examinees we can adjust this median rate to about 17.5 percent for white men from the high-density areas of metropolitan Boston. If we could also take into account the unrecorded psychiatric cases screened out *before* reaching the station's examiners, and also the subsequent recorded and un-recorded psychiatric discharges from the armed services, the overall rate would almost certainly turn out to be not less than 20 percent.

To achieve a better-fitting match to this military-age, white Boston population, we might look at the age twenty to thirty-nine males in our Midtown sample. And there we find an overall prevalence of impairment in a frequency of 19.5 percent. The chances are 95 in 100 that this rate stands somewhere between 15.1 and 23.9 percent in the corresponding segment of the Midtown population universe.

We would not be understood to attach any large significance to the seeming concordance between the Boston frequency of mental morbidity, as just worked out, and Midtown's. It is universal knowledge that initial Selective Service psychiatric examination was usually brief and superficial, and evaluation was hardly geared to a realistic formulation of psychological balances required to cope with the military environment. From the viewpoint of military manpower needs, therefore, such screening may have discarded too many men who could have been fitted to a limited service function of some kind. However, its very superficiality, and an accompanying set of intense social pressures for acceptance in the armed forces, together argue that few of these men could have been rejected except on psychiatric grounds that were sufficiently telling by the criteria of civilian experience.[59]

From this comparison of the Baltimore, Boston, and Midtown data we do *not* draw the inference that *overall* mental morbidity rates in the three populations were demonstrably alike. Although we made several adjustments in the data to enlarge comparability, remaining uncontrolled are several large intercommunity variations: (1) known differences in such elements of demographic composition as socioeconomic standing and ethnic origin—which could not be analytically controlled because of lack of necessary information; (2) known gross differences in the operating circumstances of the psychiatric examination and evaluation process; and (3) probable differences in professional criteria for differentiating the mentally impaired from others. On all these counts, it remains impossible to make any generalizations about the comparability of *overall* mental pathology in the three analyzed populations.

Nonetheless, we have introduced the two comparison populations to suggest, despite appearances to the contrary, that they offer no evidence to support a view of the Midtown mental morbidity rate as out of line with previous relevant research experience.[60]

HELP-NEED AND READINESS

Earlier in this chapter we fixed attention on the results of our Treatment Census operation. There, numbers of patients in therapeutic facilities were expressed as rates per 100,000 of the general population. We found that these rates cannot be accepted as reliable indicators of *overall* frequency of mental morbidity in that population, primarily because limited local treatment capacities place an artificial ceiling on the number of impaired people who can be accommodated as patients.

Yet this very factor of number of patients remains of intrinsic interest in its own right as a portal to a logistic problem in the distribution of treatment resources. To this end, it will be more useful if expressed as a rate relative not to the community population at large, but to the group at risk of requiring help, or more precisely, in this instance, the disability group in presumptive need of professional intervention. About this latter group the Treatment Census data could, of course, tell us nothing.

Fortunately, the Home Survey can speak to this point, in the specific form of the 389 sample adults, age twenty to fifty-nine, who fall within the Impaired range of the psychiatrists' mental health gradient scheme. On the criterion of observed or inferred *performance deficiencies* in adult roles, these people in most cases can be assumed to need professional help of some kind, at best, to relieve the distress implied by their symptoms and to improve their capacities for adult functioning, and at the least, to reduce possibilities of future deterioration under normal or crisis circumstances of life.

On the whole, therefore, we have warrant to translate the Impaired group into the broad category of *help-need.* It is hardly necessary to add that such inferred need is not circumscribed by the impaired individual, but includes as well his family, friends, work associates, employer, and the community itself, who all stand to be helped in some large or small measure by his improvement. In relation to the hobbled individual at the center of this social circle, "help" is not necessarily equated here with individual, intensive, long-term psychotherapy. For many, such treatment may not be specifically indicated, and for most, given such insurmountable realities as high costs and insufficient therapists, it is not remotely possible. Alternative kinds of professional help are still in the crawling stage of development, but it can be assumed that under pressures of acute necessity inventions not yet envisaged will presently emerge. As one example, Sanford perceptively argues "for research on the communication of mental health information. Maybe we can find a way for the gifted analyst to affect the lives of 15,000 people rather than the 150 people who now occupy his professional lifetime."[61]

In any case, we can here empirically address ourselves only to two small but important facets of the overall problem of help-need. First, we can ask the extent to which the individuals in the impaired range within the Midtown sample have ever been in the status of psychiatric patient. This was put to *all* sample respondents as follows: "We are also interested in the kinds of medical specialists people go to. Have you ever gone to any of these specialists?" Seven kinds of specialists were separately named for a yes or no reply. Fourth and fifth on this list were "nerve specialist" and "psychiatrist."[62]

All told, 222 respondents, or 13.4 percent of the entire sample, had been to one or more psychotherapists.[63] Respondents indicating they had been patients in this sense were asked only one follow-up question, inquiring when they had last been to the therapist. Where the last contact had been as recent as a month before the interview, the respondent was classified as a current patient; all others, somewhat arbitrarily, as ex-patients. On this criterion, 40 respondents were patients and 182 were ex-patients, or 2.4 and 11 percent of the sample, respectively.[64]

It must be emphasized that the classification of both types of patients is ambiguous on an important point. That is, at one extreme are those who may have seen a therapist for consultation or diagnosis only, with no subsequent treatment, and at the other extreme are those who may have been in treatment for years. Nevertheless, although a patient history in any particular case cannot necessarily be equated with exposure to treatment, in all cases it does seem to reflect the twin minimal facts that the need for seeing a psychotherapist was felt and acted upon.

In table 10–5 we report the distribution of each Impaired grade on the patient-history variable. Among the separate impairment groups the differences in ever-patient rates are relatively small, ranging from about one in four (23.3 percent) of the Marked group to about one in three (35.5 percent) of the Incapacitated.

If we conceive of the Impaired respondents in the aggregate as metaphorically approximating the form of an iceberg, then only one-twentieth (5.4 percent) of this mass is in any one month visible, however briefly, to psychotherapists in ambulatory facilities.[65] In addition, about one-fifth (21.3 percent) had once come to such professional attention, in some instances within hospital settings, but are still in a help-need condition. Finally, about three in every four (73.3 percent) of these Impaired people are completely "submerged," having never been known to any psychotherapist.[66] Here sketched for the first time, we believe, in any American population is the patient-history structure of one community's mass of mental morbidity. This structure takes the roughly delineated form of a pyramid, by far the largest part at the base never having found the way to a psychotherapist for a single session of consultation, and a small fractional part forming the peak currently visible to psychiatrists.

Of the former, we have no information revealing whether they are receiving need-directed help from other kinds of professionals. However, we did approach the entire Midtown sample for orientations to several

TABLE 10–5. HOME SURVEY SAMPLE (AGE 20–59), IMPAIRED RESPONDENTS' DISTRIBUTIONS ON PATIENT-HISTORY CLASSIFICATION BY IMPAIRMENT GRADES

Patient-history	Impairment grades			
	Marked	Severe	Incapacitated	Combined Impaired
Current outpatients . . .	5.0%	4.0%	11.1%	5.4%
Ex-patients.	18.3	25.6	24.4	21.3
Ever-patients*.	23.3	29.6	35.5	26.7
Never-patients	76.7	70.4	64.5	73.3
N = 100%	(219)	(125)	(45)	(389)

*It must not be inferred that respondents who were ever-patients were necessarily considered by Study psychiatrists as being in an Impaired state of mental health. On the contrary, of the sample's 40 current outpatients, 19 were not so regarded. And of 182 ex-patients, 99 were not so considered.[67]

relevant types of professional assistance. This was probed indirectly by means of two behavior problems posed in terms of advice solicited by hypothetical friends: (1) "We are interested in what people think about ways of handling family problems. Now let's suppose some friends of yours have a serious problem with a child. I mean a problem with the child's behavior, or difficulty getting along with others. The parents ask your advice as to what to do. What would you probably tell them to do about it?" (2) "Now let's suppose a good friend [same sex as respondent] came to you about serious trouble in his [her] marriage. He [she] asks your advice as to how to straighten it out. What might you tell him [her] to do about it?"

We have classified respondents in one of four categories: (1) those who, to either or both of the two questions, advised seeing a "psychiatrist" or a "psychologist" or their institutional equivalents; (2) all others who to either question advised "see a physician" or his institutional equivalent, for example, a pediatric clinic; (3) those remaining who to either question advised seeing some other remedial professional person, for example, a clergyman or social worker; (4) the residue of those whose reply in *both* situations failed to include any suggestion of professional help.[68]

The above two life-problem questions were open-ended, giving no hint themselves of the possibility of professional help as such. Since they left the respondent a wide range of action alternatives to choose from, we can be reasonably confident on this point: Those respondents who would specifically recommend a psychotherapist to a friend under these circumstances are probably in a state of potential readiness to apply such advice to themselves.

The results among the sample's Impaired never-patients are seen in table 10–6.

Here we note that only one in twenty (5.4 percent) is presently in a patient role with a psychotherapist, and in this specific sense is in an active state of getting what is presumably the most appropriate professional help for his needs. These will not concern us further in the following discussion.

Another one in five (21.3 percent) of these Impaired respondents has been in this patient role and presumably has seen it terminated. Relative

TABLE 10–6.   HOME SURVEY SAMPLE (AGE 20–59), IMPAIRED NEVER-PATIENTS'
DISTRIBUTION ON PROFESSIONAL ORIENTATION VARIABLE

Current patients	5.4%
Ex-patients	21.3
Never-patients (73.3%) advising:	
"See psychotherapist"	13.4
"See physician"	8.5
"See other professional".	7.2
No professional advised	44.2
N = 100%	(389)

to the psychotherapeutic professions, therefore, he is currently in an inactive status. However, on the criterion of his previous activity we can assume that henceforth he will find his way to a psychotherapist more readily than others in need of such help.

Of the entire Impaired group, another one in eight (13.4 percent) has never been in the role of a psychiatric patient but appears to be disposed to accept it. If potential demand for psychotherapy of some kind can be defined as "need combined with willingness to accept such help,"[69] then these never-patients and the ex-patients appear to be the closest, albeit crude, approximation we can reach to an estimate of the extent of such unmet potential demand. Together, these constitute 34.7 percent of the Impaired respondents and 8 percent of the entire interviewed sample.

Of all the Impaired people, 15.7 percent are never-patients who, we can infer, are either getting help from a physician or other professional, or are inclined to seek such help from these specialized directions. Finally, a little under half (44.2 percent) of the Impaired group are never-patients who appear to give no sign of orientation to professionals as a possible source of assistance. These seem to represent the large segment of help-needy who are unlikely to come to psychiatric attention, at least of their own initiative.

Among all the help-needy people, therefore, we can judge that the unmet potential demand for psychotherapy of some kind is relatively large. But even larger in number are those who, for a variety of possible reasons, apparently perceive no professional person or agency as a haven of possible relief for the disability and distress they suffer in their daily lives.

The dimensions of the social problem disclosed by these two Impaired subgroups are indirectly suggested by this glaring fact: the small summit-of-pyramid subgroup now seeing a psychotherapist is by itself sufficient to "strain the seams" of psychiatric resources to their utmost in the metropolis with by far the largest ambulatory treatment capacities, relative to population size, in the entire country. In light of this fact, policy problems of enormous proportions seem to be posed by the extent of potential demand for professional intervention here crudely estimated.

Some may find it comforting to escape these problems by rejecting the technical grounds on which the estimates rest. Strictly speaking, this is an empirical question, of course, that further research alone can answer in due time. In the meantime, however, if only the Incapacitated and Severe symptom-formation grades in the Impaired range are considered as warranting psychiatric help, the problem of meeting their unserved needs would still be pressing and huge in magnitude.

Despite the thick hedge of qualifications that surrounds the Midtown morbidity and nontreatment findings, these estimates suggest reconsideration of the entire strategy of confronting and relieving the mass of mental pathology prevalent in the population. Such reconsideration of public policy cannot be denied except at peril to the suffering, to the healing professions, to the community, and to the nation at large.

SUMMARY

1. On the yardstick of a one-day prevalence count, the Treatment Census found that inpatients hospitalized continuously for up to five years constituted 502 per 100,000 of the total Midtown population. Average length of hospitalization among these patients in public institutions is more than twice that of their counterparts in private hospitals. However, to judge from readmission cases, the frequency of relapse and rehospitalization is no different in the two patient groups.

2. On the same prevalence yardstick, 788 per 100,000 of the entire Midtown population were reported as ambulant mental patients in clinic

or office facilities. Evidence was noted warning against the inference that patient status, hospital or ambulant, necessarily indicates therapy was involved.

3. Contrary to previous assumptions, a substantial proportion of patients diagnosed as psychotic are in ambulant treatment facilities. Accordingly, hospitalization rates as used in previous studies must be rejected as an index of frequency either of total psychoses or of *treated* psychoses in an urban community population.

4. A difference of approximately four to one between Midtown and New Haven in reported prevalence of ambulant nonpsychotic patients can be largely attributed to intercommunity differences in outpatient treatment capacities, rather than to overall frequency of such conditions. A supply-demand principle consistent with these data was formulated.

5. Both the Midtown and New Haven populations are more favored than the rest of the country in their supply of psychiatric clinics and office therapists. Yet there is ample evidence from both places that this supply was insufficient in the period of study to the local demand for such services. Under such bottleneck circumstances, therefore, patient rates can only reflect the supply of therapists locally available, rather than the *overall* frequency of mental morbidity. In an attempt to measure the latter, the Home Survey was conducted in a random sample of the general population of Midtown ranging between the ages of twenty and fifty-nine. All subsequent points in the present summary refer to results of this survey.

6. As a prelude to its findings, the methods of the Home Survey were recalled. Particular attention was paid to the psychiatrists' mental health classification of survey respondents, and the issues it raises for methodologists, both in social science and psychiatry.

7. In the survey sample, an impairment rate of 23.4 percent compares with a Well frequency of 18.5 percent and a combined Mild-Moderate representation of 58.1 percent. Two forms of skepticism may be directed against the 23.4 percent morbidity rate. The first questions whether Midtown, in mental health respects, may not be a deviant population on the national scene. However, on a series of pathognomonic signs and symptoms, covered both with the Midtown respondents and a national cross-section sample of white Army men, there appeared few differences

to lend credence to this possibility.

8. A second question suggests that the Midtown morbidity range may be excessively broad relative to clinical standards. Evidence seemingly supporting this possibility is marshaled from investigations of the Baltimore and Boston populations, both presenting mental pathology rates well below that of Midtown. Close analysis of data from these two studies revealed that their deviations from the Midtown morbidity rates were not real. Accordingly, they fail to support the hypothesis that the Midtown psychiatrists' definition of mental morbidity may have been overextended in its scope.

9. Focusing on the Impaired category of sample respondents, it was assumed that they were in a state of professional help-need. Of interest was the extent to which these respondents had ever seen a psychotherapist, our criterion for a patient history. Among these Impaired people in the aggregate, only one in twenty could be considered a current patient. Another one in five were ex-patients, and roughly three in four had never come to the attention of such a specialist.

10. On the criteria of impairment and readiness for professional help, we discerned a large potential demand for such intervention. Even more numerous, however, were the Impaired never-patients who seemed unlikely of their own accord to find a way to professional help of any kind.

11. These data pose challenging questions about the community's strategy of marshaling professional services for the help-needy.

NOTES

[1]Excluded were specialized institutions for mental defectives. Also, at the suggestion of Dr. Henry Brill of the New York State Department of Mental Hygiene, patients hospitalized continuously for five years or more were not counted in our Treatment Census. Dr. Brill at that time pointed out that the chances of such a patient leaving the institution alive were slight. Even if he should be discharged after so long an absence the patient's local ties to family and extrafamily associates, frayed or broken at the time of hospitalization, would probably be moribund through attrition, death, removal to another area, and so forth. [See N. C. Morgan and N. A. Johnson, "Failures in Psychiatry: The Chronic Hospital Patient," *American Journal of Psychiatry* 113 (March 1957): 824–830.] Accordingly, for a section of a metropolis like Midtown such patients can no longer be meaningfully considered as among its bona fide residents.

In the absence of any evidence available at the time, we assumed that the number of plus-five-year patients so excluded would not be excessively large. However, a subsequent study in the state hospitals of seven states (New York excluded) and a separate study in the New York state hospitals revealed that of all patients in these institutions on a given day about 60 percent had been continuously hospitalized for five years or more. Accordingly, it is almost certain that the plus-five-year patients uncounted by our Treatment Census are numerous indeed. As to Midtown's private hospital patients, none had been continuously confined for more than three years.

[2]It must be emphasized that the Treatment Census operation was conducted in a period before the introduction of tranquilizing drugs. Of course, these have reduced average length of hospitalization. During 1955, however, of all patients in New York state hospitals about 3.5 percent received active psychotherapy, 15 percent drug treatments only, and 81.5 percent custodial care only. (Dr. Paul Hoch, report to Milbank Memorial Fund Technical Board, March 20, 1956.)

[3]In the New York state hospital system as a whole, one-third of all discharged patients relapsed and were returned to a state institution (ibid.).

[4]Throughout this volume, the term *clinics* will be used to refer exclusively to psychiatric outpatient clinics.

In the official "1954 Directory of Psychiatric Clinics in New York State," seventy-seven outpatient clinics were listed in Manhattan; thirteen others were identified in the borough through local sources. About one-third of these clinics serve the home borough alone, the remainder serving the entire city.

[5]Within the boundaries of New York City, residents of the four outer boroughs can secure professional services either in the home borough or in Manhattan. Geographically dispersed in the outlying boroughs, such services are highly centralized in Manhattan. Thus, the Manhattan resident is most unlikely to seek these services in the outer boroughs. This pattern was preeminently the case for ambulant mental patients. Accordingly, our Treatment Census could safely concentrate its coverage on office therapists and clinics in Manhattan only.

[6]Some 11 percent of these Midtowners were in the care of clinical psychologists.

[7]The method of deriving this estimate was as follows: (1) The cooperating therapists were divided into four groups according to *(a)* psychiatrists versus psychologists and *(b)* offices in or near the Midtown area versus those more distantly located in Manhattan. (2) We calculated the average number of Midtown census day patients reported by each of the above four groups. (3) We divided the noncooperating therapists into the above four groups and assumed that each of the four would have reported patients approximating the average reported by the corresponding group of cooperating therapists. (4) On this basis, it is calculated that the noncooperating therapists would have designated an additional 127 patients, to produce an estimated total of 1,086 private office patients.

For reasons we need not take space to explain, we believe that another large source of error is traceable to the underreporting of cases on the part of an unknown number of *cooperating* psychiatrists and psychologists. However, no attempt will be made here to correct for this particular source of error, since we lack any basis for estimating its magnitude. The reader will take into account this potentially large error of understatement.

[8]A. B. Hollingshead and F. C. Redlich, *Social Class and Mental Illness,* 1958. The total New Haven population figure used as denominator in calculating the rates is 236,940 and appears on page 199 of the latter monograph. A total of 1,963 New Haven patients were enumerated, but 72 were of unknown social class position. [A. B. Hollingshead and F. C. Redlich, "Social Stratification and Psychiatric Disorders," *American Sociological Review* 18 (April 1953): 167.] Elsewhere it is reported that of these 1,963 New Haven patients, 159 were found in clinics and 374 were in the care of private psychiatrists. [B. H. Roberts and J. K. Myers, "Religion, National Origin, Immigration and Mental Illness," *American Journal of Psychiatry* 110 (April 1954): 759.] These are the numerator figures used in computing the New Haven rates appearing in our table 10–2.

[9]Through the checking of our records for instances of the same patient being reported by several treatment facilities, we believe this total to be free of error from such duplication.

[10]*Annual Report for Calendar Year 1957,* Biometrics Branch, National Institute of Mental Health, p. 10.

[11]*The Functioning of Psychiatric Clinics in New York City,* New York City Committee on Mental Hygiene, 1949.

[12]The New Haven proportion has been calculated from distribution data in Hollingshead

and Redlich, *Social Class and Mental Illness,* p. 258.

[13]From the Midtown Treatment Census there is reason to believe that the cooperating office therapists in an unknown number of instances were unwilling to report a psychotic patient or to attribute a psychotic condition to a reported patient. If so, these figures relating to both the Midtown and New Haven outpatient populations may be in error on the side of understatement.

[14]Compared to the North, southern states generally have low inpatient rates. One factor contributing to this difference is that a state like New York admits blacks to its extensive mental hospital system without apparent discrimination. In southern states, relatively few Negroes are hospitalized because the necessary facilities simply are not provided. (Cf. B. Malzberg, "Important Statistical Data about Mental Illness," in S. Arieti, ed., *American Handbook of Psychiatry,* 1959, vol. 1, p. 171.)

[15]This rate has been computed from data in Hollingshead and Redlich, *Social Class and Mental Illness,* p. 258.

[16]At the time of the New Haven investigation there were no clinical psychologists known to be in private practice within its study area (personal communication from Fredrick C. Redlich).

[17]It is also of interest that of the 4,000 psychiatrists in the United States estimated by Clausen as engaged in private practice (during 1954), fully 20 percent by our calculation conduct that practice on the island of Manhattan and about 2 percent more in the rest of New York City. Approximately half (53 percent) are practitioners in *all other* American cities exceeding 100,000 people and about 25 percent serve all other American places with populations under 100,000. (J. A. Clausen, *Sociology and the Field of Mental Health,* Russell Sage Foundation, New York, 1956, p. 9.) Whether this unbalanced distribution is in the public interest constitutes a policy question outside the province of this report.

[18]Between 1947 and 1957 the number of APA members in private psychiatric practice grew from 5 to 27 in New Haven and from 330 to 910 in Manhattan. No comparable data are available for clinical psychologists in private practice. However, there are some indications that their rate of growth in Manhattan during this decade may have been faster than that of the psychiatrists.

[19]Hollingshead and Redlich, *Social Class and Mental Illness,* p. 154.

[20]*Mental Health Facilities and Needs in New York City,* Welfare and Health Council of New York City, 1956, p. 6. That this situation was still chronic three years later is revealed in a report by the Community Council of Greater New York (*Welfare and Health in New York City: 1959,* p. 30). Indicating that "both children and adults find extremely long waiting periods before they obtain service," the report added: "It is ironic, but the only sure way to get prompt psychiatric treatment is to sit on a lofty window ledge and threaten to jump."

[21]J. A. Clausen, "The Sociology of Mental Illness," in R. K. Merton et al., eds., *Sociology Today,* 1959, p. 494.

[22]E. Gruenberg, "Problems of Data Collection and Nomenclature," in C. H. Branch et al., eds., *The Epidemiology of Mental Health,* 1955, p. 68.

[23]E. Gruenberg, "Epidemiology of Mental Disorders," *Milbank Memorial Fund Quarterly* 35 (April 1957): 121.

[24]The social scientist working in psychiatry is aware that some therapists, especially those somatogenic in emphasis, regard the major syndromes of mental illness as more or less distinct disease entities. However, he also hears an impressive chorus of psychiatric dissent from this view. For example, Karl Menninger has commented: "I not only believe that no such disease as schizophrenia can be clearly defined or identified or proved to exist, but I also hold that there is no such thing as a psychosis or neurosis. My point is that no one can satisfactorily define these terms in a way which the rest of us can accept, so that if we use the terms we involve ourselves in confusion." (Karl Menninger, "Toward a Unitary Concept of Mental Illness," in *A Psychiatrist's World,* 1959, p. 517.) For further manifestations of Freud's impact on the concept of mental disease entities, see P. Hoch and J. Zubin, *Current Problems in Psychiatric Diagnosis,* 1951, to which Rennie contributed a notable paper, "Prognosis in the Psychoneuroses," pp. 66–79.

[25]Clausen, "The Sociology of Mental Illness," p. 493.

[26]United States National Health Survey, *Preliminary Report on Disability, United States,*

July-September, 1957, pp. 6–8; *Chronic Conditions and Limitations of Activity and Mobility, 1965–1967.*

[27]P. E. Sartwell, "Problems of Identification of Cases of Chronic Disease," *Milbank Memorial Fund Quarterly* 31 (July 1953): 17.

[28]To these phenomena others have applied the concept of biologic "gradient of disease." See John E. Gordon, "The World, the Flesh and the Devil as Environment, Host and Agent of Disease," in I. Galdston, ed., *The Epidemiology of Health,* 1953, p. 70.

[29]K. Menninger, "Toward a Unitary Concept of Mental Illness," in *A Psychiatrist's World,* 1959, pp. 516–528.

[30]R. H. Felix and R. V. Bowers, "Mental Hygiene and Socio-environmental Factors," *Milbank Memorial Fund Quarterly* 26 (April 1948): 130.

[31]That is, after systematic adjudication of cases in which the two psychiatrists differed in their independent evaluations. The method of adjudication was adapted to the degree of difference in judgment expressed by the two psychiatrists in rating the mental health of a given respondent. If the latter had been placed in adjoining mental health categories, he was regularly assigned to the *more favorable* of the two categories. If in certain instances he was placed in categories two steps apart, he was systematically placed in the *intervening* mental health grade. And if in a few cases he had been placed in categories three grades apart, then Rennie reviewed the respondent's data and with his associates made the final determination.

[32]F. Redlich and D. Freedman, *The Theory and Practice of Psychiatry,* 1966. See page 2 for the authors' definition of the preferred term.

[33]The parallel criterion being applied in the National Health Survey is "morbidity measured along an axis for which the scale is in terms of the effect that the morbidity has upon the lives of the people concerned." (See United States National Health Survey, *Concepts and Definitions in the Health Household-Interview Survey,* 1958; and *Disability Components for an Index of Health,* 1971.)

[34]In this context, therefore, "impairment" does *not* refer to organic damage or deficiency, although conditions of this nature were documented or seemed probable among a few interviewed respondents, constituting 1.7 percent of the entire sample.

[35]Gruenberg, "Epidemiology or Mental Disorders," p. 122.

[36]"The Predictive Value of the Brief Psychiatric Interview," *American Journal of Psychiatry* 107 (February 1951): 582–585; and "A Rationale for Psychiatric Selection," *American Psychologist* 10 (May 1955): 199–204. See also the extensive work on a health-sickness scale conducted by the Menninger Foundation, L. Luborsky, "Clinicians' Judgments of Mental Health: A Proposed Scale," *Archives of General Psychiatry* 7 (1962).

[37]This sentence was written late in 1959 and is further proof of the fallibility of foresight. In January 1973 a twenty-year follow-up investigation of the original Midtown sample was launched, under the direction of the present author.

[38]Because of the seeming disability equivalence of the Incapacitated category to hospital patients, it would have been desirable to maintain its separate identity in this discussion and in future analyses. However, the small number of cases affords too slight a base for credible statistical manipulation or inference.

[39]In the interest of readability, hereafter we will as a rule avoid reiterated corrections for sampling error. For the most part, instead, we shall discuss mental health distributions as we find them in the sample, without projecting estimates to the population universe. The reader wishing to make such projections from the total Home Survey sample of 1,660 respondents can add plus or minus 2 percent to proportions around 25 or 75 percent and plus or minus 3 percent to magnitudes around 50 percent. These limits are calculated to meet the .05 level of confidence.

[40]This arises from the unlikelihood of achieving 100 percent detection of mental morbidity cases in a community population.

[41]*Selected* here refers to the fact that obvious physical and mental misfits had already been in largest part screened out. On the other hand, it should not be overlooked that the military environment is at a considerable sociological distance from the family and community settings of these ex-civilians.

[42]This has been fully reported, authors undesignated, in *Chronic Illness in a Large City: The Baltimore Study,* 1957.

[43]"Studies in Medical Sociology: The Relation of Mental Disorders to Population Density," *New England Journal of Medicine* 23 (October 26, 1944): 571–577.

[44]*Third Annual Report,* Joint Commission on Mental Illness and Health, 1958, p. 11.

[45]N. J. Cole, C. H. Branch, and O. M. Shaw, "Mental Illness: A Survey Assessment of Community Rates, Attitudes and Adjustments," *AMA Archives of Neurological Psychiatry* 77 (April 17, 1957): 393–398.

[46]Such cases were classified in one of four categories, namely: (1) psychoses; (2) psychoneuroses; (3) psychophysiologic, autonomic, and visceral disorders; and (4) other mental, psychoneurotic, and personality disorders.

[47]*Chronic Illness in a Large City: The Baltimore Study,* 1957, p. 97.

[48]Ibid., p. 384.

[49]Ibid., p. 391.

[50]The authors report that only psychiatric consultations were sought, and for only 14 (1.7 percent) of the 809 examined sample subjects (ibid., p. 390). Given that the examiners were internists in the main, this is not exactly a reassuring index of psychiatric interest.

[51]Ibid., p. 96. Throughout the volume, the authors are critically aware of methodological problems in, and lessons to be learned from, the Baltimore investigation.

[52]This estimate assumes that the one-in-three rejection of diagnosed cases by the reviewing psychiatrist, reported for the examined sample as a whole, more or less applies to the subsample of interest here.

[53]*Chronic Illness in a Large City: The Baltimore Study,* 1957, p. 209.

[54]That is, these varyingly underrepresented groups in the studied sample were arithmetically reconstituted to accord with their representation in the population universe. In this process it was apparently assumed that the unknown mental disorder rate of *nonparticipants* from a given demographic segment would approximate the rate known for *participants* from the same segment.

[55]N. Q. Brill and G. W. Beebe, *A Follow-up Study of War Neuroses,* 1955, pp. 322–333.

[56]The region covered was eastern Massachusetts.

[57]R. W. Hyde and L. V. Kingsley, "Studies in Medical Sociology: The Relation of Mental Disorders to Population Density," *New England Journal of Medicine* 23 (October 26, 1944): 571–577.

[58]S. A. Stouffer et al., *Measurement and Prediction,* Studies in Social Psychology in World War II, vol. 4, 1950, p. 551.

[59]This probability finds particular reinforcement in the case of the Boston induction station from the fact that it was served by a corps of psychiatrists out of the area's distinguished medical schools.

[60]Since the first edition of this book was written, three mental health investigations have come to our attention that applied diverse methods to extremely different general populations, and reported impairment (or suggestive indicators) in frequencies matching or exceeding the Midtown rate: (I) G. Gurin, *Americans View Their Mental Health,* 1960, p. 278. This was a study of 2,460 adults, representing a random sample of the American population. No psychiatric evaluation of symptoms was made. But as a rough clue the authors report "readiness for self-referral" to get professional help for "a lot of personal problems." Some 23 percent of the sample "has used" or "could have used [such] help." (II) D. H. Leighton et al., *The Character of Danger,* 1963, p. 128. In their sample of a Stirling County (Nova Scotia) population the Leightons found a significantly impaired rate of 32 percent. (III) W. Ryan, *Distress in the City,* 1969, pp. 9–10. This Boston Mental Health Survey focused on estimates of the number of emotionally disturbed persons "made by reporting agencies—[and] projected from sample data." Without specifying methods, the author's summary estimate is that "about one out of every four or five . . . have emotional problems interfering with their lives, handicapping them in their work, in their social relationships, and in dealing with members of their own family."

These investigations are not regarded as providing new support to the Midtown impairment rate, but rather as additional evidence contradicting the view of that rate as "incredible" or "unprecedented."

[61]F. H. Sanford, "The Rising Tide of Mental Health," *Public Health Reports (U.S.)* 72 (July 1957): 607.

[62]This double listing was prompted by awareness that to people with limited schooling

psychiatrist is a more or less unfamiliar term, and *nerve specialist* is its colloquial equivalent. In addition, the interviewer was provided a special code for respondents volunteering. the information that they had gone to a psychologist or some other kind of trained psychotherapist, as thirteen respondents did.

[63]All but twelve of these reported this fact to the interviewer. The twelve respondents who did not do so were found on our Treatment Census records. Thus, on an extremely sensitive point of personal information, the respondents' 5.4 percent rate of known underreporting is encouragingly small. Moreover, it is probably no larger than the inferred underenumeration of their Midtown patients on the part of an unknown number of therapists collaborating in our Treatment Census operation.

[64]This, of course, is an ambulant patient rate of 24 per 1,000, contrasting with the 8 per 1,000 derived by the Treatment Census. From other evidence, we have gathered that the latter involves an error of unknown size due primarily to underreporting of cases by some office therapists. The former rate, in turn, is subject to the fluctuations of chance referred to as *sampling error.* Hence the contrast between the two rates may in part be more apparent than statistically real.

[65]This particular finding parallels the results of a 1945 study focused on 623 New York City veterans who had been discharged from military service for neuropsychiatric reasons. Of these, about 82 percent were judged to be in need of some kind of psychotherapy, but only 5 percent were getting such care. (See *Psychiatric Needs in Rehabilitation,* study by the New York City Committee on Mental Hygiene of the State Charities Aid Association, 1948.)

[66]This may be compared to the extent of certain specific unmet medical needs revealed by the California Health Survey. The latter disclosed that "a substantial amount of illness does not come to the attention of physicians. For example, about one-fifth of the rheumatism, one-fourth of the deafness and almost one-third of the asthma and hay fever reported in the survey were not medically attended." L. Breslow, "Uses and Limitations of the California Health Survey for Studying the Epidemiology of Chronic Disease," *Journal of Public Health* 47 (April 1957): 171.

The United States National Health Survey has reported that of all persons with one or more chronic somatic conditions fully half (49.7 percent) were not under medical care. "Limitation of Activity and Mobility Due to Chronic Conditions," United States National Health Survey, *Health Statistics,* ser. B, no. 11, 1959, p. 4.

More recently the Chicago Health Research Foundation has estimated that "approximately half of this country's hypertensives are undetected, and half of the detected go untreated." Quoted in *Medical Tribune,* February 3, 1971.

[67]These are nonimpaired respondents with Mild or Moderate levels of distressing symptoms who felt needy, willing, and able enough to seek psychiatric relief. That they thereby entered patienthood in no way detracts from Rennie's expert, *post hoc* "clinical opinion" that the symptomatologies he encountered in the Impaired respondent protocols resembled those of patients known to him. In logical form: not all the Impaired are patients, and not all patients are impaired. Nonetheless, the symptomatological overlap is sufficient to justify articulating the newer category heuristically to the older one, albeit with less than the complete precision some assume to be the norm in the life sciences.

[68]They answered, for example, "talk it over" with kin or friends, "work it out in the family," "would not know what to say," and so on.

[69]*Mental Health Resources in New York City,* New York City Community Mental Health Board, 1957, p. 43.

CHAPTER II

THE PRIME OF LIFE AGE GROUPS
LEO SROLE AND THOMAS LANGNER

Epidemiological investigations of mental disorder in a general population ultimately arrive at an estimated overall morbidity rate somewhat as do the laboratory scientists who isolate the first pinhead quantity of a rare element—that is, only after prolonged dredging, sifting, refining, and synthesizing of an enormous mass of raw materials.

The parallel diverges, of course, on this special limitation in the mental morbidity "quantum" estimated for a community population: It is based on a highly selected, i.e., restricted, body of information that has been (1) secured by one specific set of techniques among others possible, and (2) filtered through the particular lens complex of professional criteria and judgments of a few psychiatrists. Such a study, accordingly, must preface the morbidity rate it has laboriously and painstakingly extracted with the plain qualification: "in the independent judgments of these psychiatrists, as applied to this corpus of data, as gathered by these methods . . ."

To be sure, such a rate offers the study area the only professionally credible estimate available of the overall magnitude of mental impairment, untreated and treated, in its midst—a rare and strategic item of intelligence for a community and its leaders. However, the qualification just stated clamps severe limits on the scientific comparability of the rates derived by separate researchers in different communities.

It should be clear that these particular limits do not operate when an epidemiological investigation turns to intergroup comparisons in the "back yard" of its own circumscribed study population. Given due awareness of certain possible pitfalls, such intergroup analyses can be viewed as resting on this common base: Individuals in the various group segments of the study population have been evaluated in terms of mental health status by the *same* psychiatrists, who had weighed the *same* kinds of information, which had been secured by the *same* research methods.

Embodying the demographic variables, these groups offer accessible, more or less standardized, paths through the bewildering maze that is the social system of every large community. Both epidemiologists and sociologists have traditionally taken these paths in their special searches for clues to pathogenic forces at work in the community.

One problem often overlooked in both fields is the etiological ambiguity inherent in the fact that certain kinds of group affiliations may be individually achieved end results, rather than exogenous antecedents, of an adult's personality and mental health. To circumscribe this ambiguity, we are distinguishing two types of demographic factors, namely, the independent and the reciprocal (see chapter 7).

Age is an example of the independent type of demographic variable. That is, the individual's position in the community's social hierarchy of age is not self-selected, but is culturally ascribed, more or less on the basis of signal indicators that attest to his stage in the maturation cycle. Indeed, the escalator of age is one of the universal mechanisms to which every society differentially gears some of its indispensable functions, role assignments, and behavioral expectations. The latter can be viewed as a complex of subtle influences and gross pressures that operate from cradle to grave to canalize behavior and guide personality development. Hence, within the individual's life history, phases of the organic cycle and of the social cycle advance more or less in interlocking coordination. Inability of the individual to perform social roles culturally appropriate to his age has been conceptualized in such psychological terms as immaturity, fixation, regression, infantilism, and retardation and is itself usually taken by psychiatry as evidence of malfunction suggesting mental disorder.

Our purpose in this chapter is to view the Midtown population as internally segmented into a series of age-level groups and to test the initial hypothesis that associated with these groups are differences in mental health composition and psychiatric care.

Age, of course, is a continuum type of variable. Therefore, any division of the temporal range must be somewhat arbitrary. The mode of division we have adopted is the standard survey procedure that systematically applies equal spans of time in the predominant form of ten-year age intervals.

TREATMENT CENSUS COUNT

We might pause first to examine what our Treatment Census operation has to report from its one-day prevalence enumeration of patients in hospitals five years or less or in outpatient clinics[1]—duration unlimited.

TABLE II–I.   TREATMENT CENSUS (AGE INCLUSIVE), PREVALENCE RATES (PER 100,000 POPULATION) OF MIDTOWN PATIENTS IN HOSPITALS AND CLINICS BY AGE LEVEL

Age level	A. Public hospitals	B. Private hospitals	C. Total inpatients	D. Clinic outpatients
5–19	153	5	158	400
20–29	404	81	485	280
30–39	499	51	550	271
40–49	449	26	475	126
50–59	486	43	529	46
60–69	622	42	664	14
70 plus	1,318	129	1,447	0

If we first scan column D in table II–I, we observe that the older the group, the smaller, progressively, is the frequency of its clinic outpatients. To judge from this trend, psychiatric clinics predominantly serve Midtown's children and younger adults (that is, under age forty).

For inpatients (column C), the opposite age trend is apparent in the sharp contrast between the extremes of the range. Though heavily represented in the clinics, there are few children in the hospitals. Above age seventy, on the other hand, the psychoses of senility and other disorders diagnosed as "organic" push hospital rates to their peak. However, among the four "prime-of-life" age groups between twenty and fifty-nine, the total inpatient prevalence rates essentially define a "flat" trend.[2]

Our main interest in these particular data attaches to the very different age patterning of patients revealed as seeking and receiving admission to psychiatric clinics and to mental hospitals. Beyond such interest, left as legacy by earlier hospital studies, is this implicit assumption: Although patients represent only a portion of the unknown quantity of overall mental morbidity, they can be pressed to serve as a visible indicator reflecting differences in the latter as composite of the treated and untreated sick.

In shifting attention to the Home Interview Survey and its sample of age twenty to fifty-nine residents, we will have the means to explore this assumption, at least as it relates to the age twenty to fifty-nine patients reviewed in table II–I.

HOME SURVEY SAMPLE: MENTAL HEALTH DISTRIBUTIONS

In the Midtown Home Survey sample of 1,660 adults, our initial task is to inspect its four constituent age groups in terms of their distributions on the psychiatrists' gradient classification of symptom formation (for characteristics differentiating the Home Survey from the Treatment Census, see p. 191). To this end, table II–2 is now presented below.[3]

In table II–2, we might first note the facts that (1) in the youngest group, most recently emerged from adolescence, about 60 percent fall in the Mild and Moderate categories and (2) the proportions held by these categories remain remarkably stable across the succeeding three age columns.

We next observe that around the more or less unvarying rates of these pivotal, center-of-gravity grades of symptom formation, the frequencies of the other mental health categories *do* vary with age. Specifically, the three age strata above the thirty-year line (B,C,D) have appreciably fewer Wells than does the youngest group (A) in the sample.

Of special interest are the three symptom-formation classes subsumed under the Impaired category that defines our criterion of mental morbidity. All three of these conditions approximately double in their frequen-

TABLE II-2.   HOME SURVEY SAMPLE (AGE 20–59), RESPONDENTS' DISTRIBUTIONS ON
MENTAL HEALTH CLASSIFICATION BY AGE GROUPS

Mental health categories	Age groups			
	A. 20–29	B. 30–39	C. 40–49	D. 50–59
Well	23.6%	16.8%	19.3%	15.0%
Mild symptom formation.	37.5	37.6	37.0	33.1
Moderate symptom formation . .	23.6	22.4	20.5	21.1
Impaired	15.3	23.2	23.2	30.8
Marked symptom formation. .	9.6	14.7	11.6	16.4
Severe symptom formation . .	4.1	7.5	7.7	10.5
Incapacitated	1.6	1.0	3.9	3.9
N = 100%	(365)	(388)	(467)	(440)

cies between the extreme age groups, to produce contrasting overall morbidity rates of 15.3 and 30.8 percent, respectively; in the two middle age strata they yield an identical rate in the value of 23.2 percent.

We earlier directed particular attention to the Incapacitated respondents, whom Rennie viewed as ambulant counterparts of hospitalized patients encountered in his experience. They lend themselves, therefore, to comparison with the like-age Treatment Census inpatients reported in table II-1. We there observed a substantially flat trend in hospital patient rates of about 5 per 1,000 for all four age-strata in the twenty to fifty-nine range.

On the other hand, in the community sample presented in table II-2, we estimate that below the age forty line the incapacitation rate is approximately 13 per 1,000, and above that line it is 39 per 1,000. Clearly, prevalence rates of inpatients cannot serve as approximate indicators of intergroup differences in frequency of presumptively hospitalizable adults living in the community.

To be sure, the incapacitation rates, representing percentages small in magnitude, are particularly susceptible to chance fluctuations due to sampling. In a strict statistical sense, the latter could occasionally wipe out the difference in incapacitation rates between age groups B and C, for example. Such fluctuations are reduced, however, if the groups are enlarged by merging the two youngest age levels (A,B) and by pitting them against the combination of two oldest ones (C,D). Their difference is further enhanced when due account is taken of the evidence suggesting that people with disorders warranting hospitalization are exceptionally high mortality risks.[4] The inroads of such differential mortality would of course be reflected least in the younger age levels and most among the older people. Accordingly, it is plausible to assume that the 13:39 ratio of incapacitation, which appears when the sample age span is dichotomized, may be narrower than the real difference before mortality does its erosive work.

Returning to the inclusive impairment category in table II–2, we might mention that the difference between its frequencies in age groups A and B is statistically significant, above the .05 level of confidence, as is the difference between groups C and D. Nevertheless, we must now revive a relevant technical issue presented at some length in chapter 8. In discussing the psychiatrists' process of classifying the mental health condition of each sample respondent, we there indicated that this was done in two stages, designated Rating I and Rating II. For each respondent, the former classification was made without the psychiatrists' knowledge of his sociocultural-demographic alignments, or other information that might contaminate their judgments; Rating II was made with such additional data. Prompting this before-and-after experiment was the embattled rationale that the two ratings permit us analytically to assay, against the sample as a whole, whether information on the indicated demographic factors had detectably operated to bias or distort the Rating II mental health classifications. We have already reported that such analysis for the sociocultural type of factors has consistently given a negative reply to that question.

This test for possible judgmental bias on the part of the psychiatrists, attaching to their knowledge of respondent's *bisocial* alignments, cannot be made. It is barred by the fact that respondent's age, sex, and marital status were known to the Study psychiatrist in formulating his Rating I classification. Left open, thereby, is the critical question whether the observed age trend in the impairment rate is more or less unreal—an artifact of the Study psychiatrists' preconceptions—and, even if real, whether it is an idiosyncratic departure peculiar to the Midtown population. There are several types of collateral evidence that can be brought to bear in considering these pertinent questions.

In the first place, we have observations from three different studies of the screened but comprehensive national population of military-age service men (in the enlisted grades) during wartime. These investigations applied different criteria: (1) hospitalization rates for psychoneurosis among precombat men,[5] (2) psychiatric breakdown rates in combat units,[6] and·(3) overall psychiatric discharge rates from the service.[7]

Despite the fact that the upper age limit in the enlisted ranks of the military population was approximately thirty-seven, all three studies are consistent in reporting more psychiatric cases among the older men than among the younger. These findings parallel the difference in morbidity rates between the Midtown age groups A (twenty to twenty-nine) and B (thirty to thirty-nine) seen in table II–2.

Second, we have already called attention to shorter life expectancies known among people with mental disorders which may require hospitalization.[8] Predicating a similar tendency, perhaps not so frequent, among the greater number of people with less extreme mental disturbances, we would expect an effect on the Midtown age groups' mental morbidity rates in the following directions: To a greater extent than in younger groups A and B, the rates of older groups C and D are smaller than they would have been without the differential intervention of mortality.

On these grounds we can judge that the Midtown age trend observed in table II–2 is probably typical rather than idiosyncratic, substantive rather than artifactual; and, if anything, it may be less pronounced than it could expectedly have been had differential mortality not intruded.

HYPOTHESIZED SOCIAL PROCESSES IN THE AGE TREND OF MENTAL MORBIDITY

On this note, we can now move from the *how* to the *why* of the association between age and mental health as documented in table II–2. An obvious difficulty besetting such discussion is that age is not a pure factor, but rather a dimension along which many variables operate simultaneously and serially. Processes of premature organic degeneration may intrude in this prime-of-life sample of adults, as may loss of psychological flexibility and adaptability. Furthermore, in Midtown, as elsewhere, age differences are entangled with several other demographic variables, such as socioeconomic status, generation-in-U.S., and rural-urban background. For reasons of neatness in reporting, analytic unraveling of age from these demographic concomitants is better left to succeeding chapters. However, we can indicate here that the basic lines of the age-and-morbidity bond emerge intact from these analyses. Accordingly, under the investigator's prerogative to relate research data to provisional, hypothetical explanations suggested by his own frame of scientific reference, we will consider certain possible social mechanisms that may contribute in part toward effecting the above-mentioned bond. Of course, such formulations in no way rule out the possibility that other kinds of processes may likewise make their own contributions.

First to be emphasized is that the observed age trend in mental morbidity derives from four groups of people who were studied at the same point of time. However, to permit an excursion in speculation around the available data, let us make this simplifying but plausible assumption about the sample's youngest group (twenty to twenty-nine): If it were henceforth restudied at ten-year intervals, its current mental health composition would progressively change in the direction indicated by the successive age groups now constituting the Midtown sample. Stated differently, the relationship between age and mental morbidity revealed in table 11–2 would be essentially confirmed if it were humanly possible to study a single age-group "cohort" longitudinally over a forty-year period.

In this "as if" perspective, the age differentials in table 11–2 can be visualized as the reflection of *individual* changes in mental health. In net effect, after consideration of those persons who do not change between early adulthood and late middle age, or who improve between those two points, the residual, perhaps predominant, age changes in individuals could be postulated as follows: (1) from original wellness to the subclinical, Mild-Moderate conditions of symptom formation, or (2) from the latter to the less Impaired class, or, in turn, (3) from the latter state to the more severe forms of impairment. Through these inferred changes in time, the Well frequency would contract, the Impaired rate expand,

and the Mild-Moderate proportion remain roughly the same. Projected, nevertheless, would be a process of individual deterioration in mental health considerable in its magnitude within the study population. Without reifying this projection, let us explore it further under the theoretician's license to proceed on the formula: If Q should be real, then X (or Y or Z) could be one of its preconditions.

One's conceptual stance would undoubtedly determine which unknown (X or Y or Z) to stress in so hypothesizing. One view would of course relate the apparent mental health deterioration to the organic processes that seem to accompany adult aging. That the annual frequency of chronic somatic disorder on the national scene reportedly increases from 9.4 percent of the age twenty to twenty-four population to 31.1 percent of the age fifty-five to sixty-four population[9] appears at first glance to support this position.

Notable, however, is the fact that many of these disorders are of the type considered to be psychogenic "body language," expressing reactions to stressors in the life situation—and this body language in many cases may include the organic ravages of senility. Thus, if mental and physical health tend to wane together with progressive aging, both may be common and interdependent consequences of a third set of potent forces, namely, the individual's incessant encounters with a particularly abrasive social environment.

On the whole it seems rather doubtful that inherent processes of organic failings could be largely responsible for the impairment rate jump seen between the young Midtown age groups A and B. Nor need biological predetermination be held wholly accountable for the similar jump seen between groups C and D—any more, perhaps, than could the abbreviated longevity expectations of a century ago be explained by biological inevitability.[10]

We must leave the precise organic determinants in the age trend of mental morbidity rates to be delineated by investigators in the appropriate disciplines. Within the limiting boundaries of the Study's observational framework, we would call attention to several possible sociocultural disruptions in the transactions between the individual as an integral self and the interpersonal environment as his encompassing universe.

During the normal progression through married life, major pivotal points are first the arrival of children and then their departure from the home several decades later. A general pattern in our social system is its tendency to be casual and haphazard, if not neglectful, in preparing the individual to assume some of his most complicated social roles. Perhaps nowhere is this tendency more pronounced than at the juncture where, in many cases, the adolescent's grab-bag collection of "gutter" values and hearsay about coitus is applied for the first time in sexual intimacy with the opposite sex, and later, when he becomes a parent—as a rule without realistic forearming for the psychological intricacies and hazards of the role. It is as if he wanders onto a stage with other amateur actors and is there compelled to play a leading character part in a family drama —with little or no disciplining or direct experience in that kind of role. This may be likened to learning to swim by propulsion from a solid platform into deep water. Such a predicament in the sociocultural realm has been designated *role discontinuity* and is contrasted with *role continuity.*[11] The latter is probably seen in its most complete form in the prolonged, intensive training for the professional ministering occupations, for example, registered nurse, teacher, physician, and pastor.

Learning principally by common sense, trial and error, and the remembered example of their own parents, adults of more or less mature personality fit into the new role of parent without apparent excess of strain. On the other hand, among the immature left unprepared for the dynamic impact of their own young children, parenthood may dramatically stir up quiescent, unresolved conflicts or breach defenses that had previously contained them. Such a developmental sequence seems to be involved in postpartum disturbances among women. If so, it would appear to be a credible hypothesis that this particular manifestation is only the visible edge of a less acute but more widespread *crisis of role imbalance,* as we designate it, among relatively new fathers and mothers. Relevant to this hypothesis is the impression of Coleman and Zwerling that the maternal postpartum reaction "is more common in the community than is generally recognized."[12] Also pertinent is the report of Hornick[13] presenting clinical observations of the same kind of reaction in fathers.

Several other clues suggest support for the above hypothesis. One is the senior author's observations among adult mental patients generally that the recent critical turn of their condition is often tied up chronologically and dynamically with the emergence of unacceptable impulses toward their young children. This is paralleled by the generalization of psychiatrist Rittwagen: "Certain it is . . . that emotionally limited and infantile parents find understanding control of their children impossible. With few healthy defenses, they often crumble completely under the pressures of parenthood."[14] Also relevant, perhaps, is a study of forty-six young couples who were "average or above in personality adjustment." Referring to their reaction when their first child was born, thirty-eight couples (83 percent) reported the event as eliciting a severe or extensive emotional crisis.[15]

The pertinence of the above discussion to the specific focus of the present chapter is this: Midtown's age group A (twenty to twenty-nine) respondents are predominantly childless,[16] whereas those of age group B (thirty to thirty-nine) are relatively new parents in the main. The above formulation, in other words, may offer a plausible partial explanation for the significant difference between sample groups A and B in their frequencies both of Impaired and Well respondents. If the number of Impaired cases per 100 Well respondents is calculated, then the resulting "Impaired–Well" ratio is 65 in group A and 138 in group B. We shall have occasion to return to these groups in the chapter that follows.

Approaching their fifties parents generally enter a new stage in the social cycle of life. Often the prelude to this phase is the growing independence of the youngest child, now in the rebellion of adolescence. This is followed by the parents' more or less complete retirement from the child-sheltering and guidance function, enforced by the severing action of the offspring themselves. Several consequences may issue in the wake of this event. First, there is the change to an emptied, fundamentally "broken" home and a greatly shrunken range of parental activity. Among its other psychological functions, the parental role is generically akin to an institutional "office," into which is poured a considerable investment of personal identity and sentiment. Both roles carry leadership responsibilities that are ego buttressing and stabilizing, and both leave voids difficult to fill when they are lost.[17] Second, if the marital relationship between the parents has previously been less than mutually equilibrated, the void tends to bring out old and new strains as the couple face their change of family life alone.

Third is the anthropological fact that societies place differential value on the several age levels in the population. If China in its classical period was at one extreme in prizing the old over the new, especially in venerating the family's aged members,[18] contemporary American society is probably close to the opposite pole in tending to equate "old" with "junk."[19] Thus, when retired to the side lines as spectators of their children's own families, often under the implicit injunction that they should be seen but not heard, parents are aware that they have begun the slide of denigration in the eyes of important others.

Fourth, a century ago aging had psychological support in the continuity of "life eternal" under the religious doctrine of the immortality of one's essential self, or soul. Secularization following upon the scientific and industrial revolutions of the nineteenth century has widely toppled this pillar of religious faith. Thereby, approaching death has come to be viewed not as the curtain rising to the life beyond but as the curtain descending with the absolute closure of "finis."

On all these counts, we would suggest, the fifty to fifty-nine years of life are the opening to a period of jolting discontinuities in rapid sequence. Thus, of an American novelist who writes about "the fretfulness and decline of heart in middle-class people of middle years" it has been said that "his characters are constantly mourning as they cower beneath the assault of age on their ego." Appropriating a term from surgery, this is the beginning of years of "insult" to the individual's integrity and sense of self-worth.

When this drama of accelerating "fall" and role discontinuity is played out in adults harboring potentials for overt mental malfunction, we postulate that the consequences may in part become psychiatrically visible[20]—for example in the depression and involutional states of late middle age. The consequences may also come to medical attention in such diagnostic forms as hypertension, arthritis, arteriosclerosis, senility, and other observed somatic expressions of overwhelming psychic stress in the aging. Perhaps the magnitude of these consequences in first impact can be crudely discerned from the shift of mental morbidity rates between Midtown's age groups C (forty to forty-nine) and D (fifty to fifty-nine), as reported in table II–2. Among the former group, for example, the Impaired–Well ratio is 120, slightly under that of our respondent sample as a whole. Among the latter, significantly, this ratio rises to 205.

We have here proposed a series of hypotheses that attempt to articulate certain sociocultural observations to the age pattern of mental morbidity discerned in the Midtown sample. Further research will be required to tell us to what extent these postulated connections are real.

If these postulates should be more or less sustained, the following summarizing propositions might conceivably be in order:

1. The individual's infancy and childhood are crucial in implanting the predispositions for his subsequent mental health.

2. Among people with susceptibilities in the unfavorable direction, actual precipitations of disabling disturbance tend to cluster around points of individual shift in major social roles.

3. Where, in addition, the individual's defense-building preparation for one of these new roles is faulty, as not infrequently happens in our society, the chances are magnified that the culturally impelled shift will carry the force of both a situational crisis and a personal trauma.

4. Some of these role shifts follow from life-changing accidents and disasters that tend to befall people more or less at random in time and place. Others, given the necessary preconditions, tend to occur at more or less regular junctures in the adult social cycle.

5. One emergence of role imbalance among predisposed adults may occur when the arrival of children bestows the mantle of parenthood on shoulders unable to bear it; another may occur several decades later, when the active parental role is terminated and our contemporary values begin to condemn the individual to a castoff role of social obsolescence, deflated personal stature, and accelerating slide toward the final trauma of discontinuity; together, these two kinds of role change can be seen as major precipitating patterns that perhaps are no small links in the tangled chain of pathogenic processes at work in the Midtown population.

6. In numerous cases, the combination of a general predisposition to mental impairment and a specific vulnerability to these patterns of precipitation may be transmitted behaviorally in a direct family line (i.e., from parent to child to grandchild) in the absence of a transmitted genetic defect.[21] If so, the possibilities of mapping preventive interventions at certain regular points in the individual's social cycle would appear to be considerably enhanced.

HELP-NEED AND THE PATIENT-HISTORY VARIABLE

An earlier section of this chapter presented the Treatment Census report of age-specific rates for Midtown patients in psychiatric hospitals and clinics. From these data we learned that prevalence of hospitalized patients does not vary among the age segments within the twenty to fifty-nine range, whereas the prevalence of clinic outpatients within this chronological span decreases with age level.

When the unit being enumerated is the patient in a psychiatric facility, as was the case in our Treatment Census, then its frequency in a particular age group can only be calculated as a rate per 100,000 of the *total* population in that group. Such a rate, strictly speaking, only answers this query: Among how many people in a given group do two specific events occur in conjunction, namely (1) perception that mental impairment is present and (2) entrance into a psychotherapeutic service for the care of that disability?

In the Home Interview Survey, on the other hand, we can isolate within each age group the Impaired category of respondents, as identified by the Study psychiatrists. Although a relatively small segment of the group's total population, the Impaired respondents are a more relevant criterion in weighing the selection problems hinging on what kinds of people are getting professional attention and what kinds are not. That is, the impairment class can be considered the population at risk of needing some form of professional help. With Rennie's support on the issue, we find warrant in equating the morbidity criterion of functional impairment with the service criterion of help-need. If this is correct, we can ask how these Impaired respondents distribute themselves among three crude types of "patient histories," namely (1) current outpatients —both of clinics and office therapists, (2) ex-patients—both of hospital and ambulatory facilities, and (3) never-patients. In table 11–3 below, we present these distributions for the Impaired of each age group.

Before discussing the above data, several preliminary observations might be offered. First, a review of table 11–2 will reveal that the Impaired respondents in the two oldest age brackets (C,D) had a relatively heavier

TABLE II–3.   HOME SURVEY SAMPLE (AGE 20–59), IMPAIRED RESPONDENTS'
DISTRIBUTIONS ON PATIENT-HISTORY CLASSIFICATION BY AGE GROUPS

Patient-history	Age groups			
	A. 20–29	B. 30–39	C. 40–49	D. 50–59
Current outpatients (ambulatory)	8.9%	8.9%	5.6%	1.5%
Ex-patients (ambulatory or hospital).	25.0	26.7	18.5	19.3
Ever-patients.	33.9	35.6	24.1	20.8
Never-patients	66.1	64.4	75.9	79.2
No. of Impaired = 100%	(56)	(90)	(108)	(135)

concentration of incapacitated-grade people than did their Impaired equivalents in the youngest age groups (A,B). From this fact, we can infer that the older Impaired respondents on the whole had more urgent help-need cases than did their junior counterparts. Second, among chronic disorders generally, the chances of exposure to appropriate professionals (in this context, to psychotherapists) would in theory tend to mount cumulatively with increasing age.

If, therefore, we were plausibly to expect that the number of help-needy who had been in treatment facilities would expand progressively in successive age groups, table II–3 does not confirm the expectation. In fact, it reveals the contrary to be the case—that is, the older Impaired (groups C,D) have the larger proportions of never-patients. In succeeding chapters we shall see other instances of differential flow of the help-needy population through the clogged channels of the treatment services.

SUMMARY

The sample of Midtown adults examined by our Home Survey operation was here viewed as divided into ten-year intervals on the spectrum of age.

In the distributions of the sample's four age groups on the symptom-formation classification scheme applied by the Study psychiatrists, the following main patterned tendencies were seen:

1. The Mild-Moderate categories of symptom-formation, presumably defining the subclinical range of mental disturbance, were almost identically represented in all the age brackets.

2. The Well proportions in the three older groups (that is, above the thirty-year age line) were significantly smaller than that of the youngest adults, age twenty to twenty-nine.

3. Standing as Rennie's criterion of mental morbidity, the Impaired condition described a three-step progression in frequency along the sample's age continuum. It was least prevalent among the youngest respondents, most prevalent among the oldest, and identically intermediate in frequency among the two middle age groups.

The possibilities were considered that this age trend in mental morbidity rates was a reflection either of an atypical population or of an artifact in the classification process of the Study psychiatrists. Available evidence suggested the remoteness of such possibilities.

The sample's four age groups were studied at a single point of time, and such a cross-sectional survey is very different, operationally, from a longitudinal study of a single age cohort over a four-decade span of time. Nevertheless, it seemed to be a plausible assumption that if the latter investigation could be conducted, the basic lines of the relationship between age and overall mental morbidity would be reproduced more or less as found in Midtown and in other general populations cited.

This reasonable assumption permitted us to draw a potentially important suggestion from the Midtown age trend in frequency of mental impairment; namely, a substantial process of slippage in mental health seems to mark the path of individual progression through the twenty to fifty-nine age range.

On the chance that this inference would ultimately be sustained, it was necessary to propose hypotheses which might explain, at least in part, how such decline in mental health could come about through the prime-of-life segment of the adult years.

It was possible, of course, to hypothesize that such deterioration is first generated by the inherent trend toward organic wear and tear and toward loss of psychological flexibility that seems to accompany the approach to journey's end. With specifying elaboration of this general hypothesis being left to more appropriate disciplines, it was held here that such somatic change could hardly, in itself, be independent of the individual's weathering exposure to the particular elements of his social environment and its potential abundance of stressors.

If there is etiological "elbow room" for the influence of sociocultural factors upon mental health along the temporal course of adult aging, there was warrant to suggest hypotheses specifying the identity of several such potential factors.

The series of postulates advanced to this end did not represent an effort to include all promising sociocultural elements that might be involved. Instead, we confined ourselves to major facets of the rather powerful umbrella concept of *role discontinuity*. This refers to a variety of situations of disjunction or jolting transition in shifting from one social role to another. Many individuals in our society experience such rough stretches in the cycle of social roles. However, when this happens to human vehicles built from childhood with tendencies toward psychic malfunction, then these rough stretches may be points at which latent pathology tends to break out into overt disability.

In line with this theory, offered to account for the marked difference in mental health composition observed between the twenty to twenty-nine and thirty to thirty-nine age groups was the recent shift of the latter to the parent role—often with few specific defenses for the new psychological complexities that a young child presents to the disturbed adult.

Offered to account for a similar difference between the forty to forty-nine and fifty to fifty-nine age groups was the recent termination of the latter's active child-rearing functions, often without adequate prior preparation for the role vacuum thereby created. We further postulated that aggravating this development for such people in late middle life was the beginning of a process of social downgrading that is particularly sharp in American society. This, in recent years, has given the over sixty age segment in the population many of the stigmata of a minority group subject to social discrimination on a purely biological criterion. Also hypothesized as an aggravating factor is that the continuity between life and afterlife, historically a rock of religious doctrine and of individual support in the declining years, has largely been worn away by the tides of secularization.

All in all, compared with the situation a century ago when grandparents (1) were more completely integrated in a stronger kinship group, (2) were more highly valued by children and community alike, and (3) were sustained by expectations of the life beyond, the sixth decade of life (that is, age fifty to fifty-nine) now carries a quite different atmosphere and meaning for its occupants. Despite greatly increased longevity and higher material standards of living, this phase of life now has a built-in series of stressors that appear to be noxious for many people and functionally disabling for the predisposed in particular.

Thus, the age trend in mental health composition, as exposed by the Midtown sample, seems to be compatible with the evolution of the adult's parental role and the notion of role discontinuity as a precipitant of mental morbidity.

Also of concern in this chapter was the age representation in the traffic of Midtowners through available psychiatric facilities. From its coverage of all patients in mental hospitals and clinics, our Treatment Census could give us rates expressing the coincidence of need perceived and therapy sought, relative to the total population in each age segment. For the four age groups in the twenty to fifty-nine range, at least, these rates described a level age trend for hospital patients and a descending age trend for clinic patients.

In our Home Survey, on the other hand, the Impaired respondents represented the help-needy who are at risk of requiring psychiatric help. Calculating current outpatient rates (in clinic and office facilities) and ex-patient rates (in hospital and ambulatory services) revealed the under age forty Impaired as having higher frequencies of both than their older equivalents in symptom-formation.

The double-barreled inference to be extracted is that with less pathological provocation on the whole, younger adults in need are more likely than their senior counterparts to find their way to a treatment haven. Certainly, on the scale of age psychiatric patients are hardly representative of the population presumably in need of professional help.

NOTES

[1]From office therapists it was not feasible to secure information on age of patient or any other demographic factor except one to be discussed in chapter 15.

[2]To check this age trend in prevalence, we have also determined the age-specific, one-year incidence rates of Midtown residents admitted to a public or private mental hospital from May 2, 1953 through May 1, 1954. Since the prevalence count included patients hospitalized for the first time and also those who were repeaters, we similarly included in the annual incidence count both first admission and readmission cases. The general nature of the age trend that emerged is indicated by hospital incidence rates in the twenty to twenty-nine and fifty to fifty-nine age groups of 333 and 360 (per 100,000 corresponding population), respectively.

[3]In presenting distribution tables to follow we will not systematically introduce a statistical measure that many students might consider mandatory, that is, significance of difference between two percentages. On the whole, we are primarily concerned not with the specific size of the difference (for example, in morbidity rates) between pairs of groups, but with the general pattern and direction of the distributions across the entire spectrum of our test variables. Moreover, accreditation of statistical significance may prove to be seriously misleading if the relationship so certified in a table melts away when an additional factor is analytically introduced. On both these grounds we intend to put such seeming statistical imprimaturs to sparing use.

In the text, hereafter, a difference between two percentages will not be tagged as significant unless it is at or above the .05 level of confidence. This criterion means that the odds are at least ninety-five to five against the difference being a chance occurrence due to fluctuations inherent in sampling.

[4]M. Kramer, "The Concepts of Incidence and Prevalence as Related to Epidemiological Studies of Mental Disorders," *American Journal of Public Health* 47 (July 1957): 838.

[5]S. Stouffer et al., *The American Soldier,* 1949, vol. 1, p. 114; vol. 4, p. 512.

[6]Col. A. J. Glass, "Observations upon the Epidemiology of Mental Illness in Troops during Warfare," in *Symposium on Preventive and Social Psychiatry,* Walter Reed Army Research Institute, 1958, p. 194.

[7]E. Ginsberg, *The Lost Divisions,* 1959, p. 111.

[8]For a wider range of cases see also the study reported in "Prognosis after Recovery from Disability Due to Mental Disorders," *Statistical Bulletin,* vol. 38, Metropolitan Life Insurance Company, January 1957.

[9]S. D. Collins, K. S. Trantham, and J. L. Lehmann, *Sickness Experience in Selected Areas of the U.S.,* Public Health Monograph, 1955, pp. 8–21. This monograph reports data on 100 diagnoses, classified by severity, from five large surveys that covered three communities and thirty-six state populations. Involved were "80,768 full-time person-years of observation."

[10]For discussion of the problem in large perspectives, see Gardner Murphy, "Biological Changes in Man," *Human Potentialities,* 1958, pp. 218–242.

[11]For these concepts we are beholden to an unusual series of papers contributed by social scientists and psychiatrists. Cf. R. Benedict; "Continuities and Discontinuities in Cultural Conditioning," *Psychiatry* 1 (1938): 161–167; T. Parsons, "Age and Sex in the Social Structure of the United States," *American Sociological Review* 5 (October 1942): 604–616; L. Cottrell, Jr., "Age and Sex Roles," *American Sociological Review* 7 (October 1942): 617–620; I. Belknap and H. J. Friedsam, "Age and Sex Categories as Sociological Variables in the Mental Disorders of Later Maturity," *American Sociological Review* 14 (June 1949): 367–376; M. E. Linden and D. Courtney, "The Human Life Cycle and Its Interruptions: A Psychologic Hypothesis," *American Journal of Psychiatry* 109 (June 1953): 906–915; and M. Mead, "Cultural Discontinuities and Personality Transformation," *Journal of Social Issues,* Supplement Series, no. 8, 1954.

Particularly important are the investigations of T. S. Tyhurst, as summarized and advanced in his paper, "The Role of Transition States—Including Disasters—in Mental Illness," *Symposium on Preventive and Social Psychiatry,* Walter Reed Army Institute of Research, 1958, pp. 149–172.

[12]M. D. Coleman and I. Zwerling, "The Psychiatric Emergency Clinic," *American Journal of Psychiatry* 115 (May 1959): 980–984.

[13]E. Hornick, "The Post-partum Depression among Men," unpublished paper.

[14]M. Rittwagen, *Sins of Their Fathers,* 1958, p. 222.

[15]E. E. LeMasters, "Parenthood as Crisis," *Marriage and Family Living* 19 (November 1957): 352–355. It is of interest that inadequate preparation for the parental role was the explanation offered by most of the subjects who experienced the crisis. One mother was quoted to the effect that "we knew where babies came from, but we didn't know what they were like."

[16]Of this group, almost half (48 percent) are still single, whereas in the next older group the corresponding figure is 27 percent.

[17]It is of course no accident that in many cultures the marriage ceremony and celebration symbolically acknowledge the underlying grief of the parents of bride and groom at losing not the child but the sentiment-charged child-rearing office.

[18]M. Granet, *Chinese Civilization,* 1930, pp. 327–343.

[19]Explicitly applied first to the consumer products of industrialization, this value equation has implicitly come to be applied to human beings as well.

[20]In discussing the psychotic mother of a delinquent, Rittwagen observes that such parents "usually become overwhelmed and threatened when their children start to assert themselves and grow away from them . . . because of their need for their children's love and their own immature dependency." *Sins of Their Fathers,* p. 135.

[21]A mentally disturbed parent, locked into a morbid relationship with the child who has innocently exacerbated his pathology, will likely implant that child with a double dosage of vulnerability to his own subsequent offspring. As in congenital syphilis, each sick parent is potentially an infecting agent, through his behavior, of subsequent generations of descendants.

CHAPTER 12

MALES AND FEMALES, BEFORE AND AFTER MARRIAGE

LEO SROLE AND THOMAS LANGNER

Vive la difference! is a universal salute to the complementary biological arrangements of the two sexes. Building on these basic biological designs, cultures universally have fashioned variously differentiated and complementary social roles for males and females as they proceed together through each successive stage of the life cycle.[1] These parallel role "tracks" are so firmly mapped from early childhood onward that sex-appropriate behavior becomes a major theme in the unfolding image of one's identity, with lasting impress on personality development. Thus, organic and social forces interweave to make sex one of the primary lines of differentiation in a community population.

Clearly the question of the linkage between the sex variable and tendency toward mental disturbance is of fundamental interest and has long attracted epidemiological investigators. In general, studies of hospital patients have shown higher rates for males. On the other hand, surveys of community populations have not produced consistent results. Some report higher mental disorder rates among females,[2] whereas others yield similar rates for the two sexes.[3]

TREATMENT CENSUS FINDINGS

The Midtown Treatment Census, covering the entire age range, does not offer particular clarification on the point. Among its clinic patients, mainly adolescents and younger adults, males outnumber females in prevalence rates at almost all age levels from five upward. For Midtown hospital patients confined less than five years the situation is more complex. Specifically, males have higher rates in all age groups between five and twenty-nine, females are more numerous in the decade age levels above the age of forty, and the two sexes are evenly balanced in the thirty to thirty-nine age group.

HOME SURVEY SAMPLE: MENTAL HEALTH DISTRIBUTIONS

For a more promising test of the hypothesis that differences in mental health composition exist between the two sexes, we can refer to the Midtown Home Survey and its representative sample of the entire Midtown population in the twenty to fifty-nine age range. There we can compare the mental health distributions of males and females within each of the four decade age groups. Such comparison reveals that in no age group is there a statistically significant sex difference. Stated differently, the separate mental health distributions of males and females are essentially that of their age group as presented in table II-2. Thus, we can seemingly infer that in the defined Midtown adult population, at least, the sex factor is unrelated to the frequency of mental morbidity.[4]

It will be remembered, however, that the Study psychiatrists knew the sex of each respondent in formulating their preliminary Rating I classification. Accordingly, we are unable to assert with complete confidence that the null relationship just reported does not reflect different preconceptions held by the psychiatrists about the sexes. Of course, such prejudgments could convert a true difference into a spurious no difference. We shall deal with this problem in connection with the variable of marital status, which we can now proceed to explore.

When Midtown males and females are next analyzed in relation to the biosocial factor of groups varying in marital status, a somewhat sharper picture emerges. It should be emphasized, however, that, unlike age and sex, marital status in our view cannot qualify as an independent demographic variable relative to mental health. On the contrary, elements of mental health may be crucially involved in determining whether or not individuals choose to marry; if they do so choose, whether or not they are successful in finding a spouse; and if they are successful in this respect, whether or not the marriage is subsequently broken by divorce.[5]

Thus, far from being independent of mental health, marital status must be regarded as a factor that is very largely open to determination by personality processes. However, it is also obvious that the several variants of marital status, once established, may exert different kinds of change impacts upon subsequent mental health. If so, marital status and mental health are related to each other by a process of mutual interaction in time. On this criterion, marital status, for purposes of the present Study, must be placed in the category of reciprocal[6] demographic variables.

In order to isolate the specific change potential of each kind of marital condition, a different kind of research undertaking is required. That is, it would have to be the before-and-after type of investigation which starts with samples of individuals who are psychiatrically well delineated at the threshold of the marrying age, and are later restudied psychiatrically in terms of their intervening marital paths and experiences. The present Study, focused on a sample of individuals at one point in time, cannot empirically disentangle the specific consequences of each marital state for subsequent changes in mental health. Nevertheless, it can attempt to weigh the findings from its marital groups in terms of such concepts and knowledge as can be relevantly marshaled. One useful purpose, of course, would be to circumscribe further pockets of high mental morbidity risks in the Midtown population. Another would be to extract germane hypotheses that might be the focus of differently designed investigations in the future. New postulates, thrown off by a researcher as targets for his successors, are an indispensable part of the scientific process.

As we probe each of a series of demographic factors in the Midtown sample population, our first interest is addressed to the varying prevalence of mental morbidity. Up to this point we have learned that such morbidity on the whole tends to increase in frequency with age. Accordingly, in coming now to assess marital status and its links to mental health, the age factor must continue to be kept firmly in the picture, especially as the married group on the average is older than the unmarried and younger than the widowed.[7] Therefore, in comparing the several marital groups we must again do so only for people of like age.[8] Furthermore, there is a possibility not to be ignored that the linkage to mental disturbance of one or more marital conditions may not be the same for men and women.[9] Accordingly, to test this possibility in assessing marital status we must take into account the sex as well as the age factor.

However, when three demographic factors must be analyzed simultaneously against a fourth, i.e., mental health, the number of demographic subgroups produced becomes inordinately large and the number of sample respondents left in such subgroups diminishes correspondingly. As a result, the small number of cases in the extreme categories of the morbidity range thin out to a point of statistical instability. This can be countered only by merging the Incapacitated, Severe, and Marked symptom-formation classes into the more comprehensive Impaired category that is our inclusive criterion of mental morbidity. For economy of tabular presentation, we shall in the present chapter concentrate on this key category alone.

Turning now to table 12–1, we can there examine the impairment frequencies among sample men and women who are married.[10] Within every age group, it is amply clear, the married men and the wives are nearly identical[11] in their proportions of individuals who fall into the Impaired range of the mental health classification. It must be added that these men and women are also alike on all age levels in their frequencies of individuals classified as Moderate or Mild symptom formation, or as Well.

TABLE 12–1. HOME SURVEY SAMPLE (AGE 20–59), PROPORTION OF IMPAIRED RESPONDENTS AMONG MARRIED MALES AND MARRIED FEMALES OF LIKE AGE

	Age groups			
	A. 20–29	B. 30–39	C. 40–49	D. 50–59
Married males.	11.7%	19.6%	19.0%	25.7%
N = 100%	(60)	(112)	(142)	(136)
Married females.	13.4%	22.1%	18.1%	30.6%
N = 100%	(112)	(136)	(155)	(134)

These close similarities in overall mental health composition do not necessarily imply like effects on the mental health of the two sexes that are specifically attributable to the married condition. That is, the data may conceal the operation of several different kinds of influence which happen to add up to the same net result. For example, it has been hypothesized that, compared with her spouse, the wife, being more circumscribed in her extrafamily role outlets may be far more dependent on the marital relationship to "achieve a comparable overall satisfaction-frustration balance. . . . In highly oversimplified terms, the husband may depend on the marriage to gratify a minor portion of his needs while the wife may depend on it to gratify a major portion of hers."[12] If so, the wife would tend to be more vulnerable psychologically than the husband to conflicts generated in their relationship to each other. In that case, and other factors being equal, it could be hypothesized that marital strains are potentially more unbalancing for women than for men, a situation that might conceivably register on the former by swinging their impairment rates higher and their Well proportions lower than before marriage.

Of course, other factors are not equal. Obviously, on his part a husband is centrally involved in a career-work situation. He may depend on this as a major source of gratification, but in turn it can generate its own inherent set of pressures. In the position of primary family breadwinner, his dependence upon the work role would probably tend to make him particularly vulnerable to its manifold points of potential stress. If so, such stresses would plausibly tend to have greater impact on the husband than on his wife.

If, as is hypothesized, conflicts in the marital relationships are more serious for wives and strains in the work setting more disturbing for husbands, then the similarities in the mental health distributions of the two groups would seem to suggest that the net effects of the two different sets of potentially unbalancing forces may be of approximately the same magnitude. Accordingly, our data notwithstanding, we cannot assume as yet that the married state has in itself like mental health consequences for the two sex groups in the Midtown population.

We move now to inspect the single[13] men and women (table 12–2), with their impairment rates on each age level. The rates for wives have been transposed from table 12–1 to serve as an additional comparison group.

TABLE 12–2. HOME SURVEY SAMPLE (AGE 20–59), PROPORTION OF IMPAIRED RESPONDENTS AMONG SINGLE MALES, SINGLE FEMALES, AND WIVES OF LIKE AGE

| | Age groups | | | |
	A. 20–29	B. 30–39	C. 40–49	D. 50–59
Single men.	20.5%	30.4%	37.5%	46.1%
N = 100%	(78)	(46)	(32)	(26)
Single women	11.2%	12.1%	24.6%	25.6%
N = 100%	(98)	(58)	(57)	(43)
Married women	13.4%	22.1%	18.1%	30.6%
N = 100%	(112)	(136)	(155)	(134)

We observe first that on none of the four age levels do the single females differ significantly in impairment rates from the wives.[14]

The single men, on the other hand, reveal a strikingly different story. Relative to the morbidity rates for the single females—and to the married men in table 12–1—the impairment frequencies of the bachelors are higher by wide margins[15] along the entire axis of age. More precisely, on three age levels the impairment rate of the bachelors is consistently about twice or more that of the single women, and on one age level (forty to forty-nine) this rate is half again larger than that of the spinsters. What can account for this large contrast across the entire age range covered? Three major directions of interpretation seem open to us in attempting to answer the question posed about the observed differences between unmarried men and women: (1) The differences are an artifact of the Study psychiatrists' preconceptions; (2) the unmarried state is more pathogenic for males than for females; (3) there is a differentially selective sifting of single males and females into the Study area.

The first possible interpretation is opened by the fact that in making the Rating I mental health assignment for each respondent, the Study psychiatrists knew his/her marital status (and also age). Accordingly, we cannot test for the possibility that this key piece of information had inadvertently served to bring certain preconceptions into the psychiatrists' evaluations of respondents' mental health. Such a preconception might readily be derived from previous studies of patient populations that uniformly have shown exceptionally high rates of hospitalization for unmarried adults. This could then be projected upon a community population through the psychiatrists' assumption that nonmarriage is a potential confirming sign of personality malfunction and psychopathology.

If this assumption did enter into the psychiatrists' classification process, table 12–2 seems to tell us that it was applied to the single males but not to the single females. If so, this would appear to imply a sex bias directed only toward bachelors.

However, if such a bias were operating, the psychiatrists would be most unlikely to view the unmarried condition among metropolitan males in the age twenty to twenty-nine range as in any way a pathognomonic sign. Yet table 12–2 reveals the impairment rate among these youngest single men to be almost twice that of like-age single females. It may then be argued that the bias was directed only to bachelors above the age of thirty. If so, the impairment rates of the latter would have deviated from those of like-age spinsters to a greater extent than the difference between single males and single females in the youngest group. However, table 12–2 shows that beyond the age of thirty the bachelor-spinster differences in impairment rates are on the whole of about the same magnitude as the difference below the age of thirty. Hence the possibility of judgmental bias narrowly attached to older unmarried men finds no apparent support in the available data.[16]

By extension, parenthetically, it also appears unlikely that the Study psychiatrists were laboring under a generalized sex bias that, with knowledge of sexual identity of respondents, could have contaminated their judgments of mental health. This improbability finds a limited measure of reinforcement in a community sample study conducted by Bellin and Hardt among 1,541 people in the age range over 64.[17] Their methods in many respects paralleled those of the Midtown Home Interview Survey. Their criterion of mental morbidity was symptom formation suggestive that a respondent "may be certifiable" for admission to a state mental hospital. Certainly this is a far more exclusive criterion than that applied to the Midtown sample. Nevertheless, it is of some interest that the Bellin and Hardt study parallels the Midtown finding of no overall sex difference in morbidity rates. All in all, therefore, it seems rather unlikely that this Midtown finding conceals any distorting bias in the psychiatrists' mental health evaluations of the two sexes.

With reference again to table 12-2, a second interpretation of the data would fix on the possibility that singleness for males is somehow more pathogenic than is spinsterhood among females. Although lacking face plausibility, this is an issue to which we shall return presently. Indirect assessment of such a possibility may follow from the third, and very different, line of interpretation. This focuses on a complicated process of psychosocial selection intrinsic to mating phenomena in Western societies—one that tends to sort somewhat different kinds of individuals into the several marital groups.

We have earlier suggested that personality elements are inevitably involved in determining marital status. How, in general, do they seem to operate in relation to the unmarried? Selection criteria permit the definition of several different types of single people. One is the self-chosen, or *confirmed,* type often found beyond the age of thirty, and characterized on the whole by personalities that require the individuals, for one of a series of possible psychodynamic reasons, to avoid seeking or accepting a spouse. It can be hypothesized that this type tends to fall outside the Well sector of the mental health spectrum.

However, not all single people are of the self-chosen type. Beyond these, a key factor in the selection process hinges upon cultural forces that press upon males the active initiator role in courtship and upon females the passive secondary role. Under these culture-bound roles, males who actively seek a wife but fail to find acceptance of their overtures or proposals can be represented as the *rejected* type. It seems likely that repeated rejections of an eligible man, in the open, eager-beaver market of single women, can only result from the handicap of physical or personality deviations,[18] often accompanied by intrinsic mental disturbance. On the other hand, limited by their circumscribed and passive role in the market of eligible men, women awaiting but failing to get an acceptable proposal of marriage often are not so much rejected as *unchosen.*[19]

Now, in a community that has like numbers of single males and females, the number of bachelors, self-chosen and rejected, will force a similiar number of women into spinsterhood. Some few of the latter will be of the self-chosen type, probably corresponding in mental health composition to the parallel type among the bachelors. Similarly, among the unchosen women will be many bypassed because of physical or personality deviations that would likely make them the equivalent in mental health make-up of the rejected bachelors.

Here, we hypothesize, another cultural factor enters, namely, that many males in their active courting roles tend to choose a wife who enhances their culturally conditioned self-image of masculine dominance. As a result, we suggest that women with strong, independent personalities, or with other especially gifted native endowments,[20] are bypassed more often than their sisters with less outstanding qualities. Thus, in a community with like numbers of males and females we postulate that, compared to the rejected bachelors, the unchosen spinsters, including such "special" women will as a group be more heterogeneous in mental health composition.[21]

In a community like Midtown, or Manhattan at large, the selection processes sorting people into the several marital categories become vastly more complicated. As reported in chapter 4, here among the unmarried there is a considerable excess of females, reflecting that more young women than young men migrate to Manhattan, principally from areas beyond New York City. Because the barriers to breaking away from family and kinship ties are usually far higher for female migrants, it appears likely that on the whole these women include a larger representation of the hardy in character and mental health than do the male migrants. Among them would probably also be found the outstanding women, whose aspirations for finding an acceptable mate would seem best attainable in the metropolis.

The second phase of personality screening winnows the unmarried in-migrants who settle permanently in Manhattan and those who make the round trip back. At this point, Manhattan's unbalanced sex ratio would tend to have different sorting-out consequences for these newcomer males and females. Specifically, the more disturbed the male, the more likely would Manhattan's excess supply of single women offer him a larger chance than he would have back home of finding acceptance, rather than rejection, as a suitor. On the other hand, the more disturbed the female, the more likely would Manhattan's undersupply of single men diminish her chances of finding a husband there. In the light of the different marriage chances in the home town recently departed, the more disturbed males would tend to stay in Manhattan, whereas the more disturbed females would tend to return to their homes. In other words, this particular selection process would tend to further "purify" the remaining unmarried Manhattan females as a mentally healthier group on the whole, while enlarging representation of the disturbed within the permanently settled bachelor group.

The final stage in the sifting process occurs when the permanently settled single men and women encounter each other in the search for a spouse. The decisive factor here is again the unbalanced sex ratio, as manifested in Midtown's age twenty to twenty-nine unmarried group, where the females outnumber the males by a ratio of 125:100.

To judge from our sample, for every 100 men of age thirty to thirty-nine, 70 are married and 30 are bachelors. Hypothetically, if these 70 husbands (in every 100 males) had drawn their wives from the original 125 single women age twenty to twenty-nine just mentioned, then remaining unmarried a decade later would be 55 of the latter women (that is, 125 minus 70). By estimate from our sample, about one-fourth of these single women may finally have left the study area, and probably the City, for better husband "pickings" elsewhere.

Now let us consider the hypothetical 30 bachelors (per 100 males) and 42 spinsters (55 minus the 13 departures) in the age thirty to thirty-nine group—whose numbers are convertible into a sex ratio of 140 females per 100 males. These bachelors, as the self-chosen or rejected residue of a group that a decade earlier already had relatively many Impaired individuals and few Well, are now even more heavily unbalanced in number of Impaired relative to number of Wells. That is, in the interim the healthier men had chosen to marry, thereby depleting the representation of Well individuals among the remaining bachelors.

The age thirty to thirty-nine spinsters, on the other hand, are the residue of a group characterized a decade earlier by a relatively high Well rate and a low Impaired rate and presumably further purified since by the probable dominance of disturbed females among those departing the area.

The single women remaining are likely in largest part to be of the unchosen type. But it will be remembered that these are women now well established in careers based in Manhattan's pace-setting economy.[22] And it is postulated that they are unchosen for either of two principal reasons: (1) They have special qualities which, by cultural emphasis in mate selection, leave them unchosen by the kind of men they would accept; (2) they are affected by the sheer quantitative scarcity of eligible men, which reduces their chances of establishing after-work relationships with potential mates—even for women who, under a more favorable sex ratio, would certainly be among the chosen.

This interpretation, cast in the form of hypotheses or probability statements, rests on a formulation of personality selection mechanisms in mating. Fitted into this formulation have been observations about a series of sociocultural factors that independently of each other influence the personality selection processes. The major ones are (1) sex differentials in self-recruitment for in-migration to and emigration from the metropolis, (2) generalized sex-differentiated patterns in courtship and mate choice, and (3) a local sex ratio characterized by an excess of females.

It is probable that each of these by itself tends to have the opposite effects of *enlarging* somewhat the number of non-Well males and *reducing* somewhat the number of non-Well females who remain in the single state. Operating together in Midtown, the combined effect of these factors, we postulate, is to leave behind in the unmarried category, on all age levels, males and females who are highly contrasting in their group mental health composition.

Remaining open is the earlier question suggested by our data, namely, whether the single (unmarried) state is intrinsically more pathogenic for men than for women. Of course, to answer this question definitively would require a longitudinal study of the two groups, matched in mental health composition when they were crossing into the marrying age. According to our present formulation, the Midtown bachelors and spinsters, far from being so matched, by social selection processes have been differently "loaded" in mental health composition, even among their youngest (age twenty to twenty-nine) element. And these loadings have been so heavy as to obscure any differential effects, specific to the single state, among men and women.

Moreover, we would venture the hypothesis that if there are such differential effects specific to the unmarried state they would in the main tend in the direction of greater situational stress for women than for men originally of like mental health condition. This postulate is suggested by the probability that the compensations for lack of a family life, such as are partially provided by a career, may be intrinsically smaller for women than for men. Furthermore, unmarried women are handicapped by the cultural fact that theirs is a more restricted, insecure, and anomalous role in the extrafamily social spheres to which they must look for their major compensations.

Seeming to support this hypothesis are the indications that unmarried career women predominantly remain ready at the "drop of the right hat" to pick up the full role of domesticity. A national sample of young women (age unreported) were asked: "Which would you rather be if you had a choice: be unmarried and have a successful career; be married and have a successful career; be married and run a home?" Of the employed single women in this sample, only 7 percent chose the first alternative, another 20 percent the second, and 70 percent the third.[23]

Seeming to contradict this hypothesis, on the other hand, is a finding of the Bellin-Hardt community study of mental health among the aged in a New York upstate city.[24] With their criterion of mental morbidity, these authors report almost identical rates for unmarried men and women in the covered age range (sixty-five and over). However, let us assume that interlocking in-migration and emigration selection processes during the young adulthood of these subjects had been such as were postulated above, namely, leaving these spinsters, as a group, originally of better mental health composition than the bachelors. If so, the present *like* mental morbidity rates of the single men and women would suggest the possibility of greater deterioration among the latter since their younger adult years. Should this turn out to be the case, it would of course support the hypothesis that the unmarried state by and large may entail greater deprivational handicaps for women than for men.

From the single people we might next turn to the widowed, who appear in any numbers only among the sample females. And even here we are compelled to merge the age thirty to thirty-nine and forty to forty-nine groups[25] for comparison with the age fifty to fifty-nine widows.

For such comparative purposes let us take the sample wives of like age as our point of reference.

Premature loss of the wife role, through death of husband in the middle years of life, would certainly qualify as a situation of discontinuity in vacating a highly invested social role. We could therefore plausibly expect this role transition to belong to the order of accidental, crisis events that tend to catalyze latent mental pathology toward more overt forms of malfunction. This expectation seems to be strengthened in the finding of the Bellin-Hardt[26] investigation that the widowed (in their age population) of both sexes had higher morbidity rates than did the still married.

However, processes of psychosocial selection can also be expected to complicate the picture among Midtown widows. To the extent that wives' personalities are directly or indirectly involved in hastening their husbands' deaths, prior to the latter event such wives might have differed in mental health from the generality of wives. However, it seems unlikely that the net differential between the two subgroups would have been large at that time.

More important, we hypothesize, is the selection process that determines which widows remain in Midtown and which leave the area. Usually, with loss of husband's income and the high cost of Manhattan housing, a widow could remain on the Island only if she had a self-supporting career, adult children capable of supporting her, or an independent income.[27]

If those widows who can meet the special requirements of remaining in Midtown are also in mental health respects a more favored group than those who depart the area, then this would reduce the difference in mental health composition previously postulated between the widowed and married categories of women. When table 12–3 below is considered, we observe that this seems to have happened.

In neither age column is the difference in impairment rates statistically significant. Nor, we would add, are the widows and wives different in their scatter among the other mental health categories.

Remaining for consideration is the divorced contingent, sufficiently represented in the Midtown sample only within the thirty to forty-nine age range. For purposes of comparison, table 12–4 places this group's

TABLE 12–3. HOME SURVEY SAMPLE, PROPORTION OF IMPAIRED RESPONDENTS AMONG WIDOWS AND WIVES OF LIKE AGE (AGE 30–59)

	Age groups	
	B-C. 30–49	D. 50–59
Widows	27.6%	26.9%
N = 100%	(29)	(52)
Wives	20.0%	30.6%
N = 100%	(291)	(134)

mental health distribution beside that of the married of like age and sex.

As was found in the Bellin-Hardt study,[28] the Midtown divorced of both sexes have the highest mental morbidity rates of all four marital status categories. In fact, these are the highest rates of any demographic groups reviewed to this point. The differences between the married and divorced groups in both Impaired and Well frequencies are well within the limits of statistical confidence. The ratio of Impaired to Well, roughly 1:1 among the married people of both sexes, is 6:1 among divorced women and 10:1 among divorced men.

The elements that probably converge to produce the standout morbidity rates among the divorced of both sexes seem to be more complicated

TABLE 12–4. HOME SURVEY SAMPLE, DISTRIBUTIONS ON MENTAL HEALTH CLASSIFICATION OF MARRIED AND DIVORCED (AGE 30–49 ONLY) BY SEX .

Mental health categories	Males		Females	
	Married	Divorced	Married	Divorced
Well	24.8%	4.0%	19.2%	7.0%
Mild symptom-formation	37.8	36.0	39.9	19.3
Moderate symptom-formation . .	18.1	20.0	21.0	31.6
Impaired	19.3*	40.0*	19.9†	42.1†
N = 100%	(254)	(25)	(291)	(57)

*t = 2.5 (.02 level of confidence).
†t = 3.6 (.001 level of confidence).

than those for any other marital status group. These factors may be briefly outlined in terms of the following probabilities:

1. When adults cross into the marriage relationship, those to undergo divorce are already less favorable mental health risks than the subgroup who will remain firm in their marriage.

2. For some, divorce itself entails a crisis or role break that can be a trauma no less shattering than widowhood. For others, however, it may signify liberation from a potentially destructive predicament. In such cases, divorce would be a eugenic rather than a pathogenic development.

3. Age at divorce is usually younger than age at widowhood. Thus, the divorced more often remarry. The residual group of divorced (after this sorting process) would likely be even less favorable in mental health composition than before.

4. Unlike the widows, the female divorcees, healthy or otherwise, can usually maintain themselves in the area through supporting alimony and, having fewer dependent children, through supplementary employment.

We believe, all in all, that the selection processes (1, 3, and 4 above) cumulatively contribute most to the exceptional mental health distributions seen among the divorced males and females in table 12–4 above, especially as the specific consequences of divorcement are by no means in a uniform direction.

By way of recapitulation, a significant relationship with mental health was found for age as an independent factor, but not for sex. When marital status was taken as a reciprocal demographic factor, in conjunction with sex, and age was controlled, significant differences in mental health composition were observed (1) between unmarried men and women, (2) but not between husbands and wives, (3) between the divorced and married of both sexes, (4) but not between widows and wives. The operation of various kinds of psychosocial selection processes was hypothesized to account for the sex differences in morbidity rates within a given marital group and for the marital status differences within one or both sex groups. The effects of these selection processes hamper the effort, in a cross-section study, to assess the discrete mental health consequences of the several marital states.

Left for future longitudinal research is this general hypothesis, which the present cross-section study could not test: Sociocultural differences in adult sex roles operate in such fashion that for unmarried people of like mental health the specific subsequent mental health impact of any given marital state tends to be less favorable for the female group than for the male. This hypothesis is prompted by a more general postulate; namely, *if two groups in a society stand to any degree in a controlling-controlled relationship, then the dominant group of the two would tend to have greater access to defensive resources for protection against the potential ravages of role crises.*

HELP-NEED AND THE PATIENT-HISTORY VARIABLE

Our second interest in this mental health tour of the demographic factors is focused on their relation to the behavior of coming under the professional care of a psychotherapist.

On this variable, we have surveyor "fixes" from two different sources of data. The first source is our Treatment Census operation, here necessarily limited to Midtown's combined clinic and hospitalized (under five years) patients. Expressed in treatment prevalence rates based on the total Midtown population in each marital status group,[29] we found, by way of brief summary: (1) higher rates among the unmarried than among the married people, which hold for both sexes on all adult age levels; (2) in the unmarried group, higher rates for males than for females; (3) in the married group, almost identical rates for the two sexes.[30]

However, such rates are of uncertain significance unless they are calculated in relation, not to the total population in a given group, but to the smaller population that satisfies the criterion of present morbidity risk. For this purpose, we can return to the Home Interview Survey where the Impaired category in the mental health classification serves as the Midtown psychiatrists' approximation of this criterion. From the sample respondents we also know whether they have ever been in a professional relationship with a psychotherapist, however brief or extended. This is our criterion of patient-history.

Narrowing the focus from the sample as a whole to the Impaired respondents severely limits our analytical possibilities. Nevertheless, we have been able to divide these respondents into a younger (twenty to thirty-nine) and an older (forty to fifty-nine) group, to subdivide these by sex, and to further subdivide the two sexes into single and now married—producing eight subgroups in all. The overall lifetime ever-patient rate among the Impaired respondents is 26.7 percent. Among seven of our eight Impaired subgroups the ever-patient frequency does not vary significantly from this percent figure. However, among the Impaired younger single males we find a patient rate of 57 percent. This contrasts with the 31 percent patient frequency of the Impaired like-age husbands and with the 22 percent of the Impaired like-age single women. In both instances the difference is statistically significant above the .05 level of confidence. Given that the younger Impaired bachelors are only thirty in number, we can push the analysis no further toward isolating the factors which might explain their unusually high patient rate.

This isolated subgroup excepted, we can infer that given an impaired level of mental health, men and women, married or unmarried, on the whole tend to have had recourse to a psychotherapist to about the same extent during their lifetime.

In short, when mental health (impairment) is held constant, the patient-history variable is unrelated to the sex and marital status factors. But since the Impaired frequency is itself higher for single males than for single females or married males, they would predictably also contribute most, in relative terms, to Midtown's present patient population. This prediction, based on the data of our Home Interview Survey, seems to be borne out by the data reported earlier from our Treatment Census operation. In Midtown at least, marital status is the only demographic factor on which differences of current patient rates happen to parallel the differences in overall prevalence of mental morbidity. With the treatment procurement variable more or less uniform, differences in overall morbidity rates *are* reflected by corresponding differences in patient rates. Whether this coincidence is a general or purely local phenomenon remains an open empirical question.

SUMMARY

Data from the Midtown community sample have here served several related purposes:

1. They have provided a basis for illustrating how exceedingly complex are the links between marital status, as a demographic variable of the reciprocal type, and present mental health.

2. In the light of these complexities, they have indicated the difficulties besetting attempts to draw etiological inferences from the findings of a cross-section study.

3. Toward longitudinal studies designed to isolate the specific effects of different marital states for those previously of like mental health, they have suggested a number of testable hypotheses relating to sex differences in sociocultural stress impacts.

4. They have illuminated that, at least in Midtown, particularly high prevalence or risk of mental pathology is to be found among single men and the divorced of both sexes.[31]

5. They have revealed that given mental pathology, patient rates on the whole do not differ between the single and the married of either sex. However, given the greater frequency of such pathology among the single men, the latter proportionately contribute the most to the patient loads of psychiatric hospital and clinic facilities.

NOTES

[1]M. Mead, *Male and Female*, 1949.

[2]*Chronic Illness in a Large City: The Baltimore Study*, 1957, p. 97; G. Gurin et al., *Americans View Their Mental Health*, 1960, pp. 41–42. On a list of twelve discrete symptoms explored by the National Health Examination Survey it was found that "women had significantly higher rates for every symptom." See H. J. Dupuy et al., "Selected Symptoms of Psychological Distress," National Center for Health Statistics, Series 11, no. 37, 1970, p. 5.

[3]W. F. Roth and F. R. Luton, "The Mental Health Program in Tennessee," *American Journal of Psychiatry* 99 (March 1943): 662–675.

[4]Needless to say, this statement in no way precludes the possibility of significant intersex differences in syndromal types of mental pathology.

[5]Unless otherwise indicated, we shall hereafter use the term *divorce* generically to cover separation as well.

[6]One study of hospital patients attempted to test a hypothesis in which marital status was formulated as an independent variable. The difficulties in generalizing from the test data to this hypothesis are illustrated in the study report. See L. M. Adler, "The Relationship of Marital Status to Incidence of Recovery from Mental Illness," *Social Forces* 32 (December 1953): 185–194.

[7]These differences in age composition, unless taken into account, would of course result in impairment rates spuriously low for the unmarried and spuriously high for the widowed.

[8]This is an analytical procedure known as holding constant or controlling a factor (in this instance, age) that may obscure or distort the relationship of a second factor (in this instance, marital status) to the study's dependent variable—in this instance, mental health.

[9]This can prove to be the case, of course, although there is no difference between the two sexes as inclusive groups.

[10]The married category throughout this report will exclude the separated.

[11]None of the male-female differences in the four columns of table 12–1 is statistically significant by the norm of an .05 level of confidence or better.

[12]Irving Rosow, "Issues in the Concept of Need-complementarity," *Sociometry* 20 (September 1957): 223.

[13]The *single* rubric throughout this report will include only the never married (as reported by each respondent).

[14]However, on the age thirty to thirty-nine level the impairment-rate difference of single females and wives nears statistical significance at the not unrespectable .07 level of confidence. Here the wives are also, in large part, relatively new mothers (see discussion in chapter 11).

[15]On all age levels, the differences between unmarried males and unmarried females are statistically significant at the .001 level of confidence. It should be added that these men and women do not differ significantly in their proportions classified in the Moderate or Mild forms of symptom formation. Residually, on every age level the single women, as compared with the single men, have substantially higher proportions in the Well category of mental health.

[16]This is not to imply that the psychiatrists were unmindful of the potential psychiatric significance of nonmarriage for *both* females and males who were over thirty. The fact is that singleness in the middle years of life carried weight in their mental health evaluations only when it was accompanied by other more credible signs of disturbance and disability in interpersonal functioning. For them, in short, nonmarriage was *in itself* not a sign of disturbance or a criterion of impairment.

[17]S. S. Bellin and R. H. Hardt, "Marital Status and Mental Disorders among the Aged," *American Sociological Review* 23 (April 1958): 158. The locus of the investigation was an upstate New York urban community.

[18]One such deviation would almost certainly be insufficiently expressed career ambitions. Girls in a national sample of high school students were asked what outstanding qualities they would prefer most in a husband—after honesty and physical attractiveness. At the very top of the list, preferred by 46 percent were "brains," by 54 percent "sense of humor," and by 82 percent "ambition." H. Cantril, ed., *Public Opinion, 1935–46,* 1951, p. 431.

[19]One local newspaper columnist has referred to this type as "the odd stick—not disliked, but not sought after; not rejected, just ignored."

[20]Of this type the same columnist notes that "her 'brain' may frighten even intelligent young men off. . . . Her basic need may continue to center on finding a male mind and personality more forceful than her own." However, of this kind of "male animal" the woods are scarce, and the "wily trappers" are many.

[21]The literatures of fiction and autobiography often highlight the maiden aunt, usually as a second, *albeit eccentric,* mother. The bachelor uncle is far more rarely portrayed, and then often as a family "stray sheep."

[22]Among the Midtown sample of single women as a group, about 25 percent are in professional or semiprofessional óccupations, and 33 percent are holding middle-range managerial posts or relatively well-paid sales jobs.

[23]The balance of 3 percent replied "don't know." Cantril, *Public Opinion,* p. 431. The 7 percent electing to remain unmarried provide an estimate of the frequency of the self-chosen type among single women.

[24]Bellin and Hardt, "Marital Status and Mental Disorders," p. 158.

[25]It will be remembered from chapter 11 that these two age groups, overall, were quite similar in their mental health distributions.

[26]Bellin and Hardt, "Marital Status and Mental Disorders," p. 158.

[27]Taking another husband is also a possibility. However, this seems to be a relatively small likelihood in an area with a large surplus of younger single women. Nationally, only 30 percent of widows marry a second time.

[28]Bellin and Hardt, "Marital Status and Mental Disorders," p. 158.

[29]These population totals were in part derived from United States Census reports, published and unpublished, and in part from estimates based on our random sample of Midtown's adult population.

[30]The widowed and divorced are represented by too few patients for reliable calculation of rates.

[31]M. D. Blumenthal, "Mental Health Among the Divorced," *Archives of General Psychiatry* 16 (1967): 603–608.

Part VI

Mental Health Composition and Psychiatric Care in Midtown's Sociocultural Groups

CHAPTER 13

SOCIOECONOMIC STATUS: MEASUREMENT IN A GOLD–COAST AND SLUM AREA

LEO SROLE

In many human societies, both simple and complex, the typical family is saturated with awareness of its relative "position," "standing," "station," or "status" in the communal scheme of social rank. There are few places where this is more evident as historical fact than on the American scene.

Writers in the literary vineyards, from Chaucer to Faulkner and Marquand, have been arrested by the individual's predicaments in the halter of social class status. On a higher level of abstraction, the concept of social class has engaged social philosophers and sociological theorists at least since Plato and Aristotle. Historians like Charles and Mary Beard, Daniel J. Boorstin, and analysts of American culture ranging from Alexis de Tocqueville to Max Lerner[1] have given it an important place in their observations.

Among the field research disciplines, anthropology from its beginnings has more or less systematically taken into account the patterning of social rank in societies other than our own. The research record of sociology on this front is rather less consistent. Starting in 1889 Charles Booth, the English sociologist, published his seventeen-volume research monograph *Life and Labour of the People in London*. A pioneer work of ground-breaking significance, its natural-history purpose was "to describe the general conditions under which each class lives." In contrast with its large influence on the social work field here, the Booth monograph found only slight resonance in the research interests of American (and British) academic sociology.[2]

Although exploring all manner of social problems associated with poverty and fruitfully mapping various facets of the heterogeneous city as a community type, American sociological research by and large did not fully awaken to the systemic and dynamic implications of social class processes until two empirical developments emerged under principal impetus from the field of anthropology. These took form (some forty years after Booth's first volume) in the Middletown studies of the Lynds and in the Yankee City investigation launched by Lloyd Warner in 1931, with the present writer as a coworker and coauthor.[3] These two studies had immediate and telling impact in directing American sociology's diverted attention to social stratification as a major specialty field of inquiry. By way of delayed recognition a massive and diffuse sociological literature in the English language has since burgeoned, of such proportions that a bibliography assembled in 1968 required a 440-page book to list its 7,000 items.[4]

Given the theoretical and technical diversities that pervade this literature, and the key importance of socioeconomic status (SES) to the present Study, the writer is prompted to indicate briefly the particular formulations, conceptual and operational, that guided his treatment of this complicated demographic variable while planning the design of the Midtown investigation. This effort will probably be better served if it starts with elementary processes discernible from the broad anthropological perspective.

FUNDAMENTALS OF SOCIOECONOMIC STATUS

All human societies utilize the biosocial factors of age, sex, and marital status to harness individuals to the conjugal family as it advances in the procession of generations. Within a given society, furthermore, family units are often categorized on various sociocultural criteria that operate to sort them along various axes of subgroup formations. Socioeconomic status is one of these axes. At the root of SES differences the world over are the commonplace facts that (1) to meet its creature needs the family must perform a productive work role within the local economy, and (2) the economy is organized around a division of labor, often manifested in technically specialized work roles or occupations that elicit and channel different kinds of individual skills.

It is axiomatic that the larger the diversification in occupations, the greater is the range of individual skills called into play. Although from society to society there are differences in the evaluation of corresponding occupations and the skills required, each society itself tends to place varying values on the several kinds of occupations represented in its own economic system. Such evaluations are usually expressed in the dissimilar "returns" associated with different occupations, returns both tangible and intangible. The intangible returns include differential respect and esteem, carrying the force of community consensus, and ranging from prestige commanding great behavioral deference to stigma seen in opprobrious behavior toward the pariah.

Of course, there are direct consequences of the differences in both types of returns. For example, varying tangible returns imply differential capacity to acquire consumer goods and services in the form of creature necessities, amenities, and luxuries. In American society especially, the highly visible level and style of family consumption or standard of living, although more or less dependent on the occupation that supports it, is itself one of several scales applied by the community in assaying the relative standing of different family units. In fact, the visible pattern of consumption, among other more basic motivations, is the family's most direct mode of symbolically validating the income value attached to its breadwinner's work role.

The varying returns of different occupations, both intangible and tangible, have further consequences (1) in the privileges and restrictions their holders are dealt and (2) in the relative control—through influence and power—that their members can or cannot exercise over community processes affecting the interests and well-being of their families. Thus family, economy, and polity interweave to form a closely knit trinity in the local social system.

Interfamily similarity of income and consumption is usually reflected in the spatial differentiation of housing areas, tending to make for residential contiguity and interaction of families in like economic circumstances. Such proximity, in combination with (1) similar life interests, problems, outlooks, and attitudes arising from like economic circumstances and (2) similar standing as status[5] equals, tends to make for close associations, beyond those of kinship, in friendship circles characterized by relatively intimate behavioral congruences. In the nation's capital, by way of illustration, we are told that "Federal employees move socially within their own salary brackets." As has been observed about a lady who has lived in the District of Columbia for a long time, "everyone she knows has an income within a thousand dollars of her husband['s]."[6]

Through overlapping memberships, these friendship circles are interlocked in an extended chain or network linking most families in the community who are in broadly similar economic circumstances. To the outside observer, this network can be seen as a loosely structured, informal kind of horizontal band, or status equivalents grouping. From the inside vantage point of the family unit, this grouping tends to be seen not as an inclusive whole, but rather as a series of three expanding, progressively less clearly delineated, concentric social rings. Bounding the innermost ring is the friendship circle or circles in which the family directly participates. In the next ring are the circles whose member units are partially known and defined as "friends of our friends." In the outer ring, the largest of the three, are the many other families of similar standing which, under the necessary face-to-face conditions, would normally be considered "socially our kind" and thus potentially eligible for friendship formation.[7] These three rings comprise a partially and loosely integrated social orbit and status domain, which is locally identified in various ways, descriptive or metaphorical. Illustrative of such modes of identification for one particular status category are such terms as "high and mighty," "top drawer," "upper crust," and "the cream."

Marking off families in different status categories are divergences in standards of consumption, in values and tastes, and in behavior patterns and group identifications. As a result, there is comparatively little interaction between such families; in fact, there may be actual avoidance.[8] When interaction happens to be unavoidable or required, this "distance" is manifested as a rule in relatively brief and formal behavior.[9]

The community's several horizontal categories of families that differ in status relate to each other in a higher-lower or vertical rank order continuum. These ranked categories have been variously referred to as strata, status levels, socioeconomic groups, social classes, etc.[10]

Thus, from the twin processes of occupational specialization and differential economic and social evaluation of occupations there emerges a third process, i.e., varying elaboration of status groups and categories based on the family as their fundamental unit and arranged in a stratified order designated as a social class system.

In an earlier period of European history, the class system was of the *closed* type, marked by lifetime fixity of family position within one or another of three sharply cleavaged categories or "estates," namely, peasantry, burghers, and nobility. Through processes of evolution and revolution, the American version of the system has emerged into one preeminently, but by no means completely, *open* to change of family position. However, the broad lines of the three estates remain discernible in the apparent behavioral distinctions (I) between the manual worker (or blue-collar) class and the white-collar classes, and (2) among the latter, between the "middle" class and the "top drawer" families of inherited or acquired wealth and power.

In certain well-studied, older American communities, each of these strata has discernibly proliferated an upper and lower segment that Warner and his associates have viewed as social class groupings in their own right. However, economic changes within families and fluidity in friendship circle formation tend to make it difficult, both for community residents and scientific observers, to identify firm lines of demarcation between certain of these more limited groupings. As Lerner has more generally remarked: "To draw the profile of the American social strata is more elusive than almost anything else in American life."[11]

Apparently, we have here something roughly analogous to the chromatic spectrum of light with its bands of well-defined primary colors, the latter blending into each other at their margins to produce the secondary colors. That a continuum of shadings, rather than a series of lines, characterizes such a spectrum does not place in question the identity or identifiability of each color, secondary or primary, despite its indistinct borders.[12]

THE METROPOLITAN SITUATION

In the case of the SES spectrum, this kind of difficulty, although real enough for the field investigator, has become grossly exaggerated in the generally cogent literature of theoretical criticism. A far more serious difficulty to this investigator was the fact that the documented picture we had available on the structure and dynamics of the status system had been derived almost entirely from studies of small and relatively stable communities in New England, the South, and the Middle West regions. We had impressionistic reasons to believe that this picture applied in the main, if with touches of caricature, to the metropolis of Washington, D.C., where rank (and its well-publicized salary tag) in the huge bureaucracy of Federal government, as in the military hierarchy and in the one-industry town, is ordinarily coded and directly translated into parallel social circle clusterings and rankings of families. In contrast with such rigid patterning of status groupings in the exact mold of the economic and political hierarchies, we had the definite impression that in industrially heterogeneous metropolitan cities, like New York and Chicago, the face-to-face processes of status evaluation, friendship circle crystallizations, and resulting group formations are far more diffuse and fluid.

One facet of this difference has been noted in the following observation:

In small towns of the United States, where every man may know almost every other, participation in the daily life of the community is widely evaluated. On the basis of such community-wide evaluations the participating person and his family may be assigned to a social class. . . . In contrast to the intimate and enduring appraisals of the small town may be placed the anonymous and often fleeting appraisals of the city [where] many social contacts are segmented and the participants often strangers. Consequently, the urbanite may frequently rely upon appearance rather than reputation: status may be temporarily appropriated by the "correct" display and manipulation of symbols.[13]

Our procedural detour around this problem can be more appropriately summarized in the instrumentation section below.

CONCOMITANTS AND CONSEQUENCES OF STATUS DIFFERENCES FOR THE CHILD

We have sketched the functional evolution of social rank systems out of fundamental economic and regulative (power) processes into varyingly circumscribed but interlocking clusters or groups of informal interpersonal associations.

Around the base of similar economic roles, resources, and capabilities each of the several social class groups elaborates its own standard of consumption, a more or less coherent framework of values and attitudes, a congruent set of behavior tendencies, and common patterns of intrafamily functioning. These form a constellation, or way of life, that, together with variant constellations in other groups, are often conceived as related subculture designs within the larger cultural tapestry of the community.[14]

For us the decisive point about each status group and its way of life is that it is also the form and content of the child's "little world" —the environment, intrafamilial and extrafamilial, that guides, channels, and marks his personality development with its own indelible stamp, as it were.

The second volume of the Rennie monograph series* focuses on certain highly specific experiences of our Midtown sample respondent and tests their connections on the one hand to social class differences and on the other to the mental health variable. Here we turn to several larger concomitants and consequences of status differences that impinge with particular force on the child and seem to provide preliminary conceptual sightlines to the connections between the socioeconomic patterning of the child's world and his subsequent mental health.

An inventory of differences among children belonging to the three broad bands (i.e., lower, middle, and upper) of the American status spectrum could list research-documented items in the hundreds. For present illustrative purposes, we shall confine ourselves to only a few of these, selected because they represent relatively recent research or conceptual developments that seem to be of large potential significance.

One set of important SES correlates is suggested by William Osler's observation that "tuberculosis is a social disease with medical symptoms." Medical epidemiology has long established that certain infectious and deficiency diseases are inversely correlated with socioeconomic status. A similar relationship has been suggested for the prevalence of major chronic disorders.[15]

Whatever the etiologies of the several genera of somatic diseases, for children in different status environments they pose varyingly dis-

* Thomas S. Langner and Stanley T. Michael, *Life Stress and Mental Health*, 1963.

criminatory risks of illness and disability, with potential untoward consequences for personality development. The cumulative effect of these
differential risks on physical survival alone may be inferred from the
fact that between newly born *white* males of highest and lowest SES
parents the latter infants have an average life expectancy 7.4 *years
fewer* than that of the former.[16] If the individual survives to the
twentieth birthday, the chances of being dead by the twenty-fifth
birthday are four times greater for the low-status person than for his
status opposite.

Of particular relevance here is this reported finding:

. . . there are positive and probably etiologic relationships between low
socioeconomic status and prenatal and paranatal abnormalities which may
in turn serve as precursors to retarded behavioral development, and to certain neuropsychiatric disorders of childhood such as cerebral palsy, epilepsy, mental deficiency and behavior disorder. . . .[17]

A number of studies over the years have now uncovered a chain
of malfunctions that arise from poverty-level status, lead through
nutritional deficiencies into maternal organic complications surrounding birth and/or prematurity of birth, accompanied by infant's
low birth weight, culminating in his early death, or survival with brain
damage or central nervous system dysfunctions. The latter may also
be induced or further aggravated by postnatal malnourishment.[18]

A large literature also testifies to SES-mediated differences in
malfunctions within the child's interpersonal realm. With the interrelationship of father and mother one of the pillars in this domain,
Goode cites evidence supporting the observation that "economic factors may be of importance in marital stability."[19] This supplements
research confirming that maladjustments in husband-wife relationships increase in prevalence downward on the social class scale.[20]

That such maladjustments frequently result in broken homes has
been repeatedly noted in the literature: "Lower class families exhibit
the highest prevalence of instability of any class in the status
structure. . . . In the Deep South and Elmtown studies, from 50 to
60 percent of lower class family groups are broken once, and more
often, by desertion, divorce, death or separation . . . between marriage, legal or companionate, and its normal dissolution."[21] Evidence
on the psychiatric effects of such broken homes has been comprehen-
sively reviewed by Gregory.[22]

This carries us to the all-important parent-child dyad in the family structure. Since we must be highly selective, we shall not touch on the extensive series of studies bearing on specific infant training practices in the lower and middle classes but shall refer instead to several investigations that have focused on more global aspects of the parent-child relationship. Offering a suggestive portal to these aspects is a study reporting that middle-class children tend to feel themselves influenced in their behavior by parents perceived as a pair, whereas to lower-class children these influences are more often felt to be emanating from parents as separate individuals.[23]

For the latter child, apparently, the father-mother bond tends to be less an entity and more a case of "house divided." The potential implications of this interparental fracture for the personality of the growing child would seem to be considerable.

To a sample of 1,472 adolescents, Nye has applied a measure of child-parent adjustment. He finds that "adolescents from the higher socio-economic level families score higher [i.e., better] on feelings of being loved and secure, feelings that parents trust and have confidence in them, socialization including disciplinary relationships [i.e., more positive feelings about parents as disciplinarians], attitudes toward the parent's personality and . . . adjustment to groups outside the family."[24]

If these findings are worded in terms of children from lower-SES families, implied is a greater prevalence there of a fracture in the parent-child relationship. This inference is consistent with projective test data among lower-SES "normal" samples, where subjects "portray themselves as relatively isolated from parental figures whom they see as cold and rejecting."[25]

From his research in a lower-class metropolitan area, Miller observes:

The genesis of the intense concern over "toughness" in lower class culture is probably related to the fact that a significant proportion of lower class males are reared in a predominantly female household, and lack a consistently present male figure with whom to identify and from whom to learn essential components of a male role. Since women serve as a primary object of identification during preadolescent years, the almost obsessive lower class concern with "masculinity" probably resembles a type of compulsive reaction-formation.[26]

Employing "family rituals, as a relatively reliable index of family integration," Bossard and Boll assert: "Our overall conclusion is that family rituals increase in number, variety, richness and willing cooperation by individual family members as one moves upward in the economic scale."[27]

These sociologists see the lower-class family as having "little connection with the past. The present is composed of individuals crowded into a space too small for comfort. . . . Children see little if anything in their families to stimulate a desire to perpetuate what they see. Opportunities for emotional satisfactions in the home are few, even for adults. The rituals arising from these situations are, for the most part, rituals of expedience, to keep the home going, and to facilitate escape. . . ."

In the middle-class families, on the other hand, "the tone is one of hopefulness and optimism. . . . The rituals here show a cooperativeness, of a desire to reach these goals, as well as a genuine family 'togetherness' in a home where there is need and opportunity for it."

In a paper appropriately titled "Portrait of the Underdog," Knupfer "considers the disadvantages of low status, the restriction of 'life chances' which low status carries with it. From this point of view, the tendency of different aspects of status to 'cluster' together takes on the aspect of a vicious circle which recalls the Biblical dictum: 'to him that hath shall be given.' "[28] Knupfer then offers evidence "to show that closely linked with economic under-privilege is psychological under-privilege: habits of submission, little access to sources of information, lack of verbal facility. These things appear to produce a lack of self-confidence which increases the unwillingness of the low status person to participate in many phases of our predominantly middle-class culture, even beyond what would be a realistic withdrawal adapted to his reduced chances of being effective."

The problem, we consider, also goes deeper than a lack of self-confidence. The child of the slum, to concretize the urban version of low status, tends to find in his home few responses to his need to feel that he is valued or respected.[29] The self-image initially implanted in that important arena of his life, we can assume, is hardly a prepossessing one.

To an even lesser degree does he find this response outside the home—with the single exception of his street gang (wherein lies its potent hold on him). In a study of school children Neugarten reports that "social class differences in friendships and reputation are well established by age eleven years."[30] Lower-class children, this investigation revealed, were regarded with indifference or disfavor by schoolmates of higher status, and even more strikingly, they regarded themselves unfavorably. Moreover, they enjoyed no surcease even when they escaped to the movies, comic books, and television. In Hollywood films, "whether by omission or commission, there is an implicit but clear disparagement of anything that suggests 'dirty work' or anyone who labors. Such deprecation pervades all the popular culture media, assailing the worker (and his children) and tending to weaken his ego-image. . . ."[31]

The pieces of evidence just reviewed, among many others, all fit into a consistent picture. This picture reveals a life setting for the slum-level child heavily weighted with impoverishing burdens and deprivations of body, mind, and spirit, to an extent well beyond the more nurturing environment of the middle-class child and far beyond that of the "cushioned" upper-class child. However, what is perhaps the most serious core of the matter remains to be brought into sharper focus. In fact, this was only partially discerned when the Midtown Study was being designed.

The keystone of the democratic creed is the doctrine that, whatever their native endowments, all men are intrinsically of equal worth before God, the law, and their fellows. With considerable intensity, children tend to incorporate this canon as a bulwark in their still fragile image of themselves. As we have seen, however, in many areas of his experience the lower-class child encounters the contempt, implicit but palpable, in the nonverbal behavior of others who think of him in the symbolism of such words as rubbish, scum, dregs, riffraff, and trash. These devastating judgments inevitably force their way into his own self-evaluation processes. Thus, he is caught between grossly contradictory, mutually exclusive images of himself, torn by a conflict implanted through the agents of a society that professes equality and practices invidious discrimination.

Between the millstones of this jarring contradiction, the slum-dweller child grows into another, if related, conflict. Under the democratic guarantee of equal opportunity he may expect, given the requisite ability and effort, to rise to a social position of more comfort and respect.[32] But with economically and culturally disadvantaged parents and a school system unequipped to help him overcome his learning lags,[33] he is likely to get only the legal minimum of ten years' schooling. On the other hand, carrying no better native endowment but confronted with none of the objective barriers, his high-status schoolmate goes on to college. From that turning point forward the career opportunities are actuarially even more disparate than the differential longevity expectations of the two boys.[34]

The "poor" boy has a large chance of becoming an unskilled worker, the "rich" boy a corporation executive. By all economic criteria, with support from all the culture media, the latter is a success, the former decidedly less than that. But under the logic of equal opportunity, this difference in terminus is presumed to reflect differences in character and abilities; q.e.d., the laborer is inherently inferior to those in higher economic echelons. Thus, the contrast between the open-opportunities doctrine (seemingly validated by the successful) and his own meager career accomplishments is a second source of unresolved contention in the arena of his self-evaluation. Reinforcing each other, we hypothesize, the two conflicts have been induced at every step in the lower-class individual's life by a self-contradicting society, one that regularly feeds and uplifts him by the promise of its tenets as democratic writ, and that just as regularly cuts him down by the punishing inequalities and discriminations of its social class system. This, it is submitted, is a culturally designed approximation of the classical experiments in provoking animals to the point of paralyzing neurotic symptomatology.[35]

In a trail-blazing paper, Merton has delineated the disparity between culturally emphasized goals and socially inaccessible means to actualize them, a sociological condition of disjunction, or *anomie*, and one he postulates is conducive to behavioral deviation.[36]

The present writer has elsewhere conceptualized these phenomena of social conflict as one stream among others leading to the individual condition of self-to-group alienation, or *anomia*, and has shown that the frequency and intensity of this state vary inversely with socioeconomic status,[37] i.e., are most heavily concentrated at the lowest reaches of the social class scale. Parallel but more extensive data from the Midtown sample adults will appear in a separate publication by this author.[38]

Although not fully articulated to the social class framework, the work of psychiatrists Cleveland and Longaker has made a conceptual contribution in relating culturally derived value conflicts to the emergence of psychopathology. The intervening process of "disparagement" they locate

. . . on the level of individual development and personality integration [as a] pattern of extreme devaluation . . . which can arise . . . when the socializing agents, primarily the parents, hold out contradictory models of behavior (grounded on conflicting cultural values). . . . Disparagement can become a fixed tendency in the child to devalue certain facets of his own personality. . . . Moreover, the disparagement of self is often not confined to one's own individual capacities but radiates to disparagement of the defined behaviors and value systems of his culture. In short, it touches all that has been internalized by the individual, or with which he identifies. . . . Its corrosive implications stem from both the tendency to deny individual worth, with resultant crippling of selfhood, and to deny the worth of group values, and thus to cripple interaction.

The quoted authors delineate this situational nexus in the neurotic processes of three psychiatric patients from a single extended family.[39]

That the parents of the slum child may themselves be behaving under this self-defeating mechanism could account for the atmosphere of malaise often observed in such homes and for the affectional fractures discerned above in the father-mother and parent-child relationships. Given this kind of disarticulated family setting in infancy and early childhood, given the assaults on body, mind, and spirit in early and late childhood, and given the double-barreled, destructive conflict of self-image during adolescence, we can judge that chance and society have saddled the lower-class child with a cumulatively oppressive series of burdens. Compared with the more privileged child, we originally hypothesized that as an adult he would be more defenseless against the crises of life and therefore more susceptible to mental morbidity.

INDEPENDENT OR RECIPROCAL VARIABLE

Applying this hypothesis to our Home Survey adults brought a further problem of specification. Most previous investigations focusing on mental health as the dependent or response variable had in effect declared, as had one, that "the class status of individuals in the society is viewed as the independent or antecedent variable."[40]

The present writer from the start rejected this view as untenable. At the very least, an adult's socioeconomic status and his mental health are *concurrent* phenomena and no basis exists for assuming a priori which is antecedent and which is consequence. Moreover, realities strongly argued that sound preadult mental health is generally a favorable precondition to achieving higher adult status, just as chronic mental disturbance could make it difficult for a breadwinner even to match his parents' socioeconomic standing.

On the other hand, the adult's success or failure in meeting the standards of the SES group to which he is oriented may contribute its own discrete weight toward changing the subsequent course of his mental health development. As previously suggested, therefore, the adult's *own* status level must strictly be hypothesized as no more than a reciprocal variable relative to his current mental health.

For SES in a form that can be defended as antecedent to and independent of mental health we had to look to the status of the adult's *childhood* family, here designated as *parental SES* or *SES origin*, particularly as the weight of accumulated evidence suggests that (1) the childhood period may be crucial in shaping determinants of later mental health and (2) interfamily differences may be partially attributed to differential social class patterning of intrafamily processes and life conditions.

INSTRUMENTATION: HOME SURVEY OPERATION

Estimation of parental SES among our Home Survey sample of adults in turn raised several technical problems. Ruled out as data altogether inaccessible to us were the subjective indications of social standing, namely, (1) how member families of the community say they place each other on the social rank scale and (2) where member families behaviorally place themselves through participation in selected friendship circles, secular organizations, and religious institutions of known SES composition. These involve rating methods that have been particularly developed and systematized by Warner in his techniques of "evaluated participation."[41]

Accessible, however, were the objective indicators that themselves contribute to the community's determination of family status. For example, toward classifying respondent's own SES we used four such indicators, namely, his education, occupation, total family income, and rent—as a key to his style and standard of family living. Such yardsticks would have been preferred in any case because they are quantifiable, are simple to secure, and readily lend themselves to comparative uses in different communities.

For respondents' parents, who in largest numbers had lived in places big and small spread over the European and American continents, across a time span of a half century, neither income nor rent offered itself as a sufficiently standardized register of interfamily differences. The father's schooling, on the other hand, was somewhat less objectionable, and his occupational level was most acceptable of all for this purpose. However, for interview elicitation from the father's offspring, the latter datum in particular required a number of special precautions. First, for what stage of father's life did we want his occupation—at marriage, at retirement, at midlife? This could not be left to respondents to decide in their separate ways. And clearly it had to be specified at a stage that respondent could report from personal observation. Rephrasing the question in terms of respondent's age of observation suggested that we set this period at the *same* point in the life cycle for *all* respondents. The point we felt to be of maximum significance was the respondent at age 18 to 19, when he was near the launching of his own career and the father himself was probably near the middle of his work history.

Second, precautions had to be taken to minimize the widespread tendency to add a substantial dosage of wishful thinking in reporting occupations, for both the father and oneself. Accordingly, three separate questions were put to each respondent with reference to his and his father's occupation. In relation to the father these were: (1) "When you were about 18 to 19 years old, what kind of work was your father doing for a living?" (Here the interviewer recorded the work as described and the title of the job if named.) (2) "At that time did he work for himself or others?" (3) "About how many people did he have working for (under) him?"

Placement of father and respondent, each in his own occupational bracket, was made neither by the respondent nor by the interviewer. Instead, on the basis of the respondent's three replies and a framework of specifications developed for the purpose, office coders placed the father in one of 27 occupational rubrics. The latter were then collapsed on the line of the blue-collar–white-collar dichotomy, with each category in turn divided into a high, middle, and low grade. In the blue-collar range, these grades represented the usual skilled, semi-skilled, and unskilled kinds of manual work.

Within the white-collar range the allocations were somewhat more complicated. Into the high stratum were placed professionals and top-level executives, self-employed and otherwise. Semiprofessionals, intermediate managerial personnel, and highly specialized sales people (e.g., in real estate, stocks, insurance, wholesale trade) were assigned to the middle grade. To the lower bracket were allocated small shop (goods or services) proprietors, managers with relatively few subordinates, other sales people, and office and clerical help.[42]

The six grades were given score values from 1 to 6 proceeding upward in the scale. Fathers' schooling was similarly divided into six grades.[43] For each father the two scores, equally weighted, were summated. The distribution of 1,660 summated scores was then cut in a manner to produce six groups as equally populated as possible. This stratification will be our measure of respondent's *parental SES*.

It is readily apparent that this is an unusual yardstick in two respects. First, the lines of demarcation between the parental-SES levels emerge from the procedure of distributing families in nearly equal numbers among the six strata. On the one hand, this is an approximation of defining classes by the criterion of equally spaced intervals, an instrumentally desirable tactic whenever it is feasible. On the other hand, it lends itself readily to symmetrical mergers into fewer and larger categories when SES-origin differences must be applied as an analytical control.

Second, the six parental strata do *not* tell us how respondents' families stood in the prestige rank system of their respective home communities. This, of course, would have been beyond the practical powers of retrospective research to reconstruct. Instead, they suggest how these families would hypothetically have stood *relative to each other*, in socioeconomic respects, had they all been gathered together, at one time and place, to continue functioning as they had when their offspring-respondent was near the turn into adulthood. In effect, therefore, these families as stratified represent an analytically contrived social rank order.

However, each of the six aggregations of respondent families may not be quite as artificial as would appear at first glance. It was the writer's prediction that when economically equivalent SES classes in different Western countries were ultimately studied and compared in detail, this would be found: The specific status-linked similarities in outlook and behavior patterns would outnumber and significantly outweigh differences rooted in specific national traditions. The rationale for this prediction was the assumption that like economic and creature conditions of life, in countries within the broad Western compass, tend to evoke similar constellations of values, goals, and role patternings in both intrafamily and extrafamily settings of daily functioning.

Monographic studies of this general kind have since been made in England, Australia, Mexico, and the Soviet Union. In a summary of the Soviet study we are told: "It will perhaps come as a great surprise to many that there is a close correspondence between the pattern of experience and attitudes of Soviet citizens and their counterparts on the same level of education or occupation in a variety of other large scale industrial societies having markedly different culture and history and possessed of quite dissimilar political institutions."[44] Despite extreme differences in methods employed, the three other studies point in the same direction.[45]

Accordingly, the respondent families in each of our SES-origin strata, with their close similarities in education and occupation, would probably have shared a wide range of other common elements. Such a larger array of like characteristics would support our inference that each stratum of families has a core of homogeneity in intrafamily patterns, if not of interfamily linkages.

In moving on to the respondent's *own* status alignments we shall proceed on two separate tracks. First, to stratify respondent's own SES on the most refined and extended yardstick available to us, we have combined his total family income and dwelling rent with his education[46] and occupation.[47] Each of the former two indicators was also cut into six brackets and scored on a 1 to 6 scale. The sum of the scores for the four indicators, all given equal weight, was calculated for each respondent. The sample's distribution of these summated scores was then cut to yield twelve segments (collapsible into six or three levels as analytically required), as evenly populated as possible.

Second, to trace respondent status changes (mobility) from specific parental positions, we compare occupational level of father and of respondent.

INSTRUMENTATION: TREATMENT CENSUS OPERATION

In our Treatment Census operation we faced certain other difficulties. Working exclusively from institutional records, we found that data related to parental SES were available, in the nature of the situation, only for preadults. That did not matter, since our interest in the treatment variable in any case allotted primary relevance to the immediate own SES circumstances and settings of patients as they crossed into a therapeutic relationship. It was here in fact that we encountered problems. In the records of psychiatric hospitals and clinics, information on income or rent appeared infrequently; for the nonemployed, including housewives, occupation of family breadwinner was often missing; and for 10 percent of the adults no data on schooling were given. From office therapists it proved possible to ask only for patient's initials,[48] diagnosis, and home address. The latter item of information, in terms of verified residential buildings, was provided for 81 percent of the office patients reported to us. Together with home address of 99 percent of hospital and clinic patients, the largest possible common indicator of status we could apply to Midtown's patient population (as enumerated by our Treatment Census) was place of residence.

Other studies have given a rank order value to all homes in a small area unit with known economic characteristics, e.g., the census tract.[49] However, Midtown's extreme housing heterogeneity—even within the census tract subunit of the city block—made this expedient patently error-ridden. The only alternative, but a difficult one, was to use the individual residence as the unit of evaluation.[50] Fortunately, earlier in the Study a housing survey had been made by four volunteer businessmen who were experts in local residential properties.[51] Every tenanted building in Midtown was inspected by a team of two of these men and graded, by means of consensus judgment, on criteria of housing quality and condition of upkeep.

The validity of these judgments was later tested against the 1,660 Home Survey respondents. A Pearson coefficient of .73 was established between (1) the housing grades independently assigned to respondents' buildings by the above teams and (2) respondents' composite own SES scores as based on education, occupation, income, and rent. This is sufficiently high to warrant use of the former, divided into three categories, as a crude substitute own SES yardstick for our Treatment Census patients. As to the reported office patients of unknown address, we assumed that they were distributed among the housing categories in more or less the same manner as the office patients of known address. Actually, there may be a bias hidden in this allocation, to which we shall allude when the data are presented in chapter 16.

It should be added that to calculate patient rates in each housing category, the denominator figures needed were the total number of people living in each such grade of housing. That the United States census could not furnish. However, we did know the housing grades and total number of occupants in 2,060 randomly selected Midtown dwellings. From this sample it was possible to estimate the total population in each housing category, thereby permitting computation of patient rates per 100,000 people in each stratum.

SUMMARY

Substantively, the contents of the present chapter belong in chapters 7 and 8. However, unusual complexities and difficulties attending observation and measurement of the SES variable dictated that this discussion be held as stage setting for the data chapters that follow immediately.

To capture the essential, universal elements of socioeconomic status, its genesis was traced to this chain of fundamental processes: proliferating social division of labor, occupational specialization, differential evaluation of occupations and differential rewarding of the skills they require, economic shaping of family conditions and style of life, and the interactional sorting of economically similar families into friendship circles and status-peer groupings.

Note was taken of the evolution of the medieval European status system, closed and sharply cleavaged in structure, toward the open spectrum type of contemporary America.

The concept of the status group's way of life as a constellation or subculture was advanced and tied to the patterning of the child's world. Selected research evidence was introduced to indicate social class differences in patternings that were potentially significant for the direction of mental health development.

Focusing on the slum child, a formulation was offered of the development of conflicting self-images and evaluations, induced by self-contradictions in the doctrinal and behavioral realms of a democratic but prestige-discriminating society. These and other impoverishments of the lower-class family and environment provided the rationale for the test hypothesis that in the Midtown survey sample parental socioeconomic status and adult mental morbidity would be inversely related.

The grounds for the distinction between parental SES and own SES were defined. Discussed also were the various problems of and solutions to measuring socioeconomic status both in the Treatment Census and Home Survey operations.

NOTES

1. D. J. Boorstin, *The Americans: The Democratic Experience*, 1973; G. W. Pierson, *Tocqueville in America*, 1959; M. Lerner, *America as a Civilization*, 1957, pp. 465–540.

2. C. H. Page, *Class and American Sociology: From Ward to Ross*, 1940.

3. Robert Lynd and Helen Lynd, *Middletown* and *Middletown in Transition*, 1929 and 1937; and W. L. Warner, L. Srole, P. S. Lunt, and J. O. Low, Yankee City Series, 1941–1959, vols. 1–5. For a comprehensive account and balanced evaluation of the antecedents, contents, and repercussions of these community studies, see M. M. Gordon, *Social Class in American Sociology*, 1958.

4. See N. D. Glenn, et al., *Social Stratification: A Research Bibliography*, 1970.

5. For verbal convenience, the term *status*, when appearing without specification, will hereafter be used as shorthand reference to socioeconomic status.

6. I. Kapp, "Living in Washington, D.C.," *Commentary*, January 1957, p. 61.

7. Obviously, other criteria of eligibility also operate. Some base eligibility on inherited family lineage, a symbolic badge that may be more weighty to a rare few than economic and related circumstances. Some criteria refer to group alignments that cut across and tend to subdivide the economically grounded status-peer grouping, e.g., religious affiliation and national background. Other criteria relate to personal tastes and interests that combine into a test of aesthetic and intellectual congeniality, such as is conceptualized in Russell Lynes's typology of "highbrow," "middlebrow," and "lowbrow." (*The Tastemakers*, 1954.)

Of course, such religious, ethnic, and aesthetic criteria may draw together people of dissimilar economic characteristics, thereby interlacing and blurring the edges of adjoining economic-peer groupings. However, it is more often likely that such criteria will tend to recruit friendship circles from within, rather than from beyond, the same economic bracket.

8. "Individuals occupying certain statuses simply do not directly interact with persons in certain other statuses, or interact only minimally. . . . A 'map' of the interaction patterns of most American communities would unquestionably show definite clusters of frequent interaction, separated from other clusters by social

voids only lightly bridged by a few individuals." Robin Williams, *American Society*, 1970, p. 593.

9. "[One] type of [interstatus] insulation involves direct person-to-person interaction, but consists of formalized and limited patterns of relationships such as the constrained interaction of superiors and subordinates in rigidly hierarchical organizations." Ibid., p. 594.

However, those serving people of different social ranks learn to modulate the formality of their behavior, as enlisted men reveal in their interactions with the various ranks of officers. Similarly, a Washington columnist reports that the capital "is a place where the grocer knows precisely the standing, social and financial, of Mrs. Jones against Mrs. Smith . . . and intuitively treats each good lady with the exact degree of deference to which she is entitled."

10. In the interest of variety, we shall use these terms interchangeably.

11. Lerner, *America as a Civilization*, p. 473.

12. Implied in this question is the fallacy of discrete concreteness; that is, what does not have clear-cut boundaries does not qualify for identification as a conceptual entity.

13. W. H. Form and G. P. Stone, "Urbanism, Anonymity and Status Symbolism," *American Journal of Sociology* 57 (March 1957): 504.

14. The development of this concept in the work of the Lynds and Warner and his associates has been synthesized by C. Kluckhohn and F. R. Kluckhohn, "American Culture: Generalized Orientations and Class Patterns," in L. Bryson et al., eds., *Conflicts of Power in Modern Culture*, 1947, pp. 106–128. For related formulations see W. B. Miller, "Lower Class Culture as a Generating Milieu of Gang Delinquency," *Journal of Social Issues* 14 (1958): 5–19; and H. H. Hyman, "The Value Systems of Different Classes: A Social Psychological Contribution to the Analysis of Stratification," in R. Bendix and S. M. Lipset, eds., *Class, Status and Power: A Reader in Social Stratification*, 1966, pp. 488–499.

15. J. M. Ellis, "Socio-economic Differentials in Mortality from Chronic Diseases," in E. G. Jaco, ed., *Patients, Physicians and Illness*, 1958, pp. 30–36; "Chronic Conditions and Limitations of Activity and Mobility, 1965–1967," *Vital and Health Statistics*, Series 10, no. 61 (1971); M. Lerner, "Social Differences in Physical Health," in J. Kosa, A. Antonovsky, and I. K. Zola, eds., *Poverty and Health*, 1969, pp. 60–112; D. J. May and M. J. Wantman, "Selected Chronic Conditions: Estimates of Prevalence and of Physician Services, New York City, 1966," *Population Health Survey Research Bulletin*, RB–M8–69, 1969, p. 15. In the latter survey, the frequencies of heart conditions, hypertension, diabetes, arthritis, asthma, and bronchitis were inversely related to family income; peptic ulcer and hay fever were not. See also T. Rennie and L. Srole, "Social Class Prevalence and Distribution of Psychosomatic Conditions in an Urban Population [Midtown]," *Psychosomatic Medicine* 13 (1956): 449–456.

16. E. M. Kitagawa and P. Hauser, *Differential Mortality in the United States*, 1973, p. 71. In a comprehensive review of the evidence, A. Antonovsky writes, "The inescapable conclusion is that class [still] influences one's chances of staying alive." ("Social Class, Life Expectancy and Over-all Mortality," *Milbank Quarterly* 45 [April 1967]: 67.) For a challenge to the evidence prompting this conclusion, see C. Kadushin, "Social Class and Ill Health: The Need for Further Research," *Sociological Inquiry*, Spring 1967, pp. 323–332.

17. B. Pasamanick, H. Knobloch, and A. M. Lilienfeld, "Socioeconomic Status and Precursors of Neuropsychiatric Disorder," *American Journal of Orthopsychiatry* 26 (1956): 594–602.

282 Mental Health Composition and Psychiatric Care

18. H. Birch and J. Gussow, *Disadvantaged Children; Health, Nutrition and School Failure*, 1970; D. Amante, et al., "Epidemiological Distribution of CNS Dysfunction," *Journal of Social Issues* 26 (1970): 105–136; F. Shah and H. Abbey, "Effects of Some Factors on Neonatal and Postneonatal Mortality," *Milbank Quarterly* 49 (January 1971): 33–57; W. Shoemaker and R. Wurtman, "Perinatal Undernutrition: Accumulation of Catecholamines in Rat Brain," *Science* 171 (March 1971): 1017–1019.

19. W. J. Goode, "Economic Factors and Marital Stability," *American Sociological Review* 16 (December 1951): 802–812.

20. J. Roth and R. F. Peck, "Social Class and Social Mobility Factors Related to Marital Adjustment," *American Sociological Review* 16 (August 1951): 478–487.

21. A. B. Hollingshead, "Class Differences in Family Stability," *Annals of the American Academy of Political and Social Science* (November 1950): 39–46. See also *Journal of Marriage and the Family* 28 (November 1966), articles on marital stability and status variables, pp. 421–448.

22. I. Gregory, "Studies of Parental Deprivation in Psychiatric Patients," *American Journal of Psychiatry* 115 (November 1958): 432–442. See also E. Furman, *A Child's Parent Dies*, 1974.

23. F. Sabghir, "Relation between Consistency and Ego-Supportiveness of Influence Techniques Used by Parent and Behavior and Self-Acceptance of Children (Ph.D. dissertation, George Washington University, 1959).

24. I. Nye, "Adolescent-Parent Adjustment: Socio-economic Level as a Variable," *American Sociological Review* 16 (June 1951): 341–349.

25. J. L. Singer, "Projected Familial Attitudes as a Function of Socioeconomic Status and Psychopathology," *Journal of Consulting Psychology* 18, no. 2 (1954): 99–104. See also B. Rosen, "Social Class and the Child's Perception of the Parent," *Child Development* 35 (December 1964): 1147–1153.

26. Miller, "Lower Class Culture," pp. 5–19. A study of London slum families uncovered the identical linkages; cf. B. M. Spinley, *The Deprived and the Privileged: Personality Development in English Society*, 1953, p. 81.

27. J. H. S. Bossard and E. S. Boll, "Ritual in Family Living," *American Sociological Review* 14 (August 1949): 463–469.

28. G. Knupfer, in R. Bendix and S. M. Lipset, eds., *Class, Status and Power*, 1953, pp. 255–263.

29. In some part this may stem from the calculus of economic costs of a child relative to inadequate and unstable means and from the further fact that under lower-class fertility patterns children arrive far more frequently than they are wanted or can be accommodated into mother's economy of affect and energy.

30. B. L. Neugarten, "Social Class and Friendship among Children," *American Journal of Sociology* 51 (1946): 305–313.

31. S. Bellin and F. Riessman, Jr., "Education, Culture and the Anarchic Worker," *Journal of Social Issues* 5 (Winter 1949): 24–32.

32. This has been stated in extreme form by an inspirational nineteenth-century writer, as follows: "The road to fortune, like the public turnpike, is open alike to the children of the beggar and the descendants of kings." (A. C. McCurty, *Win Who Will*, 1872, p. 19; cited in H. M. Hodges, Jr., *Social Stratification*, 1964, p. 195.)

33. W. L. Warner, R. J. Havighurst, and M. Loeb, *Who Shall Be Educated?*, 1944.

34. B. K. Ecklynd, "Academic Ability, Higher Education and Occupational

Mobility," *American Sociological Review* 30 (October 1965): 735–746.

35. J. H. Masserman, "The Biodynamic Approaches," in S. Arieti, ed., *American Handbook of Psychiatry*, Vol. II, 1959, pp. 1686–1688.

36. R. K. Merton, *Social Theory and Social Structure*, 1949, pp. 125–129. The writer's indebtedness to this paper is apparent. The deviation Merton refers to is "in types of more or less enduring response, not types of personality organization." Emphasized in the present formulation are effects on the ego mechanisms of the child's developing character structure.

37. L. Srole, "Social Integration and Certain Corollaries: An Exploratory Study," *American Sociological Review* 21 (December 1956): 709–716.

38. L. Srole, "Anomia: Antecedents and Consequences," work in progress.

39. E. J. Cleveland and W. D. Longaker, "Neurotic Patterns in the Family," in A. H. Leighton, J. A. Clausen, and R. N. Wilson, eds., *Explorations in Social Psychiatry*, 1957, pp. 167–200. For a conceptually refined and empirical articulation of the process to SES differences in a general population sample of 500 adults, see H. B. Kaplan, "Social Class and Self- Derogation: A Conditional Relationship," *Sociometry* 34 (January 1971): 41–54.

40. A. B. Hollingshead and F. C. Redlich, *Social Class and Mental Illness*, 1958, p. 12.

41. W. L. Warner, M. Meeker, and K. Eells, *Social Class in America*, 1949.

42. In so stratifying the grades within the white-collar range, the writer was departing from the Edwards' United States Census scheme of occupational classification in the general direction taken by Warner's system (*Social Class in America*, pp. 140–141). However, in the absence of local evidence to indicate otherwise, we maintained the integrity of the blue-collar–white-collar dichotomy, as had Edwards.

43. That is, (1) some elementary school, (2) elementary school graduate, (3) some high school, (4) high school graduate, (5) some college, (6) college graduate. If father's schooling was uncertain or unknown, mother's schooling was used instead.

44. A. Inkeles and R. A. Bauer, *The Soviet Citizen: Daily Life in a Totalitarian Society*, 1959.

45. Spinley, *The Deprived and the Privileged*; O. S. Oeser and S. B. Hammond, *Social Structure and Personality in a City* [Melbourne], 1954; and O. Lewis, *Five Families*, 1959.

46. However, wives are classified by composite score of *own* schooling, occupation of husband, total family income, and dwelling rent.

47. In the present edition of this monograph attention can be called to the Kansas City investigation reported in R. Coleman and B. Neugarten, *Social Status in the City*, 1971. This investigation was directed to analysis of the status structure in the subject city by methods adapted from studies of small communities (principally by W. L. Warner and his colleagues). It empirically arrived at a measure called "the Index of Kansas City Status" (IKCS). Three of the component indicators incorporated in the IKCS (p. 81)—namely, education, occupation of head of household, and total family income—had been included in our composite measure of respondent's own SES. Also included in the IKCS were classification of "neighborhood of residence and quality of housing." These were both represented in the Midtown measure by the single indicator of household rent. However, novel in the IKCS was the inclusion of three other indicators—based on "evaluations made by Kansas Citians"—namely, "education of wife, church affiliation, and community associations [including the factor of ethnic identity]." We have found that schooling of husband and that of spouse

are sufficiently correlated (Gamma = .75) that the latter is largely redundant. For purposes of the Midtown Study, moreover, religious and ethnic affiliations stand on very different conceptual planes relative to metropolitan SES as we had observed it. Above all other considerations, our hypotheses about these affiliations as potential predictors of mental health required that they be analyzed with controls for SES as usually defined, precluding their merger with the latter.

48. These were needed to check against multiple reporting of the same patient.

49. The New Haven Study of psychiatric patients used a residential area scale of this kind, but the specific nature of the area unit employed has not been clearly identified. Hollingshead and Redlich, *Social Class and Mental Illness*, p. 390.

50. See R. W. Mack, "Housing as an Index of Social Class," *Social Forces* 29, no. 4 (May 1951): 391–399. Also, Warner et al., *Social Class in America*, pp. 143–150.

51. These were Messrs. Kurt Porges, Percival Perkins, René Hoguet, and Maurice Bloch, to whom the Midtown Study is indebted for this and other highly skilled services.

CHAPTER 14

SOCIOECONOMIC STRATA: THEIR MENTAL HEALTH MAKE-UP

LEO SROLE AND THOMAS LANGNER

Change as it may, socioeconomic status is a lifelong motif in the individual's web of daily experience. One of the dominating designs in the vast tapestry of the nation's culture, it also weaves itself into the dreams, calculations, strivings, triumphs, and defeats of many Americans from childhood on.

Accordingly, the hypothesis linking frequency of mental disorder to SES differences was inevitable, and indeed has drawn the attention of numerous investigations. Their reports provide convenient points of departure for the present chapter.

In largest numbers these researchers chose to test the hypothesis by the relatively simple expedient of enumerating psychiatric patients recorded on treatment rosters as their measure of the extent of mental morbidity. With several notable exceptions, these efforts did not explicitly distinguish between *treated* frequency and *overall* (untreated and treated) frequency of mental impairment as very different yardsticks of morbidity. They therefore applied the former but fell into the error of drawing generalizations as if they had measured the latter.

We hold that socioeconomic status as linked on one hand to *overall* frequency of mental impairment and on the other to frequency of *psychiatric treatment* among the Impaired present rather different questions that require discrete hypotheses and separate testing. In the next chapter we take up the SES-and-treatment hypothesis, where the previous studies of patient populations can claim direct relevance. To our top-priority hypothesis connecting status and *overall* mental morbidity, these limited studies do not offer tests that satisfy the criterion of relevance.

Potentially offering a more adequate test of the latter hypothesis are the investigations that have looked beyond patients inscribed on institutional records and, in search of both untreated and treated cases of morbidity, reached with a far wider, albeit crude, net into the lifestream of a general population at large. Relatively few in number, these published studies deserve brief examination for any light they can throw on the state of knowledge bearing on this particular hypothesis.

Probably the first and the largest of these was the National Health Survey conducted in 1936 under Federal auspices. Using the interview method and covering, in one of its aspects, a sample of 703,092 households (2,502,391 individuals) in 83 cities,[1] this study included a wide range of medical disabilities reported active on the day of interview. Included was the category "nervous and mental diseases," specifically "neurasthenia, nervous breakdown, epilepsy, chorea, locomotor ataxia, paresis, other diseases of the nervous system." Occupation was the SES indicator (among the employed in the age range 15 to 64), and was dichotomized on the line of the white-collar and blue-collar distinction. In frequencies of "nervous and mental disease," so defined, the data for employed females revealed no difference by occupation category. Among males, on the other hand, the white-collar rate exceeded that of the blue-collar category by about 3:2.

A check of the latter finding is at hand in several World War II studies of Selective Service male registrants, with rejections for "mental and personality disorders" as the criterion of morbidity. One of these investigations involved a national sample clinically examined during November–December 1943, with occupation again the status indicator.[2] With the exclusion of farmers, students, and the unemployed, no significant differences in psychiatric rejection rates were found among the several occupational categories there defined.

A second Selective Service study was conducted with 60,000 male registrants examined at the Boston Area Induction Station in 1942.[3] The Boston psychiatric rejection rates by socioeconomic level of registrants, as indexed by area of residence, were as follows:

Socioeconomic level	Rejected in each level
A (highest)	7.3%
B	9.2
C	9.4
D	10.0
E	12.7
F (lowest)	16.6

Clearly the lower the SES stratum, the larger was the rejection rate.

A more recent study relevant here was conducted in Baltimore.[4] From our discussion in chapter 10 it will be remembered that this investigation involved a clinical examination and evaluation of a sample of 809 men and women (approximately 30 percent of these were nonwhites) and covered a broad spectrum of some 30 somatic disorders. The mental disorder rates by income level are reported only for whites and nonwhites combined. If we assume that the nonwhites of Baltimore, as elsewhere, were highly concentrated in the lowest of the four income brackets defined, then the other income groups, inferred to be predominantly white, have mental disorder rates reported as follows:

Income level	Disorders in each level
$6,000 and over	13.6%
$4,000–$5,999	8.9
$2,000–$3,999	8.9

The four inquiries just considered had in common the distinguishing feature of covering a general population, rather than an aggregate of patients. However, on the issue of a connection between SES and overall prevalence of psychiatric disability, the findings of these studies point in almost all possible directions. In the national Selective Service investigation the correlation was practically zero; in the Boston Selective Service survey it was inverse, i.e., the lower the SES level, the higher the morbidity rate; among the Baltimore sample whites it was apparently positive, i.e., highest morbidity rate in the top-income category; and in the National Health Survey the correlation was zero among females and positive among males.

Although the four inquiries used different SES indicators—occupation, area of residence, or income—these are standard measures that are known to be highly correlated with and predictive of each other. Accordingly, it is unlikely that the contradictory findings arise from the different socioeconomic yardsticks applied. Note in particular that the same indicator, occupation, was used in the two national investigations, yet divergent morbidity trends were obtained for the males in the two samples.

In the absence of sufficient evidence to explain or reconcile the inconsistent yields in the four studies reviewed,[5] we viewed the suggested hypothesis linking socioeconomic status and overall mental morbidity in the general population as an open question.

PARENTAL SES: MENTAL HEALTH DISTRIBUTIONS

During childhood, the individual shares the socioeconomic status of his parents and its many fateful consequences. This factor of SES origin we postulated as an independent precondition related inversely to variations in adult mental health.* We look to the Midtown Home Survey and its sample, representing some 100,000 adult "in residence" Midtowners, for a test of this hypothesis.[6] From the previous chapter it will be remembered that respondents' SES origins are distributed among six strata according to composite scores derived from their father's schooling and occupational level. With the SES-origin strata designated A through F in a sequence from highest to lowest position, table 14–1 arranges the Midtown sample adults in each stratum as they are distributed on the gradient classification of mental health assigned by the Study psychiatrists.

Reading table 14–1 horizontally from left to right in order to discern the nature of the trends, we might direct first attention to the Mild and Moderate categories. It is readily apparent that the frequencies of these two mental health conditions are remarkably uniform across the entire SES-origin range. These categories, it will be remembered, encompass more or less adequate functioning in the adult life spheres, although some signs and symptoms of mental disturbance in presumably subclinical forms are present. Equally prevalent along the entire continuum of parental SES, these two mental health types emerge here as generalized phenomena, much as they did with the age variable in chapter 11.

We also note in table 14–1 that around these numerically

---

* To our knowledge, the present investigation has so far been the only one in the adult mental health field to propose and test this hypothesis.

TABLE 14–1. HOME SURVEY SAMPLE (AGE 20–59), DISTRIBUTIONS OF RESPONDENTS ON MENTAL HEALTH CLASSIFICATION BY PARENTAL-SES STRATA

Mental health categories	Parental-SES strata					
	A (highest)	B	C	D	E	F (lowest)
Well	24.4%	23.3%	19.9%	18.8%	13.6%	9.7%
Mild symptom formation	36.0	38.3	36.6	36.6	36.6	32.7
Moderate symptom formation	22.1	22.0	22.6	20.1	20.4	24.9
Impaired*	17.5	16.4	20.9	24.5	29.4	32.7
Marked symptom formation ..	11.8	8.6	11.8	13.3	16.2	18.0
Severe symptom formation ..	3.8	4.5	8.1	8.3	10.2	10.1
Incapacitated .	1.9	3.3	1.0	2.9	3.0	4.6
N = 100%	(262)	(245)	(287)	(384)	(265)	(217)

* $x^2 = 28.81$, $5df$, $p < .001$.

stable mental health categories the Well and Impaired frequencies vary on the SES-origin scale in diametrically opposite directions. From the highest (A) to the lowest (F) of the status groups the Well proportions recede gradually from 24.4 to 9.7 percent, whereas the Impaired rate mounts from about one in every six (17.5 percent) to almost one in every three (32.7 percent).[7]

These countertrends can be more efficiently communicated by converting them into a single standard value that expresses the number of Impaired cases accompanying every 100 Well people in a given group. In the Midtown sample as a whole, this Impaired-Well ratio[8] emerges with a value of 127, a norm available for comparative uses in the pages to come. In bar chart form figure 1 presents the Impaired-Well values translated from table 14–1.

With the top SES-origin levels (A and B) as our points of comparison, we observe in figure 1 that the Impaired-Well ratio is half again larger in the adjoining group C, almost twice higher in the D stratum, three times greater in the E level, and at a point of five-power magnification in the bottom (F) group. Phrased somewhat differently, the two highest strata (A and B) taken together constitute

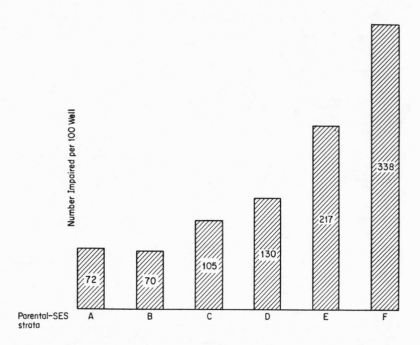

FIGURE I.   HOME SURVEY SAMPLE (AGE 20–59), IMPAIRED-WELL RATIOS OF PARENTAL-SES STRATA.

about 30 percent of the sample but account for 40 percent of the Well and for only 22 percent of the Impaired. On the other hand, the two lowest strata (E and F) taken together constitute 29 percent of the sample but account for only 19 percent of the Well and for fully 39 percent of the Impaired.[9] Through these variously expressed data a connection seems to be apparent between parental SES and mental health in Midtown's adults.

But before we accept such a conclusion, we must give precautionary consideration to this question: Could not the above differences be the result of biasing factors that intruded in the research process? Four major points of potential intrusion can be identified, namely, (1) selection of a sample unrepresentative in SES composition, (2) bias on the part of the interviewing staff, (3) status-linked differences in reporting symptoms on the part of respondents, and (4) preconceptions about social class held by the Study psychiatrists. These error potentials are too serious to be briefly dismissed and too technical for lengthy digression here. Accordingly, they are being held for evaluation in appendix E below. In fine, that evaluation presents firm evidence indicating that two of the four potential sources of bias (1, 4) had left no discernible traces of intrusion. Another possible source (2) is unlikely to have contributed significantly to such error, and the last (3) probably operated in a direction to *understate* the SES differences seen in table 14–1. On balance, therefore, the chances seem large that the connection observed between SES origin and adult mental health is authentic rather than a spurious consequence of biases brought out by the research process. If so, the data reported appear to offer an adequate test of the following hypothesis as originally stated: Parental socioeconomic status during childhood is an independent variable that is *inversely* related to the prevalence of mental morbidity among Midtown adults. However, the data produced force us to elaborate that hypothesis as follows: The stated independent variable of parental SES is related (1) inversely to the frequency of the Impaired condition of mental health, (2) directly to the frequency of the Well state, and (3) not at all to the frequencies of the Mild and Moderate types of symptom formation.

The first part of this proposition asserts that successively lower parental status carries for the child progressively *larger* risk of impaired mental health during adulthood. For those who may hold reservations about the clinical identity of the Impaired category of mental health, the second part of the proposition refers to the asymptomatic state as beyond cavil the minimal form of good mental health; and it asserts that successively lower parental SES tends to carry for the child progressively *smaller* chances of achieving the Well state during adulthood.[10]

The above proposition attributes some share of responsibility for adult mental health to differences in family socioeconomic status during childhood. Notwithstanding respondents' real differences in parental SES, however, it is altogether possible that the decisive factors influencing their current mental health had occurred not during childhood but since they have become adults.

The only approximate test of this possibility open to us here is to isolate the sample segment that has most recently turned adult, i.e., the age 20 to 29 respondents, who, on the average, are only five years removed from the end point of the teen-age phase. If childhood factors associated with parental socioeconomic status carry little weight for adult mental health, then we would expect that among these youngest sample respondents the parental-SES subgroups will emerge with relatively minor differences in Impaired and Well rates. For each of the three parental-SES "classes"[11] among the age 20 to 29 respondents the actual frequencies and the Impaired-Well ratios are seen in table 14–2.

TABLE 14–2.   HOME SURVEY SAMPLE (AGE 20–59), DISTRIBUTIONS ON MENTAL HEALTH CLASSIFICATION OF AGE 20–29 RESPONDENTS BY PARENTAL-SES CLASSES

Mental health categories	Parental-SES classes		
	Upper (A–B)	Middle (C–D)	Lower (E–F)
Well	34.1%	21.4%	12.9%
Mild symptom formation	35.5	38.1	39.6
Moderate symptom formation	20.5	23.7	27.7
Impaired	9.9*	16.8	19.8*
N = 100%	(132)	(132)	(101)
Impaired-Well ratio	29	82	154

* $t = 2.1$ (.05 level of confidence).

Table 14–2 shows that the theoretical possibility defined is not fulfilled. On the contrary, among these young people recently out of adolescence,[12] significant differences in Impaired-Well balances are plainly tied to variations in SES origin. We can therefore plausibly infer that these differences were predominantly implanted during the preadult stage of dependency upon parents and were brought into early adulthood rather than initially generated there.

PARENTAL SES AND NATURE OF SYMPTOMS

We can here take certain limited steps toward eliciting clues about the qualitative nature of these differential implantations. From the technical discussion in chapter 8 it may be remembered that the questionnaire used to structure the Home Survey interviews covered a number of symptom clusters or dimensions. Each dimension was represented by a series of specific questions ranging from three to eight in number. The number of symptomatic replies that a respondent gives under each dimension can be expressed as a score, which permits examination of the SES-origin strata in their distributions on that score range. Without detouring systematically into all the quantitative details of such psychometric data, we can here indicate the general nature of their trends.

For example, one of these dimensions had reference to signs of tension and anxiety.[13] It can be reported that there were no significant differences in tension-anxiety scores among the six parental-SES strata. In all of these groups about 30 percent reported one or another of these symptoms, i.e., score of 1, and another one-third acknowledged two or more symptoms in this series. It can therefore be inferred that tension and anxiety scores are a generalized rather than a status-linked phenomenon in the Midtown population. The same inference is indicated for the "excessive intake" dimension, which refers to partaking "more than is good for you" of food, coffee, liquor, or smoking—each asked as a separate question. Again, about one-third of the respondents in all parental-SES groups reported overindulging in two or more of the four forms indicated. (Some 23 percent of the sample replied affirmatively to the liquor question.)

However, on all other symptom dimensions there was a highly significant *inverse* correlation with SES origin; that is, downward on the parental-SES scale the symptomatic tendencies increased. This trend obtained on such types of somatization as appetite-stomach or vasolability disturbances, dyspnea, heart palpitations, frequent headaches, and back pains. The trend registered similarly on the energy-deficit dimension of neurasthenic symptoms and on the affect dimensions of depression and hostile suspiciousness. It was manifest in the series of behavioral signs suggesting self-isolating tendencies. The high inverse correlation also appeared on two character dimensions that for the Study psychiatrists carried little weight in themselves as criteria of functional impairment, namely, rigidity and immaturity. Both of these suggest difficulties in impulse control.

Moreover, on the basis of interviewers' observations there were 41 intellectually retarded individuals apparent in the sample, ranging from 5.5 percent in the lowest parental stratum to 0.4 percent in the highest.

Finally, where the protocol evidence suggested a passive-dependent character structure or a schizophrenic thought process, these were also recorded by the Study psychiatrists. The former dimension was observed with a prevalence of 40 percent in the bottom parental stratum and only 15 percent in the top. The corresponding rates of the schizophrenic thought process were 7.8 and 4.6 percent, respectively, but this difference is not statistically significant.[14]

From an unreported number of clinic patients, we might recall that Ruesch projected the following symptomatic tendencies to two of the major social classes in American society: "We can state that the lower class culture favors conduct disorders and rebellion, the middle class culture physical symptom formations and psychosomatic reactions. . . ."[15] Even if the Ruesch sample of patients offered a basis for generalization about the universes of the American lower and middle classes, as it does not, the data we have reported above suggest that the corresponding parental-SES strata in the community sample of Midtown adults do not support that generalization. A more plausible interpretation of Ruesch's observations is that (1) rebellious lower-class individuals with "acting out" character disorders tend to be shunted to psychiatric facilities by action of community authorities or agencies; (2) their status peers with psychosomatic reactions get strictly medical or no attention; (3) middle-class individuals with psychosomatic disorders tend to be referred to psychiatric outpatient services, generally on the advice of their own physician.

In all, among Midtown's parental-SES groups there appear to be no frequency disparities in signs of a schizophrenic process, in symptoms of anxiety and tension, or in tendency toward excessive intake. However, on all other pathognomonic dimensions covered there is evidence among these groups of consistent variation in frequencies of disturbances in functioning—intellectual, affective, somatic, characterological, and interpersonal.

PARENTAL SES, AGE, SEX, AND MENTAL HEALTH

A definite relationship between parental socioeconomic status and adult mental health, sound and impaired, has been tentatively established in Midtown. We emphasize the word *tentative* because the possibilities that this finding is spurious are far from exhausted. Beyond technical artifacts, the correlation observed would be spurious if it evaporates when a third factor is analytically introduced and controlled. In the chapters to follow we shall test the relationship to mental health of other independent demographic variables of the sociocultural type. In those chapters it will be systematic procedure to assess the multiple ties linking parental SES and other such factors to the Study's dependent variable.

As a first step in this direction we ask: What is the outcome when we analyze adult mental health simultaneously against parental SES, sex, and age? Chapter 12 noted that in the Midtown sample as a whole there are no significant differences between males and females in their mental health composition. This situation persists, we can report, when both age and parental SES are controlled; conversely, control of the sex factor does not affect the relationship of parental SES and mental health. In future chapters, therefore, we shall drop sex as a control variable in dissecting factors potentially entangled with mental health.

In chapter 11, it will be remembered, we saw the Impaired-Well ratio rise from 65 in the age 20 to 29 segment to 205 in the age 50 to 59 group. In the light of this clear trend, it may be that age is the dominant variable and that the observed correlation between parental SES and respondent mental health is a spurious result of the contingencies that (1) groups with low SES origins may be "loaded" with older people and (2) those of high SES origins are heavily weighted with younger people.

To test this possibility, figure 2 has been prepared. And to avoid imposing undue burdens on the graph, only the Impaired-Well magnitudes are there presented for each of 12 subgroups of respondents representing a particular conjunction of respondent age and parental SES. Of course, with so many subgroups the number of Impairment cases in each is unduly attenuated. However, we emphasize again our interest in the *direction* rather than the *size* of the Impaired-Well differences, especially when pressing our finite sample to its utmost analytic limits.

Inspection of figure 2 reveals that on all age levels the Impaired-Well values—with only one exception—are progressively larger downward on the SES-origin scale.[16] In short, the connection between parental SES and mental health persists when the age factor is held constant.

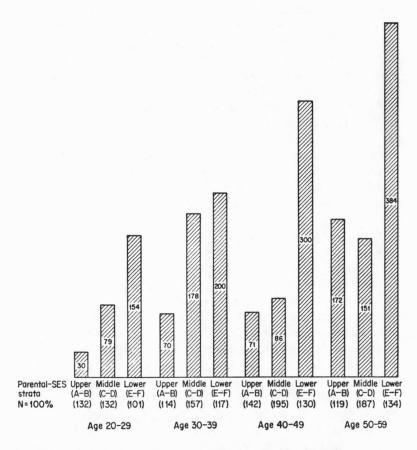

FIGURE 2.   HOME SURVEY SAMPLE (AGE 20–59), IMPAIRED-WELL RATIOS OF
LIKE-AGE RESPONDENTS BY PARENTAL-SES CLASSES

The reader may also wish to trace the age trend within like SES-origin classes. For example, proceeding from the youngest through the oldest subgroup within the upper-origin class (A–B), the Impaired-Well ratios are 30, 70, 71, and 172 respectively. Within the lower-origin class (E–F), similarly, the corresponding values are 154, 200, 300, and 384, respectively. Finally, within the middle-origin class (C–D), the age progression shows values of 79, 178, 86, and 151, respectively. The trend-deviant subgroup here appears to be the age 30 to 39 respondents who, in fact, are quite close in mental health composition to their age peers of lower-class origin.[17]

We can summarize the two trends just disentangled with the single general statement that in the Midtown sample parental SES and respondent age are *both* related, quite *separately of each other*, to the frequencies of sound (Well) and Impaired mental health.[18] Stated in more dynamic terms, we can infer first that parental-SES differences were somehow involved in differential childhood implantings of potentialities for mental wellness and impairment. By the end of the teen years these susceptibilities were already differentially crystallized in the overt mental health conditions of the several SES-origin strata. Second, we can surmise that subsequent progression through adulthood carries in its wake further precipitating or aggravating pathogenic effects for the vulnerable people *from all SES-origin groups.*

The power of the two demographic factors when joined together can be seen in the extreme contrast of Impaired-Well values between the pair of most favorable variants, i.e., upper-SES origin and age 20 to 29, and the combination of most unfavorable variants, i.e., lower-SES origin and age 50 to 59. Among the former subgroup there are 30 Impaired cases for every 100 Well respondents; among the latter there are 384—a joint magnification power, by this measure, in the order of almost 13 times.

Given the "collaboration" of SES origin and age in their impacts on adult mental health, question arises about the generality of their interrelationship. And given that approximately three-fourths of Midtown's adults are migrants from beyond the City's five boroughs, might it not be that Midtown attracts migrants of a particular atypical kind—in whom the interlocking triad of SES origin, age, and mental health happens to be an idiosyncratic conjunction? On its face, this suggestion appears to be implausible but not impossible, and therefore cannot be ignored.

To consider the question, we need of course the evidence of independent observation. Fortunately, three quite different shreds of evidence of this kind are available to be fitted together in somewhat the fashion of a jigsaw puzzle.

First, is the study at an Eastern college, that reported a "six-year mean prevalence rate of 11.5 percent for clinically significant emotional impairment," a finding supported by a 12 percent rate of "clinically disturbed cases" at a second college.[19] In the Midtown sample, the closest single counterpart of the broad college population just referred to are the 132 age 20 to 29 upper-SES-origin (A–B) respondents. Included in this subgroup, as a matter of fact, are 29 current college or postgraduate students and five wives of such current students; among the remainder, most have attended or completed college training. It is therefore pertinent to recall that the impairment rate in this delimited age-and-SES subgroup is 9.9 percent.

The second source of evidence is a wartime study focused on white enlisted men who had not yet served overseas.[20] Used were one cross-section sample of 6,869 on-duty personnel and a separate sample of 563 psychoneurotic patients in Army hospitals. On the one hand, the latter represented mental impairment as judged by the criterion of behavioral incapacity for military duty. On the other hand, because of the constant surveillance and command powers of "noncoms," officers, and Army doctors these patients probably constitute a far closer approximation of overall prevalence of impairment than do mental patients in civil life.[21]

The particular relevance of this investigation is to be seen in two of its aspects. First, it calculated the number of hospitalized psychoneurotics per 100 nonhospitalized men, producing a "PN ratio," which, in fact, suggested our own Impaired-Well measure. Second, it tested the variability of this ratio with age and education *simultaneously*. To be sure, a person's education is generally treated as an own-SES indicator, a precedent we ourselves followed. However, by reason of its direct dependence on, and high correlation with, parents' socioeconomic position, schooling level of offspring can also be considered as an alternative, crudely approximate, indicator of the latter.

In the Army study, the educational range was trichotomized into three levels, namely, high school graduation or more, some high school (short of graduation), and grade school only. In the 20 to 24 age group the PN ratios for these successive schooling levels were 29, 99, and 129, respectively. In the 25 to 29 age group the corresponding ratios were 51, 104, and 156, respectively. And in the 30-and-over age group they were 119, 214, and 284, respectively.

Thus, when age is held constant, the PN ratio progressively *increases* downward on the education scale; and when these ratios are rearranged to hold schooling level constant, they are found to *increase* progressively with each age increment.

The third source of evidence is the study conducted by Bellin and

Hardt, involving a noninstitutional community sample of 1,537 elderly people dichotomized into two age groups, 65 to 74 and over 74.[22] The focus was *overall* prevalence of mental morbidity, the latter as judged by "evidence suggestive of certifiability" to a mental hospital. With own SES, in this instance dichotomized into a high and a low stratum, the morbidity rate was larger for low-status people than for those of high SES in both age groups and larger for older people than for those younger in both SES strata.

There are gross differences in the observed population segments just cited and in the nature of the evidence drawn from them. Nevertheless, these varied pieces fit into a congruent pattern consistent with the Midtown finding that SES origin and age stand in separate but convergent relationships to adult mental health. Accordingly, this complex triad uncovered in the Midtown sample of adults gives the definite appearance of a general rather than a local or idiosyncratic phenomenon.

This has since been supported in a national survey. Employing a large sample, dichotomized by schooling and sorted into five age categories, the frequency of reported "nervous breakdown" was greater with low education among *all* age groups, and larger with progressive age in *both* schooling groups.[23]

STATUS MOBILITY AND MENTAL HEALTH

We have thus far concentrated attention on *parental* socioeconomic status, postulated as embracing overarching constellations of different life conditions during childhood. However, there is a generalized cultural mandate binding all social classes in American society. Rising from impoverished immigrant parents to the summit of an industrial empire, Andrew Carnegie gave utterance to this mandate in ringing words: "Be a King in your dreams. Say to yourself 'My place is at the top.' "[24]

A more realistic injunction and one more widely accepted is this: Whatever your status inheritance from parents as a point of departure, strive to "do better," i.e., advance beyond it. In due course, the adult settles into his own position, at a level that may be higher, lower, or more or less the same as his father's. These three parent-offspring sequences are technically designated as the variable of *intergeneration status mobility.* The status mobility variable circumscribes an extremely complicated and dynamic set of processes that operate in the individual's life history between childhood under the roof of parental-SES conditions and his own status shelter built in adulthood for his spouse and children.

What light does published research shed on the mental health aspects of such mobility differences? In their literature-synthesizing book *Social Mobility in Industrial Society*, Lipset and Bendix devote separate sections to (1) "the consequences of social mobility" for the individual and (2) varying individual orientations that spur different directions of status change.[25] In the former discussion they conclude that "studies of mental illness have suggested that people moving up in America are more likely to have mental breakdowns than the nonmobile." An examination of the New Haven study used as the principal source of this inference shows that Lipset and Bendix appear to have misread the evidence. The New Haven reports on status mobility covered 847 schizophrenics in treatment, who were found to be 88 percent nonmobile, about 4 percent upward-mobile, and 1.2 percent downward-mobile.[26] (The remainder were in the category of "insufficient family history.") Contrary to the Lipset-Bendix reading, these data do not suggest a picture of upward mobility as a major trend among the New Haven cases. More important, even if their reading were correct, trends among treated schizophrenics, whatever their direction, can hardly be generalized to apply to treated nonschizophrenics (unreported in the New Haven publications), or to untreated schizophrenics, or to the untreated with other disorders. Above all, these trends cannot be extrapolated, as Lipset and Bendix have done, to "mental breakdown" trends in the universe of "people moving up in America" as compared with trends in the universe of nonmobile Americans. In point of fact, there is some question whether it is possible to extrapolate from the New Haven treated schizophrenics to schizophrenic patients generally. In a New Orleans study, such patients were reported to be predominantly (45.7 percent) downward-mobile—in striking contrast with the New Haven cases.[27]

In further fact, single-point-of-time studies, whether of treated or overall mental morbidity, offer no basis for the inference that status mobility "may cause difficulties in personal adjustment."[28] Such investigations cannot parcel out the discrete mental health *conse-*

quences of individual changes in socioeconomic status from the specific personality *preconditions* of different self-determined mobility paths.

However, citing the *same* New Haven treated schizophrenic rates, Lipset and Bendix assert in their later section on differential motivations for mobility that "mental illness rates would seem to provide additional data for the notion that the upwardly mobile [population] tend to be deprived psychodynamically."[29] In its context, this statement seems to suggest that psychic deprivation tends to induce status climbing. But clearly no study of patients can tell us about the psychically deprived and nondeprived segments of the nonpatient population and their respective mobility tendencies.

In a relevant research paper, Douvan and Adelson preface their data report with the observation that in the large literature on social mobility

. . . only limited attention has been given to studying the motivational sources of mobility. What we do find is a general disposition to treat *upward* mobility in a vaguely invidious fashion. It would seem that, in this country, the Horatio Alger tradition and the "dream of success" motif have been pervasive and distasteful enough to have alienated, among others, a good many social scientists. The upwardly aspiring individual has apparently become associated with the pathetic seeker after success* or with the ruthless tycoon. This image of success is, much of it, implicit—assumption and attitude, and not quite conviction—but it seems to have dominated the thinking of our intellectual community.[30]

In their insightful study of a national cross-section sample of 1,000 age 14 to 16 boys, Douvan and Adelson tested their ego-theory conceptualizations on personality determinants of precareer mobility aspirations. To draw on the summary of their findings:

The upward aspiring boy is characterized by a high energy level, the presence of autonomy, and a relatively advanced social maturity. These attributes may be viewed as derivatives of a generally effective ego organization.

[In the] downward mobile boys . . . we see an apparent blocking or impoverishment of energy which should ideally be available to the ego. There is a relatively poor articulation among the psychic systems; impulses

---

* Playwright Arthur Miller has embodied the type in his *Death of A Salesman* character Willy Loman.—EDs.

threaten the ego's integrity; the superego seems overly severe and yet incompletely incorporated. These boys seem humorless, gauche, disorganized—relatively so, at least. Perhaps the most telling and poignant datum which the study locates is their response to the possibility of personal change, their tendency to want to change intractable aspects of the self, and the degree of alienation revealed by their desire to modify major and fundamental personal qualities.

The study just cited was focused on mobility aspirations among a general sample of adolescents, and their personality correlates. As contrast to this prospective approach to adult developments, in the Midtown sample of adults we are focusing retrospectively on status mobility, completed or in process, and current mental health. In the planning phase of the Study we were clear that from the latter we could not dissect (1) what the level of mental health had been at the threshold of the respondent's career and (2) what increments of mental health change were subsequently added as a specific result of the struggle for one's own place in the socioeconomic sun.

In the face of this empirical limitation we hypothesized as follows:[31]

1. Upward mobility requires not only appropriate aspirations but also efficient personal mobilization, such that to actually "make the grade," sound mental health is a decided preparatory asset and impaired health is not. Downward mobility, on the other hand, is culturally so deviant from group and typical self-expectations that it can only happen under some initial, predisposing handicap in physical or mental health.

2. In turn, given adequate preparation in the preadult stage, accomplished upward mobility and its rewards tend to have constructive consequences for subsequent adult mental health;[32] whereas the consequences of downward mobility and its deprivations would tend to be in the opposite direction.

3. However, countervailing tendencies also operate. For some people, status climbing may have costly pathogenic effects that would have been avoided had they remained stationary, i.e., nonmobile, relative to father. Similarly, downward mobility may conserve or stabilize mental health in certain special, limited circumstances, when other courses would have been taxing or damaging to the individual.

As to the relative importance of these postulated elements in the resultant current mental health of sample respondents, we believe that those subsumed under hypothesis 3 are relatively rare and partially offset those suggested in hypothesis 2. The latter, in our view, are secondary to the dominant contribution of the forces emphasized in hypothesis 1, namely, the psychosocial selection of different kinds of preadult mental health for adult replication, advance, or retreat from parental status.

In testing the relationship of status mobility, as a reciprocal-type variable, to current adult mental health, we faced a number of alternatives in choosing a common yardstick to measure SES of both the respondent and his father. The decision finally taken was that for this specific purpose occupation level by itself, though not accounting for all socioeconomic variability, is more useful in identifying specific father-offspring sequences than any two status indicators arithmetically averaged. From the previous chapter it will be remembered that a series of three questions was used with each respondent to elicit (1) the nature of his own work and (2) that of his father when the respondent was age 18. On the basis of these data, father and respondent were separately placed within the identical occupational framework of six levels, numerically scored 1 to 6. Where respondent and father have a like score, the former is classified nonmobile. If the respondent has a higher score, he is classified upward-mobile, and if a lower score, downward-mobile.

It can now be reported that the 911 sample males and never-married females[33] who could be placed in terms of both father's and own occupation were distributed among the three forms of mobility approximately in a 1:1:1 ratio. However, the mental health compositions of these three groups present significant differences in the hypothesized directions, as table 14-3 below reveals.

We note first in table 14-3 that the stable nonmobile group presents an even balance in its number of Impaired and Well members. With this as a point of comparison, we further observe that among the "climbers" there is an imbalance, with the Well outnumbering the Impaired by about 3:2. Finally, among the "descenders" the imbalance is tipped sharply to the other side, the Impaired exceeding the Well by almost 5:2.[34]

Two qualifications must be weighed in considering these trends. First, the relationship between occupational mobility and mental health would be at least partially spurious if the up-moving people were largely younger adults of higher status origins and those moving in the opposite direction were principally older adults of lower paren-

TABLE 14–3. HOME SURVEY SAMPLE (AGE 20–59), RESPONDENTS'
DISTRIBUTIONS ON MENTAL HEALTH CLASSIFICATION OF MEN AND SINGLE
WOMEN BY OCCUPATIONAL MOBILITY TYPES

Mental health categories	Mobility types		
	Up	Stable	Down
Well	21.0%	22.6%	12.7%
Mild symptom formation	41.6	37.0	33.8
Moderate symptom formation	23.8	16.8	23.4
Impaired*	13.6	23.6	30.1
N = 100%	(315)	(297)	(299)
Impaired-Well ratio	65	104	235

* $x^2 = 24.57$, $2df$, $p < .001$.

tal SES. The fact is that the climbers are split below and above the 40-year line exactly 50–50, whereas the descenders are split 40–60. The latter *are* a somewhat older group. On the other hand, the climbers are predominantly (67 percent) from blue-collar fathers, whereas the descenders are mainly (55 percent) from white-collar fathers. Thus, the two potentially masking factors approximately serve to cancel each other out.

Second, our data may actually understate the strength of the relationship. An optimal test would focus on self-supporting adults at an age when occupational change is largely over, i.e., beyond the age of 40. Among younger adults, particularly in bureaucratic organizations, further reaches of work upgrading may still lie ahead. If so, mobility tendencies among younger adults would expectedly have a lesser linkage with mental health than among older people. This inference is actually supported by a comparison of the younger (age 20 to 39) and older (age 40 to 59) male and single women respondents. That is, the contrast in Impaired-Well balance between the upward- and downward-mobile types is considerably sharper in the senior than in the junior group.

We can look more closely at the character of the changes by focusing down to the 442 U.S.-born male respondents known in terms both of own and of father's occupation. This particular segment of the population is of purified relevance because it excludes single women, who are limited in their occupational movements by an intracultural bias. Also excluded are the foreign-born males, whose mobility can be measured only by their occupational place in the American economy as compared with their father's occupational level in the economy of the homeland. Here various intercultural biases probably operate.

We might start with the high white-collar level of business executives and professionals. Sixty-three fathers have been in this stratum. Of their 63 sampled sons, 33 established themselves in the same occupational bracket; the other 30 dropped to lower levels—several in fact to the bottom of the blue-collar range. However, more than offsetting the latter were 65 men who climbed into this stratum from fathers in lower occupations. (Fifteen of these men had blue-collar fathers.) Now let us consider the respondent mental health differences selectively carried in these shifts. To be emphasized is that the number of cases involved is small and accordingly the Impaired-Well values are to be regarded as suggestive only. In figure 3 the arrow suggests the direction of mobility (horizontal arrow signifies nonmobility), and the number in the circle attached represents the Impaired-Well ratio of the men who moved in that direction.

As figure 3 indicates, the healthier sons replicated their father's top

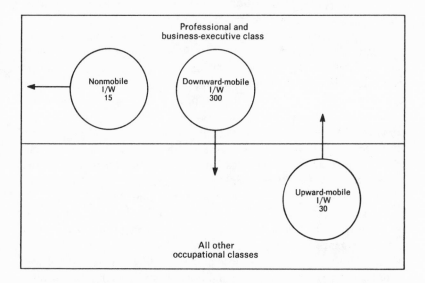

FIGURE 3. HOME SURVEY SAMPLE (AGE 20–59), IMPAIRED-WELL RATIOS OF SONS ORIGINATING IN OR ASCENDING INTO THE TOP OCCUPATIONAL CLASS.

occupational position. On the other hand, the less healthy sons more often moved down, to be replaced by far healthier men ascending from fathers at lower levels. Thus, all 63 sons of top-level fathers present an Impaired-Well value of 70, whereas for all 98 men *now* in that occupational bracket the corresponding value is 24.

At the opposite pole is the unskilled class of blue-collar occupations. Fifty of our U.S.-born male respondents were from fathers at this level. Of these sons, 14 remain in the same kind of occupation; 6 of these have impaired mental health, 3 are "well." Thirty-six other sons have climbed to higher points—14 to the low and middle white-collar strata, 6 to the executive-professional ranks—and have an approximate balance in number of Impaired and Well respondents (Impaired-Well ratio of 120). Replacing these climbers are 37 descenders from fathers in higher positions.[35] With the out-climbers healthier in composition than the nonmobile men and the in-descenders least favorable of all in mental health (Impaired-Well ratio of 240), the 51 men now in the unskilled class have an Impaired-Well ratio of 225. This compares with a value of 150 for the group of 50 offspring of unskilled fathers.

In the intervening occupational levels the mobility traffic is at once more balanced and more complicated. For example, there are 135 male respondents with fathers in the middle (managerial and semiprofessional) white-collar stratum. Of the sons, 65 (48 percent) were nonmobile, 46 (34 percent) were climbers, and 24 (18 percent) descenders. However, the latter two types of out-movers from the class were replaced by two types of in-movers, namely, 43 climbers from fathers of lower occupational standing and 26 descenders from executive-professional fathers. As net effect of these four-way counterbalancing movements, the mental health composition of American-born male respondents who are *themselves* in the middle white-collar category is little different from that of the group of men *deriving* from fathers who had been in this category.

We would emphasize again that the mental health differences reported for the three mobility types of respondents probably represent the convergence of two sets of factors: (1) original (preadult) mental health differences among those carried in different own-SES directions and (2) subsequent mental health shifts along the several mobility courses.

A longitudinal study design is required to bridge the Douvan-Adelson data from adolescents and our own from Midtown adults. To such a prospective study, both sets of data offer the hypothesis that on the whole healthier adolescents tend to be more heavily drawn into the traffic of upward-moving adults, whereas more disturbed adolescents tend to be shunted into the downward traffic. We suggest the further hypothesis that on the whole those in the ascending traffic stream are subsequently less likely to show exogenous deterioration in mental health than those in the descending stream.

It may be asked how these hypotheses are to be articulated to the postulates in the previous chapter bearing on the child of low-status families. Among sample respondents derived from blue-collar fathers we know that about two in every five have been upward-mobile on our six-level occupation scale. Whether or not these Midtowners are in this respect typical of blue-collar offspring elsewhere is not yet known; but from evidence presented in chapter 5 there are intimations that they may be more upward-oriented than their occupation peers elsewhere seem to be. Even here, however, the nonclimbers outnumber the ascenders. That there are climbers at all would seem to reflect two factors: (1) The dynamic New York economy had open places at the requisite occupational levels, and (2) the objective goads to escape to a more comfortable and respected style of life probably sort out the climbers from the nonclimbers along such personality dimensions as were delineated in the Douvan-Adelson study and were briefly sketched earlier in this chapter. The latter inference raises the unanswered question whether differences within lower-class families yield personality variations among their *own* offspring which issue in subsequent status-mobility divergences among siblings.

OWN SES AND MENTAL HEALTH

From the unraveling of father-son occupational changes we can better grasp the results when the entire Midtown sample of adults is examined for mental health composition as classified on the scale of own socioeconomic status. In figure 1 we charted the Impaired-Well ratios of the sample arranged by SES origin as indexed by father's schooling and occupation. These are reproduced in figure 4, but they

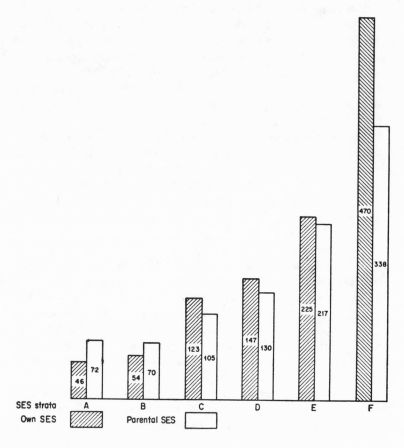

FIGURE 4. HOME SURVEY SAMPLE (AGE 20–59), IMPAIRED-WELL RATIOS OF OWN-SES AND PARENTAL-SES STRATA.

now accompany bars representing the Impaired-Well values of the entire sample when sorted by own SES as indexed in this instance only, strictly for comparison, by respondent's own education and own occupation.[36]

Reflecting the greater tendency of the Well to move upward and the Impaired downward, figure 4 for the first time reveals that own SES stands to adult mental health in a relationship even more sharply accentuated than does parental SES. In other words, if parental socioeconomic status plays any contributory part in mental health determination, own SES tends to overstate the magnitude of that contribution.

For all other purposes of classifying respondent's own SES, we inquired about his/her family income and household rent as well as his/her education and occupation. From the sum of the scores on these four indicators, the sample was divided into twelve own-SES strata, as nearly equal in numbers of respondents as possible.

In the strata at the top and bottom extremes of this twelve-way range are 7.0 and 6.5 percent of the sample, respectively. Table 14–4 gives the complete distributions of these two sets of respondents on the Study psychiatrists' classification of mental health.

TABLE 14–4. HOME SURVEY SAMPLE (AGE 20–59), RESPONDENTS' DISTRIBUTIONS ON MENTAL HEALTH CLASSIFICATION OF TOP AND BOTTOM STRATA IN TWELVE-WAY OWN-SES RANGE

Mental health categories	Highest stratum	Lowest stratum
Well	30.0%	4.6%
Mild symptom formation	37.5	25.0
Moderate symptom formation ...	20.0	23.1
Impaired	12.5*	47.3*
Marked symptom formation ...	6.7	16.7
Severe symptom formation	5.8	21.3
Incapacitated	0.0	9.3
N = 100%	(120)	(108)
Impaired-Well ratio	42	1,020

* $t = 6.0$ (.001 level of confidence).

The Moderate and Mild categories of symptom formation aside, the mental health contrast between the top and bottom strata could hardly be more sharply drawn. The story is partially told in their Severe and Incapacitated totals (5.8 and 30.6 percent, respectively) and above all in their respective Impaired-Well ratios of 42 and 1,020.

Of even larger interest perhaps is the shape of the Impaired-Well trend line across the entire range of the twelve-way own-SES continuum. This is profiled in figure 5.

Confronting data like those underlying figure 5, some investigators would defer to a statistical device (like chi square) for a yes-or-no dictum about the existence of a relationship between two vari-

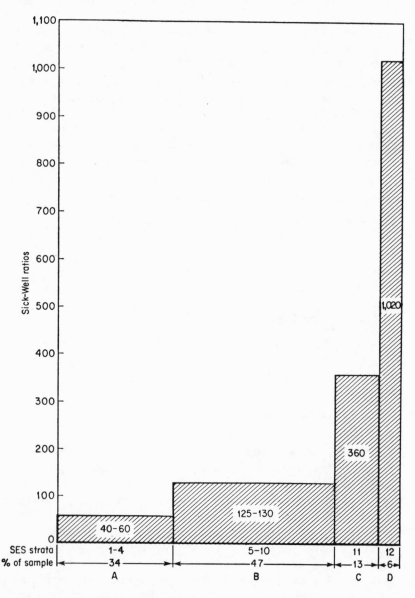

FIGURE 5. HOME SURVEY SAMPLE (AGE 20–59), IMPAIRED-WELL RATIOS OF TWELVE-WAY OWN-SES STRATA.

ables, beyond that producible by chance, and consider their work done if the answer is "yes" at a given level of confidence. Since such an answer conveys nothing whatever about the relative strength or weakness of the relationship so affirmed, other investigators apply more specialized statistical devices to measure closeness of the correlation.

However, both kinds of statistical yardsticks are completely insensitive to something potentially important in the data which are given in figure 5. That is, on the overall spread of the trend there is a wide socioeconomic span (strata 1 to 4) devoid of any notable differences in mental health composition until a line of change is crossed. Rising to the 125 to 130 level at this crossing point, the Impaired-Well ratio next remains in a flat trend across another broad span of own-SES differences (strata 5 to 10). These two large plateaus are followed toward the bottom of the own-SES range by two Impaired-Well peaks (strata 11 and 12).

The precise extent to which Midtown's mental health distributions statistically vary with differences in own socioeconomic status is of negligible moment compared to this demand of sheer curiosity: Given that each of the graph's four SES zones has its own inner similitude of mental health composition, how can these segments be concretely identified? We have already seen that the adult own-SES groupings are the residues of rise and fall of status around the parental-SES points of departure. However, our present interest in identifying the four own-SES zones is directed not to their past but rather to their present life circumstances. These are large contemporary "worlds," we can assume, that are the scene or the source of morbidity-precipitating events for the more vulnerable people in their midst. On the basis of data culled for this monograph we can indicate the approximate boundaries of these four worlds only in the most elementary economic terms.

In order of size, the largest is zone B, embracing strata 5 to 10 and roughly half of the entire sample. These six strata are quite uniform in mental health composition, with Impaired-Well ratios that stand near the whole sample's value of 127. They are broadly spread across the lesser ranks of the middle managerial and semiprofessional occupations, through the lower white-collar, the skilled blue-collar, and the higher-wage ranks of the semiskilled factory workers. The family income span, in 1954 dollars, was in the main from $3,000 to

$6,000, permitting a tolerable but hardly ample standard of consumption and certainly not permitting the accumulation of any significant reserve funds. With this "tightrope" living standard as the foundation of their claim to respectability, these respondents are close to the line of insecurity. When family crises jeopardize the economic supports of this way of life, the strain placed upon personality resources may be great.

Since these people are numerically the dominant and psychosocially the pivotal segment in the Midtown population, they have a potentially large influence on the mental health climate of the community, above all at times of collective crisis.[37]

Noteworthy also is the large representation of blue-collar respondents in this zone. In recent decades they have caught up with the lower white-collar class[38] in both income and level of consumption and now also match their mental health composition. A tantalizing question they pose is this: Has their documented economic and social progress through these decades been accompanied by an unobserved improvement in mental health, i.e., improvement sufficient to close what had previously been an unfavorable difference? This is a question to which we will return in chapter 23.

Second in sample representation (34 percent) are zone A's own-SES strata 1 to 4, covering the more affluent managerial and professional classes. Here we cross into a world characterized by a more secure, expansive, and ego-nurturing style of life, with larger buffers or cushions against the inevitable abrasions and hard knocks of human existence. It is striking that above roughly $6,000 annual income (in 1954 dollars) further increments toward $15,000 and far beyond, with all the accompanying socioeconomic correlates, do not appear to register any further gains in group mental health composition. (One 1954 dollar is about equivalent to two in 1974.) However, it can be hypothesized that without the common denominator "prophylactics" of these strata their latent store of mental pathology would probably emerge in more overt and impairing forms.

At the other side of the own-SES range we find that zone C absorbs a relatively narrow 13 percent segment of the Midtown sample. Occupationally they are semiskilled workers in the City's newer, marginal low-wage industries and workers in the more stable forms of unskilled labor, e.g., domestics, sweepers, window washers, and janitors. Weekly family income may at times reach the $60 point but more often hovers around $50. Here, we move into a zone of "struggle to keep head above water." The entire style and tone of life bear the marks of strain from constant struggle at the edge of poverty. The mental health situation here is suggested by the spike in the Impaired-Well ratio to the 360 point.

In zone D there is breakthrough to still another psychosocial realm, namely, poverty itself. Stemming in the main from parents in unskilled and semiskilled manual occupations, people in zone D are in or near the bottom bracket on every one of our four status indicators. Probably of first significance is that most of them did not complete elementary school. For some respondents this default doubtless was determined by such exogenous barriers as extreme poverty, a disabled or departed parent, or an otherwise acutely deprived family; for other respondents the default may reflect childhood endogenous disabilities, physical or mental.

Whatever the specific source of the barrier, subminimal schooling on its own account sets off a chain of other restrictions: (1) restriction largely to marginal, temporary forms of unskilled labor; (2) restriction to a low, unstable income[39] that at best is beneath the minimal necessary to shelter, clothe, and feed a family (total 1954 income in zone D households almost without exception was in a range between $15 to $40 weekly); (3) restriction to cramped quarters in the most deteriorated slum tenements.

Such noxious life burdens, together with handicapped or vulnerable personalities developed in childhood, often combine to produce a break in the intolerable struggle. Chronic poverty has at some time brought almost all zone D respondents to the City Welfare Department for financial assistance; and many belong to "multiproblem" families that are known to the police, courts, private social agencies, and mental hospitals.

From this group's mental health distribution reported in table 14–4 above, it is seen that exceedingly few (4.6 percent) are Well and nearly half (47.3 percent) are Impaired.[40] Segregated with others in like circumstances and mental health conditions, the numerically dominant Impaired of zone D doubtless help to create an unstable slum community that often carries its own pathogenic "contagion," in particular for the children in its midst. It is hardly surprising, therefore, to hear of a contemporary (1956) New York City Youth Board Survey that covered 825 children of needy families and reported that 40 percent of these children manifest "serious behavior problems." It was predicted that another 10 percent, principally in the youngest segment of the sample, would likely develop such problems.

Here the frequency of adult mental pathology is probably of unprecedented proportions. And here the environmental contamination of children very likely ensures that the epidemic shall continue to reproduce itself in the generation ahead, as it apparently has from the generation preceding.

Reviewing the four zones observed in figure 5, we can infer that certain turning points in the quality and weight of adult life conditions emerge along the status continuum represented in our twelve-way own-SES scale.

SUMMARY

In this sweep across the front defined by socioeconomic status with its multiform salients, we probed a number of discrete hypotheses with the following returns:

1. On the parental-SES range the frequency of impairment varies inversely and the Well rate varies directly.

2. This trend in Impaired-Well balance also characterizes those in the sample's youngest age group, who only recently have crossed the threshold from adolescence. It was thus possible to reject the hypothesis that SES-origin differentials in mental health had almost entirely been generated during adult life.

3. Among the several SES-origin groups no significant differences appear in the frequency of schizophrenic signs, anxiety-tension symptoms, or excessive intake behaviors. In all other pathognomonic dimensions covered, however, there is an *inverse* correlation with parental SES. These dimensions included disturbances in intellectual, affective, somatic, characterological, and interpersonal functioning.

4. Simultaneous analysis of age and status-origin against respondent mental health revealed that *both* independent variables are related to mental health, each in its own right. This suggested first that parental-SES differences had implanted varying mental health potentialities among sample respondents during childhood; and second,

that during the temporal course of adolescence and adulthood, precipitating factors had provoked overt morbidity among the more vulnerable people from all SES-origin strata. The combined power of these two demographic variables, as reflected in the index of Impaired-Well magnitudes, is substantial.

5. The hypothesis was suggested that this triad of age, parental SES, and adult mental health was specific to the kinds of people who choose to live in an area like Midtown. That is, the identified nexus lacked wider currency in the American population. Evidence from four radically different populations indicated rejection of this hypothesis. Positively stated, the complex triad isolated in the Midtown sample may well characterize larger reaches of the American people.

6. Intergeneration status mobility, as read in a single point-of-time study, is a reciprocal factor relative to adult mental health. In the Midtown sample's coverage of three mobility types, the climbers had the smallest Impaired-Well values and the descenders had the largest by far. For prospective longitudinal studies these data suggested the two-part hypothesis: (*a*) Preadult personality differences partially determine directions of status change in adulthood; (*b*) *on the whole*, upward status mobility is rewarding psychically as well as materially, whereas downward status mobility is depriving in both respects.

7. Reflecting the selective escalator effects of status mobility, own-SES shows an even stronger relationship to adult mental health than does respondent status origin.

8. Using four status indicators it is possible to divide the own-SES range into 12 finer strata. Revealed in these strata are four mental health zones, or contemporary worlds, seemingly marked at their boundaries by breakthrough points of differences in the size and security of economic underpinnings, in styles of life, in ego nurturance, and in their psychosocial atmospheres. In zones C and D, near or at the poverty level, we discern particularly heavy pathogenic weights currently bearing on the especially vulnerable people.

For targeting of social policy, Midtown zones C and D, and likely their psychosocioeconomic counterparts elsewhere on the national scene, convey highest priority claims for milieu therapy in its broadest sense. Ultimately indicated here may be interventions into the downward spiral of compounded tragedy, wherein those handicapped in personality or social assets from childhood on are trapped as adults at or near the poverty level, there to find themselves enmeshed in a web of burdens that tend to precipitate (or intensify) mental and somatic morbidity; in turn, such precipitations propel the descent deeper into chronic, personality-crushing indigency. Here, we would suggest, is America's own displaced-persons problem.

For basic research, the joint evidence of this chapter and of several collateral studies of general populations here reviewed highlights the status system as an apparatus that differentially sows, reaps, sifts, and redistributes the community's crops of mental morbidity and of sound personalities.

In no way have we claimed that the mental health effects produced by this apparatus are determined by sociocultural processes alone. Nevertheless, in line with our field of professional competence and responsibility to future investigators, we have advanced a number of hypotheses that implicate certain specific forms of sociocultural processes operating within the framework of the social class system. These hypotheses focus on the four mental health zones we have found dividing Midtown's own SES range. Distinguishing these zones, the hypotheses suggest, are economic factors linked to mechanisms of invidious discrimination that pervade the zones' respective way-of-life constellations. These postulates hold that toward one pole of the status range, in both preadult and adult life, such processes tend to penetrate the family unit with eugenic or prophylactic effects for personality development, whereas toward the opposite pole they more often work with pathogenic or precipitating effects.

These hypotheses chart paths of further necessary exploration. They can thereby lay reasonable claim to the attention of research programs of community psychiatry and psychiatric sociology.[41]

NOTES

1. David E. Hailman, *The Prevalence of Illness among Male and Female Workers and Housewives*, Public Health Bulletin 260, United States Public Health Service, 1941.

2. L. G. Rowntree, K. H. McGill, and L. P. Hellman, "Mental and Personality Disorders in Selective Service Registrants," *Journal of the American Medical Association* 128 (August 11, 1945): 1084–1087.

3 R. W. Hyde and L. V. Kingsley, "Studies in Medical Sociology: The Relation of Mental Disorder to the Community Socioeconomic Level," *New England Journal of Medicine* 231 (October 19, 1944): 543–548. Subjects were classified by place of residence, the residential unit being "the area under the jurisdiction of each local selection board." Each area was rated by criteria of "attractiveness

as a residential section." The highest (A) of the six rating categories covered "wealthy suburban communities" and the lowest (F) covered "the worst Boston slums."

4. Reported in *Chronic Illness in a Large City: The Baltimore Study*, 1957. The SES indicator employed was annual family income, as classified in four categories: Under $2,000, $2,000–$3,999, $4,000–$5,999, $6,000 and over. Overlooked in this investigation was the following consideration: to the extent that the sick are, or should be, family breadwinners, and are impaired in their earnings capabilities, their income is a variable contaminated by, rather than independent of, their mental health status.

5. It should be observed that three of the investigations had a second common characteristic—namely, psychiatric evaluation of the sample individuals was quite peripheral in emphasis to a physical examination. In the Boston Selective Service investigation, Hyde and Kingsley report that each psychiatrist examined about fifty men in a five-hour day, averaging in fact a few minutes per man. In the Baltimore study, a large number of chronic and acute somatic conditions were in the purview of the examining internists, who also made the psychiatric evaluation—if they were so inclined and scarce time permitted. Thus, the possibilities of judgmental error in the mental morbidity rates of all three studies loom large. Furthermore, when enmeshed in a variable like socioeconomic status, such an element of error can unwittingly work to bias the findings in various directions among different studies.

We can assume that validity of mental health determination in a general population study partially depends on primacy of the psychiatric focus in the research design and also upon measures for controlling potential bias in the classification process.

6. This hypothesis, it must be emphasized, cannot be tested in the patient aggregate counted by the Midtown Treatment Census nor in the patient aggregate enumerated by the earlier, parallel New Haven Psychiatric Census conducted by Hollingshead and Redlich. Both sets of patients are being held for later discussion of the treatment variable in the chapter that follows.

7. To be sure, the trend in incapacitation rates—except between the extreme strata—is not altogether consistent. It should be remembered, however, that Midtown's mental hospital patients have been drawn principally from the incapacitated group. These patients were excluded from the Home Interview Survey but were included in the Midtown Treatment Census. In the latter operation, we could determine only own SES of patients, in a form allowing delineation of three status levels. As we shall see presently, the hospitalization rates in the upper, middle, and lower of these levels are 0.2, 0.4, and 0.7 percent, respectively. Accordingly, we can infer that if the hospitalized patients could be added to the several columns in table 14–1, the trend in incapacitation rates on the SES-origin scale would probably be somewhat smoother and sharper than now appears to be the case.

In any event, the smaller the frequency values in a distribution, the more prone they are to magnify chance fluctuations due to sampling. Thus, with small frequencies some irregularity of trend is a negligible matter if the overall direction of the trend is clear. Such a trend is discernible in the above incapacitation rates, especially when corrected for the hospitalized patients.

8. Needless to say, this measure carries no claim to a place in the armamentarium of statistics. It is a supplementary reporting device for arithmetical summary of two rates and is employed for the convenience of the reader when intergroup comparisons of such paired rates become too complicated and cumbersome to juggle.

9. The intermediate (C and D) levels number 41 percent of the sample and account for 41 and 39 percent of the Well and Impaired categories, respectively.

10. Thus, parenthetically, our findings do not rest entirely on the impairment band of the Study's mental health spectrum. The frequency of impairment usually varies in a counterpoint congruence with the Well category, in such a way that a generalization about one category often applies in reverse to the other. This seesaw bond seems to reinforce the apparent significance of both mental health types.

11. The three classes are mergers of the six SES-origin strata and carry their original A to F notations. Only by such merger can the progressive shrinkage of cases in subgroups be partially compensated. The price paid, of course, is reduction in the range of SES differences.

12. Of the four age groups in the sample it will be remembered that this is also þy far the most favored in mental health composition (cf. chapter 11).

13. The five specific signs were: (1) I often have trouble in getting to sleep or staying asleep. (2) I am often bothered by nervousness. (3) I have periods of such great restlessness that I cannot sit long in a chair. (4) I am the worrying type. (5) I have·personal worries that get me down physically.

14. However, when respondents are classified according to own SES, the prevalence rates in the bottom and top strata are 7.4 and 1.8 percent, respectively, a difference that *is* statistically significant. Reflected thereby is the fact that in their own status these particular "schizophrenic thought-process" respondents tend to be lower than their parents were.

15. J. Ruesch, "Social Techniques, Social Status and Social Change," in C. Kluckhohn and H. A. Murray, eds., *Personality in Nature, Society and Culture*, 1949, pp. 117–130.

16. Among the 12 subgroups the only exception to this consistent trend is to be found on the 50 to 59 age level, where the respondents of middle-class origin stand at an Impaired-Well point somewhat below that of their upper-class neighbors. Beyond the possibilities of chance fluctuations, the explanation for this exception is not yet apparent.

17. One possible accounting for this particular exception, beyond that of sampling variability, goes back to a problem sketched in chapter 5. We there discussed the pressures of inadequate living-and-play space on Midtown families with young children and the consequent exodus of middle-class families (in particular) to city and suburban areas of less horizontal and vertical congestion. Accordingly, it seems possible that the age 30 to 39 parents of middle-class origin are a self-selected residue who have resisted these pressures bearing on the well-being of their children. If so, the question of why their age 40 to 49 SES-origin peers, with older children, do not reflect the same processes is one for which no immediate answer is at hand.

18. This means, of course, that both of these factors must be controlled simultaneously, so far as possible, in analyzing the other sociocultural variables covered in the data chapters that follow.

19. R. J. Weiss et al., "Epidemiology of Emotional Disturbance in a Men's College," *Journal of Nervous and Mental Disease* 141 (1965): 240–250; and W. G. Smith et al., "Psychiatric Disorder in a College Population," *Archives of General Psychiatry* 9 (1963): 351–361.

20. S. Stouffer et al., *The American Soldier*, 1949, vol. II, table 2, pp. 423–425.

21. If the universe of white Army men in the enlisted ranks was more general than the Midtown universe in its national, rural-urban, and ethnic-origin

dimensions, it was less general in age, sex, socioeconomic status, and in screening out of grosser pathologies at the point of Selective Service examination.

22. S. S. Bellin and R. H. Hardt, "Marital Status and Mental Disorders among the Aged," *American Sociological Review* 23 (April, 1958): table 4, p. 160.

23. H. J. Dupuy et al., "Selected Symptoms of Psychological Distress," *National Center for Health Statistics*, Series 11, no. 37, 1970.

24. Quoted in R. K. Merton, *Social Theory and Social Structure*, 1968, p. 192. So ingrained is the emphasis upon status change in the *upward* direction that it can operate as a reflex in seemingly unrelated kinds of spatial situations. Referring to changes in tenancy, for example, a prominent New York realtor reports that in Manhattan "many tenants, commercial as well as residential, have a great reluctance to move down. When they move to new quarters, the space *must be* [italics added] on a higher floor than that which they leave." (*New York Times*, April 27, 1958.) Because of street noises and lack of vistas, avoidance of quarters at low floors is of course utilitarian. However, this rationale is hardly involved in upward changes from quarters on the higher floors of Manhattan's skyscraper apartment houses and office buildings. The penthouse and the executive suite at the crown of the tower are of course physical embodiments symbolizing Carnegie's phrase, "My place is at the top."

25. S. M. Lipset and R. Bendix, *Social Mobility in Industrial Society*, 1959, pp. 65, 251.

26. A. B. Hollingshead and F. C. Redlich, "Schizophrenia and Social Structure," *American Journal of Psychiatry* 110 (March 1954): 695–701.

27. M. H. Lystad, "Social Mobility among Selected Groups of Schizophrenic Patients," *American Sociological Review* 22 (June 1957): 280–292.

28. Lipset and Bendix, *Social Mobility in Industrial Society*, p. 65.

29. Ibid., pp. 251–252.

30. E. Douvan and J. Adelson, "The Psychodynamics of Social Mobility in Adolescent Boys," *Journal of Abnormal and Social Psychology* 56. (January 1958): 31–44.

31. These hypotheses had been influenced by the promising conceptualizations of Ruesch bearing on (1) mobility motivations as emergents from "attitudes toward one's parents" and (2) the distinction between "climbers," and "strainers" as the upward aspiring who did not quite succeed. (Ruesch, "Social Techniques, Social Status and Social Change," p. 125.)

32. Some writers, Ruesch included, tend to view the consequences of upward mobility in terms of stresses that we can subsume under the concept of role discontinuity. As employed in chapter 11, this concept refers to the disjunctive predicament enveloping an individual when he acquires a rather new kind of role without adequate preparation of the requisite psychic defenses and social skills. This concept would probably apply in the main to the relatively rare instances of individuals who rise far economically in a relatively short period of time. However, our observations suggest that in most cases status mobility tendencies go back to the child's socialization in family, age-peer, and school settings. In such instances, furthermore, adolescence tends to be a period of informal apprenticeship in developing skills for the higher-status goal envisaged. Indeed, one of the major functions of high school and college life is to offer just such an apprenticeship. Thus, the usual gradual transition from parental SES to higher own status seems to us to be rather more continuous than discontinuous. See relevant data in L. Srole and A. K. Fischer, "The Social Epidemiology of Smoking Behavior, 1953 and 1970: The Midtown Manhattan Study," *Social Science and Medicine* 7 (May 1973): 341–358.

33. Married women were excluded from this analysis because intergeneration status mobility was usually accomplished in their case through their choice of husband. The wife's effect on his status movement was expected to be secondary to his own personality determinants. Indeed, when we classify wives according to occupational differences between their father and their husband, we find relatively small variations in mental health composition among the three mobility types.

34. The schizophrenic-process respondents form only a small fraction of the down-mobile group.

35. Nine of the latter fathers were in the white-collar category and two in the executive-professional class. If the latter sons represent the extreme type of downward mobility, the six sons who rose from unskilled fathers to top-drawer careers exemplify maximal upward mobility. In this particular sample of American-born males such "rags-to-riches" movement occurred once in every 75 men. It is a plausible guess that the latter is an exceptionally high rate, probably to be found in few populations outside of New York City.

36. In the case of married women, the indicators used were own education and husband's occupation.

37. As evidence of one possible facet in this crisis potentiality, the history of collective pathology is not likely to minimize the significance of industrial Germany's Nazi period.

38. It is not to be assumed that this group has been economically static. Reflecting not unionization but shortages in the local white-collar market, city-wide data on clerical office workers indicated that between 1949 and 1960 their salaries increased 59 percent in dollars and 21 percent in buying power.

39. Applying as a criterion the frequency of *steady* employment during the minor economic recession of 1958, a national survey revealed a frequency of only 50 percent among workers with less than nine years school, 75 percent among high school graduates, and 90 percent among holders of a college degree. (Unpublished study by the University of Michigan Survey Research Center and United States Census Bureau.)

40. A New York study has revealed that "67% of public welfare recipients [had] known or suspected psychological disorders." (Violet G. Bemmels, "Survey of Mental Health Problems in Social Agency Caseloads," *American Journal of Psychiatry* 121 [August 1964]: 136–147.)

41. For differential definitions of these two fields see L. Srole, "Sociology and Psychiatry: Fusions and Fissions of Identity," in P. Roman and H. Trice, eds., *Explorations in Psychiatric Sociology*, 1974, pp. 5–17.

CHAPTER 15

PARENTAL SOCIOECONOMIC STATUS: INCOME ADEQUACY AND OFFSPRING MENTAL HEALTH

LEO SROLE

In constructing the measure of respondents' parental socioeconomic status during childhood, we used as components father's years of schooling and occupational level but not family income. The latter was excluded because of the Midtown sample's enormous diversity in parental income standards for any given occupation across time and space. How, for example, could we possibly transform into a single monetary yardstick the incomes of three respondents' fathers of the very same occupation—e.g., plumber, one in Rome, Italy, during the 1890's; the second in Rome, New York, during the 1920's; and the third in Manhattan's "Little Italy" during the 1940's—even if our adult respondents could remember the actual figures approximately, if at all?

We assumed that they would more likely recall from childhood, with some vividness, as we shall see, the felt deprivational vacuums of the family's empty cupboards and pockets. Accordingly we asked a two-part question: "During the years you were growing up (age 6 to 18) did your parents (or those who brought you up) ever have a hard time making ends meet, i.e., making a living, buying what the family needed?" If the reply was "Yes," this followed: "Did they have such a hard time—often, sometimes, or rarely?" Analysis indicates the feasibility of a dichotomy counterposing the "often hard times" category against the "sometimes," "rarely" and "no/never" replies, combined into a "not often" category.

In figure 1 (page 322 below), a bar graph represents the ratios of

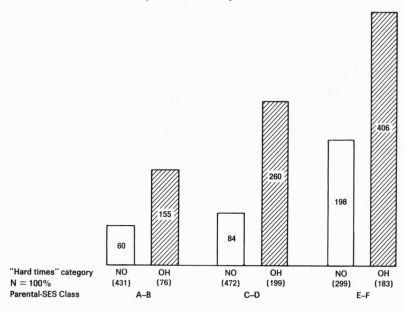

FIGURE 6. HOME SURVEY SAMPLE (AGE 20–59), IMPAIRED-WELL RATIOS OF PARENTAL-SES CLASSES DIVIDED INTO "OFTEN HARD TIMES" AND "NOT OFTEN" CATEGORIES.

number of Impaired per 100 Wells in each of the respondents' six parental-SES strata. In figure 6 these six strata are telescoped into three classes; represented are the Impaired-Well ratios when each class is split into an "often hard times" ("OH") and a "not often" ("NO") category.

We see above that whatever the father's weight of schooling and occupation (with corresponding expected standard of living), chronically insufficient income for that standard, and accompanying thwarting of legitimate expectations, are followed in his grown offspring by a tipping of the balance in their mental health composition toward a higher risk of Impairment and a lower chance of Wellness.[1]

Attention is drawn in particular to the middle (C–D) class, where the OH–NO difference of 3:1 is greater than the 2:1 difference in the lower (E–F) class. It would appear therefore that chronic financial insufficiency for a middle-class standard of living places a family in the hierarchically interstitial niche of "middle-class poor." That is a painfully anomalous, marginal position in a social class group that at best appears to be never altogether free of a lingering sense of economic insecurity, and one that seems to be somewhat more pathogenic for its children than even the NO, unpressured lower class family (I–W ratios of 260 and 198, respectively).

Similarly, grown offspring of upper-class parents who in earlier years had been chronically pressed for money to meet their normative social class prerogatives are somewhat less favorable in mental health composition than even their counterparts from middle-class families with incomes more or less approximating their class norms (I–W ratios of 155 and 84, respectively).

An excellently documented case study of this relatively rare upper-class predicament is offered us in novelist John Marquand's early life history and its life-long reverberations in his character and behavior. Marquand's parents were of "old money" Massachusetts "Brahmin" origin, originally presenting a domestic picture broadly resembling TV's turn-of-the-century "Upstairs" Bellamy family ambiance, with a full complement of "Downstairs" household staff—except that John's father, a personable but financially irresponsible man, dissipated all of his inherited, modest wealth. As a result, while John's still amply moneyed cousins were off to "fashionable" prep schools, John, in a reversal of his long-held plans, had to suffer through Newburyport's lackluster public high school, deprived, writes his biographer, of "all things [he] might once have expected but now could never enjoy. . . . there was no need for him even to look forward to anything like that. There was no money for it [he was told] and that was that. It was what happened when one's father was a failure."[2] The father's profligacy took on the proportions to the son of a hero fallen and a Paradise lost, grievous and forever irrevocable, a Horatio Alger story literally turned upside down.

"Throughout his life," adds biographer Birmingham, "John Marquand liked [as a tireless audience seeker] to make the point that much of his childhood and young manhood had been hard and poor." The resulting character disfigurations in Marquand's extreme "obsession" with money were later reflected in the fact that, even at the peak of his munificently rewarding career as a popular writer, he was an "exceptionally frugal, even tightfisted man—[manifesting] a preoccupation with thrift and spending [that] was almost neurotic. . . . He once had a violent scene with a woman he loved over an air mail stamp. To keep himself from spending money he adopted the practice of carrying no money on his person. As a result, he was a slight [the biographer's understatement] annoyance to his friends, who were forever having to make him small loans."[3]

The deeper trauma of his early family's financial stringencies are reflected in the clinically significant fact that "John had always been something of a hypochondriac."[4] In 1953, "convinced that he had an ulcer . . . he spent close to two weeks . . . undergoing a series of tests and x-rays which revealed an 'ulcerous condition' but no frank or apparent ulcer. . . . his doctor pronounced his problems largely psychosomatic."[5]

Of the early family impacts projected into Marquand's fictional works, Birmingham writes, "Failure and lost chances . . . would become linked themes in John Marquand's best [indeed almost all] novels . . . in which the villain was most often his father."[6]

Although Marquand went on to Harvard on a scholarship the College offered him, "he felt acutely embarrassed [there] at being the poor relation of a well-off [extended] family."[7] "Sometimes," during those college years, in what is pure Horatio Alger imagery, "Marquand would . . . stand quietly in the shadows," writes his biographer, "watching the bold young blades in their tail coats and silk hats . . . as they emerged from [Harvard's] Gold Coast parties [and] see himself not only as the poor relation but also the social outcast, the lonely boy with his nose pressed against the window pane, watching the shimmering life that was led by the handsome, the witty and the rich."[8]

In the light of figure 6 it is now necessary to refine the finding revealed in figure 1 to read as follows: Relative poverty and felt deprivation by the standards of one's social class reference group are heavy burdens that can descend on and distress children at all SES levels, including the topmost one, with possible adverse consequences for their subsequent mental health chances. This is not to suggest, of course, that the implicated factor is purely economic in character. Chronic parental underachievement of financial and related expectations is always mortifying to a family caught in its immobilizing web, but if it operates as a pathogenic input into children's subsequent personality development, it may itself also be a symptomatic manifestation of malfunctions, emotional and/or somatic, in either or both parents.

If so, what we have been reading in figure 6 may be the "sleeper effects" of chronic economic pressures and frustrations, compounded by mental and/or physical disabilities of parents, on children during the formative years of life. Certainly, the elder Marquand's gambling compulsions, restless itinerancy and relatively early signs of senility suggest that he played such a compounded role during his son's adolescent period.[9] A remarkably parallel case in point is Eugene O'Neill's "storm-swept" family history that is repeatedly reenacted in many of his plays. O'Neill came from middle-class parents of Irish origin who fell economically during his boyhood under the devastating weights of both parents' problems.[10]

Figure 6 seems to show cross-SES traces of the financial adequacy strand[11] in the tangle of parental characteristics that are implicated in offsprings' mental health, perhaps the first evidence of this kind on a general population-wide scale to be reported in the relevant scientific literature, evidence that in fact had been isolated too late for inclusion in the earlier (1962) edition of the present monograph.[12]

In conclusion, while it may be something of a discovery to learn that about 13 percent of A-stratum SES-origin respondents report an "often hard times" childhood, we must not overlook that the corresponding proportions in the five parental-SES strata successively lower are 16.5, 26, 33, 36.6 and 41.4 percent, respectively. Certainly the facts that this deprivational trauma is experienced among three times as many F-origin as A-origin families, and in the former at far lower, and substantively thinner, levels of accessible material resources, account in no small way for their contrasting Impaired-Well ratios (figure 1) of 338 and 72, respectively, with an OH Impaired-Well ratio (figure 6) of 406 at one extreme and an NO ratio of 60 at the opposite extreme.

After all, John Marquand, with extra-family help, did make it to and through Harvard. On the other hand, his F-origin boyhood acquaintance from a Newburyport riverfront family of clammers never got through the doors of the town's high school. And thereafter, Marquand could go "onward and upward" to a Pulitzer Prize, the cover of *Time* magazine, and a photographic appearance as "Man of Distinction" in a widely displayed liquor ad, whereas his boyhood acquaintance from the Newburyport riverfront was progressively hammered down into knee-crawling dependency on degrading welfare client hand-outs.

In these contrasting life outcomes of two boys, both traumatized and damaged by economically unsupportive and psychologically disturbed fathers, we can glimpse the vastly different compensatory forces operating at different SES-origin levels to carry them as adults to absolutely opposite kinds of career rewards and climaxes.

The converging evidence of this chapter suggests that parents' social class position and income-earning adequacy, as well as personalities, determine to an appalling extent the mental health fates of their adult children. If specific gene linkages lie hidden beneath this empirically established knot of manifestly specific parental characteristics, as some hypothesize, the sociologist must leave it entirely to the geneticist to carry on the slow and extraordinarily refractory scientific work of uncovering and clearly delineating them for us.

NOTES

1. This tipping is apparent in all six parental-SES strata, which are merged above into three classes, both to avoid crowding of graphic space and to counteract undue numerical attenuation of Impaired and Well cases when the OH–NO dichotomy is superimposed on each stratum.

2. S. Birmingham, *The Late John Marquand*, 1972, pp. 15, 28. See also W. L. Warner et al., *Yankee City*, Volumes 1–5, 1941–1959, which reports the pioneer community study of Newburyport with which the present writer was associated as field researcher and coauthor of Volume 3.

3. Birmingham, *The Late John Marquand*, pp. 12–13.

4. Ibid., p. 215.

5. Ibid., p. 243.

6. Ibid., pp. 15, 28.

7. Ibid., p. 32.

8. Ibid., p. 34.

9. Ibid., pp. 17–21, 103–105.

10. For the definitive biography see A. Gelb and B. Gelb, *O'Neill*, 1960.

11. See M. H. Brenner, *Mental Illness and the Economy*, 1973, where long-term rates of psychiatric hospital admissions and changes in the economy are found correlated. This finding seems to partially explain why some hospitalizations occur when they do, but not why the psychopathologies warranting such institutionalization have taken root in some people but not in others.

12. For a different statistical treatment of the same Midtown information see T. S. Langner and S. T. Michael, *Life Stress and Mental Health*, 1963, pp. 227–228.

CHAPTER 16

SOCIOECONOMIC STRATA: THEIR PSYCHIATRIC TREATMENT

LEO SROLE AND THOMAS LANGNER

In the Midtown sample of age 20 to 59 adults the overall prevalence of mental morbidity is inversely related to the independent variable of parental socioeconomic status and related even more closely in this direction to the reciprocal variable of adults' present (own) SES.

We must turn now to another facet of the total complex, namely, how the frequency of psychiatric care varies with socioeconomic status. In this instance we shall apply own SES rather than SES origin as our test variable. We shall do so in part because the latter information is not available in certain segments of the treatment data gathered, but principally because current status, if only in its economic aspects, is certainly the more relevant precondition of movement into prolonged professional care.

For present purposes we can first call upon the one-day prevalence data secured by our Treatment Census operation. The latter, it may be remembered, entailed the systematic effort to circumscribe the universe of Midtown residents, across the entire age range, who on May 1, 1953, were psychiatric patients in the care of public or private hospitals (institutionalized under five continuous years) or of outpatient clinics or office therapists. For reasons outlined in chapter 13, the own-SES indicator we shall use in this particular analysis is a threefold classification of the housing quality observed at the last residence recorded for each patient.

Table 16-1 presents the one-day prevalence of Midtown patients in each status group (per 100,000 of its estimated population) as

TABLE 16–1.   TREATMENT CENSUS (AGE INCLUSIVE), PREVALENCE RATES
(PER 100,000 CORRESPONDING POPULATION) OF MIDTOWN PATIENTS IN
OWN-SES STRATA BY TREATMENT SITE

Treatment site	Own SES (housing indicator)		
	Upper	Middle	Lower
Hospitals:			
Public	98	383	646
Private	104	39	18
Combined inpatients ...	202	422	664
Clinics	61	160	218
Office therapists*	1,440	596	178
Combined outpatients	1,501	756	396
Total Patients rate	1,703	1,178	1,060
N = No. of patients	(575)	(604)	(934)

* These rates are uncorrected for the unreported patients of noncooperating
office therapists. They are corrected for patients reported with addresses lacking
or verifiably false.

distributed through four kinds of psychiatric facilities, together constituting the Total Patients rate.

Given the costs of private hospitals and office therapists, there can
be no surprise that the Midtown prevalence rates for these sites *decrease* downward on the socioeconomic scale, or that the patients in
lower-cost public hospitals and clinics should *increase* downward on
this SES scale.[1] As a result of these cross tendencies, at least in
Midtown, Total Patients rate is largest at the top of the status range
and smallest at the bottom.

The latter finding is in a direction quite the reverse of that observed
in chapter 14 (table 14–1), where mental impairment was seen to be
least prevalent in the highest SES-origin stratum (A) and most concentrated in the lowest stratum (F). This is a paradox, seemingly, to
which we shall return presently.

The SES trend in table 16–1 is also in direct contradiction to that
reported for the Psychiatric Census undertaken by the New Haven
investigation. In their monograph, Hollingshead and Redlich concluded that "the lower the [socioeconomic] class, the greater the
proportion of psychiatric patients."[2]

So striking a contrast warrants careful exploration. The New

Haven authors record[3] Total Patients rate per 100,000 population in each of their several social class groups,[4] as follows:

New Haven SES Class	Total Patients Rate per 100,000
I–II (highest)	556
III	538
IV	642
V (lowest)	1,659
All New Haven	798

This series of rates,[5] as published in the New Haven monograph, hardly represents the linear progression claimed in the conclusion just cited. Instead, it appears to conform more to a dichotomy in which class V for all practical purposes stands counterposed to the rest of the SES range.[6]

As for the seeming direction of the rate differences in the above series, two observations may be in order. First, the New Haven monograph estimates that approximately 40 to 50 office patients were not reported by therapists, principally New York practitioners, who refused to cooperate[7] with the study. These commuting Connecticut patients of New York City psychiatrists were not included in the above New Haven rates. However, it seems most likely that such shielded patients were predominantly from New Haven's highest social class levels. If so, they represent a pinpointed error of under-statement, one that by our estimate could conceivably raise New Haven's combined class I–II patient rate from 556, as reported, toward 700.[8]

Several pertinent reservations also attach themselves to New Haven's class V patient count. Included in this enumeration were transients committed to a state hospital by New Haven police with key information about their home community undeterminable.[9] Not revealed is the number of such rootless transients charged to New Haven's count as class V. Moreover, the sample of New Haven's general population, drawn to estimate the city's inclusive social class distribution (for service as denominators in calculating rates per 100,000 population), explicitly included *no* transients.[10]

Second, the New Haven investigators make this observation: "Once a class V person is committed to a mental institution, the likelihood of his return to the family is small."[11] In terms of our present concern, this would seem to imply that the exceptionally high prevalence rate of New Haven's class V is in part a result of the cumulative pile-up of its unmoving sick as the more or less permanent ". 'ag he ₄p" deposit of custodial patients in public hospitals. To probe this inference we would need a New Haven counterpart of our table 16–1 above. This has not been published, but for such a purpose it is possible to regroup several New Haven tabulations[12] and convert their percentages into patients per 100,000 estimated population in each of the social class groups. These are presented in table 16–2.

TABLE 16–2.   NEW HAVEN PSYCHIATRIC CENSUS (AGE INCLUSIVE), PREVALENCE RATES* (PER 100,000 CORRESPONDING POPULATION) OF NEW HAVEN PATIENTS IN OWN SOCIAL CLASS GROUPS BY TREATMENT SITE

Treatment site	Social class group			
	I–II	III	IV	V
Hospitals:				
Public	89	242	464	1,500
Private	85	17	6	—
Combined inpatients .	174	259	470	1,500
Clinics	30	66	53	115
Office therapists	352	213	119	44
Combined outpatients ..	382	279	172	159
Total Patients rate ..	556	538	642	1,659
N = No. of patients	(150)	(260)	(758)	(723)

* Adapted from A. B. Hollingshead and F. C. Redlich, *Social Class and Mental Illness*, pp. 265, 419. Source data are used by permission of John Wiley & Sons, Inc., New York.

Inspection of table 16–2 frequencies reveals the same SES trends in New Haven as were observed for like treatment sites in Midtown (table 16–1). That is, patient rates for the low-cost facilities (public hospitals and clinics) *increase* downward on the socioeconomic scale, whereas for the high-cost services (private hospitals and office therapists) the trend is for the patient frequencies to *diminish* with descending SES. The parallel Midtown and New Haven evidence on these countertrends suggests anew that if the inescapable calculus of cost relative to financial means is not the only factor determining whether and where psychiatric care is sought and secured, it probably is one of the most important.

A closer comparison is warranted of New Haven's classes IV and

V in table 16–2. These two groups do not differ in either private hospital rate or combined outpatient frequency. However, they *do* diverge in their public hospital rates by a decisive margin of 3.2:1.

Noteworthy in the comparison next of the public hospital frequencies in tables 16–1 and 16–2 is the general *numeric* similarity of these rates between the Midtown pair of upper and middle strata on the one hand and the New Haven series of classes I–II, III, and IV on the other. Residually highlighted thereby is the sharp contrast differentiating the public hospital rate in the bottom stratum of the two communities, i.e., 646 for Midtown's lower SES group and 1,500 for New Haven's class V.

If the "permanently" hospitalized (by our definition those confined continuously for five years or more) are predominantly drawn from the lowest socioeconomic level, then the pinpointed intercommunity contrast just mentioned is in part a consequence of the facts that (1) in its patient prevalence count one investigation (New Haven) included these piled-up people in limbo and (2) the other (Midtown) excluded them on grounds that they could no longer be meaningfully considered bona fide residents of the study area.

On two lines of analysis, accordingly, the extraordinarily high public hospital rate of New Haven's class V appears to be a function, at least in part, of the accumulation and stagnation in state hospitals of the terminally confined, who mainly originate in this group.

If class V has the standout Total Patients rate (1,659) of all SES groups in New Haven, in Midtown this distinction belongs to the top stratum (rate: 1,703) at the opposite end of the socioeconomic hierarchy. Table 16–1 tells us that accounting for seven-eighths of this peak frequency are the patients reported by Manhattan office therapists,[13] who by a 4.4:1 margin outnumbered (per 100,000 local population) their fellow professionals in New Haven at the time. Office patients all told represent nearly half of Midtown's inclusive patient universe reported to us, and by their numbers they have imposed their skewed SES composition on the trend in Total Patients rates among Midtown's several SES groups.

On the other hand, with New Haven's office therapy cases numbering only about 20 percent of all local patients, Total Patients rates in that community are dominated to a greater degree by the public hospital occupants and *their* particular kind of skewed SES make-up.

In chapter 10 we offered the seemingly obvious but often overlooked point that intercommunity variations in the treatment capacities of their psychiatric facilities place different ceiling limits on their patient rates, thereby tending to conceal any real differences in their overall prevalence of mental disorder.

This can now be given the obvious amplification that intercommunity variations in the development of high-cost and low-cost psychiatric facilities will inevitably place differential ceilings on the number of people in like-SES groups who can get psychiatric care. All in all, it is difficult to avoid the conclusion that divergences in Total Patients rates among a community's several socioeconomic groups have a significance decidedly less etiological than that seemingly attributed to them at some points in the New Haven monograph's earlier chapters.

The issue of ambulatory versus hospital sites of treatment, earlier discussed, becomes programmatically sharpened when narrowed down to the psychotic patients uncovered by our Treatment Census. In table 16–3 we present Midtown's psychotic patients in each status group as they divide on the ambulatory-hospital line of psychiatric facilities.

TABLE 16–3.   TREATMENT CENSUS (AGE INCLUSIVE), DISTRIBUTIONS OF MIDTOWN'S PSYCHOTIC PATIENTS IN OWN-SES STRATA BY TREATMENT SITES

Treatment sites	Own SES		
	Upper	Middle	Lower
Outpatient	49.6%	25.2%	10.0%
Inpatient	50.4	74.8	90.0
N = 100%	(113)	(274)	(598)

As expected, of course, Midtown's large outpatient facilities, or more particularly its corps of office therapists, operate to the far greater service advantage of the high-status psychotic needing treatment than to fellow psychotics on SES levels below him. Suggested thereby is the *urgent importance of low-cost outpatient clinics and day-care, night-care, foster family, and home treatment facilities to correct this service imbalance among the more seriously impaired in the community.*

PSYCHIATRIC ATTENTION AMONG THE HOME SURVEY'S IMPAIRED RESPONDENTS

In the preceding section, patient rates yielded by our Treatment Census were calculated relative to the total number of Midtown people making up each status group. If all the afflicted came under treatment, as generally happens with a dread infection like polio, such rates could stand for the frequency of a disorder in a given group per 100,000 of its total population. With mental pathology, however, we have every reason to believe that the treated represent merely a fraction of all the impaired, whose numbers are generally unknown. Under this circumstance, the count of patient numbers is the product of at least two unknowns: (1) the *overall* frequency of the disorder and (2) the extent to which the impaired manage to get psychiatric care.

However, the count of patient numbers can break out of its besetting clouds of ambiguity if it is converted into a rate per 100 in presumptive need of professional help. Such a rate acquires significance by giving at least some rough inkling of the number and character of the help-needy who get professional attention as compared with those who go unattended. The unmet needs so uncovered, if sizable in extent, would be an action challenge to both the healing professions and the communities they serve.

In view of the specific mission assigned to the Midtown Treatment Census operation, it was felt that the treatment factor could be given only a brief glance during Home Survey interviews with a representative sample of Midtown adults. Given the hard-won wisdom of hindsight, we concede this short cut to have been an error.

In any event, every respondent in the Home Survey sample was asked whether he had ever gone to a psychiatrist or a "nerve specialist."[14] Affirming respondents were then asked only one other question, namely, when the therapist was last seen.

Such affirming respondents were subsequently pressed into service as the Home Survey's particular criterion of a patient, under a definition considerably wider than that applied in our Treatment Census operation. Those counted by the latter's methods had been admitted into a program of psychiatric care, however diverse or brief may have been the treatment content. However, by the Home Survey's broad-spectrum definition, patients included not only respondents who had received intensive treatment, but also those who in seeing a psycho-therapist had not progressed beyond (1) a consultation, (2) one or more diagnostic sessions, or (3) unsuccessful application for treat-ment. Instances such as these three indicate the Home Survey's cri-terion of a patient to be a respondent who, however briefly, secured and directed the attention of a psychotherapist to his felt need for help. This liberal definition should be taken into account as we ex-tract the patient-history variable from the Home Survey sample. We divide respondents into three categories: (1) current patients, ambu-latory of course, who had last seen the therapist during the thirty-day period preceding the interview; (2) ex-patients, covering all others who had been in either a hospital or an ambulatory service; and (3) never-patients.

We now seek the connection between this patient-history variable and socioeconomic status, not on the broad base of the inclusive community population (as in table 16–1), but only among Midtown adults who are in a mental condition of probable help-need, at the very least for professional consultation, diagnosis, or prophylaxis. These we find represented by the Home Survey's 389 (age 20 to 59) sample respondents who were judged by the Study psychiatrists to be in the Impaired category of the mental health classification scheme. In table 16–4 the own-SES yardstick is a composite derived from scored rankings of respondent's education, occupation, income, and rent. However, given the relatively small number of Impaired people, the six A to F strata used in chapter 14 must be merged into three.[15]

TABLE 16–4. HOME SURVEY SAMPLE (AGE 20–59), DISTRIBUTIONS OF IMPAIRED CATEGORY RESPONDENTS IN MIDTOWN OWN-SES GROUPS BY PATIENT-HISTORY CLASSIFICATION

	Own SES (four indicators)		
	Upper (A–B)	Middle (C–D)	Lower (E–F)
Current patients (ambulatory)..	19.1%	4.5%	1.1%
Ex-patients (ambulatory or hospital)	32.4	18.0	19.9
Ever-patients	51.5	22.5	21.0
Never-patients	48.5	77.5	79.0
N = 100%	(68)	(134)	(187)

Relative to the lower stratum's Impaired people, the current patient rate in the middle and upper group is greater by 4 and 18 times, respectively. This trend in the probable "at need" segment of the general population reveals more clearly than before the highly selective nature of the current patient traffic to the doors of the ambulatory facilities.

The ex-patients, on the other hand, are more heterogeneous in terms of service site, including as they do the clients of both ambulatory facilities and hospitals. From clues provided by our Treatment Census data, we estimate in table 16–5 that these ex-patients were divided between hospital and ambulatory sites roughly as follows on the own-SES range:

TABLE 16–5. HOME SURVEY SAMPLE (AGE 20–59), DISTRIBUTIONS OF IMPAIRED EX-PATIENTS BY TREATMENT SITE AND SES

	Upper	Middle	Lower
Ex-patients:			
Hospital	4.4%	6.0%	12.3%
Ambulatory	28.0	12.0	7.6
Total ex-patients of Impaired group	32.4%	18.0%	19.9%

Thus, within the circumscribed confines of the Impaired category of respondents, almost half (the above 28.0 percent + 19.1 percent in table 16–4) of those belonging in the upper-SES stratum are estimated to be ambulatory ever-patients, as compared with one-sixth (the above 12.0 percent + 4.5 percent in table 16–4) and one-twelfth (the above 7.6 percent + 1.1 percent in table 16–4) of the middle and lower SES groups respectively.

We can now confront the seeming paradox, posed by tables 14–1 and 16–1, where on the one hand overall prevalence of mental morbidity was seen to *expand* downward on the SES pyramid and, on the other, treatment rates (per 100,000 total population) tended to *shrink* with descending socioeconomic status. From the previous paragraph it becomes apparent that if the top SES stratum has the fewest cases of mental morbidity, these cases present an even chance of sooner or later seeking ambulatory psychiatric service. The lower status group, on the contrary, has by far the largest prevalence of Impaired respondents, but the latter have only a slight chance (1 in

12) of ever coming to the professional attention of an outpatient facility. As net effect, into the traffic going through the community's psychiatric services the inclusive upper stratum, although healthier on the whole, *pours more patients*, relative to its numbers, than does the most impairment-laden bottom SES group.

HELP–NEED AND PROFESSIONAL ORIENTATION

In what remains a significant opening discussion of the matter, the New Haven investigators[16] have extracted this important point from observations on 50 intensively studied psychiatric patients: beyond the play of economic factors, there are SES-linked divergences in orientation to psychiatry that may partially explain the varying patient rates of the several social class groups. We did not attempt to retrace their pioneering steps in this direction. However, in our Home Survey sample we did explore respondents' readiness to advise, and presumably to accept, several relevant forms of professional help in instances of behavioral disturbance. By their replies, all sample respondents have been placed in one of these four professional orientation categories: (1) those advising a psychiatrist, a psychologist, or an institutional equivalent; (2) those others recommending a physician or an institutional equivalent; (3) those remaining who would call upon a member of some other remedial profession, e.g., social worker or clergyman; (4) the residue, who made no reference to professional intervention of any kind.

TABLE 16–6. HOME SURVEY SAMPLE (AGE 20–59), DISTRIBUTIONS OF MIDTOWN SAMPLE RESPONDENTS IN OWN-SES STRATA BY PROFESSIONAL ORIENTATION

Respondent recommendation	Own SES		
	Upper (A–B)	Middle (C–D)	Lower (E–F)
Psychotherapist	51.2%	26.4%	12.3%
Physician	11.8	11.2	12.3
Other professional	6.3	10.4	12.3
No professional	30.7	52.0	63.1
N = 100%	(560)	(556)	(544)

Of course, readiness of the help-needy person to accept professional service is only one element in the highly complicated total situation that determines what, if any, steps he takes to get help. Another element is the prevailing view or attitude climate that his group tends to press upon him and his family toward taking a certain course of action. From table 16–6 we can surmise that the Impaired never-patient of the upper-SES bracket would find a majority of his status peers urging him to see a psychiatrist.* If he is of middle or lower status the predominant tendency of his peers would apparently be in a direction other than advising professional assistance. However, compared to the lower-SES stratum a substantially bigger minority of the middle-class group would suggest a psychotherapist, namely, 12.3 and 26.4 percent, respectively. These data from a large sample of community residents may supplement the New Haven observations on a small sample of psychiatric patients. Seemingly implied is that SES-linked attitude climates operate differentially to facilitate or complicate the path a help-needy person must take if he is to find his way into a patient-therapist relationship.

OUTCOME OF EXPOSING IMPAIRMENT ˙CASES TO PSYCHIATRIC ATTENTION

Our final question poses this issue: For those who do get psychiatric attention, what SES-mediated effects differentially accrue to patients from exposure to a therapist in a service setting? This is an exceedingly difficult empirical question—one not remotely contemplated when we designed the Home Survey operation. Nevertheless, a suggestive clue may emerge from the circumstance that this survey encountered 182 sample respondents who, by the criteria of our

* The *Psychiatric Dictionary*, by Hinsie and Campbell (1970), defines psychotherapy as "any form of treatment for mental illness, behavioral maladaptions, and/or other problems that are assumed to be of an emotional nature. . . . There are numerous forms of psychotherapy—ranging from guidance, counselling, persuasion, and hypnosis to reeducation and psychoanalytic reconstructive therapy." Although there are narrower definitions than this one, the authors of the present monograph emphasize that we use the terms "psychotherapy" and "psychiatric care" in the comprehensive sense just quoted, which we extend to cover the practices of clinical and pastoral psychologists, counselors, and psychiatric social workers, whether they work with individuals singly or in family or nonconsanguineous groups.

patient-history classification, are ex-patients. In 'the interest of expanding on this clue, let us assume that the reported relationship with a therapist probably would not have been arranged by, or for, these respondents unless a condition of Impaired mental health was believed to be present or imminent.

If this assumption is correct, and we have nothing to support it except plausibility, then we can take note that of these 182 ex-patients 83 are currently still in an Impaired state of mental health, whereas 99 are now functioning more or less adequately despite symptoms of underlying pathology. Of considerable interest at this point are the following differences among the ex-patients when sorted by their own-SES level:

1. Of 78 upper-SES ex-patients, the non-Impaired number 71.8 percent (the Impaired, 28.2 percent).

2. Of 50 middle-SES ex-patients, the non-Impaired number 52 percent (the Impaired, 48 percent).

3. Of 54 lower-SES ex-patients, the non-Impaired number 31.5 percent (the Impaired, 68.5 percent).

The potential clue buried in these data may be stated as follows: Within the universe of patient-therapist relationships, the chances of a successful outcome (as judged by the operational criterion of reversal from a state of Impaired to a state of non-Impaired mental health) seem to vary considerably among the several socioeconomic segments of the patient population, in a range from about 7 in 10 of the top segment to 3 in 10 of the bottom one.

If this clue should prove to be substantive, a number of factors could be adduced to explain the outcome differences. In fact, some of these variables have already been insightfully discussed in parts 4 and 5 of the New Haven monograph. Here we would only add our view that if the American patterning of socioeconomic status performs central social system functions, it also has serious dysfunctional aspects that remain a challenge to its powers of self-correction. The unequal consequences of these aspects for the development of mental health were discernible in the preceding chapter. Here we have presented clues and evidence attesting to another specific dysfunction in the social order: the conflict between the status system as it actually operates and a bedrock value on which the healing professions are founded, namely, that the sick shall have ready access to the ministrations of these professionals irrespective of their social differences.

SUMMARY

In the previous chapter our efforts were directed toward uncovering the lines of association between group mental health composition and socioeconomic status in several of its major aspects. Our point of focus in this chapter has been narrower, namely, the connection between psychiatric attention or care and adults' present (own) SES. On this level, the earlier New Haven Psychiatric Census study has made possible some illuminating intercommunity comparisons. However, our own sightings on this nexus have come from the twin vantage points provided by our Treatment Census and Home Survey operations.

Comparison of the Midtown and New Haven patient rates indicated like SES trends for like treatment sites. Notwithstanding this parallelism, the anomaly emerged that the SES trend in Total Patients rates of the two communities seemed to move in opposite directions.

Analysis suggested first that New Haven's inverse trend was beset on the one hand with some technical artifacts and, on the other, with a special tendency of the lowest (V) stratum's public hospital patients to become permanently institutionalized. In Midtown the opposite SES trend was shown to be a consequence of the numerical dominance of office therapy patients in this universe of patients and the overshadowing impact of their high socioeconomic status on the SES differences in Total Patients rates.

Thus, the relative development of high-cost and low-cost facilities in a community's treatment apparatus will variously affect people at different SES levels in their chances of securing psychiatric care.

Opposite SES trends were also encountered in comparing the Midtown Study's two field operations. The Home Survey revealed that overall prevalence of mental morbidity varied inversely with socioeconomic status. On the other hand, the Treatment Census reported Total Patients rates rising between the lower and upper socioeconomic strata. Using a broader definition of patient history as its criterion of psychiatric attention, the Home Survey Impaired respondents who satisfied this definition also showed the latter kind of SES trend. Integrating these separate findings, we observed that as we descend the continuum of socioeconomic status, Midtown's Treatment Census rates represent progressively smaller fractions of progressively larger reservoirs of mental morbidity.

In comprehensive terms, compared to the "affluent" group the "poor" have many more mentally impaired people; their help-needy people far less often get psychiatric attention; and when their impaired members do get such attention, the outcome, to judge from an elicited clue, rather less often appears to be a significant and sustained gain.

Indicated were the implications of sociological dysfunctions to be drawn from the large picture sketched in this and the preceding chapter.

NOTES

1. This SES trend of patient rates in publicly supported mental hospitals has been reported in other studies of patients, usually of the first-admission category. Cf. A. J. Jaffe and E. Shanas, "Economic Differentials in the Probability of Insanity," *American Journal of Sociology* 44 (January 1935): 534–539; R. E. L. Faris and H. W. Dunham, *Mental Disorders in Urban Areas*, 1939; C. W. Schroeder, "Mental Disorders in Cities," *American Journal of Sociology* 48 (July 1942): 40–48; R. E. Clark, "Psychoses, Income and Occupational Prestige," *American Journal of Sociology* 54 (March 1949): 433–440; R. M. Frumkin, "Occupation and Major Mental Disorders," in A. M. Rose, ed., *Mental Health and Mental Disorders*, 1955, pp. 136–160; B. Malzberg, "Mental Disease in Relation to Economic Status," *Journal of Nervous and Mental Disease* 123 (March 1956): 257–261; and B. Kaplan, R. B. Reed, and W. Richardson, "A Comparison of the Incidence of Hospitalized and Non-hospitalized Cases of Psychoses in Two Communities," *American Sociological Review* 21 (August 1956): 472–479. However, the trend was not found, at least for first-hospital-admission schizophrenics, in the study reported by J. A. Clausen and M. L. Kohn, "Relation of Schizophrenia to the Social Structure of a Small City," in B. Pasamanick, ed., *Epidemiology of Mental Disorder*, 1959, pp. 69–86.

2. A. B. Hollingshead and F. C. Redlich, *Social Class and Mental Illness*, 1958, p. 207.

3. Ibid., p. 210.

4. These groups were based on scored, differentially weighted rankings of education, occupation, and area of residence. Partly because institutional files were found to be markedly irregular in recording occupation and schooling, the Midtown Treatment Census has used only quality of residence as its indicator of patients' SES. Despite this difference and differences in dividing the socioeconomic range of the two patient populations, the Midtown and New Haven sets of data lend themselves to critical comparison of their SES trends.

5. When we undertake computations for classes I and II separately, the rates

we secure are 267 and 668, respectively, based on data (p. 199) in the New Haven monograph.

6. From notes taken of Redlich's report ("Social Class and Psychiatry," p. 181) given at the New York Academy of Medicine, March 9, 1955, it seems clear that he himself viewed the New Haven social class rates, group V excepted, as essentially describing a plateau.

7. Hollingshead and Redlich, *Social Class and Mental Illness*, pp. 22–24.

8. See also S. W. Ginsburg's review, *American Journal of Orthopsychiatry* 29 (January 1959): 195.

9. Hollingshead and Redlich, *Social Class and Mental Illness*, p. 19.

10. A. B. Hollingshead and F. C. Redlich, "Social Stratification and Psychiatric Disorders," *American Sociological Review* 18 (April 1953): 167.

11. Hollingshead and Redlich, *Social Class and Mental Illness*, p. 343.

12. Ibid., pp. 265 and 419.

13. In chapter 13 we indicated that information on 19 percent of the Midtown office patients reported to us failed to include the requested home address information needed to classify housing quality as a socioeconomic indicator. To prevent their exclusion from the rates in table 16–1, we arbitrarily assumed they were distributed on the present SES trichotomy as were the 81 percent of reported office patients for whom correct addresses were furnished. However, it seems plausible that office therapists would be more prone to shield the addresses of "top-drawer" people than of others. If so, the indicated correction we have introduced for the address-missing patients would make the office therapy rate of the Midtown upper-SES group an *understatement* of the true rate.

It is impossible to estimate the number of patients altogether unreported by the Manhattan office therapists. If these patients also are predominantly from the top rung of the socioeconomic ladder, then they represent a further error of understatement attached, with magnitude unknown, to the upper-SES rate in table 16–1.

14. The respondent was credited with a "yes" if he answered "no" but volunteered that he had been to a clinical psychologist or some other kind of certified therapist.

15. Such merger of course tends to reduce differences between groups at the extremes of the SES range.

16. Hollingshead and Redlich, *Social Class and Mental Illness*, pp. 335–356.

Steerage by Alfred Stieglitz. Courtesy The Witkin Gallery

"Remember, remember always that all of us . . . are descended from immigrants."—President Franklin D. Roosevelt

CHAPTER 17

IMMIGRANT AND NATIVE
GENERATIONS: RURAL–URBAN ORIGINS

LEO SROLE AND THOMAS LANGNER

American history is the epic of a nation hewed out of wilderness by the brawn and wits of diverse peoples gathered from the length and breadth of the Old World. Nationality and religious segments in this patchwork diversity are being held for separate examination in the two chapters that follow.

Here we want to look at the demographic architecture of the Midtown population from another angle, one that delineates a tier of groups arranged in a sequence of generations from the immigrants through successive orders of their lineal descendants. In the foundation group, of course, are all the foreign-born, designated generation I. American-born offspring of immigrants stand as generation II, and grandchildren of the foreign-born as generation III.[1] Midtowners who have four American-born grandparents are placed in generation IV; that is, the nearest immigrant forebears were great-grandparents or even more remote ancestors.[2] It is no surprise, therefore, that this oldest-in U.S. generation group is largely derived from Old American, Anglo-Saxon stock.

On this ordering of the generations, the Midtown age 20 to 59 sample adults are distributed[3] as follows:

Generation	Percent
I	35.8
II	34.5
III	15.9
IV	13.6
Unknown[4]	0.2
Total (N = 1,660)	100.0

What specific relevance to the concerns of the Midtown Study has the seeming genealogical criterion that differentiates these generation levels? In the first place, these are not categories that claim only conceptual identifiability. Rather, they are in varying respects groups that have separate identities and self-images. Certainly, immigrants—within the several nationality divisions—have their own informal associations and accessible formal organizations. So also does the Old American generation IV, as can be seen in the Colonial Dames of America, the Sons of the American Revolution, and the Society of Colonial Wars, among others.

Lerner refers to the persistent effort during the colonial period "to build an aristocracy of prior immigration."[5] Every wave of immigrants from the early English colonists onward tended to look askance on subsequent newcomers as somehow of suspect and inferior character. The invidious implications of the self-styled "patriotic societies" within the Old American group are not likely to be missed by those who are excluded on ancestral criteria. Of course, more than mere implication was involved in the congressional acts of 1921 and 1924, which drastically cut the number of newcomers, above all by discriminating against the newer sources of immigration.

As subsequent professional analyses of school textbooks in American history have shown, the facts about immigrants reported there often "were, to put it politely, uncivic, uncivil, and untrue."[6] Saveth, one of these analysts, refers to such textbooks as "miseducation by insult, whereby American children are systematically exposed to a racist evaluation of—in so many cases—their own parents and grandparents."[7]

Such grading of the generations on an inferior-superior scale was one process among others serving to widen the boundaries between these groups.

THE GENERATION–IN–U.S. HYPOTHESES

Even more important for our research concerns was a chain of other processes that hinge on these facts: Generation IV, in personality and behavior, is "at home" under the roof of American society. By contrast, immigrants on arrival are often at the farthest pole removed as strangers in the land and aliens to the patterns and nuances of American conduct. During his remaining lifetime the immigrant proceeds some distance in acculturation toward the American model; his children proceed considerably farther; and in his adult grandchildren the process is substantially but rather less than completed.

An extensive literature on the experiences accompanying this process has accumulated in the work of novelists, sociologists, and a new generation of historians. Almost without exception they portray the immigrant as one caught in the dilemma of the iron maiden type, impaled by himself when he yielded to environmental pressures on issues of central importance to his integrity and impaled by the environment when he refused to yield to these pressures under the interdictions of his "out of context" personality.

Rarely has this predicament been conveyed with more detailed insight than in Handlin's *The Uprooted*.[8] On the impact of transplantation, Handlin notes that the "shock and the effects of shock persisted for many years."[9] Among these effects,

. . . the immigrants witnessed in themselves a deterioration . . . a marked personal decline and a noticeable wavering of standards. [They] found it difficult, on the basis of past habits, to determine what their own roles should be . . . they had been projected into a situation where every element conspired to force them into deviations. . . . It was significant of such deviations—pauperism, insanity, intemperance, gambling—that they represented a yielding to the disorganizing pressure of the environment. . . . If only a small number actually plunged into [such deviations] many more lived long on the verge.[10]

In short, here was the discontinuity phenomenon, not in one role but in the immigrant's entire complex of roles—as worker, consumer, tenant, neighbor, husband, father, etc. In the light of these multiple points of potential stress, it was hypothesized that on the generation scale mental health conditions would be found most adverse of all in the Midtown immigrant group.

The predicament of the generation II child, although different, was directly chained to that of his parents. The latter saw themselves challenged and disarmed on almost every front of their new lives. However, one salient on which they could defend themselves was in the refuge of their dwelling, where they partially recreated a family regimen rooted in their traditions, perhaps now magnified and idealized.

This was the intrafamily atmosphere in which they often raised their child without serious extrafamily challenges during his preschool years. Thereafter, however, he came under the increasing pressures of peers and school to conform with American ways. Between these crosscurrents of conflicting sets of values and behavior patterns, both of which exerted powerful claims upon his identifications and loyalties, the generation II child was caught.[11] It has been said of this generation that it is their predicament to stand in both cultural worlds but to be completely at home in neither. Complicating the situation further was the unmistakable antiforeigner bias that these children encountered among people perceived as the authentic American type, including the writers of textbooks in American history. Internalizing this attitude led them to rebel with focused hostility against their immigrant parents, seen miscast as incongruous models and overbearing authorities. In culmination, they could reject themselves as well in a form that Lewin has called "self-hatred."[12]

Hypothesizing about generation II adults, on these grounds, we could expect to find their mental health composition tending in a relatively unfavorable direction. However, we also anticipated that it would be less adverse than that of generation I. Our reasoning was twofold: (1) In degrees of discontinuity there was greater disparity for the immigrant between his natal home and the new environment than there was for the generation II individual; (2) in the intergeneration conflict the American environment was openly a supportive ally of the child and an antagonist of his immigrant parent. This would intrinsically tend to tip the balance, in settling the conflict, toward the former and away from the latter. Thus, the blows of the encounter, we observed, were harder on the foreign-born parent than on his American-born child.

In framing predictions for generation III we had in mind the notable essay by historian Marcus Hansen.[13] Contrasting the second generation's conflicted rejection of the parents' traditional way of life, Hansen says of the third generation: "It has none of the bitterness or heartbreaking features of its predecessors. . . . Whenever any immigrant group reaches the third-generation stage of development a spontaneous and almost irresistible impulse arises which forces the thoughts of many people of different professions, different positions in life, and different points of view to interest themselves in that one factor which they have in common: heritage. . . ."

This statement was congruent with our own wide but unsystematic observations that, not being defensive either about their American identification or about their family tradition, generation III children are no longer conflicted in these important dimensions of the self-image. To this extent we could hypothesize that in adulthood they would appear as a group less vulnerable to the blows of life and more skilled in crisis management than would generation II.

Compared to generation IV, in turn, the only situational liability we could discern for generation III during childhood was their generation II parentage and the latter's own embattled personality development. Accordingly, it seemed plausible to advance the consistent general hypothesis that progressively upward on the generation scale, i.e., from I to IV, the group mental health trend would be toward diminishing frequencies of mental pathology.

HOME SURVEY SAMPLE: MENTAL HEALTH DISTRIBUTIONS

Our hypothesis that mental health varies inversely with generation-in-U.S. is here tested for the first time on a community cross-section population. Also for the first time, the generation variable has been refined to go beyond the usual simple dichotomy (foreign versus American birth) to encompass three categories of the native-born.

We turn now to table 17–1 below for distributions of the four Midtown generation groups on the psychiatrists' classification of mental health. Focusing first on the two intermediate mental health categories, i.e., Mild and Moderate symptom formation, we note, as in previous chapters, high consistency of their rates across the generation range. Looking next to Well and Impaired frequencies, we see that generations II and III are identical; relative to these, generation I has a somewhat larger Impaired-Well ratio and generation IV a decidedly smaller one. As cumulative effect, the Well and Impaired frequencies of the immigrants (16.1 and 26.7 percent, respectively) are completely reversed in the fourth-generation group (27.9 and 17.2 percent, respectively).

Except that the anticipated difference between generations II and III does not appear, the Impaired-Well ratios vary in the direction postulated, although hardly to the degree that had been expected. Moreover, before this modest support can be claimed for the hypoth-

TABLE 17–1.   HOME SURVEY SAMPLE (AGE 20–59), RESPONDENTS'
DISTRIBUTIONS ON MENTAL HEALTH CLASSIFICATION BY GENERATION-IN-U.S.

Mental health categories	Generation groups			
	I	II	III	IV
Well	16.1%	17.8%	17.4%	27.9%
Mild symptom formation .	36.0	37.8	36.7	32.3
Moderate symptom formation	21.2	21.5	23.9	22.6
Impaired	26.7	22.9	22.0	17.2
Marked symptom formation	14.9	13.6	11.8	8.8
Severe symptom formation	9.4	6.3	7.2	5.8
Incapacitated	2.4	3.0	3.0	2.6
N = 100%*	(593)	(573)	(264)	(226)
Impaired-Well ratio	165	128	126	62

* Four respondents are of unknown U.S.-born generation

esis as tested, we must take the precaution of inquiring about the potential play of other demographic factors.

This inquiry becomes particularly pertinent when we discover age differences among the sample's generation groups.[14] Likewise, there are some marked differences in SES origin. As we have seen in a previous chapter, frequency of impairment varies directly with respondent age and inversely with SES origin. Accordingly, we must analytically parcel out the separate effects of the latter two factors if we are to determine what residual relation remains between the generation variable, in its own right, and mental health. This can be accomplished most expeditiously by the device of "standardizing" the generation groups' populations. By this method, we recompute the mental health distributions that would result if all four groups were identical in age and SES origin with a population accepted as the standard.[15]

On this standardized basis, the mental health distributions in the several generation groups appear as presented in table 17–2. The limited support for our test hypothesis, as read from table 17–1, is here seen to be largely spurious.[16] For all practical purposes, no relation between generation and mental health remains[17] when SES

TABLE 17-2. HOME SURVEY SAMPLE (AGE 20-59), RESPONDENTS'
DISTRIBUTIONS ON MENTAL HEALTH CLASSIFICATION BY GENERATION-IN-U.S.
GROUPS AS STANDARDIZED FOR AGE AND PARENTAL SES

Mental health categories	Standardized generation groups			
	I	II	III	IV
Well	16.5%	18.1%	16.6%	24.3%
Mild symptom formation	36.5	37.9	36.8	26.4
Moderate symptom formation ...	21.7	21.0	23.9	26.3
Impaired	25.3	23.0	22.7	23.0
N = 100%	(593)	(573)	(264)	(226)

origin and respondent age are held constant.[18] This says, in effect,
that there are no mental health divergences among respondents of
different generation levels who are alike in parental SES and age. To
be sure, the latter variables in combination are highly correlated with
respondent mental health. And it may be expecting too much of a
third demographic variable to come through the fine screen of these
two with a separate relationship all its own. Yet, in the light of the
general evidence that prompted our hypotheses about the four generation groups, this is exactly what we *did* expect. In failing this expectation, the findings of table 17-2 seemed to flatly contradict the
nearly unanimous testimony of a large and diverse corps of competent observers. Accordingly, we regarded our data with special
skepticism and proceeded to probe and dissect them from a number
of possible angles.

DATA AND HYPOTHESES RECONSIDERED

There was the obvious possibility, for example, that the Study
psychiatrists had been influenced by their own observations of the
conflicted predicaments in which both immigrants and their children
were caught. If so, in classifying respondents' mental health they
could have regarded a given set of symptoms more seriously if occurring in generation III or IV individuals than if found in generation I
or II people. In that event, of course, real differences among these

groups could be more or less leveled out. However, inspection of the psychiatrists' Rating I classifications, made without knowledge of respondents' generation level, indicated trends in no way different from those reported in table 17–1. Thereby, the possibility that a judgmental bias intruded at the point of classifying mental health can be confidently rejected.

A second possibility was that the evidence prompting our hypothesis was biased in the sense that it overstated the negative aspects of the immigrant's situation and understated the positive aspects. Lerner seems to imply this view:

> The immigrant experience was . . . somber and tragic. Yet it would be a mistake to see it thus without adding that it was also one of excitement and ferment. Millions of the immigrants, after giving their strength to the new country, died with a sense of failure and frustration. But many more millions survived their ordeal, became men of influence in their communities, and lived to see the fulfillment of the American promise in their own lives doubly fulfilled in the lives of their children. "Everything tends to regenerate them," De Crevecoeur wrote of his fellow immigrants, "new laws, a new mode of living, a new social system; here they are become men: in Europe . . . they withered and were mowed down by want, hunger and war; but now by the power of transplantation, like all other plants, they have taken root and flourished!" One doubts whether this lyric description, written at the end of the eighteenth century, would have been accepted as a faithful one a century later; yet it described a process which would have meaning for many through the whole course of the immigrant experience and even more meaning for the second and third generations, who reaped the harvest of the transplanting of their fathers without having had to suffer the ordeal.[19]

This comment of course is well grounded for many immigrants in the later years of life. However, if it does not minimize the earlier ordeal which immigrants survived, it *does* seem to gloss over the turbulent childhood of the second generation. In any event, needless to say, the senior author had taken this view into account in framing the chapter's test hypothesis.

A third possibility is that the test hypothesis would have secured confirming data were the Midtown Study designed differently, i.e., had it sampled generation groups that stood as lineal kin to each other. Although it is difficult in Manhattan to draw a probability sample comprehending pairs of adult respondents who stand to each other as offspring to parent or grandchild to grandparent, there is more to this critical point than we realized when we planned the study. At that time, it was our implicit, unconsidered assumption that the sample's generation I would be more or less representative of the unsampled parents of the generation II respondents, and that the latter, in turn, would be more or less representative of the unsampled parents of the interviewed generation III group, etc. Therefore, we assumed that the sample would permit us to reconstruct the *unbroken* generation-to-generation progression in mental health.

The simplicity of this assumption is revealed when we examine our sample generation II in terms of a hypothetical average member. About 39 years old when we interviewed him (in 1954), "Mr. Two's" year of birth was 1915. His parents were born abroad, probably between 1880 and 1895, and migrated here most likely between 1901 and 1914.

In this connection it is relevant to recall that with a total population in 1900 of 76 million, the United States received in the following 15 years almost 14 million immigrants along with Mr. Two's parents. Involving an arrival rate of almost 1 million per year, this period (1901–1914) marked the flood-tide climax in a century of sustained massive immigration unparalleled in history. Dependence on the economic "crumbs" of the natives, the sheer enormity of the influx, and accelerating political disorganization of the receiving cities probably made these fifteen years the century's high point also in the survival difficulties faced by "green" immigrants.[20]

Our key question now is this: With the sample's generation II originating from immigrant parents who arrived in the climactic period 1901 to 1914, how comparable to these parents are the sample's generation I? In answer, we note that the average member of the latter group was born in 1908. In time of arrival he belongs on the whole to another chapter of American immigration history, namely, the period after congressional passage of the acts of 1921 and 1924 that ended relatively free immigration from the Western Hemisphere.

With admissions sharply reduced (to a token number of about 150,000 annually) there came a change in the make-up of the immigrants. In the first years of the twentieth century males outnumbered females by about 7:3; in the late twenties the sex ratio had changed to 5:5; and in the thirties, to 4:6. During the earlier (pre-1921) period of mass immigration the overwhelming majority of those reporting occupation had been relatively unschooled laborers from farm, village, or town. Federal sources[21] document the rapid relative increase, during the "new" period, of professional, semiprofessional, and other white-collar workers, a fact reflected in our sample generation I. Also, of this sample group only about one-third were from a farm or village. An additional 15 percent were from towns, 25 percent from small or middle-size cities, and 25 percent from big cities.[22] Finally, many of these sample immigrants were offspring of fathers who in their homeland occupations were skilled blue-collar or white-collar workers.

These and other characteristics convey a picture of decided change in make-up of the shrunken post-1921 immigration as compared with the massive immigration waves at the turn of the century that drained large rural stretches in Europe of their young people.

Certain of the known attributes of the "new" immigrants were of a nature that would probably make for an easier and faster[23] adaptation to the American metropolis than had been the case for their predecessors. Moreover, in the interim the metropolis had itself changed—from a "vast jungle" that Lincoln Steffens stamped as "the shame of the cities"—to something more nearly approaching "community." In particular, between 1910 and 1930 Manhattan reduced its impossibly engorged resident population by almost 500,000. On both counts, therefore, it doubtless could more easily and humanely accommodate the smaller company of newcomers than had been possible for the hordes who had come earlier.

All told, therefore, the *Sturm und Drang* ordeal of exile we have come to associate with the pre-1921 immigrants appears likely to have diminished for their post-1921 successors. Better equipped for metropolitan life and probably better received, our sample generation I group could plausibly be expected to appear with less wear and tear of mental health than had their predecessors by two decades at the same stage of life.

Thus, if in table 17–2 above we find no difference in mental health composition between the sample's generations II and I we can infer that were comparison possible between group II and their own parents, such a difference would likely have been found in the direction suggested by this chapter's test hypothesis.

IMMIGRANTS' PARENTAL SES, RURAL–URBAN ORIGIN, AND MENTAL HEALTH

This line of reviewing the overlooked implications of historical changes in the immigration stream led us to reexamine the generation I group. There we conducted an analytical search for respondents who would most closely exemplify the old and the new immigrant populations. From this dissection we were able to isolate two extreme types. Type O is the nearest approximation in two respects to the kind of individual who dominated the older, pre-1921 immigration; that is, these respondents are from Europe's farms, villages, or small urban places and derived from parents who were low (E–F) in our SES-origin scale. Type N, on the other hand, represents in two respects the newer element appearing in the post-1921 immigration, namely, those who came from Europe's big or medium-size cities and out of families who stood in the higher strata (A–D) of our SES-origin ranking. In table 17–3 these two types and the totality of generation I, standardized for age, are seen in their distributions according to the psychiatrists' classification of mental health.

TABLE 17–3. HOME SURVEY SAMPLE (AGE 20–59), RESPONDENTS' DISTRIBUTIONS ON MENTAL HEALTH CLASSIFICATION BY TYPES OF IMMIGRANTS AS STANDARDIZED FOR AGE

Mental health categories	Type O	Type N	Total generation I
Well	10.2%	17.9%	16.0%
Mild symptom formation	30.8	40.5	37.2
Moderate symptom formation ...	24.7	23.1	21.2
Impaired	34.3*	18.5*	25.6
N = 100%	(163)	(185)	(593)
Impaired-Well ratio	336	103	160

* $t = 3.4$ (.001 level of confidence).

Thus, had type O been predominant in our sample generation I group (as it had in the earlier period of immigration), it seems clear that the mental health difference we originally hypothesized for generations I and II would likely have received the support of the Midtown data.

The pronounced difference we see above in types O and N suggests that what is decisive among immigrants is *not* transplantation to the American metropolis per se, but resettlement in the American metropolis from a *particular kind* of overseas milieu, namely, from the low socioeconomic strata in farm, village, or town. In this perspective, "foreignness," in the nationality and linguistic sense alone, may involve certain initial difficulties for the immigrant from the middle- or near middle-class strata of European cities. But these difficulties in themselves probably are minor in significance and relatively brief in duration, at least compared to the situational and adaptational burdens that descend when the immigrant combines this foreignness of nationality with other special dimensions or meanings of the word *foreign*. Those dimensions hinge on the contrast between the involuted complexities of Manhattan and the simple way of life in Europe's rural places as delineated with great artistry in a novel like Reymont's *Peasants*[24] or in Gavin Maxwell's book[25] portraying an economically depressed Sicilian village. The contrast stretches in time from the somnolent agrarian, preindustrial order characterizing the early-nineteenth-century hamlet to the twentieth century's summit point in the industrial cosmopolis. To compress the profound historical changes of a revolutionizing century into a few adult years of an individual life cycle may exact a high price in psychological well-being, such as is intimated in the mental health distribution of type O immigrants seen in table 17–3.

If this formulation accounts, at least in part, for the mental health differences between types O and N, perhaps primarily responsible is not the character of the environment at the immigrant's point of origin in itself, but its distance in "social time" from New York and the rush with which the O-type immigrant had to accomplish his sociopsychological vault from one to the other. Thus, divergence between O and N immigrants in their Impaired-Well balance may reflect different magnitudes of role discontinuity bridged in the transition from their respective native environments.

Within the framework of the generation-in-U.S. variable, immigration from abroad, at least on the part of adults, is usually a motivated act; as such, personality differences may be associated with the distinction between the self-chosen migrants and their nonmigrant townspeople. We can assume that *self-choice* was maximally involved among generation I respondents who migrated "on their own steam" as isolated adult individuals, involved to a lesser degree among adults who migrated with family or settled with kin, and involved negligibly among those who, as children, were brought to this country by their parents. On the criterion of their present mental health composition, at least, these three subgroups of immigrants emerge without any significant differences.

This bit of evidence is suggestive but hardly conclusive on the issue, since the three subgroups may deviate psychologically in similar fashion from the nonmigrants. In part they could deviate not only by the processes of subjective selection,[26] but also as a consequence of the objective selection engineered through the screening apparatus of the United States government. By way of explanation: "The visa requirement established by the Immigration Act of 1924 is in itself an important regulative device. . . . In order to secure a visa an immigrant must have established his eligibility to enter the United States, a process requiring many documents with respect to the identity, character and financial standing of the applicant. The overseas issuance of visas has proved an effective means . . . of screening immigrants prior to entry."[27] According to an official document, beyond rejecting those "likely to become a public charge," such screening also rejects individuals who "are not mentally sound and physically fit, [or are] drug addicts and chronic alcoholics, [or are] over 16 years of age [and] cannot read and understand some language, [or] have committed a crime. . . . In short, an alien who does not measure up to the moral, mental, physical and other standards fixed by law is subject to exclusion, or [after admission] may be deported to the country from which he came."[28]

This is a formidable screen, especially for personality deviants of all kinds, both as it is directly applied to visa applicants by American overseas consulates and as an indirect restraint in discouraging applications.[29] The threat of rejection, or of acceptance and subsequent deportation, was known to be taken into grim account by potential applicants.

Under such screening, direct and indirect, this seems certain: Winnowed of those already impaired in mind or body and probably of many others representing gross risks in such directions, immigrants in the years 1924–1954 were a more selected, and more homogeneous population in mental health respects as compared to their nonmigrant fellow townspeople.

Moreover, the steady stream of returnees to the homeland[30] is evidence suggesting that the nonreturnees have been further sifted of those who could not adjust to the difficult demands placed upon the immigrant new to America and to the metropolis.

These points have been developed here on the same rationale that prompted a parallel discussion of marital status in chapter 12, that is, to underscore the probability that the sample immigrant group, including type O itself, being largely post-1921 in arrival date, is a residue of multiple winnowing processes.

On the one hand, this may shed light on a fact previously unattended in table 17–1, that among its four groups the incapacitation rate of generation I is no greater than that of the rest. On the other hand, it leads us to a reconsideration of the earlier immigrants who were the parents of our generation II respondents.

A decisive fact is that this earlier wave of immigrants arrived before establishment of the United States visa-screening apparatus. Thus, it is almost certain that they had a substantially greater representation of mental disorder risks than did the later immigrants. Also more numerous in the earlier wave of immigrants was the type O background that we now know, from our post-1921 sample immigrant group, to be particularly associated in Midtown with a high mental morbidity rate.

On both of these counts, there are ample grounds for the expectation that our generation I respondents, as an aggregate, are better off in mental health respects than the immigrant parents of our generation II had been at the same age. Second, according to our original test hypothesis, we expect that our generation II respondents are also in better mental health composition than their parents had been at the same age. Third, if indeed both sample generation I and sample generation II are healthier than the latter's unstudied immigrant parents had been, then it could have been hypothetically predicted that these two sample groups would not be far apart from each other in this respect. Of course, table 17–2 offers evidence that when respondent age and SES origin are held constant, these two generation groups are almost identical in their mental health distributions.

All in all, reconstruction in terms of the probable differential effects of selection processes on the earlier and more recent waves of immigrants, together with the direct evidence from immigrant types O and N appearing in table 17–3, represent separate lines of analysis that lead to the same conclusion: Far from rejecting the test hypothesis predicting mental health differences between immigrants and their native-born children, the data in table 17–2, historically interpreted, seem to stand in support of that hypothesis.

PARENTAL SES, THE URBAN–ORIGIN VARIABLE, AND MENTAL HEALTH AMONG THE U.S.–BORN

In table 17–2 generations II and III also appear to contradict our original hypothesized predictions for these groups. Here again, processes of self-selection may have unexpectedly intruded to complicate the picture.

Although we had always seen generation I as open to self-selection processes, we had viewed a position in generation II, III, or IV as a matter of descent and therefore independent of individual influence or choice. We had also been aware of the fact that about half of the U.S.-born people in Midtown were themselves in-migrants from birth places reaching to the four corners of the nation. To be sure, like immigration of the foreign-born, in-migration of the native-born is a motivated act, usually self-determined, and therefore amenable to the influences of subjective selectivity.

However, in the absence of census data on this point, we had simply assumed that the weightings of in-migrants among generations II, III, and IV would not be grossly different. When the Midtown sample data were in and analyzed, however, we found that this assumption had been erroneous.

Figure 7 below reveals that in generation II a minority of 30 percent are in-migrants from the rest of the country, i.e., 70 percent are native New Yorkers. On the other hand, in generation III the in-migrant proportion rises to 47 percent and in generation IV it jumps to a commanding majority of 72 percent, i.e., only 28 percent are native to the City. In short, the seemingly independent variable of generation differences among the U.S.-born respondents proves to be entwined with the reciprocal variable of in-migration from communities large and small on the continuum of American rural-urban places.

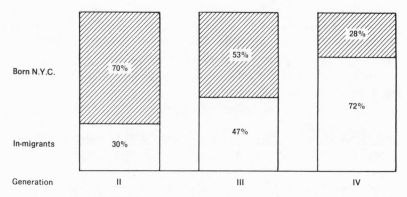

FIGURE 7.   THREE MIDTOWN AMERICAN-BORN GENERATIONS (AGE 20–59), PROPORTIONS OF IN-MIGRANTS AND NEW YORK CITY–BORN

It is possible that mental health differences selectively associated with in-migration tend to obscure the expected decrease in the impairment rate from generation II through IV. This possibility can be checked, although under some handicaps. First, generations III and IV, each with about 250 respondents, are too small to sustain analysis of the in-migration factor while also controlling for both parental SES and age. Accordingly, for this purpose we have no choice except to combine the two generations in one group. This is unfortunate because it will blur the close comparison of generations II and III that we seek to make. Even so, the merged group, i.e., III–IV, has too few respondents of low SES origin for reliable treatment of the latter.

Confining ourselves to the middle (C–D) and upper (A–B) strata, we find these countertrends in both SES-origin classes: (1) among the native New Yorkers, generation II emerges with a higher Impaired-Well ratio than does group III–IV (with age standardized in all instances); (2) among the in-migrants the reverse obtains; i.e., here generation II has a smaller Impaired-Well imbalance than do the group III–IV respondents. As illustration, we offer the Impaired-Well ratios in the four subgroup cells representing the middle SES-origin stratum in table 17–4.

If we focus only on the native New Yorkers in the left-hand column of the table, the generation difference in balances of Impaired and Well people is in the direction originally hypothesized. However, the

TABLE 17–4. HOME SURVEY SAMPLE (AGE 20–59, SES C–D), IMPAIRED-WELL RATIOS AMONG U.S.–BORN GENERATIONS BY PLACE OF ORIGIN

	Native New Yorkers	In-migrants
Generation II	140 (N = 178)	63 (N = 90)
Generations III–IV	99 (N = 68)	90 (N = 82)

in-migrant generation II respondents are the healthiest of the four subgroups, and their weight is sufficient to counterbalance the generation difference observed among the New York–born.

That the intergeneration difference among in-migrants (right-hand column above) is not in the hypothesized direction may be largely a function of differential subjective selectivity for movement to New York, operating in ways we cannot document or reconstruct as yet.[31] On this open-ended note we can at least draw this inference: Table 17–4 offers no warrant to reject the original hypothesis positing that mental health composition would be less favorable in generation II than in III.

The identification of types O and N among immigrants hinged on the factor of rural-urban community settings during childhood abroad. To round out this exploration, we can next apply the same variable[32] to the U.S.-born respondents (generations II to IV inclusive).

There are too few of these respondents reared in a farm or village community to be included while controlling for SES origin and age. Accordingly, the categories examined can cover only the broad urban range and include (1) town or small city, to be abbreviated as *town*, (2) medium or big city (excluding New York City), designated *city*, and (3) *New York City*.

Among American-born adults of low (E–F) parental-SES, mental morbidity rates, with age standardized, do not vary with the urban-origin factor so categorized. Along the remainder of the SES-origin range, however, there are noteworthy mental health differences. These are reported in table 17–5 below.

Although the relationship of impairment rates to urban origin here verges on statistical significance (slightly below the .05 level of con-

TABLE 17–5. HOME SURVEY SAMPLE (AGE 20–59), DISTRIBUTIONS ON MENTAL HEALTH CLASSIFICATION OF U.S.–BORN RESPONDENTS BY URBAN-ORIGIN TYPES AS STANDARDIZED FOR AGE AND PARENTAL SES (INCLUSIVE OF SES STRATA A–D ONLY)

Mental health categories	Urban-origin type		
	Town	City	N.Y.C.
Well	26.6%	24.7%	19.2%
Mild symptom formation	34.3	40.3	36.8
Moderate symptom formation ..	26.0	16.2	22.5
Impaired*	13.1	18.8	21.5
N = 100%	(173)	(170)	(386)
Impaired-Well ratio	49	76	112

* $x^2 = 5.51$, $2df$, $p > .05$.

fidence), the trends in both Impaired and Well frequencies are consistent in their respective directions.[33] Here we see a reversal of the trend previously observed in generation I. Among the latter, Impaired-Well values of *greatest* magnitude were isolated in low SES-origin immigrants from the smaller, principally rural, communities abroad. In table 17–5 the Impaired-Well ratios of *least* magnitude are noted in Midtown respondents from the nation's smaller urban places. The facts that their childhood communities were American and urban and that their parental-SES derivations were in the upper two-thirds of our SES-origin range together offer the reasonable inference that no adaptive problems of sharp change in environment had here been involved.

Instead, we are left with two alternative explanations for this discerned mental health trend on the American urban-origin variable. The first is that the three urban-origin types living in Midtown more or less accurately reflect mental health differences in the like-age-and-SES segment of their parent American communities. Under this assumption, then, the smaller the urban community in which American middle- and upper-status children grow up, the better are their mental health chances when they reach adulthood. If this should be the case, New York City would appear to be the least favorable place to rear such children.

The second possible interpretation proceeds from a far more complicated framework. To begin with, it asserts that in most American communities the indigenous *permanent* residents as a rule far outnumber the native-son *emigrants* who settle elsewhere. On this ground of much greater numerical strength, the indigenous residents are likely to be more representative or reflective of the community's mental health productivity than are the minority of native-son-and-daughter emigrants.

By this line of reasoning, the native New Yorkers in table 17–5 probably are not far different in mental health make-up from the population universe of New York–bred adults of the specified age and parental SES. On the other hand, the in-migrants seen in table 17–5 are less likely to be representative of mental health conditions among like-age-and-SES people in their *home* communities.

Third, this approach also takes into account the fact that emigrants from a given community, in moving to their adopted places, travel varying "distances" in the social dimensions of the rural-urban continuum.[34] In this sense, the town group appearing in table 17–5 has "traveled farther" to settle New York than has the city type. Next we can posit as a consequence of subjective selectivity that personality and mental health differences divide those who in this sense travel near ("hoppers") from those who move far ("broad jumpers"); specifically, of these two categories of emigrants from the same childhood community, the jumpers may deviate farther from the mental health composition of their common population of origin than do the hoppers.

As to how representative the three groups in table 17–5 are of their respective parent populations, by this formulation the New York–born respondents are the most representative and the town in-migrants are the least. Since we have reason to believe that such town-to-metropolis traffic[35] is an important facet of upward SES mobility, as discussed in chapter 14, it seems likely that both types of Midtown in-migrants were actually more favorable in mental health composition than were their respective back-home populations of like-age-and SES origin. Accordingly, from the town and city groups in table 17–5 we cannot generalize that the smaller the urban community in which middle- and upper-class American children live, the better are their mental health chances as adults.

In chapter 20, the senior author presents recently emerging evidence that suggests what we *can* generalize about the links between indices of community well-being and rural-urban-metropolitan differences.

TREATMENT CENSUS FINDINGS

In the Midtown Study the factor of treatment was covered, although in very different ways, by both of our major research operations. One was the Treatment Census, with its goal of enumerating all Midtown residents in the care of hospitals, clinics or office therapists at a given point of time. The other was the Home Interview Survey, in which we asked each sample respondent whether he had ever been to a psychotherapist, and if so, when. (For characteristics differentiating the Home Survey operation from the Treatment Census see chapter 10, p. 191.)

It has been our consistent effort to relate Midtown data bearing on the demographic factors to published studies that are substantively or technically relevant and challenging to the present investigation. Pertinent to this chapter is a monograph that appeared under the sponsorship and imprint of the Social Science Research Council (SSRC) and its Committee on Migrant Differentials. Entitled *Migration and Mental Disease*,[36] the monograph includes an introductory chapter by Dorothy S. Thomas, chairman of the stated SSRC committee.

Since this work presented expert views on the migration factor (both immigration and in-migration) and its links to *treated* mental disorder, we are called upon to take it into serious account by way of providing a backdrop for the Midtown treatment data.

The general mandate of the SSRC committee had been to consider in what respects migrants are different from nonmigrants. The monograph reports its examination of mental illness as one of the possible differentials. Reviewing the relevant literature up to 1953, Thomas in her introductory chapter considers that the most rounded work in this field had been done by Odegaard, the Norwegian psychiatrist, and Malzberg, the American statistician. Both of these investigators took first-admission patients of mental hospitals as their criterion of the frequency of mental illness.[37]

As indicated in the Thomas chapter, Odegaard's study[38] is probably unparalleled. He compared the public hospital rates over a forty-year span (1889–1929) of Norwegian-born immigrants in Minnesota with those (1) of the total native-born population of Minnesota and (2) of the total population of Norway, with standardization for age and sex differences. Odegaard found the Norwegian-born Minnesotans to have patient rates higher than those of U.S.-born Minnesotans; the latter, in turn, had rates higher than those of the population in Norway. In short, *both* U.S.-born and Norwegian-born Minnesotans had higher hospitalization rates than did the population of Norway. Odegaard notes that differences in

... the hospital facilities of the two countries may to some extent explain this, but of course nothing definite can be known about them. . . .[39] The discrepancies [between hospital patient rates in Minnesota and Norway] seem too large for such an explanation to be entirely satisfactory, and it is probably safe to assume that there is actually more insanity among native-born Minnesotans than in the population of Norway. This is in fact very natural, if, as we have some right to believe, there is a connection between immigration and mental disorders. During [1890–1900] about 33 percent of the native-born [Minnesotans] were actually [in-migrants] from other states in the Union, mostly the East. . . . The factors which tend to increase the incidence of mental disease in the Norwegian immigrants [to Minnesota] will therefore probably to some extent be at work in one-third of the native-born [i.e., in the U.S.-born in-migrants to Minnesota] also.

Odegaard sees two main factors as explaining "the natural . . . connection between immigration and mental disorders." One is the "mental and physical strain" of resettlement; and this, for him, applies both to the Norwegian and Yankee settlers of Minnesota. The other, more heavily emphasized element is the "prevalence of certain psychopathic tendencies in the constitution of those who emigrate. Emigration is frequently a result of the restlessness and difficulties of adaptation which may at times be a basis for a later psychotic development."

For our present purposes, the principal difficulties in Odegaard's investigation lie not in the sweeping generality of its etiological conclusions, but in the inadequacy of its data to support etiological inferences of any kind. The root difficulty is the author's assumption that variations in hospitalization rates among the three population groups under study adequately reflect differences in their overall frequencies of severe mental disorder. This assumption may perhaps be valid in some places and not in others and at some points of time and not at others. Accordingly, there is no warrant to impute varying characteristics to diverse groups on the basis of intergroup differences in hospital rates, if the validity of this assumption at the particular places studied is unknown. This precaution is especially indicated by the simple fact that variations in the bed capacities of mental hospitals and the latter's spatial distance from large population centers rather than a presumed "constitutional" etiology tend to determine the number that can be institutionalized.[40]

In a subsequent paper[41] Odegaard takes note of such criticisms. He suggests that the goal of such research is "not to obtain a higher degree of completeness by extending the concept of mental disease, but to establish some definite limitation to make it possible for various authors to compare results." For this purpose,

. . . hospital admission is, in borderline cases, the only distinctive landmark; and besides, it is not at all without clinical meaning. Practically all psychoses with definite clinical symptoms will at some time necessitate admission. At least this is so for schizophrenic and allied disorders and for general paresis, although for the depressive psychoses it may be more doubtful. For senile psychoses, and for psychoses with mental deficiency and epilepsy, on the other hand, hospitalization will frequently be dependent more upon social than upon clinical factors; and admissions for those diagnostic groups do not allow any safe conclusions as to the incidence of the disease.

To round out, if hardly to close this debate, several observations can be addressed to Odegaard's comments. First, as reported earlier (chapter 10), the Midtown Treatment Census found that in *ambulatory* care were 36 percent of all reported nonparanoid schizophrenic patients and 14 percent of all paranoid schizophrenic patients. Second, from other studies there is evidence indicating that when hospitalization does eventuate it often does so long after psychotic symptoms first appeared.[42] Furthermore, the effort to secure psychiatric treatment of any kind often depends upon social factors like a break in family or local tolerance of the symptoms, precipitating, if not a first recognition of "illness," at least a change in the previous view that the condition is "harmless."

Finally, in the whole battery of possible social elements impeding the family from committing a member to a hospital, one potentially affecting immigrants in particular is noted by Malzberg and Lee: "It is claimed that recent immigrants may sometimes be sent to hospitals for mental disease with reluctance because ot the possibility of deportation on the ground that the disease was contracted before entry into the United States."[43]

All in all, there are ample grounds for questioning confidence in the inevitability that any of the more frequent psychotic disorders "will at some time necessitate admission to a mental hospital."

Also worthy of attention is Odegaard's claim that immigration tends to recruit people predisposed to mental disorder, with the obverse implication that nonmigrants tend to be selectively less predisposed. That migrants and nonmigrants are selectively different in such characteristics as mental health seems to be a plausible hypothesis. But that such selection operates in the direction suggested by Odegaard has yet to be established.

As mentioned earlier in the present chapter, we can test this hypothesis in the Midtown sample's immigrant group by dividing it into three subgroups: (1) those who came to the United States as children and therefore are not self-selected migrants; (2) those who came as youths in the company of parents or kin, with the element of self-determination of the migratory act somewhat ambiguous; and (3) those who came unaccompanied, as youths or later, most probably a self-selected group. To corroborate Odegaard's postulate, group 3 should have the highest impairment rate and group 1 the lowest. However, the data for these three subgroups show no differences in their Impaired or Well frequencies. There is no endorsement in these Midtown data for the view that the self-recruited newcomers who initiated their own immigration to the United States have a higher rate of mental morbidity than the less selected who were brought on the initiative of others.

The main body of the SSRC monograph is the study report contributed by Malzberg and Lee. In their own opening chapter, these authors take note that from

. . . the literature on this subject, it is generally concluded that the incidence of mental disease is higher among migrants than among nonmigrants, and that the difference is attributable either to selection of poorer risks at places of [migrants'] origin or to stresses of migration and adjustment at places of destination. Most of these differences have been based on scanty or otherwise inadequate data, and even the fact of higher incidence of mental disease among migrants is not firmly established, much less the theories as to cause.[44]

Their study covered all residents of New York State who were first-admission patients in hospitals supported by the state or federal government (VA) and in state-licensed private hospitals during the three fiscal years ending June 30, 1941.[45] For the white population only, Malzberg and Lee report these average annual rates of hospital first admissions (per 100,000 population), as standardized for age:

Foreign-born males	156
Native-born males	140
Foreign-born females	143
Native-born females	118

Thus, among these four groups only the U.S.-born females deviate in their rate to any extent. Moreover, most of their deviation from the other three groups is traceable to the age range above the 60-year line.[46] There is the definite impression that many senile U.S.-born women in the pre-World War II years were placed for custodial care in nursing homes rather than in psychiatric hospitals.

With this evidence suggesting little difference in hospitalizations between immigrants and U.S.-born in the white population of New York State, Malzberg and Lee concede that

. . . rates of first admission are far from ideal indicators of the incidence of mental disease, but for our purposes they are the best available. It is impossible to determine the number of persons who each year become psychotic because many persons with psychoses may not be included in the statistics of mental disease. There are persons who would be considered psychotic by psychiatrists but who are never treated or diagnosed. Others are treated privately but never hospitalized, and their cases are not reported. [Later they elaborate that] comparisons of migrant and nonmigrant populations are affected to an unknown extent by differential ability or willingness to care for mentally ill persons at home.[47]

The reservations placed by Malzberg and Lee on hospital patients as study populations are shared by the present authors. However, to the view that such patients are "the best available" indicators of the frequency of mental illness we must counter that *best available* does not necessarily imply *good enough* for the kinds of generalizations drawn from them.

A more recent work that concentrates on the migrant-nonmigrant dichotomy straddles both horns of the dilemma posed by patient aggregates and general populations as appropriate bases for etiological generalizations.[48]

In the New Haven study alluded to in previous chapters, the scope of coverage for the first time encompassed ambulatory as well as hospital patients and used prevalence instead of incidence as the measure of frequency. For the demographic factor of concern to this chapter, the New Haven investigators report only for foreign-born and native-born above the age of 20.[49] From distribution data published, we calculate New Haven Total Patients rates of 1,169 per 100,000 immigrants and 1,005 per 100,000 of the American-born population. However, even within the adult age range immigrants are decidedly the older of the two groups, and therefore standardization for age is indispensable. Such standardized rates have not yet been reported. However, the effect of such standardization can be anticipated from the results secured when we remove cases diagnosed as disorders of senescence[50] from the patients of both New Haven generation groups. When this is accomplished, the rates per 100,000 among adult immigrants and natives are reduced to practical identity. We might note in passing that this "no difference" parallels the New York State findings.

We turn now to the Midtown Treatment Census. On the basis of institutional records, hospital and clinic patients could be classified into three generation-in-U.S. groups paralleling the Home Survey sample's I, II, and III–IV. On the patients of office therapists no data identifying generation level were secured. We are therefore extrapolating estimates of office patients from the current patients[51] identified in the Home Survey sample. Because these estimates relate to the 20 to 59 age range, in table 17–6 below we are including only hospital and clinic patients who are within this age span.

To what ends can tables like this be put? In concrete terms, they serve to map the patient traffic in terms of (1) its volume, (2) its differential group origins in the community population, and (3) its flow toward different destinations among the various types of available treatment facilities. Such information, in turn, can have important implications for policy decisions in planning service programs. By way of a single example, we know office therapists are treating psychotics in considerable numbers, diverting them from hospitalization—especially, we now discover, in generation group III–IV. Ambulatory treatment in clinics could probably serve the same pur-

TABLE 17–6. TREATMENT CENSUS (AGE 20–59 ONLY), PREVALENCE RATES
(PER 100,000 POPULATION) OF MIDTOWN PATIENTS BY TREATMENT SITE
AND GENERATION-IN-U.S.

Treatment sites	Generation groups		
	I	II	III–IV
Hospitals	504	829	298
Clinics	76	210	89
Office therapy*	430	2,058	4,811
Total Patients rate*	1,010	3,097	5,198

* Estimated.

pose for generation I and II people who cannot afford high-cost
private therapy. But, table 17–6 indicates that those clinics available
to Midtowners served *adults* of *all* generations to a negligible degree.
Clearly, such knowledge can guide plans for the expansion of treatment facilities that will inevitably come.*

There is one function table 17–6 clearly cannot serve: It cannot
offer any ground for proceeding from known demographic differences
in frequencies of *treatment* to inferences about frequencies of *illnesses*
untreated. To fix the point, we might compare tables 17–1 and
17–6 in this chapter, both having reference to the age 20 to 59
Midtown population. Among the three generation groups in table
17–6 the hospital rate of generation II is substantially highest and of
III–IV the lowest. In table 17–1, Incapacitated is a category in
Rennie's classification scheme that is the closest available approximation to the criterion of *hospitalizable*. According to that table there
are *no* significant generation differences in the proportions of these
noninstitutionalized Incapacitated people. The generation trends of
the Incapacitated and of the Hospitalized bear no resemblance to
each other.

Or, in table 17–6, let us take the clinic *and* estimated office treatment rates which, together, *rise* from 506 (per 100,000 population)
in generation I to 4,900 in group III–IV. In table 17–1, the mental
health categories designated Impaired-Severe and Impaired-Marked

* This sentence stands as written in 1961. Chapter I gives a summary account
of just such developments that followed between 1963 and 1974.

could be expected to delineate the reservoir of potential eligibility for ambulatory treatment. The joint frequency of these two categories *declines* from 24.3 percent in generation I to 19 percent in group III and 14.6 percent in group IV. In short, the two trends on the generation variable move in opposite directions.

The objection may be made that these cross-directional findings on the generation pyramid are chance or freak incongruences that are of no general significance. In rejoinder, it should be noted first that a similar phenomenon has already been reported in previous chapters for the age and socioeconomic status factors and will be encountered again in the chapter on religious groups.

Second, that treatment rates may vary in ways different from morbidity rates can be demonstrated if a criterion group of known mental morbidity cases are circumscribed and treatment rates then are shown to vary among them with differences in demographic characteristics. Equally important is that this will bring to bear data on that part of our key question which asked: What kinds of impaired people do *not* get treatment?

HOME SURVEY SAMPLE: HELP–NEED AND THE PATIENT–HISTORY VARIABLE

Toward these ends, we would now return to our age 20 to 59 Home Survey sample, where the Study psychiatrists have placed 389 respondents in the Impaired category of mental health. Despite apparent limitations, this category in the sample has served as our working criterion of potential need for professional help.

It will also be remembered that on the basis of interview material we were able to classify all sample respondents on a variable we call *patient history*. Those who had never been in one or more professional sessions with a psychotherapist are never-patients; those who had been in such a session during the previous month are designated current patients; and the remainder who had ever been to a therapist are ranked as ex-patients.

In table 17–7 below, only the Impaired in each generation group are shown in their distribution on the patient-history variable. Because of their small numbers the Impaired of generations III and IV are here combined.

TABLE 17-7.   HOME SURVEY SAMPLE (AGE 20-59), DISTRIBUTIONS OF
IMPAIRED RESPONDENTS ON PATIENT-HISTORY CLASSIFICATION BY
GENERATION-IN-U.S.

Patient history	Generation groups		
	I	II	III–IV
Current patients	0.6%	4.6%	14.3%
Ex-patients	16.5	24.4	25.5
Ever-patients	17.1	29.0	39.8
Never-patients	82.9	71.0	60.2
N = 100%*	(158)	(131)	(97)

* Three Impaired respondents are of unknown generation.

Table 17-7 indicates that among Impaired respondents the ever-patient rates increase in regular progression up the generation scale. If the increase is far sharper for current patients than for ex-patients, we can assume that among the latter are mixed the formerly hospitalized, whose rates by generation vary in a direction opposite to the probable trend in the ambulatory ex-patients.[52]

Two important questions remain open: Do these patient-history differences genuinely adhere to the generation factor independently of other demographic factors? Or are these differences largely the indirect reflection of more powerful demographic variables that are concealed in the generation factor? That these questions are decidedly in order is indicated by the facts revealed in previous chapters that ever-patient rates among the Impaired are largest in the younger and higher own-SES segments of the Midtown sample population. The latter are of course underrepresented in generation I.

To answer these questions we shall convert the data in table 17-7 by standardizing the Impaired category in each generation group to a hypothetical ideal population.[53] The results appear in table 17-8.

In this table we discern that the marked difference in current-patient rates previously observed between II and III–IV is erased. The conclusion seemingly to be drawn is that when age and own SES are controlled, the tendency of the Impaired to be treated in an ambulatory setting splits rather sharply on the line dividing the immigrants from the American-born generations. That is, among the Impaired those with the highest ever-patient rates are U.S.-born younger

TABLE 17–8. HOME SURVEY SAMPLE (AGE 20–59), DISTRIBUTIONS OF
IMPAIRED RESPONDENTS ON PATIENT-HISTORY CLASSIFICATION BY
GENERATION-IN-U.S. AS STANDARDIZED FOR OWN SES AND AGE

Patient history	Generation groups among impaired		
	I	II	III–IV
Current patients	1.1%	11.0%	13.4%
Ex-patients	13.8	25.5	22.4
Ever-patients	14.9	36.5	35.8
Never-patients	85.1	63.5	64.2
N = 100%	(158)	(131)	(97)

adults (age 20 to 39) of higher socioeconomic status. Whereas lagging far behind in such rates are the older adults (40 to 59) of lower
SES and foreign birth.

HELP–NEED AND PROFESSIONAL ORIENTATION

We have seen earlier in this chapter that among Midtown sample
adults mental health distributions do not vary with generation-in-U.S.
level when parental SES and respondent age are controlled. Furthermore, we have just observed that within the criterion Impaired category, when own SES and age are controlled, ever-patient rates are at
the same relatively high point in generations II and III–IV and substantially lower only in the immigrant group.

The question is now raised about the relative extent of *effective*
demand for professional help that exists among Impaired respondents
in the several generation groups. To this end, the effective demand
can be judged by their replies to two interview questions that were
put to all respondents. The questions inquired about the nature of the
advice the respondent would give if such counsel were solicited by a
friend concerned about "what to do" (1) with a problem child and
(2) with a problem spouse. Respondents were classified according to
the most specialized kind of professional help they would recommend
for either or both problem situations. In so doing we can assume they
reveal, by indirection, what kind of professional help they are themselves aware of and disposed to seek. In table 17–9, the Impaired

respondents in each generation group, as first sorted by own-SES class, are shown with the proportion who recommended psychotherapy in their replies.

TABLE 17–9. HOME SURVEY SAMPLE (AGE 20–59), PROPORTION RECOMMENDING PSYCHOTHERAPY AMONG IMPAIRED RESPONDENTS BY GENERATION-IN-U.S. AND OWN SES

Own-SES classes	Generation groups among Impaired		
	I	II	III–IV
Lower (E–F) .... N = 100%	12.4% (97)	13.1% (61)	10.7% (27)
Middle (C–D) .... N = 100%	9.8% (51)	32.7% (52)	40.0% (30)
Upper (A–B) .... N = 100%	—* (10)	55.5% (18)	60.0% (40)

* These cases are too few to present a meaningful percentage.

In positive orientation to or awareness of psychotherapy among Impaired respondents, lower-SES respondents in the U..S-born generation subgroups are as often remote as are the foreign-born. Among the upper-status respondents the pro-therapy proportions are far higher but again more or less uniform among the generations. With the middle-stratum Impaired cases, the pro-therapy rates split sharply on the line dividing the foreign-born from the natives. Stated differently, higher frequencies of potential demand for psychiatric care seem to be localized among the American-born Impaired people of the upper two-thirds of the own-SES range.

SUMMARY

We might now briefly retrace the new ground we have traversed in this chapter's coverage of the generation-in-U.S. variable.

1. On the foundations of the large literature reporting observations of American immigrants and their children, it was hypothesized that mental health would be most unfavorable in generation I and would

be progressively more favorable in successive generation groups from II through IV.

2. As distributed on the psychiatrists' mental health scale, the four generation groups in the Midtown sample emerged with Impaired and Well differences that leaned in the hypothesized direction. However, these differences were relatively small in magnitude except between the two anchoring groups—I and IV.

3. When the age and SES-origin factors entangled with the generation variable were controlled by standardizing, the original Impaired-Well differences observed were practically erased. With no evidence of mental health differences specifically attributable to the generation variable apart from the age and SES-origin factors, rejection of the tested hypothesis was indicated.

4. The face implausibility of this "no relationship" finding prompted a critical reexamination of our assumptions and methods. A number of these were seen to be grossly simplistic. However, reanalysis of the data in the light of the overlooked complexities suggested that (*a*) at the very least, the data do not warrant rejection of the chapter's major hypotheses; and (*b*) with considerable probability, the data seem to support these hypotheses.

5. In the course of this dissection we discovered in the sample's immigrant group that relatively frequent prevalence of mental morbidity was associated with the combination of lower parental SES and a rural-town childhood background. Conducting a similar exploration among the sample's American-born respondents (generations II to IV), we found urban-origin differences in mental health only within the middle and upper brackets of parental SES. With the urban-origin variable classifying Midtown respondents according to town, city, or New York derivation, mental health composition was most favorable in the town category and least favorable among the native New Yorkers. Two contradictory interpretations of this trend were discussed.

6. Turning to the factor of psychiatric treatment, we reviewed three studies that focused on immigrants and the native-born among psychiatric patients. Noted were differences in the findings and inferences they generated. Also brought to bear were the generation data yielded by the Midtown Treatment Census, with emphasis on their special utility and their specific limitations.

7. Returning to the Midtown Home Survey, those in the sample's

Impaired category, taken as criterion of professional help-need, were analyzed by generation groups for differences in patient history. Upward on the generation scale the ever-patient rates increased and the never-patient rates diminished. However, with standardization for own SES and age, the trend changed to a dichotomy that broke sharply on the line dividing the Impaired immigrants from the Impaired native-born groups. Compared to the latter of like age and socioeconomic status, the foreign-born Impaired people get to a psychotherapist to a considerably lesser extent.

8. On an indirect test of awareness of and disposition to seek psychotherapy among Impaired respondents, again the U.S.-born of middle and upper own-SES strata were far ahead in their pro-therapy frequencies. This roughly delineated the locus of effective demand for professional intervention among Midtown's help-needy adult residents.

NOTES

1. Placement in a generation group was made not on the judgment of the respondent but on that of the interviewer and was subsequently checked by office staff.

In classifying the Midtown sample, all U.S.-born respondents who had one foreign-born parent and the other of American birth were arbitrarily placed in generation II. This mixed subgroup numbered about one-fourth of all sample respondents assigned to generation II. Similarly, all U.S.-born respondents with both parents of native birth were placed in generation III if one to four grandparents were foreign-born. Approximately half of all sample respondents classified as generation III had from one to three U.S.-born grandparents. Because the mixed subgroups of generations II and III are not significantly different in their mental health composition from their unmixed generation peers, they will not be differentiated in the data analysis that follows.

2. In the interest of conserving interview time, the identification of such respondents' immigrant forebears was not pursued beyond the question, "About how many generations before your father's parents did his family come to the United States?" With an identical question for mother's family, the answers ranged from respondent's great-grandparents to ancestors dating back to the eighteenth century. Thus, the category of generation IV for a respondent should be understood as referring to four or more generations in the United States on *both* father's and mother's side.

3. By sample design only one age-eligible occupant was drawn from each randomly selected dwelling. Furthermore, in a metropolitan area like Midtown the chances are slight of drawing two linear kin from separate households. To our knowledge no generation II respondent is either offspring of a generation I respondent or parent of a generation III respondent.

4. Four U.S.-born respondents terminated the interview before the generation section was reached. However, the symptom coverage was sufficient in scope for mental health evaluation, permitting their retention in the interviewed sample.

5. M. Lerner, *America as a Civilization*, 1957, p. 476.

6. E. N. Saveth, "Good Stocks and Lesser Breeds: The Immigrant in American Textbooks," *Commentary*, May 1949, pp. 494–498.

7. Ibid., p. 498.

8. Oscar Handlin, *The Uprooted*, Boston, 1951. For a recent critique of the Handlin work see C. Greer, *Divided Society*, 1974, pp. 1–35, 331–333. See also T. C. Wheeler, ed., *The Immigrant Experience: The Anguish of Becoming American*, 1971.

9. Handlin, *The Uprooted*, p. 6.

10. Ibid., pp. 155–164.

11. For a field study of variations in these conflict situations among eight different immigrant groups, cf. W. L. Warner and L. Srole, *The Social Systems of American Ethnic Groups*, 1945, pp. 124–155. Cf. also I. L. Child, *Italian or American? The Second Generation Conflict*, 1943; O. Handlin, ed., *Children of the Uprooted*, 1966; J. Lopreato, *Italian Americans*, 1970.

12. K. Lewin, *Resolving Social Conflicts*, 1948, pp. 186–200.

13. M. Hansen, "The Third Generation in America," in his *The Immigrant in American History*, 1940. See also S. Koenig, "Second and Third Generation Americans," in F. J. Brown and J. S. Roucek, eds., *One America*, 1952.

14. Average age in generations I and II is 46 and 39, respectively; in both III and IV it is 36.

15. Since we shall use this device in subsequent chapters, considerations of interchapter comparability suggest that the same kind of standard population be applied throughout. To this end, it is necessary to construct a hypothetical ideal standard. In the present instance, the standard generation group is con-structed to be equally distributed among the six cells (i.e., with 16.7 percent of the group's population in each cell) that are produced when parental SES is trichotomized (lower, middle, upper) and respondent age in each SES stratum is dichotomized (20 to 39 versus 40 to 59). Calculations are then made of the mental health distributions that would have emerged from the four generations so identically constituted.

16. For the record, we would note also that no significant differences in mental health composition emerge when we sort out and compare males and females in each of the four generation groups.

17. To be sure, generation IV splits 2:2 on the Well-Mild line, whereas the other generations split roughly 1:2. Plausible explanations for this difference, at the better end of the mental health range only, do not suggest themselves. In any case, this localized deviation is hardly sufficient to revise the comprehensive "no difference" judgment.

18. As a corollary, the relationships of SES origin and age to mental health are negligibly altered when the generation variable is analytically controlled.

19. Lerner, *America as a Civilization*, pp. 87–88.

20. See the remarkable novel *Christ in Concrete* by Pietro Di Donato, 1937.

21. U.S. Immigration and Naturalization Service, *Annual Reports*.

22. Population of 500,000 or over.

23. On the average, the sample's immigrants, when interviewed, had been in the United States about twenty-five years.

24. P. Reymont, 1924.

25. *The Ten Pains of Death*, 1959.

26. The psychological processes that carry the individual toward considering and applying for emigration we shall hereafter refer to as *subjective selectivity*. The qualities distinguishing those accepted for migration (by the screening of external processes) from those rejected we shall refer to as *objective selectivity*.

Where we refer to selectivity without such specifications, we have in mind the special characteristics of migrants that are the *joint* consequences of both kinds of selection processes.

27. W. S. Bernard, *American Immigration Policy*, 1950, p. 30.

28. U.S. Department of Justice, *United States Immigration Laws*, M-50, rev. 1958, p. 2..

29. For a travel visa to the U.S., the prosecutor's stance and guilty-until-proved-innocent attitude of American consulate personnel toward applicants had come to be epitomized abroad in the cryptic phrase: "Even Columbus couldn't get a visa." For those seeking an immigrant's visa "the bureaucratic barrier and curtain of red tape" were a far more forbidding gauntlet. How this gauntlet was experienced by refugees fleeing persecution has been poignantly conveyed in Menotti's stirring opera *The Consul*.

30. In the years 1921 to 1940, some 4.6 million immigrants entered the country; in the same period 1.5 million departed, principally returnees to native lands.

31. The literature based on investigations of mental hospital patients has offered discussion of the "drift theory." The latter is addressed to the finding that the institutionalized schizophrenic rate is highest in residential areas nearest the city's central business district (R. Faris and H. W. Dunham, *Mental Disorders in Urban Areas*, 1939). The theory assumes that such concentration is the result of movement into these sections of prodromal schizophrenics from other areas.

With group balances of Impairment and Wellness as our particular criterion, the data just presented suggest that U.S.-born migrants to Midtown on the whole are healthier in mental health composition than are the area's native New Yorkers.

This, of course, does not necessarily invalidate the drift theory as an explanation for the high mental *hospitalization* rates in core-of-city residential areas.

Focusing on the psychotics who are in-migrants and probably detached from kin, as compared with those who are natives of the city and are more likely to have protective kin nearby, it is a plausible hypothesis that the former, lacking such protection, are more likely than the natives to be surrendered to institutionalization. Here again, patient rates should be pointed not to questions of etiology, but rather to forces blocking or facilitating paths to different kinds of help.

32. Rural-urban origin for all respondents was derived from replies to an interview question about size of place where "you spent most of your childhood up to the age of 16."

33. In the upper parental-SES class (A–B) the left-to-right urban-origin Impaired-Well values are 44, 66, and 97, respectively. In the middle class (C–D), the corresponding values are 56, 84, and 130, respectively.

34. By the latter criterion, a change from Boston to New York, i.e., from a smaller metropolis to a larger one, is minimal in magnitude, whereas removal from Roxborough (Vermont) to Boston, i.e., from a village to a metropolis, is assumed to be a near maximal change.

35. Sociologists have emphasized the significance of intercommunity movements as an American phenomenon. In its general outlines this formulation is indebted to S. A. Stouffer, "Intervening Opportunities: A Theory Relating Mobility and Distance," *American Sociological Review* 5 (December 1940): 845–867; and A. M. Rose, "Distance of Migration and Socio-economic Status of

Migrants," *American Sociological Review* 23 (August 1958): 420–423; G. W. Pierson, *The Moving Americans*, 1972.

36. B. Malzberg and E. S. Lee, *Migration and Mental Disease*, 1956.

37. Here we shall not be at all concerned with the controversial issues centering on the relative merits and limitations of incidence (first admissions over a span of time) and prevalence (total patients at a given point of time) as alternative measures of patient frequency when applied to hospital populations (see Appendix C).

38. O. Odegaard, "Emigration and Insanity," *Acta Psychiatrica Neurologica*, Suppl. 4, 1932. All citations here drawn from this work are as quoted in Dorothy S. Thomas's chapter in the SSRC monograph.

39. The reference here is to the bed capacities of tax-supported hospitals in Minnesota and Norway, facts known from the public records at both places.

40. Goldhamer and Marshall refer to the " 'law of distance,' whereby the frequency of [mental hospital] admissions tends to be inverse to the distance from a hospital." (H. Goldhamer and A. Marshall, *Psychosis and Civilization*, 1949, p. 63). The element of spatial accessibility seems to uncover one of many possible considerations taken into account by the prospective patient and his family in deciding whether or not to accept hospitalization when both the need is indicated and the bed space is believed to be available.

41. O. Odegaard, "A Statistical Investigation of the Incidence of Mental Disorder in Norway," *Psychiatric Quarterly* 20 (July 1946): 382–383.

42. J. A. Clausen and M. R. Yarrow, "Paths to the Mental Hospital," *Journal of Social Issues* 11, no. 4 (1955): 25–32.

43. Malzberg and Lee, *Migration and Mental Disease*, p. 47.

44. Ibid., p. 43.

45. Not covered were patients in out-of-state private hospitals or patients at in-state municipal psychiatric hospitals offering short-term treatment.

46. Cf. Malzberg and Lee, *Migration and Mental Disease*, pp. 70–71.

47. Ibid., p. 123.

48. M. B. Kantor, ed., *Mobility and Mental Health*, 1965.

49. B. H. Roberts and J. K. Myers, "Religion, National Origin, Immigration and Mental Illness," *American Journal of Psychiatry* 110 (April 1954): 761.

50. Of course, these occur largely beyond the age of 60, where adult immigrants are now far more concentrated than are the native-born.

51. The sample's current patients encompass both clinic and office cases without differentiation between the two; but since a group's clinic rate is known from the Treatment Census, by subtraction of the latter rate an estimate of the office patient rate is possible. Two limitations beset these estimates: (1) Current patients among sample respondents may be a close but not exact equivalent of the one-day prevalence measure used in the Treatment Census; and (2) such estimates are always subject to sampling variance and therefore lack assurance of precision. Nonetheless, with due caution they can serve the purpose of filling a gap in our Treatment Census data.

52. The latter, we can assume, follow the generation trend observed in the ambulatory current patients.

53. This population is equally distributed among the six cells produced by trichotomizing respondents' own-SES range and dichotomizing the age range.

Photograph by Ira Srole

"New York is a prism that refracts the spectrum of nationality groups from the entire face of our earth."

CHAPTER 18

EIGHT NATIONAL–ORIGIN GROUPS

THOMAS LANGNER AND LEO SROLE

Having probed the generation-in-U.S. levels for their connections with mental health, we can take the next step of examining the main national-origin or ethnic groups that subdivide Midtown's immigrant, second and third generations.

In the description of the Study area's population presented in chapter 4, a number of key facts about these groups were indicated. Here we can enlarge the picture somewhat by sketching in several salient background details in space and time.

It will be remembered that at the time of our field work, immigrants accounted for about one-third of Midtown's residents. According to the United States census, Germans and Irish were then the two largest nationality segments of Midtown's immigrant population, comprising 21.7 and 16.9 percent of the latter, respectively.

Next in size within this generation (I) were people born in Czechoslovakia (9.2 percent of Midtown's immigrants), in Hungary (8 percent), in Italy (7 percent), and in the United Kingdom (6.9 percent). Among the still smaller groups were immigrants from Austria, who constituted 5.9 percent of the foreign-born population. Because they were few, and of identical language, they will here be merged with the German group.

There were also people from Poland, Russia, and Lithuania who were predominantly Jewish and together added up to 5.6 percent of Midtown's immigrants. In view of their heterogeneity of national origin and small numbers, they are being held for separate analysis, with Jews of other nationalities, in the chapter on religious groups that follows.

Puerto Ricans, although few in the Study area, presented special problems. On their home island they are citizens of the United States; therefore, on arrival in New York they are citizen in-migrants rather than alien immigrants. Nonetheless, sociological students of Puerto Ricans have observed: "As established by law, the Puerto Rican is an American, but the contrast between his rural island with its Spanish heritage and the American metropolis makes him in psychological and cultural reality a foreigner in the city."[1] In this sense, we regard Puerto Ricans as an ethnic group differentiated on the same psychosocial plane as other nationality elements in the Study area. To judge from the Home Survey sample, Puerto Rican–born residents comprised about 4 percent of Midtown's generation I group in the age 20 to 59 range.[2]

Still unaccounted for by Census Bureau reckoning were people from many other countries abroad—each group too small to be handled statistically here. These "all others" plus Russians, Poles, and Lithuanians with whom they are merged in this chapter, together add to about 25 percent of the age-inclusive Midtown immigrants.

By way of brief historical perspective, between 1910 and the time of this Study the total population of the Midtown area contracted about 15 percent. Seen in terms of the generations, the immigrants diminished in absolute numbers by one-third and the second generation by about 20 percent; whereas levels III and IV (not differentiated by the Census Bureau) actually expanded by nearly one-third. Also noteworthy is that in that period the number of resident foreign-born from Germany, Austria, Ireland, Italy, Hungary, and Russia fell in each case by roughly one-half. On the other hand, in the same years people from the United Kingdom increased by 12 percent, and those from all other countries combined multiplied by about four times. Populated once by a relatively small number of large nationality groups, the Midtown scene became ethnically diversified to a far greater degree, i.e., characterized by a large number of smaller groups. When such a fractionated population must be studied in miniature cross section through a sample, analysis of ethnicity as a demographic variable presents refractory technical problems that we shall return to presently.

It is obvious that in focusing on the factor of national origin our interest is not in political entities per se. Historically, each immigrant-contributing nation-state had usually emerged from a people with an underlying communality in linguistic and other cultural traditions. Thus, nationality is a convenient, if rough, operational index of cultural differences within the broad tapestry of European civilization. Furthermore, at least for the larger of Midtown's ethnic groups, the element of common national background exerts a gravitational pull toward knitting local families into institutions and varying approximations of "community."

Social scientists are known to divide on several issues touching on the mental health implications of these national differences in what we shall call the immigrant's *ancestral culture*.[3] One view tends to see the ancestral culture as a single, more or less homogeneous whole, which is significantly different from the cultures of other European nations in two (among other) respects: (1) in the character of the built-in mechanisms that tend to generate stress—mechanisms seen as largely rooted in the culturally conditioned emotional economy of the several intrafamilial roles during childhood, and (2) in the nature of the culturally approved cathartic outlets for stress.

Relative to the ancestral cultures of the main ethnic groups represented in Midtown, there was no systematic knowledge available to us bearing on their differences in culturally patterned stress-generating and stress-ventilating mechanisms.[4] Furthermore, procurement of such knowledge was beyond reach of the methods employed in either the Home Survey or Treatment Census operations.

The literature of psychology and common observation bear out the pronounced tendency of outsiders to characterize the members of a minority group in stereotyped terms. The common-stamp attribution takes a more sophisticated form among those students who seem to assume a given people to be essentially homogeneous in their most significant cultural features.[5]

Relative sociocultural homogeneity within an ethnic group is an empirical issue that cannot be swept under the research carpet in the guise of a self-validating axiom. To be sure, this would make for seemingly tidy convenience in the research operation, but it also delays the day of full reckoning.

The Midtown ethnic groups revealed in our sample population are excellent cases in point. Approximations of complete homogeneity, at least in the sphere of religious origin, are found among local Italians[6] and Irish, who are 95 percent of Catholic background, and among Puerto Ricans, who are 89 percent Catholic. On the other hand, the ratio of Catholics to Protestants to Jews among Hungarians is roughly 6:1:3 and among German-Austrians 4:4:2.

The closest approximation to homogeneity in educational background is traced to the sample Puerto Ricans, 70 percent of whom did not go beyond primary school, and only 4 percent reached college. At the other extreme, in Midtown's sample British group[7] the corresponding proportions are 27 and 36 percent, respectively.

Or, consider generation composition itself. In the Midtown sample, representation of generation I ranges from 85 percent of the Puerto Ricans and 61 percent of the Hungarians to only 28 percent among Italians. Conversely, few or no generation III people appear among sample Puerto Ricans and Hungarians, in contrast with 33 percent among both Irish and British and 20 percent among German-Austrians.

The generation III element is itself interesting, if we dichotomize it into (1) those whose four grandparents were of like transoceanic national origin and (2) those whose grandparents were of two or more different national backgrounds, Old American included. The ratio of people in these two subgroups is about 1:2 among both Irish and German-Austrians and 1:9 among the British third generation. If the criterion is intermixing of nationality stocks, the American "melting pot" is here seen in slow but inexorable operation.[8]

If we narrow the focus to the immigrant segment in each nationality group, we find important intergroup demographic differences bearing on mental morbidity rates. For example, sample generation I Germans show only 12 percent of their members to be in the 20 to 39 age range, whereas of Puerto Rican immigrants fully 75 percent are in that age bracket. In other ethnic groups, the immigrants are more evenly balanced in age distribution.

Among the several groups of immigrants we also find differences in SES origin, i.e., parental socioeconomic status. It will be remembered that the sample's range in parental socioeconomic distribution, when its analytical control becomes necessary, is cut into three equally populated categories, designated low, middle, and high. On this criterion, generation I Irish, Italians, and Czechs are each predominantly (over 50 percent) from low-SES families; whereas German-Austrian, British, and Hungarian immigrants are in each instance more heavily derived from middle-SES parents. Of these two sets of immigrant groups, the Irish, Italians, and Czechs were in greater numbers drawn from farm, village, or town communities and the German-Austrians, British, and Hungarians from more urbanized places.

Speaking of immigrant groups in America generally, Mills, Senior, and Goldsen observe that each "is accused of 'clannishness.' Yet the immigrant group itself is almost never cohesive, but is criss-crossed by economic cleavages, intervillage rivalries, rural-urban lines, and sometimes by religious differences, educational rank, and vocation. But if the group as a whole has one visibly distinguishing characteristic, it is that all members are usually lumped together by the 'natives.' "[9]

GROUP ATTACHMENTS

One of our concerns in designing the Study was to take the question of relative cohesiveness within ethnic groups out of the realm of impression and onto an empirical footing for comparative analysis. Stereotypes aside, one could uncritically observe the impressive institutional apparatus of a given ethnic group on the metropolitan scene and conclude that it is a broadly based, effectively functioning community, with its people rocklike in their attachment to their nationality origins and traditions. Yet more complete investigation might well reveal facts of a different nature.

To meet this empirical problem in the context of the Home Survey interviews, an operational scale was devised according to which one could measure an individual's relative behavioral attachment to or detachment from his national traditions, his country of origin, and his local ethnic group. The scale consisted of a sampling of five component indicators: (1) whether or not the individual prefers his native culinary tradition; (2) whether or not he observes native secular or religious holidays, e.g., St. Patrick's day among the Irish; (3) whether or not he retains any interest in the "old country"; (4) whether or not he participates in the secular affairs of his local ethnic group; and (5) whether or not he is opposed to young people marrying out from his nationality group.

The interview questions constructed to represent these components were uniformly worded for all groups, adapted only to refer to the specific national origin of the respondent. As read, for example, to generation I, II, and III respondents of Italian descent, the questions were as follows:

1. Comparing Italian style cooking and regular American style cooking, do you like Italian style cooking (*a*) better, (*b*) just as much, or (*c*) not as much?
2. During the last year or so did you do anything at all special about *any* of the Italian holidays?
3. Are you interested at all in what's going on today in Italy?
4. Do you attend Italian-American meetings or social affairs often, occasionally, or not at all?
5. Some Italian parents feel that it is all right if a son or daughter wants to marry someone who is not Italian. Other Italian parents don't feel that way at all. How do you feel about it: is it all right or *not* all right?

Each respondent was scored from o to 5 according to the number of yes or "attached" replies he gave. For convenience in reporting, we will here designate respondents as *attached* if their score was 2 to 5 and *detached* if the score was either o or 1.[10]

The nationality attachment-detachment scale was devised in order to compare the several ethnic populations in the sample according to extent of group cohesion within each. If the scale *actually* measures what was intended, differences must appear among the generation-in-U.S. levels in only one possible direction, namely, most attachment in generation I and least in generation III. Moreover, within generation I greatest attachment must appear among those who arrived in this country as mature adults (age over 24) and least attachment among those who arrived as children (age 17 or under). The line-up of attached and detached, classified as indicated above, in the several inclusive generation segments is seen in table 18–1.

The differences in attachment rates fall into the rank order expected by our formulation.[11] With this internal evidence as a form of validation for the scale, we can determine its results when applied first to the immigrant segment (generation I) in each of the seven ethnic groups presented in table 18–2.

The number of cases in several of these immigrant groups is small. This suggests caution against drawing inferences from small differences and also prevents control for other relevant factors, namely, age at immigration, sex, years in the United States, etc. Nonetheless,

TABLE 18–1. HOME SURVEY SAMPLE (AGE 20–59), NATIONALITY ATTACHMENT-DETACHMENT RATES BY GENERATION LEVEL

Generation level	Attached	Detached	Total
Generation I arrived as:			
Mature adults (over 24).....	51.1%	48.9%	100%
Young adults (18–24)	41.4	58.6	100
Children (under 18)	33.4	66.6	100
Generation I: Total	43.2	56.8	100
Generation II: Total	23.8	76.2	100
Generation III: Total	16.7	83.3	100

we can take note that in general the lowest attachment rates are found among the British and German-Austrian immigrants, the only two ethnic groups that are in combination (1) West European (2) predominantly Protestant,[12] and (3) more heavily of urban than of rural origin. Substantially higher in attachment rates are the Czechoslovakian and Hungarian immigrants, who of course are (1) East European in language stock, (2) predominantly Catholic,[13] and (3) in the former group, at least, predominantly rural in origin.

The highest attachment frequency is found among the Puerto Ricans, probably in part a function of a circumstance that does not apply to any of the other groups; namely, they were of very recent arrival compared to the average of twenty-three years of residence in this country for generation I as a whole.

With the Puerto Ricans seemingly a special case, the immigrant groups in table 18–2 rank themselves according to their nationality detachment rates in an order roughly corresponding to the degree of sociocultural congruity between their backgrounds and the basically

TABLE 18–2. HOME SURVEY SAMPLE (AGE 20–59), ATTACHMENT-DETACHMENT RATES IN GENERATION I BY ETHNIC GROUP

Ethnic group	Attached	Detached	N = 100%
Puerto Ricans	65.1%	34.9%	(23)
Czechoslovakians	53.3	46.7	(60)
Hungarians	53.3	46.7	(45)
Irish	46.8	53.2	(79)
Italians	43.5	56.5	(40)
German-Austrians	34.7	65.3	(164)
British	27.0	73.0	(37)

Anglo-Saxon, urban, industrial, and Protestant trends that are the dominant figures in the cultural fabric of contemporary America.

Although deculturation from the old society and acculturation to the new do not necessarily move in a 1:1 relationship, we can find in table 18–2 confirmation for a generalization advanced in an earlier study,[14] that intergroup differences in acculturation tempo of immigrants depend in part on the degree of native sociocultural congruity with salient aspects of the American environment.[15]

Remaining open is the question whether the data for the generation II segments of the several ethnic groups will also fit the culture congruency postulate. In table 18–3 we present their detachment frequencies only, alongside the corresponding rates for each group's immigrant generation. Appearing with only four generation II people in the sample, the Puerto Ricans cannot be represented in the table.

Of course, in the generation II column, the range of differences

TABLE 18–3. HOME SURVEY SAMPLE (AGE 20–59), DETACHMENT RATES IN GENERATIONS II AND I BY ETHNIC GROUP

Ethnic group	Generation II	N = 100%	Generation I	N = 100%
Czechoslovakians	75.9%	(54)	46.7%	(60)
Hungarians	69.3	(26)	46.7	(45)
Irish	74.0	(92)	53.2	(79)
Italians	74.2	(93)	56.5	(40)
German-Austrians ...	84.4	(109)	65.3	(164)
British	84.4	(32)	73.0	(37)
Total for generation ..	76.2		56.8	

quantitatively possible for the detachment rates is far narrower than among the immigrants. Nonetheless, we see that British and German-Austrians again stand out with high rates among their generation II peers. In this particular sense, we can discern that the factor of cultural congruence continues to be reflected in the deculturation-acculturation tempo of generation II ethnic groups, although with considerably diminished magnitude.

The above discussion has been intended to illuminate, however briefly, something of the intragroup heterogeneity in most Midtown nationality segments and the intergroup differences in tempo of transformation from the old-country to the new-American model of man.

From the specifically Italian, or German, or Irish line of ancestral culture, for example, there was no ground for framing hypotheses relating to the expected mental health composition of corresponding nationality groups in the Midtown sample—especially as these ancestral cultures were all kindred variants of the millennial-old European civilization. Nevertheless, recommending itself was the criterion of relative congruity between the several ancestral cultures in their major contours and the overall cultural fabric of urban America. Accordingly, one of the early hypotheses entertained by the Midtown research team was this: The greater the degree of such congruity among local ethnic groups, the less would be the adaptive stresses and the better correspondingly would be the resulting mental health. An alternative hypothesis was also proposed: The faster the tempo of change among ethnic groups, with respect to shifting attachments from the old to the new cultural foundations, the greater the strain and the less propitious the mental health consequences. Under the "congruity" hypothesis, the British and German-Austrian groups, by way of illustration, would expectedly turn up with the most favorable mental health composition. Under the "tempo" hypothesis, on the other hand, these two groups would foreseeably present the least favorable mental health picture. How the data fall between these two alternatives is examined in the next section of this chapter.

HOME SURVEY SAMPLE: MENTAL HEALTH DISTRIBUTIONS

The ethnic factor is not unknown to studies in medical epidemiology. Among nationality groups resident in the United States, mortality differences have been found for such causes of death as pneumonia, tuberculosis, diabetes, and heart disease.[16] Also reported among these groups are differences in the frequency of cancer at particular sites.[17]

Previous investigations that focused on nationality background and its relation to mental disorder have been exceedingly few in number. The only one known to us that employed a general population is that of Hyde and Chisholm.[18] This study involved 60,000 consecutive selectees from homes in eastern Massachusetts, who were examined in 1941–1942 at the Boston Induction Station. The criterion was rejection for psychiatric reasons. As reported, the rejection rates for three nationality groups also covered in the Midtown Study are given in table 18-4 below.

TABLE 18–4.   SELECTIVE SERVICE PSYCHIATRIC REJECTION RATES IN THREE
NATIONAL-ORIGIN GROUPS

	Italian	Irish	Old American
Percent rejected	13.7	12.8	5.7
Percent accepted	86.3	87.2	94.3
N = 100%	(3,472)	(2,440)	(1,640)

Hyde and Chisholm indicate that the Old-American men were from communities[19] that were graded on the whole as high (B) in socioeconomic level, whereas the Italians and Irish were from communities rated as low in SES (E and F, respectively). The authors provide this information so that "corrections can be made for [nationality] differences that may be traceable to [SES]." Although they did not make such corrections, they report elsewhere that overall rejection rates for communities of B, E, and F socioeconomic levels were 9.2, 12.7, and 16.6 percent respectively. In the light of the latter, it appears offhand that if SES differences could be standardized, the Irish would have the highest rejection rate by a small margin and the Old American the lowest rate by a smaller margin than that reported. However, there are reasons for viewing these findings with serious reservations.[20]

We must now turn to the seven nationality groups represented in the Midtown sample population. For the record, we are presenting in table 18–5 the distribution of each group on the psychiatrists' classification of mental health. Covered in each group are its three generation segments, I, II, and III.

A first consideration is that if different national backgrounds exert varying impacts on mental health, they must manifest this power most clearly among people born in and shaped by these overseas societies, i.e., among the immigrant element in the several ethnic groups.

In the light of this overriding consideration, we have no choice except to narrow our comparison directly to the ethnic groupings within the immigrant generation. Although left with relatively few people in these groups, we accept the sacrifice of statistical viability in the interest of substantive insights suggested, if any.

In table 18–6 below, the several identified immigrant groups are arranged in the order of diminishing detachment frequencies as

TABLE 18–5. HOME SURVEY SAMPLE (AGE 20–59), RESPONDENTS'
DISTRIBUTIONS ON MENTAL HEALTH CLASSIFICATION BY NATIONAL ORIGIN
(GENERATIONS I, II, AND III COMBINED)

National origin	Mental health categories							
	Well	Mild symptom formation	Moderate symptom formation	Impaired	Marked* symptom formation	Severe* symptom formation	Incapacitated*	N = 100%
British	22.0%	33.0%	15.0%	30.0%	17.0%	9.0%	4.0%	(100)
German-Austrians	18.6	37.3	21.0	23.1	11.2	9.5	2.4	(338)
Irish	17.5	33.4	27.2	21.9	12.6	7.3	2.0	(246)
Italians	14.0	34.2	24.5	27.3	15.4	9.8	2.1	(143)
Hungarians	13.5	35.1	24.3	27.1	20.3	4.1	2.7	(74)
Czechoslovakians .	10.5	41.1	21.0	27.4	12.9	9.7	4.8	(124)
Puerto Ricans ...	3.7	44.5	7.4	44.4	18.5	25.9	0.0	(27)
All others	18.8	39.4	20.4	21.4	14.1	4.4	2.9	(382)
Old Americans (Generation IV)	28.0	32.0	22.2	17.8	9.3	5.8	2.7	(226)
Sample total	18.5%	36.3%	21.8%	23.4%	13.2%	7.5%	2.7%	(1,660)

* These values are subtotals of the Impaired figure.

previously seen in table 18–2. It is first observed that the British and German-Austrians, who stood highest on the detachment scale, here have the largest Well rates; whereas the most strongly attached group, the Puerto Ricans, are altogether absent from the Well ranks. Seemingly intimated here is the existence of some sort of relationship between ethnic detachment and wellness.

Beyond the category of the Well, however, there seems to be no consistent connection between mental health composition and rank order of detachment from the national-origin group. This applies to the Impaired rates as well as to frequencies of the Moderate and Mild categories of symptom formation. On the whole, therefore, these data from Midtown's immigrant generation fail to lend support to either the congruity or the tempo hypotheses defined above.

Hypotheses aside, our attention is drawn to three groups that stand out as potential deviants in this population of immigrants. We note impairment rates of 37.5 and 18.2 percent among the Italian and Hungarian immigrants respectively, with an accompanying reversal in their Moderate category frequencies, i.e., 15.0 and 31.8 percent. Before interpreting these divergences as reflecting unspecified

TABLE 18–6. HOME SURVEY SAMPLE (AGE 20–59), DISTRIBUTIONS ON
MENTAL HEALTH CLASSIFICATION OF IMMIGRANT RESPONDENTS
(GENERATION I) BY NATIONAL ORIGIN

National Origin	Mental health categories				
	Well	Mild symptom formation	Moderate symptom formation	Impaired	N = 100%
Total generation I .	16.1%	36.0%	21.2%	26.7%	(593)
British	21.6	39.7	19.0	29.7	(37)
German-Austrians .	18.3	32.9	24.4	24.4	(164)
Irish	12.5	35.0	22.5	30.0	(79)
Italians	15.0	32.5	15.0	37.5	(40)
Hungarians	13.6	36.4	31.8	18.2	(45)
Czechoslovakians .	13.3	41.7	18.3	26.7	(60)
Puerto Ricans	0.0	39.1	8.7	52.2	(23)
All others ......:.	19.2	39.7	19.2	21.9	(145)

national differences in the culture patterns of Italy and Hungary, a specifiable fact must first be taken into account.

It will be recalled that the sample respondents were stratified by socioeconomic status of parents, with the sample's distribution of parental-SES scores divided, when their analytical control was necessary, into three more or less equally populated SES-origin groups. We know that there is a link between parental SES, so classified, and the Impaired-Well mental health ratio, and that the link has survived our efforts to shake out possible spurious effects of other demographic variables.

How the populations of Italy and Hungary, at the time our respondents departed these lands, would have distributed themselves on this SES-origin continuum is of course unknown to us. But we do know how *these* foreign-born respondents were distributed (table 18–7).

TABLE 18–7. HOME SURVEY SAMPLE (AGE 20–59), PARENTAL-SES
DISTRIBUTIONS OF IMMIGRANT ITALIANS AND HUNGARIANS

Parental SES	Generation I	
	Italians	Hungarians
Lower (E–F)	50.0%	22.2%
Middle (C–D)	32.5	48.9
Upper (A–B)	17.5	28.9
N = 100%	(40)	(45)

The number of people in each ethnic group is too small to permit control of these SES-origin differences by standardization. But knowing that the lower stratum contributes disproportionately to the Impaired category of mental health, we can be sure that were such standardization possible the effect would be to substantially narrow the 2:1 divergence in impairment rates seen between Italian and Hungarian immigrants. Similarly, in place of origin the Italians are predominantly rural and the Hungarians more largely urban. In short, the above divergence in morbidity rates principally reflects the facts that the Italians are mainly type O immigrants and the Hungarians type N. It will be remembered that for *all* type O and type N immigrants in the Midtown sample, the morbidity rates were 34.3 and 18.5 percent, respectively.

The third group warranting special attention in table 18–6 are the Puerto Rican immigrants, half (52.2 percent) of whom appear in the Impaired ranks—or double the rate (26.7 percent) for generation I as a whole—a difference appearing to be statistically significant at the .01 level of confidence. With a mean age of 35, these Puerto Ricans are eleven years younger, on the average, than the sample generation I as a whole. About half of them qualify as type O immigrants. Only a few are type N. The remainder are of low parental SES and town-city origin and seem to define an "urban proletariat" type, which is relatively rare in our sample of immigrants.

Testing the assumption that the current poverty of these Puerto Ricans might be a specific source of stress contributing to their deviant mental health picture, we isolated a subsample of 252 European immigrants with family incomes identical to that of the 18 Puerto Ricans in the lowest income bracket. The morbidity rate of the former aggregate was just half (31 percent) that of the latter (61 percent).

Compared to other immigrants, who found in Midtown a main residential concentration and institutional center for their fellow nationals, the Puerto Ricans in the Study area are, geographically speaking, isolated outriders from the main body of their fellow islanders gathered elsewhere in New York City.[21] We do not know whether subjective selection factors related to mental health have operated to determine this residential self-separation from their cultural group.

Differential selection may also be involved for Puerto Rican immigrants generally. As indicated in the previous chapter, alien immigrants, before receiving an American visa, had to pass the screen of Federal statutes "barring mentally, physically and morally undesirable classes and persons likely to become a public charge."[22] Compared with this severe kind of governmental screening, the Puerto Ricans, as citizen in-migrants, are limited only by the same kinds of spontaneous self-selection as are migrants to New York from the other 49 states. The variable sifting effects on the mental health characteristics of the two forms of migratory movements also remain largely unknown.

Nor can events in Puerto Rico itself be overlooked. That island has rapidly moved from an agrarian to an urban, industrial stage of development. We are not yet informed whether such movement has there had the early unsettling psychological consequences reported from other fast-changing agrarian areas.[23]

Finally, and of particular importance for appropriate perspective, is the fact that the Puerto Ricans in New York are recent arrivals from their home island. They betray signs of the initial, transient stage of uprooted instability that marked most previous nationality groups in the decades immediately following their settlement here.[24]

Although Puerto Ricans in the Midtown sample are few in number, and perhaps atypical, they may give us a brief glimpse into an extremely complicated tangle of factors. This complex of exogenous sociocultural forces and pressures, converging with endogenous selection processes, may have created turbulent effects overtly visible in the problems of the City's Puerto Rican people. It is hoped that more specifically focused research might soon answer these speculations.[25]

In the previous chapter we found little difference in mental morbidity rates between generations I, II, and III of like age and SES origin. When we now compare generation levels within each ethnic group, generation III is represented by sufficient individuals only among the British, German-Austrians, and Irish, and their mental health distributions are uniformly like that of their generation II juniors in the same nationality group. This likewise applies when generations II and I are compared in the British, German-Austrian, and Czech groups. However, we must report that this is not the case among the Irish, Italians, and Hungarians whose mental health distributions are presented in tables 18-8 and 18-10.

Here we see that in both the Irish and Italian groups the immigrants have impairment rates significantly higher than those of the

TABLE 18-8. HOME SURVEY SAMPLE (AGE 20–59), MENTAL HEALTH
DISTRIBUTIONS OF IRISH AND ITALIAN GENERATIONS I AND II

Mental health categories	Irish		Italians	
	Generation I	Generation II	Generation I	Generation II
Well	12.5%	18.6%	15.0%	15.1%
Mild symptom formation	35.0	37.4	32.5	35.3
Moderate symptom formation	22.5	27.5	15.0	27.0
Impaired	30.0	16.5	37.5	22.6
N = 100%	(79)	(92)	(40)	(93)

second generation. However, there are intergeneration age and SES-
origin differences in each ethnic group. Standardization for these
differences is not possible among the Italians[26] but is possible among
the Irish, where we shall now merge generations II and III. The Irish
mental health distributions, so standardized, are as follows (table
18–9):

TABLE 18-9. HOME SURVEY SAMPLE (AGE 20–59), MENTAL HEALTH
DISTRIBUTIONS OF IRISH GENERATIONS I AND II (STANDARDIZED FOR AGE AND
SES ORIGIN)

Mental health categories	Irish	
	Generation I	Generations II–III
Well	11.2%	18.0%
Mild	35.6	35.2
Moderate	24.5	26.4
Impaired	28.7	20.4
N = 100%	(79)	(167)

Standardization among the Irish has reduced the intergeneration
difference in impairment rates to a margin no longer statistically significant. Were such standardization possible among the Italians, there
is reason to believe that the remaining generation difference would
also fall below the level of statistical acceptability.

We have noted that the Hungarians also appeared to be an exceptional group. The sense of this judgment can be gathered from the
mental health composition of their two generation segments (table
18-10).

TABLE 18–10.   HOME SURVEY SAMPLE (AGE 20–59), MENTAL HEALTH
DISTRIBUTIONS OF HUNGARIAN GENERATIONS I AND II

Mental health categories	Hungarians	
	Generation I	Generation II
Well	13.6%	14.8%
Mild	36.4	29.6
Moderate	31.8	14.8
Impaired	18.2	40.8
N = 100%	(45)	(26)

Here the Hungarians emerge as seeming anomalies in that the
higher impairment rate for the first time is found not among the
immigrants, as hypothesized, but among their second generation juniors. Standardization for SES origin and age composition is here
altogether ruled out by their small numbers. Nonetheless, the picture
becomes clearer if we look into the parental SES of the two generations of Hungarians (table 18–11).

TABLE 18–11.   HOME SURVEY SAMPLE (AGE 20–59), PARENTAL-SES
DISTRIBUTIONS OF HUNGARIAN GENERATIONS I AND II

Parental SES	Hungarians	
	Generation I	Generation II
Lower (E–F)	22.2%	46.2%
Middle (C–D)	48.9	46.2
Upper (A–B)	28.9	7.6
N = 100%	(45)	(26)

The seeming anomaly is here seen reduced to this fact: Hungarian
generation II has a representation in the low SES-origin stratum that
is double that of their Hungarian immigrant neighbors. Thus, if it
were feasible to standardize for parental SES, the Hungarian intergeneration divergence in impairment rates would probably be largely
eliminated.

We conclude that in no national group are there intergeneration divergences in mental health composition that cannot be traced to the operation of SES-origin and age differences.

PATIENT FINDINGS

In previous chapters the number of Midtown's psychiatric patients were reported from our two field operations. From neither of these operations do the patient data on the Midtown nationality groups permit presentation here.

It is clear that variations in treatment rates can be attributed to differences in ethnic background only if analytical controls can be applied to disentangle other, more fully documented, demographic factors like age, SES origin, and generation-in-U.S. For purposes of the Midtown Treatment Census operation, the U.S. Census Bureau does not provide total population figures for subgroups analytically refined in this multifactorial fashion.

The Midtown Home Survey, in dealing with what is called the patient-history variable among its sample respondents, is not dependent on Census Bureau figures. Its patient rates have consistently been calculated relative to the Impaired mental health category only in a specific demographic group or subgroup. However, the grand total of generation I to III individuals in the several mental health categories is relatively small among most ethnic groups isolated in our sample population. This is especially the case in the Impaired category.[27]

It is not only that the distribution on the patient-history variable of each of these Impaired subgroups is statistically unreliable. It is rather that this unreliability is only one in a related series of considerations; e.g., we know that ever-patients are more numerous among the Impaired who are (1) younger (under age 40), (2) of higher socioeconomic status, and (3) American-born. Since the ethnic Impaired segments are too small to permit analytical control for these factors, differences in their ever-patient rates would be decidedly ambiguous, even as clues to the substantive connection between ethnic background and quest for therapy. Given Midtown's population scatter through many relatively small ethnic groups, the size of our sample excludes analyses of such extreme complexity.

SUMMARY

In this attempt to test the factor of national origin, we first confined ourselves to a comparison of seven ethnic groupings within the immigrant generation. With the mental health composition of generation I *in toto* serving as yardstick, we found that four ethnic groups conformed quite closely in their mental health distributions. Relative to this norm, however, the Italian-born were higher in impairment rates, and the Hungarian-born were lower—a difference exposed as largely a product of the fact that the former were more heavily type O immigrants and the latter were predominantly type N. Most deviant of all in apparent concentration of mental morbidity were the immigrant Puerto Ricans, and consideration was given to the special factors that may be operating in New York City's newest in a long procession of nationality groups.

As second step, we directed attention to intergeneration differences in mental health within six ethnic groups. In only three of these groups were such differences found. However, were control of their accompanying divergences in SES origin and age possible, these differences would very largely disappear.

This chapter sought to trace variations in mental health composition to a factor that looms large on the Midtown scene, namely, respondent differences in national culture derivations. We could discover no firm discrete variations of this kind. Whether or not other studies will confirm this finding is an entirely open question, needless to say.[28]

We would suggest that the question can be carried to the next stage of advance only if each ethnic group subsample is large enough to permit control for the obscuring effects of more powerful demographic factors. Even so, to test definitively for the links between international differences in culture and mental health, investigations will have to move to a more appropriate site than the American metropolis, namely, to the indigenous populations in the countries of origin. Among immigrants to America alone, there are too many special complications, such as subjective and objective selection, variable age at migration, familial structure in migration, differential experiences upon arrival, stage of development in the local ethnic community—as a stabilizing or disruptive influence—and stage in familial Americanization. All these intervene to becloud observation of the unencumbered factor of national culture differences and their eugenic-pathogenic potentials for mental health.

The writers now entertain the hypothesis that unencumbered observation will *not* reveal significant international differences in these eugenic-pathogenic potentials within the European continent west of the Iron Curtain. This does not blink the cultural differences existing among the countries of this continent. This *does* reflect some skepticism about the relative weight of these differences as against two other sets of likenesses that these countries share. One overarching source of likeness is their common roots in the general 2,000-year-old European-Christian tradition. In the next chapter we shall see whether the Catholic-Protestant split in the American version of that tradition registers on the mental health criterion of concern to us here.

A more specific source of intra-European likeness is the basic socioeconomic homogeneity. With corresponding SES groups in different countries apparently go similar conditions of life, values, attitudes, and behavior patterns. In this perspective, upper-class people from different countries, conspicuously joined in the "international set," probably have more in common with each other than does each national segment of that set with co-nationals in the lower reaches of the social class range. In turn, we suggest that the lower classes in the several countries, except on the point of language, have more that culturally binds than divides them. The same probably holds for the middle classes as well.

In fine, we hypothesize as follows: Comparative studies of indigenous European populations will yield conclusive findings that do not grossly diverge, in general trend, from the necessarily inconclusive comparative data for Midtown's immigrants of the several national backgrounds here represented.

It is relevant to add in closing that within the circumscribed framework of Midtown's immigrants and their European nationality subgroups, we can test a key assumption underlying the quota differences that were legislated by the congressional immigration acts of 1921 and 1924. This was the assumption that immigrants from Western and Central European countries were preferable to those who might originate in the Southern and Eastern sections of the

Continent. If mental health of immigrants (of like SES origin and rural-urban origin) is still a meaningful index of desirability in the eyes of America's policy makers (as it was in 1921–1924), then the Midtown data plainly appear to contradict that assumption.

POSTSCRIPT

Since the preceding paragraph first saw print (1962), the restrictive and discriminatory Immigration Act of 1924 has been replaced by the Immigration Reform Act of 1965 (with revisions in 1968). The latter ended the "national origins" quota system that had favored Western and Northern Europeans against immigrants from the rest of the continent. As an immediate result, by 1972 the total number of immigrants admitted annually increased by 30 percent, with striking jumps in particular from the South European countries of Portugal, Greece, and Italy of about 500, 400, and 200 percent, respectively.

NOTES

1. C. W. Mills, C. Senior, and R. K. Goldsen, *The Puerto Rican Journey*, 1950, p. 79.

2. Or 1.5 percent of the total Midtown population. However, Puerto Ricans do not figure in the Census Bureau's count of immigrants.

3. By this term we mean the complex system of more or less traditional folkways in which immigrants from a given country were bred during the childhood years before departure for the United States.

4. As a result, there was no basis for hypothesizing the degree and direction of differences in mental pathology risk that might be expected in these groups.

5. See A. R. Lindesmith and A. L. Strauss, "A Critique of Culture-Personality Writings," *American Sociological Review* 15 (October 1950): 587–600, in particular the section entitled "Oversimplification and the Homogeneity Postulate." See also, A. Inkeles and D. J. Levinson, "National Character: The Study of Modal Personality and Sociocultural Systems," in G. Lindzey and E. Aronson, eds., *Handbook of Social Psychology*, vol. IV, 1969, pp. 418–506.

6. Unless otherwise specified, data on a particular ethnic group here refer to its three generation levels inclusively, i.e., I, II, and III.

7. This group includes immigrants and generation II and III descendants of immigrants from England, Scotland, and Wales.

8. For other criteria see N. Glazer and D. Moynihan, *Beyond the Melting Pot*, 1963.

9. Mills, Senior, and Goldsen, *The Puerto Rican Journey*, p. 82.

10. Replies to question 5 above were found in all ethnic groups to be "all right" by such overwhelming consensus as to be of little discriminative value.

For all practical purposes, therefore, most respondents with a score of 1 had given "detached" replies to all four of the items preceding 5. Stated differently, a respondent classified as attached gave an affirming reply to at least one of the first four items.

11. It might be added that among the generation I adult arrivers the frequency of detached individuals is considerably larger than we had anticipated.

12. Specifically, 79 percent of the British and 44 percent of the German-Austrians are of Protestant origin.

13. Specifically, 57 percent of the Hungarians and 73 percent of the Czechoslovakians are of Catholic origin.

14. W. L. Warner and L. Srole, *Social Systems of American Ethnic Groups*, 1945.

15. See also R. T. Berthoff, *British Immigrants in Industrial America: 1790–1950*, 1953. This valuable work by a historian focuses most heavily on the second half of the nineteenth century. Comparisons with immigrants of other nationalities are drawn throughout. Special emphasis is placed on the relative ease of the British in fitting into and advancing in the American society. The importance of intercultural congruence is indicated in these observations: "In practically every American field which they entered, the British enjoyed the highest status and rose most easily. . . . With folkways and habits of thought acceptable to Americans, they enjoyed a unique advantage over most newcomers . . . the new country must have seemed rather like the old . . . settled among the Americans, [they] passed almost unnoticed. They hardly seemed to be 'immigrants' in the usual condescending sense of the word" (pp. 122–132).

The second, and perhaps more striking theme of this work is that British immigrants were accepted by Americans "as equals . . . yet they too clung to old loyalties . . . few doubted that for a proper life the old country was, after all, the only land" (pp. 139–142).

16. M. Calabresi, "The Relation of Country of Origin to Mortality for Various Causes in New York State," *Human Biology* 17 (1945): 340–365.

17. S. Graham, "Cancer, Culture and Social Structure," in E. G. Jaco, ed, *Patients, Physicians and Illness*, 1972, pp. 31–39.

18. R. W. Hyde and R. M. Chisholm, "The Relation of Mental Disorders to Race and Nationality," *New England Journal of Medicine* 231 (November 1944): 612–618.

19. That is, Selective Service Board areas.

20. A damaging limitation appears in this particular substantive phase of the Boston Induction Station studies directed by Hyde. By way of example, the 12.8 percent rejection rate reported for the Irish refer not to all Irishmen in the sample, but to all men from "Irish communities," defined as Selective Service Board districts whose selectees were in the majority Irishmen. Counted, therefore, as "Irish" were non-Irish men living in such predominantly Irish communities, and excluded were all Irish selectees who did not reside in such unusual districts.

The extent of this exclusion may be judged from the fact that the selectees living in these Irish districts totaled 2,440, or only 4 percent of the 60,000 men from the heavily Irish region of Boston.

Compounding the difficulty is the fact that we are not told how those counted as actually Irish in the Irish districts were determined. Were they only those born in Ireland? Or did they also include the U.S.-born of Irish descent?

The root difficulty is inherited from the tradition of ecological studies—here uncritically applied—where individuals living in an area are classified not according to their own characteristics but according to the average or predominant characteristics in the overall population of the area.

21. Mr. Joseph Suarez, Director, Mental Health Services Division, Hill Health Center, New Haven, Conn., and a lifelong observer of New York's Puerto Ricans, in personal communication has commented on the significance of this point. He calls attention to a powerful institution that generally tends to keep New York Puerto Ricans dependently chained to their areas of residential concentration. This is their neighborhood grocery store, which on the one hand carries indigenous Puerto Rican staples and on the other hand extends credit to fellow immigrants whenever need arises.

Thus, in leaving the areas of high Puerto Rican density, the Midtown Puerto Ricans had removed themselves from ready access to these two important services.

22. W. S. Bernard, *American Immigration Policy: A Reappraisal*, 1950, pp. 23–24.

23. The advances in general health that have accompanied the rise in the Island's standard of living are documented in C. Senior, *The Puerto Ricans*, 1961. For a descriptive treatment of a small number of Island families harboring a schizophrenic husband or wife, see L. Rogler and A. Hollingshead, *Trapped: Families and Schizophrenia*, 1965.

24. While the rear guard of poverty-stricken New York Puerto Ricans continue to manifest such instabilities, the group's vanguard is now on the upward mobility trail taken by the City's earlier ethnic groups.

25. See J. P. Fitzpatrick, "Special Problems: Mental Illness," in his *Puerto Rican Americans*, 1971, pp. 164–166. See also A. M. Padilla and R. A. Ruiz, *Latino Mental Health: A Review of Literature*, 1973.

26. Because of insufficient cases of Italian immigrants.

27. For example, there are 12 among all Puerto Rican respondents, 20 among Hungarians, 30 among the British, 34 among Czechs, 39 among Italians. Even the Irish and German-Austrian impairment cases do not exceed 54 and 78 respectively.

28. This finding on the Study psychiatrists' classification of degree of symptom formation and functional disability would not be controverted by a finding of qualitative differences in syndromal patterns among nationality groups.

CHAPTER 19

PROTESTANT, CATHOLIC, AND JEWISH ORIGINS

LEO SROLE AND THOMAS LANGNER

In the antiphony of voices that express American society, Protestantism, Catholicism, and Judaism stand out as the nation's three great religious communions. In the hypersegmented, centrifugal social structure of Manhattan, they perform a special and generally overlooked function, as the editors of *Fortune* magazine have perceptively observed:

> So what gives New York its coherence? No city could exist for three hundred and thirty-odd years in incoherence. For one thing, surprisingly enough, it hangs together on the cord of its religions. . . . From its religions the city derives much strength and character. Protestantism's vigorous social ethic, with which the city began, is still a force in New York as throughout the nation. . . . Quite apart from the fact that Jewish intellectuality and artistic appreciation give the city a special élan, Jewish philanthropy, with its deep religious base, lifts the level of the whole community. The emergence of Catholics to higher levels in the city's social structure . . . brings to New York's amalgam the ancient firmness and cultural richness of that church. For all their differences, these three faiths are united in the conviction that the community exists to serve men.[1]

The significance for mental health of personal roots in these different religious traditions[2] is the complicated and difficult question that shall engage us in this chapter.[3]

TREATMENT CENSUS FINDINGS

Due note should first be taken of the meager research literature that bears on the above question. Until recently, such research has been confined to patients of state mental hospitals, classified by religion as inscribed on the case record. Such studies have usually categorized patients only in terms of the Jewish–non-Jewish dichotomy.[4]

Nevertheless, from the largest of these investigations, Malzberg concludes: "On the basis of the estimated population in 1950, Jews had a rate of first admissions [to New York state-supported mental hospitals] of 74 per 100,000 population compared with 102 for white non-Jews. As regards the severe mental disorders which result in hospitalization, it is therefore clear that Jews have a lower rate than non-Jews. This confirms a similar conclusion which was arrived at in three separate studies."[5]

The New Haven study signaled a considerable advance beyond the foregoing literature in that it covered one-day prevalence of patients in *all* treatment sites and also differentiated Protestants and Catholics. On the basis of published New Haven distribution data,[6] we have calculated the rates per 100,000 estimated population among the several New Haven religious groups as presented in table 19–1.

In rates of *treated* psychoses and related disorders we note only minor differences among New Haven's three religious groups.[7] This is a finding at variance with previous studies of state hospital pa-

TABLE 19–1.　NEW HAVEN PSYCHIATRIC CENSUS (AGE INCLUSIVE), DIAGNOSTIC COMPOSITION (PREVALENCE RATES PER 100,000 POPULATION) OF NEW HAVEN PATIENTS BY RELIGIOUS AFFILIATION*

	Catholic	Protestant	Jewish
Neuroses and character disorders ...	140	158	442
Alcohol and drug addictions	45	36	0
Psychoses and affective disorders ...	481	414	496
Organic disorders	120	136	68
Total Patients rate	786	744	1,006

* Adapted from B. H. Roberts and J. K. Myers, "Religion, National Origin, Immigration, and Mental Illness," *American Journal of Psychiatry* 110 (April 1954): 760.

tients.[8] On the other hand, if New Haven Protestants and Catholics are also alike in frequencies of *treated* neuroses and character disorders, Jews stand out in this category with an appreciably higher patient rate.

In certain technical aspects, the New Haven study to date has had its only counterpart in the Midtown Treatment Census operation. As in New Haven's case, the latter had no United States census data on the religious composition of the Midtown population. However, from the religious distribution of the Home Survey sample we could estimate such composition, at least in the age 20 to 59 segment of the Midtown population. In addition to this intercommunity difference in the age span of the religious group rates, the one-day prevalence counts of patients in Midtown and New Haven diverge in two other respects: (1) Midtown's hospital enumeration excluded patients continuously hospitalized for five years or more, whereas this exclusion was not applied to the New Haven hospital patients; and (2) on the Midtown patients of office therapists we could secure information about neither their age nor their religious affiliation. Accordingly, in table 19–2 we can present only prevalence rates (per 100,000 estimated corresponding population in each Midtown religious group) of age 20 to 59 patients in mental hospitals and psychiatric clinics.[9]

TABLE 19–2. MIDTOWN TREATMENT CENSUS (AGE INCLUSIVE), PREVALENCE RATES (PER 100,000 POPULATION) OF MIDTOWN PATIENTS (AGE 20–59 ONLY) IN HOSPITALS AND CLINICS BY RELIGIOUS GROUPS

Treatment sites	Catholic	Protestant	Jewish
Hospitals:			
Public	659	385	250
Private	33	61	148
Total inpatients	692	446	398
Total clinic outpatients	108	103	380

Within the indicated limitations of the Midtown patient data, we see in table 19–2 that the public hospital rate is lowest in the Jewish group, half-again higher among Protestants, and higher by over 2.5 times among Catholics. With private hospital frequencies, however, the group ranking is exactly reversed. As a result, when the two sets of inpatients are taken together, the total hospitalization rates of Protestants and Jews for all practical purposes are alike, both still being appreciably below the Catholic frequency. Thus, the Jewish-Protestant difference in public hospital rates is practically wiped out when total inpatients become the measure.

Moving next to the psychiatric clinics, we observe Protestants and Catholics with identical patient rates and Jews with a frequency almost four times greater.

Among Midtown residents known on one day to all treatment facilities, the reported patients of office therapists aggregated almost half of the total reported. These patients cannot be brought into table 19-2, but it is obvious that were they included their trend could dominate the Total Patients rates. To discern the direction of this trend, we can apply one of two alternative assumptions. First, on the common element of ambulatory treatment, we might anticipate that interreligious differences in *office therapy* rates would tend to parallel the observed differences in *clinic* frequencies. If so, the Total Patients rate probably would be highest among Jews, with the Catholic rate perhaps exceeding the Protestant frequency by a relatively small margin. Or, on the common element of high treatment costs, we might anticipate that interreligion differences in office therapy frequencies would tend to parallel the observed *private hospital* rates. In this event, the Jews would again emerge with the largest Total Patients rate; but now second position in magnitude of these rates would probably be held not by Catholics but by Protestants. There are intimations in the Midtown Home Survey supporting the second assumption and suggesting that Total Patients rates among Jews, Protestants, and Catholics may stand to each other in a ratio of roughly 7:6:5, respectively. From Treatment Census evidence, this result would reflect the fact that inpatient and outpatient rates tend to vary in opposite directions among the three religious groups.

Comparisons of New Haven and Midtown Treatment Census data should of course be undertaken with caution. With this caveat in mind, attention might be called to the fact that New Haven's interreligious differences in neurosis and character disorder rates (table 19-1)—principally treated in outpatient facilities—parallel Midtown's differences in observed clinic patient frequencies (table 19-2). That is, in both communities Jews seem to emerge with higher ambulatory treatment rates and Total Patients frequencies than either Protestants or Catholics.

What is the meaning of the seemingly convergent findings from the two studies? An anthropologist's review of the literature on this general question, published a few years before the New Haven study, concluded:

The factual residue thus appears at present to be: American Jews have a lower incidence of [hospitalized] insanity than non-Jews. . . . When it comes to the matter of neurosis, psychiatric opinion holds that Jews are more neurotic or anxiety ridden than non-Jews. . . . A. B. Brill, Abraham Myerson and Israel S. Wechsler may be mentioned as exponents of this view.

The causes of Jewish neurosis are attributed by these authorities to the taboos and inhibitions of Mosaic law, to the unconscious "incest motive" resulting from exceptionally close ties within the Jewish family, to exclusion from manual activity and "seclusion into a world of life predominantly cerebral," and to the tensions of minority life.

Generalizations by practicing psychiatrists, however, invite errors resulting from the selective nature of their experience. . . . The only empirical verification comes, as usual, from studies of college students, and these studies (conducted by psychologists) are by no means in unanimous agreement on the hypothesis of neurotic Jewish personality.[10]

HOME SURVEY SAMPLE: MENTAL HEALTH DISTRIBUTIONS BY RELIGIOUS ORIGIN

To move to new ground on the inclusive question of interfaith differences in mental health, we can proceed now to the evidence provided in the sample of 1,660 Midtown adults studied by our Home Interview Survey. Here we of course apply as yardstick the Midtown psychiatrists' classification of the mental health status of each sample respondent. Although this classification scheme lacks the nosological specificity of clinical diagnosis, the Home Survey in another direction avoids a difficulty inherent in the use of institutional records, at least when religious groups are the focus of attention. This difficulty is that at institutional intake, information about religion of the patient as a rule is rather less than carefully ascertained and recorded. By contrast, in the Midtown interviews as many as 15 separate questions were asked about the individual's religious orientation, identification, and behaviors, past and present.

We have already discussed in chapter 7 the distinction between independent and reciprocal demographic variables. Obviously, the individual's religious identification can change between childhood and adulthood, and such change may be consequences of personality processes that also work themselves out in forms subsumed under the concept of mental health. Thus, adults' replies to the interview question, "To what religious faith do you *now* belong?" must be considered in the nature of a concurrent, reciprocal, and etiologically ambiguous variable relative to their mental health. On the other hand, in replies to questions on the faith that the respondent's parents grew up in, we have his/her religious origin, potentially standing as an antecedent and independent variable to the dependent variable of his/her current mental health.

We shall presently consider changes in religious identification between parents and their adult offspring. But here we first want to classify the sample adults by religious origin and to examine the mental health distribution in each of the four religious categories shown in table 19–3.

We know that among the religious groups in the sample there are differences in age composition and socioeconomic origin. We have

TABLE 19–3.   HOME SURVEY SAMPLE (AGE 20–59), RESPONDENTS'
DISTRIBUTIONS ON MENTAL HEALTH CLASSIFICATION BY RELIGIOUS ORIGIN

Mental health categories	Religious origin			
	Catholic	Protestant	Jewish	Others*
Well	16.1%	22.6%	16.0%	22.6%
Mild symptom formation ..	35.4	36.1	41.7	30.1
Moderate symptom formation	22.2	19.8	25.8	20.8
Impaired	26.3	21.5	16.5	26.5
Marked symptom formation	13.9	12.5	11.3	17.0
Severe symptom formation	9.0	6.9	3.8	5.7
Incapacitated	3.4	2.1	1.4	3.8
N = 100%	(832)	(562)	(213)	(53)

* Almost two-thirds of these respondents had parents who were identified as Christians of the Eastern (Greek or Russian) Orthodox Church. The remaining parents were either members of non-Western religious cults or were reported as having grown up in no known religious faith. These respondents are too diverse in religious backgrounds and too few in number to be brought into subsequent analyses in this chapter.

previously found that these two demographic factors are independently related to respondent mental health. Thus, if interesting differences appear in table 19–3, there is a decided chance that these differences are not real, but rather are spurious results of intergroup variations in age and SES origin. In table 19–4, we present the mental health distributions that could be expected were the three religious-origin groups identical in these latter respects.[11]

TABLE 19–4. HOME SURVEY SAMPLE (AGE 20–59), RESPONDENTS' DISTRIBUTIONS ON MENTAL HEALTH CLASSIFICATION BY RELIGIOUS ORIGIN AS STANDARDIZED FOR AGE AND SES ORIGIN

Mental health categories	Religious origin		
	Catholic	Protestant	Jewish
Well	17.4%	20.2%	14.5%
Mild symptom formation	34.5	36.4	43.2
Moderate symptom formation	23.4	19.9	25.1
Impaired	24.7*	23.5	17.2*
N = 100%	(832)	(562)	(213)

* $t = 2.6$ (.01 level of confidence).

This standardization almost completely levels the Protestant-Catholic differences seen in table 19–3. The impairment differences observed between Jews and the other two groups in the table remain statistically significant, however. Reference to table 19–3 locates the Jewish difference specifically in smaller Severe (3.8 percent) and Incapacitated (1.4 percent) frequencies, i.e., at the end of the impairment range rather than in the Marked category.

On the other hand, in table 19–4, Jews are also seen with the lowest prevalence of Wells at a not insignificant distance from the Protestants' Well frequency. With the lowest rates both of the Well and the Impaired, Jews of course are found more heavily concentrated than Protestants or Catholics in the large subclinical range in between, namely, in the Mild and Moderate categories of symptom formation.

We might follow the matter one step further. Suppose we look at the religious-origin groups within each of the three SES-origin strata, retaining standardization for age differences. We then find in all three strata the essential mental health picture discerned in table 19–4.

However, there are differences of degree—the most suggestive appearing in the lower stratum (E–F) of SES origin. Here respondents of Protestant, Catholic, and Jewish origin have almost identical Well frequencies, but their Impaired rates are 32.0, 30.5, and 19.4 percent, respectively.

If Jews convey the most favorable group picture of mental health in the SES stratum having the highest concentration of mental morbidity, then one possible hypothesis that can be suggested for future testing is this: Midtown respondents of Jewish parentage tend to reflect some kind of impairment-limiting mechanism that operates to counteract, or in some degree contain, the more extreme pathogenic life stresses during childhood. This hypothesis appears to be consistent with the repeatedly confirmed relative immunity of Jews to such self-impairing types of reactions as alcoholism[12] and suicide.

If such a "this-far-and-no-farther" control mechanism exists, its source is a question that here can only be a subject of speculation. One factor often hypothesized by psychiatrists as potentially pathogenic is the strong Jewish family structure. However, this factor may conceivably be eugenic on balance, in the specific sense that powerful homeostatic supports are brought into play at danger points of crisis and stress that in other groups may be unbalancing for the family and impairing for the individual.

If subsequent investigation should lend support to this inference, the mechanism involved may have historical, broadly psychosocial roots, of a kind defined by the following hypothesis: A group that for thousands of years has been beleaguered by chronic environmental threats of destruction survives by developing internal processes of resistance, deep within the dynamics of the family itself, that counteract in some measure the more extreme kinds of exogenous crises and check the more extreme forms of pathological reaction.

Also potentially relevant, although stemming from another framework, is the inference Janis draws from his classic study of surgery patients:

Arousal of some degree of anticipatory fear may be one of the necessary conditions for developing inner defenses of the type that can function effectively when the external danger materializes. . . . If a person is given appropriate preparatory communications before being exposed to potentially traumatizing stimuli, his chances of behaving in a disorganized way . . . may be greatly decreased. Thus, from the standpoint of preventive psychiatry, it is of considerable importance to determine how preparatory communications can be made to serve an effective prophylactic function.[13]

To translate this formulation for the present discussion, mobilization of anxiety about the instability of the Jewish exilic environment may historically have been established as a conditioning pattern of the Jewish family structure. In one direction, such anxiety, subsequently magnified in the adult by extrafamily life conditions, may be reflected in our finding of an unusually large concentration of Midtown Jews in the subclinical Mild category of symptom formation. On the other hand, this large component of historically realistic anxiety, as generated in the Jewish family, may function prophylactically to immunize its children against the potentially disabling sequelae of the more severe pressures and traumas of existence.[14] Later in this chapter we may see other expressions of this process.

Also to be emphasized is that, like earlier studies of patients, the Midtown Home Survey shows a somewhat higher overall frequency of mental morbidity in the Catholic group than in the Protestant group. However, this difference was found to be a wholly spurious consequence of the fact that Protestants in the aggregate are younger and of considerably higher socioeconomic antecedents than are Catholics.

HOME SURVEY SAMPLE: MENTAL HEALTH AND PARENTAL RELIGIOSITY

In the section preceding we have been concerned with the respondent's religious origin as based on the faith in which his parents had grown up. This is a formal, demographic kind of classification, but it tells us nothing about the degree of parental commitment to the doctrines, commandments, and practices enjoined by their religious institution.

Seen in historical perspective, this dimension of individual commitment to the tenets of the faith—or "religiosity"—is extremely sensitive to changes in the environing society. The Protestant Reformation is an excellent case in point. The period in which our respondents' parents had been born roughly spanned the half century from 1864 to 1914. These, of course, were years that saw vast scientific, technological, and economic changes which made themselves felt along the entire broad front of Western institutions. Not the least of these impacts registered on the church and on the individual's anchoring ties to it.

We can hypothesize that this factor of relative religious anchorage or commitment had direct effects on parents' roles and on the home atmosphere, with radiating consequences for the development of the child as observed when he himself had grown into adulthood.

Interviewing each respondent, we asked this key question as a shortcut approach to his parents' religious orientation:[15] "How important would you say religion (belief in religion) was to your parents? For example, would you say it was: Very important? Somewhat important? Or not important at all?"[16]

We were of course aware that a reply to this question is essentially the respondent's judgment applied to his recall of observed words and deeds as they reflected parental attitude toward religious tradition.[17] We could assume that the judgment hinged in part on a norm or image of the "faithful" man that is specific to each church system and, in part, on the respondent's recall of modifications in this ideal among the parents' local contemporaries.

Within the Study's taxonomy of test factors,[18] parental religiosity certainly stands to the dependent variable of respondent mental health as a chronologically antecedent factor. But we deal with the respondent's *judgment* of such religiosity, and this "filter" is potentially open to influence from psychological processes related to the dependent variable. However, parental religiosity qualifies as an independent, as well as antecedent, test factor to the extent that the respondent's judgment took its measure from long and relatively close observations of parental behavior. We can produce no evidence to illuminate this issue. As a matter of the investigators' opinion, however, we will assume that respondents' reports of parental religiosity provide a reasonable approximation of independence from the dependent variable.

A final preparatory point must now be clarified. Earlier in this chapter, the respondent's religious origin was used, as determined by the criterion of descent through the religion of parents' upbringing (much as had national origin in the preceding chapter). This criterion was appropriate to our purposes of inclusive demographic classification at that point. With religiosity now the factor of central interest, we must gear this factor to identification of religious group-ings based on a more refined criterion. That is, instead of religious origin or descent of parents, we refer to this criterion as parents' *religious-group identification*, after their marriage, as ascertained from respondent replies to the interview question: "What religious faith did *you* grow up in?"

Of course, the religion a parent had experienced during his own childhood tells us nothing with certainty about his religious identifica-tion during adulthood. However, we can be confident that the reli-gious tradition which enveloped the child is a fairly reliable indicator of the religious-group identification conveyed, however minimally, by his parents. This criterion, of a specific religious identification *con-veyed* to one's children, is the basis for our present classification of respondents' parents by religious group.

With a locus in any given religious system, individuals vary in degree of acceptance of its disciplining claims upon their thought and behavior. In this perspective, parents who had stood with the "faith-ful," by the light of locally modified standards of the church at large, would likely be seen by the child as having given their religion very important weight in their lives. On the other hand, parents deviating considerably from the faithful model, while remaining more or less anchored in the church, would probably be judged as holding their religion no more than "somewhat important." Finally, parents re-maining formally identified as in the fold of the church but whose behavior suggested that its religious tenets were to them "not impor-tant at all" were probably at best peripheral, nominal members of the institution.

Let us first record how the sample respondents' parents are dis-tributed on this gross scale of reported religiosity:[19]

Very important (VI) 52%
Somewhat important (SI) 37%
Not important at all (NIAA) 11%

Table 19–5 below shows next how respondents' parents located within *each group fold* are distributed by religiosity as reported to us. We need not pause to speculate on the explanations for the differences that appear in table 19–5.[20] However, they are consistent with gen-eral observations that close conformity to the normative expectations of one's religious institution characterizes more adherents of the Catholic Church than Protestants or Jews.

TABLE 19–5. HOME SURVEY SAMPLE (AGE 20–59), DISTRIBUTIONS OF RESPONDENTS' PARENTS ON RELIGIOSITY CLASSIFICATION BY PARENTAL RELIGIOUS-GROUP IDENTIFICATION

Parents' religiosity	Parents' religious-group identification		
	Catholic	Protestant	Jewish
Very important (VI)	67.4%	40.0%	31.1%
Somewhat important (SI)	28.1	45.8	48.4
Not important at all (NIAA)	4.5	14.2	20.5
N = 100%	(805)	(541)	(190)

Furthermore, if we could assume that at some not-too-distant period in the past almost all adherents of each religious faith were in the top level of religiosity, it seems apparent that this was far from the case among the respondents' parents a generation ago. Even within the relatively stable Catholic group, one in every three parents in the eyes of their offspring stood at less than a "very important" level of religious commitment. Thus, the erosions of traditional religious anchorages among adults of a generation ago can seemingly be discerned from the data presented in table 19–5.

Our primary concern here is addressed to this question: What are the detectable consequences of parental differences in religiosity for the mental health of the children they raised to adulthood? Let us first direct this question to the Midtown sample respondents of Jewish-identified parents. In table 19–6 below they are distributed on a threefold classification of the mental health continuum.

Among offspring of the several religiosity categories of Jewish par-

TABLE 19–6. HOME SURVEY SAMPLE (AGE 20–59), DISTRIBUTIONS OF RESPONDENTS WITH JEWISH-IDENTIFIED PARENTS ON MENTAL HEALTH CLASSIFICATION BY PARENTAL RELIGIOSITY

Mental health categories	Parental religiosity		
	VI	SI	NIAA
Well	8.5%	18.5%	15.4%
Mild-Moderate	76.2	63.0	64.1
Impaired	15.3	18.5	20.5
N = 100%	(59)	(92)	(39)

ents, no significant difference in mental health composition is to be seen. In the light of the relatively small number of cases in the VI and NIAA columns of table 19–6, we must consider our evidence from the Jewish segment of the Midtown sample as statistically inconclusive.

The difficulty of insufficient sample numbers is not encountered to the same degree among respondents of Protestant-identified parentage. In fact, this group is sufficiently numerous to be examined on our present test variable as subdivided by our three-way stratification of parental socioeconomic status. In table 19–7 we present the mental

TABLE 19–7.   HOME SURVEY SAMPLE (AGE 20–59), DISTRIBUTIONS OF RESPONDENTS OF UPPER SES ORIGIN AND PROTESTANT-IDENTIFIED PARENTS ON MENTAL HEALTH CLASSIFICATION BY PARENTAL RELIGIOSITY

Mental health categories	Parental religiosity		
	VI	SI	NIAA
Well	26.7%	25.7%	27.0%
Mild-Moderate	56.5	55.0	56.8
Impaired	16.8	19.3	16.2
N = 100%	(101)	(109)	(37)

health distributions only for the respondents who are of upper-SES descent (A–B).

Mental health composition is almost identical in the three religiosity categories of table 19–7. However, when we similarly categorize respondents of Protestant-identified parents who had been in our middle or lower stratum of socioeconomic status, we find a rather different pattern of mental health composition. Since the pattern is quite similar in these parental strata, and the number of cases is relatively small in the lower of the two, table 19–8 below combines the respondents of these two SES-origin groups (C–D and E–F).

If the VI- and SI-reared respondents there are alike in their Well frequencies, the latter are better off in having a significantly lower Impaired rate, accompanied by a correspondingly higher frequency in the subclinical (Mild-Moderate) range of the continuum. Relative to these two groups, moreover, the NIAA-sired respondents have the largest impairment rate and the smallest Well representation.

TABLE 19–8. HOME SURVEY SAMPLE (AGE 20–59), DISTRIBUTIONS OF RESPONDENTS OF LOWER AND MIDDLE SES ORIGIN AND PROTESTANT-IDENTIFIED PARENTS ON MENTAL HEALTH CLASSIFICATION BY PARENTAL RELIGIOSITY

Mental health categories	Parental religiosity		
	VI	SI	NIAA
Well	20.9%	22.3%	12.5%
Mild-Moderate	51.3	60.4	50.0
Impaired	27.8*	17.3†	37.5*
N = 100%	(115)	(139)	(40)

* $t \doteq 2.1$ (.05 level of confidence).
† $t = 2.9$ (.01 level of confidence).

In short, we discern the most favorable mental health picture in the SI religiosity column and the least favorable in the NIAA segment, with the VI category standing more or less intermediate. On the yardstick of impairment rates, therefore, the pattern of relationship between parental religiosity and respondent mental health can be described as being of the general J-curve type.

Of course, the generality of this pattern remains in question when we consider that it does not seem to appear among Jewish-bred respondents or among Protestant-reared people of high SES origin. However, respondents of Catholic-identified parents have not yet been examined in this respect. Analysis reveals the presence of this distribution pattern among such Catholics on *all* three SES-origin strata. However, because the number of respondents with NIAA par-

TABLE 19–9. HOME SURVEY SAMPLE (AGE 20–59), DISTRIBUTIONS OF RESPONDENTS WITH CATHOLIC-IDENTIFIED PARENTS ON MENTAL HEALTH CLASSIFICATION BY PARENTAL RELIGIOSITY

Mental health categories	Parental religiosity		
	VI	SI	NIAA
Well	17.1%	15.0%	5.5%
Mild-Moderate	56.0	63.3	58.4
Impaired	26.9	21.7	36.1
N = 100%	(543)	(226)	(36)

ents is so small in each of these strata, we can best delineate the pattern by viewing, in table 19-9, the entire Catholic-identified group as differentiated in terms of parental religiosity.

Although the intra-Catholic differences in table 19-9 do not achieve firm statistical significance, we again see the lowest Well frequency and highest Impaired rate in the NIAA column. Moreover, the SI category again emerges with the smallest prevalence of impairment; the VI respondents in turn stand intermediate in this respect.

All in all, therefore, the J-curve pattern observed among Protestant-sired respondents of lower and middle SES origins seems to be paralleled among Catholic offspring of all SES-origin strata. We can thereby infer, first, that this is a key pattern for respondents from both Protestant and Catholic childhood homes that were of lower or middle socioeconomic position. Jews of such SES origin do not seem to fit this pattern, but because of their small numbers in these strata, we lack confidence that this negative finding in their case is statistically conclusive.

Second, we can infer that a finding of no relationship between parental religiosity and respondent mental health seems to characterize both Protestants and Jews of upper socioeconomic descent. Here, Catholics of like SES origin seem to deviate, presenting instead the J-shaped curve. However, their number in this stratum is relatively small, and we cannot be sure that this positive finding in their instance is statistically stable.

Accordingly, we are left with the residual inference that in lower- and middle-class homes, parental religiosity tends to be related to childrens' adult mental health—at least if the home had been Protestant or Catholic identified.

To be sure, the affinity uncovered in these parental-SES strata is not strikingly strong. On the other hand, this relationship has come through a measure of religiosity that rests on the narrow base of a single interview question and offers only a crude trichotomous classification. Accordingly, it is a plausible expectation that with a broader base of information and more refined classification of parental religiosity the relationship may well emerge in clearer form and enlarged magnitude.

Suggestive evidence lending support to the link between parental religious behavior and offsprings' mental health comes from a study of King and Funkenstein, who report:

... there is a constellation of psychological and sociological factors which are associated with the cardiovascular reactions of healthy subjects [male college students] in acute stress. The constellation includes the immediate emotional reaction of the subject, his attitudes in the area of religious values, his perception of parental behavior in discipline, and the *church-going behavior of his parents* [italics added]. . . . We leave it to further research to spell out the manifold implications of these associations. We do suggest that they are of sufficient strength to encourage further inter-disciplinary research among the fields of physiology, psychology and sociology.[21]

The relationship seemingly discerned in the Midtown sample poses a series of questions that cannot be answered at this time. First, why is this relationship apparently specific to the lower two-thirds of the parental-SES range and seemingly nonoperative among respondents from the upper third of that SES range? What specific elements can explain why the VI type of home in the susceptible SES strata seems to be more eugenic for offsprings' mental health than the NIAA home, and why does the SI home tend to be the most eugenic type of all? Under the secularizing pressures of industrial, urban society, are different modes of religiosity chosen by parents of broadly different types of personalities? If so, the apparent consequences of parental religiosity for offsprings' mental health may partially dissolve themselves into consequences of more comprehensive aspects of parents' characters.

On the other hand, assume broad personality similarities in a group of parents who diverge in religiosity: What consequences of the latter variable alone would flow into the intrafamily processes, e.g., into performances of parental roles, and thereby into the psychological conditioning of their offspring? What effects do variations in parental religiosity have upon family stability under crisis? For children, especially in adolescence, what are the intrafamily consequences when they veer away from the religious orientation of parents under pressure of peers and larger social influences?

By the inroads made into the religious anchorages of a large segment of the population, we see one cutting edge of the vast sociocultural changes of the past century. In particular we have seen the impacts of these historical forces on the religious moorings in the generation parental to our sample adults, and we can glimpse possible residues of such forces in the mental health of these respondents.

MENTAL HEALTH AND RELIGIOUS MOBILITY

We have been concerned about presumptive changes in religiosity among respondents' parents who had been identified with a specific religious group. Here we focus on direct evidence of a more drastic kind of change—among respondents themselves, namely, a change in their own religious-group *identification*, or what we call *religious mobility*.

For respondents' religious-group lineage we shall take their religious origin, and we shall compare this with their replies to the interview question: "To what religious faith do you *now* belong?" In table 19–10 we can ascertain the relative prevalence of religious mobility in the Midtown sample population.

TABLE 19–10.   HOME SURVEY SAMPLE (AGE 20–59), DISTRIBUTIONS OF RESPONDENTS' CURRENT RELIGIOUS GROUP BY RELIGIOUS ORIGIN

Current religious group	Religious origin		
	Catholic	Protestant	Jewish
Catholic	90.0%	4.1%	1.9%
Protestant	2.5	78.6	1.9
Jewish	0.0	0.4	75.6
None	5.8	14.2	16.9
Other	1.7	2.7	3.7
N = 100%	(832)	(562)	(213)

This table clearly shows that respondents of Protestant or Jewish origin have total religious mobility rates more than twice (21.4 and 24.4 percent, respectively) that of Catholic-derived people (10 percent). However, in all three origin groups most of the movement has been not into another group, but into the disidentified "no faith" or "unchurched" ranks.

Of particular relevance to us here is the mental health composition of the several subgroup segments that have sufficient numbers of cases. Given the number of these segments, perhaps the most summary indication of such composition might be in terms of the Impaired-Well ratio,[22] as presented in table 19–11 below.

TABLE 19–11.   HOME SURVEY SAMPLE (AGE 20–59), IMPAIRED-WELL RATIO OF SAMPLE RESPONDENTS BY RELIGIOUS ORIGIN AND CURRENT RELIGIOUS GROUP

Current religious group	Religious origin		
	Catholic	Protestant	Jewish
Catholic	163	57	. . .
N* = ...	(747)	(23)	(4)
Protestant	25	87	. . .
N = ...	(21)	(442)	(4)
Jewish	. . .	. . .	92
N = ...	(0)	(2)	(161)
None ....,.....	200	170	120
N = ...	(48)	(80)	(36)

* N is the total number of respondents in the specific cell to which the Impaired-Well ratio value refers.

As we have just seen, Protestants who changed to Catholicism and Catholics who shifted to Protestantism are small in number. But to judge from the Impaired-Well ratios as derived from so few cases, such church-to-church changers appear in a somewhat more favorable mental health condition than do the stable Protestants and Catholics. Compared to the latter and the nonmobile Jews, however, the currently unchurched respondents from all three religious-origin groups uniformly present a less favorable mental health picture.

Since religious mobility is in the realm of voluntary behavior, it seems likely in large part to be psychologically determined. Hence, table 19–11 probably tells us more about the kinds of people who change their religious group identification than it reveals about the mental health consequences of such change.

A potential programmatic utility of the data is to highlight to metropolitan religious organizations the mental health weighting of adherents they are losing to the unchurched, unreachable condition.

HELP–NEED, THE PATIENT–HISTORY VARIABLE, AND PROFESSIONAL ORIENTATION

We turn finally to the patient-history factor as applied exclusively to the population at help-need, namely, the sample respondents who are in the Impaired category of mental health. Because religious origin is the most comprehensive criterion for classification by religious grouping, it is used with the Impaired segment of the sample in table 19–12.

TABLE 19–12. HOME SURVEY SAMPLE (AGE 20–59), DISTRIBUTIONS OF IMPAIRED RESPONDENTS ON PATIENT-HISTORY CLASSIFICATION BY RELIGIOUS ORIGIN

Patient history	Religious origin		
	Catholic	Protestant	Jewish
Current outpatients	1.8%	8.3%	20.0%
Ex-patients	19.7	24.0	20.0
Never-patients	78.5	67.7	60.0
N = 100%	(219)	(121)	(35)

Of course, the ex-patients shown in the table include people who had been hospitalized, as well as those who had used ambulatory facilities. Accordingly, if the ex-patient rates are quite similar in the three columns of the table, we can be sure—from our Treatment Census data earlier reviewed—that the exhospitalized representation in the "mix" is quite different in the three religious groups.

More clear-cut are the current outpatient frequencies. We discern that among those now at risk of help-need, Jews have a current outpatient rate more than twice that of Protestants and approximately ten times that of Catholics. This illuminates the finding earlier drawn from the New Haven Study and our Treatment Census analysis that Jews emerge with higher ambulatory treatment rates than either Protestants or Catholics.[23]

From our Home Survey sample we have already seen (table 19–3) that Jews have a lower impairment rate than either of the other two religious groups. This seemed to be at direct variance with the Treatment Census finding that Jews were the highest of the three groups in Total Patients rates. The seeming paradox is set aright by the finding that between two groups of like size a low mental morbidity rate and a strong tendency to seek therapy can bring more Impaired people to a treatment facility than a high morbidity rate and a relatively weak tendency to seek therapy.

This statement stands irrespective of the fact that determinants other than mental morbidity enter into the varying motivations that lead one to treatment—especially of the voluntary outpatient type. One of these determinants is certainly the Impaired respondent's socioeconomic status. When the latter factor among the Impaired is controlled, the interreligious differences in current outpatient rates are narrowed but by no means eliminated. In most previous studies of patient populations sorted by religious groupings, lack of control for the SES variable has obscured its contribution to the large interreligious differences in patient rates.

However, that more than socioeconomic status is involved in patient rate differences may be gathered from questions put to the Midtown sample adults bearing on a dimension that we designate *professional orientation*. This was derived from our Midtown respondents through open-ended questions that posed certain psychiatric problems in a hypothetical family. One question was: "Let's suppose some friends of yours have a serious problem with their child. I mean a problem with the child's behavior, or difficulty getting along with others. The parents ask your advice about what to do. What would you probably tell them to do about it?" A similar query was phrased in terms of an advice-seeking friend with a problem spouse.

Respondents were first sorted into those who in either or both situations would recommend consulting a psychotherapist of some kind. Sorted next were all the remaining respondents who would advise seeing a physician. In the third category were placed those who at most would refer such friends to some other kind of professional person, principally a clergymen or member of a social agency staff. The residue contained all respondents whose replies to both questions contain no suggestion of professional help of any kind.

Since professional orientation is strongly related to socioeconomic status of respondents, in table 19–13 distributions on the former variable appear standardized for respondents' own SES. The criterion of classification by religion is again religious origin.

Catholics and Protestants are alike in that within each group about half could perceive no professional help as relevant for either of the stipulated problem families, and about one in eight would refer such problems to a physician. They differ in that fewer Catholics than Protestants would recommend a psychotherapist, and correspondingly more Catholics would advise other kinds of professionals, principally clergymen.

TABLE 19–13.　HOME SURVEY SAMPLE (AGE 20–59), RESPONDENTS'
DISTRIBUTIONS ON PROFESSIONAL ORIENTATION SCALE BY RELIGIOUS ORIGIN
AS STANDARDIZED FOR OWN-SES DIFFERENCES

Respondent recommends	Religious origin		
	Catholic	Protestant	Jewish
Psychotherapist	23.8%	31.4%	49.2%
Physician	13.3	12.5	7.9
Other professional	13.0	7.5	3.1
Nonprofessional	49.9	48.6	39.8
N = 100%	(832)	(562)	(213)

Jewish respondents, to a degree well beyond the other groups, see psychotherapists as the most appropriate source of help for the disturbed individuals outlined to them. In fact, they are the only group where this response is more frequent than the "no professional" recommendation.

Table 19–13 views the Midtown sample in its entirety, whereas table 19–12 views only the Impaired portion of that sample. Nevertheless, as observed in table 19–13, the religious groups' rank order of orientation to psychotherapy corresponds to their rank order of current outpatient rates seen in table 19–12. Independently of socioeconomic status, then, religious groups differ in their spontaneous awareness of and receptivity to the psychotherapeutic professions. Given a help-need condition and like socioeconomic status, these differences are manifested through intergroup variations in actually seeking the counsel of a psychotherapist. This generalization is consistent with the evidence provided earlier in the present chapter by both the Treatment Census and Home Survey operations of the Midtown Study.

It is now relevant to note the discussion on this point by the New Haven investigators of a patient population:[24]

It is our opinion that the acceptance of psychiatry probably accounts for the inordinately high rate of psychoneurosis among Jews. [25] The explanation for this must be considered in terms of the ethnic structure and the tradition of the Jewish group in addition to its religious organization. Among Jews it is generally accepted that there is no conflict between religious doctrine and psychoanalytic theory. This is in contrast to a partially supported opposition among Catholics. From the standpoint of community attitudes, the Jews exhibit a high level of acceptance of psychoanalytic psychiatry with a minimum of disturbance of their social values. The Jewish attitude is widely divergent from the Irish, as is substantiated by our finding that not a single patient of Irish birth was receiving psychotherapy for psychoneurosis. Although this explanation of the rates of psychoneurosis in terms of the acceptance of modern psychiatry appears plausible, we cannot definitely state that the actual occurrence of the illness is not higher among Jews.

The statement just quoted, on one point at least, finds support in the implication of Midtown data just reviewed that readiness for psychotherapy, or the "pro-psychiatry" attitude, among Jews contributes to their high patient rates. However, the explanation offered by the New Haven investigators for the Jewish acceptance of psychiatry seems to rest primarily on a contrast drawn from the Catholic group. We understand the New Haven authors to posit that official opposition of the church, at least to psychoanalysis, diverts Catholics from seeking psychotherapy of *any* kind. In the Jewish group, further, the lack of such hieratic and doctrinal opposition and a "minimum of disturbance with their social values" are essentially negative factors in the sense that they do *not* interpose barriers to soliciting psychiatric help.

In our view, this formulation is unduly simplified. First, Protestantism, at least in its metropolitan churches, if anything is more overtly active in articulating itself to psychiatry than are synagogues on the whole. On this basis, according to the New Haven reasoning, the pro-psychiatry frequencies of Protestants should be substantially larger than those of Catholics and at least approximate those of Jews. Table 19–14 reveals these frequencies by religious group as sorted into respondent own-SES strata.

In two of the three SES strata, the pro-psychiatry rates of Protestants and Catholics do not differ appreciably. In the upper stratum the Protestant frequency stands no better than roughly intermediate between those of Catholics and Jews. Accordingly, our data suggest that if there are differences in psychiatric orientation among the clergy of the three major religious groups, they appear to have no power to explain the variations in psychiatric readiness observed above among their respective laities.

The information in tables 19–13 and 19–14 enables us to question the New Haven formulation offered to explain the "high level of

TABLE 19–14. HOME SURVEY SAMPLE (AGE 20–59), PRO-PSYCHIATRY
FREQUENCIES AMONG RELIGIOUS-ORIGIN GROUPS BY RESPONDENT OWN SES*

Own SES	Religious origin		
	Catholic	Protestant	Jewish
Lower (E–F)	12.1%	13.8%	†
N = 100%	(381)	(137)	(11)
Middle (C–D)	23.6%	28.6%	41.3%
N = 100%	(322)	(168)	(46)
Upper (A–B)	35.6%	51.8%	63.4%
N = 100%	(129)	(257)	(156)

* Needless to say, a group's distribution on the own-SES range may deviate considerably from its scatter on the parental-SES range.

† These cases are too few to present a meaningful percentage.

acceptance of psychoanalytic psychiatry among Jews." This hypothesis emphasized the absence among Jews of clerical and doctrinal constraints to securing psychotherapy. The alternative hypothesis we would propose emphasizes not the absence of constraint but rather the presence of a positive motivating process, and looks for it not in the religious institution alone but in the spontaneous operations of the family unit as well.

Earlier in this chapter (table 19–4), we reported that in mental health composition Protestants and Catholics are little different when standardized by age and SES origin, whereas by comparison Jews have a significantly lower impairment frequency and a higher subclinical (Mild or Moderate symptom formation) rate. Furthermore, we observed that the Jewish deviation in impairment frequency was sharpest in the SES-origin stratum that is associated with the most pathogenic life conditions, namely, the lower class. We therefore indicated that the Jewish mental health distribution suggests the possible presence in the family unit of an impairment-limiting mechanism that operates to counteract or contain in some degree the more pathogenic life stresses. Consistently low rates of self-impairing alcoholism and suicide in the general Jewish population seemed compatible with this hypothesis.

We have since seen in the Midtown sample that, given an Impaired state of mental health, Jews have far higher current patient rates than Protestants or Catholics. Furthermore, Jews generally tend to deviate from the other two religious groups of like socioeconomic status in their pro-psychiatry orientation. We would now extend the postulate of an impairment-limiting mechanism to cover its manifestations in greater Jewish responsiveness to psychotherapy as an appropriate means to limit and reverse psychopathology.

It would go somewhat outside our present framework to develop the further suggestion that this mechanism may be part of a larger survival-insurance process rooted in the Jewish family and religious tradition that has found expression in these other varying forms: (1) explicit emphasis upon health as transcending fundamental ritual prescriptions when the two are in conflict; (2) mobilization of family and kin in psychological and material support of the sick individual; and (3) pragmatism in calling upon extrafamilial healing resources.[26] The fusion of all these elements may perhaps be discerned in the millennial-long affinity of Jews for the field of medicine and, more recently, for its psychiatric branch, in the several roles of explorers, healers, and patients. The Jewish group historically can be viewed in one perspective as a culture mobilized for the prevention and, that failing, for the healing of the ailments of body and mind.

Finally, we would question the inference of the New Haven investigators that opposition to psychoanalysis (as a mode of therapy) on the part of the Catholic laity is "partially supported" by the Church.

There is no question about the Church's unequivocal reactions to the antidoctrinal aspects of the psychoanalytic literature. Overlooked, however, is the impressive movement of Church spokesmen toward explicit acceptance of Freud's scientific and therapeutic contributions.

As one churchman has put it: "A Catholic will differ radically with Freud in philosophy and religion. But such differences, radical and profound though they be, should not obscure our vision nor dim our appreciation of the many fresh and brilliant insights which he brought to the understanding of the forces moving in the subconscious areas of our mental life and exercising their pull upon us."[27] Commenting on the address of Pope Pius XII to the First International Congress on the Histopathology of the Nervous System, the Vatican's official newspaper observed: "All the systems of psychoanalysis have in common certain principles, methods and psychic experiments which are in no way contrary to rational ethics and Christian morality, and therefore are not in any way touched or reproved by the Sovereign Pontiff."[28,29]

Pope Paul VI has recently declared of psychiatry in general: "First of all we must underline the paramount importance of the branch of medicine you represent. The Church has always rejoiced in seeing scientific progress wherever such programs are placed at the disposal of mankind. Of all the branches of medicine, neuropsychiatry is a privileged branch, for this area of scientific progress is striking."[30]

From another approach we postulate that two major institutional influences, among others, may operate to restrain financially capable Catholic laymen from seeking ambulatory psychiatric care more often. Psychotherapy tends to be seen as a secularized form of a central Church procedure: the confessional. In this perspective the therapist need not be a cleric, but considerations of personal comfort in the therapeutic relationship may dictate that he should be a fellow Catholic. On this line of reasoning, the Midtown Catholics' relatively low patient rates and infrequent psychiatric readiness may partially be a function of the plain fact that Catholic clinics and office psychiatrists at the time of the Study were so few in number.

Between 1950 and 1975, the number of American psychiatrists increased many times. Data are lacking on the Catholic segment of the profession, but it is the senior author's strong impression that the proportion of Catholics among U.S. psychiatrists still lags far behind the general increase in the profession's manpower.

SUMMARY

Religious differences constitute the final demographic variable explored in the Midtown data for lines of influence leading to the several facets of mental health under review in this monograph. The principal exploratory results are as follows:

1. Despite technical differences between the Midtown Treatment Census and New Haven Psychiatric Census, intercommunity comparison revealed these parallels: (*a*) For the kinds of disorders usually treated in an ambulatory facility, Catholics and Protestants yielded like patient rates that were considerably below that found among Jews; (*b*) for the kinds of disorders usually treated in hospitals, Jews and Protestants yielded like patient rates that were below that of Catholics; and (*c*) taking Total Patients rates as an inclusive yardstick, Jews stood highest in both communities.

2. Clarification of these seemingly contrary directions was sought in the Midtown Home Survey sample of 1,660 representative adults. On the chronologically antecedent criterion of parental religion, the sample's groups of Jewish, Protestant, and Catholic derivation had impairment rates of 16.5, 21.5, and 26.3 percent, respectively.

Standardization for intergroup differences in age and SES origin reduced the Protestant and Catholic groups to near identity in mental health distributions. Respondents of Jewish origin retained a significantly lower Impaired rate—one wholly explained by smaller numbers in the Severe and Incapacitated subcategories of impairment. However, they were relatively underrepresented in the Well category and overrepresented in the Mild-Moderate range of symptom formation.

Analysis further revealed that the more favorable impairment rate of the Jewish-origin group was especially characteristic of its low SES-origin members. A number of hypotheses and speculations were advanced as possible explanations of these findings.

3. Within each religious-origin group we differentiated respondent parents on a threefold gradient of religiosity, i.e., commitment to and anchorage in their faith. Reflected in the data were substantial erosions in religious moorings among respondents' parents. The Midtown evidence further suggested a J-curve type of relationship between parental religiosity and offspring mental health in Protestant and Catholic families adhering to the lower two-thirds of the SES-origin range. Seemingly discernible here were the echoes in contemporary adults of the reverberating sociocultural upheavals generated during the nineteenth century.

4. Modeled after SES mobility (chapter 14) was the factor of intergenerational change in religious affiliation. The few converts to other religions were favorably constituted in group mental health, but those who had drifted into the "no religion" stream presented a relatively unfavorable picture of mental health.

5. Focus upon the patient-history variable among the religious groupings' Impaired respondents suggested this: In groups of similar size a combination of low mental morbidity rate and pronounced tendency to seek therapy can deliver more Impaired people to treatment services than a combination of high morbidity rate and slight tendency to seek therapy.

6. Representing the former combinations, Jews were also found

with a more widespread openness to psychiatry. Discussed were explanatory formulations of the readiness variable as offered by the New Haven and Midtown investigators.

NOTES

1. *Fortune*, February 1960, pp. 2–4.

2. To avoid unwieldy segmentation, we will not focus on the denominational branches within Protestantism and Judaism. Here, however, we might venture a brief look into our Midtown sample of adults for indications as to the specific denominations represented and their relative size. On the criterion of respondent's report of his own current religious identification, we find the major Protestant denominations in descending order of size to be Episcopalians, Lutherans, and Presbyterians, followed by Methodists and Baptists and a variety of smaller sects.

Similarly the three branches of Judaism are locally represented in a descending sequence by population size, namely, Reform, Conservative, and Orthodox. It may illuminate this denominational distribution to note that only 30 percent of the Jewish respondents are immigrants, almost 50 percent are children of immigrants, and roughly 20 percent are of generation III or beyond.

3. To avoid monotony of usage, we shall hereafter employ such terms as religion, faith, church, tradition, and persuasion as specific synonyms of "religious group" with which a respondent is personally identified.

4. Of course, it is necessary to have the total population figure in each group for use as the denominator in calculating its patient rate. The decennial United States census is the source of such information for many kinds of demographic groupings, but religion is not one of these. This deficiency has undoubtedly had crippling effects on epidemiological investigations of the religious factor along the entire range of diseases, somatic as well as psychiatric.

However, application of the Jewish–non-Jewish dichotomy was usually made possible by the availability of local estimates of the Jewish population. These figures were often little more than armchair estimates that by wide and unchallenged repetition had acquired an aura of universal acceptance.

5. Benjamin Malzberg, "Mental Disease among Jews in New York State, 1920 to 1952," *Yivo Annual of Jewish Social Sciences,* vol. X, 1955, p. 298.

6. B. H. Roberts and J. K. Myers, "Religion, National Origin, Immigration and Mental Illness," *American Journal of Psychiatry* 110 (April 1954): 760.

7. As in other research of this kind, the New Haven investigators lacked United States census data on religious composition of their community population. Estimates of this composition were apparently extracted from a special survey of a 5 percent sample of New Haven residents. Given the sampling error underlying these estimates and the rates derived from them, the above differences in treated psychosis rates seem sufficiently small to be a resultant of chance in the sampling process.

8. Of course, the New Haven study covered private as well as state psychiatric hospitals. If Protestants and Jews in some numbers preferred such institutions to state hospitals, then patient rates based on the latter alone would of course be understatements to the extent of such preference.

9. The absence of the office patients makes it pointless to analyze the remaining patients in each religious group by diagnostic category.

10. H. Orlansky, "Jewish Personality Traits: A Review of Studies on an Elusive Problem," *Commentary*, October 1946, pp. 377–383.

11. This is accomplished by the technique of standardization. In this method, the less-populated mental health categories in the Impaired range cannot be separately sustained. Accordingly, they are merged in table 19–4.

12. C. R. Snyder, "Culture and Jewish Sobriety," *Quarterly Journal of Studies on Alcohol* 16 (December 1955): 700–742.

13. I. Janis, *Psychological Stress*, 1958, p. 352.

14. Here may also be the seedbed of the Jewish community's proverbial gift, through its long history, for rising from adversity and for converting a handicap into an asset. Alexander King points to another possible consequence: "Jewish humor, as I learned at one of its very sources, was a racial anti-biotic, whose original cultures the children of Israel had carried out of Egypt, more than two thousand years ago, and whose health-preserving properties had been nurtured through the centuries in all the ghettoes and outposts of persecuted Judaism." (A. King, *Mine Enemy Grows Older*, 1958, p. 171.)

15. Originally also asked for this purpose was a question on parents' frequency of church (or synagogue) attendance—"when you were growing up." Subsequently, we recognized more fully that as a universal index of religiosity, frequency of church attendance had a number of serious deficiencies. Accordingly, it is not being employed here for this purpose.

16. If respondent indicated that father and mother differed in this respect, the interviewer recorded the specific nature of the difference. Later, with an eye on the parent likely to have had the larger influence on the home's religious atmosphere, we classified such cases according to importance of religion reported for the mother.

17. Whether this reply would have coincided with the judgments of the parents themselves, their clergyman, or their friends at the time, is information beyond access to us. Even if accessible, these judgments would not necessarily be of transcending relevance compared to the respondent's judgment from his personal vantage point.

18. Cf. Chapter 7.

19. If personal importance of religion is seen as a continuum ranging (1) from complete submission to the expectations of one's church to (2) more or less complete independence of one's church, it is clear that in this distribution about half of the parents stand at the VI range of the continuum. With benefit of hindsight, were we to test this factor again, we would enlarge the number of categories in the scale, perhaps to four, in order to sort out religiosity differences within the present VI category and to produce a closer approximation to a normal distribution curve.

In this direction, Fichter has applied the following fourfold classification of Catholics: "[a] *Nuclear*, who are the most active participants and the most faithful believers. [b] *Modal*, who are the normal, practicing Catholics easily identifiable as parishioners. [c] *Marginal*, who are conforming to a bare arbitrary minimum of the patterns expected in the religious institution. [d] *Dormant*, who have 'given up' Catholicism but have not joined another denomination." (J. H. Fichter, S. J., "The Marginal Catholic: An Institutional Approach," *Social Forces* 32 [December 1953]: 167–172.)

20. It might be added that parents' religiosity also varies inversely with their socioeconomic status. That is, the higher the SES level, the lower, on the aver-

age, is the religiosity reported. However, when both the SES and religious-group factors are analyzed simultaneously, religiosity varies more among religious groups within any given SES stratum than among SES strata within any given religious group.

More accurately stated, in all parental-SES strata such analytical control tends to eliminate the differences in religiosity distributions between Protestants and Jews seen in table 19–5 and tends to magnify the distribution differences between each of the latter two groups and the Catholics. For example, in the parental lower-SES stratum the "very important" frequencies of Catholic, Protestant, and Jewish parents are 74.0, 39.8, and 37.5 percent, respectively.

21. S. H. King and D. Funkenstein, "Religious Practice and Cardiovascular Reactions during Stress," *Journal of Abnormal and Social Psychology* 55, no. 1 (January 1957): 135–137.

22. It may be remembered that this expressed the number of Impaired cases per 100 Well respondents in a given group.

23. Cf. p. 433 of this chapter.

24. Roberts and Myers, "Religion, National Origin, Immigration and Marital Illness," p. 762.

25. For the New Haven data on treated neuroses and character disorders see table 19–1.—Eds.

26. Cf. L. Srole, "Social Conflicts in Relation to Health Education: Minority Groups," *Psychological Dynamics of Health Education*, Proceedings of Eastern Health Education Conference, 1951, pp. 90–99; M. Zborowski and E. Herzog, *Life Is with People*, 1952, pp. 114–115, 354–357; and M. Zborowski, *People in Pain*, 1969, pp. 120–132.

27. Rev. J. A. O'Brien, *Psychiatry and Confession*, Paulist Press, 1958.

28. *L'Osservatore Romano*, Sept. 21, 1952.

29. For the most systematic concordance bridging Catholic philosophy and Freud's contributions to scientific psychology and clinical psychiatry, see *Psychoanalysis and Personality: A Dynamic Theory of Normal Personality*, 1962, by Joseph Nuttin, Sr., Professor of Psychology at the Catholic University of Leuven (Belgium).

30. Addressed to Dr. Bertram S. Brown, Director of the U.S. National Institute of Mental Health, as reported in *Psychiatric News*, April 18, 1974.

Part VII

Epilogue

CHAPTER 20

THE CITY VERSUS TOWN AND COUNTRY: NEW EVIDENCE ON AN ANCIENT BIAS, 1975

LEO SROLE

In this data chapter, prepared for the present edition,* the author expands the focus beyond Midtown to encompass a far larger sociological terrain. I refer to the spectrum of community-habitat types defined at one pole by the relatively homogenous rural/"country"/village/small-town scene and, toward the other extreme, by the highly heterogenous urban/city/metropolis agglomeration. Within this greatly extended framework, the present chapter will briefly review past professional assessments of urban and country milieus as polarities, and summarize recent research evidence bearing on this issue, particularly as it relates to both somatic and mental well-being.

On a preliminary semantic note, the professional literature I must draw on for these purposes largely employs the above extreme categories of settlements, and intermediate ones as well, with little more quantitative specificity or consistency than does popular usage of terms like tall, medium, and short in referring to individual stature. I have no choice except to follow the practices of the particular sources cited, underscoring that the chapter's analytic interest, by and large, is in comparing the big city at one pole with village and town at the other.

Recorded attitudes toward the city go back at least to the Book of

* In its original version this chapter was a paper read at the Conference on Cognitive and Emotional Aspects of Urban Life held in June 1972 under the auspices of the Graduate Center of the City University of New York. Subsequently revised, it appeared as an article, "Urbanization and Mental Health," in *American Scientist* 60, no. 5 (September–October 1972): 576–583. The latter has been considerably reworked and enlarged for this edition.

Genesis and its imprecations against Sodom, Gomorrah, and "the whore city" of Babylon, site of Babel, the memorable high-rise housing development that collapsed from the weight of its builders' tongues. Keynoted later by Rousseau's romantic exaltation of "man in a state of nature," the voices of antipathy swelled as the Industrial Revolution ran its accelerating course. A collection of all writings that decried, deplored, or denounced the city would probably fill a sizable college library. Heavily represented on its shelves would certainly be works of the Romantic poets. It was the English poet George Byron who wrote, "To me the hum of human cities is torture." His contemporary Percy Shelley put it more epitaphically in even fewer words: "Hell is a city like London."

There were of course U.S. counterparts. One of the fullest treatments of native-son variations on the same theme appears in *The Intellectuals versus the City* (1962), where historians of philosophy Morton and Lucia White dip into two centuries of Americans' writings about their cities.[1]

Not all men or women of letters were nettled by the American city. For example, some, like Walt Whitman, carried on an unabashed, unabated love affair with New York. Whitman communicates his extravagant image of the object of his ardor in the line, "I find in this visit to [Manhattan] and the daily contact and rapport with its myriad people . . . the best, most effective medicine my soul has yet partaken." Such solo voices aside, the Whites call particular attention to "the volume of the anti-urban roar in the national literary pantheon . . . [that has been sounded] in unison by figures who represent major tendencies in American thought."[2]

One of the giants among these figures was Thomas Jefferson, agrarian apostle of the Enlightenment and staunch preacher of the democratic canon that people are the best judges of what is best for them. Paradoxically, despite growing multitudes electing to settle places like London, Paris, Boston, New York, and Philadelphia, Jefferson in his middle years referred to them as "the mobs of great cities," which were "cancers on the body politic." He later reluctantly conceded that cities were economically necessary for a developing country like the United States. But near the end of his long life he could write: "City life offers you . . . vice and wretchedness. New York, for example, like London, seems to be a Cloacina of all the depravities of human nature."[3,4]

The Whites' cast of U.S. anti-urbanists include, among others, Emerson and Thoreau, Theodore Dreiser and John Dewey, Frank Lloyd Wright and pioneer urban sociologist Robert Park, to whom I shall return below.

The Whites note that "those figures form a body of intellectual lore and tradition which continues to affect the thought and action about the American city today."[5] Long-term observers of the proceedings in Congress or any state legislature have hardly known a year in which each of these elected bodies has not reflected this "lore and tradition," although rarely, until recently, in explicit terms.

John Lindsay has commented that "we *do* make public policy out of private prejudices," and in particular "the federal government, which has historically established our national priorities, has never really thought the American city was 'worthy' of improvement."[6] An illustration of the point is to be found in a *New York Times* editorial (April 20, 1973). It caustically noted that on the issue of appropriating already authorized funds for expanding urban mass transportation facilities, "the anti-urban forces [in the House of Representatives] succeeded in denying [such funds] to cities poisoned by exhaust fumes and immobilized by collapsing transportation systems. . . . The single-minded claque of an America of roaring highways brushed aside all rational arguments, in total lack of concern about the inescapable fact that the nation cannot prosper while its cities are being strangled."

In 1975, this congressional tendency was vented with unprecedented force on New York in particular. At the time of the city's severest fiscal crisis, and request for federal backing of its credit, the local press reported this response from the nation's capital: "A deep-rooted Congressional hostility to New York City [surfaced] in dozens of cloakroom interviews in which legislators were openly critical not only of New York's municipal management . . . but also of the city itself. . . ."

Subsequently, on a head-of-state visit abroad, the President responded to New York's crisis with a public castigation, reflecting, according to some Washington observers, that "Mr. Ford's real constituency [is] . . . anti-city Middle America." This led the *New York Times* (September 15, 1975) to comment editorially: "When a multibillion dollar private corporation is skidding into bankruptcy, alarm arouses the Administration out of do-nothingness. But when the nation's largest city is in trouble, the Administration adopts the three blind mice as its policy-making model. Indeed, Mr. Ford seems to gloat over New York's distress."

Urban sociologists and historians will doubtless mark this episode as revealing a level of animus toward the "city of cities" that was at an all-time high of explicit political expression.

A Texas writer reflected a broader view of national attitudes toward the Empire City:

New York's [fiscal] fate has inflamed a confused hostility that runs deep and bitter, that cuts across class and racial lines, that knows no geographic boundaries. Much of that hostility is a prejudice against the city's very character. Its accents are not our accents, its neighborhoods are not our neighborhoods, its life style not our life style. . . . But the hostility is more than that—it is the historic prejudice provinces have for their capital city. . . .

Like a magnet [capitals] both attract and repel, they draw from their provinces both love and hate. Although Washington may be our political capital, in every other way New York has been America's center, and we, in terms of geography and power, its provinces; it has told us what to wear, how to act, what to think, what to buy.

We need New York because it is our nation's center of excellence, the stage for the best talent in America, whether that talent be in business, the arts, communication, or finance. We also need New York because it has been our safety valve. Not only has it given our best talents their big chance, it has also taken off our hands millions of people down to their last chance. Each time some poor soul spends his last dollar on a Greyhound ticket to New York City we can cross one more human problem off our ledger books, and New York has one more person on its overburdened welfare rolls. New York is more than just any city—it is a symbol of both the best and worst in America.*

Someone else has summed up the great city as "a volatile compound of every virtue and every vice-versa known to men." Militant anti-urbanists, on the other hand, see only what is apparently wrong with the city, dismiss all that is right or excellent, and shrug off what is improving or improvable. Moreover, with anti-urbanists vocal, intellectually influential, and politically muscular, much of what has been considered wrong with the city—and in some particular ways

---

* William Broyle, "The Capitol Letter," *Texas Monthly*, reprinted with permission in *New York* magazine, January 12, 1976.

getting worse—may be self-fulfilling prognoses that their biases have helped to bring about. Included, by way of one more illustration, are federal failures to regulate the traffic in guns,[7] controls most heavily opposed by the rural citizenry.[8]

If the present writer here focusses on anti-urbanism as a sociopolitical ideology, it is not out of uncritical, pro-city partisanship, but to the end of tracing its relevance to central scientific concerns of this study. To state my thesis in advance: For over a century, American theory and research on the psychological consequences of small-town versus big-city life, springing from a substrate of anti-urban aversion, have sharpened ancient stereotypes that distorted national perceptions, flouted democratic values, and at times disfigured legislated policies.

I call attention not merely to philosophers like Emerson, Thoreau, or Dewey. I am referring more specifically to social scientists and psychiatric thinkers in this country and elsewhere. Almost from its beginnings as an empirical discipline, sociology was transfixed with the industrial city, its growth pains and problems and, above all, its loss of qualities believed to have been distinctively embodied in the small, pre-industrial community.

Robert Park is an especially interesting case in point.[9] He grew up in a small nineteenth-century town, became in turn a newspaperman, a student of philosophy, then of social theory, and went on to lead the University of Chicago department of sociology. In the 1920's and 1930's, that department was a colossus in American urban sociological thought and research. Park characteristically saw the metropolis as a kind of transient hotel wrought large, "a world in which man is henceforth *condemned to live*" (italics added), reflecting, say the Whites, "his disappointment over the fact that a return to the rural past was impossible."[10] Wendell Bell, a contemporary urbanologist, considers that Park and his students "gave a one-sided and partially false picture of the nature of urban life in its exaggerated portrayal of personal and social disorganization."[11] Summing up, sociologist S. H. Aronson writes: "The Chicago School brought the prestige of science to the support of an anti-urban tradition in America that long antedated the development of sociology. . . ."[12]

Park and his followers, like so many others, were misled in part by nostalgic idealization of what Marcel Proust called "remembrance of things past," and in part by Alfred North Whitehead's "fallacy of misplaced concreteness." By their central, but not exclusive, interest in the social pathology of the city, Chicago sociologists were drawn to study behavioral disorders in slums, rooming-house sections, and deteriorating areas adjoining the expanding central business district— all worthy research targets in their own right. But when they converted their findings about these problem-ridden core areas into generalizations about the genus metropolis as an entity, they were, of course, exceeding the reach of their data. This tendency probably reached its culminating expression in the thought of Louis Wirth,[13] one of Park's Chicago successors.

The anti-city bias endemic in articulate segments of American society was also in part cause and in part effect of an old and related tendency within psychiatry as well. In the United States, the tradition was started in the late eighteenth century by Dr. Benjamin Rush, "upper-crust" Philadelphian, signer of the Declaration of Independence, friend of Thomas Jefferson, and author of the first American textbook on psychiatry.[14] He there advanced his considered opinion that cities are "pestilential to the morals, the health, and the liberties of man." His psychiatric successors, medical superintendents of American mental hospitals, in the middle of the nineteenth century drew upon the premorbid social settings of their patients for empirical support of Rush's thesis.

In those years, the mental hospital population was rapidly increasing, coinciding with industrialization and urbanization in the northeastern states. Moreover, the inflow of patients from rural areas in those states lagged behind those from the cities. These trends seemed to confirm the anti-urbanists and persuade others as well that city living is intrinsically conducive to mental disorder.

Reflecting a closely related bias, antebellum southern hospital superintendents noted higher mental hospital rates among freed Negroes in northern cities than among rural southern slaves. These statistics were taken up by the anti-Abolitionists to support the position that for blacks slavery was psychologically "salutary," whereas they were especially prone to insanity in "the unnatural condition" of freedom. These ideologues neglected to mention the fact that if the northern states grudgingly admitted black patients to their mental hospitals, the southern states were adamently opposed,[15] largely accounting for regional differences in Negro rates.

In the post–Civil War era, northern hospitals found recent Irish immigrants from seaboard cities filling their wards. Given these rising admissions, prominent hospital superintendents proposed segregation of all Irish patients in state almshouses, which of course lacked any semblance of therapeutic pretension. Mounting patient rates persuaded them that "the Irish race is especially prone to mental illness, preeminently incurable," and, moreover, they "aggravate" the condition of fellow patients of other national origins.[16]

By the early decades of the twentieth century, nativist anti-Irish fever had abated. But cresting mental hospitalizations of migrants from southern and eastern Europe prompted a political movement to bar the immigration of these newcomers in particular. Such hospital reports, reflecting their writers' "intense dislike for their immigrant patients," were used in congressional hearings "to build up the notion of the innate inferiority" of these recent settlers. The hearings culminated in the Quota Laws of 1921 and 1924 that discriminated against applicants from countries in southern and eastern Europe.[17]

Thus, mental hospitalization differentials between urban and rural populations, blacks and whites, immigrants and natives, heated up simmering prejudices, spilled into the legislative mills, and there were turned into national policies discriminatory against large segments of the American population, above all those living in cities.[18] It is no surprise, therefore, that a leading member of the House of Representatives a decade ago wrote that congressional "legislation is often a travesty of what the national welfare requires."[19]

In the light of such heavy political fallouts, it is necessary to emphasize anew that conclusions of the kind just reviewed, drawn from rates of admissions to mental hospitals, also violate a fundamental "law" of evidence. From the social characteristics of state hospital patients (those in high-cost private institutions were rarely included), generalizations were extracted about the pathological predispositions of corresponding social groups in the general American population.

Past professional prejudices and evidential fallacies aside, what is the current situation in the age-long controversy about the respective effects of small town and big city life on the well-being of their residents?

THE PHYSICAL HEALTH SITUATION

Let us start with recent research on somatic health as measured by disease-specific morbidity and mortality rates. In the past, morbidity and mortality rates of the acute infectious diseases have almost always been higher in the city than anywhere else. And it has been widely accepted, almost as a law of the urban condition, that they would continue so. However, this "law" is now being rewritten. In recent decades national morbidity studies have shown that rural-metropolitan differences in the frequencies of such illnesses have been steadily shrinking.

For example, we can refer to one of the recent National Health Interview Survey Reports (1974) on acute disorders in the United States.[20] As defined there, "an acute condition is a condition which has lasted less than three months and which has involved either medical attention or restricted activity." General types included are respiratory (accounting for more than half the total), infective, digestive, injuries, and "all others." The rate is expressed in the "number of acute conditions per 100 persons per year."

The place-of-residence spectrum is divided nationally into three U.S. Census Bureau populations: (1) All Standard Metropolitan Statistical Areas (SM),* (2) Non-SM–Nonfarm population (NF), (3) Non-SM–Farm population (F).

If we exclude the injury category (because it represents etiologically an entirely different order of malfunction than the predominantly infectious conditions), the rates for the three populations, by my calculations, are 167, 165, 142, respectively, there being no difference between the two nonfarm populations.

However, when we compare the frequencies in the SM and NF groups by age we find:

1. Below age 5, the metropolitan rate is somewhat higher than that of the NF population, as it is in the 25 to 44 range as well.
2. Within ages 5 to 24, the SM and NF frequencies are almost identical.
3. In the entire age range beyond 45, the metropolitan rates are actually somewhat *lower* than the nonfarm frequencies.

Thus, from a comparative disadvantage in the pre-school years, the metropolitan frequencies tend to become progressively more favor-

* The federal definition, somewhat simplified, is as follows: "The SM contains a central city with population over 50,000, and includes the surrounding county and adjacent counties that are metropolitan in character and economically and socially integrated with the county of the central city." The nation's 243 SM's in 1970 had an average population of 575,000, varying in a range from about 75,000 to over 11,000,000.

able (relative to the other nonfarm group) upward on the adult life span.

I would next turn from the acute conditions, as defined above, to those of longer duration and assigned by the National Center for Health Statistics to the "chronic" category. Since it has been widely held that physical stress and strain, wear and tear, are intrinsic to the city's tempo and style of life, we might expect the metropolis to produce correspondingly higher morbidity rates of such presumptively stress-related, "chronic" conditions as rheumatoid arthritis, hypertension, heart disease, etc.

The most recent NCHS Report (1974) covers the prevalence of all chronic conditions associated with "limitations of activity."[21] The reported age-adjusted rates (per 100 population), with community size again trichotomized, as we see in the following, fail to support the expectation:

$$
\begin{array}{ll}
\text{SM} & 12.2 \\
\text{NF} & 13.5 \\
\text{F} & 13.2 \\
\end{array}
$$

Moreover, for the age group over 65, where the urban "wear and tear" theory would predict the greatest differences in frequencies, the theory seemingly is contradicted by these rates:

$$
\begin{array}{ll}
\text{SM} & 40.5 \\
\text{NF} & 47.5 \\
\text{F} & 47.8 \\
\end{array}
$$

Here, the expected differences are reversed—the metropolitan population has the lowest frequency, farm areas the highest.

NCHS in the early 1960's extended its Health Examination Survey to a large national sample of children 6 to 12 years old. One of the key questions prompting the investigation was: "In general, is country living more healthful for children than city living?" Two widely accepted indicators of physical well-being were used, namely, height and weight, with analytical control for the first time applied to a most "weighty" predictor, namely, socioeconomic status of parents.

Popular images (e.g., as projected in Norman Rockwell's illustrations) have long contrasted the tall, sturdy rural lad with his shorter, stringier peer on the city streets. How closely do these images fit the present facts? The NCHS concludes: "The data very strongly suggest that for children growing up in the 1950's and 1960's in the U.S. it makes no difference on the average either in the rate of growth or size attained at any age as to whether they live in the middle of the big city, in the country, or in a suburb, as long as one takes into account the major detectable socioeconomic factors."[22]

Wrapping it all up, a definitive summary of U.S. health trends between 1900 and 1960 concluded a decade ago as follows: "As mortality from the communicable diseases shrinks to ever lower levels, differences in the general level of health and well-being between city and country have narrowed almost to the vanishing point . . . over the years, life in the cities has taken on a healthier complexion. Thus, life expectancy in New York City in 1901 was about seven years less than in the United States for males and almost six years for females. Today [1960] differences in life expectancy between residents of New York City and the entire nation are relatively insignificant."[23]

The post-1960 evidence reviewed above suggests that by measures of physical health indices the cities have pulled up to the smaller places, and among their older people have perhaps forged ahead.

For New York City in financial crisis at the time this book went to press the situation was summed up as follows in a *New York Times* editorial (January 7, 1976):

New York City in 1975 was healthier than ever before in history. For the first time, fewer than 1% of the city's population died last year. . . . Because the city is so large, has so diversified a population, and has so many of its citizens below the poverty line, the progress here is all the more remarkable.

The city's declining death rate is a particularly impressive accomplishment because the proportion of its population over 65 has been increasing steadily since 1960. . . . The forces that lengthen life are [reflected in] the latest statistics on increasing longevity in New York City.

THE SITUATION IN MENTAL HEALTH

A drug company ad in a psychiatric journal pictures a curb-side view of two looming-downward skyscrapers with the large-type caption "Anxiety Canyon," followed below by the line, "[Drug brand name] can help you control the excessive anxiety that so often accompanies the impersonal, oppressive climate of urban living."

Two psychiatrists, in a recent book for professionals, state axiomatically, without qualification or citation of a single supporting fact or source: "Psychiatric disorders occur at a significantly higher rate in cities compared with rural areas."[24]

A writer of popular works on environmental health has a chapter entitled, "The Crude Art of Cracking Up," in his book *Crisis in Our Cities: Death, Disease and the Urban Plague*.[25] He there discusses several mental health studies. Of the present investigation he writes: "The Midtown study shows that the mental illness rates in a crowded residential area of Manhattan are probably much higher than currently accepted figures for the country as a whole." Attentive reading of the original (and this) edition of the present work "shows" nothing of the kind. In fact, we explicitly warn against interpreting our data as supporting such a conclusion or inference.

The readiness to alchemize a belief into a presumed fact about the city, as manifested in the preceding examples, can take other judgmental forms. One basic limitation in the relevant research literature had been this: Mental health studies of general populations in urban and rural habitats were generally done by different investigators, using diverse kinds of methods, data, and diagnostic criteria. Thus, firm generalizations about urban-rural differences could not be made because such studies lacked sufficient comparability.

However, a series of nine independent investigations have by now been conducted, each with the distinction of having the same personnel researching mental health in both a rural and an urban place, all located, as it happens, in the Eastern Hemisphere. Although the scientific methods, concepts, and judgmental criteria applied were inadequately reported, they presumably were the same in each pair of communities. If so, a seemingly sound basis for comparing the intrapair differences is for the first time present.

Drs. Bruce Dohrenwend and Barbara Dohrenwend have performed a singular scholarly service in scanning the literature over a thirty-year period, and have summarized and assessed findings from the nine "twin" investigations they have uncovered.

These are presented in their chapter "Psychiatric Disorder in Urban Settings" appearing in the 1974 edition of the *American Handbook of Psychiatry*.[26] Table 20–1 below is drawn from that chapter (p. 428), as reproduced from my *American Scientist* article, with additions here of percentage signs and national context of each pair of studies.

The Dohrenwends offer this summary judgment about the entire

TABLE 20–1.   TOTAL PREVALENCE OF PSYCHIATRIC DISORDERS REPORTED FOR INVESTIGATIONS INCLUDING BOTH AN URBAN AND A RURAL SITE (PERCENT IN EACH SAMPLE)

Disorders in urban site	Disorders in rural site	Urban % minus rural %	Author(s)
0.8	1.7	−0.9	Kato (Japan)
1.1	1.1	0.0	Lin (Taiwan)
1.11	1.03	+0.08	Kaila (Finland)
1.28	1.07	+0.21	Kaila (Finland)
3.0	2.7	+0.3	Tsuwaga et al. (Japan); Akimoto et al. (Japan)
13.5	11.7	+1.8	Piotrowski et al. (Poland)
45.0	40.0	+5.0	A. H. Leighton et al. (Nigeria)
18.1	13.0	+5.1	Piotrowski et al. (Poland)
34.1	20.2	+13.9	Helgason (Iceland)

set of intrapair divergences: "On the basis of this evidence—and it is the best we have available—there appears to be a tendency for total rates of psychiatric disorder to be higher in urban than in rural areas." About the perceived "tendency" of higher disorder rates among the urban sites in the set, they make this comment: "The consistency in direction of most of the urban-rural differences reported in these studies, despite the diversity of time,* place and method of assessing disorder suggest that the results be taken seriously."

The Dohrenwends ask us to take the results seriously on the criterion of consistency in direction of "most" of the intrapair differences. (In the third column a plus sign denotes the urban rate is higher, minus that the rural rate is higher.) I suggest that before fixing on the plus-minus direction of these nine differences, the analyst must first take into account their magnitude and probable statistical reliability. To do so, we can proceed stepwise down the above table and note as follows:

1. In the first pair, the urban rate is the more favorable one (i.e., has the smaller of the two frequencies), but to a degree so slight as to deny any claim to statistical credibility.

2. In the second pair, the two rates are identical.

* This refers to the fact that three of the nine investigations were published in 1942, one in 1953, and five between 1963 and 1969.

3. In the next four pairs, the urban rates *are* higher, but by margins of far under 1 percent in three instances, and by under 2 percent in the fourth case. These differences are thin to the point of being statistically ephemeral, because they certainly belong well within the range of sampling error alone. In other words, that *each* of the four differences happens to fall in the same "plus" direction is as much a matter of chance as the separate 50–50 probability that each of four successive children in a family will be female.

The inter-rate divergences between the paired Leighton communities in Nigeria (like Piotrowski's in Poland) can on the surface be viewed as of marginal statistical substance. However, Leighton warns that his urban sample numbered only sixty-four people, which "did not give us a random sample of the town's eight sample areas," together housing a population of 80,000. Impaired by an inadequately small and nonrandom sample, the Nigerian urban rate lacks credentials both of representativeness and comparability.

We are thus left with only the Helgason pair, and perhaps Pietrowski's (5.1 percent difference), to take seriously for *both* magnitude and direction of their respective rural-urban rate differences. Let us now identify and briefly describe the city in each of those two pairs. Helgason's urban site is Reykjavík, Iceland's capital, a fishing and shipping center lacking any other industry to speak of, with a population (at the time of the study) of 65,000 largely drawn from the rest of that volcanic and glacial ("fire and ice") island at the edge of the Arctic Circle. Piotrowski's urban place is Plock, a town of 37,000 in the early stages of industrialization, situated in the heartland of predominantly agrarian Poland.

How far can we legitimately generalize from these two remaining sets of twin studies? That they cover settlements in the Old World makes it hazardous to extrapolate their findings to communities in the New. This is especially so because we now know there are pronounced differences between psychiatrists of the two hemispheres in their criteria and modes of diagnostic classification.[27] Furthermore, in any typology of exclusively Eastern Hemisphere urban places, Reykjavík and Plock not only are out of the region's socioeconomic "main stream," but in size they fall into one of its classes of smaller and least urbanized cities. As for being representative of mainstream North American cities that are a primary interest in these pages, they are probably even further afield.

All in all, the "tendency" extracted by the Dohrenwends from the nine pairs of rural-urban studies falls far short of persuasive support by criteria both of statistical substance and generalizability.*

Such twin investigations of mental health in general populations have not yet been made in North America. However, there is one pair of related studies that if not "twins" may be considered "kin." I refer to the researches in Midtown Manhattan and Stirling County,† a rural area of Nova Scotia,[28] directed not by the same investigator, but by two psychiatrists with unusually homogeneous professional vitae.

Specifically, Drs. Thomas Rennie and Alexander H. Leighton had been contemporary residents in the Johns Hopkins Department of Psychiatry under the leadership of Adolph Meyer. In the early fifties, both were Cornell professors, Leighton in the Ithaca, N.Y., campus Department of Sociology and Anthropology, Rennie in the University's New York City–based Medical College. Although their investigations were administratively autonomous, staffed separately and (in terms of disciplines represented) somewhat differently, until Rennie's death in 1956 each served as an ad hoc consultant to the other's operation.[29]

The two staffs pursued independent searches for a validated series of psychopathological signs and symptoms, but both gravitated toward the same two recently reported sources of candidate symptom questions, namely the Army's (World War II) Neuropsychiatric Screening Adjunct and the Minnesota Multiphasic Personality Inventory. It is not surprising, therefore, that among the Midtown and Stirling interview instruments' two large series of psychological signs and symptoms, many were identical, some quite similar, and some were represented in one instrument but not in the other.

While Rennie and Leighton were both key members of the Meyer "school" of psychiatry, in modes of classifying mental health status

---

* For the Dohrenwends' response to this critique and my rejoinder see Appendix G.

† Stirling County (hereafter "Stirling") is a code name for an area of 970 square miles that could encompass 44 Manhattans, but in 1950 contained a population of 20,000 (96 percent white, therefore close to Midtown's corresponding figure of 99 percent). The principal sources of livelihood were fishing, lumbering, and subsistence farming. Its rural contrasts with metropolitan Midtown could hardly be more extreme. For example, in residents per square mile the latter's population density was 75,000 and Stirling's was 20.

on the basis of their overlapping sets of symptom information there were several divergences between the two, involving technicalities that, with some exceptions, are irrelevant here. The first relevant divergence was this: Under Rennie's scheme the time framework implied in almost all of his symptom questions was "in recent weeks prior to the interview." His classification therefore referred to respondent's "current" mental health status. On the other hand, Leighton's symptom time reference and classification "procedure was focussed on estimating the probability that an interviewed individual was or had been suffering from a psychiatric disorder *at any time during his adult life* [author's italics]. There is no precise way of using the evaluations to estimate the *current prevalence* [italics added] of psychiatric disorder at the time of the survey."[30]

The original use of such different time frameworks by itself would have deprived the Stirling and Midtown prevalence results of any basis for comparison. However, the Stirling psychiatrists subsequently conducted "a review inspection of our interview protocols. [This] suggests that if we went back and used these to estimate current prevalence . . . [it would be] our conclusion from all available information . . . that at least half of the adults in Stirling County are *currently* [italics added] suffering from some psychiatric disorder defined in the American Psychiatric Association's *Diagnostic and Statistical Manual* [1952]."[31] Although lacking precision, this inferential conclusion seemingly brought the two investigations to approximately similar time frameworks for sighting mental health status frequencies.

The second interstudy divergence was this: Under Rennie's scheme, classification involved placement of all sample respondents along a single six-way continuum of symptom formation, with discerned or inferred "impairment in social functioning" as the landmark defining the boundary line of mental morbidity.

As indicated in the Stirling monograph quotation given above, Leighton's criterion of mental morbidity was a "psychiatric disorder defined in the [APA] *Diagnostic and Statistical Manual* of 1952." Leighton considered this as providing landmarks for defining "a psychiatric case."[32] Rennie regarded his "impaired" category as covering symptomatic equivalents of psychiatric patients observed in his long hospital and clinical experience.[33]

Therefore, Leighton's "psychiatric case" and Rennie's counterpart of "socially impaired" psychiatric patients might be taken to approach, if hardly to achieve, approximate equivalence. Given such seeming approach, the two studies may lend themselves to cautious comparison. On this guarded assumption, we can now note that the Midtown current impairment rate was 23.7 percent and its Stirling equivalent was estimated as "at least half" of the interviewed sample. Let us accept this "least" 50 percent figure as the Stirling rate, representing a prevalence frequency about twice that of Midtown.

However, before taking that one-to-two difference seriously, we must carefully take into account disparities in the demographic composition of the two communities that yielded the difference.

1. Although French-speaking Acadians have been natives of the county for centuries, no foreign-born elements are mentioned in the Stirling publications, whereas they constitute fully one-third of the Midtown sample. Excluding the immigrant generation lowers the Midtown impairment rate to about 22 percent.

2. On the basis of scattered bits of information available in the Leighton reports I gather this decided impression: In socioeconomic class composition, about 95 percent of Stirling's adult population more or less approximate the lowest 30 percent of the SES distribution in Midtown's American-born respondents.

   a. If that is so, we can take this 30 percent subsample of the Midtown native-born population, numbering 315 respondents, as a rough match of the Stirling sample.

   b. The mental impairment rate of this narrowed Midtown segment is slightly over 33 percent.

3. The Midtown sample confined itself to the prime-of-life age 20 to 59 range. The Stirling sample set no upper age limit, with the result that 27 percent of its members were over the age of 59.

   a. When the Stirling age 60-plus segment is excluded, the distributions of the two native-born subsamples across the 20 to 59 adult span are quite similar, as are their sex ratios.

   b. By this exclusion we can match the Stirling sample to Midtown's age distribution, just as we "matched" Midtown to Stirling's nativity and SES composition.

   c. The Leighton reports do not make it possible to exactly calculate the current "psychiatric disorder" frequency in the matched Stirling under-age-60 groups. However, on the basis of a Stirling volume graph[34] I estimate that excluding the elderly would probably lower the Leighton's estimated Stirling disorder rate by roughly 5 percent, i.e., from 50 percent to about 45 percent.

We started with unstandardized, estimated morbidity rates of 24 percent and 50 percent for Midtown and Stirling, respectively. By crudely matching the two subsamples to each other we have a foundation of demographic comparability in race, nativity, age, sex and socioeconomic class, and thereby have narrowed that 26 percent gap in estimation by approximately one half, i.e., to the 12 percent difference between 33 percent and 45 percent. By the test of significance of difference between two proportions, this 12 percent deviation would be statistically significant at the .01 level of confidence. On balance, taking appropriate qualifications into account, we appear to have a noteworthy residual difference in estimated mental morbidity rates, yielded by two studies that were kindred rather than twin research operations.

Compared to the nine sets of investigations reviewed by the Dohrenwends, the Midtown and Stirling studies as a pair have several advantages of their own:

1. They are both sited in North American places.

2. Midtown stands at the extreme metropolitan end of the rural-urban range, whereas the nine East Hemisphere urban sites are dispersed across cities of considerable variation along the lower end of the urban population–size spectrum. We could expect that the polar sociological contrasts between Stirling and Midtown afford an optimal test of hypotheses about the effects of community size on their residents' emotional well-being.

3. Unlike the Eastern Hemisphere set of twin investigations, the roughly comparable Midtown and Stirling morbidity rates have been here derived by conservatively estimated sample matching, a procedure applied to narrow intersample differences in demographic composition. Given the near universality of such differences between small and large localities, particularly in demographic respects relevant to mental health, analytical controls are as essential for intersample as for intrasample comparisons.

With such controls applied to data from two investigations conducted in the early 1950's, we find, perhaps for the first time in a long-tilled field, that a resident metropolitan population emerges with a lesser prevalence of mental impairment than a demographically matched sample of ruralites.[35]

However, Midtown and Stirling are each a single case drawn from a universe of communities at opposite poles of the North American continuum of local habitat types. Therefore, in the absence of independent supporting evidence, it would be inappropriate to generalize from them to their respective parent universes.

The passage of time, however, has brought us relevant independent evidence from two more recent investigations. The first is reported in the U.S. National Center for Health Statistics document entitled *Selected Symptoms of Psychological Distress* (1970). That report is based on the Health Examination Survey of a national probability sample of 6,672 adults who, in 1960–1962, were medically examined and interviewed in mobile clinics.

For the first time in any NCHS investigation, the interview included twelve self-reported symptoms of the kind used in the Midtown Manhattan and Stirling County studies. Ten were validated against the other two, namely, self-reported nervous breakdown, experienced or felt impending, and all of the ten presented "moderate to high correlations" with the two nervous-breakdown items.

Moreover, for the first time in any mental health investigation known to me, the entire community-size variable was divided into five categories, ranging from "giant metropolitan statistical areas" (cities and their fringe suburban areas with total populations of 3,000,000 and over), "other very large metropolitan statistical areas" (populations 500,000 to 3,000,000), other "standard metropolitan statistical areas" (50,000 to 500,000), "other urban areas" (2,500 to 50,000), to rural areas (of less than 2,500). It has also been possible to split the latter into predominantly farm or nonfarm areas.

Counting the actual and near nervous-breakdown items as one symptom and giving each symptom present a score of one produced a respondent score range of 0 to 11, and permitted the determination of age-adjusted mean symptom scores. These group mean scores for the rural-metropolitan variable do not appear in the report mentioned above, but have been made available to me, controlled for sex, by Dr. Harold Dupuy of the NCHS. I am presenting them in table 20–2 for the white segment of the national sample to match the almost totally white populations of Midtown and Stirling.

In the men's column, a dichotomy is apparent, with the three largest (SMSA) categories of cities showing the lowest scores and the three smallest categories of localities the highest scores. The differences between the two sets of males are not wide; but they are reinforced by the identical dichotomy among the women, where the differences between the two sets of community places are substantial.

To my knowledge, the data in table 20–2 are the first of their

TABLE 20–2. NCHS NATIONAL HEALTH EXAMINATION SURVEY (1960–1962), WHITE AGE-ADJUSTED MEAN PSYCHOLOGICAL SYMPTOM SCORES BY SEX AND POPULATION-SIZE LOCALITIES IN A SAMPLE OF THE U.S. POPULATION

	Men	Women
Giant metropolitan statistical areas	1.53	2.73
Other very large metropolitan statistical areas	1.65	2.77
Other standard metropolitan statistical areas	1.63	2.70
Other urban areas	1.98	3.26
Rural areas, nonfarm	1.90	3.14
Rural areas, farm	1.81	3.25

kinds to be drawn from a national sample with the entire metro-politan-rural spectrum delineated. Scores in the two extreme categories confirm the different morbidity rates of the matched Midtown and Stirling samples both in direction and relative magnitude.

I must add that the above scores have been standardized for age, sex, and race, but not for differences in socioeconomic mix. Relevant here, however, is that the symptom mean scores break dichotomously at the 50,000 population-size line. This suggests the unlikelihood that linear SES variations can be large enough to appreciably reduce the noteworthy parallelism between (a) the U.S. extreme locality-type symptom-score differences, and (b) the demographically matched Midtown-Stirling morbidity rate differences. Helgason's reversed crude rate findings from Reykjavík and rural Iceland hardly stand up as a credible challenge to the parallel metropolitan-rural trends here uncovered for the first time in the three largest and most analytically controlled investigations ever conducted on the North American continent.

The second investigation referred to above is of a totally new kind, involving a survey of all pharmacists in the predominantly white, Anglo-Saxon population of New Zealand, a member nation of the British Commonwealth. Each pharmacist was asked "to list every tranquilizer prescription by strength, client sex, and prescribed daily dosage . . . that he filled on an average day."[36] Webb and Collette add that the information provided was "adjusted and aggregated for each [community] to provide an index of the average number of prescriptions filled." Part of their data appeared in the above cited article; part, yet to be published, was conveyed to this writer in a personal letter from Webb.

The Webb-Collette unpublished data classify size of corporate places in six categories of population numbers from under 1,000 to over 100,000. I have the authors' permission to note this overall finding: Per capita psychotropic drug prescription rate varies inversely with size of locality, the rural rate being over twice that of the biggest cities.

On the issue of SES differences among New Zealand localities the Webb–Collette article notes previous studies that "found no association between socioeconomic status and psychotropic drug use [rates]. Furthermore, any supposed effects of socioeconomic status on physician utilization would most likely have only limited influence in the New Zealand context, for all prescribed pharmaceuticals are free and only a token charge is made for physician services."[37]

Because the NCHS and New Zealand investigations are to my knowledge the first of their respective kinds, their findings must be viewed with appropriate caution. It is suggestive, however, that the general rural-urban trends in the above two, relatively recent, surveys are similar. Moreover, as already noted, their data also coincide with the morbidity rate differences I have extracted from approximately matched demographic segments of the Midtown and Stirling sample populations, in studies conducted some years earlier.

THE SITUATION IN SUICIDE RATES

We have reviewed evidence on rural-urban differences in the prevalence of somatic and mental morbidity, with new trends visibly emerging in both. We can complete this survey by briefly scanning recent data on two forms of destructive behavior. These involve violence against the self, and crimes against others, with the frequencies of each type often regarded as indicators of differential community well-being.

Violence against the self has been measured by suicide rates, per 100,000 population, as reported by physicians on death certificates. Like other "official" statistics, this too is beset by major, and as yet refractory, deficiencies.[38]

Specifically, such figures cannot be regarded as even close approximations to the true incidence of suicide. However, if the unknown margins of underreporting have not shifted radically over recent decades, then a trend in a time series of reported suicide frequencies may roughly parallel the trend in the true suicide rates.

On that tentative, open-ended assumption, let us first consider reported suicide frequencies between 1929 and 1959. In the former year, available reported rates, as then dichotomized simply for rural and urban places, were 11.0 and 17.4 respectively. By 1959, however, the former frequency was down slightly to 10.0, whereas the urban rate had fallen by almost 40 percent to 10.7.

According to a personal communication from the Mortality Statistics Division of the National Center for Health Statistics, more recent corresponding information is not yet available. But we do have approximations suggesting further marked changes by 1967.

1. In that year, the reported age-adjusted suicide frequency for the United States was 11.1.

2. In the same year, according to the Urban Institute,[39] the average corresponding rate for eighteen large cities was 12.7.

3. However, eight of those cities had rates lower than the 11.1 national frequency, with New York's 7.7 standing as the lowest of all.

The narrow category of large cities in 1967 and the broader category of urban places in 1959 are not comparable. On the surface, however, it would appear that in 1967 at least eight of the listed large cities were continuing the falling trend of reported urban suicide rates that obtained in the period 1929–1959.

Fuller data may or may not substantiate this observation. If they do, and our previously mentioned underlying assumption is not contradicted by appropriate evidence, this conclusion would be in order: the peak rates of suicide characterizing the biggest cities since medically certified data were first assembled have been largely, if not yet completely, levelled.

THE SITUATION IN CRIME RATES

Finally, there is new evidence on frequencies of a related kind of violent behavior. For as long as police registers have been the source of national (FBI) Uniform Crime Report statistics,[40] the latter have consistently shown that cities, and above all the largest cities, have been the most crime-ridden places on the entire national scene.[41,42] This applied to both adult and juvenile delinquencies.

However, at this writing we have the first results of a pair of investigations of high school boys in Philadelphia and in a "nonmetropolitan county" in Oregon. Both followed the careers of their subjects from the age of 15 to age 18. A preliminary NIMH summary of findings reports as follows:

In the days when the United States was primarily a country of farms and small towns it was generally believed that teenage delinquency was almost entirely confined to cities. Even today many people think that teenage boys who live outside metropolitan areas get into substantially less trouble than their city cousins, and that when they do their scrapes are usually minor.

Perhaps surprisingly, studies made in recent years have shown that there is no basis for this common assumption—non-metropolitan youths have just about as many run-ins with the law as [racially matched] metropolitan youths, and the causes of these confrontations are often of roughly equal seriousness in both towns and cities.[43]

Police registers share with mental hospital records the serious deficiency that they reveal "only the tip of the iceberg." Hospital enumerations miss the disabled who are untreated or are treated as outpatients, whereas FBI compilations miss the crimes unreported to or by the police authorities.[44]

A technical advance in measuring the overall incidence of crime is being made in current surveys by the Census Bureau for the U.S. Law Enforcement Assistance Administration (LEAA). These involve not police reports, but interviews with large population samples and the confidential testimony of respondents who are surviving victims[45] of one or more crimes.

The first of these surveys is questioning a National Crime Panel of people from 60,000 households in 26 major American cities and hundreds of smaller areas. The second covers 22,000 residents and 2,000 business men in each of thirteen selected cities, varying in size from Portland, Oregon (population 383,000), to New York. Made available at the time of this writing are only the preliminary results of the investigation for the latter range of medium-to-largest cities.[46]

In announcing these findings, the *New York Times* (April 21, 1974) opened its article with the following observations:

Johnny Carson jokes about it, Europeans are horrified by it and New Yorkers are sure of it: New York is the crime capital of the United States of America. . . . Last week the nearly universal preconceptions were challenged . . . according to a Federal report, New York is significantly safer than any other major American city and some of the smaller ones as well.

To summarize the results briefly:

1. The LEAA frequencies, even with homicides excluded, on the average exceed the FBI compiled rates by 260 percent.

2. With specific reference to crimes of violence against persons, i.e., assault, robbery, attempted rape and rape, the annual "victim report" rate per 1,000 residents (age twelve and over) was at a low of 36 in New York and at highs of 59, 63, 67, and 68 in Portland, Philadelphia, Denver, and Detroit, respectively.

3. New York was also lowest of the covered cities in frequencies of "household victimization" (breaking and entering for thefts of property) per 1,000 households.

Further results and technical assessments of the two ground-breaking surveys will be issued in the years ahead, in particular with findings from small urban and rural places. At this writing, however, "nearly universal preconceptions" about heaviest frequencies of force-involved criminal incidents, at least in the middle-to-top size range of cities, seem to be approaching resemblance to Humpty Dumpty's "great fall."

It has been implicit in anti-urbanist thinking that the larger the community the higher the rates of such overlapping forms of pathology as somatic illness, mental disorder, suicide, juvenile and adult crime. To be sure, serious reservations have long been registered about the accuracy of measurement techniques applied to all of these manifestations of individual and community dysfunction. However, in recent years methods applied to four of these indices have been appreciably improved.

We must assume that varying margins of underreporting remain in all of them. Even so, it is a striking fact that all five indicators are sounding the same *new* message in *unison*: The traditional linear correlation—the bigger the place, the worse it is—seems "no longer operative." In the face of this unanimity, it seems the time has come to redraw the contrasting millennia-old city versus country images to fit the recently emerging facts.

Parenthetically, it is ironical that this historical turnabout in the apparent well-being of American city dwellers has surfaced at a time of deepening crisis in the fiscal affairs of their municipalities. The current political responses at the federal level to this widespread crisis have potentially important sociopsychological and policy implications for the future of the city. These are being held for discussion in concluding chapter 23.

The traditional image of rural and small-town America seems also in process of being redrawn. In the past decade a little noticed series of nonfiction works have appeared[47] documenting that our smaller places (both here and abroad) are not, and probably never were, benign havens of untroubled "serenity, tranquility, and stability." One disillusioned ruralite among the many who did not escape to the city speaks of "shattered cherished myths." Another deflates "the fantasy of the city dweller about the superiority of rural life over urban life." A third, foreshadowing the New Zealand study discussed just above, notes: "Our drug stores sell a lot of tranquilizers and pep pills." A distinguished historian-reviewer of one of these books comments on its revelations as follows:

The reality of rural life, and it comes through in this book with authenticity, is harsh. Discomfort, isolation, dependence on the whims of nature, the bare revelations of life and death, the inevitable predacity of living beings, the need for social intercourse but the treachery of social pressure, the unrelenting rhythm of hard work—all these form the other side of the coin of which we prefer to see only the side showing the image of the noble savage. Many people cannot tolerate this kind of life. Mental illness is often high in rural areas.[48]

Another reviewer of the same book sums it up succinctly: "On the whole, I'd prefer hell. Or even Philadelphia."

At both ends of the rural-metropolitan continuum we seem to be breaking through ancient stereotypical barriers and confronting current existential realities that, on the whole, big cities are no more Shelley's "Hell"[49] than our open places are Rousseau's approximation of "Paradise Regained."

NOTES

1. See also the subsequent works: A. L. Strauss, ed., *The American City: A Sourcebook of Urban Imagery*, 1968, and J. B. Quandt, *From the Small Town to the Great Community: The Social Thought of Progressive Intellectuals*, 1970.

2. M. White and L. White, *The Intellectuals versus the City*, 1962, p. 2.

3. Ibid., p. 19.

4. Jefferson was of course a Virginia aristocrat, and according to his biographer Dumas Malone: "He was a highbrow, built his home on a mountain top, didn't like to rub shoulders with people. . . ." (*New York Times*, January 9, 1975).

5. White and White, *The Intellectual versus the City*, p. 3.

6. *The City*, 1969, p. 5.

7. The Federal Gun Control Act of 1968 (banning mail-order sales) "has failed . . . to reduce the illegal use of firearms. . . . the appalling slaughter [a threefold increase in homicides since 1968] so plainly attributable to the uncontrolled traffic in firearms will not abate until ownership of guns is effectively regulated by Federal laws which can and will be enforced." (*New York Times*, editorial, January 3, 1975.) On the same issue, one New York City Congressman expressed the view that "we are literally out of our minds to allow 2.5 million new weapons to be manufactured every year for the sole purpose of killing people."

8. Recent opinion polls have shown 75 percent of adults favoring a law that would require a police permit to buy a gun. Regardless of size of community only about one in five opposed such a law—except in rural areas where the opposition was almost twice as large.

9. R. H. Turner, *Robert E. Park: Selected Papers*, 1967.

10. White and White, *The Intellectuals versus the City*, p. 162.

11. "The City, The Suburb, and a Theory of Social Choice," in S. Greer et al., eds., *The New Urbanization*, 1968, p. 136. See also E. Mayo, *Human Problems of an Industrial Civilization*, 1933, p. 141.

12. "The City: Nostalgia, Illusion and Reality," in I. Howe and M. Harrington, eds., *The Seventies*, 1972, p. 432.

13. L. Wirth, "Urbanism as a Way of Life," *American Journal of Sociology* 44, no. 1 (1938): 1–24.

14. B. Rush, *Medical Inquiries and Observations upon the Diseases of the Mind* (1798), 1972.

15. N. Dain, *Concepts of Insanity in the United States: 1789–1865*, 1964, pp. 105–108.

16. Ibid., pp. 99–104.

17. W. S. Bernard, *American Immigration Policy: A Reappraisal*, 1950, pp. 23–24. Bernard notes that "the use of out-dated population statistics was the most flagrantly discriminatory device of any employed in quota calculation, and it made particularly obvious the motives which were behind the quota legislation."

18. For exploitation of a related form of institutional statistics, see K. Weis and M. E. Milakovich, "Political Misuses of Crime Rates," *Society* 11 (July–August 1974): 27–33.

19. H. Bolling, *House out of Order*, 1965.

20. National Center for Health Statistics, *Acute Conditions, July 1972–June 1973*, series 10, no. 98, (1974).

21. National Center for Health Statistics (NCHS), *Limitation of Activity and Mobility Due to Chronic Conditions 1972*, series 10, no. 96 (1974), p. 6. See also NCHS, *Rheumatoid Arthritis in Adults*, series 11, no. 17 (1966), table 7, p. 20, and NCHS, *Hypertension and Hypertensive Heart Disease in Adults*, series 11, no. 13 (1966), p. 17.

22. National Center for Health Statistics, *Height and Weight of Children*, series 11, no. 13 (1966), p. 17.

23. M. Lerner and D. W. Anderson, *Health Progress in the U.S.: 1900–1960*, 1963, pp. 105–106.

24. P. M. Insel and R. H. Moos, eds., *Health and the Social Environment*, 1974, p. 8.

25. L. Herber, *Crisis in Our Cities*, 1965, p. 140.

26. S. Arieti, ed., 1974, pp. 424–447. The authors generously made available a prepublication draft of their chapter.

For earlier summaries of the relevant literature see A. R. Mangus and John R. Seeley, *Mental Health and Mental Disorder*, 1955, pp. 209–214; Eleanor Leacock, "Three Social Variables and the Occurrence of Mental Disorder," in A. H. Leighton et al., eds., *Explorations in Social Psychiatry*, 1957, pp. 308–340; and S. C. Plog, "Urbanization and Psychological Disorders," in S. C. Plog and R. B. Edgerton, eds., *Changing Perspectives in Mental Illness*, 1969, pp. 288–311.

27. Diagnostic differences of this kind exist even between two psychiatric communities having so much in common, and so advanced, as London and New York. See J. E. Cooper et al., *Psychiatric Diagnosis in New York and London*, 1972. See also M. Kramer, "Cross-National Study of Diagnosis of the Mental Disorders," *American Journal of Psychiatry*, Supp. (April 1969): 1–11.

28. D. C. Leighton et al., *The Character of Danger*, 1963. See also A. H. Leighton, *My Name Is Legion*, 1959, and C. C. Hughes et al., *People of Cove and Woodlot: Communities from the Viewpoint of Social Psychiatry*, 1960.

29. Leighton was named director of the Midtown Study in 1956, when the latter's data gathering and mental health classification processes were both completed. He continued as director of the Stirling investigation.

30. D. C. Leighton, et al., *The Character of Danger*, p. 356.

31. Ibid.

32. Ibid., pp. 46–47.

33. In Rennie's clinical view, being in outpatient psychiatric treatment was by itself no necessary sign of "impairment in social functioning."

34. Ibid., p. 260.

35. For the Leightons' comparison of the Stirling and Midtown studies see their chapter "Mental Health and Social Factors" in A. M. Freedman and H. I. Kaplan, eds., *Comprehensive Textbook of Psychiatry*, 1967, pp. 1520–1525.

36. S. D. Webb and J. Collette, "Urban Ecological and Household Correlates of Stress-Alleviative Drug Use," *American Behaviorial Scientist* 18 (July 1975): 752–772.

37. Ibid., p. 755.

38. For a full critique see J. M. Henslin and J. C. Campbell, "Sociology and the Study of Suicide: Issues and Controversies," in P. M. Roman and H. M. Trice, eds., *Explorations in Psychiatric Sociology*, 1974, pp. 159–184.

39. M. J. Flax, *A Study in Comparative Urban Indicators*, 1972, p. 39.

40. For a fuller discussion of the shortcomings of police reporting of crimes, see Weis and Milakovich, "Political Misuses of Crime Rates," pp. 27–33.

41. Personal observations suggest that in the absence of competitive press, radio, and TV coverage of crimes, nonreporting of such events, both to and by the local police, is substantially greater in small places than in the metropolis.

42. *Social Indicators, 1973,* published by U.S. Department of Commerce, Social and Economic Statistics Administration, 1974, pp. 45, 55.

43. NIMH Research Report No. 5, "Teenage Delinquency in Small Town America, 1974," 1975, pp. 1–7. Also, M. E. Wolfgang, "Crimes in A Birth Cohort," *Proceedings of the American Philosophical Society* 117, no. 5 (1973): 404–411; F. L. Richmond, "Rural Delinquency and Maturational Reform: Extent and Character of Official Deviancy" (unpublished report of Marion County Youth Study, 1974).

44. Recent studies have shown that the high overall correlation between city size and (FBI-reported) rates of violent crime is almost entirely accounted for by intercity differences in such census-type indices as unemployment rate, racial composition, and proportion of families with female heads, all three closely associated with poverty. These findings suggest that high crime rates are not intrinsic to the city as such, but rather to the poverty that tends to be more densely concentrated within it.

45. According to NCHS latest age-adjusted figure (1970) the U.S. annual homicide rate of 7.6 per 100,000 population, while the largest in the world, is too small to significantly affect the findings of the LEAA surveys.

46. U.S. Department of Justice National Crime Panel Surveys, *Crime in the Nation's Five Largest Cities,* advance report, April 1974, and *Crime in Eight* [Other] *American Cities,* advance report, July 1974.

47. I would cite the following in particular: Page Smith, *As A City Upon A Hill: The Town in American History,* 1966; R. Blythe, *Akenfield: Portrait of an English Village,* 1969; E. Morin, *The Red and the White: Report from a French Village,* 1970; E. Rosskam, *Roosevelt, New Jersey: Big Dreams in a Small Town and What Time Did to Them,* 1972; and Raymond Williams, *The Country and the City,* 1973.

48. Lawrence Wylie in *Trans-Action,* May 1970, p. 59.

49. In B.J.L. Berry, *The Human Consequences of Urbanization,* 1973 (The Making of the Twentieth Century Series), the author identifies himself (pp. 32, 58) with the revisionist view of the city as formulated in an earlier version of the present chapter. Berry joins in a critique of the long tradition of unfavorable evaluations of the metropolis that preceded and followed the Park-Wirth-Chicago school of thought.

CHAPTER 21

SUMMING UP, 1975
LEO SROLE

Whatever their separate particularities of time, place, characters, and reporting styles, a novel like James Joyce's *Ulysses*, for example, and a research monograph like the present one, are each, in Émile Zola's phrase, "a study of humanity." Their overarching subject matter is accompanied by a common undergirding framework. To illustrate:

1. His *Ulysses*, Joyce indicates, is the odyssey of Stephen Dedalus, Leopold Bloom, and their familiars as they criss-cross each other's paths through the central sections of Dublin on one noteworthy but unsingular day of their lives. To be sure, the Midtown investigation randomly corralled a far larger company of characters; and what we learned emerged during our encounters as we joined each in his or her Manhattan home for several hours of one particular, seemingly commonplace day.

2. Joyce, like his contemporary, Sigmund Freud, plumbed each of his character's interior, meandering streams of affect-laden ruminations. Ours was a somewhat related two-pronged quest, that of the psychiatrist's diagnostic inquiry into manifestations of underlying emotional distress and that of the sociologist delineating the landscape contours of the respondent's past and present family and community environs.

3. Both sets of "explorers," to use the term Freud applied to himself, wrestled with problems of synthesis—to extract larger patterns of coherence and meaning in the volatile confluences at the junctures of their subjects' interior and exterior lives.

4. Joyce cast himself as his own protagonist in the character of Stephen Dedalus. Except for the preformulated stimuli-questions conveyed through our interviewers, the Midtown researchers were strictly sideline observers

of our sample respondents. In turnabout, however, one or another of us could well have written a "documentary" novel on the investigators working through a host of procedural issues and interdisciplinary strains as they confronted so many diverse kinds of subjects, on matters at once so intimate, so psychologically complex, and so broad in social scope.

5. Novelists and behavioral scientists are all dedicated to serving illuminating social purposes. But in the course of observation, synthesis, and report writing, both sets of professionals themselves undergo subtle and sometime significant changes. The observers in the end, like Joyce-Dedalus, are altered by immersion in their subjects as representatives of large classes of human beings. Certainly the present author can testify, at least for himself, to the following effect: When the 1962 edition of this volume was at last in hand, he recognized that his research experiences in Midtown had penetrated to deeper personal levels than the purely cognitive.

In the above senses, then, the two kinds of craftsmen tend to move through a parallel but largely tacit sequence of stages. I suggest, therefore, that this covert agenda would have been shared little differently had Joyce in his time happened to place his characters on the east bank of the Hudson River rather than on the River Liffey, and had we later chosen to conduct our study in Midtown Dublin instead of Midtown Manhattan.

This monograph has crowded a large canvas with the minutiae of many research concerns and findings. It is now time to step back from our pointillistic closeup of that canvas to highlight its major motifs in an equivalent of the short coda that closes a long and intricately woven musical composition.

Unlike most previous investigations of the same general kind,[1] this report, in data chapters 4 to 6, has sketched the huge amphitheater in which our studied subjects were engaged as natural actors. There they projected themselves both as individuals and as a social aggregate with multiple interlocking lines of collective identity.

New York is a leviathan among world cities, and Midtown is a large and integral segment of the photogenic island-hub of that metropolis. In synoptic form we delineated (1) the high-density, compact features of Midtown as a residential habitat; (2) the enormous diversity in the socioeconomic, cultural, and geographical origins of its all-white population; and (3) the great complexity in its network of institutions and in its psychosocial qualities as a community. Midtown, in these and other specific respects, was found at time of study to be a close counterpart of Manhattan's non–Puerto Rican, white population, numbering some 1,250,000 people, and to resemble high density, "gold-coast-and-slum" sections of others of our biggest cities.

Nor, Senator Goldwater to the contrary notwithstanding,[2] can the city in any way be perceived except as one of the most vital organs of the entire national body sociopolitic. On the contrary, emphasizes one novelist, "The island of Manhattan . . . touches all of us on the surface, but also lies at the buried, troubled questioning center of American life."[3]

TECHNICAL ACCOUNTABILITY

The scientist is required to be as forthright and critical in describing the working methods he has applied, and their limitations, as in reporting his findings. Scientists tend to be silent about the paths on the way to and from their final blueprint design and to make the final route look smoother and neater than was actually the case. False leads, miscalculations, obstructions, blind alleys, and other forms of waste motion are often unacknowledged, although inevitable to exploratory research in still partially dark areas. Moreover, even when tidied up and selectively telescoped, such brief working accounts are often relegated to the "back room" of the report's appendixes.

In this monograph, three early chapters (7 to 9) have devoted some sixty-five pages to setting out our technical problems, dilemmas, and reasons for our resolving decisions. We there emphasized limitations in our methods that we were aware of from the start, steps taken to counteract or at least estimate the effects of potential sources of error, oversights we discovered only in the rear-view mirror of hindsight, and the hedges we had to plant around the generalizations extractable from our findings.

Such accountings and caveats there, and in subsequent chapters, were intended to serve our readers further, so far as we could do so objectively, by making them parties to the role of "our own most persistent critics." That the original edition of this monograph has been assigned as a case study in graduate courses on research methodology suggests that perhaps our section "Strategy and Tactics" is serving as an example of technical openness and self-criticism.

One reviewer of the original edition seemed to support that inference: "The authors are at some pains—they seem almost obsessive compulsive—to examine the weaknesses and biases of their procedures honestly. Indeed, it may well be as a case study in self-conscious research methodology that this book will have its greatest value; the chapters on [research] design are as subtle in their self-questioning as the musings of a Dostoevsky character."[4]

We need only add here that the Midtown Study has been among the first investigations in its field to make the following combination of advances in operating methods:

1. A shift in focus from an inpatient aggregate to a large sample of a community's general population, although we also covered Midtown's inpatients and outpatients in our Treatment Census Operation.

2. In primary mode of data gathering, a change from census-type counts of institutional case records to multihour, face-to-face interviews with sampled subjects.

3. A shift from incidence to prevalence as the more defensible measure of frequencies of mental morbidity.

4. From reliance on psychiatry's embattled diagnostic categories of disorder, a turn toward classifying mental health on an innovative, inclusive gradient of degrees of symptom formation.

5. In breadth of statistical analysis, a shift from the traditional cross-tabulation of one or two potential predictors of mental health toward controlled analysis of up to five of such explanatory variables simultaneously.

MENTAL HEALTH IN THE MIDTOWN SAMPLE AS ENTITY

Skimming the top layer of the Home Interview findings, how did our sample of the Midtown population "shape up" on the Study psychiatrists' continuum of mental health differences? Compressed into a single sentence, the subclinical forms of symptom formation (the Mild and Moderate categories) constituted almost a 60 percent majority of the sample adults, and on either side of this modal group were the segment of Well individuals, approximating somewhat under

20 percent of the sample, and the morbidity segment of Impaired people, representing somewhat more than 20 percent of the sample. It was impossible, however, to judge the significance of this distribution except in the comparative perspective of findings from other relevant populations. Unfortunately, no other urban study known to us has tried to estimate the frequency of Wellness or of the subclinical forms of symptom formation, ruling out comparative analysis on these levels. However, several investigations have reported on the overall (i.e., untreated and treated) frequency of mental disorder, and these offer at least the potential for comparison with the Midtown morbidity findings.

Such comparison was especially indicated, given that previous studies of patients, i.e., treated morbidity only, could seem to imply that the Midtown overall morbidity rate was inordinately high. If so, one ready interpretation might be that the assessment "screen" applied by the Midtown psychiatrists to identify the Impaired individuals had been unduly coarse.

Seeming to support this view were previous investigations of the overall prevalence of mental disorder in rather less than representative samples of Baltimore and Boston. Both of these studies reported overall morbidity frequencies of about 11 percent, representing half the Midtown sample's Impaired rate of 23.4 percent. Suffice it to recall that when known gross errors in underreporting mental disorder cases were corrected, and differences in population composition had been adjusted, the Baltimore and Boston frequencies were shown to approximate the Midtown sample's rate.

However, if these corrected rates from Baltimore and Boston did not stand as a challenge to the credibility of Midtown's estimated impairment frequency, neither could they be read by themselves as lending support to the plausibility of the Midtown estimate. All in all, the Midtown sample's roughly 2:6:2 distribution among the Well, the subclinical, and the Impaired bands of the mental health spectrum had to be tentatively considered specific to *this* sample population, as screened through the particular methods, data, and psychiatric judgments brought to bear in this investigation. It must be added, however, that in the years since publication of this monograph's original edition, the consensual tendency in the psychiatric literature has been to regard the Midtown sample's Impaired rate, given our criteria of impairment, as a scientifically credible estimate.

MENTAL HEALTH IN MIDTOWN'S COMPONENT GROUPS

To the present researchers, the Home Interview Survey "held out the ultimate hope of uncovering clues to the differential quality of various group environments" (p. 10). For this purpose we systematically combed through an array of constituent groups within the Midtown Home Interview sample, including the following classes of groups:

Age levels—four (20–29, 30–39, 40–49, 50–59)
Genders—two
Marital statuses—four (never married, married, separated-divorced, widowed)
SES-origin strata (i.e., SES of respondent's childhood family)—six
Own-SES strata in 1954—six
Own-SES mobility types—three (upward, downward, stable)
Generation-in-U.S. aggregates—four (immigrants, children of immigrants, grandchildren, and great-grandchildren)
National-origin groups—eight
Religious-origin communities—three
Degree-of-religiosity subgroups within each religious community—three

In searching through these ten categories and their forty-three component segments, the test yardstick we applied to all was of course the compositional distribution of each group segment on the psychiatrists' mental health gradient scale—in particular, intergroup differences in relative number of Impaired per 100 Well.

The most clear-cut and pervasive finding raked out from this meticulous search was this: Respondent SES-origin and current age level share almost equally strong input relationships, independent of each other, to adult mental health make-up. Specifically, age 20 to 29 and high SES-origin respondents were most heavily loaded with the Well, whereas the age 50 to 59 and the low SES-origin respondents, especially those from poverty-level childhoods, were most heavily weighted with the Impaired.

Interestingly, the powerful trinity of age, SES, and mental health composition came through in consistent fashion when we pieced together four independent sources of age-fragmented evidence. One was based upon psychiatric observation of the national college population universe (age 18 to 22). The second emerged from a large sample of American enlisted men in the age range 18 to 37. The third derived from an investigation of "senior citizens" (over 64) in an upstate New York city. And the most recent is reported from a large national cross-section sample in which frequency of "nervous breakdown" varied simultaneously with both age and years of schooling (an SES indicator). In effect, therefore, the Midtown Home Interview sample, together with these four highly contrasting sources of evidence, suggests that the triadic constellation of SES origin, age, and adult mental health may well be a generalized phenomenon in the national population at large.

At first scan, similar links to mental health also appeared within the Midtown generation-in-U.S., national-origin, and religious-origin categories. But these relationships, with two exceptions, largely "washed out" when intergroup comparisons were made with the effects of age and SES origin analytically controlled. The two exceptions were (1) respondents from Jewish families whose impairment rate was somewhat below those of like age-and-SES non-Jews, and (2) immigrants from impoverished, rural places abroad, whose Impaired-Well ratio was the highest of any group or subgroup of like age in the entire Midtown sample.

Stated differently, within the age 20 to 59 Midtown sample's population universe there appear to have been two relatively eugenic group settings during childhood, namely, families in the upper third of the SES-origin spectrum and Jewish families across the rest of the SES range, and one setting during "prime of life" adulthood, i.e., the age 20 to 29 decade of that forty-year expanse of the life cycle. On the other hand, the most pathogenic group environments in childhood seem to have been families in the lower third of the SES-origin range, especially those in the lowest sixth of that range, and above all those originating in poverty-stricken rural areas overseas, with the single most pathogenic group during the "prime of life" years appearing to be those in the last decade of that span (i.e., age 50 to 59).

THE STUDY'S MASTER HYPOTHESIS

From this capsule overview, we might now reexamine the following statement on page 119:

The Midtown Study phrases the following general proposition as its most fundamental postulate: Sociocultural conditions, in both their normative and their deviant forms, operating in intrafamily and extrafamily settings during childhood and adulthood, have measurable consequences reflected in the mental health differences to be observed within a population.

This hypothesis, in far simpler form, dates to at least the end of the eighteenth century, but then and since the postulate has largely been restricted to contextual conditions operative during *adulthood*. Our findings on Midtown's four adult age levels seem to be consistent with the proposition so delimited.

However, our hypothesis was broadened to also include sociocultural influences on adults that had operated decades before, during their formative *childhood* years. This early life-history emphasis of the postulate was tested, perhaps for the first time in a general population, within the Midtown sample and, as already noted, was confirmed in our mental health findings on respondents' SES origin, overseas-rural provenience, and religious origin. No subsequent study known to us has attempted to replicate coverage of the latter two childhood factors.

POST HOC HYPOTHESES

Mechanisms that might partially explain these empirical results have been suggested in the appropriate data chapters above. Hypothesized on the pathogenic side were the following three overlapping, but not coterminous, sets of social processes:

1. The multiple, interwoven deprivations imposed on children of indigent parents. In the past decade notable investigations pointed on this front have been reported by a number of social scientists.[5]

2. The stigmatize-rejection mechanisms rooted in the evaluative apparatus of the society's prestige rewarding and penalizing system. From childhood onward, these have been directed in most extreme forms at blacks, but they comprise a pathogenic pattern that cuts across all color lines and there ensnares and demeans the poor, the disabled, the aged, and other nonmainstream categories. Recent work has appropriately focused upon the "self-esteem" consequences of such systemic tendencies for their outcaste objects.[6]

3. Role-transitions and their potentially jolting impact on vulnerable

personalities among children as well as adults. These transit points have been incorporated into the focus of a fast growing literature on "life events" as potential psychological stressors.[7]

All three processes stand arraigned as social system dysfunctions, exacting a huge human toll and economic price, and calling for societal self-correctives, such as are discussed in the closing chapter.

DISCLAIMERS AND CLAIMERS

To be emphasized here are the following further observations. Nowhere in this monograph have the Study's social scientists regarded the above three noxious intrusions into the individual life stream of millions of people as precluding the simultaneous operation of pathogenic somatic factors, either as primary or secondary contributions to the emergence of mental disorder. No less emphatically, these intrusions are far from encompassing the entire universe of exogenous sociocultural factors that can be implicated as potentially damaging for the personality development of the child. Nevertheless, they represent discernible orders of social experience that together may account for a substantial portion of dysfunctional inputs into family units. There they can strain or dislocate the intricate balancing mechanisms of parents—strain that can ultimately yield mental disturbance in their children. Underlying this observation is our basic formulation that mental morbidity is in part immediate manifestation of an impaired ego, damaged by an earlier malfunctioning intrafamily structure that, in turn, had been rendered defective, at least partially, by disruptive intrusions from or defaults by mainstream community and national social networks.

"This may be," to quote the poet, "the unkindest cut of all."

REVIEW ON MENTAL HEALTH SERVICES

Chapters 10 to 19 above included Study information secured both from our Home Interview and Treatment Census[8] operations on delivery of mental health services to Midtown's residents.

Having uncovered a frequency of mental impairment far beyond that estimated by earlier investigations, the above-mentioned Midtown information exposed (1) the enormous disparity between this previously unmeasured reservoir of need for therapeutic help and the gross quantitative inadequacy of the services available, and (2) the discriminatory dimensions of that disparity. In brief, we emphasized, "those *most* in need of such services had by far the *least* access to them."

It is now appropriate to ask: What has since happened on this front? In the years just before the Midtown Study was launched, an estimated annual total of one million Americans had one or more contacts (as a patient) with a mental health professional in a hospital, clinic, or office. A decade later the number had doubled, by 1970 it had doubled again, and by 1975 it probably reached a total of five million. This represents a jump in a quarter century from 0.7 percent to 2.4 percent of the national population, largely made possible by NIMH-supported tripling in the number of practicing psychiatrists and allied professionals per 100,000 people.

With the advent of psychotropic drugs in the mid-fifties, followed by the establishment of community mental health centers in the decade since 1965, came large-scale shifts in the sites of treatment. In 1955 about 77 percent of what the NIMH Biometrics Division calls "patient care episodes" were attended in mental hospitals, predominantly state supported. By 1975 that figure had fallen to about 40 percent, with over half of these now treated by the psychiatric inpatient services of local general hospitals.

In the latter year, new, tax-supported, community mental health centers probably accounted for over 20 percent of all patient care episodes, with the remaining 40 percent treated principally by the enlarged cadre of office therapists and to a relatively small extent by privately supported outpatient clinics.

The simultaneous expansion of the system, and large-scale shift of primary treatment sites from distant state institutions to accessible local facilities, for the first time brought such services close to home for millions. These developments were made possible by the combined backing of the electorate, their congressional representatives, leaders of the mental health professions, and federal, state and community authorities and agencies.

According to NIMH directors previously cited, researches of the early 1950's, including the Midtown Study, provided evidence that helped to spark, support, and accelerate these unprecedented developments. Melvin Sabshin, Medical Director of the American Psychiatric Association, addressing the APA's 1975 Institute on Hospital and Community Psychiatry, made the following further observations relevant here: "The need to rectify imbalances in this country's mental health delivery system provided the moral fuel and force for the community mental health legislation of the 1960's. These imbalances . . . discriminated against the poor, the old, the very young . . . ,"[9] and, the Midtown Study had added, the foreign-born.

The huge and rapid transformations mentioned did not happen without adaptational strains, resistances, and slippages. These are still rife in 1975 and may be further exacerbated if federal funding in the years immediately ahead continues to drop below the level legislatively set as national goals in the late 1960's.

On a closing note about community mental health as a social movement, Sabshin concluded that it "has a history now, rather than being a hope, a prayer, and a vague plan, as it was in 1963."

It was the Midtown Study's unanticipated privilege to have contributed to that history and, hopefully, to continue that role in the future.

NOTES

1. An outstanding exception in this genre is C. C. Hughes et al., *People of Cove and Woodlot: Communities from the Viewpoint of Social Psychiatry*, 1960, volume 2 in the Stirling County Study series of monographs.

2. The Senator from the last continental state to join the Union, a state harboring a population less than one-fourth of New York City's, has offered the Procrustean proposal that this metropolis in its entirety "should be sawed off the continent and set adrift in the Atlantic."

3. H. Gold, *Salt*, 1963.

4. E. Z. Friedenberg, *Commentary*, December 1962, pp. 545–547.

5. See in particular: J. G. Eisenberg, T. S. Langner, and J. C. Gersten, "Differences in the Behavior of Welfare and Non-Welfare Children in Relation to Parental Characteristics," *Journal of Community Psychology* 3 (October 1975): 311–340; V. L. Allen, ed., *Psychological Factors in Poverty*, 1970; R. Sennett and J. Cobb, *The Hidden Injuries of Class*, 1972.

6. S. Coopersmith, *The Antecedents of Self-Esteem*, 1967.

7. One of the early delineations of this focus was offered by J. S. Tyhurst, "The Role of Transition States—Including Disasters—in Mental Illness," in *Symposium on Preventive and Social Psychiatry*, Walter Reed Army Institute of Research, 1958, pp. 149–172.

For one of a number of recent investigations in this area see G. W. Brown, et al., "Life Events and Psychiatric Disorders: Nature of Causal Links," *Psychological Medicine* 3, no. 2 (1973): 159–176.

8. For our critique of previous patient enumeration investigations based on the Midtown Study's Treatment Census operation results, see Appendix G.

9. M. Sabshin, quoted in *Psychiatric News*, November 19, 1975.

CHAPTER 22

PSYCHIATRIST'S COMMENTARY

STANLEY T. MICHAEL

This monograph was written by sociologists and is based on sociological data gathered in a random sample of the community. But it is a sociological study with medical orientation. The central reference point is an estimate of mental health; its central theme the etiology of mental illness; its programmatic concern the amount, quality, and adequacy of psychiatric treatment. Although conducted by psychiatrists and clinically oriented sociologists, the Study was not clinical. Subjects were not seen by trained medical personnel, nor were medical and laboratory examinations performed in a clinical setting. Nevertheless, the fundamental orientation toward psychiatric problems has resulted in a significant contribution to the psychiatrist who, bearing down on the individual case, may formulate only a general impression of the total social and epidemiological setting of his patient.

Not infrequently, the clinician recognizes psychopathology in relatives and other significant persons related to his patient. He may not know the extent of the psychopathology, but he is aware that most of these persons have never had psychiatric care. How severe is this unknown psychopathology? What behavior is the psychiatrist to expect from these other untreated significant persons in relation to his patient? Can he treat his patient as though everyone else around him were mentally well? The clinician has to formulate pragmatic answers to these questions. He will have to continue to meet the impact of the environment on the psychopathology of his patient. In this respect the findings of the Midtown Study can be of significant assistance by providing information not only on the prevalence of psychopathology in the community as representing his patient's broader environment, but also by estimating the frequencies of psychopathology in specific demographic situations and circumstances.

The design of the study provided for simultaneous estimates of treated and untreated psychopathology as well as the enumeration of known patients in psychiatric treatment. The information was gained from two sources: the respondent himself and the treatment facilities —hospitals, outpatient clinics, psychiatrists in private practice and psychologists. Through this integrated approach, information about prevalence of clinical morbidity, previously available only from clinical studies, assumed a new dimension in its relatedness to the total psychopathology· in the community. Not only are we beginning to recognize the distribution of treated and untreated psychopathology, but also the various conditions which were previously only vaguely implied or suspected of being related to psychopathology and treatment are becoming more clearly understood. Reference is here made particularly to the relationship between socioeconomic status and the prevalence of psychopathology and its treatment. The relatedness of attitudes toward psychotherapy and such sociocultural factors as socioeconomic status, religion, or generation-in-U.S. is an enlightening contribution.

The concept of sociogenesis of mental illness deserves special comment. In the discussion of the conceptual design of the Study in chapter 7, it was suggested that mental illness is multidetermined; however, since such factors as constitutional predisposition, biological determination, and psychogenesis are not fully understood in their theoretical preconceptions, nor accessible as data pertinent to this particular study, it was decided to report and analyze only sociogenic factors. There is no intention to disavow or conceal the etiological importance of the non-sociogenic factors, but the influence of these would remain largely undetermined and open to speculation. As a consequence of the decision to cover only the sociogenic factors, the reader who is not mindful of the formulation and design of the report may be impressed with a sense of sociogenic overdeterminism. This impression is further strengthened by the fact that the manuscript was written by sociologists whose orientation pervasively influenced the terminology and structural composition of the language of the book. The selection and formulation of concepts to be analyzed, the data suitable for such analysis, the framework of presentation, the arguments relevant to the claims, the supporting data in the tables, the new hypotheses extracted, and the form and outline of the book were all contributed by the sociologists.

The proposition presented in chapter 7 that sociocultural conditions may "have measurable consequences" for mental health is a plausible hypothesis and worthy of testing. The method of choice for this investigation consisted of description and enumeration of demographic variables which carried an etiological potential relative to mental health. In the conceptual formulation, the mental health of the respondent (as represented by the psychiatrists' ratings) was considered the outcome and therefore was made the dependent variable. Conditions prevailing earlier in the life history were assumed to possess a potential for influencing adult mental health.

The caution and reservations necessary in the interpretation of pathogenic potential in a matter as complex as the etiology of mental illness impose severe limitations on generalizations from the findings, especially if these should be interpreted as constituting the total information. The pitfalls involved in statistical correlation of two or several biological variables are numerous not only because of the nature of the biological phenomena themselves, which in their complexity pose formidable sampling impediments, but also because of the multiplicity of interpretations of the implied associations, which may be spurious even when statistical validity is beyond question.

The partial applicability and incompleteness of the sociogenic hypothesis may be best demonstrated by analysis of an example. It has been shown in chapter 14 that parental socioeconomic status as an antecedent factor is related to the mental health of the offspring, the best mental health occurring in respondents whose parents were in the high SES groups, and relatively unsatisfactory mental health in respondents whose parents were of low SES. The inference is presented that "these differences [in mental health] were predominantly implanted during the preadult stage of dependency upon parents." If one chooses to be oblivious of constitutional factors, this hypothesis might be acceptable, cautiously as it is worded. However, there are other possible interpretations:

1. The parents of the upper-SES groups had good mental health, which was passed down to their children—our respondents—by inheritance of a

constitution promotive of good mental health. In contrast, the parents of low SES had poor mental health, which was passed on to their descendants through hereditary predisposition to poor mental health. Such a hypothesis, not proved, nor necessarily exclusive of other factors, offers a satisfactory interpretation of the data based completely on constitutional heredity.

2. A second hypothesis, sociogenic in nature, might be derived from a biological hypothesis that living organisms tend to return to homeostasis and from deviation and pathology toward normal physiology. It is not the parents' low SES which is pathogenic in the direction of poor mental health; rather, respondents are born in all SES groups with equal potential for good or poor mental health, but the conditions in the families of high SES tend to favor the evolution of the positive potential in the offspring, which in the families of low SES remains unexploited.

3. The statistical correlation may be interpreted by still another hypothesis, as may be inferred from the data regarding social mobility and mental health (chapter 14, pages 285 ff.). It would seem from the data presented that respondents who are upward-mobile in SES have better mental health than respondents who are downward-mobile. Mental health, as represented by the Impaired-Well ratios of the various socioeconomic groups, has a greater direct correlation with the respondents' own SES as compared with the SES of the respondents' fathers. This may be demonstrated by the steepness of the regression curve of the Impaired-Well ratios correlated with the respondents' own SES, which is greater than the curve of the Impaired-Well ratios related to parental SES (Figure 14–4). These two observations would seem to suggest the possibility that a respondent's mental health determines his SES. In other words, and in the terminology used in the design of the investigation, the SES of the respondent becomes the dependent variable and a consequence of the respondent's own mental health, which thus becomes the antecedent variable. The same would apply to the respondent's parents, resulting in the observed correlation between parental SES and respondent's mental health.

4. The statistical correlation between parental SES and the mental health of respondents could be interpreted also as contingent upon the fact that respondents' SES and parental SES are highly intercorrelated. Given that respondents' mental health is closely related to own SES as a primary phenomenon, then parental SES may be tied to the former by its own relatedness to respondents' current socioeconomic status.

It is not intended here to estimate the extent to which each one of these hypothetical factors contributed to the relatedness of SES and mental health, nor is it possible from the available data. However, accepting the premise established in chapter 8 that this report will be confined solely to the sociogenic findings, we must never lose sight of the ever-present alternative interpretations which, even though indeterminate and unknown, may be potential modifiers of the sociogenic impact.

The association of increasing severity of mental symptomatology with increasing age of the respondents is a finding which must also be hedged with numerous qualifying, cautionary, and conditional statements. The age of the respondent was known to the rating psychiatrist. It would have been very difficult, indeed frequently impossible, to gauge the significance of certain symptoms without the knowledge of the age milieu in which the symptoms operated. The age factor was taken into account and was represented in the psychiatrists' rating judgments. If on statistical count the symptoms of the older respondents still averaged to be more severe and more incapacitating, it can be inferred that on the basis of symptoms alone, without knowledge of the age of the respondents, the mental health ratings of the older respondents would have been even worse, as the respondents would not have been credited with the compensations with which they countered the insidious decline in health due to aging.

The possibility must not be overlooked that the symptomatology on which the mental health rating was based was not necessarily of the same quality in the various age groups. Part of the matrix which formed the basis of the rating scale consisted of psychosomatic symptoms and illnesses. By definition, psychosomatic conditions were rated as moderate symptoms and were not considered adequate to elevate the rating beyond the designation "moderate symptom formation," even though the psychosomatic illness might be in a terminal phase as, for example, hypertension complicated by cerebrovascular disease and hemiplegia, conditions which certainly interfere with life adjustment. However, the presence of a psychosomatic condition did not preclude a more severe rating if other symptom complexes so indicated.

In early adulthood, psychosomatic conditions are not necessarily taken seriously. In contrast, the impact of recurring incidence with age, the unrelenting progress of relapse and remission, the chronic and increasing residues after each attack, as for instance in arthritis, impresses on the older respondents the extent of their incapacity, which in turn is more readily reported to the interviewer as age increases.

Psychosomatic symptoms increase with advancing age and no

doubt contributed substantially to the more severe average mental health ratings in the groups of more advanced age. The prevalence of respondents whose psychosomatic symptoms were considered to be primary contributors to the mental health rating, outbalancing all other symptoms, and who were consequently designated as psychosomatic types was 5.2 percent in the age group 20 to 29, 11.8 percent at 30 to 39, 11.6 percent at 40 to 49, and 17.9 percent at 50 to 59. While undoubtedly change in role function, especially that of a parent respondent in relation to growth of children and their departure from the home, may contribute to conflict and stress and to the development of psychopathology in the older age groups, decline in biological vitality ,with concomitant loss of ability to cope with adversities, increasing physical debility, and illness cannot be disregarded as significant determinants of the increase in mental symptomatology observed in the respondents of advancing age.

There is, in addition, the question of differentiation of the types of psychiatric symptoms according to age level. Is there a difference in the quality of symptoms in respondents of the youngest age group as compared with those of the oldest? Reports attesting to a high incidence of neurotic symptoms in the twenties with steeply falling curves in the next decade[1,2] raise the question whether the greater morbidity of the older age groups may not be based on symptoms of a more severe quality, perhaps even psychotic, in addition to the already mentioned psychosomatic symptoms. The problem of the quality of symptoms as related to age raises a challenging issue for future research.

The higher incidence of psychosomatic conditions in the older age groups of the community sample leads yet to additional speculations in relation to psychiatric therapy. The more advanced medical clinics accept psychotherapy as the treatment of choice in psychosomatic conditions. However, the populace in general is more likely to consider its psychosomatic conditions physical and seek treatment with a general practitioner or a specialist in internal medicine. Indeed it has been estimated that 30 to 60 percent of patients seeking medical help for presumed medical conditions[3] are essentially afflicted with psychosomatic or psychoneurotic illness and consequently should receive psychiatric treatment. If the proportions of our respondents who had psychosomatic conditions increased with age, is it not possible that these respondents are receiving therapy for their psychosomatic conditions from general practitioners and other medical specialists? If so, our statistical evaluation, which indicates that respondents of the older age group are receiving less psychiatric therapy in relation to their need than are respondents of the younger age groups, may have to be reevaluated by further investigation. These respondents may be in a therapeutic relationship which, though ostensibly consisting of medicinal and physical therapy, is basically psychotherapy in disguise in the form of relationship therapy, directive encouragement, and supportive therapy. The presence and importance of such nonspecific, auxiliary psychiatric therapy must not be underestimated, even though from the viewpoint of the psychiatrist such treatment may be deemed inadequate because of its inability to provide understanding of the psychodynamic causes of the illness.

There are still other considerations which may contribute to the interpretation of the abrupt decline in rate of outpatient therapy in the older age groups of our respondent population. As has been cited,[4] the national annual frequency of chronic somatic disorder increased from 9.4 percent of the age 20 to 24 population to 31.1 percent of the age 55 to 64 population. The rate of somatic illness increases threefold from young adulthood to late middle age. Not only does frequency of illness increase with age, but so does the severity of incapacity resulting from such somatic illness. In youth somatic illness is not the rule and is not usually anticipated as a source of interference in life adjustment. It is also overcome with reasonably assured expectancy of early recovery because of the relatively vigorous physiological defense forces of the young patient. In contrast, with advancing age somatic illnesses, especially those with a chronic and recurring course, become increasingly important as a factor around which the patient must modify his life. Indeed, lapses in conformity in social behavior which would be ill tolerated in young adults are readily excused in the aged if attributable to somatic illness. Both the patient and society are apt to seize on somatic disability for explanation of social malfunction rather than dwell on psychoneurotic interpretations. Since the emphasis shifts with age to somatic disability, which in its own right is increasingly more threatening to social and even physical survival, it is likely that the resources, time, and effort of the patient will be preferably oriented toward somatic therapy rather than psychotherapy.

The data presented in this volume seem to be unequivocal in their indication that certain demographically defined groups of the population are influenced for or against psychotherapy by sociocultural factors. Age is essentially a somatic factor grossly related to somatic development and illness. But in our study it is also a sociocultural factor, especially in relation to psychiatric therapy, as the era of psychotherapy is relatively recent, and the older age groups have not been exposed to its impact at a time when their emotional pliability might have allowed for its acceptance. It would seem that with the sociocultural influences established as factors affecting the quest for psychotherapy in the various age groups, the next step for investigation is the unraveling of the complex relationships between age, sociocultural factors, and somatic illness—all these bearing on psychiatric symptoms and their treatment by psychotherapy.

The uncovering of mental and emotional symptoms in four-fifths of the sample representing an urban population suggests that either a degree of psychopathology is the norm in the statistical sense of population average or that mental mechanisms which by psychodynamic derivation can be considered pathological may be a mode of normal adjustment.

The individuals in the Impaired category of mental health, derived from the original psychiatric ratings containing the suffix "with interference in life adjustment," are represented as being analogous to patients in psychiatric therapy. Such a designation clearly demonstrates the difficulty in dissociating the hitherto clinical approach to mental health from concepts necessary or desirable for the estimate of mental health in a nonpatient community population. When it is urged that the mental ratings "Marked" and "Severe" are comparable to the clinical conditions of patients in ambulatory treatment, and the rating "Incapacitated" to the clinically hospitalized, the distinction is presented only as an attempt to anchor our conceptualizations in relation to known degrees of psychopathology.

If the degree of severity of psychopathology in the above ratings of the community sample is comparable to that of patients, what are the factors which sustain these respondents in the community and prevent them from succumbing to the load of symptoms which drives their peers into ambulatory treatment or a hospital? Do the symptoms of these untreated respondents have an unusual protective quality? Do these respondents have compensatory devices which counteract the pressures of the symptoms? Are they equipped with special, socially motivated assets or symptoms which prevent them from seeking therapy? A well-organized defense mechanism, a systematized paranoid state, or a devotion to a system of physical culture or to a religious healing cult may possibly be sustaining individuals with large loads of psychopathology in the community. On the other hand, passive-dependent tendencies; depressive, hypochondriacal, or hysterical symptoms; or introspective rumination may incline others to collapse of defense and to the seeking of therapy. The number of symptoms or their severity may provide an indication of severity of psychopathology, but the degree of interference in life adjustment or the appearance as a patient for psychotherapy is determined also by a socially directed quality of the symptoms in both their positive and their negative senses.

The proposition that those in the Impaired mental health category are in risk of needing help evolved during the analysis of the data. It was not one of the criteria in the original rating process—indeed no estimate was made of the need for therapy of the respondent during the rating process. It may not have been possible to estimate the need for therapy from the data available to the rating psychiatrist, but this investigation does indicate that it is desirable that any future study of psychopathology in an untreated community population be designed to provide more definite answers on the need for therapy, the desirability of therapy, and its acceptability to the respondent.

The data and interpretations reported here are committed in the direction of revelation of etiological relationships between selected demographic variables and mental pathology. As the data evolved, we learned too that certain demographic variables influenced attitudes of the respondents toward psychiatry and psychotherapy. Undoubtedly psychopathology and demographic variables also influence the respondents' attitudes which are related not to psychiatry directly, but rather to all social interactions and ultimately to the structure of the social order itself.

Psychopathology is destructive to the individual and may interfere in his enjoyment of life. Psychopathology of the individual may also interfere in the lives of others. In order to understand and cope with these noxious forces with adequacy and appropriateness, we must know more about them. This volume is intended as a contribution toward that needed understanding. The data presented provide new knowledge and a springboard for future research in social psychiatry, and hopefully will lead to the redefinition of some of our psychiatric concepts and insights.

NOTES

1. M. Shepherd, "The Epidemiology of Neurosis," *International Journal of Social Psychiatry* 5, no. 4 (1960): 276.

2. M. Shepherd and E. M. Gruenberg, "The Age of Neuroses," *Milbank Memorial Fund Quarterly* 35, no. 3 (1957): 258.

3. R. Kaufman et al., "Psychiatric Findings in Admissions to a Medical Service in a General Hospital," *Journal of Mt. Sinai Hospital* 26, no. 2 (March–April 1959): 160–170.

4. S. D. Collins, K. S. Trantham, and J. L. Lehmann, *Sickness Experience in Selected Areas of the U.S.*, Public Health Monograph, 1955, pp. 8–21.

CHAPTER 23

SOCIOLOGIST'S PERSPECTIVES: PAST AND FUTURE, 1975

LEO SROLE

Further important social implications in the Midtown findings emerge when they are placed in historical perspective.

W. H. Auden, in a work of poetry, indelibly stamped the twentieth century above all its predecessors as "The Age of Anxiety," an imputation that has found few challengers even in the ranks of psychiatry. That historical tag is actually a contemporary version of the older notion that the Industrial Revolution and its corollaries were responsible for a continuing deterioration in general mental health from a presumed high level in the presumably carefree pre-industrial period.[1] On the American scene, the seeming increase of state mental hospital patients after the industrial quickening of the mid-nineteenth century was widely regarded as supporting that nostalgic view of the period preceding.

The most sophisticated research to challenge the reality of a temporal trend surmised from raw totals of mental hospital patients is that of sociologists Goldhamer and Marshal, in a study conducted several decades ago.[2] Using first admissions of psychotics to Massachusetts hospitals, and applying age-specific rates, the investigators found no increase between 1840 and 1940 in these frequencies among those below the age of 50. In other words, for the largest category of hospitalized disorders by far there was a flat (i.e., unchanging), rather than an upward, trend of rates within the 90 percent of the population who, through most of the century covered, were under age 50.

This report did discernibly little to diminish acceptance of the long-standing axiom about the historical increase in the frequency of mental disorder. However, the Massachusetts hospital patient finding, for reasons already demonstrated above, itself lacks credibility as an indicator of the trend in overall frequencies of emotional disability within the population at large.

For trend discernment purposes, a time series of studies of such populations is needed. Unfortunately, investigations of this kind have been few in number, technically diverse, and, even if they had been comparable, they were conducted over too short a period to permit sighting of longer range trends. Yet authoritative calls for such information continue to be made. For example, the Director of the National Institute of Mental Health has recently observed that the effects of NIMH programs since the agency's establishment in 1948 "could be best assessed if we could state clearly whether there is [now] more or less mental disorder in the population [than in 1948]."[3]

A point of departure toward responding to such questions may be found by taking another look at our own Midtown respondents. This monograph, in chapters 14 and 15, has documented that parents' SES during one's childhood has pronounced consequences for mental health. If that is a firm fact, as other investigations have since confirmed, then we may have the basis for a retrospective extrapolation of the direction of previous changes in general mental health. To be specific: the latter is the "unknown" in an algebra-like equation for which we have "known" trends of two other related kinds, documented on a national basis in government reports of the past 35 to 45 years.

The first "known" is the historical trend in the economic and other components of socioeconomic status. The second "known" is the direction of long-term changes in the physical health of the American people.

If we demonstrate in the following pages that socioeconomic and physical health trends are concordantly linked, and if we accept the view that a population's mental health tends to be interwoven with its somatic health, then the temporal trend in our unknown could reasonably be extrapolated from the direction of like changes in the two "knowns."

To restate the equation in statistical terms: If three variables are correlated with one another at a given point of time, and the previous known historical trends of two of these are found to be parallel, then the undocumented course over time of the third variable can be plausibly extracted from the similar trends of the other two variables.

The *overall* expansive direction of America's recent economic evolution has been personally observed by every perceptive adult. But the longer sweep of that movement may not have been generally or accurately appreciated. In the following capsule review I am necessarily dependent upon such details as are reported in available government and other publications, often in less comprehensive coverage than the reader and I would have preferred.

In the national economic domain let us start, by way of accessible illustration, with the average annual salary paid full-time, mainly skilled, employees in the bellwether durable-goods manufacturing industry. In inflation-free, constant (1973) dollars such wages ascended from $1,600 in the pre–World War II year of 1940 to over $10,000 in 1973.[4] Supplemented in recent decades by working wives, the gross *real* income of such families has multiplied by about seven times. Looking at family income in the *entire* labor force, excluding the substantial boost in fringe benefits, and subtracting the growing take of taxes (partially flowing back in expanded public services and subsequent income supplementing payments), the remainder can be translated into "disposable income per capita." In the same constant dollars, such work-generated income climbed from $2,000 per *man, woman, and child* in 1940 to about $4,800 in 1973, a total jump of 140 percent, or an average annual increase in spendable money of 4.1 percent. At the same time, the hours of work needed to pay for standard items of consumer goods and services fell between 1939 and 1973 by about 50 percent.

Accompanying these strides has been the secular contraction in the proportion of American families with incomes "below the minimum adequacy level," as defined in constant dollars by the Social Security Administration.[5] From 45 percent in 1935, this figure fell to 28 percent in 1950, to 15.6 percent in 1965, and to an estimated 12.7 percent in the economic recession year of 1975.

The cumulative gains in real income in part reflect shifts within the occupational hierarchy. Large-scale unionization of blue-collar industries in the 1930's and 1940's carried their skilled and semi-skilled workers' wage levels up to (or above) those of lower-white-collar families. Moreover, there have been broad shifts in the proportion of the labor force (1) holding white-collar jobs, up from 31 percent in 1940 to 50 percent in 1975, and (2) doing unskilled work, down from 40 percent to 22 percent in the same period.

One effect of the wide gains in buying power on the standard of living can be read on a crude but representative gauge like stability and quality of housing. The heavy investment in home ownership rose between 1940 and 1973 from 43 percent of all families to 65 percent. And in the same period the proportion of households living in qualitatively substandard units fell from about 49 percent to 7 percent.

Another large part of the increase in family discretionary spending has been salted into additional increments of children's education. The climb between 1940 and 1973 in years of schooling completed has been steep. For example, the proportion of persons 20 to 24 years old who had graduated from high school almost doubled from 44 percent to 84 percent. Similarly, the proportion of persons 25 to 29 years old with college degrees more than tripled in the same period, going from about 6 percent to almost 20 percent.[6]

The above advances were of course already under way, if at a lesser annual momentum, in the first three decades of the century.[7] Thus the overall effects of such long-term socioeconomic strides in education, occupation, working conditions, and disposable income on the standard and quality of family living have been predictably profound.

To sight one such effect, let us turn to our second "known," namely the domain of physical health, where available data in some instances go back to 1900. The best known yardstick here is of course average life expectancy at birth. In 1900 it was 46 years for males and 48 for females; by 1974 the corresponding figures were 68 and 76, a phenomenal jump of 22 years and 28 years respectively.

Part of these gains are explained by a drop in the infant mortality rate during the same period from 140 (per 1,000 live births) to 19. (In 1870 it had been 300.) But the increments in lives saved continued far beyond the first twelve months after birth. For example, we might look at the average years of life remaining to those who have achieved age 30. In 1900 their further life expectation if male was 33, if female 35. By 1971 the corresponding figures were 40 and 47, respectively, an average life-extending dividend for men of seven extra years over their own grandfathers' expectancy at age 30, and for women of twelve years over their own grandmothers' at similar age!

These increases in years of expected life of course reflect drops in a number of major disease-specific death rates. For example, the TB death rate fell from 46 per 100,000 population in 1900 to 1 in 1973. Especially noteworthy is that most of this drop came well before the initial large scale use of anti-TB drugs, when the annual rate had already descended to about 10.

As for mortality from the chronic disorders of later life, it has been generally assumed that these have been continuing to increase. However, between the only available baseline year of 1949 and 1973, the age-adjusted rate of cancer mortality, excluding cancers sited in the cigarette-vulnerable respiratory tract, has receded, just as death rates for heart disease have fallen back from 292 to 248, and for stroke from 87 to 64.[8]

V. R. Fuchs, an eminent medical economist, has accounted for these long-term changes in the mortality picture in the following broad terms:

For most of men's history life was short and uncertain. It depended primarily upon such basic economic conditions as adequate supplies of food, water and shelter. . . . [In particular] from the middle of the eighteenth century to the middle of the twentieth century rising real incomes resulted in unprecedented improvements in health in the United States and other developing countries.[9]

Fuchs adds however that the long link in the general population between per capita income—"above a certain minimum [i.e., poverty] level"—and life expectancy has recently largely disappeared. And surprising perhaps is that education has now apparently displaced income as a primary influence on physical well-being. He notes:

One of the most striking findings of recent research on the socioeconomic determinants of health in the United States is the strong positive correlation between health and length of schooling. This result holds for several types of health indexes ranging from mortality rates to self-evaluation of health status. It also holds *after allowing for the effects* [italics added] of such other variables as income, intelligence, and parents' schooling.

This relationship may reflect a chain of causality that begins with good health and results in more schooling. In the most detailed investigation yet undertaken of this subject, however, Michael Grossman has shown that the reverse hypothesis—that more schooling leads to better health—stands up well under a number of critical tests. One of Grossman's most interesting findings concerns the relationship between schooling and premature death. Suppose you were studying, as he was, a group of white men in their thirties and you wanted to predict which ones would die in the next ten years. According to his results, educational attainment would have more predictive power than any other socioeconomic variable—including income and intelligence, two variables that are usually highly correlated with schooling.[10]

We shall have to await publication of Grossman's report[11] to assess his arresting findings on these facets of socioeconomic status.

In any event, it is beyond question that rising standards of living and improvements in physical health are trends that are joined and have marched together since the turn of the century, and long before. Fuchs emphasizes further: "During most of the period medical care (as distinct from public health measures) played an insignificant role in health, but, beginning in the mid-1930's, major therapeutic discoveries [e.g., antibiotics] made significant contributions independently of the rise in real income."[12]

A broad spectrum world history of the twentieth century, sponsored by UNESCO, elaborates:

Improvement in the economic situation, living conditions and nutrition of the masses of the people must be credited with much of the reduction in mortality and improvement in health. . . . Inadequate diets not only meant deficiency diseases in extreme cases, but general lack of resistance to [other] diseases. . . . The advances [in health] achieved in the industrially developed countries during the years under review were intimately bound up with the rising levels of real income enjoyed by the people of these societies.[13]

Deprivations of elementary creature necessities and debilitations of physical health add up to a form of slavery[14] that cripples and locks personality development of the young into chains cutting off subsequent escape from that state. Coles documents the full force of this point when he refers to "the frightened children [of the poor] who years later are adults plagued by defeat, futility, hate and loss of the *freedom* [italics added] to change with changing circumstances."[15]

In this light it seems little less than an unarguable inference that the historically documented progress of a very large part of the population from poverty and near poverty toward higher standards of living and physical health carried with them similar changes in mental health over time.[16]

The Midtown data, although gathered in 1954, can be viewed as supporting this inference. Specifically, in the light of the known socioeconomic strides of the past century, we can assume that the parents of our D-origin respondents (p. 321 above) had in the main come up from E- and F-like childhood family backgrounds. We can also assume that had these D-origin sample members themselves been reared in E or F stratum settings, then their mental health composition would likely have approximated that of their E and F class-origin contemporaries in the Midtown sample.

On these assumptions we can hazard the estimates that our 384 D-origin respondents of 1954 had numerically about 20 percent fewer Impaireds and 40 percent more Wells than they otherwise would have had. These estimates must be assessed in the light of several additional considerations. They are based on inferrable socioeconomic movements among Midtown respondents' parents above poverty and near-poverty levels in the decades just preceding and following 1900. However, such gains were appreciably slower and smaller than those that are known to have followed in the decades after 1935.

Thus, it can be argued that the above estimated mental health improvements in our D-origin respondent group would have been significantly larger had the post-1935 socioeconomic and physical health changes been under full steam at the turn of the century. If so, our estimated mental health gains may be understatements of the probable mental health trend in children of the post-1935 years, and in any case, would represent the progress of only *one* parent-to-child generation in the past hundred-year processional of the generations.

Although it contradicts a long and predominant train of professional and popular thought, the position buttressed by the circumstantial evidence presented above is not without other knowledgeable advocates.

For example, confronting the characterization of our era as preeminently an "age of anxiety," a distinguished contemporary historian of the eighteenth century onward documents that "within this last [i.e., twentieth] century enormous burdens of anxiety have been lifted off the shoulders of men and women, particularly in the industrialized West, *to a degree that they can scarcely appreciate* [italics added]."[17] And from a cross-cultural perspective, an eminent anthropologist similarly rejects that characterization in an article pointedly entitled "One Vote for 'This Age of Anxiety.' "[18]

Reinforcing the position joined by such advocates is the fact that the intertwined scientific, technological, and democratic revolutions launched in the eighteenth century and accelerated in the two centuries following, powered a series of advances in facets of the human condition other than those discussed above. Among other thrusts they (1) forced the legal emancipation of American blacks from slavery; (2) freed women to a large, although still incomplete, degree from their dependent, constricting domestic role and de jure status as chattels; (3) transformed American society from the European model once relatively closed to spacial and vertical SES mobility into one open for unprecedented degrees of self-actualizing movement in both dimensions; (4) expanded the time and means for self-recreating leisure; (5) turned around a laissez faire state to provide public funding for a variety of social programs, targeted principally at persons in need;[19] and most recently (6) raised the scientific foundations of general medical and psychiatric care.

It is almost a truism, however, that there can be no new benefits without new costs. With the above massive humane gains have come a number of secondary side effects, including psychological strains inherent (for some) in adapting to rapid change, tensions generated by the heightened competitiveness and insecurity of a more fluid status system, erosions in the doctrinal and moral areas of the religious sphere, and loosening in the cathected qualities and supportiveness of interpersonal relations. To this incomplete list must be added overpopulation, economic and social devaluation of the aged, and uncontrolled technological defilement of the natural environment.

The many who have embraced the traditional view of a "decline and fall of mental health in the West" did so in part because of almost exclusive fixation on such adverse side effects, which they saw as particularly rampant in the expansive city. Conspicuous among those manifesting such preoccupations have been both sociologists and psychiatrists. In contrast have been two other sets of professionals. First have been the economists, who were themselves preoccupied with charting the primary socioeconomic movements of the Industrial Revolution, without regard, until recently,[20] for its adverse secondary effects. Second are a small number of diverse kinds of observers who have emphasized the sociopsychological gains accompanying socioeconomic advances. For example, A. H. Raskin, an editor of the *New York Times*, speaking of post-1935 developments among newly unionized skilled and semi-skilled blue-collar employees, saw their economic advances as bringing "a new sense of economic emancipation and dignity to millions of workers."

The most powerful leverage for improving human health is exemplified in the macro-economic evolution reviewed in this chapter and was distilled in the axiom of journalist-statesman Theodore Herzl near the turn of the century, namely, that "whoever would change men must first change the conditions of their lives."

Among health professionals there has long been a division of labor between those who work directly with the individual sick, primarily physicians, and those who address themselves to focal points in the community environment that contain health hazards, primarily milieu-altering, disease-preventing public health specialists.

In his "Message to Congress on Mental Illness and Retardation" (February 5, 1963), President Kennedy extended the reach of the latter specialty into the mental health field in these words:

An ounce of prevention is worth more than a pound of cure. For prevention is far more desirable for all concerned. It is far more economical and it is far more likely to be successful. Prevention will require both selected specific programs directed especially at known causes and the *general strengthening of our fundamental community* [italics added], social welfare, and educational programs which can do much to eliminate or correct the harsh environmental conditions that often are associated with mental retardation and mental illness.

Twelve years later what can be said about movement in the interim toward preventing mental disabilities? A number of recent innovations fall under the rubric of "secondary prevention," generally defined in the public health field as "early case finding" and intervention at the first manifestations of a potential disability.

Chapter 11 above discusses social role transit points as hurdles in the life cycle where vulnerable personalities experience distress and difficulties in effecting the transition. An example is the child first entering school, when reading, learning and related emotional problems may first be visible to a professional, i.e., the first grade teacher. Early malfunctions manifested here tend to have "snowballing" effects on subsequent learning failures, dropping out of school, work handicaps, and spiraling emotional disabilities across the entire life span.

Imaginative experimental interventions at this level in the school system have been demonstrated by psychiatrists Kellam and Schiff in a Chicago poverty area.[21] The professional skills required for such intervention have been illustrated by the innovators mentioned. But training for such secondary prevention specialists seems to be lagging far behind the needs calling for them.

At the other end of the schooling cycle are the local programs that help young people with problems or special needs through the transition from school to work. One impressive example is to be found in the broad social spectrum of sixteen sponsoring community organizations that have joined to form a coalition called "The Industry-Education Coordinating Council of New York City." Operating the programs under this federation are a total of sixty-eight school system bureaus and other nonprofit agencies, government or private. An illustration is the High School Redirection project that "offers students who may be potential dropouts an alternative work-study program format leading to a regular high school diploma, and including individual and group counselling."

Still farther into the life cycle is the point at which an adult worker's emotional-behavioral tendencies are disrupting both his productivity and relationships with his associates and supervisor. Isolation from his disaffected coworkers aggravates his condition until he is usually suspended from his job. Dean H. J. Weiner has developed an innovative strategy of intervening in the unionized work setting, through the on-the-spot shop representative of the union involved.[22] On the basis of a demonstration try-out, the New York City Central Labor Council and the Columbia University School of Social Work are conducting training courses for union counsellors, shop stewards, and other officers of 500 constituent union locals having a combined membership of 1.25 million workers.

Such union personnel have had the sole responsibility of communicating worker grievances to management. Now they are also charged with addressing themselves to the worker whose behavior is placing his/her job in jeopardy. They do so by providing the worker with emotional support, counselling, mediation with management to avoid suspension, and, if still necessary, referring him/her to an appropriate mental health service. This intervention strategy has also been adopted by the United Automobile Workers' union locals in Detroit and by several other unions on a national basis.

The common element in all three of the above resourceful developments is that they reach out to people at risk where they are still functioning in their regular extrafamily settings, arresting, if possible, the need to see a therapist, and facilitating, if necessary, referral to such a specialist. In working through established institutions like the school and the work place, they represent secondary prevention at its best, and offer models for other kinds of community institutions to constructively serve their members in new ways.

The above three illustrations of secondary prevention in action are of narrow-gauged dimensions in that they reach out in pinpointed fashion to help already distressed individuals in an early stage of maladaptive behavior.

Broad-gauged *primary* prevention, on the other hand, is directed toward correcting what Knowles has referred to as our persisting "great social problems." He continues:

> In attacking the causes, rather than simply trying to alleviate the symptoms, of these problems, [we] have learned that what lies at the root of most social pathology is human *powerlessness*—the powerlessness of the poor, of the undernourished, of the uneducated, and of those who receive unequal treatment because of their race, color or sex—to claim a fair share of life's opportunities and rewards. Promotion of social justice should be a concern—as long as we have a society [still] characterized by severe inequities.[23]

Fundamental to the power sharing called "freedom of choice" is a social system that universalizes these elementary ingredients of self-actualizing personality development: the right to equal respect for the inalienable dignity of all individuals without exception, no less than the right to more equitable fulfillment of the creature essentials and amenities of the human estate. Both ingredients call for top-priority attention to that 12 percent powerless segment of the American population which, a decade after the trumpeted and short-lived "War on Poverty," is still hanging onto the ledge below the minimum subsistence line.[24] That segment, estimated 27 million in absolute number of individuals at this writing, is increasingly concentrated in urban and rural enclaves that exacerbate the already epidemic prevalence of emotional and behavioral disabilities documented in chapter 14. These handicapped millions clearly present the most serious challenges to our socioeconomic inventiveness, to our psychotherapeutic ingenuity, and to America's two-century-long claim to being above all a moral society.

Two recent and promising developments toward ending the pariah'dom of poverty have been (1) the "income maintenance" proposal, still languishing in Congress, to place an adequately supportive income floor under the substandard earnings of "the working poor"; and (2) the West European concept of "supported work," now being programmatically demonstrated, tested, and evaluated in thirteen American states. The latter program provides subsidized employment to the many "nonworking poor" now caught in the "welfare trap," i.e., those unemployable in the competitive labor market because of physical, educational, mental, or emotional disabilities.

Answering to the call for improvers of the human condition have been the social *macro-changers*, preeminently the ideological, scientific, political, and technological innovators who in modern times sparked and propelled the Western democratic and industrial revolutions. Recently a new breed of macro-changers has emerged, concentrating not on solutions to immediately pressing problems but on identifying and catalyzing public discussion of alternative solutions to large, long-range social problems, imminent and forseeable. One manifestation of this development is to be seen in the formation of the World Future Society,[25] which has issued a ground-breaking report: *The Next Twenty-five Years: Crisis and Opportunity*.[26]

Joining the recognized macro-changers have been a growing establishment-shaking army of activists who have mobilized in an array of advocacy groups like the civil rights, women's liberation, environmental conservation, mental health, senior citizen, and consumer-protection movements. Their already discernible impacts on change are in various degrees accelerating, although a sociologist would parenthetically remark that they have not been joined with comparable activism from their natural allies, our religious institutions.

Finally are the unsung, anonymous legions of lay *micro-changers* who, on the model of Alcoholics Anonymous, manifest in their daily lives the person-to-person approach, "I actively care."

Macro-changers, organized activists, and "on my own" micro-changers are all indispensable to a society of concerned citizens who contribute to making a community that cares,[27] one that incorporates the common core of all psychotherapies, and that in the aggregate can energize the "critical mass" of what can freely be called "a layman's health-enhancing, therapeutic community."

There are many promising indications for the future that this care-sharing personal orientation is part of a changing humanistic ethic that has struck new roots, among other places, in the current generation of young people. For example, social psychologist Kenneth Kenniston notes that the overall educational composition of American young adults today is "absolutely unprecedented in world history. . . . No one can guess the full impact of these wide educational gains. But they certainly mean that a large segment of society will be more capable of dealing with complexity . . . and *more concerned with the society around them*" (italics added).[28]

Taming and bending the physical environment to sustain and enhance the human estate has fully engaged man since he acquired the art of making fire hundreds of millennia ago. From a state of passive, fatalistic, total obeisance to social arrangements as an immutable given, the average man, collectively speaking, has now progressed far in his power to remake his society, a development that can be measured in the span of a few short centuries. Most noteworthy is that the sweep of this movement has recently accelerated enormously, above all in the decade since 1965.[29]

If the Midtown investigation has in any way illuminated the need for and realistic potentials for an activist lay society committed to individual and collective well-being, it will have partially repaid the debts owed to all the micro-changers who made the study possible. This would include most conspicuously the 1,660 Midtowners, in the aggregate and each in his or her own individual way, who for us opened the vistas to both the past and the future that are sketched in this and successor study monographs.[30]

NOTES

1. One mid-nineteenth-century thinker dated the turning point from the democratic revolution, rather than the industrial. He proclaimed: It is our "free institutions which promote insanity." (D. C. Hayden, "On the Distribution of Insanity in the United States," *Third Literary Messenger* 10 [1844]: 178.)

2. H. Goldhamer and A. Marshal, *Psychosis and Civilization*, 1949.

3. Bertram S. Brown, "A National View of Mental Health," U.S. Department of Health, Education and Welfare Publication no. (NIH) 74–661, 1974, p. 5.

4. All of the 1940–1973 income and occupation figures below are derived from *Fortune* magazine graphs, April 1975, pp. 92–96.

5. W. J. Cohen, *Social Policy for the Nineteen Seventies*, U.S. Department of Health, Education and Welfare Indicators, May 1966.

6. Schooling figures are from *Social Indicators, 1973*, U.S. Department of Commerce, Social and Economic Statistics Administration, 1974, pp. 100 and 107.

7. A medical observer has written, "Let it be recalled that there were all sorts of improvements in general socioeconomic status in New York City, as in other cities, between 1900 and 1930." (W. McDermott, "Medical Institutions and Modifications of Disease Patterns," *American Journal of Psychiatry* 122 [June 1966]: 1398–1406.)

8. Graph in *Fortune*, April 1975, p. 94.

9. V. R. Fuchs, *Who Shall Live?* 1974, pp. 30, 31, 54.

10. Ibíd., pp. 46–47.

11. M. Grossman, "The Correlation between Health and Schooling," Conference on Research in Income and Wealth, *Household Production and Consumption*, National Bureau of Economic Research, forthcoming.

12. Fuchs, *Who Shall Live?*, p. 54.

13. Caroline F. Ware et al., *The Twentieth Century*, 1966, p. 472.

14. A Belgian playwright identifies the malaise usually accompanying poverty as rooted in the "feeling that . . . without money, one is someone who, in a sense, does not quite have the right to live; someone who, in a sense, does not exist; someone who fluctuates between being and nothingness." (Félicien Marceau, quoted in the *New York Times*, February 28, 1960.)

15. R. Coles, "What Poverty Does to the Mind," *Outlook*, April 1968.

16. Lest a simplistic theory of economic causation be read into this formulation, the view expressed is an elaboration of an ancient Jewish proverb: "It is not that a full purse is necessarily good [for mental health] as that an empty one is almost certainly bad." Bronowski offers us an apt paraphrase: "The good life is more than material decency, but it must be based on material decency." (*The Ascent of Man*, 1973).

17. J. H. Plumb, *In the Light of History*, 1973, p. 199.

18. Margaret Mead, *The New York Times Magazine*, May 20, 1956.

19. Data on federal expenditures for "selected programs for low-income persons" in the U.S. are a relevant yardstick. Information as to the magnitude of such outlays in 1929 is not at hand, but predictably they were minuscule. Data are available for the years 1968 and 1973, and they show outlays of $13 billion and $32 billion, respectively. When social security and other benefits for the general population are added under the rubric of "total social welfare programs," the corresponding figures are $60 billion and $122 billion, respectively. (A. M. Skolnik and S. R. Dales, "Social Welfare Expenditures, 1971–72," *Social Security Bulletin*, December 1972; and A. M. Skolnik and S. R. Dales, "Social Welfare Expenditures, 1972–73," *Social Security Bulletin*, January 1974.)

20. See A. M. Okun, *Equality and Efficiency: The Big Tradeoff*, 1975.

21. S. Kellam et al., *Mental Health and Going to School*, 1975.

22. H. J. Weiner et al., *Mental Health Care in the World of Work*, 1973.

23. J. H. Knowles, *Rockefeller Foundation Annual Report for 1973*, 1974.

24. For the definitive work on poverty alleviation in the decade since 1964

see R. D. Plotnick and F. Skidmore, *Progress against Poverty*, 1975. See also M. Pillsuk and P. Pillsuk, *How We Lost the War on Poverty*, 1973.

25. The Society is an association of a wide spectrum of professionals that defines itself as "an impartial clearinghouse for a variety of different views and does not take positions on what will happen or should happen in the future." See *The Futurist: A Journal of Forecasts, Trends and Ideas about the Future* 10 (October 1975).

26. Edited by A. A. Spekke, 1975.

27. That ever-refreshing octogenarian and psychiatric missionary Karl Menninger recently told a conference on "Toward a Caring Society": "We must help people learn to care more for one another, personally and through institutions like government, the mass media and business. . . ." (Reported in the *New York Times*, November 13, 1975.) Dr. Menninger might have added this pragmatic note, provided in a 1975 report of the National Institute of Mental Health (Office of Program Planning and Evaluation, June 1975): Mental impairments that in greater or lesser measure arise from the "care-lessness" of others exact a heavy price in direct and indirect costs that in the United States added up to a $36.5 billion estimated total in 1974.

28. K. Kenniston in a *New York Times* interview, February 4, 1971.

29. Manifestations of the power of this current is that it swept two American presidents out of the land's most powerful office by nonelectoral processes of resolute public opposition.

30. T. S. Langner and S. M. Michael, *Life Stress and Mental Health*, 1962, and L. Srole and Anita K. Fischer, eds., "Mental Health in the Metropolis Revisited: *The Midtown Manhattan Longitudinal Study*, 1954-1974," work in progress. For a preliminary technical and data report see L. Srole, "Measurement and Classification in Socio-Psychiatric Epidemiology: Midtown Manhattan Study (1954) and Midtown Manhattan Restudy (1974)," *Journal of Health and Social Behavior* 16 (December 1975): 347-364.

Part V

Appendixes

APPENDIX A

ACKNOWLEDGMENTS

A large-scale investigation passes through a series of stages that begins with planning for mobilization and ends years later when, objective achieved, it disbands. Without the contributions, large and small, of those named below, this objective would not have been reached.

During the years prior to procurement of support for the Midtown Study, Dr. Rennie consulted a number of knowledgeable people who helped him to crystallize its focus "in broad general terms," as he put it. Among Cornell Medical College colleagues these included Drs. Oskar Diethelm, Alexander H. Leighton, Allister M. Macmillan, Leo Simmons, Wilson Smillie, and Emerson Day. Also important in this stage were Drs. Dorothy Bask, John Clausen, Ernest Gruenberg, Herbert Goldhamer, Molly Harrower, Marie Jahoda, Msgr. George A. Kelly, Ann Kent, Seymour Klebanoff, Lawrence Frank, Raymond Mangus, Louis McQuitty, Melly Simon, Livingston Welch, and, of particular note, Harry Alpert.

We here distinguish four categories of staff personnel who were engaged in the Midtown Study: (1) senior investigators, who (with some exceptions) participated in the planning phases and subsequently had major responsibility to one or another of the four field operations; (2) research aides, principally performing office functions of processing and tabulating field data; (3) interviewers for the Home Survey operation; and (4) volunteers, who carried out miscellaneous field, library, and office functions.

Senior investigators are listed in the order of their appointment to the Study staff. Immediately following each member's name is given his/her self-defined professional identification, dates of inception and termination of services, and major research responsibility or assignment. Except for the psychiatrists, all members listed were engaged on a full-time basis during the periods indicated.

Thomas A. C. Rennie (psychiatrist), 1952–1956: Director, Midtown Study.
Leo Srole (sociologist), 1952–1960: Director, Home Survey operation.
Marvin K. Opler (anthropologist), 1952–1958: Director, Ethnic Family studies.

Margaret Bailey (psychiatric social worker), 1952–1955: Treatment Census operation.

Freeda Taran (psychiatric social worker), 1952–1955: Treatment Census operation.

Arthur Weider (clinical psychologist), 1952–1955: questionnaire committee for the Home Survey operation.

Eleanor Leacock (anthropologist), 1952–1955: Assistant Director, Ethnic Family studies.

Price Kirkpatrick (psychiatrist), 1952–1955: mental health evaluation of the Home Survey sample.

Guy La Rochelle (psychiatrist), 1952–1954: Home Survey operation.

Vera Rubin (anthropologist), 1953–1955: Assistant Director, Ethnic Family studies.

Thomas S. Langner (sociologist), 1953–1962: Assistant Director, Home Survey operation; Director, Data Processing and Statistical Analysis for Home Survey and Treatment Census operations.

Stanley T. Michael (psychiatrist), 1954–1962: mental health evaluation of Home Survey sample.

Alexander H. Leighton (psychiatrist), 1956–1962: Director, Midtown Study.

In a special category was Dr. Irwin Bross, Cornell Professor of Biometrics (now of the Roswell Park Memorial Institute), who was a frequent technical consultant to the Midtown staff through the whole of its planning phase. In the years following, he continued as a regular advisor on methodological problems relating to sampling and analysis designs. His role as incisive critic and catalyst while we pushed our way through a host of complexities and difficulties cannot be adequately conveyed in this brief note of indebtedness to him.

The following list of research aides includes those predoctoral people who were employed by the Study for one or more years: Ann Jezer Avins, Betty Bunes, Elliott Camerman, Michel DiLiscia, Allyn Falls, Muriel Grant, Ira Greiff, Jerold Heiss, India Hughley, Merton Hyman, Harold Jarmon, Barbara Kennedy, Dolores Kreisman, Arnold Levine, Anita Lowell, Frances Libby, Sally Pinkerton, Thomas Rick, Irving Silverman, Amorita Suarez, Jan Snaauw, Alice Togo, and Malcolm Willison.

The social workers and social scientists next named completed 25 or more Home Survey interviews: Ruth Balter, Joseph Borello, Marjorie Cantor, Rosemary Dempsey, Helen Halley, John Kupyn, Claire Marck, Robert Marsh, Irene N. Norton, Jess Osterweil, Edmond Pollack, Florence Rothman, Edwin Seda, Esther Shaw, Sol Siegel, Elsie Siff, Ada Slawson, Robert M. Slawson, Janet Sperber, Isidore Weider, and Rosalind Zoglin. Shepard Wolman and Edwin Fancher were supervisors of the interviewing staff. Graduate students in the New York School of Social Work, under the guidance of Margaret Bailey, were instrumental in pretesting several versions of the interview questionnaire.

A total of 99 voluntary workers were secured for the Study through Mrs. Margaretta W. Treherne-Thomas, Director, Volunteer Department of the New York Hospital-Cornell Medical Center. The volunteers listed below met the criterion of contributing in excess of 500 working hours: Renee Apfelbaum, Maurice Bloch, Tillie Drucker, Lewis Faron, Warren Fox, Leila Freedberger, Mrs. Leonard Frutkin, Mrs. Howard Harris, Rene Hoguet, Percy Perkins, Kurt Porges, Eva Profeta, Samuel Reber, and Mrs. Mary J. Kempner Thorne. Special volunteers were Judith Bernays Heller, Esther A. Srole, and Philip C. Haydock.

Grateful acknowledgment is expressed to the publishers who generously granted permission to draw on extensive passages from the following sources:

Hamilton Basso, *The View from Pompey's Head,* Doubleday & Company, Inc., New York, 1954.

Dorothy Barclay, *Understanding the City Child,* Franklin Watts, Inc., New York, 1959.

John A. Clausen, *Sociology and the Field of Mental Health,* Russell Sage Foundation, New York, 1956.

————, "The Sociology of Mental Illness," in R. K. Merton et al. (eds.), *Sociology Today,* Basic Books, Inc., New York, 1959.

E. J. Cleveland and W. D. Longaker, "Neurotic Patterns in the Family," in A. H. Leighton et al. (eds.), *Explorations in Social Psychiatry,* Basic Books, Inc., New York, 1957.

The Commonwealth Fund, *Chronic Illness in a Large City: The Baltimore Study,* Harvard University Press, Cambridge, Mass., 1957.

Oscar Handlin, *The Uprooted,* Little, Brown & Company, Boston, 1951.

Granville Hicks, *Small Town,* The Macmillan Company, New York, 1946.

A. B. Hollingshead and F. C. Redlich, *Social Class and Mental Illness,* John Wiley & Sons, Inc., New York, 1958.

Irving L. Janis, *Psychological Stress,* John Wiley & Sons, Inc., New York, 1958.

Max Lerner, *America as a Civilization,* Simon and Schuster, Inc., New York, 1958.

B. Malzberg and E. S. Lee, *Migration and Mental Disease,* Social Science Research Council, New York, 1956.

E. B. White, *Here Is New York,* Harper & Brothers, New York, 1949.

Thomas Wolfe, *The Web and the Rock,* Harper & Brothers, New York, 1939.

The photo research for the present edition is by Ann Novotny, Research Reports, New York City, N.Y. Photographers are Aero Service; James P. Blair, National Geographic Society; James Carroll, Nancy Palmer Photo Agency; Gerry Cranham, Rapho-Guillumette; Jim Jowers, Nancy Palmer Photo Agency; Lee Lockwood, Black Star; George Novotny; Bill Ray, Black Star; Ira Srole; Alfred Stieglitz; Burk Uzzle, Magnum. Illustrations are by John Huehnergarth and Saul Steinberg.

Other notes of appreciation have already appeared at appropriate points in the chapters above. Our greatest debt of gratitude is reserved for the many unnamed residents of Midtown who freely gave themselves in the service of research and the commonweal.

ADDENDUM

In January 1967, the Midtown Study was reactivated (NIMH grant 13369) for follow-up investigation, with Leo Srole as Director and, since 1970, Anita Kassen Fischer as CoDirector. Since that date, the Study directors have had the cooperation of Professors William Lhamon and Stanley Michael of the Cornell University Medical College. To Columbia colleagues, in particular Professors Lawrence C. Kolb and Viola W. Bernard, we also owe grateful acknowledgments for their counsels.

The present edition of this book could not have been completed without the invaluable administrative and secretarial assistance of Renee Biel.

For the making of this edition we also acknowledge the editorial ministrations of Robert L. Bull and Despina Papagoglou of the New York University Press.

APPENDIX B

THOMAS A. C. RENNIE'S PUBLICATIONS IN SOCIAL PSYCHIATRY

"The Rehabilitation Clinic of the New York Hospital," *Cornell University Medical College Quarterly,* November 1943.

"National Planning for Psychiatric Rehabilitation," *American Journal of Orthopsychiatry,* vol. 14, no. 3, 1944.

"A Plan for the Organization of Psychiatric Rehabilitation Clinics," *Mental Hygiene,* vol. 28, no. 2, April 1944

"Experiments in a Psychiatric Rehabilitation Clinic for Ex-service men," *Journal of Medical Sociology, City of New York,* vol. 3, no. 24, June 10, 1944.

"Rehabilitation of the Psychoneurotic," *Proceedings of the Annual Meeting of the National Council on Rehabilitation,* New York, June 1944.

"Community Organization for Meeting Problems of Psychiatrically Disabled Veterans" (with L. E. Woodward), Round Table on Rehabilitation, *American Journal of Orthopsychiatry,* vol. 14, no. 4, October 1944.

"Psychiatric Rehabilitation Therapy," *American Journal of Psychiatry,* vol. 101, no. 4, January 1945.

Jobs and the Man (with L. E. Woodward), Charles C. Thomas, Publisher, Springfield, Ill., 1945.

"The Rehabilitation of the Psychiatric Casualty" (with L. E. Woodward), *Mental Hygiene,* vol. 29, no. 1, January 1945.

"The New York Hospital Offers a Pattern for Rehabilitation," *Modern Hospitals,* vol. 64, no. 4, April 1945.

"Psychiatric Rehabilitation Resources," *Proceedings of the American Neurological Association,* 1945.

"Psychiatric Rehabilitation Techniques: Current Therapies of Personality Disorders," *Proceedings of the American Psychopathological Association, 1946.*

"Mental Hygiene," *Social Work Year Book,* 1947.

"Toward Industrial Mental Health: An Historical Review" (with Gladys Sockhamer and Luther E. Woodward), *Mental Hygiene,* vol. 31, no. 1, January 1947.

Mental Health in Modern Society (with L. E. Woodward), The Commonwealth Fund, New York, 1948.

"Vocational Rehabilitation of the Psychiatrically Disabled" (with Temple Burling and Luther E. Woodward), *Mental Hygiene,* vol. 33, no. 2, April 1949.

"The Veterans Administration Shows the Way," *Mental Hygiene,* vol. 35, no. 3, July 1951. Presented at the Annual Conference of the National Association for Mental Health, New York, November 17, 1950.

"Rehabilitation Problems and Services in the Community" (with Mary F. Bozeman). Presented at the Conference of the National Rehabilitation Association, October 25, 1950. Published in Conference Proceedings.

Vocational Rehabilitation of Psychiatric Patients: A Study of Post-hospital Vocational Work (with Temple Burling and Luther E. Woodward), The Commonwealth Fund, New York, 1950.

Vocational Services for Psychiatric Clinic Patients (with Mary F. Bozeman). Published for The Commonwealth Fund by Harvard University Press, Cambridge, Mass., 1952.

Introductory chapter to American edition of *Mental Health and Human Relations in Industry,* by Thomas Ling, M.D., Paul B. Hoeber, Inc., New York, Medical Department of Harper & Brothers, 1954.

"Social Psychiatry: A Definition," *International Journal of Social Psychiatry,* vol. 1, no. 1, Summer 1955.

"The Rehabilitation of the Mentally Ill," *The Elements of a Community Health Program,* 1955.

"Social Class Prevalence and Distribution of Psychosomatic Conditions in an Urban Population" (with Leo Srole), *Psychosomatic Medicine,* vol. 18, no. 6, November–December 1956.

INCIDENCE VERSUS PREVALENCE OF TREATED MENTAL DISORDER

The largest morbidity study ever undertaken has been that conducted by the United States National Health Survey (NHS) of the Federal Public Health Service. Within its broad reach the NHS covered 12 categories of "acute" somatic conditions, for example, infectious diseases, and 17 kinds of chronic disorders.

This authoritative government investigation has uniformly applied the *incidence* measure to the acute illnesses, which are relatively brief in duration, and the *prevalence* yardstick to the chronic conditions, characteristically of prolonged duration.[1]

That prevalence is the indicated measure of choice for chronic illness is further seen in the unequivocal statement of medical epidemiologists working in the field of cardiac disorders: "The cardinal statistic in the epidemiology of rheumatic heart disease is the overall prevalence rate."[2]

Although mental disorder in many instances tends to become chronic, the dominant tendency of researchers in this field, transfixed by the acute diseases as seemingly appropriate analytical models, has long been to embrace the unequivocal and unqualified position that "the incidence rate is the fundamental epidemiological ratio."[3] The extremity of this position is reflected in one professional book review[4] of the New Haven Psychiatric Census monograph by Hollingshead and Redlich.[5] In the latter work, the epidemiological aspect was largely carried out in terms of prevalence, with minor utilization of the novel Yale modification of the incidence yardstick. Yet the reviewer dismissed the voluminous New Haven prevalence findings as seemingly beneath discussion and focused almost entirely on the slender incidence data from New Haven.

The key to this bias is the reviewer's contention that incidence is a "measure of the amount of mental illness generated during a standard period." As do advocates of the prevalence yardstick, the proponents of the incidence measure tend to use *treated* psychiatric cases as if they represented the totality of mentally impaired people, or at least an acceptable approximation of that universe. However, the incidence partisans, proceeding from the model of the acute somatic disorders, also seem to assume (1) that mental disturbance generally has a specific point of onset, (2) that admission to treatment (usually to a mental hospital) tends to occur at a time not distant from the point of onset, and (3) q.e.d. the number of such "first" admissions during the course of a given year can be accepted as a measure of the amount of mental impairment *generated* during that period.

These assumptions do not stand up under critical inspection. First, like other chronic disorders, mental disorder as a rule proliferates slowly from a more or less asymptomatic stage. In other words, the break into an open psychosis, far from being the onset of the dysfunctional process, is no more than a culmination; the neuroses and character disorders, to complicate matters, may present no sharply delineated break of any kind. Unlike the acute illnesses, therefore, point of onset in mental morbidity is often beyond determination or highly equivocal.

Second, even with the psychotic break as a definable landmark, the manifest disorder may be severe and brief or mild and prolonged. The former type generally gets to treatment more often than the latter. One study, focused on chronic first-admission hospital patients, found that only 29 percent entered the institution within a year of presenting unmistakable psychotic symptoms, whereas 46 percent entered three or more years after such symptoms had appeared.[6] Similarly, Clausen reports: "In our own research on the families of mental patients, we have encountered instances in which an accepting and nurturant wife has been able to sustain a schizophrenic spouse for 5–10 years before [securing treatment]."[7] From a study of hospitalized patients, C. A. Whitmer has indicated that not psychosis as such leads to institutionalization, but rather a turn of the overt but harmless psychotic toward "dangerous or unmanageable behavior that threatened the family or the community." [Personal communication.] In short, if a point of "illness onset" *were* definable it would bear little regularity of proximity relative to initiation of treatment as a second point of time.

Furthermore, institutional files, being what they are, often default in recording whether or not a patient (particularly if he is in short-term treatment) is a first admission. Most serious of all, the first-admission criterion of "illness onset" crumbles completely when we see that it refers to cases new only to a particular institution or hospital system. Many Treatment Census patients listed as a first admission in the New York state hospital system were variously found to have been treated for years previously by an office therapist, an outpatient clinic, a private hospital, a public hospital in another state system, or some combination of these. The effort to equate such a New York state hospital first admission with "onset of illness" descends to the level of the unfathomable.

Even if all of the above deficiencies were not involved, there is still the question of the meaning of differences in incidence (of treatment) rate between two populations. By way of one example, the incidence rate is usually calculated with the number of newly treated cases during a given *year* as the numerator and the total population resident in the area on *any given day* as the denominator. Now let us imagine two urban areas each with 100,000 residents on the United States decennial census day. Area A has an annual incidence of 100 hospitalized patients and area B of 150 such patients—a seemingly meaningful difference.

However, area A is a stable section of homeowners only, with little population turnover; that is, it actually housed few more than 100,000 people all told during the course of the study year. Area B, on the other hand, is entirely a section of short-lease apartments, apartment hotels, and rooming houses with large inflow and outflow of transient residents. During the year this area may actually have housed a total of 150,000 people. Thus, area A's 100,000 residents during the year yielded 100 patients, and B's 150,000 residents during the year yielded 150 patients, the two now defining an *identical rate* of 100 per 100,000 population at risk.

The fact is, however, that the United States population census has *not* provided more than a *prevalence* count of residents as of a *single* day. Accordingly, the conventional annual incidence rate rests on an inappropriate population base as its denominator value. On all these critical grounds, among others, we reluctantly concluded that use of the incidence rates produced by the Midtown Treatment Census would be indefensible.

As this monograph abundantly shows, the patient prevalence measure is itself an inadequate foundation of evidence.for generalizing about *overall* (untreated and treated) prevalence of mental illness.

NOTES

[1] *Health Statistics from the U.S. National Health Survey: Diabetes,* ser. B, no. 21, 1960; and *Acute Conditions,* ser. B, no. 23, 1960.

[2] J. Stokes, III, and T. R. Dawber, "Rheumatic Heart Disease in the Framingham Study," *New England Journal of Medicine* 225: 26, (Dec. 27, 1956): 1228.

[3] M. Kramer, "A Discussion of the Concepts of Incidence and Prevalence as Related to Epidemiological Studies of Mental Disorders," *American Journal of Public Health* 47: 7 (July, 1957): 827.

[4] *American Sociological Review,* August 1959.

[5] A. B. Hollingshead and F. C. Redlich, *Social Class and Mental Illness,* 1958.

[6] N. C. Morgan and N. A. Johnson, "Failures in Psychiatry: The Chronic Hospital Patient," *American Journal of Psychiatry* 113: 2 (March, 1957): 824–830.

[7] J. A. Clausen, "Ecology of Mental Disorders," in *Symposium on Preventive and Social Psychiatry,* Walter Reed Army Institute of Research, 1958, p. 107.

INTERVIEW SUMMARY FORM FOR STUDY PSYCHIATRISTS

The interview schedule used to interview the Midtown sample respondents was sixty-five pages long and cannot be reproduced here in its entirety. The Interview Summary form was prepared by direct transfer of the respondent's specific replies to the psychiatrically relevant questions selected from the inclusive interview protocol.

Also presented below are the original code numbers for each question. Not accounted for is the additional ("spillover") information offered by the respondent and transferred to the Summary form for the psychiatrists.

PART A

W13–1. Height 4' or less 2. (4'1"–4'4") 3. (4'5"–4'8") 4. (4'9"–5') 5. (5'1"–5'4") 6. (5'5"–5'8") 7. (5'9"–6') 8. (6'1"–6'4") 9. (6'5" and over)

W14–1. Weight 89 lb or less 2. (90–109) 3. (110–129) 4. (130–149) 5. (150–169) 6. (170–189) 7. (190–209) 8. (210–249) 9. (250–299) 0. (300 or over)

W15–1. Age 20–24 yrs. 2. (25–29) 3. (30–34) 4. (35–39) 5. (40–44) 6. (45–49) 7. (50–54) 8. (55–59)

W15–X. Male Y. Female

W16–1. Married 2. Never married 3. Widowed 4. Divorced 5. Separated

N27–1. Married once 6. Twice 7. Three or more times

N28–1. Under 15 when married 2. (15–19) 3. (20–24) 4. (25–29) 5. (30–34) 6. (35–44) 7. (45–59)

W18–1. Health excellent now 2. Good 3. Fair 4. Poor

W18–7. Health now same as 4–5 yrs ago 8. Health now better 9. Health not as good

W19–43. Conditions (arthritis, asthma, bladder, colitis, diabetes, hay fever, heart condition, hypertension, neuralgia, nervous breakdown, epilepsy, ulcer, skin trouble)

R5–1. Appetite poor 2. Fair

R5–8. Stomach upset pretty often 9. Nearly all the time

R6–1. Headaches often 2. Sometimes
R6–6. Sleep trouble often 7. Sometimes
R7–1. Hands damp often 2. Sometimes
R7–6. Hands tremble often 7. Sometimes
R8–1. Shortness of breath often 2. Sometimes
R8–6. Heart beats hard often 7. Sometimes
R9–1. Cold sweats often 2. Sometimes
R9–7. Dizziness a few times 8. More than a few times
R10–2. Fainting a few times 3. More than a few times
R10–6. Nervousness often 7. Sometimes
R11–9. Other ailments_____
R14–6. Smoke too much
R15–6. Drink coffee too much
R16–6. Drink liquor too much
R17–2. Eat too much
R17–6. Feel weak all over
R18–1. Such restlessness, can't sit long in a chair
R18–5. Bothered by sour stomach several times a week
R18–0. Memory is not all right
R19–1. Every so often feel hot all over
R19–5. Periods of days, weeks, months when couldn't get going
R19–9. Pains in back interfere with work
R20–1. Often have hard time making up my mind about things I should do
R20–5. Often have a clogging in my head or nose
Q 29 A. No. of med. specialists seen _____

R25–3. Childhood health poor
R25–8. Birth defects _____
R26–5. Childhood trouble—sleep
R26–9. Childhood trouble—stammer or stutter
R27–1. Childhood trouble—upset stomach fairly often

Childhood Fears of

R27 Strangers 6. Little 7. Much
R28 Thunder 2. Little 3. Much
R28 Being left alone 8. Little 9. Much
R29 High Places 2. Little 3. Much
R29 Animals 8. Little 9. Much
R30 Being laughed at 2. Little 3. Much
R31 Being bawled out 2. Little 3. Much

R45–2. Is worrying type

B11–1. Dated opposite sex more often than others did 2. About same 3. Less often
B14–7. Liked school very much 8. All right 9. Disliked 0. Hated

G5–1. One should do everything perfectly
G5–5. One drink is one too many
G5–9. Never show feelings to others
G6–1. Never change mind
G6–5. Always be on guard with people
G7–1. Often, old ways are best ways
G7–5. Prefer to go out by myself
G7–9. Feel somewhat apart even among friends
G8–1. Keep my opinions to myself
G8–5. Feel people are against me
G8–0. Not had my share of good luck
G9–1. Most of the time in high spirits 3. Low spirits 4. Very low spirits
G40–2. Life gives a lot of pleasure—Disagree
G40–5. People talk behind your back
G40–9. Nothing turns out right for me
G41–1. In marriage the woman sacrifices more than the man
G41–5. At times a person feels he is a stranger to himself
G41–9. The unmarried can be just as content as the married
G42–1. Most people think a lot about sex
G42–5. Personal worries get me down physically
G43–1. Sometimes wonder if anything is worthwhile
G44–1. Can't enjoy myself when alone
G44–5. High buildings, tunnels, bridges make me tense (nervous)
G44–9. One should retire at same time each night
A5–1. I rarely make a mistake
A5–5. Don't care what others think of me
A5–9. When I want something very much I want it right away
A6–1. Am a gambler at heart
A6–5. No one really understands me
A6–0. I don't always take good care of my health
A7–6. Often worry—loneliness
A10–6. Often worry—old age
A11–1. Often worry—atom bomb
A11–6. Often worry—personal enemies
A12–1. Often worry—health
A24–1. Better do things on spur of moment than plan ahead
A24–5. No right and wrong, only easy and hard ways to make money
A24–9. Grief and sorrow not for adults
A25–1. Better to keep away from family
A27–2, 3, 4, 5, 6 Hospitalized conditions _____
A29–2, 3, 4, 5, 6 Clinic conditions _____

Interviewer's Observations

A34 R's interest at start 1. Lack 2. Mild 3. High
A34 R's interest at close 5. Lack 6. Mild 7. High
A34 R's tension level at start 9. Nervous 0. Sporadic nervous X. Mostly relaxed

A35 R's tension level at close 1. Nervous 2. Sporadic nervous 3. Mostly relaxed
A35 Distractions during interview 5. Much 6. Some 7. None
A36 R's attitude 1. Hostile 2. Suspicious 3. Friendly 4. Solicitous
A36 Responses 6. Inappropriate, irrelevant, rambling 7. Vague, facetious, dull 8. Alert 9. Overtalkative (appropriate content)
A37 Affect or mood 1. Depressed 2. Apathetic 3. Normal 4. Cheerful
A37 Alertness-intelligence 6. Dull 7. Slow 8. Average 9. Above average
A38 Appearance 1. Sloppy 2. Untidy 3. Neat 4. Overly neat
A38 Physical defects 6. Muscular tic 7. Stutter 8. Memory difficulties 9. Cosmetic deformity 0. Gross physical difficulty X. Other

Scores on Symptom Dimensions

Immaturity M52–0 1 2 3 4 5 6 7 8 9
Rigidity M53–0 1 2 3 4 5 6
Frustration-Depression M54–0 1 2 3 4 5
Excess intake M55–0 1 2 3 4
Tension-Anxiety (Short form) M56–0 1 2 3 4 5
Neurasthenia M57–0 1 2 3
Appetite-Stomach M58–0 1 2 3
Headaches M59–0 1 2 3
Vasolability M60–0 1 2 3
Other organs M61–0 1 2 3 4 5
Suspicious M62–0 1 2 3 4
Withdrawal M63–0 1 2 3 4
Adult Anxiety Dimension M64–0 1 2 3 4 5 6 7 8 9
    M64–10 11 12 13 14 15 16 17 18
Childhood Anxiety Dimension M65–0 1 2 3 4 5 6 7 8

PART B

W8–1. One in household 2. two 3. three 4. four 5. five 6. six 7. seven 8. eight 9. nine 0. ten+
W9 Kin composition 1. Husband 2. Wife 3. Father 4. Mother 5. Children 0. Other Kin X. Non-kin
W17–1. No children 2. One 3. Two 4. Three 5. Four 6. Five-Eight 7. Nine-Twelve
R11 Race 1. white 2. Negro 3. Other

R30 As child feared family quarrels 8. Little 9. Much
R32–1. No brothers 2. One 3. Two 4. Three-Four 5. Five+
R32–7. No sisters 8. One 9. Two 0. Three-Four X. Five+
R33–1. First sibling 2. Second 3. Third 4. Fourth 5. Fifth 6. Last 7. Other _____ 8. No sibs
R36–2. Not raised by both parents

R37–1. What'happened—death of father 2. Death of mother 3. Divorce 4. Separation 5. Desertion by father 6. Desertion by mother 7. Father in hospital 8. Mother in hospital 9. Lived away from parents 0. Other

R38–1. R's age at separation—under 1 yr. 2. (1–3) 3. (4–6) 4. (7–9) 5. (10–12) 6. (13–15) 7. 16+

R39–1. Raised by remaining parent 2. Grandparent 3. Step-parent 4. Foster parents 5. Aunt-Uncle 6. Institution 7. Other

R40–2. Remaining parent remarried

R41 R's age when parent remarried. 1. Under 1 yr. 2. (1–3) 3. (4–6) 4. (7–9) 5. (10–12) 6. (13–15) 7. (16+)

R42–1. Got along with substitute parent(s) well 2. Not so well 3. Not at all

R43–5. Poor health—Mother 6. Father 7. Both

W44–50 Kin's psychosomatic conditions⎯⎯⎯⎯⎯⎯⎯⎯⎯⎯⎯⎯⎯⎯⎯

R44 Parents worrying type 5. Mother 6. Father 7. Both

R45–5. R takes after—Mother 6. Father 7. Both 8. Other ⎯⎯⎯⎯⎯⎯⎯⎯⎯

R46–1. Discord between parents—often 4. Never

R46–7. R had discord with parents often 0. Never

R47–1. Disagreement over free time 6. Religion

R48–1. Disagreement over food 6. Money

R49–1. Disagreement over going out with girls (boys) 6. Schoolwork

R50–1. Disagreement over what to do when sick 6. Deciding things for self

B5–1. Disagreements mainly with father 2. Mother 3. Both

B6–1. Parents had no problems while R 6–18 yrs. 2. Unemployment 3. Work 4. Financial 5. Father-mother conflict 6. Illness 7. Myself 8. Siblings 9. Other kin 0. Father inadequate X. Mother inadequate Y. Housing

As child felt that—

B7–7. Parents behind the times

B8–1. Father spends too little time with me. 5. Mother wants to run children's lives 9. Home is where people get in each other's way

B9–1. Parents always proud of children 5. Mother does not understand me 9. Parents don't practice what they preach

B10–1. Father wants to run children's lives 5. Parents want me to do things better than other children 9. I'm happy only when at home

B12 R's educ. 1. None 2. Gs 3. Hs 4. HSG 5. Col 6. Col grad 7. Postgrad

B15 Father's educ. 1. None 2. Gs 3. Hs 4. HSG 5. Col 6. Col grad 7. Postgrad

B16 Mother's educ. 1. None 2. Gs 3. Hs 4. HSG 5. Col 6. Col grad 7. Postgrad

B17 Spouse's educ. 1. None 2. Gs 3. Hs 4. HSG 5. Col 6. Col grad 7. Postgrad

B18 During R's childhood parents had hard time making ends meet 5. Often 6. Sometimes

B21–7. Mother worked full time 8. Part time

B22 Father's occupation when R 8–9 yrs. ⎯⎯⎯⎯⎯⎯⎯⎯⎯⎯⎯⎯⎯⎯⎯⎯⎯⎯⎯

B23 Father's occupation when R 18–19 yrs. ⎯⎯⎯⎯⎯⎯⎯⎯⎯⎯⎯⎯⎯⎯⎯⎯⎯⎯

B24–2. Father's occupational aspirations for R ⎯⎯⎯⎯⎯⎯⎯⎯⎯⎯⎯⎯⎯⎯⎯

B26–2. Mother's occupational aspirations for R ⎯⎯⎯⎯⎯⎯⎯⎯⎯⎯⎯⎯⎯⎯⎯

G22–1. One address since age 18 2. Two 3. Three 4. Four 5. Five 6. Six 7. Seven 8. Eight 9. Nine 0. Ten+

G26–1. Income under $65/month 2. ($65–99) 3. ($100–199) 4. ($200–319) 5. ($320–429) 6. ($430–539) 7. ($540–649) 8. ($650–749) 9. ($750–859) 0. ($860–1,299) X. (1,300+)

G32. Number of neighbors visited 1. (none) 2. (one) 3. (2–3) 4. (4–5) 5. (6–9) 6. (10+) 7. (Other)_____

G33–2. Would like more friends

G34. No. of close friends 1. (none) 2. (one) 3. (2–3) 4. (4–5) 5. (6–9) 6. (10–14) 7. (15+) 8. (Other)_____

G35–1. No leisure activities 2. Mass media 3. Reading 4. Music 5. Arts 6. Outdoor activities 7. Spectator sports 8. Volunteer 9. Other hobby. 0. Self-improvement X. Other_____

G37 Active in organizations 1. One 2. Two 3. Three 4. Four 5. Five+

G38–2. R attends meetings

A7–1. Often worry—cost of living

A8–1. Often worry—getting ahead

A8–6. Often worry—my work

A9–1. Often worry—overwork

A9–6. Often worry—marriage

A10–1. Often worry—children

A14–1. Problems with children: physical health 2. Bad companions 3. Delinquent 4. School 5. Child-parent conflict 6. Sib conflict 7. Poor adjustment 8. Habit disturbances 9. Generalized concern 0. Other _____

A15–2. Received advice for child

A16–1. Received advice from relatives 2. Friends 3. Church 4. School 5. Court 6. Doctor 7. Psychiatrist or guidance clinic 8. Psychologist or counselor 9. Social agency 0. Recreational leader X. Other _____

A23–1. R known to Dept. of Welfare 2. Court 3. Mental hospital 4. Social agency 5. Not known 6. Cannot be identified by SSE 7. Not cleared by SSE 8. Known to our Treatment Census 9. Not known to our Treatment Census 0. Seen by Team psychiatrist

A32–1. Interviewer SES rating 1. (A) 2. (B) 3. (C) 4. (D) 5. (E) 6. (F)

A30–5. Hospital plan: Blue Cross 6. Blue Shield 7. HIP 8. Insur. co. 9. Other

R. has seen:	Last 30 days	1–12 mos. ago	1–5 yrs.	6–10 yrs.	11+ yrs.
R21–2. Nerve specialist	5	6	7	8	9
R22–2. Psychiatrist	5	6	7	8	9
R23–2. Psychologist	5	6	7	8	9
R24–2. Other therapist	5	6	7	8	9

G22–1. One address since age 18 2. Two 3. Three 4. Four 5. Five 6. Six 7. Seven 8. Eight 9. Nine o. Ten+

G26–1. Income under $65/month 2. ($65–99) 3. ($100–199) 4. ($200–319) 5. ($320–429) 6. ($430–539) 7. ($540–649) 8. ($650–749) 9. ($750–859) o. ($860–1,299) X. (1,300+)

G32. Number of neighbors visited 1. (none) 2. (one) 3. (2–3) 4. (4–5) 5. (6–9) 6. (10+) 7. (Other) _____

G33–2. Would like more friends

G34. No. of close friends 1. (none) 2. (one) 3. (2–3) 4. (4–5) 5. (6–9) 6. (10–14) 7. (15+) 8. (Other) _____

G35–1. No leisure activities 2. Mass media 3. Reading 4. Music 5. Arts 6. Outdoor activities 7. Spectator sports 8. Volunteer 9. Other hobby. o. Self-improvement X. Other_____

G37 Active in organizations 1. One 2. Two 3. Three 4. Four 5. Five+

G38–2. R attends meetings

A7–1. Often worry—cost of living

A8–1. Often worry—getting ahead

A8–6. Often worry—my work

A9–1. Often worry—overwork

A9–6. Often worry—marriage

A10–1. Often worry—children

A14–1. Problems with children: physical health 2. Bad companions 3. Delinquent 4. School 5. Child-parent conflict 6. Sib conflict 7. Poor adjustment 8. Habit disturbances 9. Generalized concern o. Other _____

A15–2. Received advice for child

A16–1. Received advice from relatives 2. Friends 3. Church 4. School 5. Court 6. Doctor 7. Psychiatrist or guidance clinic 8. Psychologist or counselor 9. Social agency o. Recreational leader X. Other _____

A23–1. R known to Dept. of Welfare 2. Court 3. Mental hospital 4. Social agency 5. Not known 6. Cannot be identified by SSE 7. Not cleared by SSE 8. Known to our Treatment Census 9. Not known to our Treatment Census o. Seen by Team psychiatrist

A32–1. Interviewer SES rating 1. (A) 2. (B) 3. (C) 4. (D) 5. (E) 6. (F)

A30–5. Hospital plan: Blue Cross 6. Blue Shield 7. HIP 8. Insur. co. 9. Other

R. has seen:	Last 30 days	1–12 mos. ago	1–5 yrs.	6–10 yrs.	11+ yrs.
R21–2. Nerve specialist	5	6	7	8	9
R22–2. Psychiatrist	5	6	7	8	9
R23–2. Psychologist	5	6	7	8	9
R24–2. Other therapist	5	6	7	8	9

ERRORS, ARTIFACTS, AND BIASES IN THE MENTAL HEALTH DISTRIBUTIONS AMONG SES–ORIGIN GROUPS

Several potential sources of error in the research process may conceivably have contributed to the Well and Impaired trends reported in table 14–1.

One potential source of error could intrude from the interviewers if, for example, they performed their inquiring role in such fashion that the information secured tended to make upper SES-origin respondents look better in mental health than they actually were, and lower SES-origin people worse than they were. We can adduce no direct evidence offering a guarantee that this kind of systematic bias was absent.

However, given that we had fully anticipated this possibility we can outline the steps we took to control and minimize it. It will be remembered that our interviewers were all professionals highly experienced in the interviewing art and thus aware of its fallibility.

Moreover, in their own social class origins (or SES group served in a professional capacity), the interviewers were chosen to cover almost the entire status spectrum. Thus, so far as it was practicably possible, it was our policy to assign each interviewer to respondents of the SES range and ethnic background closest to his family or professional experience. It is our opinion, based on our supervision of the interviewers, that the special leaning they harbored was a rather consistent one, combining both empathy for and clinical objectivity toward the respondent.

Hardly serving to dilute this predilection was their knowledge that according to a blueprint of our research design we intended to reinterview a subsample of our respondent population. Although the blueprint did not finally work out in the form originally anticipated, it was foreseen by the interviewers as affording a technical opportunity to check the respondent information they were reporting.

On several grounds, therefore, it seems unlikely that our carefully selected and specially trained staff of professional interviewers had, wittingly or unwittingly, systematically or significantly, distorted the essential facts of the case about their respondents.

Another potential source of bias in the data may be sought among the respondents themselves. That is, to explain the SES connection uncovered (table 14–1) in these terms, it would have to be assumed that high SES-origin respondents tended to censor their answers to the symptom questions, whereas the lower SES-origin respondents in turn were more truthful in replying to these queries.

However, two considerations argue against this assumption. The first is the general observation that denial of symptoms, somatic as well as mental, tends to be a conspicuous mechanism among individuals of lower-class background; whereas people of higher-class rearing are able in a professional setting to confront and report their symptoms more readily and fully. Indeed, Hollingshead and Redlich have observed that "denial or partial denial of psychic pain appears to be a defense mechanism that is linked to low status."[1]

Second, we have reason to believe that several aspects of the Midtown Study's own public image—i.e., its sponsorship by a nationally known medical college and its "community health" focus—carried greater weight with higher SES-origin people than with lower-status respondents. Thus we sensed that the former, more often than the latter, accepted the interview in terms of its medical framework and conscientiously gave candid replies to its questions as a matter of both personal and civic responsibility. These orientations also become manifest when we examine the interview protocols. There it is quickly apparent that compared with their lower-status fellow respondents the sample's higher-SES people more often volunteered or elaborated revealing sensitive material about themselves.

The possibility we posed for evaluation here is that higher-SES people on the whole underreported their symptoms to a greater extent than did their lower-status fellows. The two considerations just presented suggest, on the contrary, that *lower*-SES respondents on the whole underreported their symptoms to a larger degree than did their upper-status neighbors.

In this light, if sample respondents as a source of error have skewed the SES-origin trend reported in table 14–1, they may well have done so by understating the frequency of mental morbidity not at the *top* of the SES-origin range but at the *bottom*. If so, the association between parental SES and respondent mental health is larger (not smaller) than table 14–1 bears witness.

A third possible source of SES bias must be considered, one emanating from the Study's evaluating psychiatrists who judgmentally classified all sample respondents on a gradient scale of symptom formation. To measure the effect of this and related kinds of socio-cultural bias, a two-stage mode of rating respondent mental health was devised for the psychiatrists. In formulating Rating I for each respondent, the psychiatrists had all symptom information except data about his functioning in sociocultural settings that might demographically identify him. In deciding Rating II, the psychiatrists additionally had the information so excepted and all other demo-graphic data about the respondent, including those revolving around his socioeconomic status. Thus, if the sample's Rating II distribu-tions, when compared with the sample's Rating I distributions, showed that the Rating II changes in certain SES-origin groups tended to be more favorable than those in other status groups, the presumption would have to be credited that the socioeconomic in-formation had perhaps contaminated the psychiatrists' judgments. Actual comparison of the "before SES knowledge" ratings (I) and the "after SES knowledge" ratings (II) reveals no status differentials in the direction of the rating changes made by the psychiatrists. We can accordingly infer that the trends in the SES-origin distributions observed in table 14–1 are not to a perceptible degree an artifact of bias on the part of the Midtown psychiatrists.

Of the three potential sources of bias in the SES-origin mental health trends, evidence has been presented that one left no discernible trace of intervention. For two other possible sources of such error evidence is not available. For one of these sources of error, namely, the interviewing staff, the possibility was likely reduced by measures of control that appear to have been more or less effective. As to the respondents themselves as a source of error, there are reasons to believe that their differentially incomplete reporting of symptoms may have operated in a direction of *understating* the SES-origin differences recorded in table 14–1.

All told, therefore, the chances seem large that the association there observed between parental SES and adult mental health is genuine, rather than a spurious result of errors and biases unlocked by the measurement process itself. Confirming findings from other investigations, presented elsewhere in this volume, seem to further enlarge these chances.

NOTES

1. A. B. Hollingshead and F. C. Redlich, *Social Class and Mental Illness*, 1958, p. 176.

RURAL–URBAN DIAGNOSTIC ISSUES*
LEO SROLE

Responding to my critique of the nine sets of rural-urban investigations presented in earlier formats, the Dohrenwends have drawn attention to another tabulation they extracted from six of the nine collected pairs of investigations. In a personal communication relating to my original paper (read to the 1972 CUNY Conference, identified on page 433 above), Dr. Bruce Dohrenwend commented: "We emphasize the consistency in the direction of the differences in table [20–1]. You emphasize their magnitude. Our general feeling, given the problems of measurement, etc., in these studies is that [such] consistencies tend to be important—but you are right that there is room for argument and difference of opinion on the matter— especially if you restrict yourself solely to the findings in table [20–1]." The latter point was subsequently amplified in a reply to my *American Scientist* article (September 1972) by Dr. Barbara S. Dohrenwend, that appeared in the January–February 1973 issue of the same journal.

She indicated there that "the results presented [in the first table] are illuminated by considering data on three broad types of psychological disorder" set forth in the second table of the Dohrenwends' *Handbook of Psychiatry* chapter (p. 429). Her letter continues: "Dr. Srole commented that the differences between percentages of all types

* See chapter 20, pp. 443-446.

of psychological disorder [combined] were very small in some of the nine studies, and suggested that these small differences probably represented nothing more than chance outcomes."

With reference to the second table alluded to above, Dr. Dohrenwend added: "A different interpretation is suggested by the inconsistency in the direction of the differences between rural and urban rates for psychoses, for neuroses, and for personality disorders. Specifically, in the clear majority of studies, psychoses were found to be more prevalent in rural areas, whereas both neuroses and personality disorders were found to be more prevalent in urban areas. Such inconsistency across different types of disorder might well be expected to result in small differences when all types are combined [as in table 20–1].

"On this reasoning I suggest that we should not dismiss differences in results for rural and for urban communities as due to chance. Instead, I think that these epidemiological findings justify the hypothesis that rural areas have higher rates for the most severe type of disorder, psychoses, while urban areas tend to have an excess of the less severe but nevertheless debilitating neuroses and personality disorders."

At the request of the editors, I submitted a rejoinder published in the same issue of the *American Scientist* that carried the above-quoted letter. One paragraph in that rejoinder read as follows: "In my article, I explicitly avoided discussion of the sub-rates of psychoses, neuroses and personality disorders . . . in part because psychiatric criteria for differentiating these three nosological types are beset with unsatisfactory margins of unreliability."

Before going on to the rest of the rejoinder, I would here make explicit the nature of the nosological difficulties just alluded to:

1. Psychoses, neuroses, and personality disorders are of course the three broadest categories in psychiatry's framework of nonorganic disorders, each subdivided into a series of diagnostic classes.

2. Unlike the readily delineated, "hard" types of etiologically specific physical disease entities, these categories of mental disorder are "soft," in the sense that they symptomatically overlap and are etiologically non-specific, leaving no clear diagnostic lines marking off one "disorder" from the others. M. H. Miller puts it that "all combinations and permutations of symptomatology are seen in clinical experience."[1]

3. Miller continues: "Compounding the effort to [differentiate] inclusive categories of neurotic versus psychotic individuals is the clinical pic-

ture presented by a *large group of patients* [italics added] who have been variously labelled 'borderline'—or 'pseudoneurotic psychotics.' "[2]

4. Others have also identified "pseudo" types among the personality disorders (e.g., "pseudopsychopathics") that present elements characteristic of neuroses and/or psychoses.[3]

5. Brill cuts more deeply when he refers to "the conventional wastebasket of the personality disorders, where much of our current lack of knowledge is gathered in one place."[4,5]

6. Such irregularities in psychiatrists' usage of the profession's conventional nosological rubrics prevail under optimal, intensive clinical explorations of patients' case histories. Spitzer and Wilson marshall the most recent research evidence as to inter-psychiatrists' agreement in applying current diagnostic categories, under *optimal* circumstances, and conclude: "In only three categories does the level of [interjudge] agreement reach satisfactory levels: mental deficiency, organic brain syndrome and alcoholism. Only fair agreement is reached for psychosis and schizophrenia. For the remaining [thirteen] categories the agreement is clearly poor."[6]

7. Babigian and associates point to an overlooked set of extraneous sources of diagnostic disagreements: "No matter how the nosological system is improved, the setting in which the diagnosis is made, the focus of the psychiatrist (diagnostic versus therapeutic) and the attitudes toward mental disorder, particularly psychosis, will continue to be major factors in the classification procedure."[7]

8. On the international level, R. M. Spitzer notes that "psychiatrists throughout the world use the same diagnostic terms [in clinical practice] when they have entirely different concepts and definitions of those terms."[8] This consideration adds an additional cloud overhanging the comparability of diagnosis-specific rates yielded by the psychiatrists of different countries whose results the Dohrenwends have called to our attention.

9. In field studies of general populations, usually involving one interview session, such accumulated diagnostic difficulties are magnified many times over. Indeed, in the Midtown study, Rennie considered the traditional psychiatric categories to be inappropriate for the kinds of symptomatic information gathered in our respondents' home interviews. Karl Menninger, one of the giants in contemporary psychiatry, has gone farther and denied their appropriateness or usefulness even in optimal clinical circumstances. He refers to them as "obsolete handles which have been so long used, arranged, rearranged, reordered, disputed and at last, we hope, discarded."[9]

10. For community population studies that *do* apply the three main diagnostic rubrics of clinical psychiatry, the above listed difficulties open the door "wide as a barn" to the play of judgmental bias, and especially to long-standing stereotypes about psychological differences between rural and city people. In historical perspective, the psychiatric literature abounds

in such preconceptions, with mounting evidence that social characteristics of examinees artifactually influence the diagnoses assigned by their examiners.

11. To control such biases in twin field studies of the kind reviewed by the Dohrenwends the obvious, if hardly perfect, solution is to have each subject's interview protocol assessed by psychiatrists who are "blind" to his or her place of residence and related identifying data.

Despite the cumulative weight of the above diagnostic difficulties, I have followed the Dohrenwends' suggestion to reexamine the second table in their *Handbook of Psychiatry* chapter. That tabulation presents the separate rates of psychoses, neuroses, and personality disorders reported for each rural and urban site.

Of course, the number of subjects in each of these nosological categories is a fraction of the number of "total disorders" presented in the Dohrenwends' first table. With smaller numbers in each category, greater differences between the two studies in each linked pair of investigations are required if they are to be viewed as statistically meaningful.

In this light, my *American Scientist* rejoinder summarized the Dohrenwends' second table as follows: "For none of the three mental disorder types, in my judgment, do the separate rural-urban rate differences of the [six pairs of] reviewed studies fall outside the range of probable chance variations, with the exception of the Helgason investigations in Iceland."

It continued: "Professor Dohrenwend urges 'the hypothesis that rural areas have higher rates for . . . psychosis, while urban areas tend to have an excess of . . . neuroses and personality disorders.' This hypothesis has been with us for some time. Yet I must submit that the comprehensive evidence corralled by the Dohrenwends, the isolated Iceland case excepted, supports only the null 'no difference thus far' conclusion."

I am most grateful to the Dohrenwends and to the editors of the *American Scientist* for stimulating the above interchanges on an issue central to chapter 20.

NOTES

1. H. M. Miller, "Neuroses, Psychoses and the Borderline States," in A. M. Freedman and H. I. Kaplan, eds., *Comprehensive Textbook of Psychiatry*, 1967, p. 590.

2. Ibid., p. 591.

3. O. Kernberg, "Borderline Personality Organization," *Journal of the American Psychoanalytic Association* 15, no. 3 (1967),: 641–685.

4. H. Brill, "Nosology," in Freedman and Kaplan, eds., *Comprehensive Textbook of Psychiatry*, p. 582.

5. An extreme position in the perennial professional controversy swirling around the usefulness of this particular category has been taken by Drs. Richard Schwartz and Ilze Schwartz. In a paper delivered to the 1975 meeting of the American Psychiatric Association entitled "Are Personality Disorders Diseases?" they replied in the negative and urged "that personality disorders be removed from the standard [official APA] nomenclature."

6. R. L. Spitzer and P. T. Wilson, "Nosology and the Official Psychiatric Nomenclature," in A. M. Freedman et al., eds., *Comprehensive Textbook of Psychiatry*, 2nd ed., vol. I, 1975, pp. 831–833.

7. H. M. Babigian et al., "Diagnostic Consistency and Change in a Follow-Up Study of 1215 Patients," *American Journal of Psychiatry* 121 (March 1965): 901.

8. Book review in *American Journal of Psychiatry* 132 (August 1975): 881.

9. K. Menninger et al., *The Vital Balance*, 1963, p. 48.

MIDTOWN CRITIQUE OF PREVIOUS PATIENT ENUMERATION STUDIES

We here briefly review and assess what the Study's Treatment Census operation in particular had for the first time clarified. Our specific interest in the Treatment Census had been in two different facets of the patient traffic. The first had to do with the demographic sources and institutional destinations of those who have found their way to psychiatric attention. This we call the "logistic" problem, to which we shall return presently.

The other aspect is the logical problem besetting generalizations drawn from file data by enumerative studies of mental patients, principally those hospitalized. An incomplete inventory of investigations reported in English-language publications listed fifty-five of this kind that had appeared in a twenty-five-year period.[1] With few exceptions, these researchers took the characteristics of their patient aggregates as more or less accurately reflecting the characteristics of the psychotic population, untreated and treated. However, Robert Felix, the leading mental health authority in federal government at the time, declared this unequivocal view of that assumption:

The large number of prevalence and incidence studies of hospitalized psychotics are inadequate for our purposes on many counts. First of all, they deal with only part of our problem, the seriously ill. Secondly, they deal only with that portion of the seriously ill which becomes hospitalized. Third, they can deal only with those socio-environmental factors which are included on hospital records. These studies are in no sense carefully designed experiments to explore relationships or test hypotheses by means of original data. The researchers have no control over the case-finding process, over the record keeping, or even the diagnosis. Rather, they are dependent upon (1) the public's uneven willingness to give up its mentally ill members and to support them in institutions, (2) the hospitals' unstandardized record-keeping activities, and (3) the hospital staffs' varied training and skill in classifying disorders. Finally, the studies have not always been made with much perception of sound methodological principles.[2]

Several years later Gruenberg amplified this position: "I don't think that it [hospital admission] is a good definition of illness. . . . The more we get into it, the more clear it becomes that it doesn't have any substantive meaning."[3]

Despite these pointed criticisms, enumeration studies of patient records continued to be made for the express purpose of testing hypotheses that were predicated on the relationship of the entire aggregate of mental disorders (not its treated cases alone) to its general population universe.

For example, one researcher used hospital admission rates to test (and "confirm") this hypothesis: "The emotional security and social stability afforded by married life make for low incidence of mental illness. . . ." Offered in explanation for the use of *hospitalized* mental patients was this reasoning: "Data on the total incidence of mental illness are almost non-existent. The best available measure of incidence is admission rates to mental hospitals. Whether or not the proportion of the mentally ill who are hospitalized differs by marital status from the total [of] mentally ill is purely a matter for speculation. . . . Since there was no alternative, hospital admission rates were employed . . . to test the hypothesis. . . ."[4]

Here, "best available measure" narrows down to one assumed to be the *only one* available. Moreover, the suitability of this forced choice for the stated hypothesis is left dangling as a matter of pure speculation.

The New Haven investigation[5] marked a definite step forward in two respects: (1) It covered ambulatory as well as hospital patients, and (2) it framed three of its five major hypotheses in terms appropriate to the use of patient frequencies as the test yardstick. However, two of the five hypotheses referred to the totality of people in "psychiatric difficulties," and then proposed to use mental *patients* as the test population.

The New Haven monograph is exemplary in the numerous reiterations that its unit of observation is the psychiatric patient. Sporadically, however, it slips into the implication that it is studying the universe of "mental illness." Of particular interest is its claim that in comparing patients and nonpatients in each social class, "broadly speaking we compare the mentally 'sick' with the mentally 'well.' "[6] Seemingly implied is the two-part proposition: (1) All or most of the "sick" are patients, and (2) all or most of the nonpatients are well. The proposition thus offered is strictly speaking not an axiom that can be accepted as if it were self-validating on its face.

Even more striking is the New Haven conclusion: "We are impelled to infer some subtle connection between class status and psychotic illnesses that we cannot explain away by questioning whether the data are for all cases or only for those in treatment."[7] This is a clear instance of begging the question.

The inference may or may not be correct as stated in a form referring to the totality of psychotic cases. However, to suggest that the specific nature of the population from which the inference has been extracted is an irrelevant matter reflects a somewhat free reading of the laws of evidence. Such a reading is apparent in most of the literature of patient enumeration studies.

Despite the absence of supporting evidence and ample indications of face invalidity, such studies have often claimed, tacitly or explicitly, that treated cases are a valid measure of what epidemiologists want to know about the mentally impaired as a whole. Moreover, their generalizations from the former to the latter have moved from the pages of an extensive literature into the stream of scientific knowledge. Notwithstanding several dissenting voices of considerable authority, this claim, by a process of selective inattention, continued until recently to be widely if not universally accepted.[8]

From the beginning of the Midtown investigation, the writer fully shared the critical views of Felix and Gruenberg quoted above. With the Midtown Treatment Census and Home Survey operations juxtaposed, it was possible to put these views under empirical scrutiny.

As a major point of approach to our Treatment Census, we reviewed Midtown's patients in the care of clinics and office therapists. Midtown's *clinic* cases of this type exceeded New Haven's rate at the time by a margin of 2.5:1, a difference illuminated by the fact that Midtown's home borough had 2.2 as many clinics (per 100,000 population) as did New Haven. In turn, Midtown's *office* patients outnumbered New Haven's by a ratio of 4:1. Of relevance to this difference is that compared to New Haven, Manhattan had 4.4 times as many office therapists per 100,000 population.

Also pertinent is that in both communities treatment capacities of clinics and office therapists were far from meeting *manifest* demands for their services. Similarly, the state mental hospital systems serving these two communities were known to be overcrowded at the time by 25 to 30 percent above their official bed capacities.* In the light of such conditions, it was plain that hospital and ambulatory patient rates reflected intercommunity differences *not* in overall frequencies of "mental illness" but in bottleneck limitations of available professional personnel and their treatment capabilities.

If the Midtown Treatment Census could tell us nothing beyond the population of patients, the companion Home Interview Survey could elicit rough approximations of the volume of unmet need for such services. In the Impaired mental health category of the Home Survey sample we had a resident community group that entailed a risk of need for professional help. To this sample group we applied the broad criterion of "patient history"—defined by the minimum of spending one or more sessions with a psychotherapist. Among these Impaired respondents, only 26.7 percent had ever been patients in this particular sense during their lifetime. The remaining 73.3 percent had never been to such a specialist.

The latter included 29.1 percent who appeared ready to accept psychiatric or other professional intervention—offering a rough estimate of unmet and apparent readiness for helping services. Another 44.2 percent of Impaired respondents were never-patients who seemed to reflect no immediate awareness of professional help as relevant to problems of emotional disability, and thus were unlikely to enter the market for such services, at least of their own accord. In fine, the large problem of unmet need seemed to hinge in part on shortages in the supply of treatment capacities to meet ready demand and, in part, on a latent demand that is still dormant.

To generalize from studied psychiatric patients to the total population of mentally impaired, investigators should have evidence that one of two conditions obtain: (1) The untreated among the latter are

---

* In the intervening years, both hospital populations have fallen far below the overcrowding point.

relatively few in number and therefore cannot significantly affect the generalizations drawn (the 1880 national census of psychotics[9] and the Midtown Study 75 years later both offer suggestive empirical grounds for rejecting this first possibility); or (2) the untreated are indeed numerous, but are nonetheless similar to the patients in demographic and other characteristics. In tacitly accepting one or other of these possibilities as valid, previous investigators operated without a visible foundation of evidence. Here also the Midtown Study could throw some suggestive light.

In the Home Survey sample of adults, impairment rates tended to *increase* with age. Among the Impaired, on the other hand, we found that ever-patient rates tended to *decrease* with age.[10] On the scale of socioeconomic status, the Midtown Treatment Census reported that Total Patients rates (in hospital, clinic, and office facilities) *increased* upward with SES. Nevertheless, the Midtown Home Survey found that impairment frequencies *decreased* upward on the SES ladder.

This seeming contradiction was clarified by the finding *among the Impaired* that ever-patient rates *increased* upward on the SES scale. That is, at the bottom of the SES continuum, relatively many Impaired people yielded relatively few patients, whereas at the top of the continuum relatively few impairment cases yielded relatively many patients. Essentially the same countertrends of impairment frequencies and patient rates emerged from our analyses of the age, generation-in-U.S., and religious-origin variables.

In Midtown at least, the various social groups yielded mental morbidity rates that were almost the reverse of the trends in the frequencies with which help-needy people in those same groups managed to cross the threshold of a psychiatric setting. In other words, here the treated were a small and (except for sex and marital status composition) a completely unrepresentative segment of the Impaired people. Relative to the logical problem posed above, therefore, generalizations from the patients' data to the latter people were fallacious in almost topsy-turvy fashion.

As for the logistic problem raised earlier, Midtown relative to other communities was (and still is) especially favored in the size of its treatment facilities. Nevertheless, the clogged bottlenecks that actually described these services forced the splitting of the help-needy into two different traffics. More likely to appear in the patient traffic were adults who in age were younger (20 to 39), in own SES were of the upper or middle brackets, and in nativity were American-born. More heavily concentrated in the untreated stream were adults older (40 to 59), of lower SES, and of foreign birth.

In part, the demographic divergences between the two traffics seemed to be a function of self-selection, arising from their differential awareness of, orientation to, and means to secure the services of a therapist. But in some part, and here we stand entirely on the New Haven investigators' observations,[11] these demographic differences may also be a function of professional selection based on questionable assumptions about treatability, prognosis, and sociocultural congeniality.

For public policy in planning the expansion of treatment facilities, we have suggested that continuing systematic assessment of the untreated traffic is indispensable.

NOTES

1. A. M. Rose and H. R. Stub, "Summary of Studies on the Incidence of Mental Disorders," in A. M. Rose, ed., *Mental Health and Mental Disorder*, 1955, pp. 87–116.

2. R. H. Felix and R. V. Bowers, "Mental Hygiene and Socio-environmental Factors," *Milbank Memorial Fund Quarterly* 26 (April 1948): 127–128.

3. E. M. Gruenberg, "Problems of Data Collection and Nomenclature," in C. H. Branch et al., eds., "The Epidemiology of Mental Health," mimeographed (University of Utah), 1955, p. 67.

4. L. M. Adler, "The Relationship of Marital Status to Incidence of and Recovery from Mental Illness," *Social Forces* 32 (December 1953): 185. See also R. M. Frumkin, "Marital Status as a Categoric Risk in Major Mental Disorders," *Ohio Journal of Science* 54 (July 1954): 274.

5. A. B. Hollingshead and F. C. Redlich, *Social Class and Mental Illness*, 1958, p. 11. In the present volume, we take critical exception to technical epidemiological points in four chapters (1, 2, 7, 8) of the New Haven monograph. These exceptions in no way detract from our view of the remainder of the latter book as a definitive turning-point work on the unwitting intrusion of social class elements in the operating methods of psychiatric facilities.

6. Ibid., p. 197.

7. Ibid., p. 244.

8. Since publication of the present monograph in 1962, the prevalence of the claim in the literature has considerably diminished, but by no means disappeared (illustrating the lag in fully correcting scientific error). Whereas the frequency of psychiatric patients had previously been almost always equated with the freqency of "mental illness," the latter term now is generally qualified as "treated mental illness."

9. Referring to the national census of mental patients made in 1880, Malzberg reports that "there were 40,942 patients with mental disease in hospitals. In

addition, through the cooperation of physicians, a total of 51,017 patients were found outside of hospitals." (B. Malzberg, "Important Data about Mental Illness," in S. Arieti, ed., *American Handbook of Psychiatry*, vol. 1, 1959, p. 161.)

In a more recent publication, it is reported that "in 1961 for every person hospitalized for a mental disorder in England and Wales, there were two seriously disturbed people [known to general practitioners] in the community, a conclusion that is consistent with previous [British] research." (A. Little, "An Expectancy Estimate of Hospitalization Rates for Mental Illness in England and Wales," *British Journal of Sociology* 16 [1965]: 221–222.)

10. In chapter 22 (p. 476) coauthor S. Michael has advanced the possibility that older Impaired people more often than their younger counterparts secure help for their mental health problems from general practitioners. There is relevant evidence available to assess this suggestion: In the American adult population generally, the average number of physician visits per person per year varies little with age below age 65. Specifically, these reported averages are: age 25 to 34, 4.4; age 35 to 44, 4.1; age 45 to 54, 4.3; age 55 to 64, 5.1. (National Center for Health Statistics, *Health Statistics: Volume of Physician Visits*, series 10, no. 75, 1972, p. 17.)

This trend assumes added significance in light of the further national fact that the proportion of adults with one or more activity-limiting, chronic medical conditions *does* increase in the relevant NCHS categories from 7.6 in the age 17 to 44 group to 19.5 in the 45 to 64 age range. (National Center for Health Statistics, *Health Statistics: Limitation of Activity and Mobility Due to Chronic Conditions*, series 10, no. 80, 1973), p. 19.) If an age trend of mounting frequency of chronic somatic conditions is accompanied by little rise in the frequency of "doctoring," the implication is that with advancing age (in the indicated range) both primarily somatic and primarily psychological conditions tend increasingly to go unattended.

11. Hollingshead and Redlich, *Social Class and Mental Illness*.

INDEX

Abbey, H., 282
Accidents, nonvehicular rates, 94
Acculturation, of immigrants and descendants, 344-345
Activist lay society, 493
Adelson, J., 301, 306–307, 319
Adler, L. M., 257, 529
Adler, Polly, 84
Advocacy groups, and social change, 492
Affective symptoms, 293
Age factor
    biogenic elements, 226–228
    composition of study, 145–146
    demographic factors, 125, 146
    of immigrants, 63
    of in-migrants, 63
    and role change, 236–237
Aging population
    Bellin-Hardt study on, 192, 251–253, 258, 298–299
    in contemporary America and classical China, 231
    and demographic factors, 227
    and ever-patient rates, 528
    generation-in-U.S., 227, 348–349, 370–371
    in Midtown and respondent sample, 51, 146
    hospital patients in, 224–225
    incapacitated respondents in, 224–225
    as independent variable, 125, 221
    inpatient history of, 233–234
    mental health distribution in, 223–226, 228, 235
    mental health symptoms in, 475–477
    military age groups and, 226
    morbidity hypothesis and, 226–228
    in other mental health studies, 465–466

outpatients in, 477
parental role changes among, 229–230
rates of clinic patients in, 222–223
SES origin, sex, and mental health in, 294–299
somatic disorders and, 228, 476–478
summarizing propositions on, 232
Treatment Census and, 233, 237
Alcoholics Anonymous model, 492
Alcoholism, 94, 155, 195
    mortality, 94–95
Alcoholism rates, in New Haven, 402
Alexander, Franz, 119, 132
Allen, V. L., 470
Amante, D., 282
American Dream, 62, 63, 75
American Foundation for Mental Hygiene, 21
American Psychiatric Association, 86, 469–470
Anastasi, Anne, 133
Anomia, 103, 272
Anomie, Merton's theory of, 272
Anonymity, 103, 105–106
Antecedent variables, 273
Anti-urbanism, 433–439
    of Chicago urban sociologists, 437–438
    in psychiatry, 438–439
    of Romantic poets, 434
    of sociopolitical theory, 437–438
Antonovsky, A., 281
Arieti, S., 283, 458
Army's Neuropsychiatric Screening Adjunct (NSA), 153–154, 200
Aronson, E., 398
Aronson, S. H., 437
Arrow, Kenneth, 133
Aspirations, and SES mobility, 302–303
Assessment method, Mental Health